Ben Sira's God

Beihefte zur Zeitschrift für die alttestamentliche Wissenschaft

Herausgegeben von
Otto Kaiser

Band 321

Walter de Gruyter · Berlin · New York
2002

Ben Sira's God

Proceedings of the International Ben Sira Conference
Durham – Ushaw College 2001

Herausgegeben von
Renate Egger-Wenzel

Walter de Gruyter · Berlin · New York
2002

♾ Gedruckt auf säurefreiem Papier,
das die US-ANSI-Norm über Haltbarkeit erfüllt.

Die Deutsche Bibliothek − CIP-Einheitsaufnahme

Ben Sira's god : proceedings of the International Ben Sira Conference,
Durham, Ushaw College 2001 / hrsg. von Renate Egger-Wenzel. −
Berlin ; New York : de Gruyter, 2002
  (Beihefte zur Zeitschrift für die alttestamentliche Wissenschaft ;
Bd. 321)
  ISBN 3-11-017559-2

Printed in Germany
Einbandgestaltung: Christopher Schneider, Berlin
Druck und buchbinderische Verarbeitung: Hubert & Co., Göttingen

Vorwort

Dieser Sammelband führt sich zurück auf die "International Ben Sira Conference at Ushaw College in Durham (GB)", welche von 1.–4. Juli 2001 stattfand und von Dr. Jeremy Corley und mir organisiert wurde. Die Idee zur Tagung entstand ursprünglich bei der Arbeit in diversen, vom Fonds zur Förderung der wissenschaftlichen Forschung geförderten Sira-Projekten am Institut für Alt- und Neutestamentliche Wissenschaft der Katholisch-Theologischen Fakultät an der Universität Salzburg. – So hatten sich über 30 Teilnehmer aus zehn Ländern am Ushaw College eingefunden, um über die Gottesvorstellungen Ben Siras zu diskutieren.

Der vorliegende Band enthält im wesentlichen die Vorträge der Tagung und einige Zusätze.

In einem übergreifenden Block wird zunächst von Alexander A. Di Lella Gott und die Weisheit in der Theologie Ben Siras aufgegriffen, dann folgt von Oda Wischmeyer die Thematik Theologie und Anthropologie. Jeremy Corley spricht über Gott als gnädigen Vater in Ben Sira und dem Neuen Testament. Otto Kaiser unternimmt den Versuch eines Vergleichs der Ethik Siras und der des Apostels Paulus.

Im folgenden Abschnitt werden Einzelthemen des Buches Ben Sira bearbeitet. Núria Calduch-Benages thematisiert Gott als Schöpfer des Alls, Pancratius C. Beentjes verwendet die Wurzel רחם zur Darstellung von Gottes Gnade, Maurice Gilbert zeigt anhand Sir 15,11–18,14 den Zusammenhang von Sünde und Gnade auf, Friedrich V. Reiterer gibt einen Überblick über das Opferverständnis bei Ben Sira und Robert C.T. Hayward nimmt die im Buch vorkommenden Gottesnamen unter die Lupe. Jan Liesen thematisiert Gottes Lobpreis in Ben Sira und Teresa R. Brown das Väterlob. Über zwei Zugänge nähert sich Otto Mulder seiner Thematik in Sir 50: Der Hohepriester Simon und JHWH, der Gott Israels und der Gott aller. Alon Goshen-Gottstein greift ebenfalls das Väterlob auf und zieht einen Vergleich zwischen christlichem und jüdischen Kanon. Ursel Wicke-Reuter macht einen Ausblick von Ben Sira ausgehend auf die Frühe Stoa im Zusammenhang der Ethik und dem Glauben an eine göttliche Providenz. Inhaltlich verwandt spricht James K. Aitken vom göttlichen Willen und der Providenz.

In einem weiteren Block folgen Beiträge zur jüdischen Wirkungsgeschichte Ben Siras. So thematisiert David S. Levene "Theology and Non-Theology" im rabbinischen Ben Sira, und Stefan C. Reif greift die Gebetstexte Siras heraus und zieht einen Vergleich mit jenen aus Qumran und jenen aus der Zeit des Zweiten Tempels.

Der Anhang wird eingeleitet von einem Bericht Renate Egger-Wenzels über den Fund eines bisher unveröffentlichten Artikels des Salzburger Rabbiners Adolf Altmann zur Originalitätsdebatte. Dann folgt ein Beitrag von Eve-Marie Becker zu einem schlesischen Katechismus, der auch Abschnitte aus dem Buch Ben Sira aufnimmt. Wido van Peursen berichtet über den Fortgang dreier Leidener Projekte zu Ben Sira. Schließlich komplementiert Friedrich V. Reiterer seinen vorangehenden Artikel mit einem Anhang zur Opferterminologie, und Pancratius C. Beentjes bat um die Aufnahme einer Corrigenda-Liste zu seiner Textausgabe von Ben Sira in VTS 68 (1997).

An dieser Stelle bleibt mir nur noch die Aufgabe, mich bei *Dr. Jeremy Corley* auf's herzlichste für das Korrekturlesen der englischsprachigen Artikel zu bedanken und bei *Dr. Petra Ritter-Müller* für die Durchsicht der deutschen Beiträge. *Prof. Dr. Dr. h.c. mult. Otto Kaiser* ist es zu verdanken, dass dieser Aufsatzband der Sira-Tagung wiederum in der Reihe BZAW Aufnahme fand. Ihm als Herausgeber der BZAW und dem Verlag *de Gruyter* für die Drucklegung sei ein herzliches Vergelt's Gott ausgesprochen.

Salzburg im Juli 2002   Renate Egger-Wenzel
                                                    (Herausgeberin)

Inhaltsverzeichnis

Übergreifende Themen

God and Wisdom in the Theology of Ben Sira:
An Overview

Alexander A. Di Lella, O.F.M.
The Catholic University of America, Washington, DC

1. Introduction

Collecting the thousands of affirmations made about God and the many titles of God found in the OT would in no way constitute a unified theological treatise. Nor does the OT discuss "the idea of God," as would, for example, a systematic theologian today. The reason is that the biblical authors do not speak about God with a single voice or in a uniform way. For the authors and editors of the OT books the existence and presence of God, however, was simply a given in need of no proof or argument[1]. Ben Sira's affirmations about God reflect, of course, Israelite traditions found in the earlier biblical books. But there is no single OT book or passage that can be identified as his major source. As a result, what he writes about God has much of the diversity of meaning or emphasis that we find in other parts of the OT.

An important point to keep in mind is that, like any other OT affirmations about God, Ben Sira's theological statements are culturally, socially, and historically conditioned. Accordingly, these must be viewed and interpreted against the background of the author's time and place and religious circumstances. In other words, individual sayings must be seen in light of the author's overall conceptual world, and should not be considered as absolute, as if cut in stone for all peoples and times and places[2]. Nonetheless, the limi-

---

1   For a good survey of this question see Scullion, God, 1041–48; see also Vawter, God, 3–7. For the Wisdom of Ben Sira I use my forthcoming translation in the revised *NAB* OT to be published probably in 2004. The translation of Sirach in the original *NAB* of 1970 was based on the then extant Cairo Geniza MSS A-E, the Masada fragment, the Qumran fragments, the grandson's Greek, the Syriac Peshitta, and the Old Latin. In my translation, a complete revision of the 1970 Sirach, I employed the same primary sources as well as Geniza MS F that I identified; see Di Lella, Manuscript, 226–38. All other biblical quotations are taken from the *NRSV* (but the chapter- and verse-numbers follow the MT).

2   Like other OT authors, Ben Sira has his limitations regarding what Christians would consider morally acceptable behavior; e.g., the teaching of Jesus (Matt 5:43–48) over-turns Sir 12:1–6:
    If you do good, know for whom you are doing it,
        and your kindness will have its effect.
    Do good to the righteous and reward will be yours,
        if not from them, from the LORD.

tations we would find today in some OT pronouncements[3] should not hinder us from learning normative truths about God and his relationship to human beings.

The concept of wisdom likewise has no uniform meaning in the OT. A large part of Ben Sira's theology of wisdom reflects ideas and concerns he learned from Deuteronomy and especially Proverbs, his favorite book; but not surprisingly, he also reflects other OT traditions. Ben Sira, however, was no mere echo or copier of older material, for his book contains many original insights. In sum, he has put his own stamp on what he derived from the earlier biblical books and traditions. Moreover, his originality consists also in the frequency of his statements about wisdom and its origin[4]. In terms of sheer volume of material on wisdom and her glories, no other OT author has said as much as Ben Sira.

In this paper I shall address three issues: (1) Ben Sira's theology of God; (2) God, the origin of wisdom; and (3) Ben Sira's theology of wisdom.

2. Ben Sira's Theology of God

In the OT, Yahweh is described as transcendent as well as immanent (e.g., Exod 3:14; see also Hos 1:9)[5]. He is utterly beyond his creatures and beyond human comprehension (Isa 55:8–9); he has neither beginning nor end nor any rivals (cp. the Babylonian and Egyptian mythologies): "Before the mountains were brought forth, or ever you had formed the earth and the world, from everlasting to everlasting you are God" (Ps 90:2). Yahweh is "the first" and "the last" (Isa 41:4; 44:6; 48:12). He is also involved in human affairs and has a stake in the history not only of the people of Israel but also of other nations as well (Amos 1:3–2:16). The Lord holds all peoples and nations, and

---

> No good comes to those who give comfort to the wicked,
>   nor is it an act of mercy that they do.
> Give to the good person but refuse the sinner;
>   refresh the downtrodden but give nothing to the proud.
> No arms for combat should you give them,
>   lest they use these against yourself;
> Twofold evil you will obtain
>   for every good deed you do for them.
> For God also hates the wicked,
>   and takes vengeance on evil-doers.

3   For example, in Exod 4:21; 7:3; 9:12; 10:1, 20, 27; 11:10; 14:4, 8 Yahweh is said to harden Pharaoh's heart as if to imply that Pharaoh has no freedom of choice in the matter at hand.

4   See Di Lella, Meaning, 133–48.

5   See Murray, Problem, 5–25.

not just Israel, accountable for their moral decisions and actions (Deut 9:4–5; Dan 4:24–34). Through the prophets, God has revealed himself to his chosen people. Ben Sira as well as other OT authors share these different conceptions about God.

The main tenet of OT theology is, of course, that God is one, as Deut 6:4 states so succinctly: "Hear, O Israel: The LORD is our God, the LORD alone."[6] Ben Sira puts it this way:

> Raise your hand against the foreign people,
>> that they may see your mighty deeds.
> As you have used us to show them your holiness,
>> so now use them to show us your glory.
> Thus they will know, as we know,
>> that there is no God but you. (33/36:3/2–5/4)[7]

Much of the rest of Ben Sira's theology of God derives from his understanding of wisdom as fear of the Lord, which means living according to the Law of Moses. Thus, in his famous poem on free will (15:11–20), Ben Sira teaches his students the great truth found elsewhere in the OT that human beings, and not God, are the cause of sin and evil:[8]

> Do not say: "My transgression is from God."
> For what he hates he does not do.
> Do not say: "He himself has led me astray."
> For he has no need of lawless people. (15:11–12)

Then Ben Sira writes that when God created human beings, he "made them subject to their own free choice" (15:14), and he concludes:

> For great is the wisdom of the LORD;
>> he is mighty in power and he sees all things.
> The eyes of God see his works,
>> and he perceives a person's every deed.
> He did not command anyone to sin,
>> nor will be be lenient with liars. (15:18–20)

Here Ben Sira attributes to the LORD's great wisdom and almighty power his ability to know all things, and in particular the actions of human beings. Ben Sira excoriates as liars those who rationalize their sinful conduct as if it were predetermined by God or others.[9]

---

6 See Sedlmeier (Israel, 21–39) for other alternatives to this translation. He also emphasizes that the purpose of Deuteronomy is not so much to impose laws as rather to stress the relationship between God and Israel.

7 Ben Sira also stresses the God-Israel relationship; see the previous note.

8 See, for example, Deut 11:26–28, 31–32; 30:15–20; Jer 7:1–7; 21:8–10.

9 Yet in 36/33:7–15, the poem on the polarities or opposites found in creation, Ben Sira seems to affirm, esp. in vv. 10–13, that God determines the destiny of individuals irrespective of their personal moral choices. But see Skehan – Di Lella, Wisdom, 399–401; Prato, Il problema, 13–61; and Sauer, Jesus Sirach, 233–34.

The LORD holds people accountable for their actions. The LORD is a God of justice (5:1–8) as well as mercy (Sir 51:8):

> For mercy and anger alike are with him
>> who remits and forgives, but also pours out wrath.[10]
> Great as his mercy is his punishment;
>> he judges people, each according to their deeds. (16:11c–12)[11]

Ben Sira employs the metaphor of shepherd and flock to emphasize that the Lord's mercy is universal:

> [People's] compassion is for their neighbor,
>> but the Lord's compassion reaches all flesh,
> He reproves and trains and teaches them,
>> and turns them back, as a shepherd his flock.[12] (18:13)

The virtuous, or truly wise, will never be disappointed. Despite adversities that come their way to test their fidelity, Ben Sira urges his students to remain steadfast and to hope in God (2:1–3). Then he adds:

> Accept whatever happens to you;
>> in times of humiliation be patient.
> For in fire gold is tested,
>> and the chosen in the crucible of humiliation.
> Trust in God, and he will help you;
>> make your ways straight and hope in him.
> You that fear the Lord, wait for his mercy,
>> do not stray lest you fall.
> You that fear the Lord, trust in him,
>> and your reward will not be lost.
> You that fear the Lord, hope for good things,
>> for lasting joy and mercy. (2:4–9)

But God punishes those who sin by not walking the way of the Lord and disobeying the Law, thereby proving they lack wisdom. With harsh language Ben Sira pronounces a three-fold "Woe" on those Jews who compromise their faith to follow the alluring ways of Hellenistic culture:

> Woe to timid hearts and drooping hands,
>> to the sinner who walks a double path!
> Woe to the faint of heart! For they do not trust,
>> and therefore have no shelter!

---

10 This verse is rephrased in 5:6:
> Do not say, "His mercy is great;
>> my many sins he will forgive."
> For mercy and anger alike are with him;
>> his wrath comes to rest on the wicked.

11 This verse alludes to the Jewish doctrine that God judges people according to their deeds; see also 3:14–16, 30–31; 11:26; 15:17–19; 17:22–23; 29:11–13.

12 See Fogliata, A figura, 68–73.

Woe to you who have lost hope!
what will you do at the Lord's visitation? (2:12–14)[13]
The double path is the way of the Lord, which makes one truly wise, and the way of the Greeks, which the Jews were tempted to emulate for personal or social gain. It simply is not possible to reconcile the two ways; one must choose either the one or the other.

3. God, the Origin of Wisdom

Other OT authors state explicitly, of course, that human wisdom has its origin in God. A typical example is 1 Kgs 5:9: "God gave Solomon very great wisdom, discernment, and breadth of understanding as vast as the sand on the seashore." Then in Dan 1:17, we read: "To these four young men God gave knowledge and skill in every aspect of literature and wisdom; Daniel also had insight into all visions and dreams."

The author of Job asks the famous question, "Where shall wisdom be found? And where is the place of understanding?" (Job 28:12) Then after the abyss and the sea declare that wisdom is not to be found in them (Job 28:14), and that gold and silver and precious stones cannot purchase wisdom (Job 28:15–19), the poet writes:

God understands the way to it,
  and he knows its place ...
When he made a decree for the rain,
  and a way for the thunderbolt;
then he saw [wisdom] and declared it;
  he established it, and searched it out.
And he said to humankind,
  "Truly, the fear of the Lord, that is wisdom;
  and to depart from evil is understanding." (Job 28:23, 26–28)

Ben Sira adds a new dimension to this idea from Job when he explains in clear terms why God alone can be the origin of all wisdom:

He searches out the abyss and penetrates the heart;
  their secrets he understands.
For the Most High possesses all knowledge,
  and sees the things that are to come forever.
He makes known the past and the future,
  and reveals the deepest secrets.

---

13   See Di Lella, Fear of the Lord and Belief, 188–204. In 41:8, Ben Sira employs "Woe" for the fourth and final time to condemn sinners who compromise their faith: "Woe to you, O wicked people, / who forsake the Law of the Most High."

> He lacks no understanding;
> > no single thing escapes him.
> He regulates the mighty deeds of his wisdom;
> > he is from eternity one and the same,
> With nothing added, nothing taken away;
> > no need of a counselor for him! (42:18–21)

Few discrete passages of the Bible speak so clearly as this one about the extent of God's eternity and immutability, his omnipotence and omniscience as well as his wisdom and knowledge (see Dan 13:42). The almighty Creator, Ben Sira states, grants wisdom only to those who fear him:

> It is the LORD who has made all things,
> > and to those who fear him he gives wisdom. (43:33)

Ben Sira's major concern was to teach his students that wisdom is a precious gift of the Lord (1:1).

4. Ben Sira's Theology of Wisdom

The OT applies the vocabulary of wisdom to many different types of individuals and activities. People who are skilled in various arts and crafts, for example, are described as being wise or as possessing wisdom. Accordingly, we read in Exod 35:30–33:

> Then Moses said to the Israelites: See, the LORD has called by name Bezalel son of Uri son of Hur, of the tribe of Judah; he has filled him with divine spirit [רוּחַ אֱלֹהִים, or the spirit of God], with skill, intelligence, and knowledge in every kind of craft to devise artistic designs, to work in gold, silver, and bronze, in cutting stones for setting, and in carving wood, in every kind of craft.

To be noted is that this passage states clearly that Bezalel's skills and intelligence as a craftsman and artist are due to the spirit of God, and not simply to human industry and effort.

The words "wise" and "wisdom" apply to silversmiths and goldsmiths (Jer 10:9) and other professionals.[14] And 1 Kgs 5:10–13 states that "Solomon's wisdom surpassed the wisdom of all the people of the east, and all the wisdom of Egypt," for he composed three thousand proverbs and a thousand and five songs; and because he was wise, he discussed trees and plants, animals, birds, reptiles, and fishes. Even the magicians, the enchanters, and the

---

14   See Murphy, Wisdom, 920. In classical Greek, the noun *sophia* also had the meaning of skill and talent in the trades and fine arts like music and poetry; see LSJ sub verbo, and Lloyd, Revolution, 83–90.

sorcerers of Egypt (Gen 41:8; Exod 7:11) and Babylon (Dan 2:2, 12) are described as "wise."

Ben Sira writes about the skills of the physician in somewhat the same
manner:

> Make friends with the physician, for he is essential to you;
> God has also established him in his profession.
> From God the doctor has his wisdom,
> and from the king he receives his sustenance.
> Knowledge makes the physician distinguished,
> and gives him access to those in authority. (38:1–3)

Note that nothing is said about the physician's medical schooling. In these
different texts there is no moral evaluation implied in the wisdom of the
skilled persons who possess it as a gift from God.

But Ben Sira is less concerned about what we would call natural ability
and talent than a person's moral life and life style in the world of that day.
Thus, he writes:

> How great is the one who finds wisdom,
> but none is greater than the one who fears the Lord. (25:10)

Ben Sira's numerous sayings about wisdom and the wise can be reduced, in
general, to two basic types: theoretical or existential or speculative wisdom,
which resides in the intellect and is akin to the Greek concept of *sophia*; and
practical or pretheoretical or recipe wisdom, which resides in the will and enables one to make the right choices for leading an ethical life.[15] In some passages, however, the two types of wisdom may not be neatly distinguished.
But whatever the case, God alone is source of all wisdom, as is clear from the
opening couplet of the book:

> All wisdom is from the Lord
> and with him it remains forever. (1:1)

Then in the remaining verses of the poem which serves as an introduction to
the book, Ben Sira writes:

> Before all other things wisdom was created;
> and prudent understanding, from eternity.[16]
> The root of wisdom to – whom has it been revealed?
> Her subtleties – who knows them?

---

15   Berger – Luckmann (Construction, 42) employ the expression "recipe knowledge,"
      defined as "knowledge limited to pragmatic competence in routine performances."
      "Recipe knowledge" suggested to me the phrase "recipe wisdom," which has, however,
      a somewhat different meaning as is clear from my definition.
16   Ben Sira derived the content of this verse from Prov 8:22–23:
      The LORD created me [Wisdom] at the beginning of his work,
          the first of his acts of long ago.
      Ages ago I was set up,
          at the first, before the beginning of the earth.

There is but one who is wise, truly awe-inspiring,
> seated upon his throne – the Lord.
It is he who created her;
> he saw her and measured her.
He poured her forth upon all his works,
> upon every living thing according to his bounty;
> he lavished her upon those who love him. (Sir 1:4, 6, 8–10ab[17])

Though all creatures manifest the wisdom of their Creator, the Lord lavishes wisdom especially on men and women who love him, i.e., who keep the Law, as we shall see later. Thus, whatever wisdom the Greeks and Egyptians possess has its origin in God. That is why Ben Sira does not hesitate to utilize material he learned from pagan authors and to adapt their ideas to make them appear thoroughly Jewish.[18]

4.1 Theoretical Wisdom

The goal of theoretical wisdom is the enlightenment and refinement of the intellect. Though all wisdom is from the Lord (Sir 1:1), the training of the mind requires hard work and diligence, as every student knows from personal experience. Ben Sira accordingly expects his students to do their part in acquiring such wisdom, for it is a necessary component of the examined life. They are to learn by instruction and study, by reflection and discipline (23:2–3), by association with the wise (39:1–3) and avoidance of the foolish (21:13–26; 22:9–15),[19] and by travel (31/34:10/10a–13/12; 39:4).[20] But theoretical wisdom may also tempt students to go astray, for they might find the Hellenistic pagan philosophy and natural science of that day more attractive than the wisdom and lore of Israel. So in 3:21–23, Ben Sira issues a stern warning:

> What is too sublime for you, do not seek;
> > do not reach into things that are hidden from you.
> What is committed to you, pay heed to;
> > what is hidden is not your concern.
> In matters that are beyond you do not meddle;
> > for you have been shown more than you can understand.

Ben Sira's longest composition on theoretical wisdom appears in 6:18–37, a non-acrostic twenty-two-line poem, which has eight stanzas that fall quite

---

17 Regarding the Greek II addition at this point, see Gilbert, Voir, 247–52.
18 See Di Lella – Skehan, Wisdom, 46–50; and Mattila, Ben Sira, 495–99.
19 Ben Sira has much to say about the fool. In one of his most caustic poems he urges his students to make every effort to avoid contact with a fool; see Di Lella, Sirach, 159–68.
20 See Lavoie, Ben Sira, 37–60.

naturally into three groups: 3 + 3 / 3 + 3 + 3 / 2 + 3 + 2; each has a thematic unity: vv. 18–22, 23–31, and 32–37.[21] A few comments on each stanza are in order.

4.1.1

> My child, from your youth choose discipline;
>   and when you have gray hair you will find wisdom.
> As though plowing and sowing, draw close to her;
>   then wait for her bountiful crops.
> For in cultivating her you will work but little,
>   and soon you will eat of her fruit. (6:18–19)

Ben Sira emphasizes that the quest for theoretical wisdom must begin in youth, so that in old age one can become wise. The familiar agricultural images of plowing and sowing dramatize the strenuous work involved, but wisdom's fruit makes the work seem rather minimal and worthwhile.

4.1.2

> Jolting she is to the fool!
>   The stupid cannot abide her.
> She will be like a heavy stone to them,
>   and they will not delay in casting her aside.
> For discipline is like her name,
>   she is not accessible to many. (6:20–22)

Fools do not even desire wisdom because they will not accept the burdens of discipline. But without discipline, wisdom is unattainable.

4.1.3

> Listen, my child, and take my advice;
>   do not refuse my counsel.
> Put your feet into her fetters,
>   and your neck into her collar.
> Bend your shoulders and carry her
>   and do not fret at her bonds. (6:23–25)

Ben Sira now changes the imagery to the hunt. Here wisdom is the hunter, and the student is the prey.

---

21 For the textual criticism and exegesis of this splendid poem, see Skehan – Di Lella, Wisdom, 191–96.

4.1.4

With all your soul draw close to her;
    and with all your strength keep her ways.
Inquire and search, seek and find;
    when you get hold of her, do not let her go.
Thus at last you will find rest in her,
    and she will be changed into joy for you. (6:26–28)

Here the student is the hunter, and wisdom is the prey, which once captured must never be let go.

4.1.5

Her net will be for you a place of strength;
    her fetters, a robe of spun gold.
Her yoke will be a gold ornament;
    her bonds, a purple cord.
You will wear her as a robe of glory,
    and bear her as a splendid crown. (6:29–31)

Wisdom again becomes the hunter who employs a net, fetters, and a yoke. But each of these implements becomes something desirable to have: wisdom's net is the strength of self-control; her fetters, yoke, and bonds, symbols of discipline, become like a glorious robe to be worn proudly with wisdom's splendid crown.

4.1.6

If you wish, my child, you can become wise;
    if you apply yourself, you will be shrewd.
If you are willing to listen, you will learn;
    if you pay attention, you will be instructed. (6:32–33)

Here is the heart of Ben Sira's teaching: personal desire to become wise and unstinting effort in listening to teachers are essential.

4.1.7

Stand in the company of the elders;
    stay close to whoever is wise.
Be eager to hear every discourse;
    let no wise saying escape you.

> If you see intelligent persons, seek them out;
>> let your feet wear away their doorsteps! (6:34–36)

According to OT wisdom tradition, the elders are the primary teachers (Sir 25:4–6), but not the only ones. The student should seek out anyone from whom he can learn.

4.1.8

> Reflect on the law of the Most High,
>> and on his commandments meditate continually.
> Then he himself will enlighten your mind,
>> and make you wise as you desire. (6:37)

Now in this final and most emphatic stanza, Ben Sira states his principal concern: reflection and meditation on the law and commandments are essential, for it is God himself who will ultimately make the student wise.

Not all theoretical wisdom, however, is praiseworthy, for even the wicked can be clever and intelligent:

> The knowledge of wickedness is not wisdom,
>> nor is there prudence in the counsel of sinners.
> There is a shrewdness that is detestable,
>> while the fool may be free from sin.
> Better are the God-fearing who have little understanding
>> than those of great intelligence who violate the Law. (19:22–24)

Thus, even a fool or a person who is intellectually challenged but fears God is superior, in Ben Sira's view, to the one who is learned but breaks the Law.

4.2 Practical Wisdom

The goal of practical wisdom is the perfection of the will, which must make choices in day-to-day living regarding matters that are secular and political, ethical and moral, religious and spiritual. For Ben Sira, wisdom is identified with the Law of Moses and resides in Israel, more specifically "in the holy tent" in Jerusalem, as he teaches in 24:8–12.[22] In the poem of chap. 24, the speaker is personified Wisdom, an image he borrowed from Prov 8:4–36. At the end of Wisdom's speech Ben Sira adds:

> All this is the book of the covenant of the Most High God,
>> the Law which Moses commanded us

---

22 Hayward (Sirach, 31–46) shows the apologetic nature of Ben Sira's claim that Wisdom, "who is older than the universe and gives order and discipline to all that exists" (p. 46), dwells in the Jerusalem Temple.

as a heritage for the community of Jacob. (24:23)

Thus, fear of the Lord and loyalty to the Law stand out as essential, an idea articulated already in Prov 9:10: "The fear of the LORD is the beginning of wisdom,/ and the knowledge of the Holy One is insight." Ben Sira rephrases this text:

All wisdom is fear of the LORD;
and in all wisdom there is the fulfillment of the Law. (19:20)

The opposite of such wisdom is sinful pride of which Ben Sira writes:

The beginning of pride is human stubbornness
in withdrawing one's heart from one's Maker.
For sin is the reservoir of insolence,
a source which runs over with vice;
Because of it God sends unheard-of afflictions
and strikes people with utter ruin. (10:12–13)

The antidote for pride is humility and prayer:

Lord, Father and God of my life,
do not give me haughty eyes,
and remove evil desire from my heart. (23:4–5)

Right after the brief introduction to his book (1:1–10), Ben Sira has a splendid non-alphabetic poem of twenty-two bicola (1:11–30) in which he explains that fear of the Lord is wisdom. I cite only a few key passages:

Those who fear the Lord will have a happy end;
even on the day of their death they will be blessed. (1:13)
The beginning of wisdom is to fear the Lord;
she is created with the faithful in the womb. (1:14)
The fullness of wisdom is to fear the Lord;
she inebriates them with her fruits. (1:16)
The crown of wisdom is the fear of the Lord,
flowering with peace and perfect health. (1:18)
The root of wisdom is to fear the Lord;
her branches are long life. (1:20)[23]

In Ben Sira's theology, only that is true wisdom which leads to fear of the Lord and observance of the Law. He repeats this basic thesis several times. A dramatic example is the two-part poem in 14:20–15:10 with its daring imagery that underscores the intensity involved in the pursuit of wisdom. The first part is a macarism[24]; I then cite only three verses of the second part:

<hr>

23   For an analysis of this poem, see Di Lella, Fear of the Lord as Wisdom, 113–33.
24   Puech (Le livre, 420–21) shows that a fragment of 4Q525 has the same pattern of eight macarisms or beatitudes as in Sir 14:20–27 and Matt 5:3–10. See also Collins, Wisdom, 49.

4.2.1

Happy are those who meditate on Wisdom,
  and fix their gaze on knowledge;
Who ponder her ways in their heart,
  and understand her paths;
Pursuing her like a scout,
  and watching at her entry way;
Who peep through her windows,
  and listen at her doors;
Who encamp near her house,
  and fasten their tent pegs next to her walls;
Who pitch their tent beside her,
  and live in an excellent dwelling place;
Who build their nest in her leafage,
  and lodge in her branches;
Who take refuge from the heat in her shade,
  and dwell in her home. (14:20–27)

4.2.2

Whoever fears the LORD will do this;
  whoever is practiced in the Law will come to Wisdom.
She will meet him like a mother,
  and like a young bride she will receive him,
She will feed him with the bread of learning,
  and give him the water of understanding to drink. (15:1–3)

Though the reference here is to practical wisdom personified under the images of mother and bride, Ben Sira clearly intimates that Lady Wisdom will bestow also theoretical wisdom on the one who fears the Lord.

Whoever does not fear the Lord can never attain true wisdom, for "she is far from the impious,/ and liars never think of her" (15:8). But the true believer not only fears the Lord but loves him as well:

Those who fear the Lord do not disobey his words;
  those who love him keep his ways.
Those who fear the Lord seek to please him;
  those who love him are filled with his law. (2:15–16)

Ben Sira here alludes to what I call the great Deuteronomic equation: to fear the LORD = to love him = to serve him = to keep his commandments = to walk in his ways (see Deut 6:1–2; 10:12–13; 30:16).

5. Conclusions

From this brief overview of Ben Sira's theology of God and wisdom, we might suggest three conclusions. First, Ben Sira reflects much of the OT theology of God, with particular emphasis on the Lord's omnipotence and omniscience as source of all wisdom. Second, theoretical wisdom, which one acquires through discipline and study in order to refine the intellect, makes it possible for one to lead a truly human and meaningful life blessed by God. Accordingly, even though such wisdom is also a gift from the Lord, Ben Sira challenges his students to exploit their talents and exert every effort to learn all they can from their elders and teachers and from their own life experiences as well. Third, practical wisdom as fear of the Lord and observance of the Law is, in Ben Sira's theology, the heart and soul of Jewish faith and life. All believers, even the less intellectually endowed, have the radical freedom of choice to acquire or reject such wisdom. Practical wisdom does not come easily or cheaply, for it requires a person to lead an upright and moral life and to be prepared for testing; accordingly, many reject it with the result that God will hold them accountable for their decision.

Bibliography

Berger, P.L. – Luckmann, T., *The Social Construction of Reality: A Treatise in the Sociology of Knowledge* (Garden City, NY: Doubleday / Anchor, 1967).

Collins, J.J., *Jewish Wisdom in the Hellenistic Age* (OTL; Louisville: Westminster John Knox, 1997).

Di Lella, A.A., "Fear of the Lord and Belief and Hope in the Lord amid Trials: Sirach 2:1–18," in *Wisdom, You Are My Sister: Studies in Honor of Roland E. Murphy, O.Carm., on the Occasion of His Eightieth Birthday* (ed. M. Barré; CBQMS 29; Washington: Catholic Biblical Association, 1997) 188–204.

Di Lella, A.A., "Fear of the Lord as Wisdom: Ben Sira 1,11–30," in *The Book of Ben Sira in Modern Research: Proceedings of the First International Ben Sira Conference, 28–31 July 1996, Soesterberg, Netherlands* (ed. P.C. Beentjes; BZAW 255; Berlin / New York: de Gruyter, 1997) 113–33.

Di Lella, A.A., "The Meaning of Wisdom in Ben Sira," in *In Search of Wisdom: Essays in Memory of John G. Gammie* (ed. L.G. Perdue et al.; Louisville: Westminster / John Knox, 1993) 133–48.

Di Lella, A.A., "The Newly Discovered Sixth Manuscript of Ben Sira from the Cairo Geniza," *Bib* 69 (1988) 226–38.

Di Lella, A.A., "Sirach 22,9–15: 'The Life of the Fool Is Worse than Death' " in *Treasures of Wisdom: Studies in Ben Sira and the Book of Wisdom* (FS M. Gilbert; eds. N. Calduch-Benages and J. Vermeylen; BETL 143; Leuven: Peeters, 1999) 159–68.

Fogliata, M., "A figura do pastor e do rebanho em Eclo 18,13," *RCB* 14 (55/56, 1990) 68–73.

Gilbert, M., "Voir ou craindre le Seigneur? Sir 1,10d," in *Biblica et Semitica: Studi in memoria di Francesco Vattioni* (ed. L. Cagni; Istituto universitario orientale, Dipartimento di studi Asiatici, Series Minor 59; Naples: Herder, 1999) 247–52.

Hayward, C.T.R., "Sirach and Wisdom's Dwelling Place," in *Where Shall Wisdom Be Found? Wisdom in the Bible, the Church and the Contemporary World* (ed. S.C. Barton; Edinburgh: T. and T. Clark, 1999) 31–46.

Lavoie, J.-J., "Ben Sira le voyageur ou la difficile recontre avec l'hellénisme," *Science et Esprit* 52/1 (2000) 37–60.

Lloyd, G.E.R., *The Revolution of Wisdom: Studies in the Claims and Practices of Ancient Greek Science* (Berkeley: University of California Press, 1987).

Mattila, S.L., "Ben Sira and the Stoics: A Reexamination of the Evidence," *JBL* 119 (2000) 473–501.

Murphy, R.E., "Wisdom in the OT," *ABD* 6. 920–31.

Murray, J.C., *The Problem of God: Yesterday and Today* (New Haven / London: Yale University Press, 1964).

Prato, G.L., *Il problema della teodicea in Ben Sira: Composizione dei contrari e richiamo alle origini* (AnBib 65; Rome: Pontificial Biblical Institute, 1975).

Puech, E., "Le livre de Ben Sira et les manuscrits de la Mer Morte," in *Treasures of Wisdom: Studies in Ben Sira and the Book of Wisdom* (FS M. Gilbert; eds. N. Calduch-Benages and J. Vermeylen; BETL 143; Leuven: Peeters, 1999) 411–26.

Sauer, G., *Jesus Sirach: Übersetzt und erklärt* (ATDA 1; Göttingen: Vandenhoeck & Ruprecht, 2000).

Scullion, J.J., "God in the OT," *ABD* 2. 1041–48.

Sedlmeier, F., " 'Höre, Israel! JHWH: Unser Gott (ist er) ...,' " *TTZ* 108 (1999) 21–39.

Skehan, P.W. – Di Lella, A.A., *The Wisdom of Ben Sira: A New Translation with Notes, Introduction and Commentary* (AB 39; New York: Doubleday, 1987).

Vawter, B.,"The God of Hebrew Scriptures," *BTB* 12 (1982) 3–7.

Theologie und Anthropologie im Sirachbuch

Oda Wischmeyer
Universität Erlangen

1. Vorbemerkungen

1.1 Thema

Als ich für den Vortrag das Sirachbuch neu las, erregten Ben Siras Aussagen über den Tod meine besondere Aufmerksamkeit. Ich gewann den Eindruck einer *sachlichen Aporie. Der Gott Ben Siras ist der* mit sich selbst identische ewig seiende *Gott des Lebens. Der Mensch dagegen* bleibt in seiner körperlichen Individuierung der kurzen Zeitspanne seines irdischen Lebens verhaftet und *gehört in die Welt des Todes* und unter das Gesetz des Todes (14,17[1] und 41,3).[1] Diese aporetische Struktur tritt in zugespitzten Sentenzen zutage wie:

> "Tief, tief beuge den Hochmut, denn das, was den Menschen erwartet, ist Gewürm" (7,17).[2]

Dagegen heißt es über Gott:

> "Noch mehr wollen wir nicht hinzufügen, und das Ende der Rede sei: »Er ist alles.«" (43,27).[3]

Diese ungeheure Rede von Gott ist so groß, dass der Mensch weder Platz noch Würde noch Hoffnung neben diesem Gott zu haben scheint. Der aufs Höchste gesteigerte Lobpreis Gottes schafft eine tiefe Melancholie in Bezug auf den Menschen. Die Rede vom Menschen ist nämlich ohne Perspektive:

> "Denn es kann nicht Vollkommenheit beim Menschen sein, weil kein Mensch unsterblich ist" (17,30).

1.2 These

Ich fragte mich, wie Ben Sira mit dieser Aporie umgeht. Dabei kam ich zu der folgenden *These*, die ich meinen Ausführungen voranstellen will:

Ben Sira versucht, mit der ihm bewussten Aporie produktiv umzugehen, indem er dem Menschen die Aufgabe der Selbsterziehung zuweist. Die Selbsterziehung oder Zucht verbindet den Menschen mit der Weisheit, jener wich-

---

1   Gesetz hier: חוק: das Angeordnete.
2   Vgl. Ijob 25,6. Im Sirachbuch vgl. bes. 10,11.
3   הוא הכל.

tigsten Größe zwischen Gott und Mensch. In der Lebensform der Zucht und Gottesfurcht, die durch das Leben nach dem Gesetz gestaltet wird, kann der Mensch eine gewisse Nähe zu Gott erreichen.

Ben Sira versucht also, diese Aporie durch eine religiös fundierte und normierte kulturpädagogische Theorie aufzulösen. Diese Theorie setzt er durch Psychologie und ethisch-religiöse Erziehung in die Praxis um. Sein Versuch muss aber letzten Endes solange scheitern, wie die Faktizität des Todes als endgültiges Ende der menschlichen Existenz verstanden wird, denn dadurch bleiben Gott und Mensch trotz aller Selbsterziehung kategorial getrennt.

Erst die Übersetzungen des hebräischen Sirachtextes werden das Element der Hoffnung auf Auferstehung in das Sirachbuch eintragen. Das Sirachbuch hat damit Anteil an dem Schicksal der Masse frühjüdisch-griechischsprachiger Schriften: Es wird in dieser eschatologisch ergänzten Form in die große Bibliothek der Christen aufgenommen und in christlichem Sinne kommentiert. Ben Sira selbst hat diese Lösung der Aporie – die Auferstehung der Toten – noch nicht gekannt.

1.3 Hermeneutik

Ben Sira lehrt auf der Basis des Maschal und in der Form des weisheitlichen Gedichts, das sich aus Einzelstrophen zusammensetzt. Er lehrt erfahrungs- und traditionsbezogen, aspekthaft, memorierbezogen, nicht in logisch-rhetorischer Entwicklung einer These oder Theorie, sondern in der Formulierung eines ungemein umfangreichen Mosaiks einzelner kleinerer und größerer, bekannter, traditionaler und eigener neuer Gedankengänge. Der Kommentar von Patrik W. Skehan und Alexander A. Di Lella zeichnet die Materialien der Lehre Ben Siras und ihre Sprache und ihre Formen magistral nach.[4]

Diese Materialien stehen bei Ben Sira im Dienst einer kohärenten Sachkonzeption, die er in der jeweils passenden Sprachform des Hymnus, des Gebets, des Lehrgedichts usw. vorträgt. Aufgabe einer wissenschaftlichen Beschäftigung mit der Welt der Aussagen Ben Siras ist es, diese Sachkonzeption zu erheben, d.h. die *Strukturen seiner Aussagen* zu erkennen und nachzuzeichnen und darüber hinaus nach dem *Typus seiner Theologie* zu fragen. Denn dadurch werden seine Aussagen vergleichbar und einem allgemeinen Verstehen und einer sachlichen Auseinandersetzung zugeführt.

Dieser Aufgabe gilt mein Beitrag. Ich werde weder auf die Frage der weisheitlichen Tradition noch auf Fragen der Sprache und literarischen Formgebung eingehen, sondern nach den Aussagen und der daraus zu erhebenden Konzeption Ben Siras fragen. Ersteres betrifft die sprachliche Ebene

---

4   Vgl. Skehan – Di Lella, Wisdom.

der Propositionen, das zweite konstruiert die sog. Theologie Ben Siras, d.h. das Gesamtgefüge seiner Rede von Gott und dem Menschen. Diese verfremdende Darstellung leistet die Systematisierung seiner Einzelaussagen, um sie im gegenwärtigen Kontext verständlich zu machen. Die Suche nach einer "Theologie Ben Siras" ist daher eine hermeneutische und das heißt vermittelnde Aufgabe. Sie muss sich stets ihrer Abständigkeit vom Denken des Autors Ben Sira bewusst bleiben. Ben Sira selbst dachte so, wie er lehrte und schrieb. Eine "Theologie" Ben Siras rekonstruiert also nicht die Autorenintention, sondern überträgt Elemente der Autorenintention in gegenwärtige Verstehenshorizonte.[5]

Damit entfernt sich der vorliegende Beitrag von dem philologisch-historischen Verstehensmodell, dem die Sirach-Forschung mehrheitlich verpflichtet ist und deren Arbeit in dem großen Kommentar von Skehan – Di Lella einen vorläufigen Niederschlag gefunden hat. Der Beitrag verändert auch die Fragestellung meiner Monographie zu Ben Sira.[6] Dort geht es um die Kultur der Zeit Ben Siras. Die Religion in Gestalt der Gottesfurcht und der Weisheit werden in ihren kultur- und persönlichkeitsbildenden Aspekten dargestellt. Der vorliegende Beitrag dagegen fragt nach der Theologie Ben Siras, d.h. nach der Art und Weise, wie Ben Sira von Gott und von den Menschen redet und lehrt. Ben Siras Rede von Gott und von den Menschen wird *sachlich* beim Wort genommen und dargestellt, typologisch bestimmt und kritisch bedacht. Diese Art der Darstellung macht die Aussagenwelt Ben Siras lebendig und regt zu einer sachlich theologischen Auseinandersetzung über Ben Siras Theologie an, die zwischen jüdischen Theologen und christlichen Theologen unterschiedlicher Konfessionen geführt werden kann und muss. Andernfalls bleibt Ben Siras Theologie in die Grenzen historischen und kanonischen Verstehens jüdischer oder christlich-konfessioneller Prägung eingeschlossen.[7]

2. Ben Siras Theologie

2.1 Elemente der Theologie

Meine erste Frage lautet: Welche *Elemente einer kohärenten Rede von Gott* finden sich im Sirachbuch?[8]

---

5   Diesem Konzept ist die Theologie des Alten Testamentes von O. Kaiser verpflichtet: Kaiser, Gott I+II.
6   Wischmeyer, Kultur.
7   Vgl. dazu allgemein die Beiträge in Wischmeyer, Text. Hier entfalte ich das Programm einer textbezogenen Hermeneutik, die zur Sachauseinandersetzung führt. – Vgl. weiter den Beitrag von Becker, E.-M., Jesus Sirach Deutsch.
8   Explizite Theologie lehrt Ben Sira in folgenden Einzelgedichten:

Wir finden folgende thematische Elemente einer Theologie:
– *Gott als Schöpfer* und Gott des Weltalls, der Eine und Einzige, der sowohl den Kosmos als auch den Menschen erschafft und regiert
– *Gott als der Gott Israels*
– *Gott als der Gott des Rechtes*, dessen Gesetz die Lebensbedingungen für die Menschen garantiert
– *Gott als der Barmherzige*, den Menschen Zugewandte, damit aber auch als der Rächer *und der Zornige*
– *Gott als der persönliche Gott des Beters*, der Vater, Retter und Helfer.

Diese Elemente stammen aus unterschiedlichen Traditions-, Sach- und Geschichtszusammenhängen Israels, die für Ben Sira aber nicht mehr als unterschiedliche Elemente erkennbar waren.

2.2 Struktur der Theologie

Ich frage weiter nach der *Struktur*, die diesen Elementen unterliegt, d.h. nach dem Ordnungsmuster, die diese so heterogenen und ursprünglich selbstständigen Elemente kohärent macht. Sie ordnen sich für Ben Sira um die Mitte des Bekenntnisses: Er ist "der Gott des Alls" (33/36,1/1a) bzw. "Er ist alles" (43,27). Diese Rede von Gott hat die Struktur einer *holistischen* Rede, und es entsteht zunächst der Eindruck, neben dieser Rede gebe es keinen weiteren Platz für irgend etwas. Dieser Eindruck täuscht. Denn die holistische theologische Rede Ben Siras ist nicht exkludierend, sondern inkludierend. Das wird deutlich, wenn wir sie auf den kosmologischen Teil der Schöpfung beziehen. Kaum ein weisheitlicher Schriftsteller hat mehr über die Schöpfung in ihrer ganzen Breite geschrieben als Ben Sira. Dabei ist es nun wichtig, die Thematik und das Interesse Ben Siras bezüglich der Schöpfung im Einzelnen zu bestimmen.

- 15,11–20 (Gott und die Wurzel der Sünde)
- 16,4–14 (Gottes Erbarmen und Zorn)
- 16,17–18,14 (Gott als Schöpfer 16,17–23 und 24–30; Gott als Schöpfer der Menschen 17,1–16; Israel als Gottes Erstgeborener 17,17–24; persönliche Wendung 17,25–32; Vergleich Gott – Mensch 18,1–14)
- 23,1–6 (*Gebet* zu Gott als Gebieter und Herr des Lebens)
- 33/36,1–22/16 und 30/33,25/16b–27/19 (Die Ordnungsstruktur der Schöpfung Gottes)
- 32/35,1/1a–26 (Gott als Gott des Rechtes)
- 33/36,1/1a–36,27/22 (*Gebet* zu Gott als dem Einen, dem Herrn des Weltalls und dem Gott Israels)
- 39,12–35 (Die Güte der Schöpfung, darin 16–31 *Hymnus* auf die Werke Gottes)
- 42,15–43,33 (Lob der Schöpfung Gottes und Gottes selbst, *Hymnus*)
- 51,1–12 (Gott als Retter des Beters, *Danklied* des Einzelnen).

Seine Thematik ist eine doppelte, wie der große Abschnitt über die Schöpfung 42,15–43,33 zeigt (אל מעשי Werke Gottes). Neben dem klassischen Schöpfungslob, das in einem Hymnus Gottes Werke von der Sonne bis zu den "mächtigen Tieren der Urflut" (43,1–25) preist, steht die reflexive Lehre über die Struktur der Schöpfung. Ben Sira versteht diese Struktur als rationale Struktur: als Einsicht und Erkenntnis (42,18) und als Weisheit (42,21). Die Schöpfung hat also den doppelten Aspekt des Ästhetischen und des Rationalen (43,1). Der Weise antwortet auf diese Erscheinungsformen der Schöpfung entsprechend mit hymnischer Adoration und Reflexion, die sich zum Enthusiasmus und zum Schrecken steigern können (43,24f). Dieselbe Doppelstruktur unterliegt dem weisheitlichen Schöpfungsgedicht 39,12–35. Das Gedicht ist ein hymnischer Preis, der eine dialogisch-apologetische Reflexion auf die Güte und Bedeutung aller "Werke Gottes" enthält. Die These dieses Weisheitshymnus heißt: "Die Werke Gottes, sie alle sind gut" (39,33). Und dies Urteil ist nicht einfach Bestandteil hymnischen Lobs, sondern eine sorgfältig begründete These, eine Lehrmeinung Ben Siras, die er "sorgfältig bedacht" und zum Thema seines Buches gemacht hat (39,32). Die reiche, dichte und sinnvoll aufgebaute Welt des Kosmos und der Erde hat nicht nur *neben* Gott Platz, sondern ist *selbst* gerade Ausdruck des Weisheitsurteils: "Er ist alles" (43,27).

Diese holistische Rede von Gott bietet aber auch für den Menschen Platz, und zwar sowohl für den Menschen als Geschöpf Gottes als auch für Israel als Gottes "Erstgeborenen" (17,18) und schließlich auch für den Einzelnen, für die Person des betenden Weisen Ben Sira. Denn Gott hat sich in besonderer Weise mit Israel verbunden[9]: "Das Eigentum des Herrn ist Israel" (17,17). Israel ist Gottes Volk (36,17/11) und als solches Gottes Partner und sein Gegenüber. Die holistische Rede von Gott schließt also ein qualifiziertes und selbständiges und selbstverantwortliches Gegenüber Gottes in Gestalt des Volkes Israel nicht aus, sondern bedingt es geradezu. Dieser Beziehung wegen gehören auch Zorn und Erbarmen gleichermaßen zu der Rede von dem Gott des Alls (16,4–14). Denn dieser Gott ist dialogisch auf die Menschen bezogen und hat in Israel und in besonderem Maße in Israels Weisen sein Gegenüber, dem er in leidenschaftlicher Anteilnahme verbunden ist.

Dieser Gott als Gegenüber der Menschen und in besonderer Weise als Gegenüber Israels nimmt in der Form der Gesetzgebung am Leben Israels teil: als Gott des Rechts, der Recht setzt, garantiert, einfordert und durchsetzt (32/35,1/1a–26/24). Das Recht gehört zu ihm wie die rationale Struktur seiner Schöpfung. So ist auch der Raum Gottes – das All – als ein Raum der Klarheit, Ordnung und Gesetzhaftigkeit vorgestellt.

---

9 Vgl. dazu Wischmeyer, Kultur, 256f. Im "Nationalen Gebet" findet sich die Israel-Theologie in konzentrierter Form. Dabei ist die Perspektive universal-oikumenisch und kosmologisch (33/36,2/1b und 36,22/16.17).

Wie kann sich in dieser holistischen Rede nun ein Einzelner, ein Mensch artikulieren? Hat er gegenüber einem Gott dieser Dimensionen und gegenüber einem Israel, das vor Gott durch den Glanz seiner Väter und seiner Hohenpriester (Kapitel 44–45 und 50) vertreten war, einen Raum? Oder wird der Einzelne angesichts Gottes und Israels geradezu zur U-topie? In den Modi des Gebets (Kapitel 23 und 33/36 sowie 51) und der weisheitlich lehrhaften Untersuchung, die teilweise oder vollständig in der Gattung eines Hymnus auftreten kann (39,12–35 und 42,15–43,33), artikuliert sich der Einzelne vor Gott im Rahmen der Geschichte (44ff) und Gegenwart (50) Israels. Und in dieser Artikulation wird Gott der persönliche Gott des Beters, und dieser Gott des Beters und Weisheitslehrers lässt sich dann auch weitgehend aussagen und verstehen, wenngleich das Verdikt weisheitlicher Vorsicht gilt: "Wir wollen weiterhin jubeln, denn wir können ihn nicht erforschen" (43,28).[10]

Ich sagte, die holistische theologische Rede Ben Siras habe nicht eine exkludierende, sondern eine inkludierende Struktur. Das hat sich für alle genannten Aspekte der Rede von Gott zeigen lassen. Ben Siras Rede von Gott, so ungeheuer sie Gott selbst erhöht, bietet doch Platz nicht nur für die Schöpfung, auch nicht nur für Israel, sondern für den einzelnen frommen und weisen Mann in Israel, ohne das "Alles-Sein" Gottes zu beschädigen.

2.3 Typus der Theologie

Wir fragen weiter: Welchen *Typus von Theologie* vertritt das Sirachbuch? Erwägt man die einzelnen Aspekte der siracidischen Reden von Gott und die ihm unterliegende Struktur einer holistischen theologischen Rede, so wird man bei einer Definition doch ausgreifen müssen, auch wenn die Definition nicht historisch differenzieren, sondern typologisch klären soll. *Der Rahmen muss zweifellos als Schöpfungstheologie beschrieben werden. Diese Schöpfungstheologie ist aber zugleich nationale, d.h. Israel-bezogene Bundes- und Gesetzestheologie.*[11] *Das heißt: Der frühjüdische Bundesnomismus ist in den Rahmen einer weisheitlichen Schöpfungstheologie hineingestellt.* Die sachlich mögliche Spannung zwischen der universalen und holistischen theologischen Rede von dem Gott und Schöpfer des Alls und dem spezifischen Gott Israels ist Ben Sira nicht als solche bewusst. Er kann diese Spannung durch eine glückliche Metapher wie die von Israel als Gottes Erstgeborenem auflösen oder aber in der sicheren Erkenntnis, der Gott Israels sei eben der Schöpfer des Alls, beide Aspekte erklärungslos nebeneinanderstellen, so wie er das Lob der Schöpfung, der Werke Gottes, und der Väter der Vorzeit ohne Ver-

---

10 Vgl. die verschiedenen Passagen der Vorsicht im Denken, bes. 3,17ff. Allg. Wischmeyer, Kultur, 283f.
11 Zum Bund vgl. bes. 44,12.18; zum Gesetz bes. Kap. 45. Eine klassische Formulierung des Bundesnomismus: 17,12.

knüpfung aufeinander folgen lässt. Den möglichen Brückenschlag durch Adam übergeht er[12].

Die holistische Rede von Gott erweist sich in typologischer Hinsicht also als integratives Modell. Die weisheitliche Schöpfungstheologie Ben Siras ist durch ihre internationalen Quellen und Traditionen geprägt, nimmt aber zugleich die Theologie des entstehenden frühjüdischen Bundesnomismus in sich auf. Diese Rede hat eine inhaltliche und eine kompositorische Seite: *Inhaltlich* redet Ben Sira von Gott als von dem, der "alles ist". Und zugleich bindet er *kompositorisch* entscheidende theologische Traditionen der überkommenen theologischen Rede Israels zusammen:

a. die Rede von Gottes Bundesschlüssen mit den Menschen und mit Israel[13] und von Israels Vätern als Fundamenten der Gottesbünde (44,12)

b. die Rede von Gottes Gesetz für sein Volk[14]

c. die Rede von Gottes Schöpfung und Gott als dem Schöpfer des Alls.

3. Ben Siras Anthropologie

3.1 Aspekte der Anthropologie

An diesem Punkt erinnere ich an die Aporie, von der ich am Anfang gesprochen habe: an die Aporie zwischen dem ins Unermessliche erhöhten Gott und dem sterblichen Menschen. Die Analyse der Aspekte der siracidischen Theologie hat bereits ergeben, dass in der holistischen Rede Sirachs von Gott nicht nur für die Schöpfung und für Israel, sondern auch für den einzelnen Menschen durchaus Platz ist. Damit ist aber auch von vornherein deutlich, dass Anthropologie bei Ben Sira im Rahmen und *nur* im Rahmen der holistischen Gottesrede stattfindet. Sie kann sich thematisch bzw. sachlich nicht verselbständigen.

Wie sieht nun diese Rede Ben Siras vom Menschen aus? Danach ist jetzt zu fragen. Ich gehe hier weder auf die sozialen, staatlichen und rechtlichen

---

12   Adam begegnet in 49,16.
13   – Der Bund mit Noah 44,17f
      – Der Bund mit Abraham 44,19ff
      – Das Weiterbestehen der Bünde bei Isaak 44,22
      – Der Bund mit Aaron 45,15ff
      – Der Bund mit Pinchas 45,23ff
      – Der Bund mit David 45,25.
14   45,1–5
      – Das Gesetz an Mose 45,1–5
      – Das Gesetz an Aaron 45,17.

"Rahmenbedingungen der Kultur" ein,[15] wie sie das Sirachbuch zeichnet, noch auf die einzelnen "Aspekte der Kultur Sirachs,"[16] die den Menschen als ein soziales, kultivierendes und kultiviertes Wesen verstehen, sondern frage nach der Rede vom Menschen selbst.

Auch die *Rede Ben Siras vom Menschen* setzt sich aus sehr heterogenen *Aspekten* zusammen, die eine ähnliche Spannweite wie seine Rede von Gott aufweisen.

Das große Lehrgedicht über den Menschen als Geschöpf (16,24–18,14), das nach einer Einschaltung über Israel (17,17–24) in 17,25–32 mit einem "profetic call to repentance" fortgesetzt wird,[17] ist durch seine doppelte Perspektive besonders interessant und charakteristisch für Ben Siras Anthropologie. Die Gottebenbildlichkeit des Menschen nach Genesis 1 wird in Sir 17,3 ganz ernst genommen und in drei Schritten entfaltet:

a. in der Herrschaft über die Geschöpfe (17,4)
b. in der Darstellung der menschlichen Sinne und der Einsicht als besonderer Fähigkeit (17,5 und 6 parallel und 17,7 mit nochmaliger Betonung der moralischen Kompetenz des menschlichen Verstandes)
c. in der Hinordnung des Menschen auf Gott (17,8f).

Bei diesem dritten Punkt ist besondere Aufmerksamkeit nötig. Wie wird die Hinordnung verstanden, wie weit reicht sie, und was soll sie leisten?

Die Hinordnung des Menschen auf Gott besteht in Gottesfurcht, im Rühmen der Werke Gottes und in der nach-denkenden Erforschung dieser Werke. Es handelt sich also um Wahrnehmen und Verstehen Gottes des Schöpfers und seiner Schöpfung und um das antwortende Lob des Menschen. Der Mensch ist ganz von seiner Geschöpflichkeit her dargestellt und bezieht allein daraus seine Würde (17,2f) und die Aufgabe des Gotteslobs (17,8–10). Zu dieser Geschöpflichkeit, die ihre Würde und Aufgabe von Gott erhält, gehört nun auch der Rahmen des Weisheitsgedichtes von Kap. 17. 17,1 lautet: "Der Herr erschuf aus Erde den Menschen, und er lässt ihn wiederum zur Erde zurückkehren". Und 17,32 endet damit, dass Gott alle Menschen betrachtet, "die Staub und Asche sind". Sowohl 17,27ff wie 18,9f weisen auf die Sterblichkeit des Menschen hin. Das weisheitliche Lehrgedicht über die Mühsal des Menschen 40,1–10 präzisiert und verengt die anthropologische Perspektive ins Psychologische. Denn die im Alten Orient bekannte Rede von der Mühsal des Menschen, die von Melancholie und Pessimismus zeugt,[18] wird hier in jeder Hinsicht ins Psychologische gewendet. Das Leben

---

15 Vgl. dazu Wischmeyer, Kultur, 26ff.
16 Vgl. ebd. 83ff.
17 Skehan – Di Lella, Weisheit, 284.
18 Skehan – Di Lella, Wisdom, 469.

des Menschen ist von psychischer Unrast und von Angst gekennzeichnet.[19]
Erst danach werden in 40,9 auch äußere Unglücksfälle in der Form eines Pla-
genkatalogs aufgelistet. Die weiterführenden Überlegungen Ben Siras dienen
dann der rational-funktionalen Bearbeitung des "Bösen" (40,10ff). Sie ändern
aber nichts an der pessimistischen Rede vom Schicksal des Menschen. Auch
die beiden kontrastiv gearbeiteten Strophen über den Tod des zufriedenen
und des hoffnungslosen Menschen 41,1 und 41,2 gehen in dieselbe Richtung.
Auch und gerade den erfolgreichen und zufriedenen Menschen trifft das To-
desschicksal.

3.2 Struktur der Anthropologie

Finden wir nun auch eine ordnende *Struktur*, die der siracidischen Anthropologie unterliegt? Kommt Ben Sira zu einer kohärenten Anthropologie, oder
müssen wir uns auf eine traditionsgeschichtliche Analyse der Aspekte einer
Anthropologie vor dem Hintergrund der Breite und Ambivalenz alttestamentlicher Rede vom Menschen beschränken?[20]
      Wenn die Rede vom Menschen bei Ben Sira ganz und gar im Ruhm der
Rede von Gott verankert ist, so dass der Mensch ausschließlich von Gott her
beschrieben wird, nämlich als Geschöpf Gottes analog zum Kosmos, der als
Werk Gottes verstanden ist, dann leitet sich die Rede vom Menschen von der
holistischen Rede von Gott her und lässt sich als eine *referentielle Rede* vom
Menschen beschreiben. Der Mensch ist das Wesen, das von Gott geschaffen
ist, von ihm abhängt und sich zugleich bewusst auf Gott zurückbezieht. Der
Mensch ist nicht Partner Gottes. Er steht nicht im gleichberechtigten und
selbständigen Dialog mit Gott. Seine Würde liegt vielmehr im *intellektuell-
kontemplativen* und im *responsorischen Verhalten* auf Gott hin.
      Der Prototyp eines solchen Menschen ist nun der Weise in Israel. Denn
das intellektuell-kontemplative und responsorische Verhalten auf Gott hin
kann nur den allerwenigsten Menschen gelingen. Für "die Völker" (גּוֹיִם), d.h.
für die Heidenwelt, gilt, dass sie (noch) keine Gotteserkenntnis haben
(33/36,5/4). Ben Sira hofft dies für die Zukunft (36,22/16.17). Für seine
gegenwärtige Rede vom Menschen gilt aber noch, dass nur Israel Gott erkennt (36,17/11). In Israel aber sind es die *weisheitlichen Gesetzeslehrer und
ihre Schüler*, die den Herrn erforschen, der sie erschaffen hat (39,5). Und allein die Gesetzeslehrer werden "in Ewigkeit nicht vergessen werden" (39,9).
Auch die "Väter der Vorzeit" in den Kapiteln 44ff werden nach dem Verstehensmodell der Weisen beschrieben (44,4). Abschließend wird der Hohepriester Simon in diesen Zusammenhang gestellt.

---

19   Wischmeyer, Kultur, 201ff, bes. 221f.
20   Hierzu bes. Kaiser, Mensch, 1–22. Zum Stichwort Ambivalenz 3ff.

Von hierher erklärt sich die Bedeutung, die Ben Sira seiner eigenen Lehre und der Tätigkeit in seinem Lehrhaus (51,23) beimisst. Die weisheitliche Lehre der Gottesfurcht in all ihren thematischen Konkretionen und Nuancen ermöglicht es dem frommen und gebildeten Israeliten, bis zu seinem Tode richtig zu leben (1,12–20) und ewigen Nachruhm zu haben.

Bei Ben Siras Rede vom Menschen zeigt sich also eine extreme *Verengung* von der allgemeinen Anthropologie der Geschöpflichkeit hin zu einer speziellen Anthropologie des natürlich männlichen Weisen in Israel als des Menschen, der sich seinem Geschöpfsein gemäß verhält: nämlich bewusst intellektuell und kontemplativ in Relation zu Gott lebt und sich nicht autonom, sondern referentiell versteht. Wir haben also das Phänomen einer *Gruppen-Anthropologie*. Diese geteilte Anthropologie hat ihren Grund in der Abhängigkeit der Anthropologie von der holistischen Rede von Gott. Der Mensch wird ausschließlich als Gottes Geschöpf verstanden, weil er es nach Ben Siras Verständnis *ist*. Und er kann nur im reflexiven und referentiellen Nachvollzug seiner Geschöpflichkeit richtig als Mensch leben. Der Mensch kann sich weder aus dieser Geschöpflichkeit befreien oder auch nur von ihr distanzieren, noch kann er seine Würde in etwas anderem als der Betrachtung dieser Geschöpflichkeit finden. Denn seine Würde liegt eben ausschließlich in dieser Geschöpflichkeit *und* in der Fähigkeit des Menschen, diesen Umstand zu reflektieren und Gott dafür zu danken. Dies aber ist nur einem kleinen Kreis von Israeliten möglich. Für die Menge der Israeliten, für die Handwerker und Bauern in Israel, ist es unmöglich, an der Weisheit teilzuhaben (38,25). Damit können sie nicht wirklich als Menschen im Sinne der weisheitlichen Anthropologie leben. Ben Sira geht diesem Problem nicht weiter nach, weil er dafür keine Lösung hat. Vielmehr entwirft er konsequent seine Weisheits-Anthropologie, die nicht nur religionsspezifisch, sondern auch geschlechtsspezifisch und gruppenspezifisch definiert ist.

3.3 Typen der Anthropologie

Fragen wir auch hier wieder typologisch, also nach dem *Typus der Anthropologie* Ben Siras, so gilt dasselbe wie für die Theologie. Auch hier muss ein Rahmen spezifisch gefüllt werden. Der Rahmen ist die Geschöpflichkeit des Menschen. Es handelt sich um eine *theologisch begründete heteronom-referentielle Anthropologie*. Ihr Horizont ist und bleibt derjenige der Geschöpflichkeit, und d.h. der Rahmen der Perspektivenlosigkeit. Es gibt für den Menschen weder Autonomie im irdischen Leben noch eine Hoffnungsperspektive für ein zukünftiges Leben.

An diesem Punkt, der in drei Richtungen, nämlich in Melancholie, in sündige Autonomie oder in unwissendes Dahin-Leben führen könnte, nimmt die spezielle weisheitliche Anthropologie Ben Siras Stellung. Sie bezieht die

Position einer religiös-pädagogisch gefärbten *exklusiven Elite-Anthropologie*, die allein imstande ist, ein sinnvolles Leben im Rahmen der heteronomen Anthropologie zu führen. Dabei nimmt Ben Sira in Kauf, dass er nicht für die Mehrheit Israels, geschweige denn für die Menschheit als Ganze denken und lehren kann.

4. Das Verhältnis zwischen Theologie und Anthropologie

4.1 Verhältnisbestimmung

Bis hierher ist der enge Zusammenhang zwischen Anthropologie und Theologie deutlich geworden. Dies *Verhältnis* gilt es jetzt genauer zu bestimmen. *Die Rede vom Menschen als Gottes Geschöpf ist eine Teilrede im Rahmen der holistischen Rede von Gott* als dem Schöpfer, der zugleich der Gott Israels, der Gott des Rechtes, der Gott der Zuwendung zu den Menschen und schließlich der persönliche Gott des einzelnen Beters und Weisheitslehrers ist.

Daher gibt die Rede von Gott der Rede vom Menschen ihre Struktur vor. Gott wird als die umfassende Größe verstanden, deren Gestaltungskraft herrschaftlichen, schöpferischen, intellektuellen, ethisch-normativen und emotionalen Charakter trägt und damit "alles" umfasst, was Ben Sira denken kann: Gott ist der Weltherrscher, der Schöpfer, der Geber der Weisheit und des Gesetzes und der Vater und Helfer. Der Mensch wird dementsprechend lediglich auf seine responsorischen Fähigkeiten, nämlich auf seine intellektuellen und ethischen Kräfte hin angesprochen, mit denen er Gott antworten soll. Das Selbstverständnis des Weisen als des prototypischen Menschen entspricht Gott bezüglich des Intellektes und des Ethos und der Umsetzung dieser formativen Größen in der Lebensführung.

Gottes Überschuss gegenüber dem Menschen ist und bleibt aber ungeheuer: Die gesamten produktiven Schöpfer- und Erhalterkräfte Gottes und seine raumzeitlichen Herrscherfunktionen stehen dem Menschen nicht zur Verfügung.

Der Überschuss der Kräfte Gottes gegenüber dem Menschen lässt sich von daher nun vertieft folgendermaßen beschreiben: Gott ist weder von der Sünde noch vom Tod betroffen. Denn er setzt das Recht und er ist und gibt das Leben. Dem Menschen dagegen stehen ebendiese beiden Größen als grundsätzliche und bleibende Bedrohungen gegenüber: die Sünde und der Tod, d.h. die Eigenverantwortung des Menschen, der er nur mit größter Mühe nachkommen kann, und sein Ende, das unausweichlich ist. Bedenkt man dies, wird man aus dem Vergleich zwischen Theologie und Anthropologie Ben Siras ein weiteres Moment einer anthropologischen Typologie gewinnen: das

Differenzmoment. Gott ist der Gott des Lebens, der Mensch aber "kehrt wiederum zur Erde zurück" (17,1). Kapitel 18 macht diese Differenz unnachgiebig deutlich: Bei Gott dem Schöpfer sind ewiges Leben und ausschließliche Gerechtigkeit (18,1f), da er ja beides setzt. Der Mensch dagegen ist sterblich, mag er auch hundert Jahre alt werden (9f).

Die holistische Rede von Gott und die referentielle Rede vom Menschen sind auf der einen Seite *so* miteinander verbunden, dass Ben Siras Rede vom Menschen ein Teil seiner Rede von Gott ist und sich von ihr herleitet. Andererseits sind beide Bereiche doch tief voneinander getrennt.

Die Aporie, von der ich ausgegangen bin, hat sich durch die Analyse nachweisen lassen. Und es ist auch deutlich, dass Ben Sira selbst sie kennt. Denn die Rede der hellenistischen Juden in 16,17ff hat ja sachlich bzw. empirisch alles für sich: Hier wird ein Programm formuliert, das das Leben unter der Maßgabe der zukünftigen Hoffnungslosigkeit freigibt. 16,17ff entwirft eine *autonome* Genuss- und Gewaltanthropologie im Vorstellungsrahmen hellenistischen Oberschichtenverhaltens. Was kann Ben Sira dagegensetzen? Seine eigene Anthropologie bezeugt doch ebenfalls die Perspektivenlosigkeit menschlichen Lebens.

4.2 These

Hier ist nun der Punkt, um meine These zu verdeutlichen:

Ben Sira versucht, mit der ihm *bewussten* Aporie von der Sterblichkeit und der damit gegebenen Endlichkeit des Menschen nicht obsessiv, sondern produktiv umzugehen. Der *Tod* ist für ihn das unlösbare Problem und eine furchtbare Wirklichkeit:

"Im Tod wird erben der Mensch Verwesung und Würmer,
Geschmeiß und Maden" (10,11).

Der bleibenden *Lebenswirklichkeit* des ewigen Gottes kann sich der Mensch nicht nähern. Hinsichtlich des Todes bleibt also die Differenz zwischen Gott und Mensch bestehen. Anders aber ist es mit der *Sünde*. Hier hat der Mensch Möglichkeiten und Perspektiven, sein Leben auch über die Grenze der Differenz zu Gott hinaus zu gestalten. Hier eröffnet sich ihm plötzlich Selbstbestimmung und damit eine Freiheit, die sich auf keinem anderen Gebiet zeigt: die Freiheit, Gottes Gesetz zu entsprechen und an *diesem* Punkt mit dem Gott, der das *Recht* setzt, in Verbindung zu treten. Kapitel 17 ist diesem Gedanken gewidmet:

"Er legte ihnen Erkenntnis vor,
und das *Gesetz des Lebens* ließ er sie erben" (17,11).

Was heißt dies "Gesetz des Lebens" (νόμος ζωῆς)? Es ist nicht ein Gesetz ewigen Lebens, sondern jenes Gesetz, das es dem Menschen ermöglicht, "sich vom Unrecht zu enthalten" (17,14). Den Tod kann der Mensch nicht überwinden, aber von Sünde und Ungerechtigkeit kann der Mensch ablassen (17,25ff), und *darin* kann er Gott nahe sein und zunächst partiell die Grenze, die durch die Differenz gegenüber Gott gesetzt ist, überwinden. Das bedeutet für die Anthropologie Ben Siras: Durch die Befolgung des Gesetzes als des ewigen Rechtes, das Gott für Israel setzt, kann der Mensch Gott nahe kommen. Hier liegen seine Würde und seine Selbstbestimmung. Und all dies gilt offensichtlich trotz der Kautele in 18,2: κύριος μόνος δικαιωθήσεται.

4.3 Schlusstypologie

Noch einmal werde ich eine Typologie versuchen, um abschließend zu beschreiben, wie Ben Sira mit der Aporie der Endlichkeit des Menschen umgeht. Er *verdrängt* die Endlichkeit *nicht*, sondern spricht sie in den Formen des realistischen Pessimismus aus, die ihn mit der altorientalischen und israelitischen Weisheit verbinden. Hier bleibt nichts unklar, kein Schatten einer falschen Hoffnung, kein Schatten einer prätendierten Gottesnähe. *Ebenso wenig* interpretiert er die Wirklichkeit *kontrafaktisch* um und erweckt den Anschein, das Gesetz des Todes sei ihm gleichgültig und berühre ihn als Weisen in Israel nicht.

Er tut aber etwas anderes. Da er keine Perspektive über die physische Lebensspanne des Menschen hinaus sieht, misst er diesem Leben eine ungeheure Bedeutung bei, und zwar als einem ethisch gelebten Leben. Denn in dieser Lebensführung nach dem Gesetz kann der Israelit jene Nähe zu Gott, dem Gesetzgeber, erlangen, die ihm in Bezug auf sein künftiges Schicksal verwehrt ist. Während der Spanne ihres Lebens können die israelitischen Weisheitslehrer und ihre Schüler – und strenggenommen nur sie und die Priester[21] – die Differenz gegenüber Gott durch Gesetzestreue und Weisheitslehre überwinden. Diese Überzeugung unterscheidet Ben Sira fundamental von dem Christ gewordenen Juden Paulus. Paulus bestreitet gerade die siracidische Unterscheidung zwischen Sünde und Tod. Er versteht Sünde und Tod als gleichwertige Mächte, die zusammen gehören und keinem Menschen gestatten, gerecht zu sein.

Ben Sira entwirft also als analoge und adäquate Antwort auf die *holistische Gottesrede* eine *panethische Anthropologie* – beide Reden unter der Maßgabe, dass Gott der Schöpfer und der Herr Israels sei.

---

21   Vgl. Kap. 50. – Vgl. weiter einerseits Wischmeyer, Kultur, 259–65, andererseits den kritischen Beitrag von F.V. Reiterer in dem vorliegenden Band.

Und von hierher erklärt sich schließlich die hohe Bedeutung der *Weisheit* bei Ben Sira. Denn die Weisheit, verstanden als Lernen des Gesetzes und Anwendung des Gesetzes auf die Lebensführung, als Gottesfurcht und Zucht,[22] ermöglicht dem gebildeten Israeliten, sein Leben im Sinne dieser panethischen Anthropologie zu leben und damit genau jene Würde zu erlangen, die Gott dem Menschen gewährt. Die *Arbeit an dieser Weisheit* macht die Dynamik des menschlichen Lebens aus, die *Mühe des Weisen* ist der Motor, der sein Leben lebendig und nützlich und würdevoll macht, bis es mit dem Tod und damit der unendlichen Entfernung von Gott endet.

Bibliographie

Becker, E.-M., "Jesus Sirach Deutsch. Über die Chancen und Schwierigkeiten einer modernen deutschen Übersetzung," *Deutsches Pfarrerblatt* 102 (2002) 18–20.

Kaiser, O., "Carpe diem und Memento mori bei Ben Sira," in *Dubsar anta-men. Studien zur Altorientalistik* (FS W.H.Ph. Römer; eds. M. Dietrich and O. Loretz; AOAT 253; Münster: Ugarit-Verlag, 1998) 185–203.

Kaiser, O., *Der Gott des Alten Testament* (2 vols.; Göttingen: Vandenhoeck & Ruprecht, 1993, 1998).

Kaiser, O., "Der Mensch als Geschöpf Gottes – Aspekte der Anthropologie Ben Siras," in *Der Einzelne und seine Gemeinschaft bei Ben Sira* (eds. R. Egger-Wenzel and I. Krammer; BZAW 270; Berlin / New York: de Gruyter, 1998) 1–22.

Kaiser, O., "Der Tod als Schicksal und Aufgabe bei Ben Sira," in *Engel und Dämonen. Theologische, anthropologische und religionsgeschichtliche Aspekte des Guten und Bösen. Akten des gemeinsamen Symposiums der Theologischen Fakultät der Universität Tartu und der Deutschen Religionsgeschichtlichen Studiengesellschaft am 7. und 8. April 1995 zu Tartu* (ed. G. Ahn; Forschungen zur Anthropologie und Religionsgeschichte 29; Münster: Ugarit-Verlag, 1997) 85–89.

Kaiser, O., "Das Verständnis des Todes bei Ben Sira," *Neue Zeitschrift für Systematische Theologie* 43 (2001) 175–92.

Prato, G.L., *Il problema della teodicea in Ben Sira: Composizione dei contrari e richiamo alle origini* (AnBib 65; Rome: Pontifical Biblical Institute, 1975).

Reitemeyer, M., *Weisheitslehre als Gottes Lob. Psalmentheologie im Buch Jesus Sirach* (BBB 127; Berlin: Philo, 2000).

Reiterer, F.V., "Deutung und Wertung des Todes durch Ben Sira," in *Die alttestamentliche Botschaft als Wegweisung* (FS H. Reinelt; ed. J. Zmijewski; Stuttgart: Katholisches Bibelwerk, 1990) 203–36.

Sauer, G., *Jesus Sirach (Ben Sira)* (JSHRZ III/5; Gütersloh: Mohn, 1981).

Schrader, L., *Leiden und Gerechtigkeit: Studien zu Theologie und Textgeschichte des Sirachbuches* (BBET 27; Frankfurt a.M.: Lang, 1994).

Skehan, P.W. – Di Lella, A.A., *The Wisdom of Ben Sira: A New Translation with Notes, Introduction and Commentary* (AB 39; New York: Doubleday, 1987).

Wicke-Reuter, U., *Göttliche Providenz und menschliche Verantwortung bei Ben Sira und in der Frühen Stoa* (BZAW 298; Berlin / New York: de Gruyter, 2000).

---

22   Zu der protestantischen Rezeptionsgeschichte dieses Aspektes des Sirachbuches vgl. den Beitrag von E.-M. Becker in diesem Band.

Wischmeyer, O., *Die Kultur des Buches Jesus Sirach* (BZNW 77; Berlin / New York: de Gruyter, 1995).

Wischmeyer, O. – Becker, E.M. (eds.), *Was ist ein Text?* (Neutestamentliche Entwürfe zur Theologie 1; Tübingen et al.: Francke, 2001).

Ziegler, J., *Sapientia Iesu Filii Sirach* (Septuaginta. Vetus Testamentum Graecum Auctoritate Academiae Scientiarum Gottingensis editum, XII/2; 2d ed; Göttingen: Vandenhoeck & Ruprecht, 1980).

God as Merciful Father in Ben Sira and the New Testament

Jeremy Corley
Ushaw College, Durham

1. Introduction

One of the most moving and memorable of Jesus' parables is the story of the Prodigal Son (Luke 15:11–32) – perhaps better named the Merciful Father. In this tale, the father does not apply the rigorous punishment for a wayward son, as stipulated in Deut 21:18–21. Instead the father is full of compassion (Luke 15:20) as he welcomes back his long-lost son. The scene is vividly captured in Rembrandt's late painting of *The Return of the Prodigal Son*, kept at the Hermitage museum in St. Petersburg. In the gospel context (see Luke 15:7, 10), this parable illustrates the joy in heaven over one repentant sinner. Indeed, the parable could serve as a fitting reflection on Jesus' saying in Luke 6:36: "Be merciful, just as your Father is merciful."[1] This short article will compare the New Testament understanding of God as a merciful Father with Ben Sira's portrayal of God.

2. A Merciful God

In speaking of God as "merciful," Luke 6:36 restates a common biblical motif. In Jewish tradition, this term ultimately reflects the portrayal of God in the divine revelation to Moses, where YHWH is called "merciful and gracious" (Exod 34:6). The Hebrew Bible repeatedly uses this phrase or a variant to describe God.[2] For Ben Sira too, God is full of mercy; for instance, Sir 2:11 Gk. echoes Exod 34:6 in its declaration: "The Lord is merciful and gra-

---

1   Biblical quotations in this article are from the New Revised Standard Version (NRSV). This brief article will consider cases where God is compared to a father as well as instances where God is called Father. For a more extensive treatment of the topic see Strotmann, Vater.

2   The phrase of Exod 34:6 is echoed in Ps 86:15; 103:8. The later variant "gracious and merciful" is also used to describe God in 2 Chr 30:9; Neh 9:17, 31; Ps 111:4; 145:8; Joel 2:13; Jonah 4:2; cf. 1QH 18:14 (= 10:14). The later phrase is applied to a human being in Ps 112:4.

cious" (my translation).[3] Elsewhere the adjectival noun "Merciful One" is used of God in Sir 50:19 H^B; the high priest's role as representative of the people would indicate that his prayer would be for God's mercy on Israel (compare Sir 36:17–18/11–12).[4]

3. God as Father

Luke 6:36 envisages God as "your Father." Elsewhere in prayer Jesus calls God "Abba" (Mark 14:36), a term that entered into the early church's prayer (Gal 4:6; Rom 8:15). Most famously, the Lucan form of the Lord's Prayer begins "Father" (Luke 11:2), while the more liturgical Matthean form opens with the phrase "Our Father in heaven" (Matt 6:9).[5] In his well-known dictum, Joachim Jeremias overstated the matter when he claimed that "my Father" was a form of personal address to God unattested in Palestinian Judaism before the time of Jesus.[6] Admittedly, this form of address to God is not the most common in Second Temple Judaism. Nevertheless, the Hebrew Bible does sometimes employ the term Father for God, and there are some examples (including in Ben Sira) both in Palestinian Judaism and in Alexandrian Judaism.

Among the various ways that the Hebrew Scriptures depict God as Father, the most widespread is as Father of the people of Israel (Deut 32:6; Jer 31:9; Mal 1:6), for "Israel is my firstborn son" (Exod 4:22; compare Deut 1:31; Hos 11:1; 4Q504.1–2 iii 5–7). Hence Jer 3:19 expresses God's hope of recognition from his people: "I thought you would call me, My Father." Some national prayers emphasize God's paternal mercy. Thus, God is acknowledged as the people's merciful Father in Ps 103:13: "As a father has compassion for his children, so the LORD has compassion for those who fear him." Similarly, Isa 63:15–16 uses parental imagery in its appeal to God: "Where are your zeal and your might? The yearning of your heart and your compassion? They are withheld from me. For you are our father."[7] God's fatherhood of the Israelites also involves discipline as well as kindness: "When they were tried, ... they were being disciplined in mercy ... For you tested them as a parent [= father] does in warning" (Wis 11:9–10). The canticle of Tobit combines the thought of God's fatherly mercy and his paternal disci-

---

3   See the article by P.C. Beentjes elsewhere in this volume. On God's mercy in the Bible, see Davies, Theology, 240–53.
4   See Hayward, Jewish Temple, 60.
5   On this prayer see Wright, Lord's Prayer, 132–54.
6   Jeremias, Prayers, 29; idem, Theology, 64.
7   The Targum of Isa 63:16 turns the prophet's metaphor into a simile: "Thou art he whose compassions towards us are more than those of a father towards his children"; see McNamara, Targum, 115.

pline towards the Israelites: "He is our Father and he is God forever. He will afflict you for your iniquities, but he will again show mercy on all of you" (Tob 13:4–5).[8]

The Hebrew Bible also depicts God as Father of those in need. The clearest illustration is the naming of God as "Father of orphans and protector of widows" in Ps 68:6(5). Ben Sira echoes this text when he encourages his students to imitate God: "Be like a father to orphans, and in place of a husband to widows, and God will call you son" (my translation of Sir 4:10 H^A).[9] Since God is Father of the needy, the righteous sufferer in Wisdom 2 can be regarded as God's child: "He calls himself a child [or: servant] of the Lord" (Wis 2:13). Because he "boasts that God is his father" (Wis 2:16), such a person suffers persecution: "If the righteous man is God's child [= son], he will help him" (Wis 2:18).

In his time of need, Ben Sira borrows language from the royal son of God to invoke God as Father. Whereas another biblical usage of the father image restricts it to the king, who is called God's son (2 Sam 7:14; Ps 2:7), Ben Sira applies this notion to his own prayer. Thus, while Ps 89:27(26) recounts the divine promise to the Davidic ruler: "He shall cry to me, 'You are my Father, my God, and the Rock of my salvation!' ", the non-royal Ben Sira echoes this phrase in his declarative psalm of praise (Sir 51:1–12). According to 51:10 H^B the author prays: "And I extolled the LORD, 'You are my Father, for you are my mighty salvation!' "[10] The grandson's Greek version of 51:10 has: "I invoked the Lord, the Father of my lord," while the Syriac has: "And I called to my Father from on high, the Lord, mighty Saviour." Despite the textual problem here, the Hebrew text and early versions agree in testifying to Ben Sira's use of the title Father for God. Since the context mentions God's mercies (Sir 51:8 H^B), the sage regards God as a merciful Father.

The seeker for wisdom can also be regarded as a child of God, who is thus viewed as a disciplining parent. The student is urged not to despise the divine correction: "The LORD reproves the one he loves, as a father the son in whom he delights" (Prov 3:11–12; cf. Heb 12:5–10). Ben Sira employs parental language when he depicts God's compassionate dealings with the human race, including rebukes (Sir 18:13–14 Gk.). According to 18:13, the di-

---

8   This translation (NRSV) from the Greek follows Sinaiticus; Vaticanus is generally rather similar. Unfortunately, the relevant Qumran Tobit manuscripts in Aramaic (4Q196) and Hebrew (4Q200) have gaps where the title "Father" would be.

9   On Sir 4:10 see Beentjes, Waisen, 51–64, esp. 60–62. Note that Sir 4:10d Gk. (but not H^A) uses maternal imagery of God: "He will love you more than does your mother "

10   The renderings of Sir 51:10 are mine. On the poetic context see Di Lella, Sirach 51:1–12, 395–407. Note that in H^B (different in Gk. and Syr.) Sir 51:1b is ambiguous: "I give you thanks, God of my father" (cf. Exod 15:2) or "I give you thanks, my God, my Father" (cf. Sir 51:10).

vine compassion exceeds human mercy: "The compassion of human beings is for their neighbours, but the compassion of the Lord is for every living thing." Ben Sira makes use of parental or educational imagery in the following phrase: "He rebukes and trains and teaches them" (18:13c). The next verse highlights the divine teaching role in parental language: "He has compassion on those who accept his discipline, and who are eager for his precepts" (18:14).

Such an understanding may lie behind Ben Sira's prayer in Sir 22:27–23:6. In this personal prayer for self-discipline, it seems that Ben Sira also twice addresses God as Father, but in the absence of the original Hebrew the textual evidence of the early versions is divergent. In praying for discipline of the tongue, the sage invokes God: "O Lord, Father and Master of my life" (Sir 23:1 Gk.), while a comparable invocation occurs in his prayer for discipline of the passions: "O Lord, Father and God of my life" (Sir 23:4 Gk.). In both cases the Syriac reads: "O God, my Father and Lord of my life" (my translation), but it is possible that the lost original Hebrew had: "O God of my father and Lord of my life" (compare Exod 15:2).[11] An appeal for God's fatherly mercy has recently been noted in a Qumran text known as the Apocryphon (or Psalm) of Joseph (4Q372). The text includes a prayer: "My father and my God, do not abandon me in the hands of gentiles ... Your tenderness is great and great is your compassion for all who seek you" (4Q372.1.16–19).[12]

God's help is sometimes described as exceeding a parent's role in reliability (Ps 27:10; Isa 49:15). The Qumran Thanksgiving Hymns (*Hodayot*) use parental imagery for God. Developing the thought of Ps 27:10 and Isa 49:15, 1QH 17:35–36 (= 9:35–36) sees God as a compassionate Father and Mother: "My mother did not know me, and my father abandoned me to you. Because you are father to all the sons of your truth. In them you rejoice, like one full of gentleness for her child."[13] The context speaks of God's mercy: "With my steps there is bountiful forgiveness and great compassion when you judge me" (1QH 17:33–34 = 9:33–34).

The Jews were not unique in regarding God as Father, since the title is applied to other ancient Near Eastern deities. For instance, a seventh-century B.C. text from Nineveh, the *Hymn to the Moon-God*, employs the title for the lunar deity (Sin in Akkadian and Nanna in Sumerian): "Begetter, merciful in his disposing, who holds in his hand the life of the whole land ... Father begetter, who looks favorably upon all living creatures."[14] Another similar sev-

---

11   See Jeremias, Prayers, 29.
12   García Martínez, Dead Sea Scrolls, 225. See further Schuller, 4Q372 1, 349–76; idem, Psalm of 4Q372 1, 67–79.
13   This quotation and the next one come from García Martínez, Dead Sea Scrolls, 350.
14   Pritchard, Ancient Near Eastern Texts, 385–86. The following quotation from the *Prayer to Every God* is from p. 392. An Egyptian *Hymn to Amon-Re* calls him "Lord of

enth-century B.C. Assyrian text, the *Prayer to Every God*, employs parental imagery when it requests the unknown deity to stop being angry with the supplicant: "May thy heart, like the heart of a real mother, be quieted toward me; like a real mother (and) a real father may it be quieted toward me." Thus, the notion of the deity as a merciful parent is present in ancient Near Eastern texts in Mesopotamia as well as in Israel.

The title of God as Father also occurs in texts from Alexandrian Judaism, such as the Book of Wisdom (first century B.C. or A.D.), Third Maccabees (first century B.C. or A.D.) and the writings of Philo (first century A.D.).[15] For instance, Wis 14:3 speaks of God as a caring Father guiding a ship safely: "It is your providence, O Father, that steers its course." Moreover, Eleazar's prayer invokes God as a merciful Father: "King of great power, Almighty God Most High, governing all creation with mercy, look upon the descendants of Abraham, O Father" (3 Macc 6:2–3; cf. verse 8). Furthermore, in his work *De specialibus legis* 2.198 Philo calls God "the Creator and Father and Saviour of both the world and the things in the world."[16]

Utilization of the title Father for God in Alexandrian Judaism may exhibit the influence not only of the instances in the Septuagint version of the Hebrew Bible, but also of usage in pagan Greek religion. For instance, Homer's *Iliad* employs the invocation "Father Zeus" (*Il.* 7.179), while Cleanthes' *Hymn to Zeus* (line 33) also calls the same deity "Father".[17]

4. Conclusion

From our brief survey we can see that the New Testament understanding of God as a merciful Father develops a theme found not only in Ben Sira but in other texts from the Hebrew Bible, Second Temple Judaism, and even pagan religions. This understanding, frequently based on an experience of prayer being answered, provides a yardstick for human behaviour. For St. Paul, an experience of God's fatherly mercy enabled him to reveal that mercy to others: "Blessed be the God and Father of our Lord Jesus Christ, the Father of mercies and the God of all consolation, who consoles us in all our

---

truth and father of the gods" (p. 366), while an Egyptian *Hymn to the Gods as a Single God* declares: "Do (not) widows say: 'Our husband art thou,' and little ones: 'Our father and our mother'?" (p. 371).

15 From the late first century A.D., Josephus' *Antiquities of the Jews* recounts that David addressed God as "Father" (7.14.11 #380), while both Abraham and Judah referred to God as "Father of all" (1.13.3 #230; 2.6.8 #152). 3 Macc 5:7 says that the Jews invoked "their merciful God and Father."

16 Sterling, Philo of Alexandria, 99–107; quotation from p. 104.

17 See Aune, Prayer, 23–42 (esp. 30 on Homer); Cassidy, Cleanthes, 132–38 (esp. 136).

affliction, so that we may be able to console those who are in any affliction with the consolation with which we ourselves are consoled by God" (2 Cor 1:3–4). God's mercy invites our response: "Authentic knowledge of the God of mercy, the God of tender love, is a constant and inexhaustible source of conversion, not only as a momentary interior act but also as a permanent attitude, as a state of mind."[18] Ben Sira teaches: "If one has no mercy toward another like himself, can he then seek pardon for his own sins?" (Sir 28:4 Gk.). If the Lord is full of mercy (Ps 111:4; Sir 2:11), his people are called to be similarly merciful (Ps 112:4). Thus, we see that the teaching of Ben Sira and other authors in Second Temple Judaism is summed up in Jesus' admonition: "Be merciful, just as your Father is merciful" (Luke 6:36).

Bibliography

Aune, D.E., "Prayer in the Greco-Roman World," in *Into God's Presence: Prayer in the New Testament* (ed. R. N. Longenecker; Grand Rapids: Eerdmans, 2001) 23–42.

Beentjes, P.C., "Sei den Waisen wie ein Vater und den Witwen wie ein Gatte," in *Der Einzelne und seine Gemeinschaft bei Ben Sira* (eds. R. Egger-Wenzel and I. Krammer; BZAW 270; Berlin / New York: de Gruyter, 1998) 51–64.

Cassidy, W., "Cleanthes – *Hymn to Zeus*," in *Prayer from Alexander to Constantine* (ed. M. Kiley; London: Routledge, 1997) 132–38.

Davies, O., *A Theology of Compassion* (London: SCM, 2001).

Di Lella, A.A., "Sirach 51:1–12: Poetic Structure and Analysis of Ben Sira's Psalm," *CBQ* 48 (1986) 395–407.

García Martínez, F., *The Dead Sea Scrolls Translated* (Leiden: Brill, 1994).

Hayward, C.T.R., *The Jewish Temple* (London: Routledge, 1996).

Jeremias, J., *New Testament Theology* (London: SCM, 1971).

Jeremias, J., *The Prayers of Jesus* (Philadelphia: Fortress, 1978).

McNamara, M., *Targum and Testament* (Shannon: Irish University Press, 1972).

Pritchard, J.B. (ed.), *Ancient Near Eastern Texts* (Princeton: Princeton University, 1950).

Schuller, E., "The Psalm of 4Q372 1 Within the Context of Second Temple Prayer," *CBQ* 54 (1992) 67–79.

Schuller, E., "4Q372 1: A Text about Joseph," *RevQ* 14 (1990) 349–76.

Sterling, G.E., "Philo of Alexandria: Two Prayers," in *Prayer from Alexander to Constantine* (ed. M. Kiley; London: Routledge, 1997) 99–107.

Strotmann, A., *"Mein Vater bist du!" (Sir 51,10). Zur Bedeutung der Vaterschaft Gottes in kanonischen und nichtkanonischen frühjüdischen Schriften* (Frankfurt a.M.: Knecht, 1991).

Wotyla, K. (Pope John-Paul II), *Dives in Misericordia* (London: Catholic Truth Society, 1980).

Wright, N.T., "The Lord's Prayer as a Paradigm of Christian Prayer," in *Into God's Presence: Prayer in the New Testament* (ed. R.N. Longenecker; Grand Rapids: Eerdmans, 2001) 132–54.

---

18   Wotyla, Misericordia, 67 (section 13).

Die Furcht und die Liebe Gottes.

Ein Versuch, die Ethik Ben Siras mit der des Apostels Paulus zu vergleichen

Ernst Käsemann in dankbarem Gedächtnis

Otto Kaiser
Philipps-Universität Marburg an der Lahn

1. Ben Sira und Paulus: ein Beispiel jüdischer und christlicher Ethik

1.1. Wenn wir im Folgenden versuchen, die Ethik Ben Siras mit der des Apostels Paulus zu vergleichen, so stellen wir das ethische Denken eines spätbiblischen jüdischen Weisen und das eines vom Pharisäer zum Apostel Jesu Christi gewordenen Mannes nicht nebeneinander, um über den einen oder den anderen den Stab zu brechen. Statt dessen wollen wir beobachten, was sie gemeinsam haben und was sie unterscheidet. Beiden ist der Glaube an Israels Erwählung und die Unverbrüchlichkeit der Offenbarung des Gotteswillens in der Tora gemeinsam. Für beide sind die Bücher der Hebräischen Bibel verbindliches Gotteswort. Aber während es für Ben Sira keine andere Offenbarung als die am Sinai / Horeb[1] und kein anderes Leben als dieses eine, durch Geburt und Tod begrenzte gibt,[2] ist für den Apostel Paulus die Sinai-Offenbarung in den Schatten der Christus-Offenbarung getreten. Daher liegt das eigentliche Ziel des Lebens für ihn nicht in einem langen und glücklichen Leben in dieser Welt, sondern in der den Tod überdauernden Gemeinschaft mit dem in den Himmel zurückgekehrten Christus. Es geht daher im Folgenden nicht darum, Kataloge für die nach der Meinung des einen oder des anderen gebotenen oder empfehlenswerten Handlungen aufzustellen, sondern vielmehr um den Versuch, die Mittel und Motive zur Erreichung eines Gott wohlgefälligen Lebens im Horizont der von ihnen vertretenen Endziele heraus zu arbeiten. Dabei stellt sich bei beiden das Problem der menschlichen Verantwortung und damit der Wahl- und Handlungsfreiheit im Horizont des Glaubens an die göttliche Erwählung. Gewiss kann man eine Ethik ohne Metaphysik treiben und daraus den Grundsatz ableiten, es auch bei der Bearbeitung historischer Quellen bei einer reinen Phänomenologie der gebotenen wie der verbotenen Handlungen zu belassen, nur wird man auf diese

---

1 Zur Entwicklung des Torabegriffs vgl. Kaiser, Gott I, 300–28 und jetzt auch Otto, Tora.

2 Vgl. dazu Kaiser, Verständnis, 175–92.

Weise weder den Texten noch der Sache gerecht, weil die menschliche Freiheit das metaphysische Problem schlechthin darstellt.

1.2. *Das Ziel des Handelns nach Aristoteles.*[3] Ehe wir uns der Weisheit Ben
Siras zuwenden, um an ihr zu beobachten, wie er Mittel und Ziel des menschlichen Handelns bestimmt, lassen wir uns durch Aristoteles' *Nikomachische
Ethik* (EN) daran erinnern, dass die antike Ethik eudämonistischer Natur war.
Sie war keine Lehre von den Pflichten des Menschen, sondern Anweisung zu
einem gelingenden Leben und entsprach darin dem Grundverlangen des Menschen nach Glück. Daher beginnt er seine Untersuchung mit der berühmten
Feststellung, dass jede Kunst und jede Lehre, jede Handlung und jeder Ent-
schluss nach einem Guten zu streben scheint. Daher könne man das Gute als
das bezeichnen, nach dem alles strebt (EN 1094a 1–3). Er erläutert dieses
Gute weiterhin dahin gehend, dass die Vielen und die Gebildeten, die πολλοί
und die χαρίεντες, darin übereinstimmen, dass sie es als *Glückseligkeit,* als
εὐδαιμονία bezeichnen und unter ihr das *Gut-Leben,* das εὖ ζῆν, und das *Gut-
Handeln,* das εὖ πράττειν, verstehen (1095b 17–20). Die das ganze Werk umfassende Antwort auf die Frage nach der angemessenen Füllung beider Ziel-
bestimmungen ist doppelter Art, wie sie sich aus der Natur des Menschen als
eines ζῷον πολιτικὸν καὶ λόγον ἔχον, als eines Vernunft besitzenden Gemein-
schaftswesens, ergibt (pol. 1253a 1–10): Für den *Menschen als Gemein-
schaftswesen* besteht das höchste Gut in der Verwirklichung der distributiven
Gerechtigkeit (EN 1178a 9–14). Denn anders als die einzelnen Tugenden ist
sie nicht allein auf den Handelnden, sondern auf die πόλις und damit auf andere bezogen und daher nicht nur ein Teil der Tugend, sondern die ganze
ἀρετή (1130a 8–10). Für den *Menschen als Vernunftwesen* besteht das höchste Gut dagegen in der Tätigkeit, in der er Gott als dem sich selbst denkenden
unbewegten Beweger (vgl. Met. Λ 1072a 19 – 1073a 13 mit 1074b 15 –
1975a 10) am nächsten kommt, in der denkenden Betrachtung, der θεωρία
(EN 1178b 7–32). Dabei gehören für Aristoteles zum Glück in beiden Fällen
ein Leben lang währende förderliche äußere Umstände, eine ἐκτὸς εὐημερία,
wie Gesundheit, ausreichendes Ver-mögen zum Unterhalt und der Besitz von
Freunden (vgl. 1178b 33 – 1179a 11 mit 1177b 19–26). Das höchste menschliche Gut besteht für Aristoteles mithin nicht im Genießen, sondern *in einem
Tätigsein der Seele gemäß ihrer Tugend, wenn es aber mehrere Tugenden
gibt, in der besten und vollendetsten Tugend, und dies in einem ganzen Leben*
(τὸ ἀνθρώπινον ἀγαθὸν ψυχῆς ἐνέργεια γίνεται κατ᾽ ἀρετήν, εἰ δὲ πλείους

---

3   Vgl. dazu z.B. Kenny, Aristotelian Ethics, 190–214; Forschner, Glück, 1–21, ferner
    Buddensiek, Theorie, und zur allgemeinen Einführung in die aristotelische Ethik Guth-
    rie, History, 331–400.

αἱ ἀρεταί, κατὰ τὴν ἀρίστην καὶ τελειοτάτην. ἔτι δ᾽ ἐν βίῳ τελείῳ [1098a 16–18]).

2. Die Begründung der Sittlichkeit bei Jesus Sirach

2.1. *Weisheit als Mittel, die Furcht Gottes als Motiv und das gelingende Leben als Ziel des richtigen Handelns bei Ben Sira.* Die Antwort Ben Siras auf das Ziel des menschlichen Handelns ist durch seine Einbettung in die biblische Weisheit bestimmt. Für sie ist der Weise der Mann, der sich auf die Kunst des Lebens versteht, weil er Gott fürchtet und daher umsichtig handelt; denn einerseits ist die Furcht des Herrn der Weisheit Anfang (Ps 111,10; Spr 9,10), und andererseits gilt: "Der Weise hat seine Augen im Kopf, aber der Tor wandelt in der Finsternis" (Koh 2,14a). Daher kann der in der Furcht des Herrn lebende und daher umsichtig handelnde Weise dessen gewiss sein, ein langes, gelingendes und von Gott gesegnetes Leben zu erlangen (Spr 3,13–18).[4] Diesem geistigen Erbe gemäß sucht auch Ben Sira das höchste Gut weder in einer der Verwirklichung der Gerechtigkeit geltenden politischen Tätigkeit noch in einer gelehrt-meditativen Kontemplation der Gottheit. Statt dessen will er seinem Schülerkreis, der sich wohl vor allem aus Jünglingen zusammensetzte, die aus Aufsteigerkreisen stammten,[5] diese traditionellen Erziehungsziele in einer zunehmend unter den Einfluss der hellenistischen Kultur geratenen jüdischen Lebenswelt neu vermitteln:[6] Er sucht sie zu Männern zu erziehen, die dem praktischen Ideal des jüdischen Weisen entsprechen, weil Gottesfurcht das Motiv ihres Handelns und das Streben, die göttlichen, in der Tora zusammengefassten Gebote zu erfüllen, sie zu einem in allen Lebenslagen umsichtigen und mithin weisen Verhalten anleitet. Ist die Betonung des Gesetzesgehorsams als Bedingung der Weisheit nicht gänzlich neu, so hat sie doch bei ihm einen bis dahin unbekannten Nachdruck gefunden, der den älteren Quellen abgeht.[7]

Man mag sich bei seiner Empfehlung des Schreiberberufs als des körperlich am wenigsten anstrengenden und angesehensten Berufes an die Hochschätzung des βιὸς θεωρητικός bei Aristoteles erinnert fühlen. Aber Ben Siras

---

4　Die Anfechtung dieser weisheitlichen Grundüberzeugung, wie sie in der Hiobdichtung und im Koheletbuch ihren Niederschlag gefunden hat, ist Ben Sira nicht unbekannt, wird aber von ihm mit allen Kräften zurückgewiesen; zur sog. Krise der Weisheit vgl. z.B. Crenshaw, Old Testament Wisdom, 100–48 bzw. Blenkinsopp, Wisdom, 46–83 und zu Ben Sira Crenshaw, Problem, 47–64.

5　Vgl. dazu Wischmeyer, Kultur, 180f, zu den von Sirach verfolgten Zielen 272, 291 und 296–97 und zu den Grenzen seiner Erziehung 298–301.

6　Vgl. dazu Hengel, Judentum, 252–75, aber auch Collins, Wisdom, 31–35.

7　Vgl. dazu auch Blenkinsopp, Wisdom, 151–67 und besonders Collins, Wisdom, 42–61.

Bewertung speist sich aus schlichteren und traditionelleren Quellen als die des Stagiriten. Doch auch für den jüdischen Weisen bildet natürlicher Weise nicht ein vorübergehender Glückszustand, sondern ein Leben das Ziel des Handelns, das sich trotz aller als göttliche Prüfungen verstandener Leiden und Misserfolge[8] in einer von glücklichen Umständen begleiteten Dauer als von Gott gesegnet erweist (Sir 11,22–28):[9]

22   Der Segen des Herrn ist das Teil des Gerechten
     und seine Hoffnung sprosst zur rechten Zeit.
23   Sage nicht: Was brauche ich noch,
     und was fehlt mir am Glück?
24   Sage nicht: Ich habe genug,
     und was könnte mir noch schaden?
25   Am guten Tage vergisst man das Unglück
     und am Tage des Unglücks das Glück.
27   Das Unglück der Stunde lässt das Glück vergessen,
     und das Ende des Menschen zeigt, wer er gewesen.
26   Denn leicht ist es für den Herrn am Tage des Endes,
     jedem nach seinem Tun zu vergelten.
28   Vor dem Tode preise glücklich keinen,
     denn an seinem Ende wird der Mensch erkannt.[10]

Doch den Weg dazu bahnen Gottesfurcht und Weisheit. Demgemäß beginnt Ben Sira sein Lehrbuch in 1,1–10 mit einem *Lob der göttlichen Weisheit* und in 1,11–30 mit einem Hohen Lied auf die Furcht des Herrn.[11] Denn die göttliche Weisheit durchdringt den Kosmos und ist der Quell aller menschlichen Weisheit, die Furcht des Herrn aber ihre Wurzel, Fülle und ihr Kranz.[12] Dass sie darin dem alles durchdringenden λόγος der *Stoiker* entspricht, ist längst bemerkt worden: Ben Sira knüpft in seinem Lob der Weisheit an das für die stoische Kosmologie und Pneumatologie grundlegende Konzept des λόγος an und adaptiert es gleichzeitig dem biblischen Denken.[13] Das wird besonders in den beiden letzten Versen deutlich, in dem er den Gedanken der universalen Verleihung der Weisheit durch Gott an alle Menschen mit dem Erwählungs- und Bundesglauben seines Volkes ausgleicht:[14]

---

8   Vgl. 2,1–6 und dazu auch Calduch-Benages, Un giogiello, 28–44 und 45–63.
9   Zur "Gerechtigkeit am Ende" vgl. auch Marböck, Gerechtigkeit, 26–28.
10   Nach H^A 26b–c.
11   Vgl. dazu Di Lella, Fear of the Lord as Wisdom, 113–33 und weiterhin die die Frucht des Herrn unter allen Aspekten würdigende Studie von Haspecker, Gottesfurcht, und zu ihrer fundamentalen Bedeutung prägnant Wischmeyer, Kultur, 278–81.
12   Sir 1,20.16 und 18.
13   Vgl. dazu Marböck, Weisheit, 93f und weiterhin z.B. ders., Gesetz, 52–72, bes. 71; Collins, Wisdom, 54–61, bes. 61; Kaiser, Bedeutung, 335 [35] und Wicke-Reuter, Providenz, 188–223.
14   Vgl. dazu auch Kaiser, Anknüpfung (1995), bes. 65–67 = (1998), bes. 213–15.

9 Er selbst hat sie (sc. die Weisheit) gebildet, gesehen und gezählt
und ausgegossen über alle seine Werke.[15]

10 Sie ist bei allem Fleisch nach seiner Gabe,
und er gab sie reichlich denen, die ihn lieben.[16]

Das aber sind nach deuteronomisch-deuteronomistischer Tradition die, die
seine Gebote halten (Sir 1,1–10*).[17] Die Frage, inwiefern alle Menschen Anteil an Gottes Weisheit besitzen, beantwortet der Weise in 17,1–10*. Dabei
lässt sich in 17,1–10 und 17,11–22* die gleiche Spannung zwischen der krea-
türlichen und daher allgemeinmenschlichen Ausstattung des Menschen und
Israels Sonderstellung als dem Volk der Tora wie in 1,1–10 beobachten. Es
gehört zum Menschen als Kreatur, dass er nach Gottes Bild geschaffen (V. 3)
und zur Herrschaft über die Tiere bestimmt ist (V. 4), dass er nicht nur die
Sinnesorgane (V. 6), sondern auch die Fähigkeit zu vernünftiger Einsicht und
damit zur Unterscheidung von Gut und Böse besitzt. Sie wird von Ben Sira in
diesem Zusammenhang so wenig wie der Tod als Folge des Sündenfalls erklärt (vgl. Vv. 1–2 mit Gen 3,19), sondern als ursprüngliche Gabe Gottes verstanden (vgl. V. 7 mit Gen 3,6).[18] Nach den Vv. 8a–b und 9–10 ist es die Bestimmung aller Menschen, Gott zu fürchten und ihn angesichts seiner Groß-
taten zu preisen; weil er ihnen die Gottesfurcht mit dieser Absicht ins Herz[19]
gelegt hat.[20] *De facto* leiten diese Verse jedoch zu der in den Vv. 11–22
behandelten Sonderstellung Israels über. Dabei ist Israel nach den Vv. 11–12
und 17 (vgl. Dtn 32,8) das mit der Tora als dem Gesetz des Lebens beschenk-
te und durch den Bundesschluß am Sinai / Horeb zum Gehorsam auf es ver-
pflichtete Eigentumsvolk des Herrn.[21]

Er teilte ihnen Einsicht zu
und ließ sie das Gesetz des Lebens erben.[22]
Einen ewigen Bund richtete er mit ihnen auf
und unterwies sie in seinen Entscheiden.
....
Einem jeden Volk teilte er einen Herrscher zu,
aber der Teil des Herrn ist Israel.

---

15 Zu dem hinter dem von Γ gebotenen Trikolon stehenden Bikolon vgl. Segal, ‏ספר בן‎
‏סירא‎, 3 z.St.
16 V. 10c–d ist erst in ΓII bezeugt.
17 Vgl. Ex 20,6 par. Dtn 5,10; 6,5f; 7,9; 10,12; 11,1.13.22; 13,4; 19,9; 30,6.16.20, weiterhin Sir 2,15f; 7,30 und zur Sache Kaiser, Gott II (künftig als GAT II zitiert), 54–65;
Wicke-Reuter, Providenz, 160–65 und Calduch-Benages, Un giogiello, 118–20.
18 Vgl. dazu auch Collins, Wisdom, 58.
19 Zum Herzen als Zentralorgan des Empfindens und Denkens bei Ben Sira vgl.
Wischmeyer, Kultur, 212–13 bzw. Kaiser, Mensch, 6–7.
20 Vgl. weiterhin Weish 13,1–8 und dazu Gilbert, La critique, 13–52 und zuletzt Kepper,
Bildung, 147–95.
21 Vgl. dazu auch Witte, Mose, 161–86.
22 17,11c gehört zum späten, erst in ΓII bezeugten Zuwachs.

Es ist sein Eigentumsvolk, dem er in der Gestalt der *Tora* einen sicheren
sittlichen Führer verliehen hat. Das Bundesgesetz vom Sinai ist in V. 14 auf-
fallend knapp formuliert und hat vermutlich in V. a bei dem Abstehen vom
Bösen den Götzendienst und damit das Erste als das Hauptgebot und in V. b
das Gebot der Nächstenliebe als Summe aller den zwischenmenschlichen
Umgang regelnden Gesetzesbestimmungen im Sinn:[23]

> Denn er sagte zu ihnen: Hütet euch vor allem Bösen!
> und befahl ihnen, einem jeden im Blick auf den Nächsten.

Poetischer wird das zwischen dem Herrn und Israel bestehende Sonderver-
hältnis in dem Selbstrühmungshymnus in Kap. 24 ausgedrückt, der der per-
sonifizierten *Weisheit* in den Mund gelegt ist:[24] Nachdem sie sich in den Vv.
3–6 auf ihre Herrschaft über alle Bereiche der Welt und alle Völker der Erde
berufen hat, berichtet sie in den Vv. 7–12, dass sie von Gott aufgefordert
worden sei, in Jakob ihr Zelt aufzuschlagen und Israel als ihr Erbe zu betrachten. So sei es gekommen, dass sie auf dem Zion eingesetzt, Jerusalem
das Zentrum ihrer Herrschaft (ἡ ἐξουσία μου) geworden sei und sie in dem
verherrlichten Volk Wurzeln geschlagen habe. Ihr, die Hymne abschließender Lockruf verheißt denen, die ihm folgen, ewige Sättigung, weil sie durch
sie vor Sünden bewahrt werden (Vv. 19–22).[25] Kein Zweifel, ihre Gabe besteht ebenso in der Tora wie sie selbst die Tora als Inbegriff aller göttlichen
Weisheit verkörpert, wie es der Kommentar Ben Siras in den Vv. 23–29*
konstatiert.[26] Mithin kann der Weg zur Erlangung der höchsten, dem Menschen möglichen Weisheit und damit zugleich zu einem gelingenden Leben
nur im Halten der Gebote liegen, wie es schon 1,26 rät:[27]

> Begehrst du Weisheit, halte die Gebote,
> und der Herr wird sie dir geben.[28]

---

23 Vgl. mit Peters, Buch Jesus Sirach, 144 Syr. und zur Sache Smend, Weisheit, 158 bzw.
    Collins, Wisdom, 60.
24 Zum Verhältnis zwischen Spr 8,22–31 und Sir 24 vgl. Marböck, Weisheit, 55–56 und
    zur Personifikation der Weisheit in den einschlägigen biblischen Schriften Murphy,
    Personification, 222–33 bzw. ders., Tree (1990), 133–49 = (1996), 133–49 und 227–29;
    zur Funktion der Weisheit in der Schöpfung (24,5–7) vgl. Marböck, Weisheit, 61–63;
    zu der in Jerusalem (24,8–12) 63–68; zur Nachinterpretation Sirachs in Gestalt der
    Gleichsetzung von Weisheit und Gesetz (24,23–29) 77–79 und grundsätzlich 81–96
    sowie Collins, Wisdom, 42–61.
25 Vgl. auch 4,11–16.
26 Vgl. dazu auch Sauer, Jesus Sirach, 184: "Das Genießen der Weisheit ist kein Gefühl
    und keine lebensferne Sättigung. Die Weisheit befähigt zum rechten Tun, vermittelt
    durch das Gesetz."
27 נַפְשׁוֹ.
28 Vgl auch 35/32,24 H^B: Wer die Weisung hält, bewahrt sein Leben, und wer auf den
    Herrn vertraut, wird nicht zu Schanden.

So wie der Gehorsam gegenüber der Tora ein Zeichen der Weisheit ist, ist der Hass auf sie ein Zeichen von Torheit. Denn der Weise besitzt in dem Wort des Herrn eine zuverlässige Anweisung für sein Handeln, während der Tor ziellos durch das Leben irrt (36/33,2f):

> Unweise ist, wer die Weisung hasst,
> denn er schwankt wie ein Schiff im Sturm.[29]
> Ein verständiger Mann vertraut dem Wort,
> und die Weisung ist ihm wie ein Losorakel.

Es ist daher nicht verwunderlich, dass sich der Dekalog als der Inbegriff der Tora in Ben Siras Lehren spiegelt.[30]

2.2. Zum Problem des Verhältnisses zwischen der Tora und der Weisheitslehre Ben Siras.

Trotzdem fällt es auf, dass sich Ben Sira in seinem Buch nicht als Ausleger der Tora im eigentlichen Sinne betätigt. Obwohl er an einer ganzen Reihe von Stellen der Tora gemäße Lehren erteilt, zitiert und diskutiert er sie nicht, sondern überlässt es seinen Lesern, die Zusammenhänge zwischen seiner Lehre und der Tora zu erkennen. Zudem beschränkt er sich bei seinen Lehren nicht auf die Behandlung der herkömmlichen Topoi der biblischen Weisheit, sondern erweitert sie durch die Aufnahme einer ganzen Reihe von solchen, die sich der Begegnung mit der hellenistischen Kultur verdanken.[31] Gleichzeitig gibt er dem bis dahin eher peripheren Thema der Freundschaft eine ganz neue Gewichtung.[32] Die Erklärung für diesen vielfach beobachteten Befund[33] lässt sich sehr einfach mittels eines Blicks auf 1,27 und 21,11 geben. Denn nach 1,27 sind Weisheit und Zucht Erfolg der Gottesfurcht:

> Weisheit und Erziehung liegen in der Furcht des Herrn,
> und sein Wohlgefallen besitzen Treue und Demut.

---

29 Γ: aber der Heuchler schwankt wie ein Schiff im Sturm.
30 Vgl. dazu Wischmeyer, Kultur, 199 und die Nachweise unten, 66–69.
31 Vgl. dazu Marböck, Weisheit, 154–70; zum Problem konkreter Anleihen bei der griechisch-hellenistischen Literatur Middendorp, Stellung, 7–34 und dazu kritisch Kaiser, Judentum (1982), 79–85 = (1985), 146–53, und ausführlich Kieweler, Ben Sira, sowie die vorsichtige Beurteilung des Sachverhalts durch Sanders, Ben Sira, 27–59. Auf Parallelen in der demotischen Weisheit macht auch Lichtheim, Late Egyptian Wisdom, 138–66 aufmerksam; ob man sie mit Sanders, 61–106, bes. 105f auf die Kenntnis der Lehre des Phibis oder nicht doch auf den "Zeitgeist" zurückzuführen hat, mag hier offen bleiben. Dass Ben Sira grundsätzlich ein jüdischer Denker war und sich als ein solcher verstanden hat, steht jedenfalls außer Zweifel; vgl. dazu die Darstellung von Wischmeyer, Kultur, die seine Einbettung in jüdisches Leben und Denken umfassend belegt.
32 Vgl. 12,8–7; 19,6–9; 22,19–26; 25,1–11; 27,16–21; 37,1–6 und dazu Reiterer, Freundschaft.
33 Vgl. z.B. von Rad, Weisheit, 314f.

Nach 21,11 aber führt die Absicht, das Gesetz mit seinen zahlreichen Bestimmungen zu halten, zu einer Beherrschung der Triebe, weil sie die Gottesfurcht vermehrt. Wer geradezu pedantisch darauf bedacht ist, auch nicht eines
der Gebote der Tora zu übertreten, weil ihm das vom Herrn vergolten würde
(17,23; 32/35,12f/9f),[34] dessen Leben wird notwendig durch die Gottesfurcht
als die eigentliche Wurzel der Weisheit bestimmt und er selbst dadurch zu
einer umsichtigen Lebensführung erzogen. Denn:

> Wer das Gesetz bewahrt, beherrscht seine Triebe,
> und vollendete Furcht des Herrn ist Weisheit.

Der ganze Nachdruck seiner Lehren liegt daher auf der Furcht des Herrn;
denn sie bewahrt den Menschen vor Sünden und verhilft ihm dadurch zu
einem langen Leben, 1,20f:

> Die Wurzel der Weisheit ist Furcht des Herrn,
> und ihre Zweige sind langes Leben.[35]
> Die Furcht des Herrn hält Sünden fern,
> wer in ihr verharrt, wendet allen Zorn ab.[36]

So rechtfertigt es die von der Gottesfurcht geförderte und verlangte Umsicht
des Handelns, dass Ben Sira sich als Weisheitslehrer in ihren Dienst stellt
und seine Schüler und Leser zu einem umsichtigen Leben ermahnt.

2.3. *Das Leben des Schreibers als Ideal des glücklichen Lebens*. Doch neben
diesem allgemeinen Ideal eines in Gottesfurcht geführten und daher langen
und glücklichen Lebens kennt auch Ben Sira ein besonderes in Gestalt des
Lebens als Gelehrter, und d.h. entsprechend seiner kulturellen Einbettung, als
סוֹפֵר oder Schreiber. In 38,24–39,11 preist er diesen Beruf als den gegenüber
allen handwerklichen Berufen erstrebenswertesten an.[37] In ihm geht es frei-

---

34 Vgl. weiterhin z.B. 16,14 und zur Erweiterung in H^A und H^B Skehan – Di Lella, Wis-
    dom, 269 z.St.
35 Vgl. 2Q18.
36 Vgl. auch 18,17.
37 Ben Siras Preis des Schreiberberufes besitzt seine Entsprechungen in der mesopotami-
    schen und der ägyptischen Schulweisheit; vgl. z.B. das sumerische Lob der Schreib-
    kunst, bearbeitet von Römer, TUAT III/1, 20, 46–48 und das ägyptische Lob des
    Schreiberberufes des Pap. Lansing, bearbeitet von Moers, TUAT.E, 109–42. Zur Rolle
    des Schreibers und Weisen im Alten Orient vgl. die einschlägigen Beiträge in Gammie
    – Perdue, Sage. Zur Frage, ob Ben Sira selbst ein priesterlicher oder ein nicht-priester-
    licher Schreiber gewesen ist, vgl. Stadelmann, Ben Sira, 25f, der ihn als Priester ein-
    ordnete und dazu das Referat über die kritischen Stellungnahmen bei Marböck, Sir
    38,24–39,11, 49–51 und weiterhin Collins, Wisdom, 37 und schließlich die prononc-
    cierte Einordnung Ben Siras durch Wischmeyer, Kultur, 296f: "Sirachs Platz und der
    Platz seiner Schüler ist nicht der Tempel, sondern das private Lehrhaus. Sein und seiner
    Schüler Verkehr mit Gott wird nicht durch das Opfer, sondern durch die Weisheit als

lich anders als im aristotelischen βιὸς θεωρητικός nicht um eine kontemplative Gottesschau,[38] sondern um das einerseits gegenüber den praktischen Berufen (38,24–34) einfachere Leben des Schreibers und andererseits um den dadurch erzielten Bildungsvorsprung (38,34c–39,3) und die sich aus ihm ergebenden beruflichen Vorteile (39,4). Dank seiner Frömmigkeit und ihm von Gott verliehenen Weisheit (39,5–8) kann er darüber hinaus zu seinen Lebzeiten zu weltweitem Ansehen gelangen und nach seinem Tode einen bleibenden Namen und damit die neben dem Fortleben in den Kindern einzige Form des Nachlebens (39,9–11) gewinnen. Da alle Weisheit von Gott dem Herrn stammt, gehört zu den Vorteilen des Schreibers, dass er nicht nur die Schriften der Vorfahren studieren, sondern auch Reisen unternehmen kann, um auf diese Weise die Sitten anderer Völker kennen zu lernen (39,4c–d).

2.4. *Die Wahlfreiheit und Verantwortlichkeit des Menschen.* In 21,11 ist bereits das Stichwort יֵצֶר, *Trieb*, gefallen. Es bezeichnet die Antriebskraft, die zwischen der Überlegung und der Handlung vermittelt. Ihm kommt auch in Ben Siras Verteidigung der menschlichen Verantwortung in 15,11–20 eine zentrale anthropologische Bedeutung zu. In den Vv. 14–17 widerlegt Ben Sira den Vorwurf, Gott sei als Schöpfer des Menschen und Lenker seines Lebens auch für die Sünden des Menschen verantwortlich (Vv. 11f), so:

14 Als Gott am Anfang den Menschen schuf,
    da gab er ihn in die Hand seines Triebes.
15 Wenn es dir gefällt,[39] so hältst du das Gebot.
    und Treue[40] ist es, nach seinem Wohlgefallen zu handeln.
16 Vor dir liegen[41] Feuer und Wasser,
    was du begehrst, danach strecke aus deine Hand.
17 Vor dem Menschen liegen Leben und Tod;
    Was ihm gefällt, wird ihm gegeben!

Ben Sira adoptiert in Vv. 16f den von Mose in Dtn 30,15–20 an das Volk gerichteten Ruf, sich im Gehorsam oder Ungehorsam gegen die Tora zwischen Leben und Tod zugunsten seines Lebens und seiner heilvollen Zukunft zu

---

38   Zu dem sirazidischen Äquivalent in Gestalt der Anbetung des alles menschliche Verstehen überschreitenden göttlichen Handelns in 42,15–43,33 vgl. unten 50f.

39   Man sollte חפץ (gegen früher auch Kaiser) nicht mit "wollen" übersetzen; denn die Vorstellung vom Willen als einer menschlichen Eigenschaft war den alttestamentlichen Autoren so fremd wie den griechischen, die den Akt der Entscheidung intellektuell deuteten; vgl. dazu Dihle, Theory, bzw. seine deutsche Übersetzung von 1985.

40   H^A: תבונה, "Einsicht"; vgl. aber Γ, H^Bm, Syr. und Vulg.

41   H^A: מוצק, wörtlich: "ausgegossen ist "

eine Gott und die Weisen und die Schüler verbindende Größe hergestellt. So bedeutet auch Sirachs Verehrung des Hohenpriesters nicht seine Zugehörigkeit zum Priesterstand."

entscheiden. Dabei verankert er die Möglichkeit zur verantwortlichen Entscheidung wie in 17,6f in der schöpfungsmäßigen Ausstattung des Menschen: Der Mensch ist dank seines יֵצֶר, seiner ihm von Gott gegebenen Fähigkeit, seine Pläne auszuführen oder nicht auszuführen, für sein Tun verantwortlich.[42] Ihm sind zudem die göttlichen Gebote als Handlungsmaximen und Handlungsanweisungen gegeben, so dass er weiß, was Gott von ihm fordert. Er kennt auch die über dem Gehorsam gegen das Gesetz liegenden Segensverheißungen und die über dem Ungehorsam stehenden Fluchandrohungen (Dtn 28; Lev 26). Daher ist ihm bekannt, welche Folgen mit seiner Wahl verbunden sind. Mit anderen Worten: Ben Sira erinnert die, die meinen, sich angesichts ihres gottwidrigen Verhaltens mit der Entschuldigung herausreden zu können, dass Gott sie nun einmal so geschaffen habe, an die ihnen als Geschöpfen zukommende und in der Tora ausdrücklich bestätigte Verantwortlichkeit des Menschen für sein Tun und Lassen, weil er Wahl- und Handlungsfreiheit besitzt.

Allerdings bedeutet die konstitutionelle Möglichkeit der Wahl- und Handlungsfreiheit noch nicht, dass der Mensch (modern ausgedrückt) einen freien Willen besitzt; denn seine Wahlfreiheit ist durch seinen Charakter bestimmt, der ebenso angeboren wie erworben sein kann.[43] Mithin könnte der die Wahl in die Handlung umsetzende Trieb (יֵצֶר) durch Gottes unergründliche Entscheidung bereits positiv oder negativ vorbestimmt sein. Oder um es theologisch auszudrücken: der Mensch könnte dank Gottes Erwählung oder Verwerfung zur Gerechtigkeit oder Ungerechtigkeit veranlagt sein.

2.5. *Das Geheimnis der Erwählung in einer polaren, durch Gottes Providenz bestimmten Welt.* Der in seiner Bedeutung umstrittene einschlägige Text liegt in 36/33,7–15 vor. Da *Ursel Wicke-Reuter* ihn jüngst umfassend ausgelegt hat,[44] kann sich die Darlegung hier auf die knappe Feststellung beschränken, dass es in diesem Text einerseits in der Tat um das Geheimnis der göttlichen Erwählung geht, andererseits und grundsätzlich aber um den polaren Charakter aller Dinge. Ben Sira setzt mit dem ersten ein: Gottes erwählendes und damit polare Unterschiede begründendes Handeln liegt zum Beispiel darin vor, dass er den gewöhnlichen Tagen die Festtage gegenüberstellte und ihnen eine heilvolle Qualität verlieh. In analoger Weise hat er auch den Menschen verschiedene Wege zugeteilt. Die einen ließ er sich ihm nahen und heiligte sie, während er andere verfluchte und erniedrigte. Dabei mag bei den Bevor-

---

42 Die genauere Untersuchung des Begriffs behalte ich einem anderen Zusammenhang vor.

43 Zur aristotelischen ἕξις vgl. Guthrie, History, 352f und zum Problem der Determination der Entscheidung Jedan, Willensfreiheit, 88–134 und 177f.

44 Vgl. dazu Wicke-Reuter, Providenz, 224–74.

zugten an die Priester aus Aarons Geschlecht (und möglicherweise auch an Israel) und dann bei den Verfluchten an die Rotte Korach (und möglicherweise die Voreinwohner des Landes Kanaan) gedacht sein. Die Aussagen über die Verschiedenheit der den Menschen von Gott gegebenen Schicksale stehen jedoch im Rahmen einer Reflexion über die der ganzen Schöpfung wesensmäßig innewohnende Polarität. Mithin ergibt es sich nicht zwingend, dass der aus Gottes freiem Rat erfolgten Erwählung seiner Diener auch eine in Gottes Prädestination bedingte Verdammung der Verfluchten gegenüber steht. Der Betonung der Verantwortung des Menschen für seine Entscheidung und damit sein Schicksal in 15,11–20 gemäß dürften sich die Verfluchten ihre Verdammung vielmehr durch ihr eigenes Verhalten zugezogen haben. Wohl aber gibt es in dieser Welt das Gute nur als Gegensatz zum Bösen und umgekehrt das Böse nur als Gegensatz zum Guten. Und mithin setzt die Existenz von Guten zugleich die von Bösen voraus. Denn gäbe es keine Frevler, Übeltäter und Gottlosen, könnte man auch nicht von den Gerechten, Frommen und Getreuen reden.

Gott hat allerdings vorausgesehen, dass es Gute und Böse geben wird und deshalb die Welt so eingerichtet, dass für die Belohnung der Guten und die Bestrafung der Bösen vorgesorgt ist. In diesem Sinne rechtfertigt Ben Sira die Vollkommenheit der Welt in seinem Hymnus über die Güte der Werke Gottes in 39,12–35 teleologisch.[45] Gott hat die Welt in seiner Vorsehung so eingerichtet, dass alle Mittel bereit stehen, um den Guten zum Glück zu verhelfen und die Bösen zu bestrafen. Demgemäß heißt es in Vv. 24–25:

> Seine Pfade sind für die Untadligen gerade,
> für die Hochmütigen[46] aber uneben.
> Gutes hat er für die Guten von Anfang an zugeteilt,
> aber den Frevlern Gutes und Böses.

Denn natürlich partizipieren auch die Bösen an den lebensnotwendigen Gaben des Schöpfers (Vv. 26–27), *aber für die Bösen wendet es sich zum Bösen* (V. 27b). Damit leitet Ben Sira zu der in den Vv. 28–31 anschließenden Aufzählung der kosmischen, biologischen und geschichtlichen Gerichtswerkzeuge Gottes über.[47] Man wird daher auch die Welt und Geschichte bestimmende Polarität grundsätzlich teleologisch und zugleich providentiell zu verstehen haben: Auch wenn Gott aus freier Wahl ein Geschlecht und ein Volk bevorzugt, wird dadurch die Verantwortung des Einzelnen für seine Entscheidungen nicht aufgehoben. Gott hatte allerdings bei der Erschaffung der Güter und Übel bereits die Belohnung der Guten und die Bestrafung der Bösen im

---

45 Zur Struktur und der Art der Aufnahme stoischer Konzepte vgl. zuletzt Marböck, Gerechtigkeit, 28–43.
46 Lies לזדים, H^B Verlesung von ד als ר.
47 So richtig Skehan – Di Lella, Wisdom, 460 z.St.

Auge. Sie sind mithin ein Werk seiner Vorsehung, seiner *Providenz*,[48] die ihrerseits Ausdruck seiner *Omnisziens*, seiner Allwissenheit, und seiner *Omnipotenz, seiner Allmacht, sind.*[49] Dem gemäß heißt es bereits in den Vv. 19f:

19 Die Werke allen Fleisches sind vor ihm,
      und nichts ist verborgen vor seinen Augen.[50]
20 Von Ewigkeit zu Ewigkeit geht sein Blick:
      Gibt es eine Grenze[51] für seine Hilfe?
      Nichts ist zu klein und zu gering für ihn,
      und nichts zu wunderbar und zu stark für ihn.[52]

Die Frage, warum der allwissende und allmächtige Gott das vorausgesehene Unheil nicht *a priori* verhindert hat, stellt sich Ben Sira nicht. Er hält sich an die biblische Festellung, dass Gott seine Werke am Ende der sechs Schöpfungstage sämtlich als sehr gut befand (Gen 1,31a), und an die Faktizität einer Welt, zu deren Wesen die Polarität aller Dinge und also auch die von Gut und Böse, Leben und Tod gehören und in welcher der Mensch Wahl- und Entscheidungsfreiheit besitzt. Daher gibt es für ihn letztlich in der Welt *keine Übel*,[53] sondern *nur gerechte Strafen*, so dass alle Werke Gottes (wie es in V. 16 als einleitende Themenvorgabe und in V. 33 zusammenfassend heißt) gut sind:[54]

      Die Werke des Herrn sind alle gut,
      sie reichen aus für jeden Zweck zu seiner Zeit.

2.6. *Das Geheimnis der Erwählung des Gerechten und die Unergründlichkeit der göttlichen Weisheit.* Und doch bleibt dabei ein unergründlicher Rest, den auch Sirach gesehen hat. Denn der Unterschied zwischen den Guten und den Bösen erscheint häufig als so fundamental, dass sich der Gedanke aufdrängt, sie seien bereits mit ihrem so oder so geprägten Charakter zur Welt gekommen. Ben Sira hat sich offenbar entsprechende Gedanken gemacht und sie in 1,14 in die Sprache der poetischen Embryologie[55] und zugleich der prophetischen Erwählungstheologie (Jer 1,5; Jes 49,1) umgesetzt und so nur auf den Gerechten bezogen:

      Der Anfang der Weisheit ist es, den Herrn zu fürchten,
      und bei den Getreuen wurde sie im Mutterleib erschaffen.

---

48   Vgl. dazu Kaiser, Rezeption, 41–54 und Wicke-Reuter, Providenz, 80–87.
49   Vgl. dazu auch Kaiser, GAT II, 142–46.
50   Vgl. 15,19 und 17,15.
51   Wörtlich: Zahl.
52   20c–d nach H^B ergänzt; vgl. Skehan – Di Lella, Wisdom, 457 z.St.
53   Vgl. dazu auch Ursel Wicke-Reuter, Providenz, 87.
54   Vgl. auch Gen 1,31a.
55   De Wilde, Buch, 152 und Kaiser, GAT II, 219–21.

Eine gegenteilige Aussage findet sich bei Ben Sira nicht: *Es gibt für ihn also sehr wohl das Geheimnis der Erwählung, aber nicht das der Verdammung,* denn dann wäre seine ganze Ethik, wäre seine Pädagogik nur Teil eines Spieles, das Gott mit den Menschen wie mit Marionetten spielte.[56]

Nach Ben Siras Überzeugung, ist es nicht die Aufgabe des Weisen und seiner Schüler, die Geheimnisse Gottes zu erforschen,[57] sondern sich in Demut (V. 21) an das zu halten, was ihnen von Gott zu wissen gegeben und von ihnen gefordert ist (3,21–25):

> Was zu wunderbar für dich ist, sollst du nicht suchen,
> und was zu schwierig für dich ist, sollst du nicht erforschen.
> Über das, was dir übereignet ist, sinne nach,
> aber bemühe dich nicht um das Verborgene.
> Denn die Gedanken der Menschen sind zahlreich,
> und schlechte Beispiele führen in die Irre.
> Wo kein Augapfel ist, gibt es kein Licht,
> und wo kein Wissen ist, keine Weisheit.

Aber der Weise bleibt staunend und anbetend vor der gewaltigen Größe und Schönheit der Schöpfungswerke des Gottes stehen (42,15–43,26),[58] dessen Unergründlichkeit sich ihm in ihrem Geheimnis erweist (43,27–33):[59]

> 27 Mehr von diesem fügen wir nicht hinzu,
> aber der Rede Ende lautet: Alles ist nur er![60]
> Denn er ist größer als alle seine Werke.
> 29 Zu fürchten über alle Maßen ist der Herr,
> und wunderbar sind seine Machterweise.
> ....
> 31 Wer sah ihn, dass er davon künden könnte,
> und wer könnte ihn preisen wie er ist?
> 32 Die Fülle des Verborgenen ist mehr als das,
> denn wenig sah ich nur von seinen Werken.
>
> 33 Denn alles hat der Herr erschaffen,
> und seinen Frommen gab er Weisheit.

---

56 Vgl. Plat.leg. I. 644d 7b 9 – e 1; VII. 804a 4 – b 4.

57 Deshalb hat er sich auch nicht auf die damals im Kommen begriffene Apokalyptik eingelassen; vgl. dazu auch Argall, 1 Enoch, und z.B. Collins, Imagination.

58 Vgl. dazu ausführlich Prato, Il problema, 116–208, bes. 207f und zuletzt Marböck, Gerechtigkeit, 39f.

59 Vgl. auch Jüngel, Gott, 340–47, bes. 341f, wo er darauf hinweist, dass es zur Struktur des positiven Begriffs des Geheimnisses gehört, dass es nicht aufhört, Geheimnis zu bleiben, es sich aber als solches offenbart und daher vom Menschen zur Sprache gebracht werden will.

60 D.h. dem Kontext gemäß: er ist der Schöpfer aller Dinge, vgl. Kaiser, Rezeption, 50; aufgenommen von Sauer, Jesus Sirach, 299–300; vgl. auch Γ: πάντα γὰρ ἐποίησεν ὁ κύριος und Prato, Il problema, 201: "הוא אל designa il motiva per cui Dio è degno di lode. ... e perciò הכל si riferisce alle maniere con cui Deo si manifesta nel mondo."

Damit aber schließt sich die Decke über den Abgründen des Unerforschlichen; denn wir erinnern uns (1,26f):

> Begehrst du Weisheit, halte die Gebote,
> und der Herr wird sie dir geben.
> Lasse nicht ab von der Furcht des Herrn,
> denn Treue und Demut gefallen ihm wohl.[61]

3. Die Begründung der Sittlichkeit in der Verkündigung des Apostels Paulus

3.1. Paulus, der Bote Jesu Christi: Verkündiger der Gerechtigkeit durch den Glauben. Wenden wir uns dem Apostel Paulus zu, so besteht das Ziel des christlichen Handelns darin, sei es in der Auferstehung, sei es in der Umgestaltung des sterblichen Leibes in eine himmlische Lichtgestalt der vollen Gemeinschaft mit Christus teilhaftig zu werden.[62] Das Mittel zur Erreichung dieses Zieles ist der Glauben an Jesus Christus als den Erlöser der Welt (Röm 3,23–24.28; 8,12–22)[63] und seine Folge die Freiheit zur Liebe als des Gesetzes Erfüllung.[64] Sie aber ist die Bedingung für die Verleihung des ewigen Lebens durch den in Kürze als Weltenrichter erscheinenden Christus.[65]

Damit ist bereits gesagt, dass sich die geistige Situation des Judentums seit den Tagen Ben Siras unter dem Einfluss der Apokalyptik tiefgreifend verändert hat. Aus der uns bei Sirach begegnenden Unterscheidung von Gerechten und Frevlern sind inzwischen die innerjüdischen Parteien der Essener und der Pharisäer hervorgegangen, die den letzten Erweis der Gerechtigkeit Gottes in einem Endgericht über Lebende und Tote erwarten.[66] Nach dem zuvor Gesagten ist es unmittelbar einleuchtend, dass der Apostel als einstiger Pharisäer diese Bewertungen und Erwartungen grundsätzlich teilte, auch

---

61 Angesichts von 3,21–25 ist es nicht erstaunlich, dass Ben Sira von den Jenseitsvorstellungen, wie sie die henochitische Apokalyptik seiner Tage vertrat, keine Notiz nahm. Seine eschatologischen Aussagen bleiben, wie das Gebet in 33/36,1/1a–36,27/22 belegt, im Horizont der prophetischen Heilserwartungen. Zum Problem der Verfasserschaft des Gebets vgl. die Ben Siras verneinend Middendorp, Stellung, 125–32 und mit guten Gründen bejahend Marböck, Gebet (1995), 149–66, bes. 157–66. Zu den prophetischen Heilserwartungen vgl. Gowan, Eschatology, 4–58.

62 Vgl. Phil 3,10–11.20–21; 1Thess 4,13–18; 1Kor 15,20–28.50–57; 2Kor 5,1–2; Röm 6,23; 8,17–25.

63 Röm 3,23–24.28; 8,19–23.

64 Röm 13,8–10.

65 Röm 2,16; 14,22; 1Kor 11,31–32; 2Thess 2,7–12.

66 Vgl. dazu Hengel, Judentum, 319–463 bzw. Schürer, History, 381–574 und weiterhin zu den vorrabbinischen Phärisäern Schäfer, Pharisäismus, 125–75 und Hengel, Paulus, 242–48: Zur Zugehörigkeit der Qumrangemeinschaft zu den Essenern vgl. Stegemann, Qumran Essenes, 83–165; García Martínez – Trebolle Barrera, People, 50–76 und zu ebd., 77–96.

wenn bei ihm die Gerechten die sind, die ihres Glaubens an die ihnen durch Christi stellvertretenden Tod geschenkte Gerechtigkeit leben (Röm 1,16–17; vgl. Gal 3,13).[67] Die Situation des Menschen hat sich jedoch gegenüber den Erwartungen der Apokalyptiker insofern verändert, als der Apostel davon ausgeht, dass der mit der Auferstehung der Toten, dem Weltgericht und der Versetzung der Frommen in die himmlische Herrlichkeit beginnende neue Äon[68] bereits mit Jesu Auferstehung angefangen hat, so dass die Christen in der Spannung zwischen dem Noch-nicht und dem Doch-schon leben. Die Gegenwart ist in seinen Augen nur noch die kurze Spanne zwischen der Auferstehung und der Ankunft des Herrn zum Weltgericht (1Thess 4,13–18; 1Kor 7,29a). Daher fühlt er sich gedrängt, das Evangelium zu den Juden und Heiden bis an den westlichen Rand der Welt zu tragen, damit am Ende ganz Israel als das auserwählte Volk Gottes vor dem erscheinenden Christus dank seines Glaubens gerettet würde (Röm 11,25–32). Demgemäß handelt es sich bei seinen Briefen nicht um theologische Traktate,[69] sondern um der besonderen Situation der Adressaten wie des Apostels entsprechende Sendschreiben. Oder anders gesagt: Es handelt sich bei ihnen um keine Lehren,[70] sondern um die Briefe eines Missionars, Seelsorgers und Bekenners, in denen er unter verschiedenen Aspekten die Botschaft vom Gekreuzigten als die Heilstat Gottes in einer zu Ende gehenden Welt verkündet (2Kor 5,20f; 1Kor 7,29). Des Apostels Paulus Denken ist mithin trotz seiner Abhängigkeit von der jüdischen Apokalyptik vor allem christozentrisch.

Dadurch war der ehemalige Pharisäer Paulus[71] genötigt, zwischen seinem Christusglauben und der im Alten Testament verwurzelten Erwählungs- und Bundestheologie zu vermitteln, die ihren Brennpunkt in der Gesetzeserfüllung als der Bedingung des Gelingens des irdischen bzw. der Erlangung des ewigen Lebens besaß.[72] Sucht man nach einer schlüssigen Antwort, warum der Apostel Christus als des Gesetzes Ende verkündigt hat, so muss man sich außer an den Galater- zumal an den Römerbrief halten, weil er in diesem der ihm fremden, aus Juden- und Heidenchristen bestehenden Gemeinde sein Verständnis des Evangeliums in grundlegender Weise dargelegt hat,[73] so dass

---

67   Zum "vorchristlichen Paulus" vgl. unter demselben Titel Hengel, Paulus, 178–293, bes. 251–54.

68   Vgl. 1Hen 103–104; vgl. Kapp. 22 und 25; 4Esra 7.

69   Außer im Fall von Röm 1,16–11,36.

70   Eine gewisse Sonderstellung nimmt allerdings der Römerbrief ein; vgl. dazu Becker, Paulus, 358–70, bes. 361–63.

71   Zum "vorchristlichen Paulus" vgl. unter demselben Titel Hengel, Paulus, 178–293, bes. 251–54.

72   Vgl. dazu auch Rössler, Gesetz, bes. 70–100.

73   Abgesehen von dem Prolog 1,1–13, dem auf Gemeindefragen eingehenden Abschnitt 14,1–15,14, dem persönlichen Epilog in 15,15–33 und der Grußliste samt dem Briefschluss in Kap. 16.

man ihn als sein geistiges Testament betrachten kann.[74] Der Galaterbrief geht
ihm zeitlich voraus[75] und stimmt in seiner theologischen Substanz grundsätzlich mit ihm überein, ist aber nicht als das letzte Wort des Apostels in dieser
Sache zu verstehen.[76] Als Einsatzpunkt für ein angemessenes Verständnis der
Botschaft von Christus als des Gesetzes Ende empfiehlt sich des Apostels
persönliches Bekenntnis in Phil 3,2–11, das zeitlich zwischen beiden anzuset-
zen ist.[77] Denn in ihm spiegelt sich die revolutionierende und weiterhin sein
Denken bestimmende Bedeutung, die die Erscheinung des Auferstandenen
für ihn zeitlebens besessen hat. Sie hat aus dem die Tora mit ganzer Hingabe
befolgenden Pharisäer und dem mit zelotischem Eifer in Damaskus gegen die
Heidenchristen vorgehenden Verfolger Saulus[78] den Apostel der Völker Paulus gemacht, dem der Glaube an Gottes in Jesu Kreuzestod erfolgter Gerecht-
erklärung des Sünders zum A und Ω seines Lebens und Denkens geworden
ist.[79] Seither ging es ihm nicht mehr darum, dank seines als eigenes Werk
verstandenen Gehorsams gegen die göttliche Weisung die Gerechtigkeit und
das ewige Leben zu erlangen, sondern in Christus Jesus erfunden zu werden
und daher die Gerechtigkeit zu gewinnen, die dem von Gott zugerechnet
wird, der an Christus glaubt (Phil 3,4–9) und das Ziel der himmlischen Heimat, das πολίτευμα ἐν οὐρανοῖς, nicht aus dem Blick verliert (Phil 3,20–21).

3.2. *Des Apostels Berufung als Wendepunkt seines Denkens und Lebens: Phil
3,2–11.* Es wird sich zeigen, dass das in Phil 3,2–11 vorliegende Bekenntnis
sich nicht nur als Schlüssel für die Botschaft von Christus als dem Ende des
Gesetzes, sondern auch als Ausgangspunkt für das Verständnis der damit
unlösbar verbundenen Botschaft von seinem Kreuzestod zur Vergebung der
Sünde und Rettung der Sünder erweist. Im Gegensatz zu seinen judenchristli-
chen Gegnern[80] hat Paulus damals erkannt, dass das καυχᾶσθαι κατὰ σάρκα,
das Sich-Rühmen nach dem Fleisch als Zeichen des πεποιθέναι κατὰ σάρκα,
des Vertrauens auf das Fleisch, Ausdruck der Selbstgerechtigkeit ist und daher in diametralem Gegensatz zu dem Gottesdienst im Geiste steht, in dem
sich der Mensch nicht seiner selbst, sondern Christi rühmt (Phil 3,3; vgl.

---

74 Vgl. dazu z.B. Vielhauer, Geschichte, 185–87 und bes. Becker, Paulus, 368–69.
75 Zur Datierung vgl. einerseits z.B. Vielhauer, Geschichte, 110–11, der den Brief
    gleichzeitig mit dem 1. Korintherbrief ansetzt, und andererseits Becker, Paulus, 276,
    der ihn 55 n.Chr. und damit kurz vor dem Römerbrief datiert.
76 Vgl. dazu z.B. Söding, Liebesgebot, 254–58.
77 Vgl. dazu z.B. Lührmann, Brief, 11f.
78 Vgl. Gal 1,22f, vgl. V. 17; 1Kor 15,8; Phil 3,6 und dann Apg 9,1–31 und 22,3–21 und
    dazu Hengel, Paulus, 265–91 bzw. Hengel – Schwemmer, Paulus, 60–72.
79 Vgl. dazu auch Lohse, Paulus, 49–53 und 58–66.
80 Vgl. dazu Becker, Paulus, 340–50, bes. 344–49.

1,26).[81] Er selbst hatte in seinem zurückliegenden Leben alle Kriterien eines wahren Juden erfüllt: Er war zeitgerecht beschnitten, stammte aus einem benjaminitischen Geschlecht, hatte sich den Pharisäern angeschlossen[82] und in der Verfolgung der Christen besonders hervorgetan, kurz:
Er war (V. 6) nach der Gerechtigkeit gemäß dem Gesetz untadlig. Aber, so fährt er in V. 7 fort, "was für mich ein Gewinn war, das achte ich jetzt um Christi Willen für einen Verlust. 8 Und in der Tat halte ich alles für einen Verlust wegen der unüberbietbar großen Erkenntnis des Christus Jesus, meines Herren, wegen dem dies alles für mich zu einem Verlust geworden ist. Und ich halte es für einen Dreck (σκύβαλα), damit ich Christus gewinne 9 und in ihm als einer erfunden werde, der seine eigene Gerechtigkeit nicht aufgrund des Gesetzes, sondern aufgrund des Glaubens an Christus besitzt, nämlich die Gerechtigkeit aus Gott aufgrund des Glaubens, 10 um ihn zu erkennen und die Kraft seiner Auferstehung und die Gemeinschaft seiner Leiden, gleichgestaltet seinem Tode, 11 ob ich wohl zu der Auferstehung der Toten gelange."

In dieser gedrängten Sprache sind die wesentlichen Elemente seines Christusglaubens eingeschlossen: An die Stelle des Strebens nach der Gerechtigkeit unter dem Gesetz ist die Gewissheit getreten, dass Gott die Gerechtigkeit denen schenkt, welche die Botschaft von dem um ihrer Sünde willen erfolgten Tod Jesu auf sich beziehen und weiterhin danach streben, dank der Gemeinschaft mit ihm an der bevorstehenden Auferstehung der Toten teilzunehmen.

3.3. Die Taufe als Einweisung in die Gemeinschaft des Todes und die Kraft der Auferstehung Christi: Röm 6. Was die Teilhabe an den zu Jesu Kreuzestod führenden Leiden als Weg zur Partizipation an der Kraft seiner Auferstehung bedeutet, geht wohl am deutlichsten aus der kleinen Taufpredigt in Röm 6 hervor: Die Christen werden (so heißt es dort in V. 4) in der Taufe auf Christi Tod getauft und mit ihm begraben, damit sie hinfort in einem neuen Leben wandeln. Der Taufritus soll demgemäß als eine Begehung verstanden werden, die den Täufling in die *vita Christiana* einweist.[83] Als solcher leitet er ihn zu dem Verzicht auf die eigene Endlichkeit an, durch den sich ihm die Unzerstörbarkeit seiner Gottesbeziehung und damit die Gewissheit der Teilhabe an der Auferstehung Jesu Christi erschließt. Das Untertauchen im Wasser der Taufe will also von ihm so mitvollzogen werden, dass er sich damit selbst mit Christus dem Tod preisgibt. Er bejaht das über ihn im Kreuz ergangene Urteil, verzichtet damit auf seinen Selbstbehauptungswillen gegenüber Gott[84] und gelangt dadurch zur Teilhabe an der Kraft des Lebens des Auferstande-

---

81 Vgl. 1Kor 1,26–31 und zur Sache Bultmann, Theologie, 242f.
82 Vgl. dazu auch Becker, Paulus, 42–49.
83 Zum vorausgesetzten Taufverständnis vgl. Dunn, Romans 1–8, 325–28.
84 Vgl. dazu sogleich zu Röm 7.

nen, der aus und durch Gott lebt. So ist die Taufe als eine Einweisung in das Leben aus dem reinen Vertrauen in Gottes nie endende Gegenwart zu verstehen. Es soll weiterhin in dem Bewusstsein seinen Wandel bestimmen, dass er diese stetige und kräftige Gottesgewissheit nicht als einen unzerstörbaren Charakter besitzt, er ihr aber sehr wohl nachjagen kann und nachjagen muss, wenn er das Ziel der ewigen Seligkeit erreichen will (Phil 3,13f). Damaskus war für den Apostel eine der Taufe entsprechende Erfahrung. In der ihn (nach den Erzählungen zu Boden werfenden)[85] Begegnung mit dem Auferstandenen hatte sich ihm die Kraft und die Teilhabe am Leben des Auferstandenen erschlossen: Der durch die Erscheinung des auferstandenen Herrn in seinem Innersten getroffene Verfolger der Gemeinde wurde zum Apostel der den Glaubenden geschenkten Vergebung der Sünden unter den Heiden (Gal 1,11–16a).

3.4. *Die Erlösung des Menschen aus seinem Widerspruch: Röm 7,14–8,2.*
Aus dieser Begegnung mit dem erhöhten Herrn ergab sich für Paulus die Notwendigkeit, seine Stellung zur Tora neu zu bestimmen.[86] Daran, dass sie von Gott gegeben und als solche heilig und gut ist, hat er auch weiterhin nicht gezweifelt (Röm 7,12). Ebenso wenig wollte und konnte er bestreiten, dass das Gesetz erfüllbar ist (Phil 3,6). Doch welche Funktion kam ihm dann nach Gottes Absicht zu, wenn es zwar als Gottes gültiges, aber nicht letztes Wort an Juden und Heiden zu betrachten ist?

Ein erster Erklärungsversuch findet sich im *Galaterbrief.* In ihm gab er die Auskunft, dass das Mose als dem Mittler von Engeln überstellte Gesetz[87] (von Gott) um der Übertretung willen verordnet worden sei. Es übernahm in der Zeit vor Christus als der Zeit der Sünde die Aufgabe eines παιδαγωγός, eines Zuchtmeisters (Gal 3,19–22), indem es die Menschen bis zu seinem Kommen unter seine Vormundschaft stellte (vgl. Gal 4,1ff).[88] Nach der im *Römerbrief* in 2,1–3,20 erteilten Antwort diente das Gesetz dagegen dazu, die Juden angesichts der von ihnen in Wahrheit nicht erfüllten Gebote ebenso als Sünder zu überführen (2,17–24), wie die Heiden,[89] denen das Gesetz ins Herz geschrieben ist und deren Gewissen sie verklagt (Röm 2,12–16). Die in Röm 5 gegebene Antwort aber lautete, dass, nachdem Sünde und Tod durch Adam

---

85 Vgl. Apg 9,3–5 mit 22,3–6.

86 Vgl. dazu auch Dunn, Romans 1–8, LXIII–LXXII.

87 Zum jüdischen Hintergrund der Vorstellung, die in der Deutung der Naturphänomene und also auch der sie begleitenden Sinaitheophanie als Wirkungen von Elementarengeln liegt, vgl. Schlier, Brief, 109f und zum jüdischen Hintergrund z.B. Jub 2,2ff und 1Hen 60,11ff.

88 Zum Wandel des Gesetzesverständnis vom Galater- zum Römerbrief vgl. Hübner, Gottes Ich, 127–35 und speziell zu dem des Galaterbriefes Stanton, Law, 99–116.

89 Vgl. dazu Bergmeier, Gesetz, 53, der 2,14ff auf Heidenchristen bezieht.

in die Welt gekommen waren, es die Aufgabe des Gesetzes war, in der bis zum Kommen Jesu während Zwischenzeit die Sünde zu mehren (V. 20). Das klingt auch noch in Röm 7,7–13 nach, wo Paulus diese These gleichsam auslegt, indem er erklärt, dass das Gesetz im Sünder gerade durch das Verbot des Begehrens die Begierde hervorruft und damit den Sünder dem Tode ausliefert.

Diese Aussagen sind hoch paradox. Denn wenn der Mensch das Gebot halten kann und über der Einhaltung der Gebote die Segensverheißung Gottes steht (Dtn 28,1ff; Lev 26,3ff), wie kann es dann zur Kraft der Sünde, zur δύναμις τῆς ἁμαρτίας werden (1Kor 15,56)? Die Gal 3,6ff gegebene Auskunft, dass jeder Mensch, der das Gesetz nicht vollkommen hält, nach Dtn 27,26 unter dem Fluch steht, überzeugt deshalb letztlich nicht, weil Paulus von sich selbst bekannt hat, dass er untadlig nach dem Gesetz gewesen ist (Phil 3,6).[90]

Über diese Verlegenheit hilft allein Röm 7,14–25a hinweg, weil hier deutlich wird, welche Bewandtnis es mit der Sünde hat und warum das Gesetz selbst den, der seine sämtlichen Vorschriften hält, nicht zu erlösen vermag, solange er sich nicht Gott ganz übergibt, wie es nebenbei Dtn 6,5f verlangt. Die geschenkte Gerechtigkeit ist in der Tat, wie es Gal 3,16ff darlegt, das Leben aus der Verheißung, die nach Gen 12,3 auch die Völker einschließt. Röm 7,14–25a entfaltet den Röm 1,18–3,20 bestimmenden Gedanken der Unentrinnbarkeit der Verantwortung des Menschen für seine Sünde in einer Meditation über den Widerspruch, in dem sich der Christ als Mensch befindet.[91] Die in diesen Versen vorausgesetzte Situation kann man nur insofern als "adamitisch" bezeichnen,[92] als der "alte Adam" auch im Christen fortlebt und beständiger Kontrolle und Überwindung verlangt. Denn das Ich dieser Verse ist der Christ Paulus, der erkennt, dass er trotz seiner Bekehrung immer noch ein unvollkommener Mensch ist, so dass er immer neu dem Ziel der himmlischen Berufung nachjagen muss (Phil 3,12–16).[93] V. 25b ist mithin kein nachträglicher Einschub,[94] sondern eine Zusammenfassung des in den Vv. 14–25a Gesagten.[95] Hier wie in allen seinen Briefen urteilt der Christ über die Bedeutung des Gesetzes, das nun freilich die Bedeutung der göttlichen Forderung überhaupt annimmt, weil es sich für den Apostel auf das Gebot der Gottes- und der Nächstenliebe reduziert und damit mit dem νόμος γραπτὸς ἐν ταῖς καρδίαις von Röm 2,15 identisch geworden ist. Auch der Christ ist als Mensch (um es mit Rudolf Bultmann zu sagen) "der Zwie-

---

90 Vgl. dazu auch Lichtenberger, Paulus, 361–78, hier 371.
91 Vgl. dazu Hegel, Vorlesung, 223–33.
92 Bergmeier, Gesetz, 69.
93 Vgl. Michel, Brief, 239 und Dunn, Romans 1–8, 407 und 410.
94 Käsemann, Römer, 201f.
95 Vgl. Michel, Brief, 238–39; Dunn, Romans 1–8, 411 und Stuhlmacher, Brief, 105.

spalt"[96]. Auch als Christ muss er feststellen, dass er dem ihm als endlichem
Wesen inne wohnenden Trieb der Selbsterhaltung und Selbstdurchsetzung
nicht zu entrinnen und (so können wir ergänzen) Gott nicht über alle Dinge
und den Nächsten wie sich selbst zu lieben vermag.[97] Obwohl er als Vernunft
begabtes Wesen den stillen Anruf Gottes in seinem νοῦς, in seiner Vernunft,
vernimmt und im Gerichtshof seiner συνείδησις als ihn selbst anklagend erfährt (Röm 2,15) und also weiß, dass er das Gute tun soll, scheitert sein ent-
sprechendes Wollen, weil er am Ende auch in der Erfüllung des göttlichen
Gebots sich selbst will. Darin eben erweist sich die Macht der Sünde, der
ἁμαρτία, unter der Paulus nicht mehr einzelne Verfehlungen, sondern das
adamitische Schicksal des Menschen versteht, sich unbedingt selbst zu wollen[98] und nicht anders zu können. Daher ist der im Menschen selbst liegende
νόμος ἐν τοῖς μέλεσιν, das Gesetz in seinen Gliedern, eben das Gesetz, das ihn
zwanghaft dazu führt, das Gegenteil von dem zu tun, was er eigentlich will
(Vv. 21 und 23). Diesem Gesetz steht in ebenso genereller Weise der νόμος
τοῦ θεοῦ, das Gesetz Gottes gegenüber, dem der ἔσος ἄνθρωπος, der innere
und eigentliche Mensch im Gegensatz zu dem leiblich vorfindlichen, als σάρξ
bestimmten Mensch, freudig zustimmt. Dieses Gesetz wird in V. 23 parallel
als νόμος τοῦ νοός μου, als das Gesetz meiner Vernunft, bezeichnet und entspricht damit der stoischen These, dass alle Menschen von Natur aus um das
Gerechte, das Gesetz und das richtige Denken wissen (φύσει τε δίκαιον εἶναι
καὶ μὴ θέσει, ὡς καὶ τὸν νόμον καὶ τὸν ὀρθὸν λόγον [DL VII 128; SVF III,

---

96   Römer 7, 198–209, hier 202; zum Unterschied zwischen der antiken Einsicht in den
     Zwiespalt zwischen Wollen und Vollbringen und seiner jüdischen Vertiefung vgl. mit
     Stuhlmacher, Brief, 100f Eur. Hipp. 358f, 375–90 und Ov.Met. VII,17–21 mit z.B.
     1QS XI, 9–11 oder 4Esra 3,19–22.
97   So unbeliebt die deutschen Idealisten bei den Theologen auch sein mögen, so haben sie
     sich doch um den Nachweis der Vernunft in der Religion bemüht. Dabei verdient auch
     der Versuch von Schelling, Wesen, 331–416 wenigstens zur Kenntnis genommen zu
     werden. Denn hier definiert Schelling die Freiheit des Willens als Fähigkeit zum Tun
     des Guten und des Bösen. Den bösen Trieb aber erklärt er damit, dass der zwar der
     Natur als dem Grund Gottes entstammt, aber nicht seiner Person, so dass die Verant-
     wortung des Menschen ebenso wenig aufgehoben wie die Gerechtigkeit Gottes ange-
     tastet wird. Dabei steht auch er vor dem Rätsel der unterschiedlichen Charaktere, für
     die er eine vorweltliche Erklärung sucht; vgl. bes. SW I/7, 352–376; AW 5, 296–320,
     PhB 25–48 und zur Sache weiterhin ders., Zusammenhang, 467: "Nothwendigkeit ist
     das Innere der Freiheit; darum läßt sich von der wahrhaft freien Handlung kein Grund
     angeben; sie ist so, weil sie so ist, sie ist schlechthin, ist unbedingt und darum nothwen-
     dig."
98   Vgl. dazu auch Kierkegaard, Krankheit, (XI, 127) 8: "Die Verzweiflung ist eine Krank-
     heit im Geist, im Selbst, und kann somit ein Dreifaches sein: verzweifelt sich nicht be-
     wußt sein, ein Selbst zu haben (uneigentliche Verzweiflung); verzweifelt nicht man
     selbst sein wollen; verzweifelt am selbst sein wollen." Daher ist die Sünde (SV XI 189)
     GW XXIV/ XXV, 75: "vor Gott oder mit dem Gedanken an Gott verzweifelt nicht
     mehr man selbst sein wollen oder verzweifelt man selbst sein wollen."

308]).[99] Der Mensch pervertiert also den ihm bekannten Gotteswillen, indem er ihn unter dem Zwang der ἁμαρτία in sein Gegenteil verkehrt und mithin dem Tode verfällt. Denn im Kampf zwischen dem Gesetz Gottes und dem Gesetz in den Gliedern unterliegt im Menschen das erste unter dem Einfluss der Macht der Sünde. Daher sehnt sich Paulus und jeder Christ, solange er lebt, nach der Erlösung aus diesem Zwiespalt (V. 24): Ταλαίπωρος ἐγὼ ἄνθρωπος· τίς με ῥύσεται ἐκ τοῦ σώματος τοῦ θανάτου τούτου; Im Rückblick wird deutlich, warum Paulus trotz seines eigenen Bekenntnisses, dass er nach dem Gesetz untadlig war (Phil 3,6), rückblickend in der Art der Gesetzeserfüllung das Mittel der Selbstrechtfertigung und im Gesetz selbst den Stachel zur Sünde erkennt: Gottes Ehre wird der Mensch nur gerecht, indem er sich die vom Gesetz verlangte Gerechtigkeit von Gott schenken lässt, um dann trotz des inneren Zwiespalts zwischen Wollen und Vollbringen aus der Verheißung zu leben und sich selbst damit voraus auf dem Wege der Liebe zu sein. Durch seine Teilhabe an der Kraft der Auferstehung Jesu Christi weiß er, dass er zu einem neuen Leben unter dem νόμος τοῦ πνεύματος τῆς ζωῆς ἐν Χριστῷ Ἰησοῦ, dem Gesetz des Geistes des Lebens in Christus Jesus, berufen und von dem in ihm mächtigen νόμος τῆς ἁμαρτίας, dem Gesetz der Sünde befreit ist (Röm 7,22–25a[b] + 8,1–2), obwohl der Mensch im Widerspruch und mithin ein Anfänger auf dem Weg zur Vollkommenheit bleibt:[100]

22 Denn nach dem inneren Menschen habe ich Freude an dem Gesetz Gottes. 23 Ein anderes Gesetz gewahre ich aber in meinen Gliedern, das liegt im Streit mit dem Gesetz meiner Vernunft und nimmt mich im Gesetz der Sünde gefangen, das in meinen Gliedern ist. 24 Ich armseliger Mensch! Wer wird mich diesem Todesleib entreißen: 25a Dank sei Gott durch Jesus Christus unsern Herrn! 25b So diene ich also mit meiner Vernunft dem Gesetz Gottes, mit dem Fleisch jedoch dem Gesetz der Sünde. 8,1 Es gibt also keine Verdammnis mehr für die in Christus Jesus. 2 Denn das mit dem Geist gegebene Gesetz des Lebens in Christus Jesus hat dich vom Gesetz der Sünde und des Todes befreit.

Die Selbstreflexion über den Christen im Widerspruch schlägt in die Botschaft von der Erlösung durch den Christus Jesus um, der uns aus dem Gefängnis der Selbstreflexion und damit der Selbstbezogenheit befreit und unserem Leben eine unumkehrbare Ausrichtung auf die Zukunft Gottes gibt. Diese Freiheit des "Selbstentzugs" (Wolfgang Harnisch)[101] ermöglicht die Zuwendung zum Nächsten in der Liebe. Daher kann die ihm geschenkte Freiheit auch nicht zu seinem Besitz werden. Sie erschließt sich ihm vielmehr als eine Möglichkeit, die er täglich und stündlich neu aktualisieren muss. So gilt auch für das Leben des Christen, was der Apostel von sich bekannte (Phil

---

99 Diogenes, Leben, 67: "Das Recht besteht nach ihnen von Natur und nicht durch menschliche Satzung, wie auch das Gesetz und der richtige Verstand ... "
100 Übersetzung von Käsemann, Römer, 189 und 203.
101 Harnisch, Freiheit (1994), 179–95 = (1999), 169–84.

3,12): Nicht dass ich es ergriffen hätte oder dass ich schon vollkommen wäre, ich jage ihm aber nach, damit ich es ergreife, gleich wie ich durch Christus Jesus ergriffen bin.

3.5. Die Ethik des Paulus: Christus ist des Gesetzes Ende und die Liebe des Gesetzes Erfüllung (Röm 10,4 und 13,10).

Wenn es sich bei der den Christen zugesagten Erlösung um die Verleihung eines *character indilebilis* handelte, so bedürfte es in der Tat keiner weiteren Ermahnungen, weil die Christen nicht anders könnten, als dem sich in ihrer Vernunft meldenden Gesetz Gottes (Röm 7,22) zu gehorchen und ihm so die Liebe zu erwidern (2Thess 3,5), die er ihnen in der Erlösung vom Fluch des Gesetzes und des Todes erwiesen hat (Röm 5,5), um dann aus der ihm neu geschenkten Freiheit das Gesetz zu erfüllen; weil die Liebe der Inbegriff aller Gebote ist (Röm 13,9f).[102] Aber schon die Tatsache, dass es keinen Paulusbrief ohne Paränesen oder Lasterkataloge gibt, zeigt, dass die Anfechtung durch die dem Tod geweihte σάρξ auch im Christen bis zu seinem realen Tode mächtig bleibt und er sich das ʻΥμεῖς δὲ οὐκ ἐστὲ ἐν σαρκὶ ἀλλὰ ἐν πνεύματι, εἴπερ πνεῦμα θεοῦ οἰκεῖ ἐν ὑμῖν (Röm 8,9) tatsächlich immer erneut ins Gedächtnis rufen oder rufen lassen muss. Die Energie, mit der Paulus im 1. Korintherbrief enthusiastisch-libertinistischen[103] und im Galaterbrief judaistischen Tendenzen[104] entgegentreten und im Philipperbrief B (Phil 3,2-21+4,8f) die heidenchristliche Gemeinde gegen judenchristliche Apostel feien musste,[105] spricht in dieser Hinsicht für sich selbst. Es galt die jungen Gemeinden zu warnen, das kostbare Gut der Freiheit nicht zu verlieren, wie Paulus es z.B. Gal 5,1 mit dem bekannten Τῇ ἐλευθερίᾳ ἡμᾶς Χριστὸς ἠλευθέρωσεν·στήκετε οὖν καὶ μὴ πάλιν ζυγῷ δουλείας ἐνέχεσθε (Zur Freiheit hat euch Christus berufen; steht nun fest und fällt nicht wieder unter das Joch der Knechtschaft) nachdrücklich eingeprägt hat. Er musste sie in Gal 5,13 überdies daran erinnern, dass die Freiheit des Christen sich nicht im Dienst an der eigenen σάρξ, am eigenen "Fleisch", sondern in der Liebe erweist, mit der einer dem anderen dient: ʻΥμεῖς γὰρ ἐπ᾽ ἐλευθερίᾳ ἐκλήθητε, ἀδελφοί· μόνον μὴ τὴν ἐλευθερίαν εἰς ἀφορμὴν τῇ σαρκί, ἀλλὰ διὰ τῆς ἀγάπης δουλεύετε ἀλλήλοις (Denn ihr seid zur Freiheit berufen, Brüder; nicht jedoch zur Freiheit als Vorwand für das Fleisch, sondern dient einander durch die Liebe).

---

102 Dass der Gedanke, dass die Liebe Gottes durch die Liebe zu Gott erwidert sein will, dem Judentum nicht fremd war, hat Nissen, Gott, 161–67 nachgewiesen; zu seiner alttestamentlichen Wurzel vgl. Kaiser, GAT II, 54–63.

103 Der Verfasser weiß, dass damit der Reichtum des Briefes nicht erschöpft ist; vgl. dazu Becker, Paulus, 209–29.

104 Becker, Paulus, 310–12.

105 Becker, Paulus, 325–38 und 340–43.

Das "Hohe Lied der Liebe" in 1Kor 13 ist so allgemein bekannt, dass es ausreicht, an es zu erinnern und 16,14 mit seinem πάντα ὑμῶν ἐν ἀγάπῃ γινέσθω (Alles geschehe bei euch in Liebe![106]) zu zitieren. Es ist jedenfalls konsequent, dass der Apostel, der Christus als das Ende des Gesetzes[107] und das heißt: seines Mißverständnisses[108] verkündigte (Röm 10,4), gleichzeitig die Liebe zur Erfüllung des Gesetzes erklärte (Röm 13,10);[109] denn (so heißt es zwei Verse zuvor in 13,8): Μηδενὶ μηδὲν ὀφείλετε εἰ μὴ τὸ ἀλλήλους ἀγαπᾶν ὁ γὰρ ἀγαπῶν τὸν ἕτερον νόμον πεπλήρωκεν (Bleibt einander nichts schuldig außer einander zu lieben; denn wer den Nächsten liebt, hat das Gesetz erfüllt).[110]

Weil in dieser Anweisung alle nur denkbaren zwischenmenschlichen Situationen enthalten sind, konnte der Apostel auf eine ausgefeilte ethische Kasuistik verzichten. Nur wenn er zu konkreten Stellungnahmen durch Anfragen aus der Gemeinde aufgefordert oder durch Berichte über besondere Vorkommnisse in ihnen herausgefordert war, nahm er konkret dazu Stellung.[111] Sonst aber betonte er wie z.B. in Phil 4,8 das Prinzipielle: Christen haben darauf zu achten, dass sie in ihrem Leben den allgemeinen sittlichen Grundsätzen des Anstands und der Tugend entsprechen. Der Unterschied zwischen den Nichtchristen und Christen sollte eben darin bestehen, dass sie einerseits aus Liebe handeln und andererseits nicht vergessen, dass sie in einer vergehenden Welt weilen und daher in der Hoffnung auf die zukünftige Welt leben. Das hat der Apostel in 1Kor 7,28–31 auf die Formel des ὡς μή, des *als ob nicht*, gebracht:[112] Τοῦτο δέ φημι, ἀδελφοί, ὁ καιρὸς συνεσταλμένος ἐστίν. Daher sollen die, die Frauen haben,[113] sein, als hätten sie keine, und die da weinen, als weinten sie nicht, und die da sich freuen, als freuten sie sich nicht, und die da kaufen, als behielten sie es nicht, und die mit der Welt verkehren, als hätten sie nichts davon. Denn das Wesen[114] dieser Welt vergeht (παράγει γὰρ τὸ σχῆμα τοῦ κόσμου τούτου). Der Christ sollte und könnte wissen, dass alle irdischen Bindungen vorletzter Natur sind. Er sollte und brauchte sich nicht seinen augenblicklichen Stimmungen und Gefühlen auszuliefern. Er sollte und könnte großzügiger mit seinem Besitz umgehen, weil er eine Hoffnung hat, die nicht nur über seine gegenwärtige Situation, sondern auch über sein irdi-

---

106 Übersetzung Conzelmann, Brief, 352.
107 Zur Bedeutung des Wortes τέλος im Kontext vgl. Dunn, Romans 9–16, 589 mit Hinweis auf eine Parallele bei Plutarch Ad principem ineruditum 780 E: δίκη μὲν οὖν νόμου τέλος ἐστί.
108 Dunn, Romans 9–16, 597.
109 Zu Röm 13,8–10 vgl. auch Söding, Liebesgebot, 250–58.
110 Vgl. auch Gal 5,14 und dazu Söding, Liebesgebot, 207–11.
111 Das große Musterbeispiel ist der 1. Korintherbrief.
112 Dass es sich in diesen Versen vermutlich um ein Überlieferungsfragment apokalyptischer Herkunft handelt, das durch seinen Kontext christlich umkodiert ist, betont Harnisch, Christusbindung, 468f = (FRLANT 187) 218.
113 Übersetzung Lietzmann, Korinther, 34.
114 Lietzmann, Korinther, 34: "Gestalt".

sches Leben hinaus reicht.[115] Daher eben sind Glaube, Hoffnung und Liebe[116]
die entscheidenden Leitsterne seines Lebens: Die πίστις, der Glaube, weil er
ihn von seinem inneren Widerspruch befreit und damit für die Zukunft öffnet.
Die ἐλπίς, die Hoffnung, weil sie ihm in seinen Ängsten, Gebrechen und
Schwächen, seinen Niederlagen und Verfolgungen zuruft, dass diese Welt
vergeht, seine Zukunft Gott und seine Heimat im Himmel ist. Beide aber,
Glaube und Hoffnung bilden die Voraussetzung für die Möglichkeit der
Liebe, der ἀγάπη, in deren Verwirklichung der Christ seine Freiheit bewährt,
dem Willen Gottes entspricht und (so fügen wir hinzu) seinem vergänglichen
Leben Sinn gibt. Und darum ist sie unter Glaube und Hoffnung die Größte
(1Kor 13,13): Νυνὶ δὲ μένει πίστις, ἐλπίς, ἀγάπη, τὰ τρία ταῦτα· μείζων δὲ
τούτων ἡ ἀγάπη. In einer vergehenden Welt schuldet der Christ diese Liebe
allen, am meisten aber seines Glaubens Genossen (Gal 6,10): Ἄρα οὖν ὡς
καιρὸν ἔχομεν, ἐργαζώμεθα τὸ ἀγαθὸν πρὸς πάντας, μάλιστα δὲ πρὸς τοὺς
οἰκείους τῆς πίστεως (Darum laßt uns, solange wir Zeit haben, Gutes an allen tun,
besonders aber an den Glaubensgenossen).

3.6. *Das Geheimnis der Erwählung.* Fragen wir, unsere Besinnung über die
Begründung der paulinischen Ethik beschließend, ob der Christ seine Freiheit
durch seinen eigenen Entschluß zum Glauben gewinnt oder sie ihm als Gabe
göttlicher Erwählung zuteil wird, so verweist bereits alles, was wir über die
geschenkte Gerechtigkeit als Antwort auf den Selbstverzicht ermittelt haben,
in die zweite Richtung. Erinnern wir uns: Auch der Apostel weiß von keinem
Bekehrungskampf zu berichten, sondern sich statt dessen zu seinem Amt berufen: Παῦλος δοῦλος Χριστοῦ Ἰησοῦ, κλητὸς ἀπόστολος ἀφωρισμένος εἰς
εὐαγγέλιον θεοῦ (Paulus, der Knecht Christi Jesu, der berufene Apostel, ausgesondert zum Evangelium Gottes) stellt er sich der römischen Gemeinde in Röm 1,1
vor. Sollen die Christen nicht wieder auf sich selbst zurück-, sondern der
Gnade Gottes in die Arme geworfen werden (Röm 3,28), so darf auch der
Glaube nicht ihre Leistung, sondern muss er Gabe, muss er Ausdruck ihrer
göttlichen Erwählung sein. Daher lässt Paulus die Römer in Vv. 5f nicht im
Unklaren darüber, dass sein Apostelamt der Erfüllung des Auftrags gilt, zu
Ehren Jesu Christi bei allen Völkern und so auch bei ihnen als den Berufenen
Jesu Christi, den κλητοὶ Ἰησοῦ Χριστοῦ, Gehorsam des Glaubens, ὑπακοὴ
πίστεως zu schaffen. Sein das Präskript des Briefes abschließender Friedens-
gruß gilt ihnen allen, als den in Rom lebenden ἀγαπητοὶ θεοῦ und κλητοὶ

---

115 Vgl. z.B. wie Ben Sira in 14,11–16 angesichts der Unentrinnbarkeit des Todes zur
    Lebensfreude und Großzügigkeit gegenüber den Freunden auffordert und dazu Kaiser,
    Verständnis, 184.
116 Zur Herkunft und Verwendung der triadischen Formel πίστις, ἐλπίς, ἀγάπη bei Paulus,
    vgl. Conzelmann, Brief, 270–71.

ἅγιοι.[117] Fragt man, was die römischen Christen in seinen Augen als solche auszeichnete, so war es eben der Glaubensgehorsam, der durch die Verkündigung des Gekreuzigten ausgelöst, aber nicht eigentlich geschaffen wird. Denn in der Annahme oder Ablehnung der Christusbotschaft wird offenbar, wer zu denen gehört, die Gott lieben und denen alle Dinge zum Besten dienen, weil sie nach seinem Ratschluss (πρόθεσις) berufen sind (Röm 8,28). Die längst getroffene Auswahl (προορίζειν) kommt in der Berufung zum Tragen und ist mit der Rechtfertigung eins (8,29): Die er nämlich zuvor ausgesondert hat, die hat er auch berufen; und die er berufen hat, die hat er auch gerechtfertigt, die hat er auch verherrlicht. Damit ist deutlich, wie unauflösbar die Vorherbestimmung, die Berufung und die Rechtfertigung für Paulus zusammenhängen: Sie sichern den unbedingten Vorrang Gottes und damit die Freiheit des Christen von seinem *cor in se ipse incurvatum*, seinem in sich selbst verschlossenen Herz.

Trotzdem stellen die Erwählung und die Berufung der Christen für den Apostel zugleich ein geschichtstheologisches Problem dar, wie es sich aus der Abfolge der Erwählung erst der Juden und dann der Heidenvölker ergibt.[118] Die Lösung, die er dafür in Röm 9–11 gefunden hat, zeigt, dass er sich als der Apostel der Heiden zugleich als Diener der endzeitlichen Bekehrung Israels und damit als Vorläufer der Parousie,[119] der mit der Auferstehung der Toten verbundenen Ankunft Christi als des Weltenrichters verstand (1Thess 4,16ff; 2Kor 5,10; Röm 14,10).[120] So wie Paulus daran festhielt, dass das Israel gegebene Gesetz heilig und das Gebot heilig, gerecht und gut ist (Röm 7,12), mußte er als Israelit auch darauf bestehen, dass Israel von Gott im voraus ausersehen und daher auch jetzt trotz seiner Ablehnung Jesu Christi nicht verworfen sei (Röm 11,1f.28b.29).[121] Das Geheimnis der Geschichte besteht für ihn darin, dass Israel teilweise Verstockung widerfahren ist, bis die Fülle der Heiden (τὸ πλήρωμα) eingegangen ist (11,25). Dann aber soll ganz Israel (πᾶς Ἰσραήλ) gerettet werden (V. 26). Das Rätsel der Ablehnung der Botschaft von der den Sündern durch Christi Tod geschenkten Gerechtigkeit durch Israel erklärt sich dem Apostel mittels der Annahme, dass es Gottes Ratschluss sei, den Juden, die nicht an die den Heiden erfahrene Barmherzigkeit glauben wollten, ebenso wie den Heiden, die einst nicht an Gott glaubten, seine Barmherzigkeit zuteil werden zu lassen (Vv. 30f). So hätte Gott denn Juden und Heiden unter den Unglauben beschlossen, um sich im Endergebnis aller zu erbarmen (V. 32): συνέκλεισεν γὰρ ὁ θεὸς τοὺς πάντας εἰς ἀπείθειαν, ἵνα τοὺς πάντας ἐλεήσῃ (Denn Gott hat alle unter den

---

117 Zur Zusammensetzung der Gemeinde vgl. Dunn, Romans 1–8, XLIV–LIV.
118 Vgl. zum ganzen Fragenkreis auch Becker, Paulus, 486–502, bes. 495–502.
119 Käsemann, Römer, 294.
120 Vgl. Dan 7,9–14; Mk 14, 62f par Mt 26,63f.
121 Zum Privileg Israels in der Sicht des Apostels vgl. Dunn, Romans 1–8, LXX–LXXII.

Ungehorsam beschlossen, damit er sich über alle erbarme). Paulus erwartete also nichts anderes, als dass seine Botschaft von der Rechtfertigung der Sünde auch das letzte Wort in der Geschichte seines Volkes behalten werde.[122] Das πάντας bezieht sich dem Wortlaut nach auf die ganze aus Juden[123] und Christen[124] bestehende Menschheit, wobei in beiden Fällen Ausnahmen nicht ausgeschlossen sind.[125] Aber man darf die Aussage kaum im Sinne einer "Wiederbringung aller Menschen" auswerten, sondern dürfte sie angemessener dem Kontext gemäß als generalisierend verstehen.[126] Paulus hat nicht die Einzelnen, sondern Israel und die Heiden im Blick. Die Gnade besteht darin, dass sich "die Macht des Evangeliums an den Ungehorsamen" erweist.[127] "Das Ziel der Heilsgeschichte ist, dass aus der alten die neue Welt hervorgeht, in welcher der Ungehorsam Adams durch seinen eschatologischen Antityp Christus (Röm 5,19; Phil 2,8) beseitigt wird."[128] Hinter Röm 9–11 steht der Versuch des Apostels, angesichts seiner bevorstehenden Reise nach Jerusalem und seiner geplanten in den Westen der römischen Gemeinde (auf deren Hilfe er für die Verwirklichung seiner Spanienmission angewiesen war; Röm 15,23f), zu versichern, "dass sein Verständnis des Evangeliums gerade auch Israel einschließt und nicht ausgrenzt."[129] Als "Vollstrecker des gottgewollten Ausgangs der Heilsgeschichte"[130] gedachte er nach Spanien zu ziehen, um so das Evangelium bis an das Ende der Welt zu tragen und Juden und Heiden vor dem erwarteten Ende der Welt die ihr in Jesu Sühnetod erwiesene Barmherzigkeit zu verkünden.

---

122 Vgl. auch Käsemann, Römer, 301f.
123 So ist in V. 26 mit πᾶς Ἰσραήλ bedeutet mit Dunn, Romans 9–16, 681 "Israel as a whole, as a people whose corporate identity and wholeness would not be lost even if in the event there were some (or indeed many) individuals exceptions."
124 Vgl. in diesem Dunn, Romans 9–16, 680 als Erläuterung zum πλήρωμα.
125 Vgl. mit Kümmel, Theologie, 217 Röm 2,5; 9,32 und 11,22.
126 Dunn, Romans 9–16, 697: "It is the magnificience of this vision of the final reconciliation of the whole world with God which makes it possible to see here the expression of a hope for universal salvation ('universalism'). But precisely because it is so summerary in its expression and so grandiose in its sweep it would probably be wiser to assume that Paul is speaking simply in general terms." Vgl. auch Kümmel, Theologie, 216–18. – In 1Kor 15,28 geht es mit Kremer, Brief, 346 weder im stoisch-pantheistischen Sinn um die letzte Einheit von Gott und Kosmos noch im mystischen um die Einheit von Mensch und Gott, sondern um die Vollendung der Gottesherrschaft, vgl. z.B. Lang, Briefe, 227: "Die mystisch klingende Wendung 'damit Gott alles in allem sei' besagt nicht, dass Christus, die Kirche und die Welt in Gott 'aufgehen', sondern legt den Akzent auf den alles umfassenden und durchdringenden Charakter der Gottesherrschaft."
127 Käsemann, Römer, 304.
128 Käsemann, Römer, 303.
129 Becker, Paulus, 495f.
130 Käsemann, Römer, 294.

Die Erwartung, dass alle Toten und Lebenden vor den Richtstuhl Jesu Christi treten müssen (2Kor 5,10), um nach ihren zu Lebzeiten vollbrachten Taten gerichtet zu werden, hat der Apostel auch im Römerbrief nicht aufgegeben (vgl. 2,12–16 mit 14,10).[131] Der sich daraus für den Christen ergebende Appell, mit Furcht und Zittern auf ihre Rettung bedacht zu sein, steht unter einer doppelten Voraussetzung: Einerseits setzt er die Gewissheit voraus, dass auch die Entscheidung über das Heil in Gottes Händen bleibt, weil er auch noch das Wollen und Vollbringen des Menschen nach seinem Gutdünken (εὐδοκία) bewirkt (Phil 2,12f), und andererseits steht auch hinter ihm der Glaube, dass die Entscheidung bereits in Christi Tod zugunsten der Sünder gefallen ist (Röm 5,9). So bleibt es dabei: Wer das in Jesu Tod gemachte Gnadenangebot Gottes im Gehorsam des Glaubens, in der ὑπακοὴ πίστεως,

annimmt, wird gerechtfertigt, aber am Ende doch nach seinen Werken gerichtet.[132] So gibt es für den Christen zwar Heilsgewissheit: er weiß sich durch Christus gerettet, aber er besitzt angesichts des als Richter kommenden Christus keine *securitas,* keine Sicherheit, die ihn vom Tun der Liebe entbindet. Er weiß sich durch Jesu Tod erlöst, bleibt aber unter dem Aufruf so zu handeln, dass er im jüngsten Gericht besteht. Doch so lange er unterwegs ist, kann er sich in den Stunden der Anfechtung ebenso dessen trösten wie dadurch erschrecken lassen, dass auch sein Tun oder Lassen durch Gott bewirkt wird. Wahl- und Handlungsfreiheit des Menschen lassen sich nicht leugnen, ohne jedem ethischen Imperativ seinen Sinn zu nehmen. Ob der, der Wahlfreiheit auch Willensfreiheit besitzt, bleibt allerdings angesichts der freien Verfügungsgewalt Gottes, Menschen gemäß seinem Vorsatz, seiner πρόθεσις, zum Glauben zu berufen (Röm 8,28), eine Frage für sich.[133] Der Glaube versteht sich denn auch nicht als eigenes Werk, sondern als eine "geschenkte Entscheidung" (Phil 1,29). Dem entspricht es, dass der Christ sich auch die Liebe nicht als eigene Leistung zurechnen kann, sondern sie für ihn eine Gabe des Geistes bleibt; denn: ἀγάπη τοῦ θεοῦ ἐκκέχυται ἐν ταῖς καρδίαις ἡμῶν διὰ πνεύματος ἁγίου τοῦ δοθέντος ἡμῖν (Röm 5,5: denn die Liebe Gottes ist ausgegossen in unseren Herzen durch den heiligen Geist, der uns gegeben ist).[134]

---

131 Vgl. dazu z.B. Kümmel, Theologie, 203–6; Lohse, Paulus, 238–40 und zumal Becker, Paulus, 49–53.

132 Es ist verständlich, dass die Kirche weiterhin zwischen dieser Spannung zu vermitteln suchte, damit die strafende Gerechtigkeit ebenso wie die Gnade zum Zuge kämen.

133 Vgl. dazu Maier, Mensch, 351–400, bes. 399f.

134 Vgl. dazu auch Bultmann, Theologie, 330f und ders., Jesus Christus, 160: "An das Wort Gottes glauben heißt, alle rein menschliche Sicherheit aufzugeben und die Verzweiflung abzustreifen, die aus dem Versuch, die Sicherheit zu finden, entsteht, ein Versuch, der immer vergebens ist. In diesem Sinne ist der Glaube zugleich das Gebot und das Geschenk, das die Predigt anbietet. Glaube ist die Antwort auf die Botschaft. Glaube ist das Aufgeben der eigenen Sicherheit des Menschen und die Bereitschaft, Sicherheit allein im unsichtbaren Jenseits zu finden, in Gott. Das heißt: Glaube ist Si-

So bleibt die Weisheit der göttlichen Gnadenwahl dem Menschen verborgen. Nachdem er das Wagnis unternommen hat, einen Blick hinter den Vorhang zu werfen, der uns Menschen das göttliche Handeln in der Welt verbirgt, verneigt sich der Apostel daher am Ende seines Traktates über Gottes Gerechtigkeit, des Christen Freiheit und Israels bleibende Erwählung in Röm 1,16–11,36 anbetend vor der verborgenen und zugleich alle Welt lenkenden Weisheit seines Gottes (11,33–36):

> O Tiefe des Reichtums,
> der Weisheit und Erkenntnis Gottes!
> Wie unerforschlich sind seine Gerichte
> und unaufspürbar seine Wege.
> Denn wer hat erkannt den Sinn des Herrn
> oder wer wurde sein Ratgeber?
> Oder wer hat ihm etwas vorgestreckt,
> dass man es ihm erstatten müsste?
> Denn: "Aus ihm und durch ihn und zu ihm ist alles."
> Sein ist die Herrlichkeit in Ewigkeiten. Amen.

4. Der Dekalog als Kanon jüdischer Ethik bei Ben Sira und Paulus

Es bedarf nicht vieler Worte, um die Unterschiede zwischen dem in der Tradition der biblischen Spruchweisheit stehenden und in hochhellenistischer Zeit wirkenden Schreiber Ben Sira und dem in der späthellenistisch-römischen Epoche wirkenden Apostel hervorzuheben. Der schlichten Selbstverständlichkeit im Umgang des Weisen mit der Tora stehen die überaus komplexen Überlegungen des christlichen Apostels gegenüber, der als ehemaliger Pharisäer die apokalyptischen Grundanschauungen von dem nahe bevorstehenden Ende, der Auferstehung der Toten, dem Weltgericht und dem Eingang der Frommen in die himmlische Welt teilte und sie nun im Schatten der eigenen Begegnung mit dem Auferstandenen neu durchbuchstabierte. Dabei ist er zu dem Ergebnis gekommen, dass Christus des Gesetzes Ende (Röm 10,4) und die Liebe als die Zusammenfassung aller Gebote des Gesetzes Erfüllung sind (Röm 13,9f).[135] Mithin konnte er getrost erklären, dass er das Gesetz durch den Glauben nicht außer Geltung gesetzt, sondern zur Geltung gebracht habe (Röm 3,31).

Es dürfte daher nicht überraschen, dass nicht nur die materiale Ethik des Juden Ben Sira, sondern auch die des einstigen Juden Paulus grundsätzlich

---

cherheit, wo keine Sicherheit zu sehen ist; er ist, wie Martin Luther sagt, die Bereitschaft, vertrauensvoll in das Dunkel der Zukunft einzutreten."

135 Zur darin liegenden Verbindung zu Jesu Verkündigung vgl. Wenham, Paulus, 229–33.

durch den Dekalog als den Inbegriff der Tora[136] bestimmt ist. Ben Sira hat seine Gebote und Verbote ausdrücklich thematisiert,[137] Paulus sind sie bei seinen Paränesen offensichtlich gegenwärtig gewesen. Eine Ausnahme bildet bei ihm das für die Fest- und Ruhetage stehende Sabbatgebot, das er offensichtlich ebenso wie die Ritualgesetzgebung für den Christen als irrelevant betrachtete. Verlockend wäre es, den Schriftgebrauch Ben Siras und des Apostels miteinander zu vergleichen, aber diese Aufgabe würde den vorliegenden Rahmen vollends sprengen. Sie ist zudem für beide Autoren bereits gelöst.[138] Statt dessen sei hier zur Kontrolle des paulinischen Rückgriffs auf den Dekalog ein zusätzlicher Blick auf die Sprüche des Pseudo-Phokylides geworfen, der vermutlich ein älterer Zeitgenosse des Apostels war.[139] Findet sich bei beiden gegenüber Ben Sira ein Sondergut, so lässt sich daraus auf eine entsprechende ethische Diskussion in der zeitgenössischen jüdisch-hellenistischen Synagoge zurück schließen.

Die Zählung der Zehn Gebote schließt sich der in Ex 20 vorliegenden an, die das Bilderverbot als selbständiges Gebot betrachtet und zum Ausgleich das in Dtn 5 in zwei Rechtssätze aufgeteilte Verbot, den Besitz des Nächsten zu begehren, in einem einzigen zusammenfasst.[140] Dass für die Juden Ben Sira[141] und Paulus[142] Gottes Einzigkeit und damit das erste Gebot die selbstverständliche Voraussetzung ihres Denkens bildete, versteht sich angesichts seiner Bedeutung im Alten Testament und im Judentum geradezu von selbst. Zudem wurde es wohl schon zur Zeit des Apostels im täglichen Morgengebet in Gestalt des שְׁמַע יִשְׂרָאֵל (Dtn 6,4–9) vergegenwärtigt.[143] Daraus ergibt sich bereits, dass beide auch den mit dem heidnischen Gottesdienst verbundenen Bilderdienst als Götzendienst ablehnten.[144] Eine ausdrückliche Verurteilung des Meineides findet sich nur bei Ben Sira und

---

136 Vgl. dazu Otto, Dekalog, 59–68; ders., Ethik, 208–19 und Kaiser, GAT I, 308–12.
137 Wischemeyer, Kultur, 199.
138 Vgl. dazu Middendorp, Stellung, 35–91 und dazu ergänzend Marböck, Kohelet, 275–302 bzw. Koch, Schrift.
139 Benutzt wurden die Textausgabe von Denis, Fragmenta, 88–102 nach dem Abdruck in ders., Concordance, 90f und die Bearbeitungen von Walter, Dichtung, 182–216 und van der Horst, Pseudo-Phocylides, 565–82 (= Phoc.). Zur Zeitstellung vgl. Walter, Dichtung, 193 (zwischen [frühestens] 100 v. und [spätestens] 100 n.Chr.), bzw. van der Horst, Pseudo-Phocylides, 567 (nicht vor 50 v. und nach 37 n.Chr.), wobei beide für Alexandrien als Entstehungsort plädieren; zum Verhältnis von jüdisch-hellenistischen und griechischen Elementen in seiner Lehre vgl. Küchler, Weisheitstraditionen, 286–302.
140 Zur unterschiedlichen Zählung des Bilderverbots vgl. Dohmen, Bilderverbot, 213–16 und zum Verbot des Begehrens Schmidt, Zehn Gebote, 131–33 .
141 Sir 18,1–2; 33/36,5/4.
142 Röm 1,18ff, vgl. V. 21 und weiterhin Tert. Apol. 17,1–3 und 21,10 (zitiert nach der Ausgabe von Becker, Tertullian Apologeticum.
143 Vgl. dazu Hoffman, Gebet III, 43.
144 Sir 30,18f und Röm 1,23; Gal 5,20; vgl. Tert. Apol. 12,6f und 41,1.

Pseudo-Phokylides. Sie lässt sich ebenso auf das dritte wie das neunte Gebot beziehen, von denen das erste den Missbrauch des Gottesnamens und das zweite die gerichtliche Falschaussage und später die Lüge überhaupt verbietet.[145] Paulus belässt es dagegen in Röm 1,29 bei einer allgemeinen Ablehnung heimtückischer List, des δόλος κακοηθείας. Während Ben Sira die Bedeutung der Feiertage und des Tempelgottesdienstes hervorhebt und damit dem vierten Gebot entspricht,[146] stellt das Halten der jüdischen Ruhe- und Festtage durch die galatischen Gemeinden nach der Überzeugung des Apostels eine Preisgabe der christlichen Freiheit dar.[147] Dagegen gibt er die Beachtung oder Nichtbeachtung der Feste und Feiertage im Römerbrief der Entscheidung des Einzelnen anheim: er mag es damit halten, wie er will, sofern er überzeugt ist, damit dem Herrn zu Gefallen zu leben.[148] Andererseits war für Paulus wie für Sirach das fünfte Gebot, die Eltern zu ehren, so selbstverständlich wie das erste.[149] Ihre enge Zusammengehörigkeit findet darin seinen Niederschlag, dass Pseudo-Phokylides ihre Respektierung in einem einzigen Mahnwort einprägt.[150] Das bei Sirach in 31/34,26–27/22 bereits radikalisierte Verbot von Mord und Totschlag hat bei allen dreien ein Echo gefunden.[151] Dass der vom siebten Gebot untersagte Ehebruch ebenso gegen die Moralvorstellungen von ihnen allen verstieß, lässt sich belegen.[152] Besondere Aufmerksamkeit aber widmeten sie sämtlich dem damit verwandten Thema der Hurerei,[153] unter das für Paulus auch die in Lev 18,7f verbotene Ehe mit der Witwe des Vaters[154] und für ihn wie für Pseudo-Phokylides der homosexuelle Verkehr mit Knaben und Männern[155] wie der (im Gesetz noch nicht behandelte) lesbische fielen.[156] Bei Pseudo-Phokylides

---

145 Sir 23,9–11; 41,19; Phoc. 10f.
146 47,10 und 50,5–21 und Marböck, Hohepriester, 215–29; vgl. auch Mulder, Simon, 377–92 bzw. das Summary 425–28.
147 Gal 4,10; vgl. Tert. Apol. 42,4f.
148 Röm 14,5f.
149 Sir 3,1–17; 7,27f, vgl. 41,17, und Bohlen, Ehrung, und Röm 1,30.
150 Phoc. 8.
151 Sir 5,14; Röm 1,29 und Phoc. 4b, vgl. 57f.
152 Sir 23,18–28, vgl. 26,9–10;. 1Kor 6,9; Gal 5,19; Röm 2,22 und Phoc. 3a; vgl. auch Tert. Apol. 39,11f; 45,3; 46,11.
153 Sir 23,23; 26,9; 1Kor 5,1ff; 6,9; Gal 5,19; 6,18 und Phoc. 177–183; vgl. auch Tert. Apol. 50,12.
154 1Kor 6,9; Röm 1,27 und Phoc. 3b; 190f; vgl. Lev 18,22 und dazu Tomson, Paul, 97–124.
155 Röm 1,27 und Phoc. 190f; zur vermutlichen Wurzel ihrer Verdammung in Lev 18,22 und 20,13 und ihrer für die Betroffenen katastrophalen Nachwirkungen bis in die Gegenwart vgl. Gerstenberger, Buch Mose, 232 und besonders 271–72 sowie zum gesellschaftlichen Wandel in der offenen Gesellschaft mit ihren neuen Kleingruppen ders., Theologien, 252–53; zur ambivalenten Bewertung bei den Griechen Dover, Homosexualität, bes. 162–77 bzw. Reinsberg, Ehe, 163–215, bes. 212–15.
156 Röm 1,26 und Phoc. 192.

findet sich nebenbei auch das Verbot der Abtreibung,[157] das nach dem Zeugnis Tertullians selbstverständlich auch in der Alten Kirche galt.[158] Ebenso untersagte Pseudo-Phokylides die Beseitigung von Neugeborenen durch Aussetzung.[159] Und selbstverständlich galten für Sirach wie für Paulus und Pseudo-Phokylides auch das achte und neunte Gebot, die inzwischen auf Diebstahl[160] und Lüge[161] überhaupt bezogen wurden. Die sittliche Sensibilität schlägt sich besonders in dem Respekt vor dem zehnten, das Begehren nach dem Besitzes des Nächsten einschließlich seiner Frau und Kinder untersagenden Gebot nieder. Dass sie Sirach und Paulus nicht fehlte, zeigen die entsprechenden Belege.[162] Die paulinischen geben zu erkennen, dass der Apostel ein in Begehrlichkeiten verbrachtes Leben als gottwidrig und heidnisch betrachtete.[163] Und so hat auch noch Tertullian geurteilt.[164] Bei Pseudo-Phokylides verbirgt sich das Gebot hinter der Mahnung, Neid als eine widernatürliche Eigenschaft zu meiden.[165]

Wollten wir nun nach dem Handeln des von Sirach und von dem Apostel bezeugten Gottes fragen (und nur ein solches Reden entspricht der Eigenart des biblischen Glaubens), so würde es sich zeigen, dass er für beide der ist, den das Alte Testament ebenso als den אֵל קַנָּא, den eifernden, über seiner Ehre wachenden (Ex 20,5) wie als den אֵל רַחוּם וְחַנּוּן, den barmherzigen und gnädigen Gott bekennt, der langmütig und von großer Güte und Treue ist (Ex 34,6).[166] So ist er für Sirach der Gott, dessen Barmherzigkeit allem Fleisch gilt (Sir 18,13) und zugleich der, mit dessen Vergebung nur rechnen darf, wer zu ihm (im Gehorsam gegen die Tora) umkehrt (5,7). Und auch für Paulus ist er der *Vater der Barmherzigkeit* (2Kor 1,3), der ihn eben deshalb berufen hat, die ὑπακοὴ τῆς πίστεως, den Gehorsam des Glaubens zu verkünden (Röm 1,5). So stimmen der jüdische Weise, der christliche Apostel und der christliche Apologet dank ihres gemeinsamen biblischen Mutterbodens und ihres jüdischen Erbes über alle religiösen Unterschiede hinweg in den von ihnen zugrunde gelegten konkreten ethischen Normen überein. Daran zu erinnern, dass niemand, der sich mit der Religionsgeschichte des Judentums in der Zeit des späten Zweiten Tempels und des Urchristentums beschäftigt, an diesem Buch vorübergehen sollte, ist die selbstverständliche Überzeugung

---

157 Phoc. 184.
158 Tert. Apol. 9,8f.
159 Phoc. 185.
160 Vgl. Sir 5,8; 15,8; 20,25 mit 1Kor 6,10; Röm 2,21 und 13,9 und Phoc. 6.
161 Vgl. Sir 15,20; 20,25f; 41,17 und Phoc. 7 mit den freilich religiös spezialisierten Aussagen in Röm 1,25; 3,4 und 2Thess 2,11.
162 Sir 5,2; 6,1–3; 18,30–33, vgl. auch 9,9 und 23,6.
163 Röm 1,24; 6,12; 7,7; 13,14; Gal 5,16.24; 1Thess 4,5.
164 Vgl. Tert. Apol. 45,3 und 46,11.
165 Phoc. 70–73.
166 Vgl. dazu Spieckermann, Herr, 1–18.

derer, die sich hier zu der nun zu Ende gehenden Konferenz versammelt haben. In der Kirche aber gilt es darüber hinaus daran zu erinnern, dass dieses Buch ein unverzichtbarer Teil der christlichen Bibel ist. Denn jeder, der bei den Grundsätzen einer einfachen Sittlichkeit und Frömmigkeit Rat sucht, wird ihn bei Jesus Sirach finden, auch wenn er sich dabei an die Mahnung des Apostels erinnern sollte (1Thess 5,21): Prüfet alles, und das Gute behaltet.[167]

Bibliographie

Argall, R.A., *1 Enoch and Sirach: A Comparative Literary and Conceptual Analysis of the Themes of Revelation, Creation and Judgment* (SBL EJL 8; Atlanta: Scholars, 1995).

Becker, C., *Tertullian Apologeticum.Verteidigung des Christentums. Lateinisch und Deutsch* (München: Kösel 1952 bzw. 4th. ed. Darmstadt: Wissenschaftliche Buchgesellschaft, 1992).

Becker, J., *Paulus. Der Apostel der Völker* (UTB 2014; Tübingen: Mohr Siebeck, 1998).

Bergmeier, R., *Das Gesetz im Römerbrief und andere Studien zum Neuen Testament* (WUNT 121; Tübingen: Mohr Siebeck, 2000).

Blenkinsopp, J., *Wisdom and Law in the Old Testament. The Ordering of Life in Israel and Early Judaism* (rev. ed., OBS; Oxford: Oxford University Press 1995).

Bohlen, R., *Die Ehrung der Eltern bei Ben Sira. Studien zur Motivation und Interpretation eines familienethischen Grundwertes in frühhellenistischer Zeit* (TThSt 51; Trier: Paulinus-Verlag 1991).

Buddensiek, F., *Die Theorie des Glücks in Aristoteles' Eudemischer Ethik* (Hypomnemata 8; Göttingen: Vandenhoeck & Ruprecht, 1999).

Bultmann, R., *Jesus Christus und die Mythologie. Jesus Christus und die Mythologie. Das Neue Testament im Licht der Bibelkritik* (Ein Stundenbuch 47; Hamburg: Furche-Verl., 1965) = *Jesus Christus und die Mythologie, Glauben und Verstehen* (vol 4; Tübingen: Mohr [Siebeck], 1965).

Bultmann, R., Römer 7 und die Anthropologie des Paulus (1932), in *Exegetica. Aufsätze zur Erforschung des Neuen Testaments* (eds. R. Bultmann and E. Dinkler, (Tübingen: Mohr Siebeck, 1967), 198–209.

Bultmann, R., *Theologie des Neuen Testaments* (ed. O. Merk; UTB 630; 7th rev. ed.; Tübingen: Mohr [Siebeck], 1977).

Calduch-Benages, N., *Un giogiello di sapienza. Leggendo Siracide 2* (Cammini nello Spirito. Biblica 45; Milano: Figlie. di San Paolo, 2001).

---

[167] Dabei dürfte der Christ von selbst erkennen, wo der Rat des Weisen und die Lehre Christi und seines Apostels sich in der Frage der Feindesliebe von einander scheiden, vgl. z.B. Sir 12,1f.7 mit Mt 5,43 und dazu Keil, Glaubenslehre, 188f. – In der Demut vor Gott sind Juden und Christen einander näher, als es der Apostel in seiner besonderen Situation wahrnehmen konnte. Wer immer den Verzicht auf die eigene Endlichkeit leistet und daher die Freiheit zur Güte gegenüber dem Nächsten und der Furchtlosigkeit gegenüber dem Tode gewonnen hat, hat die Lehre begriffen, die ihm Gott durch die Endlichkeit seines Lebens gibt. – Für mehrfache Hilfe bei den Korrekturen danke ich meinem Freund, Herrn Pfarrer Martin Neher, Stuttgart und Maulbronn.

Collins, J.J., *The Apocalyptic Imagination. An Introduction to Jewish Apocalyptic Literature* (2d ed.; The Biblical Resource Series; Grand Rapids / Cambridge: Eerdmans, 1998).

Collins, J.J., *Jewish Wisdom in the Hellenistic Age* (OTL; Louisville: Westminster, 1997).

Conzelmann, H., *Der erste Brief an die Korinther* (11th ed.; KEK 5; Göttingen: Vandenhoeck & Ruprecht, 1969).

Crenshaw, J.L., *Old Testament Wisdom: An Introduction* (London: SCM Press, 1982).

Crenshaw, J.L., "The Problem of Theodicy in Sirach: On Human Bondage," *JBL* 94 (1975) 47–64.

Denis, A.-M., *Concordance grèque des pseudépigraphes d'Ancient Testament. Concordance, corpus des textes, indices* (Louvain-la-Neuve: Institut Orientaliste. Université Catholique de Louvain, 1987).

Denis, A.-M., *Fragmenta Pseudepigraphorum quae supersunt graece: una cum historicorum et auctorum judaeorum hellenisticarum fragmentis* (ed. M. Black; PVTG IIIb; Leiden: Brill, 1979).

Dihle, A., *The Theory of Will in Classical Antiquity* (Berkeley: University of California Press, 1982) = *Die Vorstellung vom Willen in der Antike* (Sammlung Vandenhoeck; Göttingen: Vandenhoeck & Ruprecht, 1985).

Di Lella, A.A., "Fear of the Lord as Wisdom: Ben Sira 1,11–30," in *The Book of Ben Sira in Modern Research: Proceedings of the First International Ben Sira Conference, 28–31 July 1996, Soesterberg, Netherlands* (ed. P.C. Beentjes; BZAW 255; Berlin / New York: de Gruyter, 1997) 113–33.

Diogenes Laertius, *Leben und Meinungen berühmter Philosophen. Buch I–X* (trans. O. Apelt; ed. K. Reich; Philosophische Bibliothek 53/54; 2d ed.; Hamburg: Meiner, 1967).

Dohmen, Ch., *Das Bilderverbot. Seine Entstehung und seine Entwicklung im Alten Testament* (2d ed.; BBB 62; Frankfurt a.M.: Athenäum, 1987).

Dover, K.J., *Greek Homosexuality* (London: Duckworth, 1978) = *Homosexualität in der griechischen Antike* (trans. S. Worcester; München: Beck, 1983).

Dunn, J.D.G., *Romans 1–8; 9–16* (WBC 38 A, B; Dallas: Word Book, 1988).

Forschner, M., *Über das Glück des Menschen. Aristoteles, Epikur, Stoa, Thomas von Aquin, Kant* (2d ed.; Darmstadt: Wissenschaftliche Buchgesellschaft, 1994).

Gammie, J.G. – Perdue, L.C. eds., *The Sage in Israel and in the Ancient Near East* (Winona Lake: Eisenbrauns, 1990).

García Martínez, F. – Trebolle Barrera, J., *The People of the Dead Sea Scrolls: Their Writings, Beliefs and Practices* (trans. Wilfred G. Watson; Leiden: Brill, 1995).

Gerstenberger, E.S., *Das dritte Buch Mose. Leviticus* (ATD 6; Göttingen: Vandenhoeck & Ruprecht, 1993).

Gerstenberger, E.S., *Theologien im Alten Testament. Pluralität und Synkretismus alttestamentlichen Gottesglaubens* (Stuttgart et al.: Kohlhammer, 2001).

Gilbert, M., *La critique des dieux dans le livre de la Sagesse* (Sg 13–15) (AnBib 53; Rome: Pontifical Biblical Institute, 1973).

Gowan, D.E., *Eschatology in the Old Testament* (2d ed.; Edinburgh: Clark, 2000).

Guthrie, W.K.C., *A History of Greek Philosophy VI: Aristotle: An Encounter* (Cambridge: Cambridge University Press, 1981).

Harnisch, W., "Christusbindung oder Weltbezug? Sachkritische Fragen zur paulinischen Argumentation in 1. Korinther 7," in *Antikes Judentum und Frühes Christentum* (ed. B. Kollmann; FS H. Stegemann; BZNW 97; Berlin / New York: de Gruyter, 1999), 457–73 = in *Die Zumutung der Liebe. Gesammelte Aufsätze* (ed. U. Schönborn; FRLANT 187; Göttingen: Vandenhoeck & Ruprecht, 1999), 206–23.

Harnisch, W., "Freiheit als Selbstentzug. Zur Begründung der Ethik im Denken des Paulus (1. Korinther 6,12–20)," in *Freiräume leben – Ethik gestalten* (ed. S. Dimpker; FS S. Keil; Stuttgart: Quell, 1994), 179–95 = in *Die Zumutung der Liebe. Gesammelte*

Aufsätze (ed. U. Schönborn; FRLANT 187; Göttingen: Vandenhoeck & Ruprecht, 1999) 169–84.

Haspecker, J., *Gottesfurcht bei Jesus Sirach. Ihre religiöse Struktur und ihre literarische und doktrinäre Bedeutung* (AnBib 30; Rome: Pontifical Biblical Institute, 1967).

Hegel, G.W.F., "Vorlesung über die vollendete Religion (1827)," in *Vorlesungen über die Philosophie der Religion III: Die vollendete Religion* (ed. W. Jaeschke; Philosophische Bibliothek 461; Hamburg: Meiner, 1995) 223–33.

Hengel, M., *Judentum und Hellenismus. Studien zu ihrer Begegnung unter besonderer Berücksichtigung Palästinas bis zur Mitte des 2. Jh. v.Chr.* (WUNT 10; 2d ed.; Tübingen: Mohr [Siebeck], 1969; 3d ed. 1988).

Hengel, M., "Der vorchristliche Paulus," in *Paulus und das antike Judentum* (eds. M. Hengel and U. Heckel; WUNT 58; Tübingen: Mohr Siebeck, 1991) 177–293.

Hengel, M. – Schwemmer, A.M. eds., *Paulus zwischen Damaskus und Antiochien. Die unbekannten Jahre des Apostels* (WUNT 108; Tübingen: Mohr Siebeck, 1998).

Hoffman, L.A., "Gebet III: Judentum," *TRE* 12, 42–47.

van der Horst, P.W., "Pseudo-Phocylides (First Century B.C. – First Century A.D.)," in *OTP* 2 (ed. J.H. Charlesworth; New York: Doubleday, 1985), 565–82.

Hübner, H., *Gottes Ich und Israel. Zum Schriftgebrauch des Paulus in Röm 9–11* (FRLANT 136; Göttingen: Vandenhoeck & Ruprecht, 1984).

Jedan, Ch., *Willensfreiheit bei Aristoteles?* (Neue Studien zur Philosophie 15; Göttingen: Vandenhoeck & Ruprecht, 2000).

Jüngel, E., *Gott als Geheimnis der Welt. Zur Begründung der Theologie des Gekreuzigten im Streit zwischen Theismus und Atheismus* (4th ed.; Tübingen: Mohr Siebeck, 1982).

Käsemann, E., *An die Römer* (HNT 8a; Tübingen: Mohr Siebeck, 1973). FN 94, 100, 110, 122, 127, 128, 130

Kaiser, O., "Anknüpfung und Widerspruch. Die Antwort der jüdischen Weisheit auf die Herausforderung des Hellenismus," in *Pluralismus und Identität* (ed. J. Mehlhausen; Veröffentlichungen der Wissenschaftlichen Gesellschaft für Theologie 8; Gütersloh: Kaiser / Gütersloher Verlagshaus, 1995), 54–69 = in *Gottes und der Menschen Weisheit* (ed. O. Kaiser; BZAW 261; Berlin / New York: de Gruyter, 1998) 201–16.

Kaiser, O., *Die Bedeutung der griechischen Welt für die alttestamentliche Theologie* (NAWG.PH 2000/7; Göttingen: Vandenhoeck & Ruprecht, 2000).

Kaiser, O., *Der Gott des Alten Testaments. Theologie des AT I: Grundlegung* (UTB 1747; Göttingen: Vandenhoeck & Ruprecht, 1993). = GAT I

Kaiser, O., *Der Gott des Alten Testaments. Wesen und Wirken. Theologie des AT II: Jahwe, der Gott Israels, Schöpfer der Welt und des Menschen* (UTB 2024; Göttingen: Vandenhoeck & Ruprecht, 1998). = GAT II

Kaiser, O., "Judentum und Hellenismus. Ein Beitrag zur Frage nach dem hellenistischen Einfluß auf Kohelet und Jesus Sirach," *VF* 27 (1982) 68–86 = in *Der Mensch unter dem Schicksal. Studien zur Geschichte, Theologie und Gegenwartsbedeutung der Weisheit* (ed. O. Kaiser; BZAW 161; Berlin / New York: de Gruyter, 1985) 135–53.

Kaiser, O., "Der Mensch als Geschöpf Gottes. Aspekte der Anthropologie Ben Siras," in *Der Einzelne und seine Gemeinschaft bei Ben Sira* (eds. R. Egger-Wenzel and I. Krammer; BZAW 270; Berlin / New York: de Gruyter, 1998) 1–22.

Kaiser, O., "Die Rezeption der Stoischen Providenz bei Ben Sira," *JNSL* 24/1 (1998) 41–54.

Kaiser, O., "Das Verständnis des Todes bei Ben Sira," *NZSTh* 43 (2001) 175–92.

Keil, G., *Glaubenslehre. Grundzüge christlicher Dogmatik* (Stuttgart et al.: Kohlhammer, 1986).

Kenny, A., *The Aristotelian Ethics: A Study of the Relationship between the Eudemian and Nichomachean Ethics of Aristotle* (Oxford: Clarendon Press, 1978).

Kepper, M., *Hellenistische Bildung im Buch der Weisheit. Studien zur Sprachgestalt und Theologie der Sapientia Salomonis* (BZAW 280; Berlin / New York: de Gruyter, 1999).

Kierkegaard, S., "Die Krankheit zum Tode. Der Hohepriester – der Zöllner – die Sünderin," in *Gesammelte Werke* 24/25 (trans. E. Hirsch; Düsseldorf: Diederich, 1954).

Kieweler, H.V., *Ben Sira zwischen Judentum und Hellenismus. Eine kritische Auseinandersetzung mit Th. Middendorp* (BEATAJ 30; Frankfurt a.M. et al.: Lang, 1992).

Koch, D.-A., *Die Schrift als Zeuge des Evangeliums. Untersuchungen zur Verwendung und zum Verständnis der Schrift bei Paulus* (BHT 69; Tübingen: Mohr Siebeck, 1986).

Kremer, J., *Der Erste Brief an die Korinther* (RNT; Regensburg: Pustet, 1997).

Küchler, M., *Frühjüdische Weisheitstraditionen. Zum Fortgang weisheitlichen Denkens im Bereich des frühjüdischen Jahweglaubens* (OBO 26; Fribourg: Universitätsverlag, 1979).

Kümmel, W.G., *Die Theologie des Neuen Testaments nach seinen Hauptzeugen Jesus, Paulus, Johannes* (2d ed.; GNT 3; Göttingen: Vandenhoeck & Ruprecht, 1972).

Lang, F., *Die Briefe an die Korinther* (NTD 7; Göttingen: Vandenhoeck & Ruprecht, 1986).

Lichtenberger, H., "Paulus und das Gesetz," in *Paulus und das antike Judentum* (eds. M. Hengel and U. Heckel; WUNT 58; Tübingen: Mohr Siebeck, 1991) 361–78.

Lichtheim, M., *Late Egyptian Wisdom in the International Context: A Study of Demotic Instructions* (OBO 52; Fribourg et al.: Universitätsverlag, 1983).

Lietzmann, H., *An die Korinther I.II* (4th ed.; suppl. by W.G. Kümmel; HNT 9; Tübingen: Mohr Siebeck, 1949).

Lohse, E., *Paulus. Eine Biographie* (München: Beck, 1996).

Lührmann, D., *Der Brief an die Galater* (2d ed.; ZBK.NT 7; Zürich: Theologischer Verlag, 1988).

Maier, G., *Mensch und Freier Wille. Nach den jüdischen Religionsparteien zwischen Ben Sira und Paulus* (WUNT 12; Tübingen: Mohr Siebeck, 1971).

Marböck, J., "Das Gebet um die Rettung Zions. Sir 36,1–22 (G: 33,1–13a; 36,16b–22) im Zusammenhang der Geschichtsschau Ben Siras," in *Memoria Jerusalem* (FS F. Sauer; ed. J.B. Bauer and J. Marböck; Graz: Akademische Druck- und Verlagsanstalt, 1977) 95–115 = in *Gottes Weisheit unter uns. Zur Theologie des Buches Sirach* (ed. I. Fischer; Herders Biblische Studien 6; Freiburg et al.: Herder 1995) 149–66.

Marböck, J., "Gerechtigkeit Gottes und Leben nach dem Sirachbuch. Ein Antwortversuch in seinem Kontext," in *Gerechtigkeit und Leben im hellenistischen Zeitalter* (ed. J. Jeremias; BZAW 296; Berlin / New York: de Gruyter, 2001) 21–52.

Marböck, J., "Gesetz und Weisheit. Zum Verständnis des Gesetzes bei Jesus Sirach," in *Gottes Weisheit unter uns. Zur Theologie des Buches Jesus Sirach* (ed. I. Fischer; Herders Biblische Studien 6; Freiburg et al.: Herder, 1995) 52–72.

Marböck, J., "Der Hohepriester Simon in Sir 50. Ein Beitrag zur Bedeutung von Priestertum und Kult im Sirachbuch," in *Treasures of Wisdom* (FS M. Gilbert; eds. N. Calduch-Benages and J. Vermeylen; BETL 143; Leuven: Peeters, 1999) 215–29.

Marböck, J., "Kohelet und Sirach. Eine vielschichtige Beziehung," in *Das Buch Kohelet. Studien zur Struktur, Geschichte, Rezeption und Theologie* (ed. L. Schienhorst-Schönberger; BZAW 254; Berlin / New York: de Gruyter, 1997), 275–302.

Marböck, J., "Sir 38,24–39,11: Der schriftgelehrte Weise. Ein Beitrag zur Gestalt und Lehre Ben Siras," in *Gottes Weisheit unter uns. Zur Theologie des Buches Jesus Sirach* (ed. I. Fischer; Herders Biblische Studien 6; Freiburg et al.: Herder, 1995) 25–51.

Marböck, J., *Weisheit im Wandel* (BBB 37; Bonn: Hanstein, 1971) = (2d ed.; BZAW 272; Berlin / New York: de Gruyter, 1999).

Michel, O., *Der Brief an die Römer* (14th [5th] ed.; KEK 4; Göttingen: Vandenheock & Ruprecht, 1978).

74 Otto Kaiser

Middendorp, Th., *Die Stellung Jesu Ben Siras zwischen Judentum und Hellenismus* (Leiden: Brill, 1973).

Moers, G., "'Weisheitstexte' in ägyptischer Sprache. Der Papyrus Lansing: Das Lob des Schreiberberufes in einer ägyptischen 'Schülerhandschrift' aus dem ausgehenden Neuen Reich," in *TUAT Ergänzungslieferung* (ed. O. Kaiser; Gütersloh: Gütersloher Verlagshaus, 2001) 109–42.

Mulder, O., *Simon, de hogepriester, in Sirach 50* (Almelo: Mulder, 2000).

Murphy, R.E., "The Personification of Wisdom," in *Wisdom in Ancient Israel* (FS J.A. Emerton; eds. J. Day et al.; Cambridge: Cambridge University, 1995) 222–33.

Murphey, R.E., *The Tree of Life: An Exploration of Biblical Wisdom Literature* (ABRL; New York: Doubleday, 1990) = (2d ed.; Grand Rapids: Eerdmans, 1996).

Nissen, A., *Gott und der Nächste im antiken Judentum. Untersuchungen zum Doppelgebot der Liebe* (WUNT 15; Tübingen: Mohr Siebeck, 1974).

Otto, E., "Der Dekalog als Brennspiegel israelitischer Rechtsgeschichte," in *Alttestamentlicher Glaube und Biblische Theologie* (FS H.D. Preuß; eds. J. Hausmann and H.-J. Zobel; Stuttgart et al.; Kohlhammer, 1992) 59–68.

Otto, E., *Theologische Ethik des Alten Testaments* (Theologische Wisschenschaft 3/2; Stuttgart et al.: Kohlhammer, 1994).

Otto, E., *Die Tora des Mose. Die Geschichte der literarischen Vermittlung von Recht, Religion und Politik durch die Mosegestalt* (Berichte und Sitzungen der Joachim-Jungius-Gesellschaft der Wissenschaften e.V., Hamburg 19/2; Göttingen: Vandenhoeck & Ruprecht, 2001).

Peters, N., *Das Buch Jesus Sirach oder Ecclesiasticus* (EHAT 25; Münster: Aschendorff, 1913).

Prato, G.L., *Il problema della teodicea in Ben Sira: Composizione dei contrari e richiamo alle origini* (AnBib 65; Rome: Pontifical Biblical Institute, 1975).

von Rad, G., *Weisheit in Israel* (Neukirchen-Vluyn: Neukirchener Verlag, 1970).

Reinsberg, C., *Ehe, Hetärentum und Knabenliebe im Antiken Griechenland* (Beck's archäologische Bibliothek; München: Beck, 1989) = (2d ed.; 1993).

Reiterer, F.V. ed., *Freundschaft bei Ben Sira. Beiträge des Symposions zu Ben Sira – Salzburg 1995* (BZAW 244; Berlin / New York: de Gruyter, 1996).

Römer, W.H.Ph., "'Weisheitstexte' und Texte mit Bezug auf den Schulbetrieb in sumerischer Sprache," in *TUAT III/1* (ed. O. Kaiser; Gütersloh: Gütersloher Verlagshaus, 1990) 17–109.

Rössler, D., *Gesetz und Geschichte. Untersuchungen zur Theologie der jüdischen Apokalyptik und der pharisäischen Orthodoxie* (WMANT 3; Neukirchen-Vluyn: Neukirchener, 1960).

Sanders, J.T., *Ben Sira and Demotic Wisdom* (SBLMS 28; Chico: Scholars Press, 1983).

Sauer, G., *Jesus Sirach: Übersetzt und erklärt* (ATDA 1; Göttingen: Vandenhoeck & Ruprecht, 2000).

Schäfer, P., "Der vorrabbinische Pharisäismus," in *Paulus und das antike Judentum* (eds. M. Hengel and U. Heckel; WUNT 58; Tübingen: Mohr Siebeck, 1991) 125–75.

Schelling, F.W.J., *Philosophische Untersuchungen über das Wesen der menschlichen Freiheit und die damit zusammenhängenden Gegenstände* (ed. Th. Buchheim; Philosophische Bibliothek 509; Hamburg: Meiner, 1997) = (Darmstadt: Wissenschaftliche Buchgesellschaft, 1997).

Schelling, F.W.J, "Ueber den Zusammenhang der Natur mit der Geisterwelt. Ein Gespräch. Fragment. Aus dem handschriftlichen Nachlaß," in *Ausgewählte Werke. Schriften von 1806–1813* (Darmstadt: Wissenschaftliche Buchgesellschaft, 1976) 429–538.

Schlier, H., *Der Brief an die Galater* (10th ed.; KEK 7; Göttingen: Vandenhoeck & Ruprecht, 1949).

Schmidt, W.H., *Die Zehn Gebote im Rahmen alttestamentlicher Ethik* (EdF 281; Darmstadt: Wissenschaftliche Buchgesellschaft, 1993).

Schürer, E., *The History of the Jewish People in the age of Jesus Christ: (175 B.C. – A.D. 135)* (vol 2; rev. and ed. G. Vermes; Edinburgh: Clark 1979).

Segal, M.Z., ספר בן־סירא השלם (3d ed.; Jerusalem: Bialik, 1972).

Skehan, P.W. – Di Lella, A.A., *The Wisdom of Ben Sira: A New Translation with Notes, Introduction and Commentary* (AB 39; New York: Doubleday, 1987).

Smend, R., *Die Weisheit des Jesus Sirach erklärt* (Berlin: Reimer, 1906).

Söding, Th., *Das Liebesgebot bei Paulus. Die Mahnung zur Agape im Rahmen der paulinischen Ethik* (NTAbh.NF 26; Münster: Aschendorff, 1995).

Spieckermann, H., "Barmherzig und gnädig ist der Herr ...," *ZAW* 102 (1990) 1–18.

Stadelmann, H., *Ben Sira als Schriftgelehrter. Eine Untersuchung zum Berufsbild des vormakkabäischen Sōfēr unter Berücksichtigung seines Verhältnisses zu Priester-, Propheten- und Weisheitslehrertum* (WUNT 2/6; Tübingen: Mohr Siebeck, 1980).

Stanton, G., "The Law of Moses and the Law of Christ – Galatians 3:1–6:2," in *Paul and the Mosaic Law* (ed. J.D.G. Dunn; WUNT 89; Tübingen: Mohr Siebeck, 1996) 99–116.

Stegemann, H., "The Qumran Essenes – Local Members of the Main Jewish Union in Late Second Temple Times," in *The Madrid Qumran Congress. Proceedings of the International Congress on the Dead Sea Scrolls, Madrid 18–21 March, 1991* (eds. Trebolle Barrera, J.C. and L. Vegas Montaner; STDJ 11; Leiden: Brill, 1992), 83–165.

Stuhlmacher, P., *Der Brief an die Römer* (NTD 6; Göttingen: Vandenhoeck & Ruprecht, 1989).

Tomson, P.J., *Paul and the Jewish Laws. Halakha in the Letters of the Apostle to the Gentiles* (CRINT 3/1; Assen / Maastricht: van Gorcum et al., 1990).

Vielhauer, Ph., *Geschichte der urchristlichen Literatur. Einleitung in das Neue Testament, die Apokryphen und die Apostolischen Väter* (2d ed.; de Gruyter Lehrbuch; Berlin / New York: de Gruyter, 1978 [1985]).

Walter, N., "Pseudepigraphische jüdisch-hellenistische Dichtung: Pseudo-Phokylides, Pseudo-Orpheus, Gefälschte Verse auf Namen griechischer Dichter," in *Poetische Schriften* (JSHRZ IV/3; Gütersloh: Gütersloher Verlagshaus Mohn, 1983).

Wenham, D., *Paulus. Jünger Jesu oder Begründer des Christentums?* (Paderborn et al.: Schöningh, 1999).

Wicke-Reuter, U., *Göttliche Providenz und menschliche Verantwortung bei Ben Sira und in der Frühen Stoa* (BZAW 298; Berlin / New York: de Gruyter, 2000).

de Wilde, A., *Das Buch Hiob* (OtTSt 22; Leiden: Brill, 1981).

Wischmeyer, O., *Die Kultur des Buches Jesus Sirach* (BZNW 77; Berlin / New York: de Gruyter, 1994).

Witte, M., "Mose, sein Andenken sei zum Segen (Sir 45,1) – Das Mosebild des Sirachbuches," *BN* 107/108 (2001) 161–86.

Einzelthemen

God, Creator of All (Sir 43:27–33)

Núria Calduch-Benages
Pontifical Gregorian University, Rome

1. Introduction

In his programmatic study on the fear of God in Ben Sira, Haspecker considers the use of the divine attribute "Creator" as a characteristic element of the book: "Der Schöpfergedanke nimmt im Gottesbild der Weisheitslehre und der spätjüdischen Religion einen recht breiten Platz ein. Der Schöpfertitel ist dementsprechend in dieser Zeit sehr geläufig. Das bedeutet jedoch nicht, dass er eine abgegriffene Münze ohne klares Profil geworden ist. Vielmehr ist wenigstens bei Sirach die Verwendung dieses Titels durchaus charakteristisch."[1] In his contribution to the Festschrift for Gilbert,[2] Reiterer has undertaken an analysis of the non-material levels of creation. Before embarking on this specific theme he gives an exhaustive listing of vocabulary pertinent to creation in general which allows us to distinguish seventeen instances in which Ben Sira utilises the title "Creator" or "Maker" with regard to God: בּוֹרֵא (3:16b)[3], עֹשֶׂ(וֹ)ה (7:30a; 10:12b; 35/32:13a; 36/33:13c; 38:15a; 43:5a, 11a; 46:13a; 47:8c), יוֹצֵר (51:12d), ὁ κτίστης (24:8a), ὁ κτίσας (24:8b); ὁ ποιήσας (4:6b; 39:5b, 28d; 47:8d). It goes without saying that these titles make up only a very small part of the vast number of references to the creational activity of God (nearly one hundred instances).

The goal of this study is to analyse the image which Ben Sira offers of God as Creator in Sir 43:27–33. Even though this text does not contain specifically the title Creator / Maker, it is a key passage in the theological construct of the sage, especially with regard to the relationship between creation and praise. Before turning our attention to this text, we will first present briefly three different ways of approaching the theme of creation, followed by an overall vision based on the most significant texts on creation in the book.

---

1 Haspecker, Gottesfurcht, 302.
2 Reiterer, Ebenen, 92.
3 Reiterer, Ebenen, 122, erroneously reads בורא in 39:29b.

2. The Creator and His Work in Ben Sira

2.1 Three Approaches to the Theme of Creation

On a par with the three major topics of the book: wisdom, fear of God and Law (cf. 19:20) the theme of creation stands out as one of the favourite subjects of Ben Sira. It has been studied from various perspectives.[4] In 1975 Crenshaw wrote his well-known article "On the Problem of Theodicy in Sirach: on Human Bondage". While positively evaluating the study of Sir 16:24–17:14; 39:12–35; 42:15–43:33 by Marböck, Crenshaw pointed out that the texts under consideration had not yet been examined "for the light they throw upon the problem of theodicy."[5] In the same year Prato published his doctoral thesis on the problem of theodicy in Ben Sira[6] filling the gap mentioned by Crenshaw. Prato presents a detailed analysis not only of the pericopes under consideration, but also of all texts concerning the principle of double aspect (*composizione dei contrari*) which is related to the theme of creation (*richiamo alle origini*), e.g. 15:11–18:14; 36/33:7–15; 40:1–17; 41:1–13 and also 4:20–6:17; 9:17–11:28. In the context of theodicy creation is considered for two main reasons: to explain how things were at the beginning (in origin) and to understand the various functions assigned by the Creator. This dynamic vision of creation, according to which the created realities reveal themselves more by how they function than by what they are, already existed in the Old Testament tradition. The novelty of Ben Sira, according to Prato, consists in applying this concept of creation to the complex problem of theodicy in all its aspects.

Twelve years later Burton defended a doctoral thesis in Glasgow in which he set out "to examine the formative influences on Sirach's doctrine of creation and the significance of that doctrine in Sirach's thought."[7] As this thesis remains unpublished and is not readily available I give here a short outline of this work. It starts with a comparative analysis between on the one hand Ben Sira and on the other hand the primordial history (Gen 1–11), Deutero-Isaiah, some Psalms, Wisdom literature and early Jewish apocalyptic, then follows a study of the principal texts on creation in Ben Sira (1:1–10; 15:14–20; 16:24–17:14; 18:1–14; 24; 36/33:7–30/33:27/19; 39:16–35; 42:15–43:33) and it concludes with the presentation of a scheme in which creation is the structuring element both for the thought and the book of the sage. The book would consist of eight blocks of creation tradition which together with the eulogy on Simon (in Sir 50), the personal prayer and the autobiographical

---

4   Reiterer, Review, 48–54, section 9: "Wisdom, Law and Creation" and section 10: "Creation and Intertestamental Literature".
5   Crenshaw, Problem, 51.
6   Prato, Il problema.
7   Burton, Ben Sira, 1.

poem (in Sir 51) constitute the pillars on which the message rests. Burton conceives Sirach's doctrine of creation as a bridge connecting God and Wisdom with human beings. He concludes: "It can be said that Sirach has a distinct doctrine of creation running throughout his whole text, which gives it both form and authority."[8]

Seven years later Perdue dedicated a chapter in his book on wisdom theology to the theme 'creation and wisdom' in Ben Sira.[9] He comes to the conclusion that the book presents a rhetorical structure, at times linear and at times concentric, which betrays a well-defined thematic development: "from creation to history to realisation in the new Jerusalem."[10] According to Perdue Ben Sira constructs his world view by means of metaphors. For instance, the creative activity of God is expressed by the metaphor of the divine word; the creation of mankind is depicted with images of artistry, and personified Wisdom is associated with the metaphor of fertility. This series of images evokes the image of a sovereign God who, seated on his celestial throne, rules over creation and directs providence by means of his divine word.[11]

2.2 Creation in Ben Sira: Synthetic Overview

From the very beginning of his book the sage emphasises that the Lord, who alone is wise (1:8), after having created wisdom before anything else (1:4) generously distributed her to all living beings and to those who love him (1:9–10). In Sir 24 personified wisdom explains how she roamed the world (24:5–6) before ὁ κτίστης ἁπάντων ('the Creator of the universe') commanded her to settle in Israel (24:8cd). Wisdom, however, is not just the first creature of God who presides over the order of creation, but she is the Law revealed to Israel by Moses: "All this is the book of the Covenant of the Most High, the Law which Moses prescribed for us, as an inheritance for the assemblies of Jacob" (24:23). In this way Ben Sira outlines the harmony and unity that exists between the natural law of creation and the Law revealed in Sinai; both are manifestations of divine wisdom.

In the long section on the origin of sin, human freedom and divine retribution (15:11–18:14) Ben Sira articulates his thoughts in answer to some foolish arguments. In reply to the last objection of the fool in 16:17–23 he

---

8   Burton, Ben Sira, 219.
9   Perdue, Earth, 243–90, esp. 248–90.
10   Perdue, Earth, 289.
11   Perdue, Earth, 290: "These metaphors provide the means by which Ben Sira conveys his understanding of creation. Placed within the rhetorical structures of language, they provoke the imagination to shape a world of beauty and justice in which God rules as creator and sustainer."

formulates a poem on the creation of the universe and human beings (16:24–17:14). His answer comes in the shape of a midrash on the creation accounts in Genesis (Gen 1:1–2:4a and 2:4b–24). In line with the sapiential tradition he offers a theology of creation which endorses divine justice. He juxtaposes the celestial beings and the human beings. The stars live in perfect order in the cosmos and in total obedience to the Creator (16:26–30), and so should the people, who are endowed with freedom and intelligence so that they are responsible for their works, capable of discerning good and evil, and free to accept or reject the commandment of God (17:1–14). It is remarkable that in 17:11–14 the argument moves from creation to the Sinaitic revelation, which Ben Sira considers to have a universal range.[12] God gave to human beings the Law and an eternal covenant, two elements which are characteristic of the chosen people. The concentration of Sinaitic references at the end of the poem gives the impression that the theophany in Sinai is present in a visible form in the order of creation, or, in the words of Collins: "Sirach allows no interval between the creation and the giving of the Torah. Rather, he implies that the law was given to humanity from the beginning."[13] Law is thus part of God's universal wisdom, which is manifest in creation.[14]

In 36/33:7–15 Ben Sira has recourse to creation in order to explain the motive of the double aspect. As there are polarities in the order of the universe (ordinary days, festive days), so there is also a differentiation with regard to human beings (some the Lord blesses and exalts, others he curses and humiliates). This free diversification by God seriously questions the disciple who might not dare to voice his preoccupation: "Why does one human being have better luck than another, if all have been created from clay?" The answer of the sage (God is like a potter who moulds the human being as he wants) does not satisfy the disciple, because it implies that the human being is deprived of freedom. The sage then is obliged to continue and refine his discourse on theodicy. God created everything in contrasting pairs in a perfect and harmonious balance: evil and good, death and life; according to his own choice a human being becomes a sinner or a pious person. In reality, God has not predestined any person, but has arranged that the result of a person's free choice puts him / her on the right or wrong way. This is how Crenshaw understands it, when he affirms: "The decision of what is better is really a discerning of the appropriate time, which Sirach, in contrast to Qoheleth, thinks is open to man."[15]

In 39:12–35, classified by Liesen as a didactic hymn or a hymnic wisdom poem,[16] Ben Sira takes up again his preoccupations concerning divine

---

12   Cf. Wénin, De la création, 147–58, esp. 155–58.
13   Collins, Seers, 376.
14   Cf. Marböck, Gesetz, 6.
15   Crenshaw, Problem, 53.
16   Cf. Liesen, Full of Praise, 39.

justice, divine wisdom and divine providence, situating them in the context of the goodness and profound meaning of creation. If we leave aside the introduction (39:12–15) and conclusion (39:32–35), the hymn consists of three strophes. In the first strophe (39:16–21) Ben Sira describes the work of God in terms of creation and salvation with special emphasis on the aspect of time. In verse 16 he introduces the theme which he wants to develop: the usefulness of all created reality in so far as it depends on divine dispositions. Appealing to the proper function of and the right time for each thing, the sage responds in verse 21 to two objections that question God's control of the universe: "For what is this?" and "This is worse than that". In the second strophe (39:22–27) the goodness of all the work of God is corroborated by a distinction between the just (good) and the sinners (wicked). Some works are destined for salvation and others for punishment. Indeed, the same works are good for the just and bad for sinners. This is the case with the natural elements, with food and with clothing. The argumentation of Ben Sira has a built-in problem here inasmuch as the concept 'work of God' is used with two different meanings: on the one hand it signifies the creational work of God, by which he orders the world, on the other hand it signifies each created element in the world (see the list in 39:26). In the third strophe (39:28–31) Ben Sira enumerates the cosmic elements which were created for vengeance and judgement and which faithfully obey the Lord's commandment. These personified elements could correspond to a pedagogical intention of the sage, viz. to motivate the disciples to praise the Lord and to accomplish their task in their time. By this personification Ben Sira seems to return to his initial understanding of the 'work of God', but even when the logic of his thoughts remains unconvincing, Ben Sira intends the wisdom poem on the goodness of creation more as a celebration than an argument.[17]

3. Sir 43:27–33: Text and Context

3.1 Translation and Textual Notes

The most important text on creation is the long hymn in 42:15–43:33 of which we consider the final part in some detail here. Sir 43:27–33 is missing in the Masada Scroll (except for some characters at the end of 29b and 30b)[18] and in the Syriac version (which skips 43:11–33). Thus our translation is

---

17 Cf. Liesen, Full of Praise, 276.
18 Cf. Yadin, Ben Sira Scroll, 192.

based mainly on the Hebrew text from MS B (and Bmg.)[19] and only when this is lacking or corrupt the Greek version is adduced.[20]

43:27   *More things like these we shall not add;*
        the last word is: "He is all."

43:28   *Let us praise him still, since we cannot fathom (him):*
        He is greater than all his works.

43:29   *Awesome is the Lord, very much*
        and his power is admirable.

43:30   *You who are praising the Lord, raise your voice*
        as much as you can, for there is still (more).
        You who are exalting him, renew your strength
        and do not tire, for you cannot fathom him.

43:31   *Who has seen him and can describe (him)?*
        and who will praise him as he is?

43:32   *There are (still) many things hidden;*
        I have seen only a little of his works.

43:33   *All the Lord has made*
        and to the pious He has given wisdom.

43:27a. MS B: לא נוסף. Gk.: μὴ ἀφικώμεθα translates סוף (to finish) instead of יסף (to add), forming an inclusion with 30d.

43:27b. MS B: הוא הכל. Gk.: Τὸ πᾶν ἐστιν αὐτός. Lat: *Ipse est in omnibus.*

43:28a. MS B: נגד[לה]. Bmg.: נגלה. Reconstruction of MS B on the basis of Gk.: δοξάζοντες (cf. 43:30a).

43:29a. MS B: נו[ר]א ייי מ[א]ד מאד. Cf. Gk.: φοβερὸς κύριος καὶ σφόδρα μέγας. The adjective μέγας echoes the ὁ μέγας of 28b.

43:29b. MS B: ונפלאות דבריו. Bmg.: גבורתו. Mas: (יו)תו[... Adopting the variant of Bmg.: גבורתו (Gk.: ἡ δυναστεία αὐτοῦ), we read ונפלאת גבורתו, since it fits the context better. The text of the Masada scroll is badly damaged. While Yadin admits the difficulty in determining whether the first character is a *yod* or a *tau*, he decides for a *tau* following the reading in Bmg.[21]

43:30a. MS B: [מגד]לו[ני ייי ה]רימו קול. Cf. 43:28a.

43:30b. MS B: בכל תוכלו כי יש עוד. Mas: אל ש[... Supposing that the fragment is correctly placed, Yadin reconstructs: [בכל תוכלו כי י]ש אל (cf. Ps 58:12). His interpretation differs greatly from MS B, which

---

19   Cf. Beentjes, Book of Ben Sira. Without apparent reason Beentjes omits Sir 43:29–30 from the text of Masada (120 and 173), while he includes it when describing the contents of the scroll: col. VI: Sir 43:8c–30 (19).

20   Cf. Ziegler, Sapientia.

21   Yadin, Ben Sira Scroll, 192; Skehan – Di Lella, Wisdom, 490. Cf. by contrast, Prato, Il problema, 139 and Burton, Ben Sira, 187–88.

according to him "has given rise to many difficulties."[22] Taking into account the notable difference in meaning between MS B ("... for there still is")[23] and Mas ("... for God is") and the fact that the Gk.: ὑπερέξει γὰρ καὶ ἔτι is closer to MS B than to Yadin's reconstruction of Mas, we prefer to follow MS B.

43:30c. MS B: כח תחליפו מרומים. Bmg.: כח החליפו מרוממיו. We prefer to follow Bmg.: the form מרומים (MS B) seems to be an error for מרוממיו, part. polel of רום 3rd per. sg. suffix (Gk.: καὶ ὑψοῦντες αὐτόν) and the imperative החליפו (Gk.: πληθύνατε) combines better with 43:30a than the future תחליפו of MS B.[24]

43:30d. We fill out the text of MS B: כי לא ת׳ with Bmg.: [כי לא תח]קרו. In Gk.: οὐ γὰρ μὴ ἀφίκησθε, cf. 27a.

43:31ab. Missing in MS B. On the basis of Gk.: τίς ἑόρακεν αὐτὸν καὶ ἐκδιηγήσεται; καὶ τίς μεγαλυνεῖ αὐτὸν καθώς ἐστιν; Segal makes the following reconstruction: מי חזה אותו ויספר ומי יגדלנו כאשר הוא.[25] Against the majority of textual witnesses Skehan follows the reading of MSS S 336 542 753: τὶς γὰρ ἑόρακεν.[26]

43:32a. The text of MS B is badly damaged. On the basis of Gk.: πολλὰ ἀπόκρυφά ἐστιν μείζονα τούτων, Segal reconstructs ... רוב נ[סתרות מ]אלה and the edition of Ben Ḥayyim proposes רוב נ[פ]ל[א וחז]ק מ[ן]אלה.[27]

43:32b. MS B: ראיתי (I have seen). In Gk. (ἑωράκαμεν, we have seen) the inclusion with 42:15b disappears. The edition of Beentjes reads ראתי instead of ראיתי (possibly an error of transcription).[28]

43:33ab. The text of MS B is badly damaged. On the basis of Gk.: πάντα γὰρ ἐποίησεν ὁ κύριος καὶ τοῖς εὐσεβέσιν ἔδωκεν σοφίαν, Segal reconstructs: את הכל [עשה] ייי ו[ל]חסידים נתן חכמה[29]. Instead of חסידים, Kahana and Di Lella read אנשי חסד (cf. 44:1a).[30]

---

22   Yadin, Ben Sira Scroll, 192.

23   According to Penar, the word עוד is a substantive, which means "eternity" and which is used as a divine epithet: "the Eternal", cf. 43:28. Cf. Northwest Semitic Philology, 73–74. In this case MS B and Mas have parallel readings.

24   Skehan – Di Lella, Wisdom, 490 and Prato, Il problema, 140.

25   Segal, ספר בן סירא, 290.

26   Skehan – Di Lella, Wisdom, 490.

27   Segal, ספר בן סירא, 290 and Book of Ben Sira, 52. Prato follows Segal's proposal, but eliminates the possible lacuna in the text, cf. Il problema, 140. Wright follows Book of Ben Sira, cf. Fear, 210, n. 68.

28   Beentjes, Book of Ben Sira, 77.

29   Segal, ספר בן סירא, 290. Thus also Prato, Il problema, 140.

30   Kahana, דברי, 85; Skehan – Di Lella, Wisdom, 496.

3.2 Sir 43:27–33 in the Context of the Hymn on Creation

Although the majority of interpreters agree in considering Sir 43:27–33 as a
well-defined literary unit, the problematic character of 43:26 escapes no one.
Sir 43:26 is notoriously difficult to integrate into the text both for its position
and for its meaning. After the wisdom of God which dominates the ocean and
after the sailors who narrate fantastic stories about maritime creatures and sea
monsters (43:23–25), unexpectedly the figure of a messenger or angel appears. This figure is usually interpreted as a personification of the word of
God: "because of him the messenger succeeds (מלאך MS B),[31] and by his
words he will do (his) will". For Perdue the messenger is every element of
creation that successfully accomplishes its God-given task. According to him
Sir 43:26 contains a summary statement which initiates the epilogue of the
hymn: 43:26–30.[32]

The obviously conclusive character of 43:27 (note that at the same time
it introduces the invitation to praise in vv. 28ff.) is a sufficient indication for
the delimitation of the text. First, the unexpected use of the first person plural
(also in v. 28)[33] after a very protracted hymn creates a break and changes the
tone of the discourse. In this way, the hearers perceive that the sage is pre-
paring for the conclusion. A similar strategy is employed in 2:18, where the
sage concludes his exhortations with a first person plural remark: "Let us fall
into the hands of the Lord and not into the hands of people." Second, the
contents of 43:27 clearly indicate that the hymn has finished. The sage not
only affirms that he is not going to add any other explanation to what he said
before, but also attempts to sum it up in one single phrase: "He is all" (הוא
הכל) which forms an inclusion with 43:33a: "all the Lord has made" (את
הכל [עשׂה ייי]). This is his last word (cf. Qoh 12:13).

Sir 43:27–33 is, therefore, the conclusion of the hymn on creation
(42:15–43:33) and serves the same purpose as Sir 50:22–24 in relation to the
praise of the fathers (44:1–50:24).[34] In both texts an invitation to praise
(43:30; 50:22) and the gift of wisdom (43:33; 50:23) figure prominently. Besides the conclusion (43:27–33: praise to the Creator) the hymnic composition consists of an introduction (42:15–25: the power of God in creation)

---

31   Some prefer to read מלאכה (work) instead of מלאך. Cf. Hamp, Sirach, 118: "Um sei-
      netwillen läßt er *die Schöpfung* ihr Ziel erreichen und durch *sein* Wort vollzieht er *sei-
      nem* Willen" and Burton, Ben Sira, 184: "For his own sake He makes his work to pros-
      per".

32   Perdue, Earth, 283. Likewise Hamp, Sirach, 118.

33   Cf. also 2:18; 8:5–7; 24:23; 33/36:1/1a–36:17/11; 43:24b; 43:32 Gk.; 44:1; 48:11 Gk.
      and 50:22–24 Gk. On the use of the first person (singular and plural) in the book, cf.
      Liesen, Self-References, 63–74.

34   On 42:15–43:33 and 44:1–50:24 with regard to the structure of the book, cf. Marböck,
      Hohepriester, 215–16.

and the central part (43:1–26: the marvels of creation).[35] Although this division is widely accepted, there remains some discussion as to the central part of the hymn. For instance, in view of the content matter Minissale, Di Lella and Goan prefer to divide 43:1–26 into two strophes: 43:1–12 (about the sky) and 43:13–26 (about the atmospheric phenomena), thus obtaining a more balanced strophic division of the whole.[36] Argall refines this division and distinguishes between the meteorological phenomena (43:13–22) and a strophe on the abyss and the sea (43:23–26).[37] Perdue subdivides 42:15–25 into three strophes: an announcement of the intent to praise (42:15–17), the unfathomable wisdom of God (42:18–21), the beauty and purpose of the created works (42:22–25); furthermore he subdivides 43:1–25 into two strophes: the wonder of sky and moisture (43:1–22) and the teeming life of the expansive Deep (43:23–25).[38]

Accepting the tripartite structure of Sir 42:15–43:33, several points of correspondence can be seen between the introduction and the conclusion of the hymn (cf. the hymnic frame in 39:12–15, 32–35). First, the announcement in 1st per. sg. with which the sage introduces his new discourse in 42:15 corresponds to the announcement in 1st per. pl. in 43:27 with which he communicates that the discourse is finished. Second, Ben Sira's plan to narrate what he had seen (חזיתי) in 42:15b, corresponds to the recognition in 43:32b that actually he has seen very little (מעט ראיתי).[39] Third, God's revelation of the mystery of hidden things in 42:19b (חקר נסתרות, ἴχνη ἀποκρύφων) corresponds to Ben Sira's acknowledgement in 43:32a that many things in creation remain hidden (רוב נסתרות, πολλὰ ἀπόκρυφά). Fourth, God plumbs (חקר) the abyss and the human heart (42:18), but a human being cannot fathom (חקר) God (43:28, 30). These terminological correspondences not only manifest the internal unity of the hymn and its fine composition, but also reveal something of the pedagogy of the sage. Through accurate contemplation of creation and humble recognition of one's limitations, Ben Sira leads his disciples to his final goal, i.e. praise of the Creator.

---

35   Cf. Prato, Il problema, 141–45.
36   Minissale, Siracide, 201–8; Skehan – Di Lella, Wisdom, 491–96; Goan, Creation, 82.
37   Argall, 1 Enoch, 147–51.
38   Cf. Perdue, Earth, 278.
39   The acknowledgement of the sage in 43:32, even when it seems to contradict the affirmation of 42:17: "not even the saints of God (i.e. angels) can narrate his marvels (נפלאות)", in fact only emphasises how difficult it is for human beings to understand the works (מעשי) of God (the same idea is expressed by the rhetorical questions in 43:31). Cf. by contrast, the Latin version: *Nonne Dominus fecit Sanctos enarrare omnia mirabilia sua?*

4. Sir 43:27–33: Praise to the Creator

4.1 From the Works to the Creator

In the central part of the hymn Ben Sira lists one by one the works of God
(מעשׂי אל) with lyrical descriptions of their beauty while at the same time
pointing out their specific functions in the universe. First, the sage contemplates the firmament where the brilliant stars are situated, and the two main
lights (the sun and the moon) which govern the seasons, and the rainbow
which spans the heavenly vault. Then he comes to natural phenomena: light-
ning, clouds, hail, thunder, wind, storm, snow, frost, north wind, ice, heat and
morning dew. In the end the terrible ocean is mentioned, a symbol par excellence of anti-creation, which has to bow before the power and wisdom of
God. It is noteworthy that the descriptions of the stars (43:1–12) are inter-
larded with explicit mentions of God (except in case of the moon) celebrating
his marvellous creational activity (43:2b, 5a, 9b, 10a, 11a, 12b). As in 16:26–
30 the ever obedient celestial beings in their perfect harmony are Ben Sira's
favourite teaching material. From 43:12 onwards direct references to God
disappear completely and only indirect references are used (his anger, his
power, his word, his wisdom ...).

In 43:27–33 the image of the Lord as Creator takes on a special emphasis: he is no longer considered in relationship to each of the works (as in
43:1–12) but as he is himself. The Lord appears (implicitly or explicitly) at
least once in each of the verses of 43:27–33 (in total 17x). Thrice his name is
mentioned explicitly (43:29a, 30a, 33a) and thrice the personal pronoun 3rd
per. sg. is used (43:27b, 28b, 31b). "His works" are mentioned in 28b, 32b
and "his power" in 29b. Furthermore, God is referred to with the direct object
"him" (43:30c, 30d, 31a, 31b). In 28a, 31a he is understood to be the direct
object of the verbs נגדלה, נחקור and ויספר respectively and in 33b he is the
subject of נתן. First, this insistence on God takes on the shape of a series of
attributes: his omnipresence (he is all), his greatness (greater than all his
works), his transcendence (he is very awesome) and his omnipotence (his
power is admirable). All the attributes are expressed in an emphatic way (all,
greater than, very much, admirable). This is a way to praise the Creator and
to show indirectly the limitation of a human being as creature (43:30–31).
The two affirmations of 43:29a in Gk.: φοβερός κύριος καὶ σφοδρὰ μέγας are
reminiscent of 1:8: εἷς ἐστιν σοφός φοβερὸς σφόδρα, where, also in a context
of creation – especially in connection with wisdom –, Ben Sira depicts God
as the only one who is wise and very awesome, capable of doing things that
are beyond human beings: to dominate the universe and to know wisdom.
Second, the insistence on the Creator is indirectly manifest in the limited
experience of a human being who cannot fathom him (חקר), nor see him

(חזה), nor describe him (ספר). According to Sauer "das Gottesbild ist verfei-
nert – und damit in eine größere Distanz gerückt worden."[40] Precisely for this
reason, from the fact that God is unfathomable, invisible and beyond description, a human being's only possible response is to praise him constantly. Notwithstanding his conviction that no one can praise God as he deserves (lit.:
כאשר הוא, as he is), the sage invites to praise him unceasingly, without tir-
ing, as much as one can. Third, the focus on God is evident in the two actions
which the sage ascribes to God (making everything and giving wisdom to the
pious). These verbs not only summarise the entire hymn, but also establish a
link with the opening hymn of the book, where God grants wisdom to those
who love him (1:10).

Alonso Schökel comments that in Sir 43:27–33 Ben Sira "sube de las
obras al Creador que las sintetiza y supera todas."[41] In other words, Ben Sira
changes the perspective: first he contemplates the marvels of creation, finding
traces of the Creator in them, then he contemplates the Creator of all, inviting
everyone to join him in a celebration of praise.

4.2 The Concept of Totality

In 43:27–33 Ben Sira accentuates in a special way the concept of totality. The
word כל appears, among other occurrences, in the beginning of the text (27b)
as a divine attribute: "He is all" (הוא הכל)[42] and in the end referring to his
creational activity: "all (את הכל) the Lord has made" (33a). Argall affirms
that the word "all" in 43:33a should be understood as referring to the polarities of creation.[43] His interpretation of Sir 43:33a is based on his reading of
42:24a (namely instead of שׁוֹנִים 'different' in MS B he follows Yadin's
reconstruction of Mas שְׁנַיִם "two", cf. Syr. and Gk.). It seems best, however,
not to change the text and to understand that what Ben Sira wants to
underline in 42:24a with כֻּלָּם שׁוֹנִים is the variation and diversity of creation
instead of its polarity. With regard to 43:33a, the dominant idea of הכל is the
totality of creation inasmuch as it is a work of God: there is nothing in the
universe which has not been created by God. Regarding this word it is
noteworthy that in other parts of the book God is designated as "Creator of
all" (18:1; 24:8a; 51:12d Heb.)[44] and as "God of all" (36/33:1; 50:22a Gk.).[45]

---

40   Sauer, Hintergrund, 320.
41   Proverbios, 304.
42   Kaiser understands the personal pronoun as a predicate and הכל as subject and he
     translates: "Alles ist nur er" instead of "Er ist alles". Cf. Rezeption, 49–50 and Sauer,
     Jesus Sirach, 296.
43   Argall, 1 Enoch, 152.
44   Sir 18:1 is text-critically problematic: "He who lives eternally created all things in the
     same way" (Heb. missing). Skehan – Di Lella follow the Syr. "judged" (ܐܬܪܥܝ =

Another occurrence of הכל comes in the expression "all his works" (כל
מעשיו) in 43:28b. It recalls 42:16, 24 in the introductory part and it is also reminiscent of 1:9; 36/33:15; 39:16, 33. Yet another occurrence of הכל shows
that the word "all" is not exclusively used for God and his creation. Ben Sira
also applies it to human beings in his exhortation to praise God with all their
strength (lit.: as much as you can, בכל תוכלו).[46]

The concept of totality is a possible link between the wisdom of Ben
Sira and Stoicism. Since the publication of the article by Pautrel (1963),[47] the
relationship between Ben Sira and Stoic doctrines has not received much attention in biblical research until recent times. In 1998 Kaiser wrote an article
about the Stoic concept of providence (πρόνοια) and its reception in the book
of Ben Sira (cf. n. 42), and last year Wicke-Reuter completed a doctoral thesis on the same subject under the direction of Kaiser.[48] It is the phrase of
43:27b "He is all" with its possible pantheistic connotation, probably derived
from Stoicism, that continues to attract the attention of interpreters and commentators.[49]

The expression (הוא הכל – τὸ πᾶν ἐστιν αὐτός) to which Beauchamp
dedicated an interesting article,[50] already posed difficulties to the commentators of the 19th century when the Hebrew fragments had not yet been discovered. While Fritzsche (1859) affirmed without restriction: "Von panthe-
istischer Fassung der Worte kann lediglich keine Rede sein", Edersheim
(1888) considered the expression as "evidently a spurious addition by the
younger Siracide."[51] The line of Fritzsche is followed by Smend, Eberharter
and Duesberg,[52] and there have even been some interpreters like Peters and
Hamp who thought that Ben Sira wanted to contradict the pantheistic ideas of
Hellenism with 43:27b (cf. e.g. the postulates of the mystery religions: *Her-
mes omnia solus et ter unus; Isis una quae es omnia*).[53] By contrast, Fuss and
Hengel speak of an "undeniable pantheistic tone" and of "almost 'pantheisiz-

---

ἔκρινεν) instead of the Gk. (ἔκτισεν). Cf. Wisdom, 280 and Prato, Il problema, 293, n.
216.

45   For the meaning of this title (אלהי הכל) in 36/33:1, cf. Zappella, L'immagine, 419–
20.

46   The insistence on "all" is also characteristic of the wisdom poem Sir 39:12–35, where
כל appears 13x (πᾶν, πάντα, 14x), always (except in 39:19) referring to the works of
God in creation.

47   Pautrel, Ben Sira, 535–49 and also Winston, Theodicy, 239–49.

48   Wicke-Reuter, Providenz. Cf. also Marböck, Gerechtigkeit, 39–43: he studies the concept of totality in Ben Sira and in Stoicism and the plausibility of a contact between the
two.

49   Cf. Mattila, Ben Sira, 493–95.

50   Beauchamp, Sur deux mots, 15–25.

51   Fritzsche, Weisheit, 257; Edersheim, Ecclesiasticus, 209.

52   Smend, Weisheit, 411; Eberharter, Buch Jesus Sirach, 143; Duesberg, Il est le Tout, 31.

53   Peters, Buch Jesus Sirach, 371; Hamp, Sirach, 118.

ing' features" respectively.[54] The majority of commentators (among others Box – Oesterley, Pautrel, Marböck, Minissale, Di Lella, Crenshaw),[55] although admitting that there may be a possible Stoic influence on the choice of words (especially in Gk.), maintain that the immediate context (in 43:28 Ben Sira affirms that God is greater than all his works) and also the idea of God the only Creator, which permeates the entire book, eliminate every possible trace of pantheism. Thus Beauchamp concludes his study: "Le vrai tout, c'est lui seul. En dehors de Dieu, il n'est rien qui mérite le nom de tout."[56]

The interpretation given by Spicq (1941), taken up by Di Lella in his 1987 commentary, expresses best what the meaning of τὸ πᾶν ἐστιν αὐτός and its Hebrew equivalent should be: "que toute la création dans son ensemble et dans les moindres détails ne s'éxplique que par Dieu, qui en est la source et le soutien permanent."[57] A similar interpretation is found in the Latin version: *Ipse est in omnibus.* "He is all" means that God is present in all created reality; each of his works carries the same divine stamp but manifests it in its own way.[58] The works of God, both taken as a whole and individually, are a faithful reflection of their Creator.[59]

4.3 The Invitation to Praise

"Let us praise (him) still" (עוד נגדלה) is what the sage exclaims in 43:28. This invitation to praise, which is typical of the hymnic style, stands out for its use of the 1st per. pl. (in agreement with 43:27) and the use of the cohortative. The plural testifies to the communion of the sage with his readers (disciples) and his active participation in what he proposes; as a good pedagogue he practises what he preaches. His invitation to praise has been accompanied from the beginning by the practice of the same (42:15: "I want to remember the works of God and to narrate what I have seen"). Ben Sira invites others to do what he has done and continues to do till the end of the book (51:1: "I praise you, my God and Saviour"). The cohortative gives emphasis to the in-

---

54 Fuss, Tradition, 307 and Hengel, Judaism, 146.
55 Box – Oesterley, Book of Sirach, 478; Pautrel, Ben Sira, 543; Marböck, Weisheit, 150; Minissale, Siracide, 207; Skehan – Di Lella, Wisdom, 495; Crenshaw, Book of Sirach, 834.
56 Beauchamp, Sur deux mots, 25. Cf. Wicke-Reuter, Providenz, 222–23.
57 Spicq, L'Ecclésiastique, 798.
58 Calduch-Benages, En el crisol, 249–50.
59 Cf. Marböck, Weisheit, 150: "Die Ordnung, die Herrlichkeit, die Weisheit sind nur verschiedene Weisen des Wirkens Gottes, der überall am Werk ist"; Prato, Il problema, 201: "[...] הכל si riferisce alle maniere con cui Dio si manifesta nel mondo"; Kaiser, Rezeption, 50: "[Alles ist nur ER] bezeichnet ihn aber auch gleichzeitig als den, den all seine Werke bezeugen"; cf. also Reitemeyer, Weisheitslehre, 33.

tention of the sage and at the same time marks the end of the discourse. The invitation of the sage to praise God is also found in other hymnic texts: in the poem celebrating the goodness of God's works in its beginning and end (39:15, 35), in the hymn to the fathers: between Aaron and Joshua (45:25 Heb.) and after the praise of Simon the high priest (50:22). It should be noted that, in contrast to 43:28, in all these texts the invitation to praise is formulated with the traditional hymnic imperative in 2nd per. pl. as in, e.g., Ps 96:1–3.

This hymnic invitation, which appears to be a general address (directed to all), actually becomes more particular in 43:30. By means of a participle with vocative meaning the sage addresses a certain group: "you who are praising the Lord", "you who are exalting him" (cf. 2:7–9); this is the group of those who have accepted and put into practice the proposal of the sage. Two texts in the book may clarify the identity of these persons. In 17:6–10 Ben Sira discusses the many creational endowments of human beings: intelligence, discernment of good and evil, inner and outer senses. All these were given "so that they would glorify his marvellous works and praise his holy name" (17:9–10). In other words, Ben Sira holds that human beings are created in order to praise God; their greatness consists therein.[60] That one needs in order to praise God "ojos y oídos que perciben, mente que comprende, boca que proclama"[61] goes together well with 15:9–10 where praise is a wise person's response to the gift of wisdom from God (cf. 1:10b). Likewise, in 43:30 "you" designates this group of disciples who love / fear the Lord and who have opted for the way of wisdom. Ben Sira exhorts them to praise for such is the principal task of a sage, and the most adequate way of responding to the mysteries of creation.

Praise also figures in a rhetorical question cast in 3rd per. sg.: "who will praise him as he is?" (43:31b), which is meant to contrast, again and with more emphasis (cf. 43:28, 29, 30), the human limitation with the unfathomable mystery of God. Ben Sira himself too is subject to this limitation, due to his human condition. So even when he is full of praise (cf. 39:12, 35) he too cannot praise God as He deserves.

All persons who are involved in the process of learning wisdom, also partake in an interaction with God through praise: "we" (the sage and his hearers), "you" (disciples), "who?" (anonymous person who can be any human being). The same distinction and interaction of persons (with some variations) occur in 39:12–15, 32–35.[62] All persons involved face an insurmountable difficulty which sets limits to their praise and forces them to make

---

60   Morla Asensio, Eclesiástico, 91: "La finalidad de la maestría divina en crear un ser aparentemente perfecto es la alabanza. El camino privilegiado del que goza el hombre para manifestar su grandeza es la alabanza".
61   Alonso Schökel, Proverbios, 201.
62   Cf. Liesen, Full of Praise, 97 (cf. 95).

considerable efforts, i.e. the impenetrable greatness of the mystery of God
and his works in creation. Therefore, the sage urges himself and the others to
praise the Lord still more.

4.4 The Mysteries of God in Creation

The tension between the unfathomable mysteries of God in creation and the
impossibility of human beings to understand them (cf. Job 5:9; 9:10; 11:7; Isa
40:28) is a constant in the book of Ben Sira. The rhetorical questions of
43:31: "Who has seen him and can describe him? and who will praise him as
he is?" are to be answered negatively: no one! These questions contradict the
situation which emerges from the context, for after having contemplated and
described (part of) the wonders of the Lord, Ben Sira not only praises the
Creator, but also invites others to join him in his praise. The same contradiction can be found in Sir 1:1–10. In Sir 1:1–4, also with the help of rhetorical
questions, Ben Sira affirms that no one can completely understand (lit.:
measure, ἐξαριθμέω and explore, ἐξιχνιάζω) the works of God in creation, for
to no one has the root of wisdom been revealed, nor does anyone know her
secrets (τὰ πανουργεύματα αὐτῆς).[63] In 1:9–10, however, the Lord grants
(χορηγέω, supply) wisdom to those who love him (τοῖς ἀγαπῶσιν αὐτόν).[64]
There exists, therefore, a group of persons, who thanks to their profound relationship with God succeed in obtaining wisdom. They are not mentioned
explicitly in Sir 18:4–7 (Heb. missing), which is very close to 43:27–33 and
1:1–10 in form and content matter:

18:4 To no one has he given power to proclaim his works,
and who can explore his mighty deeds?
18:5 Who can measure the power of his greatness?
and who can fully recount his mercies?
18:6 It is not possible to diminish nor to add,
nor is it possible to explore the wonders of the Lord.
18:7 When a human being finishes, then he begins,
and when he halts, then he remains stupefied.

Again the rhetorical questions and frank affirmations of the sage insist on the
impossibility for a human being to comprehend, God (κράτος μεγαλωσύνης
αὐτοῦ) and his works in creation (τὰ ἔργα, τὰ μεγαλεῖα, τὰ θαυμασία). These
cannot be proclaimed nor recounted (18:4: ἐξαγγέλλω; cf. 42:17; 43:31, ἐκ-

---

63   Argall (1 Enoch, 70–71) reconstructs: מַעֲרֻמֶיהָ, "her parts" (cf. 42:18: where πανουρ-
     γεύματα translates מַעֲרֻמִים). Likewise Segal: ספר בן סירא, 3.
64   In Syr.: ܪܚܡܘܗܝ (= τοῖς φοβουμένοις αὐτόν): this reading is preferred by Haspecker,
     Alonso Schökel and Marböck. Cf. Haspecker, Gottesfurcht, 51–52; Alonso Schökel,
     Proverbios, 146; Marböck, Weisheit, 21.

διηγεῖσθαι) nor explored (18:4, 6; cf. 1:3; 42:18, ἐξιχνιάζω).[65] To this limitation another one is added: the impossibility to recount his mercies (18:5: ἐκδιηγήσασθαι τὰ ἐλέη αὐτοῦ). Notwithstanding this insistence on human limitations, the end of the poem (18:14) reveals that those who have chosen to follow the way of wisdom and to keep the Law (lit.: "the ones who receive instruction" and "who are eager for his decrees") are the recipients of divine pedagogy and mercy. It goes without saying that Ben Sira and his disciples belong to this category.

A halo of mystery surrounds the activity of the Creator in the universe. In 11:4cd Heb. the sage justifies his exhortation not to ridicule a poor person nor anyone's bitter day with a double affirmation: "for the works of the Lord are marvellous (פלאות – θαυμαστά) and his actions are hidden (נעלם – κρυπτά) from human eyes". In 16:21 Gk. he affirms: "and [as] a hurricane which a human being cannot grasp, [thus] the majority of his works [remain] concealed (ἐν ἀποκρύφοις)."[66] These texts manifest the existence of a series of mysterious realities in creation which a human being cannot grasp. Also in 3:21–24, in an exhortation to humility and intellectual modesty, the sage mentions "wondrous things" (21a: פלאות – χαλεπώτερα, cf. 21b: ἰσχυρότερα) as well as "secret things" (22b: נסתרות – τῶν κρυπτῶν) which are better left alone,[67] because they transcend the limits of human comprehension. To try to identify with precision these wondrous and secret things is difficult, since the exhortation of Ben Sira remains very general and vague. Although the majority of interpreters suspects a polemic against cosmogonic and theosophic speculations from Greek philosophy, commentators like Prockter and Wright discover allusions to mystic and apocalyptic currents within Judaism. More precisely Wright, in his study of the social context of the book of Ben Sira in the light of *1 Enoch and Aramaic Levi*, interprets the "wondrous things" as the secrets of creation and the "secret things" as the future events (cf. 42:19; 48:25).[68]

The image of God as creator of unfathomable mysteries clashes with the image of Sir 42:18–19: God who explores (חקר – ἐξίχνευσεν) the abyss and

---

65   Cf. 6:27 (ἐξιχνεύω) and 24:8 (ἐξιχνιάζω) referring to wisdom.
66   Gk. has added an image which does not exist in the Hebrew text (MS A): "If I sin, no eye will see me, or if I deceive in all secrecy (בכל סתר), who will know [it]?".
67   Cf. 3:21b in MS A: מכוסה, "hidden things" and in MS C: רעים, "bad things". Against Skehan (cf. Skehan – Di Lella, Wisdom, 159), Argall prefers the reading of MS C (cf. 1 Enoch, 74–75) especially because of the inclusion with 34/31:24b (רעות). Cf. the solution of Wright, Fear, 208, n. 63: in 3:21ab he follows MS A for the verbs and MS C for the adjectives.
68   Cf. Prockter, Torah, 245–52 and Wright, Fear, 208–12, here 209–10. Argall discovers in the secret things of 3:22b an allusion to Deut 29:29a [Heb. 28a]: "The hidden things [נסתרות] belong to the Lord our God" (cf. 1 Enoch, 75–76) which was already noted by von Rad, Weisheit, 372, n. 6.

the human heart, understands (יתבונן – διενοήθη) all their secrets בכל
מערומיהם – ἐν πανουργεύμασιν αὐτῶν), declares (מחוה – ἀπαγγέλλων) the
past and the future, and reveals (מגלה – ἀποκαλύπτων) the most hidden mysteries (חקר נסתרות – ἴχνη ἀποκρύφων).[69] The fact that God reveals his deepest secrets, if not all then at least part of them (cf. 43:32), implies that someone will be the recipient of this revelation, and will therefore be able to know
them. In 39:7 Ben Sira notes that one of the main tasks of the sage is "to
meditate on the mysteries of God" (lit.: ἐν τοῖς ἀποκρύφοις αὐτοῦ)[70]. A last remark regards Sir 4:18. Here it is Lady Wisdom who as a good teacher, after
having put the disciple to the test, announces her recompense: "and I shall reveal my secrets to him" (וגליתי לו מסתרי).[71] If the pedagogy of God and the
pedagogy of Lady Wisdom coincide, it is evident that the revelation of God
will not come to naught: there always will be some persons, like Ben Sira and
his disciples, who will be disposed to receive it and pass it on to others.

4.5 The Experience of the Sage

Conscious of his limitations Ben Sira recognises that many things remain
hidden and indecipherable, and that he has seen only a few of the works of
the Lord (cf. 42:15). The use of the verb "to see" (ראה – ὁράω) is reminiscent
of two other autobiographical texts, viz. 16:5 and 31/34:11/10b. In a context
of controversy with his opponents about sin, freedom and retribution (15:11–
16:14) Ben Sira emphasises his teaching by presenting himself as a witness
for it: "Many things like these my eyes have seen" (16:5), and in the text on
travelling (31/34:9–17/15a) he appeals again to his own experience: "I have
seen many things on my travels" (31/34:11). Both in these texts and in 43:32
the insistence of the sage on giving witness to what he has seen and
experienced personally corresponds to a clear pedagogical objective. Ben
Sira knows that the testimony of the master's life is an enormously effective
way of impressing the disciple.

In 43:32 the many hidden things contrast with the little which Ben Sira
has seen; likewise, the hidden part of creation (the invisible things) contrasts
with the visible works. In contemplating the universe Ben Sira recognises
that he has not exhausted the fullness of this unfathomable reality. The same

---

69   Cf. Beauchamp, Sur deux mots, 24: "Cet arrière-fond [the cosmology of the book of
     Enoch] donne un sens fort à l'ἀποκαλύπτων de Si 42,19. Toute la cosmologie de Ben
     Sira manifeste à la fois le sens enthousiaste du mystère et la volonté de le contenir".
70   According to Liesen, the expression "on his secrets", in combination with the verb
     διανοεῖσθαι, probably refers to the wisdom of God and more concretely to his Law, cf.
     Full of Praise, 83–84.
71   In Gk.: καὶ ἀποκαλύψει αὐτῷ τὰ κρυπτὰ αὐτῆς (cf. 14:21 Gk.). Cf. Calduch-Benages,
     Sabiduría, 45.

idea occurs in Job 26:14 with regard to the foregoing verses: "these are but the fringes of his works; we have heard only a whisper of him; who will understand the thunder of his mighty deeds?" Ben Sira has only touched the fringes of his works, has heard only a whisper, has perceived a spark (cf. Sir 42:22). This fragile and veiled perception of the mystery has brought him to praise the Creator.

Instead of insisting more on the human limitations, Ben Sira concludes his hymn by directing attention towards the Creator. Sir 43:33 contains two affirmations about God which provide an interpretative key for the entire hymn. The first one: "All the Lord has made" (43:33a) is of indubitably biblical origin (cf. Gen 1:1–2:4a; Isa 44:24; 45:7)[72] and can be considered as a confession of faith in God the Creator of the entire universe. According to Burton 43:33a is a summary statement which not only concludes the final part of the hymn but also resumes the whole doctrine of creation in Ben Sira.[73] The second: "and to the pious ($\tau o \hat{\iota} \varsigma \ \epsilon \dot{\upsilon} \sigma \epsilon \beta \acute{\epsilon} \sigma \iota \nu$) he has given wisdom"[74] complements the first by inserting two key concepts of the book (piety / fear of God and wisdom) which are thus linked to the creational work of God. The importance attributed to "the pious ones" is noteworthy: through the divine gift of wisdom (cf. 1:10) they acquire a special ability that renders them capable to see part of the works of God and to understand part of the hidden secrets in creation. Ben Sira (and also his disciples) having but followed the tracks of his predecessors, presents himself as one of these pious ones. The implications of the second affirmation of 43:33 have to be seen in the light of what follows: "I wish to praise the men of goodness / piety / fidelity (אנשי חסד), our forefathers, each one in his own time" (44:1). The wisdom which Ben Sira received is the same wisdom which had come to the heroes of the faith, the faithful par excellence in history. In this way, the personal testimony of Ben Sira acquires more weight, because it is backed up by the weight and authority of tradition. Ben Sira consciously presents himself, therefore, as a model to be imitated.

5. Conclusion

In the 2nd chapter of his book on wisdom in Israel, von Rad dedicates some pages to the "Limitations of Wisdom". At a certain point, after having praised

---

72 Cf. Burton, Ben Sira, 36–38: "The הכל of creation in Sirach and Deutero-Isaiah".
73 Cf. Burton, Ben Sira, 189.
74 According to Argall, the expression ἔδωκεν σοφίαν is a technical term (cf. Sir 6:37d and *1En.* 5:8; 82:2) which goes together with the phrase "reveals the most hidden secrets" of 42:19b, cf. 1 Enoch, 72 and Wright, Fear, 210.

the audacity with which Israel tried to understand the wholly unfathomable presence of God, and after having recognised that the sages offered a moving instruction on the mystery of divine government, he notes: "Das Geheimnis Gottes ist geradezu zu einem Lehrgegenstand geworden."[75] Summarising our study of 43:27–33 we could say the same about the entire creation. For Ben Sira and his disciple creation has not only become an object of teaching, but also a motive for praise. In contemplation of the wonders of creation Ben Sira both enjoys and learns from the wisdom of God. Although aware of his limitations, his fine aesthetic and religious sensibility instils in him the desire to praise the creator of the universe with all his strength.

If creation in its immensity and harmony is the privileged area where God and human beings meet, what image of God does the sage present in these verses? First, God is the absolute Creator of all created reality, which according to the classification of Reiterer includes both "die materielle Ebenen der Schöpfung" (human beings, animals, elements of the universe, concrete persons and many other realities) and "die immaterielle Ebenen" (Wisdom, negative forces such as evil and the devil). It follows then that God, who is greater than all his works, is present in all and in each one of them. Second, he is an awesome and mighty God, who inspires great respect and who is capable of realising those tasks which are beyond human beings. Third, he is an impenetrable God, invisible, defying description, unfathomable, for, no matter how hard a human being tries, he cannot penetrate God's mystery, and cannot even praise him duly. And finally, he is a wise God who not only created Wisdom but who also poured her out on all his works; a wise God who is especially generous to the pious ones to whom he gives Wisdom. In this way, these can perceive something of his works and know part of his mysteries. This is the experience which Ben Sira wanted to inculcate: praise God, the Creator of all, for there always will be reasons to praise him.

Bibliography

Alonso Schökel, L., *Proverbios y Eclesiástico* (Los Libros Sagrados 8.1; Madrid: Cristiandad, 1968).

Argall, R.A., *1 Enoch and Sirach: A Comparative Literary and Conceptual Analysis of the Themes of Revelation, Creation and Judgment* (SBLEJL 8; Atlanta: Scholars, 1995).

Beauchamp, P., "Sur deux mots de l'Ecclésiastique (Sir 43,27b)," in *Penser la foi. Recherches en théologie aujourd'hui. Mélanges offerts à Joseph Moingt* (eds. J. Doré and Ch. Theobald; Paris: Éditions du Cerf, 1993) 15–25.

---

75   Von Rad, Weisheit, 146–47.

Beentjes, P.C., *The Book of Ben Sira in Hebrew: A Text Edition of All Extant Hebrew Manu-scripts and A Synopsis of All Parallel Hebrew Ben Sira Texts* (VTSup 68; Leiden: Brill, 1997).

The Book of Ben Sira / ספר בן סירא. *Text, Concordance and an Analysis of the Vocabulary* (The Historical Dictionary of the Hebrew Language; Jerusalem: Academy of the Hebrew Language and the Shrine of the Book, 1973).

Box, G.H. – Oesterley, W.O.E., "The Book of Sirach", in *APOT*, vol. I (ed. R.H. Charles; Oxford: Clarendon, 1913) 268–517.

Burton, K.W., *Ben Sira and the Judaic Doctrine of Creation* (Typewritten manuscript, Ph.D. dissertation, University of Glasgow, 1987).

Calduch-Benages, N., *En el crisol de la prueba. Estudio exegético de Sir 2,1–18* (ABE 32; Estella: Verbo Divino, 1997).

Calduch-Benages, N., "La Sabiduría y la prueba", *EstBib* 49 (1991) 25–48.

Collins, J.J., *Seers, Sibyls and Sages in Hellenistic-Roman Judaism* (JSJSup 54; Leiden: Brill, 1997).

Crenshaw, J.L., "The Book of Sirach. Introduction, Commentary, and Reflections", in *The New Interpreter's Bible*, vol. V (Nashville: Abingdon, 1997) 601–867.

Crenshaw, J.L., "The Problem of Theodicy in Sirach: On Human Bondage", *JBL* 94 (1975) 47–64.

Duesberg, H., "Il est le Tout. Siracide 43,27–33", *BVC* 54 (1963) 29–32.

Eberharter, A., *Das Buch Jesus Sirach oder Ecclesiasticus* (HSAT 6/5; Bonn: Hanstein, 1925).

Edersheim, A., "Ecclesiasticus", in *The Holy Bible: Apocrypha*, vol. 2 (ed. H. Wace; London: John Murray, 1888) 1–239.

Fritzsche, O.F., *Die Weisheit Jesus-Sirach's* (Kurzgefasstes exegetisches Handbuch zu den Apokryphen des Alten Testaments 5; Leipzig: Hirzel, 1859).

Fuss, W., *Tradition und Komposition im Buche Jesus Sirach* (Typewritten manuscript, Th.D. dissertation, University of Tübingen, 1963).

Goan, S., "Creation in Ben Sira", *Milltown Studies* 36 (1995) 75–85.

Hamp, V., Sirach (Die heilige Schrift in deutscher Übersetzung. Echter Bibel: Das Alte Testament 13/2; Würzburg: Echter, 1951).

Haspecker, J., *Gottesfurcht bei Jesus Sirach. Ihre religiöse Struktur und ihre literarische und doktrinäre Bedeutung* (AnBib 30; Rome: Pontifical Biblical Institute, 1967).

Hengel, M., *Judaism and Hellenism. Studies in their Encounter in Palestine during the Early Hellenistic Period*, vol. I (Philadelphia: Fortress, 1974).

Kahana, A., הספרים החיצונים כרך ב' דברי שמעון בן־סירא (2d ed.; Tel Aviv: Masada, 1955–56).

Kaiser, O., "Die Rezeption der stoischen Providenz bei Ben Sira", *JNSL* 24 (1998) 41–54.

Liesen, J., *Full of Praise. An Exegetical Study of Sir 39:12–35* (JSJSup 64; Leiden: Brill, 2000).

Liesen, J., "Strategical Self-References in Ben Sira", in *Treasures of Wisdom: Studies in Ben Sira and the Book of Wisdom* (FS M. Gilbert; eds. N. Calduch-Benages and J. Vermeylen; BETL 143; Leuven: Peeters 1999) 63–74.

Marböck, J., "Gerechtigkeit Gottes und Leben nach dem Sirachbuch. Ein Antwortversuch in seinem Kontext", in *Gerechtigkeit und Leben im hellenistischer Zeitalter* (ed. J. Jeremias; BZAW 296; Berlin / New York: de Gruyter, 2001) 21–52.

Marböck, J., "Gesetz und Weisheit. Zum Verständnis des Gesetzes bei Jesus Ben Sira", *BN NF* 20 (1976) 1–21.

Marböck, J., "Der Hohepriester Simon in Sir 50. Ein Beitrag zur Bedeutung von Priestertum und Kult im Sirachbuch", in *Treasures of Wisdom: Studies in Ben Sira and the Book of Wisdom* (FS M. Gilbert; eds. N. Calduch–Benages and J. Vermeylen; BETL 143; Leuven: Peeters, 1999) 215–29.

Marböck, J., *Weisheit im Wandel. Untersuchungen zur Weisheitstheologie bei Ben Sira* (BBB 37; Bonn: Hanstein 1971).

Mattila, S.L., "Ben Sira and the Stoics: a Reexamination of the Evidence", *JBL* 119 (2000) 473–501.

Minissale, A., *Siracide (Ecclesiastico)* (Nuovissima versione della Bibbia 23; Rome: Paoline, 1980).

Morla Asensio, V., *Eclesiástico. Texto y comentario* (El mensaje del Antiguo Testamento 20; Estella: Verbo Divino, 1992).

Pautrel, R., "Ben Sira et le Stoïcisme", *RSR* 51 (1963) 535–49.

Penar, T., *Northwest Semitic Philology and the Hebrew Fragments of Ben Sira* (BibOr 28; Rome: Pontifical Biblical Institute, 1975).

Perdue, L.G., "'I Covered the Earth like a Mist': Cosmos and History in Ben Sira", in *Wisdom and Creation: The Theology of Wisdom Literature* (ed. L.G. Perdue; Nashville: Abingdon, 1994) 243–90.

Peters, N., *Das Buch Jesus Sirach oder Ecclesiasticus* (EHAT 25; Münster: Aschendorff, 1913).

Prato, G.L., *Il problema della teodicea in Ben Sira: Composizione dei contrari e richiamo alle origini* (AnBib 65; Rome: Pontifical Biblical Institute, 1975).

Prockter, L.J., "Torah as a Fence against Apocalyptic Speculation: Ben Sira 3:17–24", in *Proceedings of the Tenth World Congress of Jewish Studies* (Jerusalem, August 16–24, 1989), Division A: The Bible and Its World (ed. D. Assaf; Jerusalem: Magnes Press, 1990) 245–52.

von Rad, G., *Weisheit in Israel* (Neukirchen-Vluyn: Neukirchener Verlag, 1970).

Reitemeyer, M., *Weisheitslehre als Gotteslob. Psalmentheologie im Buch Jesus Sirach* (BBB 127; Berlin: Philo, 2000).

Reiterer, F.V., "Die immateriellen Ebenen der Schöpfung bei Ben Sira", in *Treasures of Wisdom: Studies in Ben Sira and the Book of Wisdom* (FS M. Gilbert; ed. N. Calduch-Benages and J. Vermeylen; BETL 143; Leuven: Peeters, 1999) 91–127.

Reiterer, F.V., "Review of Recent Research on the Book of Ben Sira (1980–1996)", in *The Book of Ben Sira in Modern Research: Proceedings of the First International Ben Sira Conference 28–31 July 1996 Soesterberg, Netherlands* (ed. P.C. Beentjes; BZAW 255; Berlin / New York: de Gruyter, 1997) 48–54.

Sauer, G., "Der traditionsgeschichtliche Hintergrund von Ben Sira 42,15–43,33", in *Verbindungslinien* (FS W. Schmidt; eds. A. Graupner, H. Delkurt, and A.B. Ernst; Neukirchen-Vluyn: Neukirchener Verlag, 2000) 311–21.

Sauer, G., *Jesus Sirach: Übersetzt und erklärt* (ATDA 1; Göttingen: Vandenhoeck & Ruprecht, 2000).

Segal, M.Z., ספר בן־סירא השלם (2d rev. ed.; Jerusalem: Bialik, 1958).

Skehan, P.W. – Di Lella, A.A., *The Wisdom of Ben Sira: A New Translation with Notes, Introduction and Commentary* (AB 39; New York: Doubleday, 1987).

Smend, R., *Die Weisheit des Jesus Sirach erklärt* (Berlin: Reimer, 1906).

Spicq, C., "L'Ecclésiastique", in *La Sainte Bible*, vol. 6 (eds. L. Pirot and A. Clamer; Paris: Letouzey et Ané, 1941) 529–841.

Wénin, A., "De la création à l'alliance sinaïtique. La logique de Si 16,26–17,14," in *Treasures of Wisdom: Studies in Ben Sira and the Book of Wisdom* (FS M. Gilbert; eds. N. Calduch-Benages and J. Vermeylen; BETL 143; Leuven: Peeters, 1999) 147–58.

Wicke-Reuter, U., *Göttliche Providenz und menschliche Verantwortung bei Ben Sira und in der Frühen Stoa* (BZAW 298; Berlin / New York: de Gruyter, 2000).

Winston, D., "Theodicy in Ben Sira and Stoic Philosophy", in *Of Scholars, Savants and Their Texts. Studies in Philosophy and Religious Thought* (FS A. Hyman; ed. R. Link-Salinger; New York: Lang, 1989) 239–49.

Wright, B.G., "'Fear the Lord and Honor the Priest'. Ben Sira as Defender of the Jerusalem Priesthood", in *The Book of Ben Sira in Modern Research: Proceedings of the First International Ben Sira Conference 28–31 July 1996 Soesterberg, Netherlands* (ed. P.C. Beentjes; BZAW 255; Berlin / New York: de Gruyter, 1997) 189–222.

Yadin, Y., "The Ben Sira Scroll from Masada. With Notes on the Reading by Elisha Qimron and Bibliography by Florentino García Martínez", in *Masada VI: Yigael Yadin Excavations 1963–1965. Final Reports* (eds. J. Aviram, G. Foerster and E. Netzer; Jerusalem: Israel Exploration Society and The Hebrew University of Jerusalem, 1999) 151–252.

Zappella, M., "L'immagine di Israele in Sir 33(36),1–19 secondo il ms. ebraico B e la tradizione manoscritta greca. Analisi letteraria e lessicale", *RivB* 42 (1994) 409–46.

Ziegler, J., *Sapientia Iesu Filii Sirach* (Septuaginta. Vetus Testamentum Graecum auctoritate Academiae Scientiarum Gottingensis editum, XII/2; 2d ed; Göttingen: Vandenhoeck & Ruprecht, 1980).

God's Mercy:

'Racham' (pi.), 'Rachum', and 'Rachamim' in the Book of Ben Sira

Pancratius C. Beentjes
Catholic Theological University, Utrecht

Every scholar who wants to investigate a specific word or theological theme throughout the Book of Ben Sira is immediately confronted with a severe methodological problem. Since a substantial part (ca. 35 %) of this work has not yet been recovered in Hebrew, one always has to consult the Ancient Versions of the Book of Ben Sira, viz. the two Greek witnesses (Gk. I, and Gk. II), and the Syriac.[1] To what extent, however, do these Ancient Versions offer solid information in such a way as to reconstruct a reliable Hebrew text?

Let us take the Hebrew noun רחמים ('mercy') as an example. According to Mandelkern, this word is found thirty-nine times in the Hebrew Bible.[2] In the majority of cases (64,1%) it is rendered οἰκτιρμος by the Septuagint. Six times (15,1%) it has been translated ἔλεος, whereas χάρις and μήτρα are found two times each; σπλάγχνα and ἔντερα have one hit each.[3] Is there any similarity to be detected between these statistics from the Septuagint and the Greek translation of the Book of Ben Sira which is the work of his grandson to be dated about 132 (or 117)[4] BCE in Egypt? Let us have a look at the following chart, where all relevant data have been put together.[5]

---

1   Gk. I is the grandson's Greek translation of the original Hebrew text of Ben Sira; Gk. II is the expanded Greek translation based on an expanded Hebrew text. The Latin translation of the Book of Ben Sira actually is the Vetus Latina, because Jerome did not make a new translation of the deuterocanonical books of the Old Testament to be included in the Vulgate. More details: Skehan – Di Lella, Wisdom, 55–59.

2   Mandelkern, Concordantiae, 1087–88.

3   οἰκτιρμος: 2 Sam 24:14; 1 Kgs 8:50; 1 Chron 21:13; 2 Chron 30:9; Neh 1:11; 9:19, 27, 28, 31; Hos 2:21; Zech 1:16; 7:9; Pss 25:6; 40:12; 51:3; 69:17; 77:10; 79:8; 103:4; 106:46; 119:77 , 156; 145:9 (Dan 1:9; 9:9, 18 Th.); ἔλεος: Deut 13:18; Isa 47:6; 54:7; 63:7, 15; Jer 42:12; χάρις: Gen 43:14; Dan 1:9; μήτρα: 1 Kgs 3:26; Am 1:11; σπλάγχνα: Prov 12:10; ἔντερα: Gen 43:30. In Jer 16:5, and Lam 3:22, there is no Greek equivalent of the Hebrew רחמים.

4   Skehan – Di Lella, Wisdom, 8–9.

5   Text editions consulted: Facsimiles; Beentjes, Book of Ben Sira; Vattioni, Ecclesiastico; Ziegler, Sapientia; de Lagarde, Libri.

No		Hebrew	MS	Greek	Syriac	Vetus Latina
1.	Sir 3:18b	רחמים	A	χάρις	ܐܝܬܪܐ	gratia
2.	Sir 3:19a	רחמים	A	ὑψηλοὶ	ܐܝܬܪ̈ܘܗܝ	potentia
3.	Sir 5:4c	רחום	A	------	ܗܘ ܐܝܬܪܗ̈ ܗܘ	------
4.	Sir 5:6a	רחמים	A, C	οἰκτιρμός	------	miseratio
5.	Sir 5:6c	רחמים	A, C	ἔλεος	ܐܝܬܪܐ	misericordia
6.	Sir 15:20c	רחם pi'el	A, B	------	ܡܪܚܡ	??
7.	Sir 16:11c	רחמים	A	ἔλεος	ܐܝܬܪܐ	misericordia
8.	Sir 16:12a	רחמים	A	ἔλεος	ܐܝܬܪ̈ܘܗܝ	misericordia
9.	Sir 16:16a	רחמים	A	ἔλεος	ܐܝܬܪ̈ܘܗܝ	------
10.	Sir 36:17a	רחם pi'el	B	ἐλεέω	ܪܚܡ	miserere
11.	Sir 36:18a	רחם pi'el	B	οἰκτίρω	ܡܪܚܡ	miserere
12.	Sir 50:19b	רחום	B	ἐλεήμων	------	??
13.	Sir 51:8a	רחמים	B	ἔλεος	ܡܪܚܡܢܘܬܗ	misericordia

First, attention should be paid to the fact that the noun רחמים which is found eight times in the Hebrew text of the Book of Ben Sira is rendered οἰκτιρμος only once in the grandson's translation (5:6a) as opposed to the fivefold use of ἔλεος which seems to be preferred by him (5:6c; 16:11c, 12a, 16a; 51:8a). In both cases, the grandson takes his own line which is quite different from the Septuagint's translation technique.[6] For in the Septuagint, ἔλεος in about seventy-five per cent of the occurrences is the standard rendering of the Hebrew noun חֶסֶד.[7] This statistical outcome, however, does not apply to the Book of Ben Sira. Leaving aside the fourteenfold כי לעולם חסדו (Sir 51:12a–o), חֶסֶד is found twelve times (Sir 7:33; 37:11; 40:17; 41:11; 44:1, 10; 46:7; 47:22; 49:3; 50:24; 51:3, 8), but has only five times (41,7 %) been translated ἔλεος by the grandson (44:10; 46:7; 47:22; 50:24; 51:3).[8]

Second, with regard to the Syriac translation of the Book of Ben Sira, the matter becomes even more complicated. Here the root ܪܚܡ and its derivations appear to be the rendering of several Hebrew verbs (e.g. אהב, חנן, חמל) and nouns (e.g. חן, חבר, רע).[9]

---

6   For a comparison of the grandson's Greek translation to the extant Hebrew Ben Sira texts, see Wright, Difference; Minissale, La versione greca.

7   Glueck, Wort hæsæd; Sakenfeld, Meaning; Clark, Word Hesed; Zobel, חֶסֶד.

8   See Calduch-Benages, En el Crisol, 283–84: 'Apéndice 2: El Uso de ἔλεος / חסד, רחם y derivados'.

9   Winter, Concordance, 575–80; Barthélemy – Rickenbacher, Konkordanz, 68*.

With this kind of problem in mind, it is an endless task to make firm statements about how to reconstruct the missing Hebrew parts of the Book of Ben Sira. This can be demonstrated with the help of text editions and commentaries which on the basis of the Greek and the Syriac offer a retranslation of the missing Hebrew parts. Let us take ἔλεος in Sir 2:9b as an example of how it has been retranslated into Hebrew. M. Segal has rendered it חֶסֶד, which is also Fritzsche's suggestion.[10] A. Kahana in his text edition, however, prefers רחמים, whereas S. Hartom with ישועה follows the Syriac (ܚܢܢܗ). This latter option seems also to be Smend's one, and is preferred by Haspecker as well.[11] H. Herkenne, on the contrary, opts for חמלה in his commentary.[12]

Another striking example would be Sir 17:29. In Segal's text edition רחמים has been chosen to render ἐλεημοσυνη, whereas this Greek noun in the Book of Ben Sira usually is the rendering of צדקה (Sir 3:14, 30; 7:10; 12:3; 16:14; 40:17, 24). Segal's choice in 17:29 is the more surprising, since ἐλεημοσυνη nowhere in the Septuagint is the rendering of Hebrew רחמים.

This short overview is solid proof enough not to mingle with one another all these textual witnesses too easily.[13] Therefore, this contribution will confine itself to the Hebrew root רחם and its derivations in the Book of Ben Sira as far as they bear upon God. For that reason the noun רֶחֶם ('womb') has not been included, since none of the Ben Sira passages involved (Sir 40:1; 49:7; 50:22; 51:5) has a direct bearing on God.

Nos. 1–2: Sir 3:18–19[14]

Both the first and the second occurrence of רחמים in the Book of Ben Sira raise serious text critical problems Whereas H.P. Rüger labels Sir 3:18 according to MS C as the primary textual witness, since it uses biblical

---

10 Segal, ספר בן סירא, 8; Fritzsche, Weisheit, 21. In Sir 2:7, 18; 18:5, Segal has also retranslated ἔλεος with חֶסֶד. In Sir 18:11, 13, however, we find רחמים as his rendering of ἔλεος.

11 Kahana, דברי שמעון, [17]; Hartom בן־סירא, 17; Smend, Weisheit, 20; Haspecker, Gottesfurcht, 236.

12 Herkenne, De Veteris, 57.

13 "Die beiden wichtigsten nichthebräischen Textzeugen, die griechische Übersetzung des Enkels und die altsyrische Übersetzung (Peschitta) sind für die Rekonstruktion des ursprünglichen hebräischen Wortlautes von keinem allzu großen Wert. Es sollte eigentlich außer Frage stehen, daß dort, wo keine hebräischen Textzeugen zur Verfügung stehen, eine Rekonstruktion des hebräischen Wortlautes abgesehen von einzelnen Ausdrücken aussichtslos ist"; Schrader, Leiden, 54.

14 For the context of these lines, see especially: Argall, 1 Enoch, 73–78; Prockter, Torah, 245–52.

idiom, L. Schrader contends that, on the contrary, the reading of MS A must be considered the original one because of its peculiar, non-biblical vocabulary (מעט being used as a verb; עולם meaning 'world').[15] According to Hebrew syntax and the grandson's Greek translation, in my view one should prefer the reading of Sir 3:17a according to MS A, whereas one should follow the text of Sir 3:17b–18 according to MS C as being more original. This means that רחמים in 3:18b (MS A) is not authentic. Most probably it was the wording of Sir 3:19a (כי רבים רחמי אלהים), a line not handed down in MS C, which in MS A caused the change from חן into רחמים in Sir 3:18b.

The Hebrew text of Sir 3:19, being one bicolon, has got a complicated continuation in both the Greek (3:19–20), and the Syriac (3:20). Their common factor is found in 3:19b (Heb.), 3:19b (Gk.), 3:20b (Syr.).[16] This colon is essential for the entire section (3:1–29). First, because by means of an *inclusio* (ענוה, 'humility' / ענוים, 'the humble ones') in the first strophe (3:17–19) it lays emphasis upon the attitude with which one should behave oneself. Second, Sir 3:19b being the conclusion of the introductory strophe, is an appropriate point to bring to the fore what subjects should be investigated by students ('what is authorized', 3:22a) and what things should be forbidden to them ('Things too marvelous for you', 3:21; 'what is beyond you', 3:23). R. Argall has convincingly argued that Sir 3:1–29 'is not a polemic against Greek learning, as is often asserted by scholars', but is 'fully intelligible as an intra-Jewish debate over the correct interpretation of Torah'.[17]

Nos. 3–5: Sir 5:4c; 5:6a–c[18]

It can hardly be coincidence that quite a lot of pericopes in the Book of Ben Sira dealing with theodicy are introduced by a specific expression: 'Do not say'.[19] As compared to other Biblical wisdom literature, the Book of Ben Sira contains a remarkably large number of passages in which this formula is used.[20] In these instances, Ben Sira as a matter of fact enters into argument

---

15 Rüger, *Text*, 30–31; Schrader, *Leiden*, 42–43. Surprisingly enough, Schrader does not refer to the same verb being used in Sir 19:1 (MS C.), 35/32:8 (MS B.), 48:2 (MS B.).

16 See Prato, "La lumière interprète", esp. 330–32.

17 Argall, *1 Enoch*, 78; Prockter, *Torah*, reaches similar conclusions.

18 Beentjes, *Ben Sira* 5:1–8, 45–59.

19 Mostly אל תאמר: Sir 5:1b, 3a, 4a, 4c; 15:11a; 16:17; 34/31:12c. Other formulae found are: ואמרת (5:6a) פן תאמר (15:12a); אין לאמר (39:21a, 21c, 34a [Bm]); אל לאמר (39:34a); μὴ εἴπῃς (7:9a); οὐκ ἔστιν εἰπεῖν (39:17a).

20 A similar use of the formula 'Do not say' as in the Book of Ben Sira is to be found only in Qoh 7:10; Prov 20:22; 24:29. Qoh 5:5; Prov 3:28; 20:9; 24:12; 30:9 must be left out in this outline, because the introductory formulae used there have a different function.

with opponents of his days, either real or fictive ones, about crucial issues relating to God. The mere fact that Ben Sira so frequently uses this particular debate-formula ('Do not say') indicates that the issue of theodicy was both vehemently debated in his days and was also a major theological issue for him personally.

Sir 5:4c–d according to MS A contains a bicolon which has not been handed down in MS C: 'Do not say: "YYY is merciful, and he will blot out all of my iniquities"'. This bicolon has unanimously been considered as a secondary or inauthentic element. Though all Ben Sira scholars assume that there must be a direct connection between Sir 5:4c–d and 5:6a–b, two completely different hypotheses circulate relating to the status of 5:4c–d. There is a group holding the view that Sir 5:4c–d is a mere doublet – or a later textual form – of Sir 5:6a–b,[21] whereas another group of scholars has come to the conclusion that in Sir 5:4c–d we are confronted by a *retroversion* from the Syriac text of Sir 5:6a–b.[22]

When Sir 5:1–8 has been stripped of its commonly accepted doublets (2a, 2d, 4c–d), there is left over a passage which is composed of exactly ten distichs.[23] What feature exactly defines Sir 5:1–8 as a more or less independent literary passage? A more accurate inspection of the אל-utterances can be helpful.[24] For, within this group of prohibitives, the particular formula אל תאמר strikes the eye. First of all, it is the only אל-formula which, throughout this pericope, has been repeated several times (5:1b, 3a, 4a [4c; cfr. 6a]). One must attach some importance, in the second place, to the fact that nowhere else in the wider context is the formula אל תאמר used by the author again.[25] The opening formulae אל תאמר in Sir 5:1–8, therefore, are a structural element which to a high degree offer to this passage both coherence and unity.

Whereas the first half of 5:1–8 has been united with the help of אל תאמר, has the second half been unified with the help of the prohibitive אל תבטח (5:5a, 8a). When compared with the rest of the prohibitive-clauses, the prohibitive אל תבטח of 5:5a and the phrases depending upon it (vv. 5b–6d) fill more distichs. It therefore deserves special attention now, whether an explicit function and sense must be attributed to this larger number of lines. The

---

21   Smend, Weisheit, 49; Peters, Buch Jesus Sirach, 52; Rüger, Text, 36.
22   Lévi, L'Ecclésiastique, vol. 2, 25; Prato, Il problema, 367–68; Di Lella, Hebrew Text, 108–13.
23   Elsewhere in the Book of Ben Sira, this feature appears to be a structural literary principle; see Haspecker, Gottesfurcht, 113–18; 181–85; Peters, Buch Jesus Sirach, 332, 341, 363.
24   Prior to Sir 5:1–8, statements introduced by אל + *yiqtol* are found in 4:20b, 22a, 22b, 23a, 23b, 25a, 25b, 26a, 26b, 27a, 27b, 27c, 28c, 28d, 29a, 30a, 31a. Subsequent to 5:1–8, similar prohibitive constructions with jussives/vetatives are found in 5:9a, 14a, 14b, 15b; 6:1a.
25   The first occurrence after 5:1–6 is to be found in 11:23–24.

formula אל תבטח which verse 5a and 8a have in common at the same time,
however, reflects a difference: its position in the two stichs involved. In verse
8a this prohibitive has its place immediately at the opening of the first stich –
as is the case in nearly all occurrences in Sir 5:1–8 –, while in verse 5a, however, it holds a different construction. Here an expression with a noun (אל
סליחה) opens the first stich, whereas אל תבטח is closing it. In consequence
of that *reversio*, with the help of the root סלח in vv. 5a–6b a *chiasm* has been
created, whereby 'to forgive' and 'forgiveness' become a central issue of the
entire passage.[26]

In fact, verse 5 marks a distinct turning-point. From here on, a series of
changes and gradations is introduced into the remarks and thoughts of those
addressed. While the sinner's utterances are the centre of the first part of the
passage (5:1b, 3b, 4), in the second part (5:5–8) it is the author who responds
to all this. Not only the *inclusio* of verse 5a and verse 8a (אל תבטח) – which
in fact takes up the entire rebuttal of the author –, but also the emphasis of
סליחה at the opening of verse 5 play a functional role. The word סליחה is effective now as a kind of 'theological lens' which determines the focus of the
second part. For, the author is not only emphasizing this crucial term explicitly as the *first* word of his rebuttal, he also has worked the same root into the
passage another time, then being the *final* word or thought of the person addressed within the entire pericope.

The noun רחמים too has an intriguing function within this second part of
the pericope.[27] Not only is רחמים the first word of the sinner in his *final* remark (5:6a), it is also the first word of the subsequent כי-clause (5:6c) in
which the author amplifies that the problem is much more complicated than
the sinner apparently supposes. There is no question of God's mercy being
merely mechanical. For that reason, the author in 5:6c–d and 5:7c–d is
unfolding a theodicy which even tends to a negative content, that must be
considered here, however, a rhetorically-justified exaggeration. The two כי-
clauses, in which God's punishing anger has been stressed (6c, 7c), also
therefore function as a framework to an almost prophetical summons from
the author to the sinner (לשׁוב אליו, 5:7a) to change his way of life
immediately and drastically.[28]

---

26   The verb סלח occurs elsewhere in the Book of Ben Sira only in Sir 16:11c–d.
27   Both Rüger, Text, 36 and Schrader, Leiden, 47 mark Sir 5:6 according to MS A as be-
     ing the more original text form, since the inversion of the words רבים רחמיו in MS C
     is considered an adaptation to 2 Sam 24:14 / 1 Chron 21:13. Text critical problems of
     Sir 5:1–8 are discussed in detail by Di Lella, Hebrew Text, 108–15.
28   In my article "Ben Sira 5:1–8", 56–57, I opposed the common view that the כי-clause
     of Sir 5:4b is attributed to the author. There I defended the thesis that these words
     should be put into the mouth of the *sinner*. Now I would like to admit that my view was
     not correct; it must be Ben Sira who is speaking in 5:4b.

No. 6: Sir 15:20c[29]

God's mercy is discussed again in the so-called 'Discourse on sin'[30] which is composed of two parts:
(I) 'Human Responsibility and Divine Justice' (15:11–16:14);
(II) 'Man and Divine Providence' (16:17–18:14).[31]
Both parts are opened by the characteristic formula 'Do not say ...'. Immediately following after this specific opening, Ben Sira reports his opponent's words, which both times are introduced by the identical exordium: 'From God ...' (15:11; 16:17). That we have to do with an important issue here indeed, can not only be inferred from the large extent of the discourse, but also from the fact that it is introduced by a poem on Wisdom (Sir 14:20–15:10). For it is a characteristic feature of the Book of Ben Sira that each new section is introduced by a paragraph in which wisdom is the main theme.[32]

The structure of Sir 15:11–20 is well-organized.[33] Ben Sira starts putting into words what is in the mind of his contemporary opponents: 'From God is my sin' (v. 11a); 'It is he who led me astray' (v. 12a). Since Ben Sira has prefaced these utterances with the introductory formula 'Do not say', he can immediately react to those two remarks with two motivation-clauses (כי) in which he has a first try to disprove the statements of his adversaries: 'God does not do what he hates' (v. 11b); 'He has no need of violent persons' (v. 12b). In the next line, on the one hand he firmly underlines his own point of view by stating 'God hates evil and abomination' (v. 13a) which refers to v. 11b ('to hate'), whereas the second colon – 'he does not let it happen to those who fear him' (v. 13b) – not only recalls an important issue from the poem on Wisdom (15:1), but also calls to mind one of the book's central themes ('to fear the LORD'). So, in a negative paragraph (vv. 11–13), on the one hand the problem has briefly been described, whereas on the other hand some starting-points for further reflexion have been touched on. In v. 14, the heart of the matter, viz. the human will, is brought to the fore and is elaborated in vv. 15–17. As a positive counterpart of the negatively formulated opening paragraph (vv. 11–13), vv. 18–19 hold some strong statements about God's power and omniscience. Since it is of great importance to Ben Sira not to give rise to any misunderstanding, he ends up with a conclusion (v. 20) which explicitly reverts to both motivation-clauses (v. 11b; v. 12b). It can

---

29   Di Lella, Hebrew Text, 129–34; Rüger, Text, 81; Prato, Il problema, 222–23.
30   Description called forth by Haspecker, Gottesfurcht, 142: 'Traktat über die Sünde'.
31   Sir 15:11–18:14 has been analyzed in detail by Prato, Il problema, 209–99; Wicke-Reuter, Providenz, 106–87.
32   Sir 1:1–2:18; 4:11–19; 6:18–37; 14:20–15:10; 24:1–29; 35/32:14–36/33:15, and 38:24–39:11.
33   Hadot, Penchant mauvais; Maier, Mensch, 84–97; Prato, Il problema, 234–47.

hardly be an accident that the collocation 'deceitful persons' (v. 20b) has also been used at the end of the poem on Wisdom (15:8b).

Sir 15:11–20 is a theologically explosive passage. The great number of doublets, triplets, and marginal readings which accompany this Hebrew text are solid proof that various attempts have been made to alter Ben Sira's argumentation by smoothing, polishing, amplifying, or even changing his text. Ben Sira explicitly states it is beyond doubt for him that human beings have their own free will. In particular Jewish scholars emphasize that Sir 15:11–20 is the first text in the history of Judaism in which the doctrine of free will has been brought out so amply and pointedly. Ben Sira makes serious efforts to explain to his opponents that their way of reasoning is wrong. He wants to demonstrate that it is a misconception to pose the question: 'Why does God allow evil?'. The only correct question to be asked would be: 'Why do *human beings* allow evil?'. Human beings have not been called into existence to be marionettes which are only set in motion by God and are kept on the lead like a dog. On the contrary, God has allotted mankind an innate responsability, its own determination or inclination.

Sir 15:20c–d (MS A), just as the identical 15:20d–e (MS B), are considered a younger textual form, whereas the older text is to be found in 15:20a–b (MS A) and 15:20a.c (MS B).[34] Since Sir 15:20c–d is not present in Greek or in Old Latin, is only partially found in Syriac, and moreover has a horrible Hebrew grammar (וְלֹא מְרַחֵם), the authenticity of this bicolon is highly questioned. According to Lévi and Di Lella, this colon must be a retroversion from the Syriac (ܘܠܐ ܡܪܚܡ).[35] Di Lella's argumentation, however, is very complicated and makes great demands on the imaginative faculty. It should not be left unnoticed, however, that in Biblical Hebrew the participle *Pi'el* מְרַחֵם is used as a predicate of God at least three times: Isa 49:10; 54:10; Ps 116:5.[36] This aspect might have influenced a mediaeval copyist and should therefore have been part of the reflection.

---

34   According to Rüger, Sir 15:20b (MS B.) is a further development of the older Hebrew textual form. The Greek text of Sir 15:20 is a rendering of the older textual form, whereas the Syriac translates both the older and the younger textual form, leaving out, however, an equivalent to the final colon in Hebrew (וְעַל מִגְלָה סוֹד; cf. Prov 11:13; 20:19); Rüger, Text, 81.

35   Lévi, L'Ecclésiastique, vol. 2, xxxi; Di Lella, Hebrew Text, 133–34; Lévi's reference to Isa 33:18 is puzzling.

36   Maybe Isa 49:15 should also be read מְרַחֵם; see BHS and the commentaries.

Nos. 7–9: Sir 16:11–14

Following two examples by means of which Ben Sira demonstrates that only a positive attitude towards God and his commandments can safeguard life,[37] the first part of the extensive 'Discourse on sin' is concluded in 16:11c–14 with a firm statement about the interrelationship between human behaviour and divine retribution. Here we can hear, in fact, the echo of some introductory lines (Sir 15:14–17) where it is said that God has given to humankind a free will to nake one's choice either for good or for evil. Now at the end of the first part (16:11c–d) the author lays stress upon the fact that God will respond according to that choice:

(1) 'For mercy and anger alike are with him,
(2) who remits and forgives,
(3) but upon the wicked alights his wrath' (16:11c–d).

The similarity between this statement and Sir 5:6c–d is striking. Since Sir 16:11c–d, however, is metrically overloaded, one cannot but assume that this threefold sentence has been adjusted to 5:6c–d. Most probably, the final words of 16:11d (ועל רשעים יגיה רגזו) do not belong to the original text. First, the Hebrew text switches from participles (ונושא וסולח) to imperfect (יגיה). Second, as opposed to נוח ('to rest upon') of Sir 5:6d which fits into its context very well, the verb נגה ('to shine') in Sir 16:11d is rather strange. Third, one should pay attention to the rendering ἐκχέων ὀργήν in the grandson's Greek translation of 16:11d. Just as is the case with the participles ונושא וסולח in the Hebrew text, it seems that ἐκχέων ὀργήν goes back to a participial construction in the original Hebrew. As the collocation ἔκχεον ὀργήν shows up in Sir 36/33:8 and there is the rendering of שפוך חמה, one is tempted to assume that this collocation was originally found in 16:11d too.

Whereas רחמים in 16:11c is accompanied with אף ('anger'), in 16:12a it is with תוכחת ('reproach, reprimand'), apparently one of Ben Sira's favourite words[38], which serves as the opposite of רחמים. Sir 16:12b ('He judges a person according to his deeds'), which can be considered the sequel of 15:19b ('He perceives a person's every deed'), emphasizes God's activity as a judge. Here we meet one of the few instances in the Hebrew Ben Sira where the verb שפט is applied to God (Sir 36/33:8; 32/35:22a/18b); no less than eleven

---

37 Sir 16:1–4 (wicked children are undesirable); Sir 16:5–11b (historical overview of wicked people).

38 Sir 16:12; 35/32:17; 41:4; 48:7. The noun תּוֹכַחַת, which is found 24 times in the Hebrew Old Testament, in 75% of the occurrences is used in wisdom literature: 16 times in Proverbs, 2 times in Job. With respect to Sir 16:12, Barthélemy – Rickenbacher, Konkordanz, 422 erroneously refer to ἐλεγμός instead of ἔλεγχος.

times in his book this verb refers to the activities of human judges.[39] Sir 16:13 holds an antithetic parallelism: the deeds of the evildoer (עָוֶל) as opposed to the desire of the righteous.[40] In the final bicolon (16:14), however, two *positive* statements conclude the first part of the 'Discourse on sin'.[41] Sir 16:15–16 are considered secondary by a vast majority of scholars. These lines, which originate from Gk. II, but have not been handed down by the Vetus Latina, serve as a biblical illustration of what has been argued in 16:11–14.[42]

It can hardly be a coincidence that the issue of God's mercy is found exactly at the *end* of the first part of the 'Treatise on sin' (16:11c–14), where Ben Sira discusses divine retribution. The same subject is dealt with at the end of the *second* part of the 'Treatise on sin' (18:11–14). It is a great pity indeed that after Sir 16:26 no extended Hebrew text is left till 30:11 apart from some lines in the anthological MS C (18:31–33; 19:1–2; 20:5–7, 13, 30; 25:8, 13, 17–24; 26:1–3, 13, 15, 17). For it could have been very interesting to investigate the exact Hebrew vocabulary of 18:11–14, which concludes a hymn of praise on the Lord as righteous and merciful judge (18:1–14).[43]

Nos. 10–11: Sir 36:17–18/11–12

Sir 33/36:1/1a–36:22/17 has handed down a prayer for deliverance in which God is supplicated to take action in favour of his people.[44] The authenticity of this plea has been explicitly disputed by Th. Middendorp, whereas J. Marböck, on the contrary, has adduced conclusive evidence that this prayer must be considered authentic, since many specific elements which show up in this plea for deliverance are also to be found in other parts of the Book of Ben Sira.[45] The prayer may be divided into four strophes: (I) 33/36:1/1a–5/4; (II) 33/36:6/5a–12/9; (III) 33/36:13a/10a–36:19/13; (IV) 36:20/14–22/17.

---

39   E.g. Sir 4:15, 27; 8:14; 10:1–2; 46:11, 13.

40   There is no need to change תַּאֲוָה ('desire, longing') into תִּקְוָה ('expectation, hope').

41   For the translation of this bicolon see: Eberharter, Ekkli 16,14.

42   See Philonenko, Sur une interpolation.

43   As far as I am aware, there has never been a monograph or a special study devoted to Sir 18:1–14. The analysis of Sir 18:1–14 by Wicke-Reuter, Providenz, 175–81, is far from exhaustive. That Sir 18:1–14 deserves a full investigation is also prompted by Marböck who compares both structure and vocabulary of Sir 18:1–13 with those of Sir 1:1–10; Marböck, Weisheit, 26–27.

44   Since in early Greek codices some pages have been exchanged the verse numbers of this prayer have a completely different notation in the Greek translation: Sir 36/33:1–13a; 36:16b–22; see Haspecker, Gottesfurcht, xxiv–xxv. The Hebrew is sometimes numbered Sir 33/36:1–17 (see Ziegler / Rahlfs).

45   Middendorp, Stellung, 125–32; Marböck, Gebet.

The verb רחם *pi.* is found twice in this lament: v.17a/11a; v.18a/12a; both lines belong to the third strophe. It is precisely this third strophe which displays some specific features. First, whereas the other three strophes all have a kind of conclusive statement, the third strophe has not:

33/36:5/4	כי אין אלהים זולתך	(end of the first strophe)
33/36:12/9	אין זולתי	(end of the second strophe)
36:22/16–17	כי אתה אל [עו]לם	(end of the fourth strophe).[46]

Second, the distribution of the possessive suffix ך is striking. Whereas it is used three times in the first strophe (vv. 2/1b, 3/2, 5/4) and is found nowhere in the second one, it shows up no less than six times in the third (vv. 17a/11a, 18a/12a, 18b/12b, 19a/13a, 19b/13b [2x]) and seven times in the fourth strophe (vv. 20a/14a, 20b/14b, 21a/15a, 21b/15b, 22a/16a, 22b/16b [2x]). This means that after a relatively long absence since v. 5 the first occurrences of the possessive suffix ך are just found in the lines which open with the verb רחם *pi.* This can hardly be coincidence.

Third, as opposed to the first, second, and fourth strophe which hold rather general supplications, the third strophe has a particular focus, which becomes more and more specific:
– the tribes of Jacob (v. 13a/10a);
– the people called by your name (v. 17a/11a);
– Israel, the firstborn (v. 17b/11b);
– your holy city (v. 18a/12a);
– Jerusalem (v. 18b/12b);
– Zion (v. 19a/13a);
– your temple (v. 19b/13b).

Fourth, as opposed to all remaining instances where רחם and its derivations are used to speak *about* God's mercy, in Sir 36:17–18/11–12 we come across the only two occurrences in the Book of Ben Sira where the root רחם functions in a *direct* address to God. Both the twofold repetition of the imperative 'show mercy' and the abundant use of the possessive suffix ך serve as Ben Sira's rhetorical device to evoke God's compassion. In the Greek, this aspect has further been strengthened by the additional vocative κύριε at this particular point of the prayer (36:17a/11a).[47]

---

46 Sir 33/36:1/1a–36:22/17 to a high degree has been influenced by Deutero-Isaiah; see Beentjes, Relations.
47 The same phenomenon is also found in 36:22a/16a (Gk.).

No. 12: Sir 50:19b[48]

Almost at the end of the panegyric on Simon, the High Priest, one comes across רחום for the second time in the Book of Ben Sira, the first occurrence being 5:4c. Curiously enough, to date it has hardly been noticed that רחום has been used here by Ben Sira in a way rather different from all those biblical instances which commentators are used to enumerate almost mechanically (Exod 34:6; Deut 4:31; Neh 9:17, 31; 2 Chron 30\:9; Joel 2:13; Jonah 4:2; Pss 78:38; 86:15; 103:8; 111:4; 112:4; 145:8).[49] Whereas from a syntactical point of view, רחום in all these occurrences, as well as in Sir 5:4c, is either a nominal predicate or an adjective, its syntactical function in Sir 50:19b is different, since רחום is used here as a proper name.[50] That this is indeed the function of רחום here is proved beyond doubt by at least three similar collocations appearing within the same context: לפני עליון (50:16d; 50:17c), לפני קדוש ישראל (50:17d). And it is no accident, of course, that רחום has been used in combination with תפלה ('prayer').

No. 13: Sir 51:8a[51]

Among modern scholars it is especially Th. Middendorp who has disputed the authenticity of Sir 51:1–30.[52] Most recently, Schrader expressed a similar opinion.[53] A majority of scholars, however, hold Smend's view that – in spite of the subscription in Sir 50:27–29 – one should consider Sir 51:1–12 authentic because of its language, form and contents.

Sir 51:1–12 'may be classified as a declarative psalm of praise of the individual who has survived a major peril'.[54] At a crucial turn of this prayer

---

48   Recently, a monograph on Ben Sira ch. 50 has been published: Mulder, Simon. It is a
      doctoral thesis written under my supervision, which has been defended at the Catholic
      Theological University at Utrecht, the Netherlands, in November 2000. An abridged
      English edition is being prepared. See also: Marböck, Hohepriester; Hayward, Jewish
      Temple, 38–63; 73–84; 171–75.
49   Only a few Hebrew dictionaries mention רחום in Sir 50:19 as a special case: Gesenius
      – Buhl, Handwörterbuch, 754: "als Name Gottes Sir 50,19"; Zorell, Lexicon, 766;
      Koehler – Baumgartner, Lexikon, 1133: "als Name Gottes Sir 50,19".
50   In just a few Bible translations רחום in Ps 78:38 is treated as a proper name; see *Traduction Oecuménique de la Bible* (TOB) and the Dutch *Nieuwe Vertaling 1951* (NBG).
51   See Di Lella, Sirach 51:1–12; Gilbert, L'action.
52   Middendorp, Stellung, 114–16.
53   Schrader, Leiden, 58–74.
54   Di Lella, Sirach 51:1–12, 396.

we find רחמים: 'But I remembered the mercies of YYY, and his evidences of grace from of old' (Sir 51:8ab). I fully agree with Di Lella that 'the whole bicolon is a minor rewrite of Ps 25:6':[55]

| Sir 51:8 | וחסדיו אשר מעולם | ואזכרה את רחמי ייי |
| Ps 25:6 | כי מעולם המה | זכר־רחמיך יהוה וחסדיך |

I would like to add, however, another Biblical reference, viz. to Isa 63:7. This reference actually is prompted by the striking resemblance between Sir 51:7 and Isa 63:5a:

| Sir 51:7 | ואצפה סומך ואין | ואפנה סביב ואין עוזר לי |
| Isa 63:5a | ואשתומם ואין סומך | ואביט ואין עזר |

Since Isa 63:7 has both the verb זכר and the word pair רחמים / חֲסָדִים, and moreover opens a prayer, Isa 63:5–7 cannot be denied as a potential background for Sir 51:7–8.

As a matter of fact, Sir 51:8 is the *only* text in the Hebrew Book of Ben Sira where רחמים and חֶסֶד / חֲסָדִים are found as a word pair. It might be an indication that the author has indeed adopted biblical phraseology here, since this word pair is used quite often in biblical poetry, e.g. Isa 63:7; Ps 25:6; 40:12; 51:3; 69:17; 103:4; Lam 3:22. As opposed to the Hebrew and Syriac, the Greek of Sir 51:8 not only has an additional vocative (κύριε),[56] but also converted the possessive suffixes from third to second person: 'I remembered *thy* mercy, O Lord, and *thy* benefit of old'.

Conclusions

1. In the Hebrew portions of the Book of Ben Sira, the verb *racham* and its derivations are exclusively used for God.
2. It can hardly be a coincidence that quite a lot of passages in the Book of Ben Sira dealing with the Hebrew root *r-ch-m* cause text critical problems It is an indication that we have to do with a very explosive theological issue, both in Ben Sira's days and during the process of copying the Hebrew manuscripts for many centuries after him. Four occurrences at least are with certainty to be considered secondary: Sir 3:19a; 5:4c; 15:20c; 16:16a.
3. Once רחמים is used to replace the synonymous and more original חֵן (Sir 3:18b).

---

55   Di Lella, Sirach 51:1–12, 404.
56   This was also the case in Sir 36:17a/11a (Gk.).

4. Whereas in the Hebrew Bible both *racham* (pi.) and *rachamim* are quite often accompanied by *chèsèd*,[57] in the Hebrew Ben Sira texts such a combination is found only once (Sir 51:8), maybe as a result of adopting biblical idiom.

5. The Hebrew Ben Sira on the one hand presents collocations which are known from the Hebrew Bible, such as רחמים רבים (Sir 3:19; cf. 2 Sam 24:14; 1 Chron 21:13), רחמים רבים (Sir 5:6a; cf. Ps 119:156), רחום יי (Sir 5:4c; cf. Deut 4:31; Ps 78:38)[58], רב רחמים (Sir 16:12a; cf. Pss 51:3; 69:17; Isa 63:7b), רחמים וחסדים (Sir 51:8; cf. Ps 25:6; Isa 63:7b). On the other hand, however, the Hebrew Ben Sira has some features of its own, such as רחמים ואף (Sir 5:6c; 16:11c), the imperative רחם על *pi.* (Sir 36:17a/11a; 18a/12a), and רחום used as a proper name (Sir 50:19).

6. The Greek translation of the Hebrew text, being the work of Ben Sira's grandson, does not allow us to draw reliable inferences relating to the original tongue of those passages dealing with God's mercy which have not been discovered in Hebrew yet, since the grandson takes his own line offering a translation technique which is quite different from the one which is presented by the Septuagint relating to the root *racham* and its derivations.

7. It is intriguing that two times God's mercy is related to סוד ('secret'), the first time with reference to the humble to whom God reveals his plan (Sir 3:19b), the second time with regard to 'him who reveals a secret' (Sir 15:20d).[59]

Bibliography

Argall, R.A., *1 Enoch and Sirach: A Comparative Literary and Conceptual Analysis of the Themes of Revelation, Creation and Judgment* (SBL EJL 8; Atlanta: Scholars, 1995).

Barthélemy, D. – Rickenbacher, O., *Konkordanz zum hebräischen Sirach mit syrisch-hebräischem Index* (Göttingen: Vandenhoeck & Ruprecht, 1973).

Beentjes, P.C., "Ben Sira 5,1–8: A Literary and Rhetorical Analysis", in *The Literary Analysis of Hebrew Texts* (vol. VII., ed. E.G.L. Schrijver, N.A. van Uchelen & I.E. Zwiep; Amsterdam: Publications of the Juda Palache Institute, 1992) 45–59.

---

57   E.g. Ps 103:4; Jer 16:5; Hos 2:21; Zech 7:9, and the examples mentioned in the paragraph discussing Sir 51:8.

58   In the majority of instances, however, the collocation רחום וחנון is found: e.g. Exod 34:6; Pss 86:15; 103:8; 111:4; 112:4; 145:8; Joel 2:13; Jonah 4:2.

59   As far as the Book of Ben Sira is concerned, a special investigation into the use and function of סוד, together with terms like מסתר (4:18), κρύπτειν / κρυπτός and μυστήριον would be welcome.

Beentjes, P.C., *The Book of Ben Sira in Hebrew: A Text Edition of All Extant Hebrew Manuscripts and A Synopsis of All Parallel Hebrew Ben Sira Texts* (VTSup 68; Leiden: Brill, 1997).

Beentjes, P.C., "Relations between Ben Sira and the Book of Isaiah", in *The Book of Isaiah / Le Livre d'Isaïe* (ed. J. Vermeylen; BETL 81; Leuven: Peeters, 1989) 155–59.

Calduch-Benages, N., *En el crisol de la prueba: Estudio exegético de Sir 2,1–18* (ABE 32; Estella: Verbo Divino, 1997).

Clark, G.R., *The Word Hesed in the Hebrew Bible* (JSOTSup 157; Sheffield: Sheffield Academic Press, 1993).

Di Lella, A.A., "Sirach 51:1–12: Poetic Structure and Analysis of Ben Sira's Psalm", *CBQ* 48 (1986) 395–407.

Di Lella, A.A., *The Hebrew Text of Sirach: A Text-Critical and Historical Study* (Studies in Classical Literature 1; The Hague: Mouton, 1966).

Eberharter, A., "Zu Ekkli 16,14", *BZ* 6 (1908) 162–63.

Facsimiles of the Fragments Hitherto Recovered of the Book of Ecclesiasticus in Hebrew (Oxford – Cambridge: Oxford and Cambridge University, 1901).

Fritzsche, O.F., *Die Weisheit Jesus-Sirach's* (Kurzgefasstes exegetisches Handbuch zu den Apokryphen des Alten Testaments 5; Leipzig: Hirzel, 1859).

Gesenius, W. – Buhl, F., *Hebräisches und Aramäisches Handwörterbuch über das Alte Testament* (17th ed.; Leipzig: Vogel, 1921).

Gilbert, M., "L'action de grâce de Ben Sira (Si 51,1–12)", in *Ce Dieu qui vient: Études sur l'Ancien et le Nouveau Testament offertes au Prof. Bernard Renaud à l'occasion de son 70ième anniversaire* (ed. R. Kuntzmann; Paris: Cerf, 1995) 231–42.

Glueck, N., *Das Wort ḥæsæd im alttestamentlichen Sprachgebrauche als menschliche und göttliche gemeinschaftsgemäße Verhaltungsweise* (BZAW 47; Giessen: Töpelmann, 1927) (ET: *Hesed in the Bible*. Cincinnati: Hebrew Union College, 1967).

Hadot, J., *Penchant mauvais et volonté libre dans la Sagesse de Ben Sira (L'Ecclésiastique)* (Brussels: Presses Universitaires, 1970).

Hartom, E.S., " הספרים החיצונים כרך ד בן־סירא " (3d ed.; Tel Aviv: Yavneh, 1969).

Haspecker, J., *Gottesfurcht bei Jesus Sirach: Ihre religiöse Struktur und ihre literarische und doktrinäre Bedeutung* (AnBib 30; Rome: Pontifical Biblical Institute, 1967).

Hayward, C.T.R., "The New Jerusalem in the Wisdom of Jesus Ben Sira", *SJOT* 6 (1992) 123–38.

Hayward, C.T.R., *The Jewish Temple. A Non-Biblical Sourcebook* (London / New York: Routledge, 1996).

Herkenne, H., *De Veteris Latinae Ecclesiastici Capitibus I–XLIII* (Leipzig: Hinrichs, 1899).

Kahana, A., הספרים החיצונים כרך ב" דברי שמעון בן־סירא (2d ed.; Tel Aviv: Masada, 1955–56).

Koehler, L. – Baumgartner, W. (eds.), *Hebräisches und Aramäisches Lexikon zum Alten Testament* 4 vols. (Leiden: Brill, 1967–90).

de Lagarde, P., *Libri Veteris Testamenti Apocryphi Syriace* (Leipzig / London: F.A. Brockhaus / Williams & Norgate, 1861; repr. phototypica ed. Bad Honnef am Rhein: Proff, 1965).

Lévi, I., *L'Ecclésiastique ou La Sagesse de Jésus, fils de Sira. Texte original hébreu édité traduit et commenté. Deuxième partie (III,6, à XVI,26; extraits de XVIII, XIX, XXV et XXVI; XXXI,11, à XXXIII,3; XXXV,19, à XXXVIII,27; XLIX,11, à fin.)* (vol. 2; Bibliothèque de l'École des Hautes Études; Sciences Religieuses 10/2; Paris: Leroux, 1901).

Maier, G., *Mensch und freier Wille: Nach den jüdischen Religionsparteien zwischen Ben Sira und Paulus* (WUNT 12; Tübingen: Mohr [Siebeck], 1971).

Mandelkern, S., *Veteris Testamenti Concordantiae Hebraicae atque Chaldaicae* (Tel Aviv: Schocken, 1969).

Marböck, J., "Das Gebet um die Rettung Zions Sir. 36,1–22 (G: 33,1–13a; 36:16b–22) im Zusammenhang der Geschichtsschau Ben Siras", in *Memoria Jerusalem: Freundesgabe für Franz Sauer* (ed. J.B. Bauer – J. Marböck; Graz: Akademische Druck- und Verlagsanstalt, 1977) 95–115 = repr., *Gottes Weisheit unter uns. Zur Theologie des Buches Sirach* (ed. I. Fischer; Herders Biblische Studien 6; Freiburg: Herder, 1995) 149–66.

Marböck, J., *Gottes Weisheit unter uns. Zur Theologie des Buches Sirach* (ed. I. Fischer; Herders Biblische Studien 6; Freiburg: Herder, 1995).

Marböck, J., "Der Hohepriester Simon in Sir 50. Ein Beitrag zur Bedeutung von Priestertum und Kult im Sirachbuch", in *Treasures of Wisdom: Studies in Ben Sira and the Book of Wisdom* (FS M. Gilbert; ed. N. Calduch-Benages and J. Vermeylen; BETL 143; Leuven: Peeters, 1999) 215–29.

Marböck, J., *Weisheit im Wandel. Untersuchungen zur Weisheitstheologie bei Ben Sira* (BBB 37; Bonn: Hanstein, 1971; repr. in BZAW 272; Berlin / New York: de Gruyter, 1999).

Middendorp, Th., *Die Stellung Jesu Ben Siras zwischen Judentum und Hellenismus* (Leiden: Brill, 1973).

Minissale, A., *La versione greca del Siracide confronto con il testo ebraico alla luce dell'attività midrascica e del metodo targumico* (AnBib 133; Rome: Pontifical Biblical Institute, 1995).

Mulder, O., *Simon, de hogepriester, in Sirach 50* (Almelo: privately published, 2000).

Peters, N., *Das Buch Jesus Sirach oder Ecclesiasticus* (EHAT 25; Münster: Aschendorff, 1913).

Philonenko, M., "Sur une interpolation essénisante dans le Siracide (16,15–16)", *Orientalia Suecana* xxxiii–xxxv (1984–1986), 317–21.

Prato, G.L., "La lumière interprète de la sagesse dans la tradition textuelle de Ben Sira", in *La Sagesse de l'Ancien Testament* (ed. M. Gilbert; BETL 51; 2d ed.; Leuven: Peeters, 1993) 317–46.

Prato, G.L., *Il problema della teodicea in Ben Sira: Composizione dei contrari e richiamo alle origini* (AnBib 65; Rome: Pontifical Biblical Institute, 1975).

Prockter, L.J., "Torah as a Fence against Apocalyptic Speculation: Ben Sira 3:17–24", in *Proceedings of the Tenth World Congress of Jewish Studies* [Jerusalem, August 16–24, 1989], Division A: The Bible and Its World (ed. D. Assaf; Jerusalem: Magnes Press, 1990) 245–52.

Rüger, H.P., *Text und Textform im hebräischen Sirach: Untersuchungen zur Textgeschichte und Textkritik der hebräischen Sirachfragmente aus der Kairoer Geniza* (BZAW 112; Berlin / New York: de Gruyter, 1970).

Sakenfeld, K.D., *The Meaning of Hesed in the Hebrew Bible: A New Inquiry* (HSM 17; Missoula: Scholars Press, 1978).

Schrader, L., *Leiden und Gerechtigkeit: Studien zu Theologie und Textgeschichte des Sirachbuches* (BBET 27; Frankfurt a.M.: Lang, 1994).

Segal, M.Z., ‏ספר בן־סירא השלם‎ (2d rev. ed.; Jerusalem: Bialik, 1958).

Skehan, P.W. – Di Lella, A.A., *The Wisdom of Ben Sira: A New Translation with Notes, Introduction and Commentary* (AB 39; New York: Doubleday, 1987).

Smend, R., *Die Weisheit des Jesus Sirach erklärt* (Berlin: Reimer, 1906).

Vattioni, F., *Ecclesiastico: Testo ebraico con apparato critico e versioni greca, latina e siriaca* (Testi 1; Naples: Istituto Orientale di Napoli, 1968).

Wicke-Reuter, U., *Göttliche Providenz und menschliche Verantwortung bei Ben Sira und in der Frühen Stoa* (BZAW 298; Berlin / New York: de Gruyter, 2000).

Winter, M.M., *A Concordance to the Peshitta Version of Ben Sira* (Monographs of the Peshitta Institute Leiden; Leiden: Brill, 1976).

Wright, B.G., *No Small Difference: Sirach's Relationship to its Hebrew Parent Text* (SBLSCS 26; Atlanta: Scholars Press, 1989).

Zappella, M., "L'immagine di Israele in Sir 33(36),1–19 secondo il ms. ebraico B e la tradizione manoscritta greca. Analisi letteraria e lessicale", *RivB* 42 (1994) 409–46.

Ziegler, J., *Sapientia Iesu Filii Sirach* (Septuaginta. Vetus Testamentum Graecum auctoritate Societatis Litterarum Gottingensis editum XII/2; Göttingen: Vandenhoeck & Ruprecht, 1965).

Zobel, H.-J., "חֶסֶד / hesed". *TDOT* V. 44–64.

Zorell, F., *Lexicon Hebraicum et Aramaicum Veteris Testamenti* (Rome: Pontifical Biblical Institute, 1940).

God, Sin and Mercy: Sirach 15:11–18:14

Maurice Gilbert
Pontifical Biblical Institute Rome

There are various ways to see how Ben Sira understands God's attitude to sin.

A first way has the advantage of every synthesis. It puts together all the texts where Ben Sira approaches the theme. Johannes Marböck[1] used this way in 1994, when he collected all the data of the book about the forgiveness of sin. One could also offer a general view of the Ben Sira's thought on sin, repentance, and forgiveness, as Roland E. Murphy[2] proposed in 1998.

A second way consists of analysing only one text, preferably a central one, where the whole theme is dealt with in a general fashion. This is the way followed here, with a reading of Sirach 15:11–18:14. This long text has the advantage of following in a concrete manner Ben Sira's reasoning. Such a choice is based on the structure of this text, which Josef Haspecker[3] was the first to propose in 1967. Some commentators did not follow him: Alexander A. Di Lella[4], for instance, in 1987, read these chapters with a different structure, and Randal Allen Argall[5] did similarly in 1992. I will follow Gian Luigi Prato[6] and Ursel Wicke-Reuter[7], who, in 1975 and 2000 respectively, returned to Haspecker's explanation, with new insights, of course, but not full agreement. Since these scholars have carefully analysed the Hebrew text of Ben Sira, for 15:11–16:26a, and seeing that their agreement most often coincides with the proposals Patrick W. Skehan[8] made in 1987, it is useless to do again the textual criticism of these verses. Only the main points on which they disagree will be mentioned. Moreover, the influence of the Stoic philosophers on Ben Sira will not be studied here, because such a study was recently done by Ursel Wicke-Reuter, exactly as the comparison between 1 Enoch and Sirach was done by Argall. Here it is rather to set forth the logical development of Ben Sira's reasoning which will be our task. Let me lastly make the clarification that neither the additions nor the specific readings of the Greek version where we have the Hebrew text will be considered.

---

1 Sündenvergebung, 480–86, inserted in his collected essays Gottes Weisheit, 176–84.
2 Sin, 260–70.
3 Gottesfurcht, 143–144.
4 Skehan – Di Lella, Wisdom, 267–86.
5 1 Enoch, 136–38, 226–32.
6 Il problema, 209–99.
7 Göttliche Providenz, 106–87. Cf. also Liesen, Self-References, 72–73.
8 Cf. Skehan – Di Lella, 267–71, 276–80.

1. Sir 15:11–16:14: Human Freedom and Retribution

1.1. Is God Responsible for Moral Evil? (15:11–13)

Ben Sira starts the discussion with his own definite position: "Do not say" (15:11a) and "(Be careful) not to say" (15:12a)[9].

The objection is put in two forms: "From God (comes) my sin" (15:11a) and "It is he who trips me up." Human moral evil, "my sin", is in question. The opponent thus acknowledges the perversity of his doing, but he makes God liable for it, and this means that he excludes his own responsibility. Therefore, he denies the freedom of his action and, ultimately, his guilt. Ben Sira, as his starting point (15:11–13), confines himself to a general refutation of God's liability in human moral evil. In this refutation we can observe a syllogism[10]: God hates the evil act and the abominable deed (15:13b); now he does not do what he hates (15:11b); therefore – and here comes the basic statement of Ben Sira – we cannot say that God is responsible for human faults (15:11a, 12a).

But Ben Sira does not prove his "minor" premise: God does not do what he hates. For Ben Sira, it is a primary truth, and if we put it in a positive manner, it becomes: God only does what he likes and he only likes what is good. Since Plato[11], Greek philosophers had excluded divine responsibility for moral evil accomplished by man.

However, Ben Sira adds another reason to his refutation: wicked people are not necessary (15:12b), and he completes this with: God does not provoke moral evil in those who fear him. In other words, if sinners are necessary, then God should occasion the sin of just people. This means that the just man proves that sin is not necessary and, because a God-fearing man loves God and is loved by God, we understand that God hates evil (15:13a) and therefore does not do it (15:11b). Briefly, if God is responsible for man's sin, there would not be any just people, any God-fearing men. This is a kind of proof *ab absurdo,* based on the fact that there really are God-fearing men.

1.2. Man Is free to Make His Own Choices (15:14–17)

If God is not responsible for human sin, the responsibility must lie with man himself.

Recalling the creation of man at the beginning (15:14), a theme analysed by Prato in 1975, Ben Sira put his answer at the universal level. Now, from

---

9   Cf. Sir 5:1–6; 7:9.
10   So Wicke-Reuter, 114.
11   *Rep.,* II, 379a–380d; X, 617e; *Tim.,* 42de.

the moment of his origin, man was "given" over to the power of his *yétsèr*. After the study of Jean Hadot[12] done in 1970, we know that such a word does not mean for Ben Sira a "bad inclination", as in rabbinism, but simply "inclination" or "deliberation" according to the Greek version. The meaning of free will must not be excluded: for Ben Sira, it seems, God leaves man free in his choices.

The following three verses repeat that man, in his action, indicates his preferences: the same verb "to prefer" returns in verses 15:15, 16, 17. However, after the general statement of 15:14, the next two verses (15:15, 16) directly address the opponent of 15:11a, 12a, who represents, of course, the disciple of the master of wisdom. To keep precepts, which means to put into practice the divine commandments, falls within the competence of man's preferential choice (15:15a). I accept the reading of MS A, confirmed by the margin of MS B and I understand, with Prato and Wicke-Reuter[13], that man's choice has something to do with "intelligence": by this I mean it is wise to do what is pleasing to God and is manifest through his precepts. Choice presupposes an alternative, or two possibilities which man meets: either fire which destroys or water which gives life.

Then 15:17 comes back to the universal frame of 15:14, but now Ben Sira bases his general statement on Deut 30:15, 19, a text which speaks about the free offer of the covenant. This is the very text of the Pentateuch which also indicates the consequences of the free choice which Israel is invited to make. Similarly Ben Sira adds in 15:17b this idea of consequences of man's free choice. This is properly the theme of retribution: man chooses what eventually will be given to him, either life or death. In a word, man is responsible for his choices: if he prefers to observe the divine precept, he will receive life, and if he prefers not to observe it, death will be given to him.

Therefore responsibility for sin does not fall on God, but on man who has received freedom, and who must accordingly accept the consequences of his choices.

1.3. Under God's Eyes (15:18–20)

Man can choose and God will repay him according to his free choices. The following verses (15:18–20) look back to the Lord: he is able to repay. His wisdom amply suffices[14] to do so, for, not only is his vigour mighty, but above all he sees everything, particularly (15:19) human actions; three synonymous verbs follow each other here: he sees, he observes, he considers (this

---

12   Penchant mauvais, 91–103.
13   Prato, 221–22; Wicke-Reuter, 116.
14   Cf. Liesen, Full of Praise, 190–91.

last verb means, in effect, that he knows). So, whatever is the choice decided by man, it cannot escape God's eyes.

Now "he never has ordered man to sin" (15:20a), because the precept he gave him, and which is pleasing to him, should lead man to life. To transgress the precept is to sin and this leads to death. Moreover, God hates sin (15:13a) and therefore never orders anyone to commit it. He who claims, as does the opponent (15:11a, 12a), that his sin comes from God is a liar and God does not validate either his opinion or his practice.

In order to better understand the answer of Ben Sira, let us start again from the objection. The sinner cannot make God responsible for his own sin (15:11–13). The responsibility falls on man, who is free to choose (15:14). He who chooses evil will get fire and death in retribution (15:15–17). This retribution is unavoidable, for God sees and knows every human act and he is all-powerful. But since he never commands man to sin, it follows that the sinner, liable for his action, will be repaid accordingly: fire and death will reach him. This last assertion must be explained and made more explicit (16:1–14). In the meantime, one can already assert that the opponent's thesis is a lie, because in denying human freedom, it made God guilty. Nor does the Lord's ability to repay man according to his free choice confirm the opponent's thesis.

1.4. Argument *ad hominem*: Your Descendants (16:1–4)

The link of 16:1–4 with its context does not become immediately evident. Ben Sira again speaks directly to his disciple. He presumes that the fear of God dwells in him. The day of his marriage, he will hope to get children, the much-desired blessing. But, says Ben Sira, if he is to have depraved sons without fear of God, there is no cause to rejoice. Implicitly the theme of retribution is present here. If these sons are wicked, it is because they had made a free choice for sin and they will receive the consequences. Their father, who is now a young fellow, should not rely on their destiny to insure his own honor. Ben Sira does not make explicit his mind, except by saying (16:4) that a band of wicked men can make desolate a city; on the other hand, ony one intelligent person (according the Greek version) or one wise, God-fearing person (as we read in the Hebrew MSS A and B) is sufficient to populate a town. This is perhaps an allusion to Abraham at Sodom (Gen 18–19). In a word, those who choose to do wrong will receive devastation. So Ben Sira thinks that to have only one son or even not to have any is better than to beget numerous wicked offspring. His thought is based on his view of choice and its consequences, and so corrects the rash wish of a disciple to be blessed with descendants without regard to their goodness – a group of wicked sons is a disaster. Here the retribution is collective, but the principle is the same: he who freely chooses to do wrong will get bitter fruits.

1.5. Historical Proofs (16:5–10) and Conclusion (16:11–14)

Sir 16:5 links what Ben Sira just said with the following argument. He saw with his own eyes what he tried to explain in 16:1–4 about offspring, and his own ears have heard still more striking events which he now will briefly summarize: these events are narrated in the Bible.

If we take the Hebrew text, verse 16:6 has to be taken as a general principle[15] and therefore not as a reference to the punishment of Korah, Dathan, Abiram and their followers (Num 16:35). In fact, Sir 16:7 clearly begins with an explanatory *'asher* which introduces three verses having a similar structure. The first, 16:7, where the Greek version sees an allusion to the giants of Gen 6:4, seems rather to refer to Gen 14:1–16, which relates the expedition of four great kings who in the end were defeated by Abraham and his men. The next verse, 16:8, alludes to Sodom's inhabitants, and 16:9, to the Canaanites. These three verses therefore follow the chronological order and all of them refer to pagan people. On the other hand, 16:10 is clearly distinguished by its introductory "in a like manner" and by its different structure: its alludes to Israel's rebellion in the desert (Num 11:21; 14:27–38; Deut 2:14–16; Sir 46:8b): thus the Lord equally punished by death Israelites as well as pagans. Their sins were pride (16:8, 10), iniquity (16:9) or abuse of their strength (16:7). All were groups or peoples.

Ben Sira concludes his reasoning with five distichs, 16:11–14[16]. There he comes back to the topic of the one person: in 16:3c, 4a, he had extolled the superiority of one wise or God-fearing person, and here in 16:11, he emphasizes that even one stiff-necked person will not go unpunished. Saying this, Ben Sira is returning to the opponent of 15:11: this man is liable for his sin and he will pay the consequences. The following verses, 16:11c–14, assert first that the Lord is at one time merciful, at another time inflicting punishment, according to the deeds of everyone (16:11c–12). Then Ben Sira makes a distinction between a guilty person, who will not escape with his prey or plunder, and the just man: the desire (MS A) or the hope (Greek version) of this one will not be abolished (16:13): he will obtain his reward (16:14a). Ben Sira concludes by asserting again what he had said in 16:12b (cf. 15, 17b): everybody is judged according to his deeds (16:14b).

Let me summarize. If the full text of 15:11–16:14 is read as is suggested here, two main ideas are set forth: man is free in his choices and he will be

---

15   This was already the opinion of Oesterley, Wisdom, 109.
16   There were also five distichs about the offspring.

repaid accordingly. About God, Ben Sira says three things: 1. He is not responsible for human sin, because he does not do that which he hates; 2. He sees how human beings do act; 3. He repays everybody according to his deeds. This last affirmation is then proved either by Ben Sira's experience in the conduct of offspring, bad or good, or by biblical narratives. It is only at the end of this pericope that he mentions mercy and forgiveness as God's characteristics (16:11c–12).

2. Sir 16:17–18:14: God is Also Merciful

2.1. Does God See Me? (16:17–25)

Ben Sira has exonerated God from any responsibility for human sin, because sin arises from human free will. But Ben Sira thinks also of retribution for sin.

It is precisely on this point that the opponent returns to the charge: how can God "up there" see me among such a huge crowd of humans? Saying this, the opponent denies individual providence: God cannot be concerned with everybody, for he is too far away and human beings are too numerous[17].

Ben Sira's answer, introduced by "behold"[18], covers two verses, 16:18–19[19]: God can visit not only the earth but also the universe in its uttermost parts, and when he does they shudder. This means that immensity does not stop him. When he looks at the most secret parts of the universe – the mountains' bases or the world's foundations – they really tremble. These cosmological images – thunder-storm and earthquake – are used as an a fortiori argument to prove that no one human being can hide from God's gaze. Ben Sira lays claim to a cosmic theophany which involves, through these images, a judgment. A fortiori, no human being can escape from divine judgment.

But the opponent insists (16:20–22), without having truly understood the meaning of Ben Sira's answer: "But[20] he will not bother about me"[21]; moreover he continues: "Who considers my paths?" As a matter of fact, he is speaking about his evil deeds as well as his good ones (16:21–22)[22]. Two the-

---

17   On this expression of Sir 16:17d, cf. Zorell, Lexicon, 731, col. A; Alonso Schökel, Diccionario, 666, col. B.
18   Cf. Gen 27:37.
19   With Prato, 215–16, and Wicke-Reuter, 143–44. But Skehan, 268–69, and Liesen, Full of Praise, 239–43, see in Sir 16:17–22 only one intervention of the opponent.
20   *Gam* is adversative: cf. Wicke-Reuter, 144; cf. also Ps 129:2; Job 18:5.
21   For the expression, cf. Sir 16:24b; Hag 1:5, 7.
22   On 16:22a: "Who will tell him (that)?", cf. Job 31:37 for the double accusative; on 16:22b: "When I practice the precept", cf. Prato, 228–29 and 263, and Alonso Schökel, Diccionario, 330, col. A.

ses are implied here: the first is the principle that God observes individual choices (cf. 15:18–19) to repay them accordingly (cf. 15:17): here again divine providence towards the individual is questioned; the second thesis – and this is new – affirms that there is no importance if man acts either well or badly[23], because God ignores personal choice, and therefore what kind of hope remains for the man who does right? Here the opponent takes a position in favor of indifferentism in moral affairs[24]. Let me stress that he does not deny the value *in se* of a moral action: he acknowledges the difference between sin and the just deed; he denies only that God knows individual moral action and that God repays it as such. Therefore the connection between God and the moral deed of an individual is here disregarded or, at least, questioned[25].

First of all, Ben Sira reacts in a very direct way: the utterances of the opponent are stupid; the man who speaks like this has no understanding. Then, against the lack of wisdom showed by this objector, he calls upon his disciples in a solemn way he never uses elsewhere to introduce his reflections or his teaching[26]: let them carefully listen to what the wisdom of the master inspires in him (cf. Prov 1:23b); he will speak with measure and discretion: such are the explanations he will give in the following verses.

It is possible that Ben Sira has perceived in the last objections more discouragement than in theoretical statements. This is why his developed answer will give at the same time theological grounds and also words full of consolation and encouragement. In this, his second part (16:17–18:14) is distinguishable from the first one (15:11–16:14): it is a moderate and modest answer.

2.2. Man amidst Creatures (16:26–17:14)

From 16:26b the Hebrew text is lacking. We will use from here on the Greek version, but it brings some textual problems on which scholars are divided. However most often their readings converge.

According to the general structure proposed by Haspecker and accepted by Prato and Wicke-Reuter, the pericope Sir 16:26–17:14 is the beginning of the developed answer of Ben Sira to the objections put forward in 16:17, 20–22. As in 15:14–17, this answer is based on the creative action of the Lord. On this point, according to the structure, the two parts of 15:11–18:14 are framed in a similar way.

---

23   Cf. Job 35:6–7, but in another context.
24   In Sir 16:22a, the expression "an act of justice" is unique; cf. Isa 32:17.
25   Cf. the many questions in Sir 16:17, 20–22.
26   Sir 39:12–15 introduces a hymn; cf. Liesen, Full of Praise, 95–143.

In 16:26–17:10, Ben Sira draws his inspiration from the first pages of Genesis, but freely. The literary structure of his rereading is fairly clear, although scholars do not agree on one point: is 16:29–30 connected with the preceding verses[27] or with the following[28]?

First of all, Ben Sira looks to the universe with its various elements which he does not mention in detail, except that in 16:27–28 he seems to refer to the stars. All that follows concerns the earth. In 16:29, vegetation is probably alluded to and in 16:30, animals. From 17:1 on Ben Sira refers only to man. Ben Sira's plan is logical[29]: he begins with creatures which have no end (16:27), then he continues with those whose life ends with their return to the earth (16:30b; 17:1b).

The Lord is the chief actor. He creates (16:26a; 17:1a) the universe and man. From this point of view, we can understand why 17:1 is seen as the beginning of the second section of this passage. But when he creates, God gives to each series of his works a function; moreover, the scope of this function is to assure order in creation: no one, in any case, is to disturb his neighbour or his fellow; it must be so for each element of the universe – Ben Sira probably thinks about stars and planets – as for each human being, in an analogous manner.

Possibly 16:29–30 is a necessary transition between the cosmos and man, because these verses already refer to the earth, with vegetation and animals, before referring to man on the earth.

Again, between the universe and man, there are still other analogies. To each cosmic element, particularly to the stars, God gave a perpetual task (16:26–27ab). Now, without specifying what kind of task or by which means each element will carry it out, Ben Sira is satisfied with laying stress on the perfect accomplishment of their tasks: each cosmic element effects its task "without weakness[30] or fatigue" (16:27c), "without any withdrawal" (16:27d), without disturbing encroachment on the field and task of any neighbour (16:28a), in perpetual obedience to the divine command (16:28b).

On the other hand, about man Ben Sira is more precise. Even if, contrary to the cosmic elements, his days are numbered (17:1b–2a), man was made as God's image (17:3b) and therefore he received power over everything that covers the earth (17:2b), particularly over the animals, beasts and birds: God in fact put in them the fear of man, their master (17:4). In all this, in spite of his short life, man still looks like the Creator's delegate: he received his power from God himself.

---

27   So Prato, 216, Skehan – Di Lella, 276 and 281, and Wicke-Reuter, 147 and 152.
28   So Wénin, De la création, 149. For more details on this difference, cf. Prato, 267, n. 130, and Wénin, 148, n. 6.
29   Cf. Prato, 269.
30   Cf. Prato, 270, n. 138. Differently Skehan, 276, Wicke-Reuter, 147, and Wénin, 148.

In order to put into practice this received power, man was granted personal means (17:6–7) for a definite goal which is mentioned in 17:8–10. But here the text of Ben Sira is quite uncertain. First of all, there are good reasons for putting at the beginning of 17:6 a verb like "He (God) formed"[31]. Even then, there seems to be confusion in the transmission of 17:8–10, at least, 17:9–10, the order of which is disputed[32]; the main difficulty comes from 17:8b, which seems to be repeated in 17:9 and in the addition of Greek II at 17:8c: on this problem, the Syriac version gives no help. Lastly, in 17:8a, do we have to read "eye"[33] or "fear"[34]? Prudence therefore is called for.

According to 17:6 man received sensory organs in order to communicate: tongue, eyes, ears, but also a heart to think, to reflect, to conceive, to plan. According to 17:7 – even if the preceding verse has already made reference to it – God bestowed on man intelligence and wisdom (according to the Syriac version) which implies discernment (cf. 17:6b?); but, at the moral level, which wisdom never excludes, God indicated to men the difference between evil and good. Then if man is able to see that difference – which the objection of 16:21–22 had supposed – he is indebted to God for that. Ben Sira thinks perhaps of Gen 2:9, 16–17 where it is said that God forbade man to eat the fruit of the tree of knowledge of good and evil[35].

In 17:8 there are two ways of understanding the text. If in 17:8a we read that the Lord "put the fear of him in their hearts", then the sentence is similar to what we read in 17:4a and we must conclude that God wanted a kind of hierarchical order: animals fear or revere man, and man fears or reveres the Lord. On the other hand, if we read in 17:8a that the Lord "set his eyes upon their hearts" (RSV) or that he "kept watch over their hearts" (NEB)[36], then we have to understand that God, after having shown men what is good and what is evil, observes what will be their choice, i.e. what will be the result of their discernment; in this line of interpretation, 17:8a logically continues 17:7b. All things considered, I prefer this second solution.

---

31 Divine action, according to the Syriac version: cf. Prato, 277, and Wicke-Reuter, 153, n. 42. Differently Skehan, 277, Wénin, 149, and Hadot, 105–20, who follow the Greek version.

32 Ziegler, Sapientia, 202, followed by Prato, 217, 279–80, and by Wénin, 149, reads 17:10.9, with the Latin version. Skehan, 277, 279, and Wicke-Reuter, 154, prefer to read 17:9–10, with the Syriac version.

33 With the great majority of the manuscripts and the Latin version: so Prato, 217, 279–80, Wicke-Reuter, 154, and Wénin, 149.

34 So Ziegler, 202, and Skehan, 277 and 279.

35 Cf. Wénin, 153.

36 So already Oesterley, 116. For different translations, cf. Di Lella, in his review of the book of Hadot, 573. The nearest text is Jer 40:4 (LXX 47:4); I would not translate "in their hearts", as do Prato, 217, Wicke-Reuter, 154, and Wénin, 149.

The infinitive at the beginning of 17:8b is generally understood as expressing purpose[37], but P.W. Skehan translated it "showing"[38], like a Latin gerundive, and I agree with him. Indeed Ben Sira is still referring to the plan of the Creator as he realized it; God gave to men everything that is necessary for their discernment and choice; he does not appear to them directly, but he observes them. What he shows to them is the greatness of his works: all of them, faithful to his word, always accomplish their tasks; they are for men a path to him, a way of theodicy inviting man to make a good choice. And whatever the order of the following verses may be, 17:9–10 or 17:10, 9, the Creator's project is that men, seeing his works, come to praise his holy name: for Ben Sira, praise is the noblest act that human beings are called to practice (cf. 15:9–10; 39:14–15).

In 17:11–14 Ben Sira goes further, because God's story with mankind has added a new chapter with the revelation at Sinai. Ben Sira is indeed referring now to the Sinai theophany. He sees in it a divine intervention completing the Creator's work and having a universal significance. That revelation granted to Israel is a supplementary knowledge for mankind to whom the Creator had already given a previous one (17:7a, 11a): creating men, he had indicated to them the difference between good and evil, but now, at Sinai, he indicates his own decisions, his precepts (17:7b, 12b). He had given to them sensory organs, but now, thanks to these, men are able to see and hear the divine glory itself (17:6, 13); previously they were able to perceive that glory only through its works (17:8b).

In 17:14 the decalogue is summarized in two sentences. The first, in direct style, could refer to the first table of the ten commandments, and 17:14b to the second[39]. But it also may be that both parts of that verse only refer to the commandments towards our neighbour. In any event, the last phrase of this pericope, while mentioning precepts which stress how to deal with one's neighbour, recalls 16:28a where Ben Sira said that no cosmic creature disturbs its neighbour.

Between stars and men, there is the difference that man received the capacity to choose personally (17:6–7). God helps him make a good choice, not only showing to him what is good and what is evil (17:7b), but also stressing at Sinai the evil to be avoided towards his neighbours. The Lord does his utmost in order that man be able to decide freely to respect his neighbour. On the other hand, because cosmic creatures perpetually obey the divine word which gives to them a specific task, none of them ever disturbs its neighbour: everyone keeps its place and performs its function. What will happen with

---

37   So Prato, 217, Wicke-Reuter, 154, and Wénin, 149, like the most usual translations.
38   So Skehan, 277. For biblical Greek, cf. Zerwick, Graecitas biblica, § 391–92; for biblical Hebrew, cf. Joüon, Grammaire, § 124 o.
39   Cf. Prato, 282, Di Lella, 282–83, and Alonso Schökel, Vision, 241.

man? The Lord made everything so that man also can hold his place and perform his part faithfully, obedient to the divine word (17:14).

The opponent thought in a concrete way. Ben Sira answers also in a concrete way, not as a philosopher: he takes his answer from the Bible and places
it in the context of biblical history, with its universal value. He had already
answered in a similar fashion in 16:6–10. Everyone has received from God
whatever is necessary for him to perform his function in the world, doing
good. This is true also of the opponent. His moral indifference (16:21–22)
does not correspond to the human vocation he has received from the Lord.

However, the opponent said (16:17), does the Lord give his attention to
every individual? Ben Sira has already answered in 17:8a: "He keeps watch
on their hearts", and in 17:14, he has stressed that everyone received precepts
demanding respect for his neighbour. But a more explicit answer would be
welcome: it is found in 17:15–23.

2.3. Under God's Eyes (17:15–23)

When Ben Sira had his first confrontation with the opponent, after his appeal
to the creative action of God, he mentioned that God looks at human deeds
(15:18–19) and then he dealt with retribution (16:1–14). Here the passage
17:15–23 is framed in the same way: after appealing to the creation, completed with the Sinai revelation (16:26–17:14), he speaks again of God's eyes
on human actions and also of future retribution (17:15–23).

The passage can be divided into two parts. In 17:15, 17bc, 19 Ben Sira
underlines that the Lord sees the paths of all men. The framing verses, 17:15,
19, are complementary and repeat some expressions of the opponent: he
claimed to be hidden from God's eyes (16:17a) and asked who could have interest in his ways (16:20b); now Ben Sira retorts that human ways are always
before the Lord (17:15a, 19b) and that they are never hidden from his eyes
(17:15b, 20a). The central verse, 17:17bc, inspired by Deut 32:8[40], makes a
distinction between Israel, of whom the Lord directly takes charge, and the
other peoples, over each one of which he himself appointed an authority: it
seems that Ben Sira alludes here to members of the heavenly court. In one
case as in the other, directly or indirectly, nobody escapes from divine control. The opponent argued about the crowd of human beings (16:17cd); now
Ben Sira answers that an order exists, which is established by God, each people having its place and thus its function, always submitted to the divine control.

---

40   Cf. Prato, 284–87.

The second part (17:20, 22ab, 23) makes a distinction between evil human deeds and good ones[41]: the first are not hidden from God's eyes (17:20), but the others are precious for him and he keeps them like a seal, as a part of himself (17:22). Judgment shall come where everyone will receive what he deserves (17:23). Contrary to 16:6–10, where punishments were recalled according to past biblical history, Ben Sira speaks only about judgment and retribution in the future.

2.4. Conversion and Praise – Human Weakness and Divine Mercy (17:24–18:14)

With N. Peters[42] and, above all, with J. Haspecker[43], we can consider 17:24–18:14 as one unit. There are twenty-two verses.

The first verse, 17:24, in fact, opens the entire text which follows[44]. The reason is that, between the divine judgment in the future and the present moment, there is room for conversion. Ben Sira thinks again of the opponent who lost hope (16:22b). At the end of his answer to the first objections, he had opposed God's mercy and forgiveness to the divine wrath repaying the guilty (16:11cd–12a). Only now he comes back in full force, till 18:14, on divine kindness towards men, without any reference to God's wrath. Lastly, for Ben Sira[45], God himself gives to the sinner a way back (17:24a); the same idea is repeated in the conclusion (18:13d): like a shepherd, the Lord brings back his flock and encourages those who have lost hope (17:24b).

Now Ben Sira addresses the opponent directly (17:25–26a, c). These two verses include seven imperatives. Each of the three first stichoi has two of them: three times Ben Sira calls the opponent to turn towards the Lord, not only to come back to him (17:25a, 26a), but to implore him (17:25b); then each of these three stichoi calls on the same opponent not to sin any more (17:25a, 26a) or at least to diminish the number of his offences (17:25b); finally, in 17:26c, "hate abomination strongly" is an allusion to 15:13a, when Ben Sira, answering the first objections, asserted that the Lord hates evil and abomination; here, in 17:26c, he calls the opponent to reproduce in himself the divine behaviour. Do we have to understand abomination as referring to idolatry? This is a matter of discussion[46], in connection with the divine command quoted in 17:14a. In any case, these seven imperatives prove an

---

41   In Sir 17:22a, Prato, 217 (read 17:22 instead of 17:21), translates *eleêmosunê* by alms; but this is too precise: cf. Sir 40:17; Gen 47:29: "kindness and goodness".
42   Buch Jesus Sirach, 145.
43   Gottesfurcht, 144, 254 and 341.
44   Cf. the same use of *plên* in Sir 29:8.
45   As, later, for Wis 12:19cd.
46   Cf. Prato 282, 289, and Wicke-Reuter, 164, 173–74.

earnestness on the part of Ben Sira. Up till now, he tried to convince the opponent how much the latter's position contradicts the biblical message. Only in these two verses does Ben Sira address that man who lost hope (16:22b; 17:24b). This one had tried to justify his behaviour with theoretical statements which Ben Sira considers untenable; the message of which Israel is the bearer has been amply set forth by Ben Sira. But it also seemed to him that from this message the opponent should end concretely by being converted. It is this conversion which the wise man urges on this discouraged fellow.

If Ben Sira insists so forcefully, it is because time is pressing. Only a living man can praise God. Praising is the most beautiful act that man is able to perform (cf. 17:10), but, because Ben Sira has no idea of an afterlife, man is called to praise the Lord during his time on earth (17:27–28). In order to accomplish this call, before it is too late, let the sinner convert! The same perspective of death comes again in 17:30 and 18:12, but it was already mentioned in 17:1–2a as a dimension of human existence.

The following verse, 17:29, is a hinge, I think, between 17:24–28 and 17:30–18:14. From now on the tone is hymnic, celebrating God's mercy and forgiveness towards those who return to him, specially towards the one whom Ben Sira has just invited to conversion (17:25–26a, c). God's forgiveness is again mentioned in 18:12b, in the conclusion, and his mercy in 18:11b, 13ab, 14a.

I divide 17:30–18:14 into two parts. From 17:30 till 18:7, Ben Sira contrasts human weakness with God's eternity and justice (17:30–18:2a); afterwards, he recalls human unfitness to praise the entire work of God, particularly his deeds of mercy (18:4–7). In such a reading, we have eight verses divided into two groups of four verses each. Then, from 18:8 till 18:14, Ben Sira continues to insist on human weakness, which justifies God's mercy; first, man's weakness is underlined in 18:8–11; after that, in 18:12–14, the divine mercy receives the emphasis. Again, if we read these verses in that way, we find eight verses in two groups of four verses each. Let us see in detail this passage with such a structure.

17:30–18:2a. It seems to me that 18:1–2a have to be joined to 17:30–32, and not with the following verses. In this sub-unit, there are some textual problems[47], but the essential meaning is discernible. Man is mortal; he also meditates evil[48], which is worse; like the sun which retires every evening, man is not continually luminous. Now the Lord inspects the stars. What will happen to men who are dust and ashes? All of these, stars and men, without

---

47   For Sir 17:30a, Prato, 289–90, is inclined to accept the reconstruction of Smend, Weisheit, 162 : "for there is not as (in) God in man"; Skehan – Di Lella, 278, 280, 285, read *tauta*, with the Syriac version; Wicke-Reuter, 171, following Sauer, Jesus Sirach, 549, understands *panta* as "perfection".

48   Cf. Hadot, 131–36. For the expression of Sir 17:31bα, cf. *Test. Sim.* 2:14; *Test. Benj.* 3:6; Matt 9:4.

exception[49], are created by the everlasting living God, the only one who should be acknowledged as just. Man's finitude and culpability are therefore contrasted with God's eternity and justice. This is one reason[50] for the Lord to forgive the one who is converted and returns to him.

18:4–7. A contrast between man and God is still perceived when man tries to praise the Lord and his works, particularly the wonders of his mercy (18:5b). Man is unable to make such a praise. This is the meaning of the rhetorical questions of 18:4–5[51]. God's marvels are above man's comprehension and he remains abashed. Therefore, even praise of God, to which the living man should dedicate his life (17:10, 27–28), will always be imperfect and will always leave him dissatisfied.

18:8–11. In 17:30–18:2a, man was seen in his cosmic surroundings: death made him different[52]. Here, his limited time is emphasized: what is a life of one hundred years[53] in comparison with eternity? This is another reason for the Lord to be patient and to pour out his mercy on men. The initial questions of 18:8–9 recall Pss 8:5; 144:3 and Job 7:17–18, but here they highlight the inconsistency and relative insignificance of such a noble but frail being.

18:12–14. Man's weakness is that he has to die: "their issue is miserable". God sees that and understands. Therefore he multiplies his acts of forgiveness (cf. 17:24). More than a man acting mercifully toward his neighbour (cf. 17:14b), God shows his mercy to all flesh: like a shepherd towards his flock, God's pedagogy has as its purpose to bring back the lost ones (cf. 17:24). Verse 18:14 concludes with this point: the Lord is merciful to those who accept his pedagogy for conversion (18:13cd)[54]; according to Ben Sira, such persons in fact search for the Lord (cf. 35/32:14a) and pay attention to his commands, i.e. they show eagerness to put them into practice.

Therefore, in these four sub-units, we find a continual contrast between man and God, but with varying nuances. In 17:30–18:2a and 18:8–11, Ben Sira lays stress upon human weakness, whereas in 18:4–7 and 18:12–14, he underlines the divine greatness. On the other hand, in 18:8–11 and 18:12–14, he ends by magnifying God's mercy and pardon, as he had announced in 17:24. He had opened his poem with an urgent call for conversion addressed

---

49 This could be the nuance of *koinê*; not *simul*, "at the same time", of the Latin version, which made difficulty for Augustine: cf. Gilbert, Jesus Sirach, 898.
50 Cf. *gar* in Sir 17:30a.
51 In Sir 18:4a, Skehan, 278 and 280, sees a question, with Greek II, Latin and Syriac versions.
52 Cf. the contrast between Sir 16:26–28 and 17:1.
53 Sir 18:9a of Greek I is equal to two stichoi in Hebrew: so Segal, ספר בן סירא, 107; Hartom, בן־סירא, 66, like Prato, 218 and Skehan, 279. On the other hand, Wicke-Reuter, 171, sees in Sir 18:9a only one stichos and takes 18:9b from Greek II.
54 Wicke-Reuter, 176 and 180, without any explanation, omits Sir 18:13cd.

to the opponent who has lost hope. Now, at the end, the insistence on the mercy and forgiveness of the Lord, who himself realizes the return of those who are converted and come back to him, truly becomes an encouraging message which the opponent greatly needed.

In proceeding in this way, Ben Sira differs from his answers to the first objections. There he proposed a refutation based on theology and on experience. Here, after his reflections on the deeds of the Creator who observes and shall judge every human being, he proceeds to the concrete situation of the present moment: let the opponent drop his untenable assertions and be converted, because, even if man's dignity is great, his misery is obvious. The Lord knows this well and therefore he is patient and merciful, he forgives and helps the lost one to come back. Finally, this poor man must understand that pity and pardon are not elementary tolerances, but basic characteristics of God as Creator and Lord of Israel. Ben Sira had already called to mind these divine characteristics which, by the way, he had mentioned in 16:11c–12a; the opponent does not seem to have taken them into account: his image of God was falsified and his objections were the proof of it.

3. Conclusion

The long text which was just analysed is the only one where Ben Sira deals so explicitly with God, sin and mercy. The structure of the whole, as it was observed by J. Haspecker, seems also to me convincing: the parallelism between 15:11–16:14 and 16:17–18:14 shows that Ben Sira touched two complementary aspects of the problem.

In 15:11–16:14, God must be exonerated from any responsibility for human sin. God does not do what he hates. Man in fact is the one responsible, for he, right from the beginning, received from God freedom to choose between good and evil. God observes human choice and shall repay accordingly. Ben Sira's personal experience, as well as the testimony of the biblical tradition, prove that the guilty are punished. Of course, the Lord of Israel is merciful, but nobody should deny that he punishes sinners in one way or in another.

In 16:17–18:14, the starting point is a double objection: God is not concerned with individual persons nor with their actions, good or evil. If this is so, is there still hope for one who does good? Ben Sira's answer first of all shows that man received from God everything that is necessary to carry out his function in the world and to keep his place among his fellows. God looks on the paths of men who are thus endowed and he shall repay them as they deserve, according to their deeds, good or evil. However, the guilty man's conversion is always a possibility during this life: God himself brings back those who repent and he gives courage again to those who have lost hope. For the Lord also sees and understands the weakness of man who is destined to die and who is prone to evil, man who is unable to estimate the marvels done by God, especially his wonders of mercy. Therefore the Lord multiplies his acts of forgiveness, his mercy towards all flesh and brings back to himself, like a shepherd his flock, those who turn towards him. Hope, therefore, is never lost.

At the speculative level, the affirmation of human freedom is the best answer to the question about responsibility for sin, and the dignity of man as well as his finitude are acknowledged as obvious. However, in order to justify such assertions, Ben Sira does not lean on philosophy: the starting point of his reflection is the biblical message about creation and the Sinai revelation, this last having, in his sight, a universal value[55].

4. Appendix: The Hebrew Text of Ben Sira 15:11–16:26

15

כי את אשר שׂנא לא עשׂה	11 אל תאמר מאל פשׁעי
כי אין צורך באנשׁי חמס	12 פן תאמר הוא התקילני
ולא יאננה ליראיו	13 רעה ותעבה שׂנא ייי
ויתנהו ביד יצרו	14 אלהים מבראשׁית ברא אדם
ותבונה לעשׂות רצונו	15 אם תחפץ תשׁמר מצוה
באשׁר תחפץ שׁלח ידיך	16 מוצק לפניך אשׁ ומים
אשׁר יחפץ ינתן לו	17 לפני אדם חיים ומות
אמיץ גבורות וחוזה כל	18 ספקה חכמת ייי
והוא יכיר כל מפעל אישׁ	19 עיני אל יראו מעשׂיו
ולא החלים אנשׁי כזב	20 לא צוה אנושׁ לחטא

16

ואל תשׂמח בבני עולה	1 אל תתאוה תואר נערי שׁוא
אם אין אתם יראת ייי	2 וגם אם פרו אל תבע בם
ואל תבטח בעקבותם	3 אל תאמין בחייהם
ומות ערירי מאחרית זדון	כי טוב אחד מאלף
וממשׁפחת בגדים תחרב	4 מאחד נבון תשׁב עיר
ועצמות מאלה שׁמעה אזני	5 רבות כאלה ראתה עיני

55 I thank James H. Swetnam who helped me with the English translation of these pages.

ובגוי חנף נצתה חמה	6 בעדת רשעים יוקדת אש
המורים [עולם] בגבורתם	7 אשר לא נשא לנסיכי קדם
המתעברים בגאותם	8 ולא חמל על מגורי לוט
הנורשים בעונם	9 ולא חמל על גוי חרם
הנאספים בזדון לבם	10 כן שש מאות אלף רגלי
תמה זה אם ינקה	11 ואף כי אחד מקשה ערף
ונושא וסולח ועל רשעים יניח רגזו	כי רחמים ואף עמו
איש כמפעליו ישפט	12 כרב רחמיו כן תוכחתו
ולא ישבית תאות צדיק לעולם	13 לא ימלט בגזל עול
וכל אדם כמעשיו ין[מ]צא לפניו	14 כל העושה צדקה יש לו שכר
ובמרום מי יזכרני	17 אל תאמר מאל נסתרתי
ומה נפשי בקצות רוחות	בעם כבד לא אודע
ותהום וארץ [ברדתו עליהם עמודים] בפקדו ירגשו	18 הן השמים ושמי השמים
בהביטו אליהם רעש ירעשו	19 אף קצבי הרים ויסודי תבל
ובדרכי מי יתבונן	20 גם עלי לא ישים לב
או אם אכזב בכל סתר מי יודע	21 אם חטאתי לא תראני עין
ותקות מה כי אצוק חוק	22 מעשה צדק מי יגידנו
וגבר פותה יחשב זאת	23 חסרי לב יבינו אלה
ועל דברי שימו לב	24 שמעו אלי וקחו שכלי
ובהצנע אחוה דעי	25 אביעה במשקל רוחי
	26 כברא אל מעשיו מראש

Bibliography

Alonso Schökel, L. (ed.), *Diccionario hebreo-español* (2d ed.; Madrid: Trotta. 1999).

Alonso Schökel, L., "The Vision of Man in Sirach 16:24–17:14," in *Israelite Wisdom: Theological and Literary Essays* (eds. John G. Gammie et al.; FS Samuel Terrien; Missoula: Union Theological Seminary Scholars, 1978), 234–45.

Argall, R.A., *1 Enoch and Sirach: A Comparative Literary and Conceptual Analysis of the Themes of Revelation, Creation and Judgment* (SBLEJL 8; Atlanta: Scholars, 1995).

Di Lella, A.A., Review of Jean Hadot, *Penchant mauvais et volonté libre*, in *Bib* 54 (1973) 571–74.

Gilbert, M., "Jesus Sirach," *RAC* 17. 878–906.

Hadot, J., *Penchant mauvais et volonté libre dans la Sagesse de Ben Sira (L'Ecclésiastique)* (Brussels: Presses Universitaires, 1970).

Hartom, E.S., בן־סירא " ד כרך החיצונים הספרים (3d ed. Tel Aviv: Yavneh, 1969).

Haspecker, J., *Gottesfurcht bei Jesus Sirach. Ihre religiöse Struktur und ihre literarische und doktrinäre Bedeutung* (AnBib 30; Rome: Pontifical Biblical Institute, 1967).

Joüon, P., *Grammaire de l'hébreu biblique* (Rome: Pontifical Biblical Institute, 1923).

Liesen, J., "Strategical Self-References in Ben Sira", in *Treasures of Wisdom: Studies in Ben Sira and the Book of Wisdom.* (FS M. Gilbert; eds. N. Calduch-Benages and J. Vermeylen; BETL 143; Leuven: Peeters, 1999) 63–74.

Liesen, J., *Full of Praise. An Exegetical Study of Sir 39:12–35* (JSJSup 64; Leiden: Brill, 2000).

Marböck, J., *Gottes Weisheit unter uns. Zur Theologie des Buches Sirach* (ed. I. Fischer; Herders Biblische Studien 6; Freiburg: Herder, 1995).

Marböck, J., "Sündenvergebung bei Jesus Sirach. Eine Notiz zur Theologie und Frömmigkeit der deuterokanonischen Schriften," *ZKTh* 116 (1994) 480–86.

Murphy, R.E., "Sin, Repentance, and Forgiveness in Sirach," in *Der Einzelne und seine Gemeinschaft bei Ben Sira* (eds. R. Egger-Wenzel and I. Krammer; BZAW 270; Berlin / New York: de Gruyter, 1998) 260–70.

Oesterley, W.O.E., *The Wisdom of Jesus the Son of Sirach, or Ecclesiasticus* (CBSC; Cambridge: Cambridge University, 1912).

Peters, N., *Das Buch Jesus Sirach oder Ecclesiasticus* (EHAT 25; Münster: Aschendorff, 1913).

Prato, G.L., *Il problema della teodicea in Ben Sira. Composizione dei contrari e richiamo alle origini* (AnBib 65; Rome: Pontifical Biblical Institute, 1975).

Sauer, G., *Jesus Sirach (Ben Sira)* (JSHRZ III/5; Gütersloh: Mohn, 1981).

Segal, M.Z., השלם בן־סירא ספר (2d rev. ed.; Jerusalem: Bialik, 1958).

Skehan P.W. – Di Lella, A.A., *The Wisdom of Ben Sira: A New Translation with Notes, Introduction and Commentary* (AB 39; New York: Doubleday, 1987).

Smend, R., *Die Weisheit des Jesus Sirach erklärt* (Berlin: Reimer, 1906).

Wénin, A., "De la création à l'alliance sinaïtique. La logique de Si 16,26–17,14," in *Treasures of Wisdom: Studies in Ben Sira and the Book of Wisdom* (FS M. Gilbert; eds. N. Calduch-Benages and J. Vermeylen; BETL 143; Leuven: Peeters, 1999) 147–58.

Wicke-Reuter, U., *Göttliche Providenz und menschliche Verantwortung bei Ben Sira und in der Frühen Stoa* (BZAW 298; Berlin / New York: de Gruyter, 2000).

Zerwick, M., *Graecitas biblica Novi Testamenti exemplis illustratur* (Rome: Pontifical Biblical Institute, 1966).

Ziegler, J., *Sapientia Iesu Filii Sirach* (Septuaginta. Vetus Testamentum Graecum auctoritate Societatis Litterarum Gottingensis editum XII/2; Göttingen: Vandenhoeck & Ruprecht, 1965).

Zorell, F., *Lexicon Hebraicum Veteris Testamenti* (Rome: Pontifical Biblical Institute, 1984).

Gott und Opfer

Friedrich V. Reiterer
Universität Salzburg

1. Vorbemerkungen

1.1 Belege

Wer sich mit dem Thema Opfer in Ben Sira umfassend beschäftigt, hat eine
große Anzahl von Stellen und Stichworten zu behandeln. In alphabetischer
Reihenfolge konnten folgende (deutsche) Schlagworte gesammelt werden:
Abgabe, Altar, Brandopfer, Dienst, Dienst tun, (beruhigender) Duft, Erst-
linge, Fasten, Fett, Fettstücke, Gabe, Geben, Gebet, Gedenkopfer, Götzen,
Götzenbild, Heilsopfer, Milchlamm, Opfer, Opfern, Opferanteile, Opfer-
fleisch, Opfergabe, Opferholz, Opferstücke, Priester, ewiges Priesteramt,
Priester sein, Schaubrote, Schlachtopfer, Schuldopfer, Speiseopfer, Sühne,
Sühnen, verbrennen / räuchern, Weihen, Weihrauch, Weihrauchfeuer, Weih-
rauchwolken, Wohlgeruch, Zehnter[1].

1.2 Verteilung im Buch

Die Verteilung auf die drei Teile des Buches Ben Sira (1–24; 25–43; 44–51)
ist nicht gleichmäßig:
  Im ersten Teil des Buches (1–24) konzentrieren sich die Vorkommen auf
die Kap. 3; 7; 21 und 24. Bezeugt sind insgesamt ca. 15 Stichworte mit der
Konzentration auf Kap. 7.
  Im zweiten Teil (25–43) finden sich Belege in den Kap. 30; 34/31;
35/32; 38; 39 und 41. Innerhalb der Belegpassagen erscheinen insgesamt ca.
37 Stichworte mit der Konzentration auf die Kap. 34/31 und 35/32.
  Im dritten Teil (44–51) stehen die Belege wie im zweiten Teil in sechs
Kap.: 45; 46; 47; 49; 50 und 51. Leicht höher als im vorhergehenden Abschnitt ist die Anzahl der Stichworte (insg. ca. 41), wobei die Konzentration
auf Personen zu erwähnen ist.

---

1   Vgl. die Sammlung der Belegstellen und der deutschen, griechischen, hebräischen und
     syrischen Termini im Anhang.

1.3 Methodische Grundsätze

Rezeption

Wie aus den Worten des Enkels[2] ersichtlich, hat sich der Großvater vor der schriftstellerischen Tätigkeit intensiv mit dem Gesetz, den Propheten und den übrigen Schriften beschäftigt. Dabei hat er für die Einarbeitung der ihm schriftlich vorliegenden Offenbarung eine eigene Methode entwickelt. Er bringt viele – ja mehr oder weniger ununterbrochen – subtile Anspielungen und erwartet offensichtlich von den Hörern bzw. Lesern, sie seien imstande, die Hinweise zu erkennen und das Gemeinte auf dem Hintergrund der angedeuteten Ausgangstexte zu interpretieren.

Dort wo klar ist, um was es geht, hat er eine andere Art der Anspielungen: durch Nicht-Erwähnen bzw. zumindest zum Teil gezieltes Verschweigen zeigt er an, worauf er Gewicht legt. Demnach besteht der erste methodische Schritt in sorgsamem Studieren des vorliegenden Textes, vor allem in Hinblick auf die Relation zu Passagen aus dem protokanonischen Alten Testament.

Dichtung

Eine besondere Rolle spielt die Berücksichtigung der poetischen Formung als dichterisch Gestalt gewordene Absicht des Autors. Es ist nicht nur wichtig, *dass etwas* und *was gesagt* bzw. geschrieben wird, sondern vor allem auch *wie* dies geschieht. Wichtige Elemente sind hierbei die poetische Struktur, die Beziehungsgeflechte, die gegenseitige Zuordnung der einzelnen Teile innerhalb der Gedichte. Daneben ist sorgsam auf die gewählten Worte zu achten.

Überlieferung

Da sich die Stichworte quer durch das Buch ziehen, wird man mit allen Problemen der Überlieferung des Buches Ben Sira konfrontiert: Die Überprüfung der griechischen und der syrischen Übersetzung wird von der Fragestellung geleitet, wieweit diese in den angegebenen Fällen dazu beitragen, den vermutlichen hebräischen Ausgangstext besser zu verstehen. Bei Abweichung vom vorliegenden H-Text muss man damit rechnen, dass es Fehler in der Übersetzung geben kann. Dies scheint aber der eher seltene Fall zu sein. – Viel bedeutsamer ist die Vermutung, dass eine abweichende Version in Γ oder Syr auf eine von der erhaltenen unterschiedliche H-Basistexte verweist. Dass es schon anfänglich mehr als eine Version gab, halte ich für sehr wahrscheinlich. – Die schon sehr früh anzusetzende Aufspaltung der Überlieferung begründet wohl auch gar manche Unterschiede, die in den verschiedenen H-Traditionen vorliegen. Wenn Γ und Syr parallel gehen, nehme ich diese Zeugnisse für sehr gewichtige Hinweise auf einen gemeinsamen Aus-

---

2   Vgl. das Vorwort des Enkel, der die griechische Übersetzung des Sirabuches erstellte.

gangstext. Dies ist vor allem deswegen von Bedeutung, weil der hebräische Text nicht vollständig erhalten ist[3] und an den nur in Γ und Syr erhaltenen Stellen die Parallelität auf Ursprünglichkeit hinweist. Die aussagekräftigsten Folgerungen lassen die Übersetzungen (von Γ und Syr) jedoch über sich selbst machen, nämlich über die Übersetzungsgewohnheiten: Dies betrifft den Umgang mit der Vorlage, und deren Verständnis vom Inhalt der Übersetzungsvorlage. Dies ist besonders dann wertvoll, wenn man die Zeitsituation der Übersetzenden spüren kann.

Schlussfolgerungen
Folgende These ist grundlegend: In jeder Sprache gibt es neben den grammatischen Regeln auch terminologische Fixpunkte. Mehr oder weniger unverrückbar, oder zumindest sehr schwer veränderbar ist die terminologische Festlegung in Bereichen, in denen eine geprägte Fachsprache vorliegt und auch unverzichtbar ist. – Wenn man nun solche Gebiete nennen will, in denen die Ausdrucksweise keineswegs austauschbar ist, dann gehört der kultische Bereich dazu. Daher ist anzunehmen, dass man im Zusammenhang des Kultes keineswegs die Worte frei wählen kann.

Jeder Mensch muss von etwas leben. Den Priestern sind für die Lebenserhaltung nach protokanonischen Zeugnissen Teile von Opfern zugewiesen. Wenn es Vorschriften gibt, die den Priestern lebensnotwendige Gegenstände zuteilen, ist es ausgeschlossen, dass diese Materialien keine präzise Bezeichnung besitzen oder die Bezeichnungen austauschbar sein könnten.

Die letzten zwei Überlegungen führen also zu folgendem Schluss: Man kann davon ausgehen, dass man festen Boden unter den Füßen hat, wenn man die Kultterminologie der Untersuchung zugrunde gelegt.

1.4 Begründung der Stellenauswahl

Wie schon ein flüchtiger Blick zeigt, überfordert eine detaillierte Behandlung der vielen Belege einen Artikel. Daher müssen für die Untersuchung vorentscheidende Überlegungen zur Auswahl der Stellen angestellt werden. Auswahlkriterien für die Stellenauswahl sind folgende:

Es gibt grundlegend unterschiedliche Zugänge zur Beantwortung des gestellten Themas: man kann eine Antwort in Form einer terminologischen Untersuchung suchen oder man kann sich auf inhaltliche Aussagen über das Verhältnis Gottes zu den Opfern konzentrieren. Man kann generell die theologische Rolle des Kultpersonals, genauer der Priester, erheben und in jenen Zusammenhängen für die Fragestellung bedeutsame Ausführungen analysieren. Im folgenden werden daher für die erste Fragestellung zwei Stellen aus

---

3   Vgl. die Belege bei Reiterer, Bibliographie, 26–38.

Kap. 7 gewählt (unten 2.), für den zweiten Schritt eine Einheit aus 34/31 und 35/32 (unten 5.). Der dritte Teil wird sich mit Passagen aus dem Lob der Väter beschäftigen (unten 6.).

Kein gewählter Abschnitt thematisiert den Kult an sich. Elemente des Kultes erscheinen daher eher zufällig und geradezu nebenbei erwähnt. Die Verwendungen sind daher nicht im Sinne von Fachausführungen zu sehen, belegen aber gerade deshalb den Standard nicht speziell reflektierter und daher allgemein anerkannter und als selbstverständlich anzusehender Vorstellungen. Sie zeigen die in der alltäglichen Verwendung des Normaljudäers (also nicht des Kultbediensteten) undiskutierte und allgemein verbreitete Bedeutung. Es ist anzunehmen, dass auch die Hörer ihren Lehrer verstehen und auf der gleichen Verständnisebene wie er sind. Dann hat man die damals weit verbreitete Wortbedeutung vor sich. Darüber hinaus sind folgende Kriterien berücksichtigt worden: im Kap. 7 wie im Lob der Väter ist auch ein H-Text erhalten. Dies trifft für die wichtigsten Passagen in Kap. 35/32 zwar nicht zu, doch ist letztere Stelle theologisch gewichtig. Zugleich erhebt sich die Forderung, auch die griechische und syrische Übersetzung dort genauer zu behandeln, wo es hebräische Vergleichstexte gibt.

2. Die Opfer in Kap. 7

2.1 Die Abgrenzung und Struktur von Sir 7

Auf den ersten Blick scheint in Kap. 7 eine unstrukturierte Anhäufung von Sprüchen vorzuliegen. Eine genauere Analyse fördert aber strukturelle und inhaltliche Entsprechungen zu Tage.

Mittels Derivaten von עשה wird zwischen V. 1 (אל תעש) und 36a (בכל מעשיך) eine äußere Rahmung hergestellt. Die thematischen Berührungen zwischen den Kola 2 und 36b unterstützen diese Abgrenzung. Die vier Kola 1.2 und 36a.b bilden für sich genommen einen allgemein gültigen Grundsatz über die Ablehnung des schlechten Verhaltens, der unabhängig vom übrigen Gedicht stehen könnte, vielleicht auch einmal gestanden hat:

2 הרחק מעון ויט ממך   1 אל תעש לך רעה ואל ישיגך

36b ולעולם לא תשחת   36a[4] בכל מעשיך זכור אחרית

---

4   1 Verübe für dich nicht Schlechtes, damit er (Gott) dich nicht belangt,
     2 halte dich fern von Verschuldung, damit er/sie sich von dir wegbeugt.
   36a Bei all deinen Taten denke an den Ausgang,
     und nie und nimmer wirst du Schaden leiden.

Bei allen Unterschieden zwischen H und Γ ist doch soviel klar, dass an den in H belegten Positionen auch ein Γ-Text steht. In 1 und 36a wird in Γ allerdings eine andere Alternative geboten als in H. Der H-Text bietet eine Anlehnung an eine figura etymologica (חעש – מעשיך), welche nach hebräischem Stilempfinden gut klingt. Worte gleicher Wurzel gelten für Γ eher schwerfällig. Daher bietet Γ als Antithese: *tun* (ποίει) versus *Rede* (ἐν ... τοῖς λόγοις):

1	Μὴ ποίει κακά καὶ οὐ μή σε καταλάβῃ κακόν	2	ἀπόστηθι ἀπὸ ἀδίκου καὶ ἐκκλινεῖ ἀπὸ σοῦ
36a	ἐν πᾶσιν τοῖς λόγοις σου μιμνῄσκου τὰ ἔσχατα	36b	καὶ εἰς τὸν αἰῶνα οὐχ ἁμαρτήσεις[5]

Beide Varianten ergeben eine aus zwei Stichen bestehende allgemein gültige Sentenz, die in sich verständlich und sinnvoll ist. Sie bräuchte den jetzigen Kontext nicht.

In 6a–d.27–28.31a–d stehen inhaltlich und strukturell aufeinander hingeordnete Paare. Es fällt auf, dass – ausgenommen 17a[A.C] – von V. 1 bis V. 20 alle in erster Position stehenden Kola mit אל (nicht; in 6c steht פן) beginnen. Die negierte Reihe ergibt so einen großen Abschnitt (7,3–20), die nicht negierte Reihe von Sprüchen bildet den zweiten Teil (7,21–35).

2.2 Die Strophengliederung in Sir 7

Auf der Basis der eben festgestellten großen Gliederungsabschnitte (7,3–20 bzw. 7,21–35) sollen nun die eher lose verbunden erscheinenden Einzelsprüche nach übergreifenden Gesichtspunkten befragt werden, womit man eine strophische Gliederung erhält. Tatsächlich lassen sich folgende thematische Schwerpunkte finden:

Im ersten, also dem negierten Teil, stehen:
die Strophe 7,4–7 mit 5 Stichen; sie beschäftigt sich mit Themen aus dem öffentlich-politischen Bereich. In 7,8–10, konstruiert aus 7 Stichen, geht es um Fragen der persönlichen Frömmigkeit. Einstellungen, die abzulehnen sind, werden in 7,11–17b anhand von 7 Stichen aufgereiht. Das engste soziale Umfeld binden 7,18–20, bestehend aus 3 Stichen, zusammen.
Demnach umfasst 7,3–20 die vier folgend angeführten Strophen:

Vv. 7,4–7   5 Stichen

---

5   1 Verübe keine Schlechtigkeiten und kein Übel wird dich treffen,
     2 Halte Abstand vom Ungerechten und er bleibt von dir weg.
    36a Bei all deinen Worten denk an die Endergebnisse
    36b und nie und nimmer wirst du dich vergehen.

Vv. 7,8–10   3 Stichen
Vv. 7,11–17   7 Stichen
Vv. 7,18–20   3 Stichen

Im zweiten, nicht negierten Teil stehen folgende Unterabschnitte: Die Strophe 7,21–28, bestehend aus 8 Stichen, handelt positiv vom engen sozialen
Bereich. Mit der individuellen Erfüllung religiöser Pflichten beschäftigen
sich 7,29–31 in vier 4 Stichen. Das öffentliche Sozialverhalten steht in 7,32–
35, strukturiert aus 4 Stichen, im Mittelpunkt. Demnach setzt sich 7,21–35
aus den drei folgend angeführten Strophen zusammen:

Vv. 7,21–28   8 Stichen
Vv. 7,29–31   4 Stichen
Vv. 7,32–35   4 Stichen

Die Strophen sind teilweise chiastisch aufeinander hingeordnet: auf der Basis
der Öffentlichkeit argumentieren die Strophen 1 (Vv. 7,4–7) und 7 (Vv. 7,32–
35). Mit Aspekten des persönlichen Verhaltens im individuellen Bereich der
Frömmigkeit beschäftigen sich die Strophen 2 (Vv. 7,8–10) und 6 (Vv. 7,29–
31). Fragestellungen aus dem engsten sozialen Umfeld stehen in den Strophen 4 (Vv. 7,18–20) und 5 (7,21–28) im Mittelpunkt. Die Strophe 3 hat im
zweiten Abschnitt kein Pendant.

So ergibt sich folgende Strukturierung

	negativ 1. Abschnitt: Vv. 7,3–20		*positiv* 2. Abschnitt: Vv. 7,21–35
öffentlich-politischer Bereich	1. Strophe: Vv. 7,4–7	⇔	7. Strophe: Vv. 7,32–35
persönliche Frömmigkeit – religiöse Pflichten	2. Strophe: Vv. 7,8–10	⇔	6. Strophe: Vv. 7,29–31
verwerfliche Einstellungen	3. Strophe: Vv. 7,11–17	⇔	---
engstes soziales Umfeld	4. Strophe: Vv. 7,18–20	⇔	5. Strophe: Vv. 7,21–28

Aus dieser Strukturanalyse wird deutlich, dass die 2. Strophe (7,8–10) und
die 6. Strophe (7,29–31)[6] einander thematisch berühren und daher für die
vorliegende Untersuchung einschlägig sind.

  Die Struktur zeigt zugleich auch, dass diese beiden Passagen als eigene
Strophen eine relativ hohe Eigenständigkeit besitzen, so dass es möglich ist,
diese aus dem Kontext zu lösen und für sich selbst zu untersuchen, ohne dass
der Inhalt verfälscht wird.

---

6   Sauer, Jesus Sirach, 92f, behandelt 7,29–31 als eigene Einheit und ordnet sie nicht in
    ein größeres Ganzes ein.

2.3 Die Strophe 7,8–10

Im H^A erhaltenen Text fehlt der Stichos 9:

8b.a   אל תקשור לשנות חט   כי באחת לא תנקה

10b.a   אל תתקצר בתפלה   ובצדקה אל תתעבר

Die Parallelität von Γ und Syr belegt aber, dass es erstens einen Stichos 9 gegeben hat und dass dieser zweitens im Wesentlichen über die Übersetzungen
auch zugänglich ist.

2.4 Die Strophe 7,29–31[7]

Diese Strophe bietet einen, trotz der Bruchstückhaftigkeit im großen und
ganzen verständlichen hebräischen Text.

29b.a   בכל לבך פחד אל   ואת כהניו הקדיש

30b.a   בכל מאודך אוהב עושך   ואת משרתיו לא תעזב

31b.a   כבד אל והדר כהן   ותן חלקם כאשר צוותה

31d.c[8]   לחם אבירים ותרומת יד   זבחי צדק ותרומת קדש

Sie konkretisiert den allgemeinen Grundsatz (7,1–2.36), was man an Positi-
vem tun soll, um dem Bösen aus dem Weg zu gehen. Vereinfachend kann
man feststellen: den Schöpfer fürchten und lieben, sowie den Priester mit den
ihm zustehenden Gaben versorgen. – Man trifft also auf Belege, die für die
vorliegende Untersuchung von großer Aussagekraft sind.

2.4.1 Die religiöse und kultische Terminologie in 7,9–10.29–31

Das Belegmaterial:

V. 9a: (Opfer)gaben δῶρον; ܡܘܗܒܬܐ; opfern προσφέρω; ܩܪܒ;

V. 9b: [Opfer] in Empfang nehmen προσδέχομαι; ܩܒܠ;

V. 10a.14b: Gebet תפלה; προσευχή; ܨܠܘܬܐ;

---

7   Vgl. zu diesem Abschnitt Haspecker, Gottesfurcht, 295–312; Snaith, Ben Sira's, 168f;
Stadelmann, Ben Sira, 55–68; Olyan, Ben Sira's, 261–86; Perdue, Wisdom, 243–90.
256f; Calduch-Benages, En el crisol, 196–99.

8   Die graphische Darstellung bedeutet: die Konsonanten in Umrissform ohne Kursivschreibung sind Buchstaben, die in den Handschriften schlecht oder kaum lesbar sind.
Auf diese Weise umgeht man die textkritischen Zeichen wie Punkte oder Striche bzw.
zusätzliche Kleinschreibung bei unsicheren Worten. Die Konsonanten in Umrissform
mit Kursivschreibung sind Ergänzungen von mir.

Vv. 29b.31a: Priester כהן; ἱερεύς; ܟܗܢܐ;

V. 30b: Diener משרת; λειτουργός; ܡܫܡܫܢܐ;

V. 31b: Anteil חלק; μερίς; ܘܢ (!);

V. 31c: (1) "Wunderbrot" לחם אבירים; ܠܚܡܐ ܕܡܠܐܟܐ;

ἀπαρχή (Erstlingsopfer) und περὶ πλημμελείας (Schuldopfer)

(2) die Handabgabe ותרומת יד; δόσις βραχιόνων

V. 31d: (1) gesetzliche Schlachtopfer זבחי צדק; θυσίαν ἁγιασμοῦ;

(2) heilige Abgabe תרומת קדש; ἀπαρχὴν ἁγίων.

2.4.2 Einzeluntersuchung

In der anschließenden Untersuchung stellen einzelne Worte bzw. Wortverbindungen den Ausgangspunkt dar. Methodischer Ausgangspunkt ist weiters, dass die Kultsprache geprägt und daher nicht willkürlich veränderbar ist. Gibt es Varianten, muss man mit einem beabsichtigten Eingriff rechnen. Durch den Vergleich der Aussagen in terminologisch vergleichbaren Passagen lässt sich der Inhalt und die Intention der sirazidischen Formulierungen erheben.

בכל לבך in 7,29a

Neben der bei Sira gegebenen Phrase בְּכָל־לֵב (16mal) ist im protokanonischen Alten Testament viel häufiger בְּכָל־לְבָב (29 mal) und dies wieder in direkter Parallele zu וּבְכָל־נֶפֶשׁ (Dtn 4,29; 6,5; 10,12; 11,13; 13,4; 26,16; 30,2.6.10; Jos 22,5; 23,14; 1Sam 12,20; 1Kön 2,4; 18,48; 2Kön 23,25; 2Chr 15,12; 34,31) belegt. Die Phraseologie ist demnach fest in der Tradition verwurzelt. – Alle protokanonischen Vorkommen von בְּכָל־לֵב bzw. בְּכָל־לְבָב stehen in positiven und direkt oder indirekt auf JHWH bezogenen Kontexten.

Verba im Kontext von בְּכָל־לֵב bzw. בְּכָל־לְבָב:

Wenn mit בְּכָל־לֵב bzw. בְּכָל־לְבָב ein Verhalten zu Gott oder zu einem ihm zustehenden Bereich, wie z.B. die Gebote, qualifiziert wird, werden folgende Verba verwendet: אהב in Dtn 6,5; 13,4; 30,6; בטח in Spr 3,5; דרש in Dtn 4,29; 2Chr 15,12; 22,9; Jer 29,13; Ps 119,10; הלך אַחֲרֵי in 1Kön 14,8; הלך ב in 2Kön 10,31; הלך לִפְנֵי in 1Kön 2,4; 8,23; 2Chr 6,14; חלה פָּנִים in Ps 119,58; ידה in Ps 9,2; 86,12; 111,1; 138,1; ידע in Jos 23,14; 2Chr 32,31; נטע in Jer 32,41; נצר in Ps 119,2.69; עבד in Dtn 10,12; 11,13; 1Sam 12,20.24; Jos 22,5; עלז in Zef 3,14; עשׂה in Dtn 26,16; 2Chr 31,21; קרא in Ps 119,145; שׂבע in 2Chr 15,15; שׁוב אֶל in Dtn 30,10; 1Sam 7,3; 1Kön 8,48;

2Kön 23,25; 2Chr 6,38; Jer 3,10; 24,7; שוב עד in Joël 2,12; שמע in Dtn 30,2 und שמר in 2Kön 23,3; 2Chr 34,31; Ps 119,34.

An keinem der protokanonischen Belege kommt der Gedanke vor, Gott sei aus ganzen Herzen zu *fürchten*, wie Sira formuliert.

פחד אל in 7,29a

Unbestritten ist *Gottesbeachtung* (= Gottesfurcht) im Sinne des intensiven Ernstnehmen Gottes, die Anerkennung an sich und die daraus resultierenden Verhaltensweisen einschließend eines der zentralsten Themen des Buches Ben Sira. Um diese Form der Anerkennung Gottes auszudrücken, stellt Sira aber Derivate von ירא mit אל (6,16b; 35/32,12b), אלהים (9,16b; 10,20b. 22b[A].24b; 40,26b), ייי (10,22b[B]; 15,1a.13b; 16,2b.4a; 26,3b; 35/32,16a; 36/33,1a; 40,26c; 43,2b[B]; 50,29b) oder עליון (6,37a; 43,2b[A]) zusammen.

Während Ps 36,2 [אֵין־פַּחַד אֱלֹהִים] von Furcht im Sinne von Schrecken und Angst spricht ("der Böse sagt zu sich selbst: ich kenne kein Erschrecken vor Gott"), gibt es doch auch weniger scharfe Bedeutungsnuancen von פחד. Nach Ps 119,161 hat der Beter keine Angst vor den politisch Mächtigen, er "fürchtet (פחד) nur dein (Gottes) Wort". Man wird, wie der Hinweis auf die den Beter "grundlos verfolgenden Fürsten" (שָׂרִים רְדָפוּנִי חִנָּם) zeigt, aufgrund der Bedeutung von פחד mit außergewöhnlich großem Nachdruck rechnen müssen. Unter diesem Aspekt ist auch auf Spr 28,14 hinzuweisen: "Wohl dem Menschen, der stets Gott fürchtet" (מְפַחֵד). Mit wenigen Ausnahmen schließen die Belege für פחד ausdrücklich Angst und Schrecken ein[9]; wenn dies nicht explizit der Fall ist, dann ist doch entschiedener Nachdruck und undiskutierbare Ernsthaftigkeit gemeint.

Nie steht פחד im engen, selten im weiteren Zusammenhang mit Opfer. Man kann auf Hos 3,4f verweisen. Nach einer Zeit, in der es keinen König, keinen Fürsten und keine *Opfer* gibt (Hos 3,4), werden die Israeliten in sich gehen, zu "Gott umkehren und ihn suchen", und schließlich "werden sie zu JHWH hin beben" (וּפָחֲדוּ אֶל־יְהוָה; Hos 3,5). – Im Kontext von Gen 31 wird auch von einem (Kult-)Mahl gesprochen (V. 54), welches der Abmachung zwischen Laban und Jakob gesicherte Einhaltung garantieren sollte. Als erstes rief Laban אֱלֹהֵי אַבְרָהָם וֵאלֹהֵי נָחוֹר als Richter an, während es von Jakob heißt: וַיִּשָּׁבַע יַעֲקֹב בְּפַחַד אָבִיו יִצְחָק (Gen 31,53). Diese Gottesbezeich-

---

9   Vgl. u.a. Dtn 11,25; 1Sam 11,7; 1Chr 14,17; 2Chr 17,10; 20,29; Mi 7,17: Völker, die JHWH sein Volk in der eschatologischen Wende begleiten sehen, werden sich "zu JHWH, unserem Gott (אֱלֹהִים), beben(d wenden; פחד) und vor dir sich fürchten (ירא)".

nung unterscheidet sich deutlich von der knapp vorher angeführten und betont das Angst erregende Element.

Während die Thematik der Angst in der Gottesvorstellung belegbar ist, konnte kein Beleg gefunden werden, der der Formulierung in Sir 7,29a ähnlich ist. Weiters kann diese Formulierung auch nicht mit Hilfe einer Rückübersetzung aus Γ oder Syr erklärt werden. Man wird sirazidische Eigenprägung vor sich haben.

Was will aber die ungewohnte Phraseologie und dieser scharfe Ton? – Da Sira zwar oft von der Gottesachtung spricht, aber keine solche Tonart anschlägt, wird man den Grund für diesen Ausbruch von Schärfe im konkreten Kontext suchen: Das, was anschließend über bzw. zugunsten der Priester gesagt wird, ist nicht nur zur Kenntnis zu nehmen, sondern wird bei Ignorierung die erschreckende Seite Gottes aktivieren.

הקְדִּישׁ in 7,29a

Wenn man "heiligen" und "Priester" in der traditionellen Zusammenstellung hört, denkt man daran, dass Personen nur dann Priester sein können, wenn sie speziell von einer dazu befähigten Person – wie Aaron – durch das "Heiligen" dazu befähigt worden sind (vgl. u.a. Ex 28,3.41; 29,1) oder dass eingesetzte Priester sich für den Dienst speziell vorbereiten, will sagen "heiligen", vgl. u.a. Ex 19,22.

In Sir 7,29a ist beides nicht der Fall! "Heiligen" ist offensichtlich eine ehrfürchtige Haltung des Hörers sirazidischer Unterweisung den Priestern gegenüber. Das Heiligen ist eine aktive Haltung des den Priester Verehrenden, wie das interessante Kausativ הקְדִּישׁ (= heilig sein lassen) zeigt. Es geht darum, dass man den Priester Priester sein lässt und seine Position anerkennt; vgl. Ez 48,11.

לחם אברים in 7,31c

Die Verbindung von לחם mit dem – bei Sira defektiv geschriebenen – אברִים ist in Ps 78,25 belegt:

וּדְגַן־שָׁמַיִם נָתַן לָמוֹ	וַיַּמְטֵר עֲלֵיהֶם מָן לֶאֱכֹל	Ps 78,24
צֵידָה שָׁלַח לָהֶם לָשֹׂבַע	לֶחֶם אַבִּירִים אָכַל אִישׁ	Ps 78,25[10]

Im Kontext des Psalms steht die Constructusverbindung לֶחֶם אַבִּירִים ("Brot der Starken"?) in entfernter Parallele zu מָן ("Manna") und דְגַן־שָׁמַיִם ("und Korn / Brot vom Himmel") aus V. 24 und צֵידָה in 25b. Während die Parallele מָן und דְגַן־שָׁמַיִם auf das Eingreifen Gottes und das Wundersame deutet, ist in V25 das direkte Parallelwort צֵידָה aufschlussreich und handgreif-

---

10 "Er ließ Manna auf sie regnen als Speise und Brot vom Himmel er gab ihnen. Brot der Starken aß ein jeder; Proviant gab er ihnen zur Sättigung".

lich konkret: צֵידָה ist die typische "Reiseverpflegung"; vgl. z.B. Gen 42,25; 45,21 (Josef gibt sie seinen Brüdern); Ri 20,10; 7,8 (Verpflegung für einen Kriegszug bzw. vom Krieg nach Hause); 1Sam 22,10 (Proviant für David vom Priester Ahimelech).

Vermutlich wurde die Wortverbindung gewählt, um die Thematik rund um die Priester geschickt mehrdimensional darzustellen: demnach geht es neben der Ernährung auch um die Ernährten. In Anspielung auf den Psalmenvers wird die göttliche Sphäre, in die der priesterliche Dienst fällt, ins Spiel gebracht, zugleich das Eindrucksvolle und Gewichtige des Priesters. Allerdings kann man solche Worte auch nicht als eine plumpe Anbiederung an die Priesterschaft interpretieren. Diese schillernde, mehrdeutige und doch in gewisser Weise recht klare, bestärkende und zugleich sich zurücknehmende Art der Argumentation ist eine typische Eigenart Ben Siras. Demnach ist festzuhalten, dass es sich bei לֶחֶם אַבִּירִים um einen religiös bedeutsamen, aber schwer deutbaren bzw. beabsichtigt mehrdeutigen, für den Kult aber keineswegs zentralen Ausdruck handelt.

תרומת ... in 7,31c

תְּרוּמָה ist ein gebräuchlicher und häufig verwendeter Opferterminus. Da Sira den status constructus תרומת bietet, ist ein Substantiv zu ergänzen. Vorgeschlagen wird dafür יָד[11]. Diese Wortverbindung findet man dreimal im AT, nämlich in Dtn 12,6.11.17: Handopfer, meistens interpretiert als Handerhebungsopfer, sind damit gemeint. Die Wortwahl entspricht der auch andernorts beobachtbaren Gegebenheit, dass Sira seltene Formulierungen bevorzugt.

צדק יִ𝔥ℨ𝔍 in 7,31dα

Auch diese Constructusverbindung ist nicht vollständig erhalten, wobei die Lesbarkeit der Vorlage unterschiedlich bewertet wird[12]. Die Constructusverbindung im Kontext kultischer Aussagen, in der צדק das zweite Glied darstellt, lässt das mit ʸ endende Wort mit großer Wahrscheinlichkeit auf יִ𝔥ℨ𝔍 ergänzen. זִבְחֵי־צֶדֶק ist dreimal im protokanonischen AT belegt: Dtn 33,19; Ps 4,6; 51,21. An allen drei Stellen geht es um rechtmäßige bzw. rechtmäßig dargebrachte Opfer. – Deutlich wird der Bezug zu eingehaltenen gesetzlichen Normen.

נתן חלק und צוה in 7,31b

Die folgende Argumentation setzt voraus, dass die allgemein anerkannte Ergänzung des unvollständig erhaltenen Textes ותן]לקם durch eine Auffüllung

---

11   Vgl. u.a. Peters, Buch Jesus Sirach, 73; ספר, 10.

12   Nach ספר ist nur das ʸ sicher zu erkennen.

zu נתן ʃ נת ‏ؚחלקם richtig ist. Es wird nun überprüft, wieweit und in welchem Sinne "den Priestern einen Anteil geben" und ein dahingehend einschlägiger Befehl Gottes im gemeinsamen Kontext vorkommen bzw. auf welche Intention die Phrase נתן חלק bzw. צוה im kultischen Kontext weist.

נתן חלק

Im protokanonischen AT wird die Phrase נתן חלק nicht in Zusammenhang mit Aussagen verwendet, die צוה, also einen einschlägigen Befehl Gottes, einschließen,. Es kommt also keine Stelle vor, wo es – gleich wie hier – befohlen wird, den Priestern "ihren Teil" zu geben.

Wenn man von נתן חלק ausgeht und נתן auf ein menschliches Objekt gerichtet ist, trifft man auf folgende Angaben:

Es wird einmal festgehalten, dass das "Land an Josua als Anteil (Jos 15,13; vgl. Jos 18,7) vergeben" wird. Weiters liest man, dass dem Stamm "Levi kein Land als Anteil" zu geben ist (Jos 14,4). Die Belege, auf die man mit Hilfe dieser Phrase stößt, führen im Hinblick auf Sir 7,31b also nicht weiter, da in 31b ausdrücklich den "Priestern" ein חלק von den durch Sira Angesprochenen zu geben ist. Es bleibt noch die schwierige Formulierung in Lev 6,10, wo zwar die Worte נתן und חלק stehen, aber nicht in dem Sinne von Verb und allein dazugehörendem Objekt, da נתן mit doppeltem Objekt konstruiert wird. Die Bezüge hinsichtlich der doppelten Objekte sind zu präzisieren: מֵאִשַּׁי[13] לֹא תֵאָפֶה חָמֵץ חֶלְקָם נָתַתִּי אֹתָהּ. Worauf bezieht sich das enklitische Personalpronomen in אֹתָהּ? Da חֵלֶק maskulin ist, kann nur das in Lev 6,7 stehende הַמִּנְחָה gemeint sein: "Backe (das Speiseopfer) nicht gesäuert. Als ihren (der Priester) Anteil gab ich es (das Speiseopfer) von meinem Feueropfer". Demnach meint חֵלֶק jenen Teil von מִנְחָה, der zugleich als אִשֶּׁה nicht gesäuert gebacken werden darf. Gleichzeitig ist klar, dass Gott nicht die ganze מִנְחָה dem Priester zueignet. Nur ein wie die Gabe an Gott nicht zu säuernder und gebackener Teil (חֵלֶק) fällt davon den Priestern zu. – Wenn mittels אֹתָהּ (enklitisches possessives ה-, das mit dem femininen מִנְחָה korreliert) auf diese Gabe Bezug genommen wird, dann wird die Formulierung wieder unscharf. Denn eigentlich müßte man dann annehmen, die (ganze) מִנְחָה stünde den Priestern zu.

---

13 Vgl. Lev 6,9–10: וְהַנּוֹתֶרֶת מִמֶּנָּה יֹאכְלוּ אַהֲרֹן וּבָנָיו מַצּוֹת תֵּאָכֵל בְּמָקוֹם קָדֹשׁ בַּחֲצַר אֹהֶל־מוֹעֵד יֹאכְלוּהָ לֹא תֵאָפֶה חָמֵץ חֶלְקָם נָתַתִּי אֹתָהּ מֵאִשָּׁי קֹדֶשׁ קָדָשִׁים הוּא כַּחַטָּאת וְכָאָשָׁם ("Das Übrige sollen Aaron und seine Söhne als ungesäuertes Brot an einem heiligen Ort, im Vorhof des Offenbarungszeltes, essen. Man soll den Anteil an meinen Feueropfern, den ich ihnen gebe, nicht gesäuert backen. Es ist etwas Hochheiliges wie das Sünd- und das Schuldopfer".)

Trotz bleibender Unschärfe wird deutlich, dass die Phrase נתן חלק besagt, dass Gott selbst den Aaroniten einen Anteil vom Speiseopfer gibt. Der
Geber ist *Gott*. – Bei Sira sind die Bezüge anders: die *Hörenden* werden aufgefordert, den Priestern deren Anteil zu geben.

צוה als Ausgangspunkt

Wenn man vom Stichwort צוה als Auftrag ausgeht, verbindlich Gaben im
Kult zur Verfügung zu stellen, stößt man in Lev 10,13 auf eine inhaltlich
relevante Stelle. Für Priester sind nach Lev 10,12 zum Essen vorgesehen "der
Rest des Speiseopfers von den JHWH gewidmeten Feueropfern (הַמִּנְחָה
הַנּוֹתֶרֶת מֵאִשֵּׁי יְהוָה)" und "die ungesäuerten Brote (מַצּוֹת)". Beide werden
als Hochheiliges (קֹדֶשׁ קָדָשִׁים) bezeichnet: "An einem heiligen Ort sollt ihr
sie (= הַמִּנְחָה) essen, denn sie (= הַמִּנְחָה) ist das, was dir und deinen Söhnen
gemäß dem חֹק (der Vorschrift)[14] von den Feueropfern des Herrn zugewiesen
ist; so ist es mir befohlen worden (צֻוֵּיתִי)"[15]. Es heißt, dass die Zuweisung von
Stücken des אִשֶּׁה an die Priester eine bestehende, gültige und konkrete Vorschrift (חֹק) ist, deren Erfüllung direkt von JHWH aufgetragen wurde: כִּי־כֵן
צֻוֵּיתִי / "denn so wurde mir befohlen". Das Passiv ist ein passivum divinum,
wodurch klar ist, dass JHWH den Befehl selbst erteilt. Das sirazidische
Stichwort צוה weist auf gleiche Zusammenhänge hin.

Der nicht erwähnte אִשֶּׁה

Die terminologischen Anspielungen weisen auf Stellen, in denen kultische
Gaben erwähnt werden, welche bei Sira nicht ausdrücklich genannt werden.
Das trifft für den zuvor erwähnten אִשֶּׁה zu, der in Sir 7,31 nicht, wohl aber in
Sir 45,21f; 50,13 erwähnt wird.

אִשֶּׁה wird häufig – dessen ungeachtet, dass אִשֶּׁה vielleicht selbst eine
bestimmte Form eines Opfers gewesen ist – als ein summarischer Oberbegriff
verwendet, mit dem speziell jene Opfer zusammengefasst werden, die teilweise verbrannt werden und von denen den Priestern und deren Familien
Anteile aufgrund der bestehenden Vorschrift (חֹק) zustehen. – Vermutlich
klangen den Zuhörern Siras aufgrund der Kenntnis biblischer Stellen oder religiöser Praktiken Zusammenhänge im Ohr, die man heute nicht mehr gewärtig hat, und die daher wieder ins Bewusstsein geholt werden müssen. Deswe-

---

14   Eigenartigerweise wurde חֹק in der EÜ lediglich verschlüsselt berücksichtigt: חָקְךָ
     וְחָק־בָּנֶיךָ הוּא מֵאִשֵּׁי יְהוָה ist zufolge EÜ: "was dir und deinen Söhnen von den Feu-
     eropfern des Herrn zusteht".
15   וַאֲכַלְתֶּם אֹתָהּ בְּמָקוֹם קָדֹשׁ כִּי חָקְךָ וְחָק־בָּנֶיךָ הִוא מֵאִשֵּׁי יְהוָה כִּי־כֵן צֻוֵּיתִי (Lev
     10,13)

gen wird die Frage gestellt, ob es Konnotationen zwischen den von Sira erwähnten חֵלֶק und אִשֶּׁה gibt, die damals bekannt gewesen sind und für die an-
stehende Untersuchung von Bedeutung sind.

חֵלֶק und אִשֶּׁה

In Dtn 18,1 wird ein Zusammenhang zwischen אִשֶּׁה und חֵלֶק hergestellt:
"Die levitischen Priester – der ganze Stamm Levi – sollen nicht wie das
übrige Israel Landanteil und Erbbesitz (חֵלֶק וְנַחֲלָה) erhalten. Sie sollen sich
von den Opferanteilen JHWHs (אִשֵּׁי יְהוָה), d.h. von seinem Erbbesitz
(וְנַחֲלָתוֹ[16]), ernähren. Der Stamm Levi soll inmitten seiner Brüder leben, aber
keinen Erbbesitz (נַחֲלָה) haben. JHWH selbst ist sein Erbbesitz (נַחֲלָתוֹ), wie
er es ihm zugesagt hat. Und das ist das Recht (מִשְׁפָּט), das die Priester
gegenüber dem Volk haben ..." (Dtn 18,1–3). Der Autor weist darauf hin,
dass חֵלֶק wie auch נַחֲלָה im Sinne von Grund- und Bodenanteil den Priestern
nicht zusteht. Im gleichen Atemzug werden ihnen aber אִשֵּׁי יְהוָה als ein entsprechender Anteil zugewiesen. Wie oben in Lev 10,13 trifft man auf eine
Aufzählung von Opfern, die offensichtlich als אִשֶּׁה anzusehen und von denen
ausdrücklich Stücke dem Priester zu geben sind[17]. Es ist darauf acht zu geben, dass bei der Benennung der erlaubten Gabe nur נַחֲלָה aus dem ersten
Wortpaar aufgenommen wird. נַחֲלָה bezeichnet die den Priestern zustehende
Gabe als Geschenk bzw. Erbteil.

Die alleinige Verwendung von נַחֲלָה wird darin ihren Grund haben, dass
die Abhängigkeit von JHWH unmissverständlich klar zum Ausdruck kommt:
Erbe setzt in sich einen Vererbenden voraus und impliziert, dass man den
Vererber nicht zwingen kann, das Erbe nach den Vorstellungen des Erb-
nehmers zu verteilen.

חלק als Ausgangspunkt

Sira fordert aber: "Gib deren (der Priester) Anteil" (ותן חלקם)! Wer die Bücher von Exodus bis Josua im Ohr hat, verbindet mit absolut gesetztem חֵלֶק
im Zusammenhang mit JHWH und Priester die Information, dass die Priester
keinen Anteil am Land, das Gott vergibt, zugewiesen bekommen. An dessen
Stelle erhalten sie Stücke von bestimmten Opfern. Das ist ein Anrecht bzw.

---

16   Es handelt sich um ein hervorhebendes bzw. explikatives וְ.

17   Um sich eine Vorstellung davon zu machen, welche Teile es konkret waren, die ein
Priester erhalten hat, sei die Auflistung aus Dtn 18,3–4 vorgestellt: vom Schlachtopfer
(זֶבַח) stehen ihnen eine vordere Hälfte (זְרוֹעַ), die Halsstücke (לְחָיַיִם), der Labmagen
(קֵבָה), weiters Teile von Korn (דָּגָן), Wein (תִּירוֹשׁ), Öl (יִצְהָר) und der Schafschur (גֵּז)
zu.

eine (einfache) Vorschrift (מִשְׁפָּט in Dtn 18,3; חֹק in Lev 10,13f) oder eine "für immer gültige Vorschrift" (חָק־עוֹלָם in Ex 29,28; Lev 6,11; 7,34; 10,15; 24,9; Num 18,8.11.19). Der Grund liegt darin, dass "JHWH selbst der Anteil" ist, den die Priester (z.B. Aaron und seine Söhne) zugewiesen erhalten.

Genau auf der gleichen Argumentationsebene sieht man Sira im Kontext Aarons, nämlich in 45,22:

πλὴν ἐν γῇ λαοῦ οὐ κληρο-νομήσει	ܠܐ ܢܩܘܡ ܒܐܪܥܐ ܕܥܡܐ ܘܠܐ	אַ[...] לֹא יִנְחַל 22a
καὶ μερὶς οὐκ ἔστιν αὐτῷ ἐν λαῷ	ܘܠܐ ܐܝܬ ܠܗ ܡܢܬܐ ܒܥܡܐ	וּבְתוֹכְכֶם לֹא יַחֲלֹק 22b נחלה
αὐτὸς γὰρ μερίς σου καὶ κλη-ρονομία	ܡܛܠ ܕܗܘ ܚܘܠܩܟ ܘܝܪܬܘܬܟ ܡܢ ܓܘ ܒܢܝ̈ܐ	אַשִׁי[...]ל[..] 22c[18]
		19ל[...] 22d[19]

Die in Γ und Syr textlich gut erhaltene, durch H^B weitgehend unterstützte Passage hält fest, dass der Priester keinen Landanteil erhalten hat, weil JHWH der den Priestern zustehende Anteil ist. Gott seinerseits versorgt die Priester in Form von Opfern. Unwahrscheinlich erscheint, dass Sira in H das Substantiv und damit den geprägten Fachterminus חֵלֶק gebraucht hatte. Das Verb חלק (ܦܠܓ; vgl. auch als einschlägiges Übersetzungswort in Sir 16,16b; 44,2a.23e) scheint gesichert.

Zwischenergebnis

חֵלֶק ist im Pentateuch terminus technicus[20] für den den Israeliten zugewiesenen "(Land-)Anteil"[21]. Natürlich hat Ben Sira dieses Faktum gekannt; vgl. 45,22. Mit dem Stichwort חֵלֶק verbindet man traditionell Anteil an Grund und Boden für nichtpriesterliche Israeliten[22]. Trotzdem fordert Sira das Ge-

---

18   Vgl. aber den Vorschlag von ספר z.St.: [יי].

19   Vgl. ספר z.St.:ישראל ....

20   Das gilt auch, wenn das Wort mit "Erbe" (נַחֲלָה) einen Doppelausdruck bildet; vgl. die Parallele in Num 18,20; Dtn 10,9; 12,12; 14,27.29; 18,1.

21   Vgl. die als selbstverständlich hingestellte Ansicht von Reicke, Erbe, 423: "Die Leviten haben keinen *ḥelæq* 'Anteil' an Palästina, d.h. Anrecht auf Bodenbesitz (Num 18,20; Deut 10,9; 12,12; 14,27.29; 18,1; Jos 14,4; Jos 18,7); Gott ist ihr Anteil (Num 18,20, *ḥælqeka wenaḥalateḳā*, zu Aaron gesagt; sonst allerdings nur *naḥalāh*; z.B. Ez 44,28). Das enthält zunächst als realen Inhalt die Aussage, dass die Priester das Recht auf gewisse 'Anteile' an Opfern haben (Lev 6,10; vgl. Deut 18,8). Dahinter steht aber die ideale Vorstellung, dass Gott der Frommen 'Teil', d.i. ganz persönlicher Besitz, ist, wie sie in dem Namen [*ḥilqîjāh(û)*] 'JHWH-ist-mein-Teil' zum Ausdruck kommt"; vgl. auch Tsevat, חָלַק, 1017–18.

22   Da Gleiche gilt für den Beitrag von Schmid, חלק, 577–78.

genteil des Tradierten: den Priestern ist ein חֵלֶק zu geben! Da חֵלֶק (wie das Wortpaar חֵלֶק וְנַחֲלָה) in der Bedeutung von Anteil an Grund und Boden fest geprägt ist, fragt es sich, wie man dann Sira in seiner Zeit wirklich richtig verstehen konnte, wenn er fordert, dass den Priestern ihr חֵלֶק zu geben ist? Ist dies ein krasser Widerspruch innerhalb des sirazidischen Werkes? Will er mehrdeutig sprechen? Oder ändert er die ihm vorgegebene Tradition, indem er חֵלֶק anstelle von allein stehender נַחֲלָה sagt (letztere könnte das Priestererbe als Opfergabenanteil meinen), wobei er aber immer annehmen muss, dass seine Zuhörer auch die Veränderung der Wortbedeutung mit vollziehen, da sie ihn ansonsten missverstehen müssten?

חלק bei Ezechiel und תרומת קדש

Ben Sira verwendet die beiden Worte חֵלֶק und תְּרוּמָה in nahem Kontext: 7,31b bzw. 7,31c.d. Damit zeigt er an, dass die damit bezeichneten Gegebenheiten nach seinem Verständnis einander nahe stehen. Diese Parallelisierung ist im Pentateuch nicht in der gleichen Art gegeben. Jedoch trifft sich Sira terminologisch mit Ezechiel. Es ist zu erwarten, dass die Beantwortung der oben gestellten Fragen durch Einbeziehung Ezechiels, der in der Sekundärliteratur in dieser Frage kaum eine Rolle spielt, möglich ist. Auffällig ist, dass חֵלֶק und תְּרוּמָה nur in Ez 45,7; 48,8.21, parallel verwendet werden. Die Constructusverbindung תְּרוּמַת הַקֹּדֶשׁ (vgl. Sir 7,31d: d.h. im Unterschied zu Sira mit einem determinierenden ה) begegnet ausgenommen Ex 36,6 nur bei Ezechiel (Ez 45,6.7 [2mal]; 48,10.18 [2mal].20.21 [2mal]). Diese Beobachtung ist zwar markant, aber nicht exklusiv, denn die beiden Substantiva bilden darüber hinaus noch zweimal eine Constructusverbindung, in der das nomen rectum immer im Plural und auch mit einem determinierenden ה verknüpft erscheint: כֹּל תְּרוּמֹת הַקֳּדָשִׁים (Lev 22,12) und בִּתְרוּמַת הַקֳּדָשִׁים (Num 18,19). In Ez 47,13–48,23 steht die Anordnung, dass das Land (אֶת־הָאָרֶץ) unter die zwölf Stämme (לִשְׁנֵי עָשָׂר שִׁבְטֵי יִשְׂרָאֵל) als Erbschaft zu vergeben ist ("ihr weist unter euch ... als Erbe zu"; תִּתְנַחֲלוּ). Hierbei bekommt Josef einen doppelten Landstrich (חֶבֶל). In Ez 45,1–8 werden nur sieben Stämme namentlich genannt, wobei eigenartiger Weise eine Bezeichnung des Landanteiles vermieden wird. Der Autor behilft sich damit, dass jeder angeführte Stamm[23] je "ein Eintel" (אֶחָד) zugewiesen bekommt.

---

23 In Ez 48,1–7 werden Dan, Ascher, Naftali, Manasse, Efraim, Ruben und Juda angeführt.

חֵלֶק in Ez 48[24]

"Neben dem Gebiet Judas liegt von Osten nach Westen das Land, das ihr (dem Herrn) als Abgabe (תְּרוּמָה) entrichten sollt, 25000 Ellen breit und genauso lang wie die anderen Anteile (חֲלָקִים) von Osten nach Westen. In der Mitte dieses Stückes liegt das Heiligtum. Das Land, das ihr dem Herrn als Abgabe entrichtet, hat eine Länge .... Die heilige Abgabe soll, wie folgt, eingeteilt werden: Den Priestern soll ein Stück gehören (תְּרוּמַת־הַקֹּדֶשׁ לַכֹּהֲנִים) ... Das Heiligtum des Herrn (מִקְדַּשׁ־יְהוָה) soll in der Mitte liegen" (Ez 48,8–10).

In Ez 48,8[25] wird also ein Landstrich, angrenzend (עַל גְּבוּל) an den Stamm Juda (יְהוּדָה), erwähnt, der zuerst als eine Abgabe (תְּרוּמָה) bezeichnet und gleich anschließend mit den Anteilen (חֲלָקִים) der übrigen Stämme gleichgesetzt wird. Jetzt erscheinen also die Fachausdrücke תְּרוּמָה und חֵלֶק! – "Mitten in" (בְּתוֹכוֹ) diesem Bereich hat "der Tempel" (הַמִּקְדָּשׁ) "zu sein" (vgl. den bekräftigenden Assertiv וְהָיָה). Ez 48,9 bestätigt nochmals, dass dieses Gebiet "Gabe" (תְּרוּמָה) "für JHWH" (לַיהוָה) ist. Die angegebenen Teile des heiligen Landes werden im weiteren ausdrücklich "für die Priester" (לַכֹּהֲנִים; Ez 48,10) bestimmt und zwar als "heilige Gabe" (תְּרוּמַת־הַקֹּדֶשׁ; so auch in Ez 48,20.21), was wohl nichts anderes besagt, als dass ausschließlich Priester als Besitzer in Frage kommen[26].

Begründung des Landanteiles für Priester

In Ez 48,11 wird weiters festgehalten, dass (nur) die "zadokitischen (מִבְּנֵי צָדוֹק) Priester" (לַכֹּהֲנִים) als "geweiht" (הַמְּקֻדָּשׁ) anzusehen[27] und deshalb für den Dienst an JHWH geeignet wie auch zuständig sind, weil sie "nicht"! (לֹא) wie die Israeliten und die Leviten abgeirrt waren.

Mit dem bekräftigenden Assertiv וְהָיְתָה ([die Gabe] "wird sein") bestärkt der Schreiber, dass deswegen "für diese" (לָהֶם; nämlich die Priester) die "JHWH-Gabe" (תְּרוּמִיָּה[28]) vorgesehen ist. Im Kontext (vgl. oben Ez

---

24 Vgl. neuerdings Konkel, Architektonik, 13–224; vgl. Rudnik, Heilig, passim.
25 Der Text ist wahrscheinlich älter als das ebenso einschlägige Kap. 45.
26 Die Formulierung kann das Missverständnis aufkommen lassen, die Priester könnten *autonom* über dieses Gebiet verfügen. In diesem Sinne ist die Anweisung nicht gedacht! Daher wird die Feststellung aus V. 8 nahezu identisch wiederholt: "Mitten in" (בְּתוֹכוֹ) diesem Bereich hat "der Tempel (הַמִּקְדָּשׁ) JHWHs (יְהוָה) zu sein (וְהָיָה)"; vgl. den bekräftigenden Assertiv.
27 D.h. in diesem Zusammenhang: aus dem profanierten Bereich anderer Menschen herausgenommen.
28 Hier wird ein hapax legomenon תְּרוּמִיָּה verwendet. Es fällt auf, dass י mitten im Wort unmotiviert verdoppelt ist. Das ist zu erklären, wenn man das Schluß-ה bei תְּרוּמָה

45,8) ergibt sich, dass es sich um eine Landgabe (תְּרוּמַת הָאָרֶץ) handelt. In deren Mitte befindet sich das speziell für JHWH vorgesehene Land für den Tempel (Ez 45,21 מִקְדַּשׁ הַבַּיִת בְּתוֹכֹה). Es ist wegen der JHWH-Widmung "Allerheiligstes" (קֹדֶשׁ קָדָשִׁים = ist Näherbestimmung der JHWH-Gabe und vorerst nicht des Priesterlandes) und ausschließlich von den Priestern zu nutzen.

Dass dieses Gebiet zu den ehemals einflussreichen Leviten in Beziehung steht, zeigt sich daran, dass – nahezu beiläufig – erwähnt wird, dass daneben das Gebiet der Leviten liegt. Es ist interessant, dass auch für deren Gebiet (V. 14) die gleiche bedeutungsvolle Folge gilt: Wie beim Land der Priester können diese keineswegs so darüber verfügen wie die Israeliten über das ihnen zustehende Land: die Leviten dürfen es auch "nicht verkaufen" (לֹא יָמֵר) bzw. "nicht weitergeben" (לֹא יַעֲבוּר). Es gehört zum "Sonderland" (רֵאשִׁית הָאָרֶץ) und es handelt sich um für "JHWH Heiliges" (כִּי־קֹדֶשׁ לַיהוָה), allerdings nicht "Allerheiligstes". So wird also der Unterschied bzw. die Neuordnung begründet, die darin besteht, dass die zadokitischen Priester die führende Rolle übernehmen.

In diesem Kontext ist תְּרוּמַת־הַקֹּדֶשׁ eine pointiert Formulierung, die das spezifisch für den Priester vorgesehene Stück Land, ausgezeichnet durch den Tempel darinnen, bezeichnet. Dieser Landesteil ist zugleich hochheilig (קֹדֶשׁ קָדָשִׁים), was vom allgemeineren קֹדֶשׁ לַיהוָה zu unterscheiden ist.

Was ist תְּרוּמַת הַקֹּדֶשׁ?

Nach Ex 36,6 ist es die Sammelbezeichnung für jene Gaben, die die Israeliten nach der Aufforderung durch Mose für die Errichtung und Ausstattung des Heiligtums spendeten, wie z.B. Stoffe, Gold, Silber usw. Damit sind keine Opfergaben im kultischen Sinne gemeint. Es sind Gaben, die dem Heiligtum zur Verfügung gestellt werden. Eine Widmung für Priester tritt am Rande in den Blickpunkt.

---

analog z.B. den lamed-he-Verben behandelt sieht. So kommt es zum Zusammenfallen des ה und י zu einem verdoppelten Buchstaben (י). Wo kommen aber י und ה her? Ich vermute eine spezielle, durch den Inhalt veranlaßte Wortbildung, die auf unübertreffbare Weise die sachliche Verbindung der תְּרוּמָה ("Abgabe") und יָה (die Kurzform für JHWH) in ein Wort gießt: תְּרוּמְיָה. Die Elberfelderbibel hat das Problem gespürt und sensibel übertragen: "Sonderweihgabe". Die vermutete Bedeutung "Steuer" (Gesenius, Wörterbuch, 889) ist gegen den Duktus des Kontextes gerichtet (es geht um ein Land, nicht um Steuern). Die von Fohrer, Wörterbuch, 305, angegebene Bedeutung "Abgabe" erklärt den Unterschied zu תְּרוּמָה nicht. Ebenso wenig kommt die im Kontext vorgenommene Konzentration auf JHWH und seinen heiligen Bereich zum Ausdruck.

תְּרוּמַת הַקֹּדֶשׁ in Ez 45,6–7[29]

In Ez 45,1 ist תְּרוּמָה לַיהוָה ein Landstrich, der bei der durch Losentscheid durchgeführten Landverteilung für JHWH reserviert bleibt: "Wenn ihr das Land im Erbteil (בְּנַחֲלָה) verlost, sollt ihr eine Abgabe für den Herrn (תְּרוּמָה לַיהוָה) ... absondern. Es soll gegenüber seiner ganzen Umgebung heilig sein (קֹדֶשׁ־הוּא)". Weiter heißt es: "Von diesem abgemessenen Stück (וּמִן־הַמִּדָּה הַזֹּאת; = Land) sollt ihr wiederum ein Stück ... abmessen, es ist Hochheiliges (קֹדֶשׁ קָדָשִׁים). Das als heilig (קֹדֶשׁ) ausgewiesene Stück des Landes (מִן־הָאָרֶץ) ist für die Priester (לַכֹּהֲנִים), die den Dienst im Heiligtum verrichten (מְשָׁרְתֵי הַמִּקְדָּשׁ) und sich dem Herrn nähern dürfen, um Dienst zu tun (לְשָׁרֵת). Es ist der Platz für ihre Häuser und die Weidefläche für ihre Herden[30]. Ein Stück ... ist für die Leviten, die den Tempeldienst verrichten. Es ist ihr Eigentum (לַאֲחֻזָּה)[31]; dort bauen sie ihre Städte und wohnen darin. Und der Stadt sollt ihr als Eigentum einen Raum von fünftausend Ellen Breite und fünfundzwanzigtausend Ellen Länge zuweisen, entlang der Abgabe für das Heiligtum (תְּרוּמַת הַקֹּדֶשׁ). Das soll dem ganzen Hause Israel gehören" (Ez 45,3–5).

Im Rahmen der Sammlung von Zwischenergebnissen ist einmal festzuhalten, das das eben beschriebene Land im Besitz der Priester ist. Als Priester werden – anders als in Ez 48 – *nicht* die Nachkommen Zadoks auf besondere Weise hervorgehoben. Der Landteil wird mit dem aus Ez 48 bekannten Fachausdruck תְּרוּמַת הַקֹּדֶשׁ bezeichnet. Dieser Landteil wurde in Ez 48,12 als Allerheiligstes (קֹדֶשׁ קָדָשִׁים) in dem Sinne verstanden, dass er nur den Priestern zukommt. – In Ez 45,3 wird die Näherbestimmung קֹדֶשׁ קָדָשִׁים für den Tempel (הַמִּקְדָּשׁ; vgl. V. 4) reserviert.

---

29 Der Abschnitt Ez 45,1–8 bietet eine vor allem das Kultpersonal berücksichtigende Weiterentwicklung von Ez 47,13–48,22. Es zeigt sich, dass es eine einschlägige Traditionsbildung gibt. Es ist unklar, wann dieser Vorgang sein Ende erreichte. – Warum sollte ausgeschlossen sein, dass auch Sira in diese Entwicklung eingebunden war?

30 Der H-Text וּמִקְדָּשׁ לַמִּקְדָּשׁ ist vielleicht nach dem Vorschlag von Zimmerli, Ezechiel, 1141f, auf וּמִגְרָשׁ לְמִקְנֶה zu emendieren.

31 In dieser Terminologie treffen sich die Ezechielstelle mit Lev 25,32–34 und Num 35,2–5, wo in betonter Weise die Leviten erwähnt werden. Die Belege sprechen dafür, dass es Probleme um Besitz und Einfluss innerhalb der verschiedenen Gruppierungen (Leviten, Aaroniten, Zadokiten), welche für sich das Priestertum in Anspruch nahmen, gab. Bezeichnenderweise geht es um den Besitzanspruch (אֲחֻזָּה Lev 25,32.33.34; Num 35,2 bzw. קִנְיָן Jos 14,4), nicht um das "Erbe" (נַחֲלָה Jos 14,3) oder den "Anteil" (חֵלֶק Jos 14,4), welche den Leviten ausdrücklich abgesprochen werden (Jos 14,3f). Offensichtlich versuchte man das Problem des Priesterbesitzes auch an anderen Stellen zu lösen. – Sira scheint auf der Seite der Zadokiten zu stehen.

Für die vorliegende Untersuchung ist bedeutsam, dass es beim für Priester nutzbaren Land um ein Thema geht, das so wichtig ist, dass sich verschiedene Entwicklungsstadien erhalten haben. Die Notizen im Buch Ezechiel zeigen eine vom Pentateuch abweichende Einstellung zum Bodenbesitz der (zadokitischen) Priester. Es ist nicht anzunehmen, dass sich einschlägige Diskussionen beruhigt haben und dann verschwanden. Die gleiche Fragestellung in Ben Sira weist darauf hin, dass sie großes Gewicht beibehielten.

Zusammenfassung

Alle Ausdrücke, die Sira verwendet, können im protokanonischen AT belegt werden. Wer aber die protokanonische alttestamentliche Tradition kennt, der stellt verblüfft fest, dass der Weisheitslehrer mehr oder weniger durchwegs in Spannung mit der Hauptlinie jener Tradition steht.

Dies beginnt mit dem Aufruf zur "Gottesachtung" (herkömmlich "Gottesfurcht") in 7,29a. Bei einem Autor, für den die Gottesachtung die wichtigste Haltung Gott gegenüber darstellt, ist es sehr einleuchtend, dass er ein geprägtes und markantes Vokabular dafür besitzt; vgl. oben (2.4.2.). Umso stärker erregt der Umstand Aufmerksamkeit, dass er in terminologisch äußerst auffälliger Form davon abweicht. Er wählt das Verb פחד. Wer innerhalb des Sira-Buches פחד untersucht, stellt fest, dass es sich um ein scharfes Wort handelt und es vor allem um Fürchten, um richtige Angst geht, der man tunlich entkommen möchte: das Schlechte *fürchten* (Sir 4,20); *Angst* vor dem Tod (Sir 9,13; 4); *Angst* vor Schande (Sir 42,12). An keiner anderen innersirazidischen Stelle kommt das Vokabel in die Nähe der von Sira häufig erwähnten *Achtung vor Gott*. Durch Siras Formulierung wird der Hörer paukenschlagartig aus der alltäglichen Sprachverwendung gerissen und darauf hingewiesen, dass etwas kommt, das ohne weitere Anfrage zu akzeptieren ist.

Fortgesetzt wird diese Reihe Aufsehen erregender Argumentationen mit der auf den Zuhörer gerichteten Aufforderung, den *Priester zu heiligen*. Sira verfremdet wieder. Er kennt die traditionelle Formulierung, dass man für den priesterlichen Dienst *ausgesondert*, d.h. *geheiligt* werden muss. Diesen Akt kann doch nie und nimmer ein gewöhnlicher Israelit vornehmen, sondern nur JHWH oder speziell von ihm dafür Beauftragte.

Sira trägt nun seinen Hörern auf, die Priester zu heiligen. Man kann nicht umhin, *heiligen* im Sinne von *ehren* zu verstehen, womit sich die geradezu dramatische Wortwahl weit vom gefüllten Wortsinn entfernt. Es entsteht der Eindruck, dass Sira für einen einfachen Akt der Anerkennung eine überzogene Formulierung gebraucht. – Was will er damit erreichen?

Die Vermutung legt sich nahe, dass Sira versucht, die Position der Priester zu sichern. Sein Anliegen ist jedoch nicht das Priesterliche am Priester, sondern etwas, was sich aus dem Kontext des Gedichtes ergibt, nämlich die politische Bedeutung des Priesters[32]; vgl. oben die Struktur des Gedichtes.

Einen weiteren Beleg für Sira als Grenzgänger in der überkommenen Tradition stellt die Aufforderung dar, dem Priester sei sein Anteil zu geben. Sira wählt dafür Fachausdrücke, die zum Repertoire der *Landanteile der Stämme Israels* gehören. Die gegen die Tradition stehende Behauptung, dass dies sogar in einem ausdrücklichen Befehl Gottes so geregelt sei, will das durchsetzen, was ohne die Autorität Gottes nicht akzeptiert würde.

Ich sehe hier einen für damalige Hörer gut verständlichen Hinweis auf die faktischen Realitäten. Die von Sira gemeinten Priester hatten offensichtlich Landbesitz. Die Zeiten hatten sich gewandelt. Sira begründet und argumentiert unter Bezugnahme auf eher unscheinbare Passagen in Ezechiel so, dass die neue Lage der Offenbarung entspricht. Auch schon zur Zeit Ezechiels[33] war es so, dass Priester – im Gegensatz zur Überlieferung im Pentateuch – eben doch Landanteile besaßen.

Man kann die Gruppe der Priester, welcher Sira nahe stand, genauer präzisieren. Es ist die Linie der zadokitischen Priester. Schon die ezechielischen Passagen beschäftigen sich mit dem zadokitischen Priestertum. Dazu passt dann auch, dass in Sir 51 just Zadok Anlass zum Lobpreis wird und das noch in prominenter Position. Es werden in diesem Gedicht neben den an zweiter Stelle erwähnten Abraham und Isaak, für die Gott als Schützer auftrat, nur Gott, David und Zadok, denen er eine Position verlieh, erwähnt:

"Danket dem Schöpfer des Alls,	denn seine Huld währt ewig.
Danket dem Erlöser Israels,	denn seine Huld währt ewig.
Danket dem, der Israels Versprengte sammelt,	denn seine Huld währt ewig.
Danket dem Erbauer seiner Stadt und seines Heiligtums,	denn seine Huld währt ewig.
Danket dem, der dem Haus David Macht verlieh,	denn seine Huld währt ewig.
Danket dem, der *Zadoks Söhne zu Priestern erwählt* hat,	denn seine Huld währt ewig.
Danket dem Schild Abrahams,	denn seine Huld währt ewig.
Danket dem Fels Isaaks,	denn seine Huld währt ewig".

Auf diesem Hintergrund erhebt sich die Frage, ob gerade Priester aus der zadokitischen Tradition Landeigentümer waren? Aber warum berührt Sira gerade der Landbesitz der Zadokiten? Ist er selbst Mitglied einer solchen Familie? Das würde sein besonderes Interesse an manchen die Priester betreffenden Fragen und das Verständnis dafür, welche gesellschaftliche Aufgaben den

---

32 Es ist Stadelmann, Ben Sira, 63f, Wright, Fear, 193, zuzustimmen, dass Ben Sira die Position der Priester hochhält und diese sogar noch stärken will. Die genannten Autoren haben aber die Motivation, die Sira zu seinem Engagement treibt, nicht weiter zu erheben versucht. Als Begründung überzeugen die Hinweise auf den Kult nicht.

33 Man würde heute differenzieren, dass auch Autoren am Werk waren, die zu seinem Anhängerkreis gehörten. Wieweit diese Stellen vor Sira entstanden sind, ist damit nicht beantwortet.

Priestern in den turbulenten Zeiten zukommen könnten, gut verständlich machen[34].

Zur Zeit Siras war bekannt, welche Opfer bzw. welche Opferteile traditionell dem Priester zustehen. Von diesen lebt er und seine Familie. Es ist auffällig, dass Sira Opfer nennt, die traditionell nicht zu dieser Kategorie zählen.

Bis jetzt ist es nicht gelungen zu klären, was *das Brot* (vielleicht im Sinne von Lebensunterhalt) *der Starken* wirklich ist. Unabhängig davon qualifiziert die Bezeichnung *Brot der Starken* nicht die Opferart, sondern die Menschen, welche Empfänger sind. Dabei bleiben mehrere Deutungsebenen offen: geht es um Personen, die an sich schon stark sind und deren Kraft zu erhalten ist, oder solche, die erstarken sollen? In der Krisenzeit um Ben Sira wird man darin eine Feststellung mit politischen Implikationen sehen. Priester haben eine die Gesellschaft stabilisierende Rolle[35]. Diese ist zu bewahren.

In diesen Kontext des verschleiert Konkreten passt auch die *Handgabe*. Was damit bei diesen dürftigen Angaben präzise gemeint ist, erscheint schwer oder gar nicht definierbar. Eines ist gewiss: die Hand ist kein Abstraktum, keine Willenskundgebung oder Absicht, sondern etwas *Handgreifliches*. Es mag sich die Erfahrung dahinter verbergen, dass man sich um die konkreten Gaben zu drücken begann und im gleichen Atemzug darauf hinwies, dass man der Einstellung nach ja ohnedies auf Seiten des in der Tradition Überlieferten stünde. Sira will offensichtlich konkrete Gaben.

In diesem Zusammenhang sollte man auch über die dem Gesetz entsprechenden Fleischopfer nachdenken. Was hat ein Priester davon, wenn die Fleischopfer tatsächlich dem Gesetz entsprechen? – Natürlich sind es dann Gaben, die tatsächlich korrekte (צדק) Opfer darzustellen. Aber im sirazidischen Kontext geht es ja nicht um die Opfer an sich, sondern darum, dass diese der Priester erhält. צדק ist demnach nicht nur die Qualifikation der Opfer, sondern bedeutet zugleich den Auftrag, die Opfer entsprechend der gerechten Ordnung (= צדק) dem Priester zukommen zu lassen. Es scheint wiederum ein Zeitproblem angesprochen zu sein. Man kann vermuten, dass ein Hinweis gegeben wird, dass die Opfer entweder ausgeblieben sind oder dass schlechte Ware als Opfer gebracht wurde[36].

---

34 Vgl. die Qualifizierung der zadokitischen Priester als Allerheiligstes in Qumran (1QS 5,6; 8,5f.8f.11; 9,5b–6; 11,8); vgl. darüber hinaus Baumgarten, Scrifice, 152.154; Gärtner, Temple, u.a. 18; Klinzing, Umdeutung, 50–93; Stadelmann, Ben Sira, 106f; Hayward, Sacrifice, passim; ders., Dead Sea Scrolls, passim.

35 Interessanterweise rechnet Calduch-Benages, Fear, 92, die Priester nicht zu den Autoritäten des Volkes; vgl. ebenso Minissale, Ben Siras Selbstverständnis, 108–14.

36 Unter diesem Gesichtspunkt scheint es sehr unwahrscheinlich, dass Sira "die unauflöslichen Vorrechte der Priesterschaft" (Kieweler, Ben Sira, 55) wahren will. Es geht doch um deren Existenzsicherung. Und dafür hat Sira inzwischen eine Alternativlösung gefunden.

Zu guter Letzt kann ein Priester tatsächlich vom קדש תרומת leben, wenn es sich um ein Landstück handelt. Der Priester wird unabhängig und ist nicht mehr auf die allem Anschein nach nicht mehr regelmäßig und auch nicht in bester Qualität dargebrachten Opfergaben angewiesen. Es handelt sich jedoch um eine Gegebenheit, die weit von der andernorts dezidierten Feststellung, was die Lebensbasis der Priester ist, abweicht.

Aber was gibt diese Passage für die Opfer und JHWH ab? – De facto nichts. Hier sind die Opfer unter dem Gesichtspunkt behandelt, dass sie die Erhaltung der Priester gewährleisten. Es ist weder gesagt, dass sie von Gott gewollt oder angenommen werden, es wird auch nicht gesagt, zu welchem religiösen Zweck sie dargebracht werden. Bei Gott spielen sie nach diesem Beispiel eigentlich keine Rolle, wie auch Gott – so hart dies klingen mag – für die Opfer eigentlich auch keine Relevanz hat[37].

Die Perspektivenverschiebung wird durch Sir 7,10 nochmals unterstrichen. Dort wird ausdrücklich betont, dass es keineswegs um die Menge der Opfer geht. Worum geht es denn dann? Ist dies eine Aufforderung, wenig opfern? – Nein, es wird wohl etwas ganz anderes erwartet. Gefordert wird Gebet (7,10a). Diese Form der persönlichen Begegnung mit Gott überbietet offensichtlich die Opfer, die dem Empfinden nach in der Durchführung auch ihren Sinn haben. (Ein Opfer kann ich auch darbringen, wenn ich gar nichts von Gott halte!). – Neben dem Gebet steht die Wohltat, die Liebestat, die Tat am Nächsten. Mit diesem Gedanken endet der Abschnitt (7,10b).

Deutet sich da eine Perspektivenverschiebung an: Opfer (u.a. zur Erhaltung der gesellschaftlichen Strukturen) ja, aber die Guttat am Nächsten ist wichtiger?

Für seine damaligen Hörer wohl unmissverständlich zeigt die Wortwahl in verschlüsselt-aufdeckender Weise, wie Sira die Position der Priester sieht.

3. Die griechische Übersetzung (Γ)

8a.b	μὴ καταδεσμεύσῃς δὶς ἁμαρτίαν	ἐν γὰρ τῇ μιᾷ οὐκ ἀθῷος ἔσῃ
9a.b	μὴ εἴπῃς Τῷ πλήθει τῶν δώρων μου ἐπόψεται	καὶ ἐν τῷ προσενέγκαι με θεῷ ὑψίστῳ προσδέξεται
10a.b	μὴ ὀλιγοψυχήσῃς ἐν τῇ προσευχῇ σου	καὶ ἐλεημοσύνην ποιῆσαι μὴ παρίδῃς

---

37 Zurecht ist schon festhalten worden, dass der Kult selbst in Siras Denken *keine* besondere Rolle spielt; vgl. Marböck, Weisheit, 87: "Die positive Empfehlung der Abgaben für die Priester in 7,29–31 wird nicht als kultische, sondern als soziale Pflicht betont im Zusammenhang des Verhaltens gegen verschiedene Menschengruppen"; auf 127 sind dies "religiöse Pflichten"; vgl. in diesem Sinne auch Perdue, Wisdom, 251, FN 225 u.ö; Haspecker, Gottesfurcht, 304.

29a.b	ἐν ὅλῃ ψυχῇ σου εὐλαβοῦ τὸν κύριον	καὶ τοὺς ἱερεῖς αὐτοῦ θαύμαζε
30a.b	ἐν ὅλῃ δυνάμει ἀγάπησον τὸν ποιήσαντά σε	καὶ τοὺς λειτουργοὺς αὐτοῦ μὴ ἐγκαταλίπῃς
31a.b	φοβοῦ τὸν κύριον καὶ δόξασον ἱερέα	καὶ δὸς τὴν μερίδα αὐτῷ καθὼς ἐντέταλταί σοι
31c.d	ἀπαρχὴν καὶ περὶ πλημμελείας καὶ δόσιν βραχιόνων	καὶ θυσίαν ἁγιασμοῦ καὶ ἀπαρχὴν ἁγίων

3.1 Der Befund

Der heute vorliegende griechische Text des Sirabuches, der allein schon durch die außergewöhnliche Wortwahl[38], aber auch durch seine poetische Straffheit auf seine Qualität aufmerksam macht, geht im Bereich der Kultterminologie in 7,9.10.14.29.31a.b.dβ mit der Übersetzung der übrigen LXX parallel.

Daher stechen besonders jene Beispiele in die Augen, wo dies nicht der Fall ist und legen eine genauere Untersuchung nahe.

3.2 Die positionsgleichen Worte אבֵים לֶחֶם und ἀπαρχή in 7,31c

Das Verhältnis von ἀπαρχή zu לֶחֶם.

Mit ἀπαρχή nimmt Γ ein im Kult traditionelles Wort auf. Allerdings wird ἀπαρχή nie als Übersetzungsvokabel von לֶחֶם, auch nicht, wenn לֶחֶם als terminus technicus der Opfersprache dient, gebraucht. In der LXX wird ἀπαρχή zur Übersetzung von רֵאשִׁית (Erstlingsopfergabe[39]) verwendet, weiters für תְּרוּמָה als Pflichtbeitrag[40] und vor allem – mit unterschiedlichen Bezügen – für (allgemeine) Opfergabe[41]. Dass ἀπαρχή das bevorzugte Vokabel für תְּרוּמָה ist und die Übersetzer bei Zusammentreffen von רֵאשִׁית und תְּרוּמָה das gleiche Wort noch einmal verwenden, zeigt Ez 20,40: אֶת־תְּרוּמֹתֵיכֶם וְאֶת־רֵאשִׁית – τὰς ἀπαρχὰς ὑμῶν καὶ τὰς ἀπαρχάς. Erwähnenswert ist, dass im Kontext von תְּרוּמָה ausdrücklich festgehalten wird, dass sie *für den Pries-*

---

38 Vgl. Ziegler, Wortschatz, 450–63 bzw. 274–87; Reiterer, Urtext, 242–49 und die umfassende und sehr sorgfältig gearbeitete Untersuchung von Wagner, Septuaginta-Hapaxlegomena, passim.

39 So in Ex 23,19; Lev 2,12; 23,10; Num 15,20f; 18,12; Dtn 18,4; 26,2.10; 1Sam 2,29; 2Chr 31,5; Neh 10,38; Ez 44,30; vgl. Tob 1,6; Jdt 11,13.

40 So in Ex 25,2.3.5; 36,6; 38,24.

41 Lev 22,12; Num 5,9; 18,8.11.29; 31,29; Dtn 12,6.11.17; 2Chr 31,10.12.14; Esra 8,25; Neh 10,40; 12,44; 13,5; Ez 45,1.6f.13; 48,8ff.12.18.20f; Mal 3,8.

ter – wie bei Sira לחם – bestimmt ist (Num 5,9; Neh 13,5); und dies ist eine immerwährende (וּלְבָנֶיךָ לְחָק־עוֹלָם; Num 18,8) Vorschrift.

Als Schlussfolgerung ist daraus zu ziehen: Der Übersetzer hatte entweder eine andere Vorlage oder er wusste mit der ihm vorliegenden, nämlich לחם אבי׳ם, nichts anzufangen. Da Syr den Text von H^A bestätigt und keine schlüssigen Hinweise auf eine andere H-Vorlage gegeben sind, wird man annehmen, Γ versucht mit dem ihm dunklen Wort zurecht zu kommen. – Der Übersetzer entschied sich für eine gebräuchliche, aufgrund der Allgemeinheit banale Formulierung aus der Kultsprache. Die Wahl scheint ihm deswegen leicht gefallen sein, weil er zugleich hervorheben kann, dass es sich bei ἀπαρχή um ein Opfer handelt, bei welchem dem Priester ein Anteil zusteht.

3.3 καὶ περὶ πλημμελείας in 7,31c

Grammatisch wird περὶ πλημμελείας vom Verb δός (7,31b), das einen Akkusativ erwarten lässt, gelenkt und steht auf der gleichen Ebene wie die vorangehenden und nachfolgenden Akkusativ-Objekte ἀπαρχήν und δόσιν.

πλημμελεία als Übersetzungswort
Es fällt auf, dass bei der Übersetzung z.B. im Buch Leviticus und Numeri nicht die gleiche Wortwahl vorliegt. In Lev – anders als in Num – wird πλημμελ* zur Wiedergabe von אָשָׁם bevorzugt. Innerhalb der LXX spricht diese Beobachtung dafür, dass verschiedene Übersetzer am Werk waren.

Im Rahmen der kultischen Vorkommen wird das Substantiv אָשָׁם in der LXX mehrfach verbal und nicht mit einem Substantiv übertragen; u.a. Lev 5,6.15.25. Es ist auffällig, dass in Leviticus Formulierungen gewählt werden, die τῆς πλημμελείας verwenden, auch wenn man den Genetiv nicht erwarten würde. Man findet schwerfällige Formulierungen, die so gestaltet werden, dass τῆς πλημμελείας vorkommen kann:

Der Nominalsatz הוּא כַּחַטָּאת וְכָאָשָׁם lässt sich zugegebenerweise nicht leicht ins Griechische übertragen. In Lev 6,10 steht: ὥσπερ τὸ τῆς ἁμαρτίας καὶ ὥσπερ τὸ τῆς πλημμελείας. Der Wille, τῆς πλημμελείας unverändert zu lassen, führt zu ungewöhnlichen Konstruktionen. Als Objekt zum Verb φέρω, das gewöhnlich ein Akkusativ- oder ein Dativobjekt regiert, steht in Lev 5,15.25 τῆς πλημμελείας ("er bringt das Schuldopfer": οἴσει τῆς πλημμελείας). Ein weiteres Beispiel für die in der LXX greifbare Vorstellung, dass τῆς πλημμελείας als festliegende und nicht veränderbare Größe anzusehen ist, liegt in Lev 14,12 vor, wo der Übersetzer προσάγω zwar mit doppeltem direktem Objekt (gewöhnlich mit doppeltem Akkusativ) konstruiert, bei dem das erste Objekt αὐτόν (= τὸν ἀμνόν, "den Widder") ist, das zweite τῆς πλημμελείας (*"als Schuldopfer"*).

Aus den Beobachtungen ergibt sich, dass (einige) Übersetzer in τῆς πλημμελείας eine feststehende Größe sehen. Τῆς πλημμελείας gilt als unveränderbarer Fachausdruck. Der Übersetzer von Γ, der ein hervorragendes und zum Teil ausgefallenes Griechisch verwendet, kannte natürlich den normalen Nominativ πλημμελεία. Daher musste er in 7,31c über den grammatischen Genetiv, der für einen Akkusativ steht, stolpern. Er versucht die Härte durch die Verwendung der – an sich unnötigen – Präposition περί zu entschärfen: durch *"in Bezug auf"* drängt er den Leser dazu, selbst etwas zu ergänzen und lenkt dadurch von der Sperrigkeit ab.

3.4 δόσιν βραχιόνων in 7,31c

Die Formulierung δόσιν βραχιόνων lässt vermuten, dass in der hebr. Vorlage eine *Constructusverbindung* stand, die etwas mit einer Gabe und mit Händen zu tun hat. Oben wurde auf תְּרוּמַת יֶדְכֶם verwiesen. Allerdings steht in der Übersetzung der protokanonischen Belegstellen τὰς ἀπαρχὰς ὑμῶν (Dtn 12,6) bzw. τὰς ἀπαρχὰς τῶν χειρῶν ὑμῶν (Dtn 12,11.17). Von hier kann der Sira-Übersetzer nicht beeinflusst sein. Er geht einen durchaus eigenständigen Weg.

Δόσις zählt nicht zu den Fachausdrücken des Opferkultes und wird nur von Sira (vgl. 7,31; 32/35,12/9) in diesem Sinne verwendet.

Im Rahmen von Opfern steht βραχίων vornehmlich als Wiedergabe von שׁוֹק ("Schenkel", durchwegs in einer Constructusverbindung), einmal זְרוֹעַ (in keiner Constructusverbindung)[42].

Als Ergebnis lässt sich registrieren, dass δόσιν βραχιόνων zwar innersirazidischem Sprachgebrauch folgt, nicht jedoch dem geprägten Übersetzungsusus der LXX. Wenn man eine Vorlage sucht, wird man ein Beispiel in Erwägung ziehen, wo שׁוֹק in einer Constructusverbindung als nomen rectum aufscheint. Das ist aber in keinem der Belege der Fall: immer ist שׁוֹק nomen regens[43]. – Da nach dem erhaltenen H-Text zu schließen die Vorlage des Übersetzers der üblichen Ausdrucksweise entsprach, sind die Abweichungen auf den Übersetzer zurückzuführen. Dieser ist mit seiner Vorlage frei umgegangen.

---

42 Zum Beleg sei auf folgende Stellen verwiesen: in Ex 29,22; Lev 7,32f; 8,25f; 9,21; Num 18,18 שׁוֹק הַיָּמִין – τὸν βραχίονα τὸν δεξιόν (die rechte Schenkelkeule); in Ex 29,27; Lev 7,34; 10,14f; Num 6,20 שׁוֹק הַתְּרוּמָה – τὸν βραχίονα τοῦ ἀφαιρέματος (die Keule des Erhebungs- / Darbringungsritus); in Num 6,19 זְרוֹעַ – τὸν βραχίονα (Vorderschenkel?).

43 Vgl. Ex 29,22.27; Lev 7,32.33.34; 8,25.26; 9,21; 10,14.15; Num 6,20; 18,18; Ps 147,10; Jes 47,2.

3.5 θυσίαν ἁγιασμοῦ in 7,31d

Die Überprüfung der Vorlagen für θυσία in der LXX führt zu folgendem Ergebnis:

θυσία dient 146mal zur Wiedergabe von מִנְחָה. Rechnet man dann noch
die Constructusverbindungen hinzu, in denen מִנְחָה vorkommt (מִנְחַת קְנָאֹת
[2mal]; מִנְחַת זִכָּרוֹן [3mal]; מִנְחַת בִּכּוּרִים [2mal]; מִנְחַת הַתָּמִיד [1mal];
bzw. die Präpositionsverbindung מִנְחָה בִּצְדָקָה [1mal]), ergibt sich eine
155malige Verwendung.

Als Übersetzungwort für זֶבַח steht θυσία 78mal; hervorzuheben unter
den Vorkommen in einer Constructusverbindung ist vor allem זֶבַח שְׁלָמִים,
wo 46mal θυσία begegnet; weiters sind זִבְחֵי־צֶדֶק (3mal); זֶבַח תּוֹדָה (7mal);
זֶבַח מִשְׁפָּחָה (1mal); זִבְחֵי תְרוּעָה (1mal) zu nennen; dadurch ergibt sich eine
Gesamtzahl von 136maligem Vorkommen. 8mal steht θυσία für אִשֶּׁה; 6mal
für עֹלָה und 1mal für בָּשָׂר (בְּשַׂר הַמִּלֻּאִים). θυσία wird demnach nicht wirklich markant und spezifisch verwendet und dient als gebräuchliches Übersetzungsvokabel für unterschiedliche Vorlagen, wozu auch זֶבַח gehört.

In H[A] steht nun צדק זבחי; da die Ergänzung zu זבחי gesichert erscheint, entsprechen sich wie in der traditionellen Übersetzung זבחי (allerdings steht der Pl.[44]) und θυσία.

Ein weiteres Problem liegt im Genetiv-Objekt ἁγιασμοῦ. Man liest in
1Sam 16,5 davon – übrigens auch recht singulär –, dass man sich zu heiligen
habe, wenn man ein Opfer darbringen will. Diese Heiligung ist aber in sich
keine Opferart. Es ist auch keine Qualifizierung eines Opfers. Die Aussage,
dass es ein Opfer zur Heiligung (ἁγιασμοῦ würde wohl ein Derivat von קדש
voraussetzen) gibt, ist im protokanonischen AT nicht belegbar.

Was ist belegbar? – Bei den zahlreichen Vorkommen von ἁγίασμα
(66mal) in der LXX handelt es sich um die Beschreibung einer "objektiven"
Vorgabe. Mit ἁγίασμα wird die Begegnung mit jener Sphäre qualifiziert, wo
Gott sehr dicht erfahrbar ist. Gemeint sind der Bereich des Heiligen (קֹדֶשׁ)
oder das Heiligtum (מִקְדָּשׁ). Für die individuelle Heiligung wird ἁγίασμα nie
verwendet.

---

44 In der LXX entspricht dem *Plural constructus* זִבְחֵי an 28 Stellen auch eine *plurale*
Übersetzung im Griechischen (vgl. Ex 29,28; Lev 7,32.34; 10,14; 17,5.7; Num 10,10;
25,2; Dtn 12,6.11.27; 32,38; Jos 22,27; 1Sam 10,8; 2Chr 30,22; Jes 1,11; 43,23.24;
56,7; Jer 6,20; 7,21; Am 4,4.7; Hos 4,19; 9,4; Ps 49,8; 50,19; 105,28; Spr 17,1).
Immerhin 9mal bietet die griechische Version anstelle eines *Plurals* den *Singular* (vgl.
Dtn 33,19; Jos 22,23; 2Chr 33,16; Hos 8,13; Ps 4,6; 27,6; 51,21; 107,22; Spr 7,14);
dazu zählen just alle Belege für זִבְחֵי־צֶדֶק – θυσίαν δικαιοσύνης (Dtn 33,19; Ps 4,6;
51,21).

Offensichtlich ändert sich die Vorstellung in späterer Zeit, was sich schon in der Wortwahl andeutet, da statt ἁγίασμα nun ἁγιασμός verwendet wird: Gott selbst ist der Heilige (ἅγιος) und er kann die Heiligung (2Makk 14,36) gewährleisten, was das Gegenteil von Befleckung bedeutet. Die Heiligung (ἁγιασμός) ist eine von Gott geschenkte Qualifikation, die ganz Israel auszeichnet (2Makk 2,17).

3.6 Zusammenfassung

Es fällt auf, dass man auf zwei gegensätzliche Gegebenheiten trifft:
Die vermutliche H-Vorlage und die Übersetzung bewegen sich in 7,9.10.14.29.31a.b.dβ zum Teil ganz und gar im Bereich des Üblichen: so bei *Opfergaben, opfern, (Opfer) annehmen, Gebet, kultischer Diener und Priester*. Das scheint ein Beleg dafür zu sein, dass die erhaltene H-Vorlage an den untersuchten Stellen doch relativ sicher die gleiche ist, die den (griechischen und syrischen) Übersetzungen vorgelegen war. Unter diesem Gesichtspunkt bezeugt Γ den H-Text. Keineswegs beantwortet diese Beobachtung die Frage danach, warum dies nur bei den einfachen, keineswegs markanten Worten und Vorstellungen zutrifft.

Es gibt Hinweise, dass der Übersetzer – zumindest partiell – die geprägte Terminologie der LXX gekannt hat, allerdings scheint er sich entweder nicht konsequent an diese gehalten zu haben, oder er besaß nur Teilkenntnisse. Wenn es richtig ist, dass er teilweise vom Hörensagen Bekanntes und nicht mehr selbst Erlebtes weitergibt, ist es verwunderlich, dass er bei den speziellen Fachausdrücken markant abweicht. Diese müsste er ja in der konservierten Form unverändert verwenden.

Wenn man annimmt, dass der Priester von den Gaben, die ihm zugesprochen sind, leben musste, kann man sich schwer vorstellen, wie dies auf der Basis des in der Γ-Übersetzung Gesagten praktisch ausgeführt worden sein sollte. Man nehme δόσις βραχιόνων als Beispiel. Wenn damit ein spezieller Anteil an einem Opfer bezeichnet wird, wie ist es dann möglich, dass diese Bezeichnung nie in der LXX vorkommt? Wenn der Priester von dem, was ihm in der Tradition zugesichert wird, tatsächlich leben musste, dann muss man diese Teile ja auch korrekt benennen können!

Diese Beobachtung vermittelt den Eindruck, dass der Übersetzer von Γ mit verschiedenen Fachausdrücken nichts (mehr) anfangen konnte. Das weist darauf hin, dass er in seinem Alltag nicht mehr mit dem Kult im klassischen Sinne konfrontiert wurde. Dort, wo der Übersetzer lebte, gab es den klassischen Kult nicht mehr, weswegen die Terminologie auch nicht wirklich korrekt gewärtig ist. Da der Übersetzer die Vorlage nicht verstand, hielt er unaustauschbare Gegebenheiten für nicht besonders wesentlich. Daher hatte er auch keine Scheu, das, was er andeutungsweise verstand, so zu formulieren, dass ihm seine Zeitgenossen auf die je eigene Art folgen konnten.

Es geht dem Übersetzer ins Griechische also um die Zuhörer oder Leser. Aber auch die Zuhörer beschäftigte anderes als die klassischen Opfer. Wahrscheinlich wurden diese übertragen verstanden: es handelt sich z.B. um kein *heiliges Opfer*, sondern ein *Opfer zur individuellen Verbesserung*, eben zur (in einem neuen Sinne) *persönlichen Heiligung* (θυσία ἁγιασμοῦ)[45]. Opfer sind also ein Beitrag zur Erhaltung der Priester und für die individuelle Heiligung da und nicht für Gott. Es liegen gravierende geistig-theologische Veränderungen vor.

4. Die syrische Übersetzung (Syr)

7,8b.a	ܠܐ ܬܬܢܐ ܠܡܚܛܐ ܚܛܗܐ	ܡܛܠ ܕܒܚܕܐ ܠܐ ܐܚܝܬ
7,9b.a	ܠܐ ܬܐܡܪ ܕܢܣܒ ܒܣܘܓܐܐ ܕܩܘܪܒܢܝ	ܕܡܩܪܒ ܐܢܐ ܠܡܪܘܡܐ ܡܩܒܠ
7,10b.a	ܠܐ ܬܬܚܡܣ ܒܨܠܘܬܟ	ܬܬܚܦܛ ܠܡܥܒܕ ܦܘܩܕܢܐ
7,29b.a	ܒܟܠܗ ܠܒܟ ܕܚܠ ܡܢ ܐܠܗܐ	ܘܠܟܗܢܘܗܝ ܝܩܪ
7,30b.a	ܒܟܠܗ ܠܒܟ ܝܩܪ ܒܪܝܟ	ܘܡܫܡܫܢܘܗܝ ܠܐ ܬܫܒܘܩ
7,31b.a	ܥܒܝܕܘܗܝ ܠܗ ܘܝܩܪ ܐܦ ܠܟܗܢܘܗܝ	ܘܗܒ ܠܗܘܢ ܙܕܩܝܗܘܢ ܐܝܟ ܡܐ ܕܐܬܦܩܕܬ
7,31c	ܠܚܡܐ ܕܩܘܪܒܢܐ ܘܪܫܝܬܐ ܕܐܕܪܐ	

Es ist schon festgehalten worden, dass die syrische Version jenen Sprachgebrauch belegt, wie er auch an typischen Vergleichsstellen in der Übersetzung der Peschiṭta gegeben ist; vgl. den Befund oben (2.4.1). Hier werden demnach nur einige der in den vorausgegangenen Untersuchungsschritten ausführlicher behandelten Passagen befragt.

4.1 ܘܗܒ ܠܗܘܢ ܙܕܩܝܗܘܢ ܐܝܟ ܡܐ ܕܐܬܦܩܕܬ in 7,31b

Syr interpretiert "und gib ihnen (den Priestern) deren Rechtmäßiges, wie dir befohlen worden ist" (ותן חלקם) vom Kolonende her: כאשר צוותה. Dem Priester steht etwas zu, worauf er rechtlichen Anspruch hat. Dies zu geben, ist befohlen worden. Aus der syrischen Wortwahl ergibt sich nicht, dass das zu Gebende mit dem Kult in Verbindung steht.

45 Sauer, Jesus Sirach, 93, notiert richtig, dass Stellen wie diese zur Stärkung der innerjüdischen Tradition gegen einen gefährlichen Hellenismus beitragen sollten. Allerdings kann ich der Argumentation Sauers bei folgender Beurteilung der griechischen Tradition nicht folgen: "Es ist anzunehmen, daß die in Alexandrien wohnenden Juden von Zeit zu Zeit auch den Tempel in Jerusalem aufsuchten, um dort Opfer darzubringen und die Nähe Gottes zu erleben. Dazu möchte Ben Sira ermuntern". – Wie ist bei solchen Gepflogenheiten soviel – in Γ belegbare – Unkenntnis denkbar?

4.2 Die positionsgleichen Worte zu לחם אבי־ים

Ließ schon der Versuch, den hebräischen Wortsinn von לחם אבי־ים zu erheben, Fragen offen, so zeigt die Übersetzung einerseits, dass sie wahrscheinlich die gleiche Vorlage hatte, und andererseits, dass auch der Übersetzer mit dieser Wortverbindung nichts Rechtes anzufangen wusste. In Ps 78,24 wird לֶחֶם אַבִּירִים mittels ܠܚܡܐ ܕܡܠܐܟܐ wiedergegeben. Damit wird jene Phrase gewählt, mit der sowohl nach Lev 3,11.16 als auch Num 28,24 לֶחֶם אִשֶּׁה übertragen wird, nämlich ܠܚܡܐ ܩܘܪܒܢܐ bzw. ܩܘܪܒܢܐ ܕܠܚܡܐ. Sicher erscheint, dass das Wort "Brot" vorgegeben war und dass Syr kultische Implikationen sieht.

4.3 ܩܘܪܒܢܐ ܕܐܝܕܝܟ in 7,31c

Es wurde schon gesagt, dass תְּרוּמַת יָד in Dtn 12,6.11.17 belegt ist. Auf den ersten Blick befremdet daher, dass die gleiche Phrase im Deuteronomium (ܩܘܪܒܢܐ ܕܐܝܕܝܟܘܢ) nicht auf dieselbe Weise wie in Ben Sira übersetzt wird (ܩܘܪܒܢܐ ܕܐܝܕܝܟ): Syr unterstützt nur, dass das in H[A] nicht erhaltene Wort tatsächlich יָד ist. Die Überprüfung der Übersetzung von תְּרוּמָה in der Peschitta ergibt jedoch, das die Wortwahl ohne erkennbares System zwischen ܩܘܪܒܢܐ und ܦܪܫܬܐ wechselt, sodass man nicht behaupten kann, Syr sei ein von H abweichender Text vorgelegen.

Dem syrischen Übersetzer ist die kultische Welt fremd geworden. Er hat generell keine große Nähe zur alttestamentlichen Welt des Kultes, was sich auch in der Übersetzung im protokanonischen Teil zeigt. – Was ergibt sich daraus? Die Überlieferung ist an solchen Passagen eher zufällig und beiläufig als gezielt formuliert. Dies läßt vermuten, dass es auch kein Interesse an einer tendenziösen Veränderung der Opferbeschreibungen gibt. Wenn dies richtig ist, dann erscheinen diese Passagen sehr zeugnisfähig für das damalige Kultverständnis.

5. Opfer in Sir 31/34,21/18a–32/35,22/20a

Im angegebenen Abschnitt ist der hebräische Text erst ab 32/35,11/8 erhalten. Die Kernaussagen über bestimmte Opferarten befinden sich indes im nicht hebräisch erhaltenen Teil.

5.1 Die Abgrenzung und Struktur des Abschnittes

Die Beschreibung der untergliedernden Strophen kann von folgenden Beobachtungen ausgehen:

Es gibt thematische Parallelführungen, da die Argumentation in Sir 31/34,21ff/18f; 32/35,1/1a–5 und 32/35,14f/11f je bei den Opfern den Ausgang nimmt und dann zum Verhalten gegenüber dem Nächsten wechselt.

Die Einheiten beschäftigen sich inhaltlich mit unterschiedlichen Aspekten der Gewichtung, Bedeutsamkeit und Schwerpunktsetzung der Opfer.

Die Strophen 31/34,21–23 und 32/35,1/1a–5 stehen sich darin nahe, dass konkrete Opferarten angeführt werden.

Die Kleinen Einheiten 31/34,21–31 und 32/35,14/11–21/18a treffen sich bei folgenden Themen:

Opfer	31/34,21ff/18f; 32/35,14/11–15/12
Soziale Gesichtspunkte	31/34,24/20–30/25 [darin Vv. 28/23–30/25 bildliche Erläuterung]; 32/35,16/13–19/15b
Summe	31/34,31/26; 32/35,21c/18a–22/20a

Die mittlere Strophe 32/35,1/1a–13/10 besitzt in sich eine weitere Strukturierung. Nach dem Hinweis auf Opfer (32/35,1–5/3) folgt eine Behandlung der Einstellung des Opfernden in 32/35,6ff/4f und dann eine erste Summe in 32/35,9/6 bzw. wieder ein Gedanke zur Haltung des Opfernden in 32/35,10/7–12/9 mit einer weiteren Summe in 32/35,13/10.

Diese Beobachtungen führen nun zu folgendem Ergebnis:

31/34,21/18a–31/26			32/35,1–13/10			32/35,14/11–21/18a
21–23	Opfer von unrechtem Gut	1–5	Opfer – Gesetz – soziales Verhalten	14–15	keine aus sich wirkenden Opfer
24–27	größeres Vergehen: Falsches Sozialverhalten	6–8	Ia: Einstellung des Opfernden	16–21b	Klage von Waise und Witwe
28–30					Klage aller Bedrängten
		9	Ib: *Summe*: Rechtschaffenheit führt zu annehmbaren Opfern		
		10–12	IIa: Großzügigkeit und Freudigkeit		
31	*Summe*: Keine Erhörung	13	IIb: *Summe*: Gott erstattet vielfach	21c.22	*Summe*: Gott erhört sie, nicht die Opfer

5.2 Inhaltliche Globalbeschreibung

Der Inhalt von Sir 31/34,21/18–31/26
Eingangs (31/34,21ff/18f) wird nachdrücklich betont, dass Gott kein Gefallen an Opfern findet, die von unrechtem Gut stammen.

Mit geradezu dramatischen Vergleichen wird beschrieben (31/34,24/20–26/22.28/23–30/25), dass soziale und mitmenschliche Vergehen um vieles schlechter sind[46].

Als allgemein gültigen Grundsatz hält Sira daraufhin fest, dass es in solchen Fällen keine Erhörung gibt, wollte man auch noch so versuchen, sich Gott durch Fasten und Gebet wohlgefällig zu stimmen.

Der Inhalt von Sir 32/35,1/1a–13/10

In 32/35,1/1a–5/3 werden verschiedene Opferarten, Gesetzeserfüllung und soziales Verhalten untereinander verglichen und durch den Hinweis auf Gottes Wohlgefallen daran, dass man sich vom Bösen abwendet, eine erste Zwischensumme angedeutet.

Die Akzeptanz von Opfern wird in Vv. 6/4–8/5 nicht der Korrektheit der Opfergaben, sondern mit der Rechtschaffenheit des Opfernden begründet. Die darauf folgende Summe (V. 9/6) notiert, dass Gott Opfer von rechtschaffenen Menschen annimmt.

Die Einstellung des Opfernden, der großzügig und frohgemut seine Gaben zu bringen hat, ist ein weiterer wichtiger Aspekt (Vv. 10/7–12/9). Es geht wiederum nicht um die Beschaffenheit der Opfertiere, sondern um die Beschaffenheit des Menschen, der diese Opfer darbringt. Als Summe wird dann festgehalten, dass man in diesem Fall Vielfaches von Gott erhalten wird.

Der Inhalt von 32/35,14/11–22/20a

Die dritte Strophe setzt Opfer mit Gott als Richter und sozialem Verhalten in Beziehung.

Wiederum (Vv. 14/11–15/12) werden die Opfer nicht unter dem Gesichtspunkt der Durchführung oder der Beschaffenheit der Opfertiere usw. gesehen, damit sie Wirkungen haben. Hier wird als Argument angeführt: Wenn das alltägliche Verhalten des Opfernden zum Mitmenschen außer Acht gelassen wird, erst recht, wenn dieses falsch ist, stimmen die Opfer Gott nicht gnädig,. In V 15/11b.12 nimmt der Autor das Thema, Gott als Richter auf. Weil er Richter ist, kümmert er sich um falsches Sozialverhalten. Vom göttlichen Richter wird aber nicht nur das Verhalten an sich bewertet, sondern vor allem die darin sich zeigende Einstellung des Opferwilligen. Daher ist die Intention, in der die Opfer dargebracht werden, eine Frage, die sich vor Gott als dem Richter zu bewähren hat.

Es finden sich Kriterien (Vv. 16/13–20/16), die eine Grundlage für Gottes Entscheidung bilden: Weil er ein Gott des Rechts ist (wo sind jetzt die Opfer?), lässt er sich nicht bestechen, er ist nicht parteiisch, hört aber auf den Bedrängten.

---

46 Vgl. Vattioni, Il sacrificio, 157–60.

Die abschließende Summe (Vv. 21/17–22/20a) hält fest, dass klagende Bitten erhört werden. Sie haben die Wirkung, dass Gott derart Erhörung gewährt, wie man sie sonst aufgrund von Opfern findet.

Nicht zu übersehen sind vor allem in der ersten und der dritten Strophe die mehrfachen Anspielungen auf Grobheiten, Ungerechtigkeiten und massive Benachteilung von Schwächeren durch Stärkere. Darin sind Hinweise auf die konkreten Erscheinungen zur Zeit Siras zu sehen, in der sich offensichtlich Benachteiligungen zu häufen beginnen.

Da diese üblen Zustände so eng mit den traditionellen religiösen Aktionen in Verbindung gebracht werden, kann man nicht davon ausgehen, dass die Seleukiden die direkten Verursacher sind, denn diese haben gewiss kein Opfer dargebracht.

Die Benachteiligungen gehen offensichtlich von judäischen Landsleuten direkt aus. Sira nennt diese nicht beim Namen, sondern umschreibt sie mit deren Verhalten, sagt allerdings ganz deutlich, wie die Perspektiven sind: Gott wird diesem Missbrauch einen Riegel vorschieben.

5.3 Das Thema Opfer in 32/35,1–5/3[47]

Zufolge der poetischen Analyse ergibt sich, dass die behandelte Passage nicht nur in drei Kleine Einheiten zu gliedern ist, sondern dass 32/35,1–5/3 zuerst eine formal, dann aber auch eine inhaltlich herausgehobene Position in der Mitte des Gedichtes besitzt. Die Relationen Opfer – Gesetz – soziales Verhalten werden in grundsätzlicher Art behandelt. Daher konzentrieren wir uns auf diese Strophe, die zugleich auch den Interpretationsschlüssel bietet.

1 ὁ συντηρῶν νόμον πλεονάζει προσφοράς
2 θυσιάζων σωτηρίου ὁ προσέχων ἐντολαῖς
3 ἀνταποδιδοὺς χάριν προσφέρων σεμίδαλιν
4 καὶ ὁ ποιῶν ἐλεημοσύνην θυσιάζων αἰνέσεως
5 εὐδοκία κυρίου ἀποστῆναι ἀπὸ πονηρίας
καὶ ἐξιλασμὸς ἀποστῆναι ἀπὸ ἀδικίας.

Sir 32/35,1/1a–2/1b
In 32/35,1/1a–2/1b liegt ein synonymer Parallelismus vor, der chiastisch aufgebaut ist. Es entsprechen sich also die Außen- und die Innenglieder. Die Außenglieder werden mit der Thematik Gesetz (ὁ συντηρῶν νόμον; ὁ προσέχων ἐντολαῖς), die Innenglieder mit der Thematik Opfer (πλεονάζει προσφοράς; θυσιάζων σωτηρίου) gebildet.

Es wird nicht angegeben und es wird nicht gesagt, aus welchem Anlass die Opfer dargebracht werden und wie die Opfertiere beschaffen sind. Es wird nur festgehalten, und zwar in terminologischer Übereinstimmung mit

---

47   Vgl. Haspecker, Gottesfurcht, 189f; Winter, Ben Sira, 121ff; Stadelmann, Ben Sira, 68–138 (für ihn umfasst die Einheit die Vv. 1–7); Krammer, Auswirkungen, 68–74.

der LXX-Wortwahl, dass das Ziel eigentlich nicht in den Opfern selbst besteht, sondern in den Rahmengliedern. D.h. dass jener, der νόμος (Offenbarung / Religion) einhält und danach lebt bzw. die Einzelvorschriften beachtet (V. 1aα und V. 2bβ), derjenige ist, der in Wirklichkeit die Opfer vermehrt oder eine Heilsgabe (σωτήριον) darbringt.

Für einen Griechen klingt in σωτήριον (terminus technicus der Übersetzung für שְׁלָמִים) auch σωτηρία (vgl. im Hebräischen die Nähe von שְׁלָמִים zu שָׁלוֹם) mit. Das bedeutet in diesem Kontext, dass das Leben nach der Religion und die Einhaltung der Gesetze ein Weg ist, um zum *Heil* zu kommen. Es geht im Kern um Soteriologie.

Sir 32/35,3f/2
Wiederum liegt ein synonymer Parallelismus vor, bei dem sich die Glieder A und B entsprechen:

3 A ἀνταποδιδοὺς χάριν   ⇔   4 A' καὶ ὁ ποιῶν ἐλεημοσύνην
   B προσφέρων σεμίδαλιν   B' θυσιάζων αἰνέσεως

Es werden folgende Ebenen einander gegenübergestellt:

Liebespraxis (χάρις)   *Opferdarbringung* (σεμίδαλις[48]).
aktive Wohltat[49] (ἐλεημοσύνη)   *Darbringung eines Dankopfers.*

Den Opfern werden Liebestaten (χάρις; wahrscheinlich im Sinne der Einstellung) einerseits, und andererseits Wohltaten (ἐλεημοσύνη[50]) vorangestellt. Jene, welche Wohltaten am Nächsten vollbringen, sind es, die Opfer darbringen. Die Liebestaten sind die eigentlichen Opfer. Die Wohltaten haben die Opfer abgelöst und ersetzen sie. Daher kann der Autor auch verschiedene Opfer nennen, an deren Stelle jetzt das Wohlverhalten zum Nächsten tritt. Sira zählt klassische Opferarten auf. Interessanterweise sind keine Opfer dabei, bei denen der Blutritus im Vordergrund steht.

Ein Blick auf Sir 3,14 zeigt, dass eine gute Tat, die allerdings in der Praxis eine große Belastung darstellen kann (z.B. die Fürsorge für beschwerlich gewordene Eltern), wahrhaft jene Wirkungen hervorbringt, welche man den Opfern zugeschrieben hatte: "Wohlverhalten gegen den Vater[51] (צְדָקַת אָב, ἐλεημοσύνη γὰρ πατρός; ܪܚ ܐ ܘ) wird nicht ausgelöscht werden, sondern als ein Sündopfer (וּתְמוּר חַטָּאת; ἀντὶ ἁμαρτιῶν; ܐ ܘ) wird es eingepflanzt bleiben".

---

48   Öfters Übersetzung von סֹלֶת, eigentlich *Grieß, Feinmehl*; es handelt sich um ein Speiseopfer.
49   Öfters Übersetzung von תּוֹדָה; vgl. aber auch תְּהִלָּה.
50   Ob man dazu Almosen sagen darf, erscheint unwahrscheinlich. Es geht um vieles mehr.
51   Vgl. zur grammatischen Bestimmung Bohlen, Ehrung, 58.

Sir 32/35,5/3

Im dritten Schritt, der oben als ein vorbereitendes Summarium bezeichnet wurde, werden nun Opfer nicht erwähnt. Es kommt aber ein ansonsten im Kontext der Opfer zentrales theologisches Thema zur Sprache: Wie kommt man in den Zustand des Wohlgefallens bei Gott? Das bewirkten einst die Opfer.

Sira hebt als einen Merksatz hervor, dass der Mensch dann Wohlgefallen erlangt, wenn er sich von den Schlechtigkeiten distanziert (ἀφίστημι). Die Abwendung vom Bösen bedeutet tatsächlich echte Sühne. Auf diese Weise wird das jetzt erreicht, wozu ursprünglich Opfer da waren.

Als Summe dieses Abschnittes ergeben sich folgende Aspekte, die sich als eine Steigerung darstellen: ausgehend von der Gesetzeserfüllung führt die Argumentation zur Wohltat / Liebestat und dann zum Wohlgefallen bei Gott. Wenn man die Verbindung von Heil (σωτήριον in V. 2/1b) mit Sühne (ἐξιλασμός; V. 5b/3b) ernst nimmt, zeigt sich eine Bewegung, die im Kern die wichtigsten Elemente des Heilswirkens anspricht. Heil bedeutet: Sündenvergebung. Sündenvergebung geschieht in diesem Kontext durch die Wohltat am Nächsten und diese Tat am Nächsten gipfelt in der – wie man heute sagen könnte – Nächstenliebe. Diese Art des Denkens ist nun der Schlüssel zum Verständnis, wie Sira zu den Opfern steht.

Sira registriert die Opfer, er kennt die klassische Opferterminologie. Er wertet sie nicht ab. Er legt aber auch kein besonderes Gewicht auf diese. Die Opfer verlieren an Bedeutung. Die nun entstandene Leerstelle wird durch die wohlwollende Zuwendung zum Mitmenschen neu gefüllt[52]. Von da aus ist es auch verständlich, dass Sira die Qualifikation, Beschaffenheit und Einstellung des Opfernden in das Zentrum stellt[53].

Wenn man von hier ausgeht und zurückfragt, wie Sira zu diesem Ergebnis kommt bzw. wie er allgemein zu den Opfern steht, kann man 31/34,21ff/18f anführen. Dort wird festgehalten, dass die Opfer, wenn sie dargebracht werden, an sich in Ordnung sein müssen. Die Annahme durch Gott erfolgt aufgrund der persönlichen Qualifikation des Opfernden. Ein schlechter Mensch, der außerhalb des JHWH-Religion steht, kann keine Opfer darbringen, die von Gott angenommen würden. Das Opfer an sich führt

---

52   "Der, der unter Beachtung des Gesetzes Opfer darbringt, handelt recht. Hier wird ganz deutlich zum Ausdruck gebracht, daß Ben Sira nicht die Opferpraxis an sich kritisiert, sondern die Art und Weise der Darbringung" (Sauer, Jesus Sirach, 244f) hebt zuwenig hervor, dass die Qualifikation des Opfernden die neue Norm für die Annehmbarkeit der Opfer darstellt.

53   Auf dieser Linie ist auch die Weiterentwicklung zu sehen im Aristeasbrief, in Qumran und bei Philo (z.B. die Hochschätzung der Essener, weil "sie sich als höchste Verehrer Gottes erwiesen haben, nicht indem sie Tiere als Opfer schlachten, sondern indem sie sich vornehmen, ihre Sinne heilig zu halten" (ἐπειδὴ κἂν τοῖς μάλιστα θεραπευταὶ Θεοῦ γεγόνασιν, οὐ ζῷα καταθύοντες, ἀλλ᾽ ἱεροπρεπεῖς τὰς ἑαυτῶν διανοίας κατασκευάζειν ἀξιοῦντες); Cohn, Quod, Nr. 75; S. 21f).

nicht nur Vergebung! Wenn einer als Sünder oder schlechter Mensch einzustufen ist, kann er auch noch so viele Opfer darbringen, so werden diese doch keine positive Wirkung bei Gott haben. Es gibt kein *opus ex operato*. Vorauszusetzen ist vielmehr die Integrität dessen, der ein Opfer darbringt.

5.4 Zusammenfassung

Anders als in den klassischen Opfertexten, wo es z.B. darum geht, dass die Opfer regelmäßig zu bestimmten Tageszeiten dargebracht werden oder dass die Opfertiere korrekt sind, spielen diese Gesichtspunkte keine entscheidende Rolle.

Die Thematik "Korrektheit und Entsprechung mit Regeln" wird aufgenommen, aber nicht zur Beschreibung der Opfertiere, sondern des Opfernden. Diese haben korrekt, anständig und redlich zu sein. Gott will Anstand und Wohltaten, nicht (kultische) Opfer.

6. Sündenvergebung

Mehrfach ist schon die wichtige Frage nach der Sündenvergebung[54] angeklungen. Es ist jetzt Zeit, Siras Stellungnahme zu diesem Thema darzustellen.

6.1 Aarons Opfertätigkeit führte zur Entsühnung der Israeliten

Man braucht nicht einmal einen Beleg zu erbringen, so selbstverständlich ist es, dass die Opfer der Priester[55] unter anderem die Sündenvergebung bewirken konnten. Das liest man auch bei Sira: "Mose hat ihn (Aaron) in sein Amt eingesetzt und ihn mit heiligem Öl gesalbt. So wurde ihm ein ewiger Bund gewährt und auch seinen Nachkommen, solange der Himmel steht: den Dienst zu tun, für Gott Priester zu sein und sein Volk in seinem Namen zu segnen. Er hat ihn erwählt aus allen Lebenden, damit er Brandopfer und Fettstücke darbringe, den beruhigenden Duft des Gedenkopfers aufsteigen lasse und für die Israeliten Sühne erwirke (ולכפר על בני ישראל). Er gab

54 Vgl. zum Thema Marböck, Sündenvergebung, passim.
55 Vgl. in diesem Kontext Till, Fragmente, 216; Vawter, Messianism, 83–99; Roberts, Proverbs, 2–17; Snaith, Ben Sira's, 172f; Beentjes, Jesus Sirach; Olyan, Ben Sira's, 261–86; Stone, Figures, 259–70; Petraglio, Il libro, 115–27; Ruß, Brand- und Sühneopfer, 125; Hayward, Jewish Temple, 63–71.

ihm seine Gebote und Vollmacht über Gesetz und Recht. So unterwies Aaron
sein Volk im Gesetz und die Israeliten im Recht" (Sir 45,15–17).

Aaron wurde also von Mose eingesetzt. Er brachte Opfer dar. Diese
tilgten die Sünden (Sir 45,16: ולכפר על בני ישראל) und befreiten die
Israeliten von ihren Lasten vor Gott. Allerdings, so deutet Sira an, war schon
von allem Anfang an ein anderer Akzent besonders bedeutungsvoll.

Sira will aber auch darlegen, dass es sich um keine wirkliche Neuerung
handelt, sondern dass es zu Beginn des aaronitischen Priestertums so war.
Aaron herrschte über die Gesetze: וימשילהו בחוק ומשפט (Sir 45,17). Es gehört vom Anfang an zu den wesentlichen Aufgaben der Priester, nicht nur die
Opfer darzubringen, sondern das Volk in den Vorschriften zu unterweisen
(וילמד את עמו חק).

Die Priester gehören zum Leitungspersonal und bilden sich selbst ihr
Urteil. Diese Befähigung wird besonders zu Siras Zeiten wichtig, da es wegen der allgemeinen Turbulenzen schwer geworden war, den rechten Weg zu
finden. Weiters sind sie legitimiert, dem Volk rechte Vorschriften zu geben.

6.2 Pinhas' priesterlicher Dienst erwirkte Sündenvergebung

"Ferner Pinhas, der Sohn Eleasars: Er bekam als dritter das hohe Amt, weil er
sich einsetzte für den Gott des Alls und für sein Volk in die Bresche trat, als
er dem Antrieb seines Herzens folgte und für die Israeliten Sühne erwirkte"
(ויכפר על בני ישראל; 45,23)[56].

Pinhas[57] zeichnet als hervorragendste Qualifikation *nicht* von allem Anfang an die Priestereinsetzung aus. Diese ist erst die Folge seines außergewöhnlich kompromisslosen Einsatzes für JHWH. Man erinnere sich an die
Szene in Num 25,6–8, wo vom Geschlechtsverkehr (wahrscheinlich eine Art
kultischer Vereinigung) eines Israeliten mit einer Midianiterin berichtet wird.
Weil dies einen Abfall vom JHWH-Glauben darstellte, wurden beide von
Pinhas getötet.

Wegen des unwiderstehlichen Eintretens für Gott wird ihm eine ganz besondere Auszeichnung zuteil: der Heilsbund (ברית שלום; vgl. Num 25,12;
Jes 54,10; Ez 34,25; 37,26). Es ist auffällig, dass keine Anspielung auf Opfer
zu finden ist. Pinhas ist ein bleibendes Vorbild, allerdings nicht wegen seines
Amtes, sondern wegen des Zeugnisses in seinem Leben[58]. Dieser Hinweis

---

56   Vgl. Murphy, Sin, 265f.
57   Vgl. dazu Stadelmann, Ben Sira, 146–76.282ff; Petraglio, Il libro, 142–49; Lust, Text,
     41f; Aitken, Studies, 85–89; Pomykala, Davidic Dynasty, 132–44; Priest, Ben Sira
     45,25, 111–18.
58   Daher kann ich der an sich überzeugenden Argumentation Marböcks, Sündenverge-
     bung, 178, an dieser Stelle dann nicht folgen ("Hier erhält bereits das hinter dem mitt-

will den politisch bedeutsamen Priestern zur Zeit Siras ein Beispiel vor Augen führen, an dem man sehen kann, wie Priestertum als öffentliches Amt richtig ausgeführt wird. Insbesondere aufgrund der Γ-Tradition verweist Di Lella darauf, "that Phinehas is leader not only in religious affairs but also in the political realm"[59].

6.3 Die Bitte für die Priester (Sir 45,26)

Nach dem Spruch über Pinhas geht Sira spontan und unerwartet auf die konkrete Situation ein und wendet sich an die damals lebenden Priester[60]:
"Er (= Gott) gebe euch Weisheit des Herzens (חכמת לב), sein Volk in Rechtschaffenheit (ἐν δικαιοσύνῃ) zu lenken, damit euer Glück nie endet noch euer hohes Amt bis in fernste Zeiten (Sir 45,26)." Daraus wird klar, dass der Priester eine Ausnahmestellung (כבוד; Sira scheint sich selbst nicht dazu zu zählen) innehat. Diese zeigt sich in der persönlichen Weisheit (חכמת לב)[61] und in der speziellen Qualität (ἐν δικαιοσύνῃ) für religiös-politische Führungsaufgaben, welche dem Wohlergehen (טובכם) der Priester dient. Man würde erwarten, dass die Basis für das Wohlergehen der Priester u.a. mit den Opfern zusammenhängt. Opfer werden jedoch nicht erwähnt.

Da Sühne die Tilgung der Sünden bedeutet, fragt man sich, was zu tun ist, damit Sühne eintritt. Nachdrücklich wird festgehalten, dass mitmenschlich rechtes und hingebungsvolles Verhalten (צדקה; ἐλεημοσύνη) die Sünden sühnt (תכפר חטאת): "Wasser löscht loderndes Feuer, so sühnt Mildtätigkeit Sünde"[62] (Sir 3,30).

Die Betonung derartiger Guttaten stellt aber keine ideelle These dar, deren Umsetzung man erst lange überlegen muss. Nein, es geht um das ganz konkrete und jederzeit den persönlichsten Bereich betreffende positive Verhalten am Mitmenschen, insbesondere auch an Familienmitgliedern. Über die Sünden vergebende Kraft dieser Guttat liest man: "Sie lässt deine Sünden

---

lerischen Eintreten des Pinhas stehende Ethos, der Antrieb bzw. die Bereitwilligkeit seines Herzens ... kultisch-sühnende Kraft"), wenn diese Worte in dem Sinne gemeint sind, dass der Kult dadurch neu interpretiert wird. Die Voraussetzungen für den Kult und vor allem für den Akteur haben sich nämlich geändert.

59 Auch der Hinweis von Box – Oesterley, Book of Sirach, 489, ist wertvoll, dass die Gefahr politischer Intrigen, mit welchen politische Tätigkeiten sehr häufig gekoppelt sind, durch Sirach bekämpft werden will.

60 Vgl. dazu Stadelmann, Ben Sira, 173–76.

61 Vgl. den Hinweis auf die Parallelität zu Simon den Hohenpriester bei Marböck, Hohepriester, 217.

62

πῦρ φλογιζόμενον ἀποσβέσει ὕδωρ   אש לוהטת יכבו מי 🄰

  καὶ ἐλεημοσύνη ἐξιλάσεται ἁμαρτίας   כן צדקה תכפר חטאת

schmelzen (עוניך לחשבית כפור; ἀναλυθήσονταί σου αἱ ἁμαρτίαι) wie Wärme den Reif" (Sir 3,15b)[63].

Sira geht also davon aus, dass der Mensch durch sein Wohltun bei Gott Vergebung findet. Dieses Verhalten kann nicht nur äußerlich sein, sondern fließt aus der Bereitschaft, sich von Innen her dem Mitmenschen zuzuwenden. Nur jener Mensch, der bereit ist, dem anderen alles zu vergeben, erfährt seinerseits von Gott die gleiche Vergebung und damit Tilgung der Sünden:

"Obwohl er (der Mensch) nur ein Wesen aus Fleisch ist, verharrt er im Groll, wer wird da seine Sünden vergeben" (Sir 28,5)?

"Vergib deinem Nächsten das Unrecht, dann werden dir, wenn du betest, auch deine Sünden vergeben" (Sir 28,2).

Es gilt also: Der Boden und die Voraussetzung für die von Gott geschenkte Sündenvergebung ist die Wohltat am Nächsten und die mitmenschliche Güte.

7. Zusammenfassung

Im Rückblick ist notierenswert, dass in Sir 7,29–31 zwar die Priester erwähnt werden, nicht jedoch die Sündenvergebung. Im Spruch über Pinhas (Sir 45,23–25d) und im anschließenden Segenswunsch für alle (zur Zeit Siras lebenden) Priester (Sir 45,25e–26c) wird die Sühne angesprochen, nicht jedoch die Opfer. Dort, wo am häufigsten verschiedene Opferarten erwähnt werden (Sir 31/34,21/18a–32/35,22/20a), kommt darüber hinaus kein Priester vor. Wenn man den Blick auf die Opfer richtet, sind zwei Betrachtungspunkte zentral: Wie war es – erstens – einst, was wollte Gott, und – zweitens – wie sieht die konkrete Gegenwart aus?

7.1 Siras Blick in die Vergangenheit

Einst spielten die Opfer eine wichtige Rolle. Sie regelten viele Fragen im religiösen Leben. In einem nahezu nostalgischen Rückblick werden die früheren Zeiten vor Augen geführt. Jene Gegebenheiten bleiben noch Modellfälle: Was damals an Wirkung erzielt wurde, das muss auch in Siras Zeit erreicht werden.

Sira legt großen Wert auf die Tatsache, dass die Persönlichkeiten der großen Vergangenheit integere Menschen waren, die äußerlich wie innerlich

---

63   Vgl. Bohlen, Ehrung, 173–79: "Der theologische Beitrag des Ben Sira besteht also in der erstmaligen Subsummierung der vom Dekaloggebot eingeforderten Elternehrung unter den Begriff der sündentilgenden und im Einsatz dieses Theorems als ethischem Motivationsimpuls" (179).

Vorbilder darstellten. Damals stimmten noch die Relationen. Daher sind die
Opfer in jener Zeit solche gewesen, wie sie Gott wollte. Aber schon damals –
so Siras Akzentsetzung – ging es nicht um Opfer um der Opfer willen, sondern um die Persönlichkeiten, welche diese darbrachten.

7.2 Siras Blick in seine Gegenwart

Zur Zeit Siras sind Opfer dargebracht worden. Ob dies allerdings mit der
Selbstverständlichkeit der Fall war, wie dies von früher berichtet wird,
scheint sehr zweifelhaft. Wenn die Priester von den Opfern leben, dann liegt
darin eine Gefahr. Wer die Darbringung der Opfer nicht als eine selbstverständliche religiöse Pflicht zur Wiederherstellung des guten Verhältnisses zu
Gott ansieht bzw. auf das Gottesverhältnis wegen der zeitgeschichtlich be-
dingten neuen hellenistischen Lebensformen überhaupt kein großes Gewicht
legt, der kann bei Bedarf durch die Opfergaben auch das Leben bzw. das politische Verhalten der – an sich einflussreichen – Priester steuern: wenn keine
Opfer, dann keine Abgaben, dann kein Lebensunterhalt.

Sira hält allerdings nichts von den Opfern an sich, denn die neuen Ent-
wicklungen sind nicht zu billigen. Und nun etwas Zentrales: man hat einst
gesagt, die Sündenvergebung setzt korrekte Opfer voraus. Ohne dass Sira
eine Opferkritik übt, hält er fest: Sündenvergebung ereignet sich konkret auf
andere Weise. Nicht die Opfer vergeben Sünden, sondern Gott. Und Gott
schaut auf andere Gegebenheiten als auf Opfer und vergibt auf dieser Basis
die Sünden. Wenn nicht die Einstellung und das Verhalten der Opfernden den
Ansprüchen Gottes gerecht wird, sind die Opfer nicht wirkungsvoll!

Dies sieht man daran, dass Vergebung nicht durch die den Regeln entsprechende Darbringung von Opfern geschieht, sondern durch den Umgang
mit dem Nächsten. Darin zeigt sich die rechte Einstellung zu JHWH. Man
möge sich nicht täuschen, so Siras Argument, Gott ist Weltenlenker und
Richter (damit verbindet er geschickt die weltpolitische Dimension [Seleuki-
den] und die innerjüdische Lage [Sympathisanten und sonstige Nutznießer
der Umbruchszeit]) und er akzeptiert nur die richtige religiöse Einstellung
und den rechten Umgang mit den Schwächsten in der Gesellschaft. Gerade
jene wird er erhören.

Es geht aber nicht an, das die Priester in Abhängigkeit geraten und dadurch steuerbar werden. Die Priester haben nämlich eine zentrale Aufgabe in
der Bildung und Leitung des Volkes zu erfüllen. Das System, wonach die
Priester von den Opfern leben und so gleichsam von Gott ernährt werden, hat
sich nicht bewährt. Denn Opfernde, zumal wenn sie einflussreich waren,
hatten offensichtlich erkannt, dass sich hier eine wirkungsreiche Manipulati-
onsmöglichkeit der Priester eröffnet.

Es ist zwar richtig, dass in diesem Fall das Opfer missbraucht wird, indem es zum politischen Mittel degradiert wird. Der Blick auf Gott geht verloren. Gottes Ehre und Sündenvergebung waren nicht die erstrangigen Güter für Menschen, die die Opfer für ihre Ziele ausnutzten. Aber die Klage darüber ändert weder die Realitäten noch kann davon ein Priester oder dessen Familie leben.

Sira sieht nun einen Ausweg aus der Gefahr der neuen Lage und vertieft die Sichtweise der Opfer. Das Verständnis, wonach der *Anteil* des Priesters nur einen Anteil an Opfern bedeutet, ist eine einseitige Interpretation. Denn, wenn man sich an jene Passagen hält, wie sie Ezechiel für die zadokitischen Priester vorgesehen hat, ändert sich die Situation grundlegend. Deren Lebensgrundlage ist Grund und Boden, von dem sie leben konnten. Diesen Besitz hat man ihnen wiederzugeben. Dadurch werden sich die Priester auch wieder frei spielen können. Der traditionelle Opferanteil tritt als Lebensquelle für Priester in den Hintergrund und im Gegensatz dazu rücken der Charakter und die Verhaltensweise des Opfernden in den Mittelpunkt. Voraussetzung dafür ist aber, dass Gott und die Opfer in einem neuen Verhältnis definiert werden. Ohne die Opfer abzuschaffen, legt Gott selbst darauf Wert, dass sich ein von ihm angenommenes Leben und die Sündenvergebung vor allem auch ohne Opfer vollzieht. Angenommen werden aber nur solche Menschen, die integer sind und sich durch Wohltaten an den Mitmenschen auszeichnen!

Bibliographie

Aitken, J.K., *Studies in the Hebrew and Greek Text of Ben Sira with Special Reference to the Future* (Ph.D. diss; Cambridge: University Press, 1995).

Baumgarten, J.M., "Sacrifice and Worship among the Jewish Sectarians of the Dead Sea (Qumran) Scrolls," *HThR* 46 (1953) 141–59.

Beentjes, P.C., *The Book of Ben Sira in Hebrew: A Text Edition of all Extant Hebrew Manuscripts & A Synopsis of all Parallel Hebrew Ben Sira Texts* (VTSup 68; Leiden: Brill, 1997).

Beentjes, P.C., *Jesus Sirach en Tenach; een onderzoek naar en een classificatie van parallellen, met bijzondere aandacht voor hun functie in Sirach 45:6–26* (diss.; Nieuwegein: Self publishing house, 1981).

Bohlen, R., *Die Ehrung der Eltern bei Ben Sira. Studien zur Motivation und Interpretation eines familienethischen Grundwertes in frühhellenistischer Zeit* (TThSt 51; Trier: Paulinus, 1991).

The Book of Ben Sira / סירא בן ספר. *Text, Concordance and an Analysis of the Vocabulary* (The Historical Dictionary of the Hebrew Language; Jerusalem: Academy of the Hebrew Language and the Shrine of the Book, 1973).

Box, G.H. – Oesterley, W.O.E., "The Book of Sirach", in *APOT*, vol. I (ed. R.H. Charles; Oxford: Clarendon, 1913) 268–517.

Calduch-Benages, N., *En el crisol de la prueba. Estudio exegético de Sir 2,1–18* (ABE 32; Estella: Verbo Divino, 1997).

Calduch-Benages, N., "Fear for the Powerful or Respect for Authority?," in *Der Einzelne und seine Gemeinschaft bei Ben Sira* (eds. R. Egger-Wenzel and I. Krammer; BZAW 270; Berlin / New York: de Gruyter, 1998) 87–102.

Cohn, L. – Reiter, S., "Quod omnis probus liber sit," in *Philonis Alexandrini opera quae supersunt* (vol. VI; repr. 1915; Berlin: de Gruyter, 1962) 1–45.

Fohrer, G. et al., *Hebräisches und aramäisches Wörterbuch zum Alten Testament* (3d ed.; Berlin / New York: de Gruyter, 1997).

Gärtner, B., *The Temple and the Community in Qumran and the New Testament* (Monograph series. Society for New Testament Studies 1; Cambridge: Cambridge University, 1965).

Gesenius, W. – Buhl, F., *Hebräisches und aramäisches Wörterbuch über das Alte Testament* (17th ed.; Berlin / Göttingen / Heidelberg: Springer, 1962).

Haspecker, J., *Gottesfurcht bei Jesus Sirach. Ihre religiöse Struktur und ihre literarische und doktrinäre Bedeutung* (AnBib 30; Rome: Pontifical Biblical Institute, 1967).

Hayward, C.T.R., "Behind the Dead Sea Scrolls: The Sons of Zadok, the Priest, and Their Priestly Ideology," *Toronto Journal of Theology* 13 (1997) 7–21.

Hayward, C.T.R., *The Jewish Temple. A Non-Biblical Sourcebook* (London / New York: Routledge, 1996).

Hayward, C.T.R., "Sacrifice and World Order: Some Oberservations on Ben Sira's Attitude on the Temple Service," in *Sacrifice and Redemption: Durham Essays in Theology* (ed. St.W. Sykes; Cambridge: Cambridge University, 1991) 22–34.

Kieweler, H.V., *Ben Sira zwischen Judentum und Hellenismus. Eine kritische Auseinandersetzung mit Th. Middendorp* (BEATAJ 30; Frankfurt a.M. et al.: Lang, 1992).

Klinzing, G., *Die Umdeutung des Kultus in der Qumrangemeinde und im Neuen Testament* (SUNT 7; Göttingen: Vandenhoeck & Ruprecht, 1971).

Konkel, M., *Architektonik des Heiligen. Studien zur zweiten Tempelvision Ezechiels* (Ez 40–48) (BBB 129; Berlin et al: Philo, 2001).

Krammer, I., *Die Auswirkungen des Verhaltens zum Mitmenschen auf die Beziehung zu Gott im Buch Ben Sira* (unpublished diss.; Salzburg, 1997).

Lust, J., "The Diverse Text Forms of Jeremiah and History Writing with Jer 33 as a Taste Case," *JNSL* 20 (1994) 31–48.

Marböck, J., "Der Hohepriester Simon in Sir 50. Ein Beitrag zur Bedeutung von Priestertum und Kult im Sirachbuch", in *Treasures of Wisdom: Studies in Ben Sira and the Book of Wisdom* (FS M. Gilbert; eds. N. Calduch-Benages and J. Vermeylen; BETL 143; Leuven: Peeters, 1999) 215–29.

Marböck, J., "Sündenvergebung bei Jesus Sirach. Eine Notiz zur Theologie und Frömmigkeit der deuterokanonischen Schriften," *ZKTh* 116 (1994) 480–86 = in *Gottes Weisheit unter uns. Zur Theologie des Buches Sirach* (ed. I. Fischer; Herders Biblische Studien 6; Freiburg: Herder, 1995) 176–84.

Marböck, J., *Weisheit im Wandel. Untersuchungen zur Weisheitstheologie bei Ben Sira* (BBB 37; Bonn: Hanstein, 1971; repr. in BZAW 272; Berlin / New York: de Gruyter, 1999).

Minissale, A., "Ben Siras Selbstverständnis in Bezug auf Autoritäten der Gesellschaft," in *Der Einzelne und seine Gemeinschaft bei Ben Sira* (eds. R. Egger-Wenzel and I. Krammer; BZAW 270; Berlin / New York: de Gruyter, 1998) 103–16.

Murphy, R.E., "Sin, Repentance, and Forgiveness in Sirach," in *Der Einzelne und seine Gemeinschaft bei Ben Sira* (eds. R. Egger-Wenzel and I. Krammer; BZAW 270; Berlin / New York: de Gruyter, 1998) 260–70.

Olyan, S.M., "Ben Sira's Relationship to the Priesthood," *HThR* 80 (1987) 261–86.

Perdue, L.G., *Wisdom and Creation: The Theology of Wisdom Literature* (ed. L.G. Perdue; Nashville: Abingdon, 1994).

Peters, N., *Das Buch Jesus Sirach oder Ecclesiasticus* (EHAT 25; Münster: Aschendorff, 1913).

Peters, N., *Der jüngst wiederaufgefundene hebräische Text des Buches Ecclesiasticus, untersucht, herausgegeben, übersetzt und mit kritischer Note versehen* (Freiburg: Herder, 1902).

Petraglio, R., *Il libro che contamina le mani. Ben Sirac rilegge il libro e la storia d'Israele* (Theologia 4; Palermo: Augustinus, 1993).

Pomykala, K.E., *The Davidic Dynasty Tradition in Early Judaism. Its History and Significance for Messianism* (SBL Early Judaism and its literature 7; Atlanta: Scholars Press, 1995).

Priest, J., "Ben Sira 45,25 in the Light of the Qumran Literature," *RevQ* 5 (1964–1966) 111–18.

Reicke, B., "Erbe," in *BHH* 1. 423–25.

Roberts, C.H., "Proverbs – Wisdom of Solomon – Ecclesiasticus," in *The Antinoopolis Papyri* (idem; vol. 1; London: Egypt Exploration Sociation, 1950) 2–17.

Rudnik, Th.A., *Heilig und Profan: Redaktionskritische Studien zu Ez 40–48* (BZAW 287; Berlin / New York: de Gruyter, 2000).

Ruß, R., "Brand- und Sühneopfer forderst du nicht. Ps 40,7 – Heute von Opfer und von Sühne reden?," *BK 49* (1994) 125.

Sauer, G., *Jesus Sirach: Übersetzt und erklärt* (ATDA 1; Göttingen: Vandenhoeck & Ruprecht, 2000).

Schechter, S. – Taylor, Ch., *The Wisdom of Ben Sira. Portions of the Book Ecclesiasticus, from Hebrew Manuscripts in the Cairo Genizah Collection Presented to the University of Cambridge by the Editors* (Cambridge: University Press, 1899; repr. Amsterdam: Philo, 1979).

Schmid, H.H., "חלק *ḥlq* teilen," in *THAT* 1. 576–79.

Schreiner, J., *Jesus Sirach 1–24* (NEchtB AT 38; Würzburg 2002).

Segal, M. Z., ספר בן סירא השלם, (3d rev. ed.; Jerusalem: Bialik, 1972).

Skehan P.W. – Di Lella, A.A., *The Wisdom of Ben Sira: A New Translation with Notes, Introduction and Commentary* (AB 39; New York: Doubleday, 1987).

Snaith, J.G., "Ben Sira's Supposed Love of Liturgy," *VT* 25 (1975) 167–74.

Stadelmann, H., "Gottes- und Priesterverehrung und die Abgaben an die Priester (7:29–31)," in *Ben Sira als Schriftgelehrter. Eine Untersuchung zum Berufsbild des vor-makkabäischen Sōfēr unter Berücksichtigung seines Verhältnisses zu Priester-, Propheten- und Weisheitslehrertum* (idem; WUNT 2/6; Tübingen: Mohr, 1980).

Stone, M.E., "Ideal Figures and Social Context. Priest and Sage in the Early Second Temple Age," in *Ancient Israelite Religion* (FS F.M. Cross; eds. P.D. Miller, P.D. Hanson and S.D. McBride; Philadelphia: Fortress, 1987) 575–86 = in *Selected Studies in Pseudepigrapha and Apocrypha. With Special Reference to the Armenian Tradition* (SVTP 9; Leiden et al.: Brill, 1991) 259–70.

Till, W., "Saidische Fragmente des Alten Testamentes," *Muséon* 50 (1937) 175–237.

Tsevat, M., "חָלַק," *ThWAT* 2. 1017–20.

Vattioni, F., "Il sacrificio dei fanciulli in Sir 34(31),24?," in *Sangue e antropologia riti e culto: Atti della V. Settimana [di Studi Sangue e Antropologia], Roma, 26 novembre – 1 dicembre 1984* (ed. F. Vattioni; Collana "Sangue e antropologia" 5; Roma: Pia Unione Preziosissimo Sangue, 1984) 157–60.

Vawter, B., "Levitical Messianism and the New Testament," in *The Bible in Current Catholic Thought* (ed. J.L. McKenzie; St. Louis University Theology Studies 1; New York: Herder, 1962) 83–99.

Wagner, Ch., *Die Septuaginta-Hapaxlegomena im Buch Jesus Sirach. Untersuchungen zu Wortwahl und Wortbildung unter besonderer Berücksichtigung des textkritischen und übersetzungstechnischen Aspektes* (BZAW 282; Berlin / New York: de Gruyter, 1999).

Winter, M.M., "Ben Sira in Syriac. An Ebionite Translation?," in *Studia Patristica XVI. Papers Presented to the Seventh International Conference on Patristic Studies Held in Oxford 1975* (TUGAL; ed. E.A. Livingstone; Berlin: Akademie-Verlag, 1984) 121ff.

Wright, B.G., "'Fear the Lord and Honor the Priest'. Ben Sira as Defender of the Jerusalem Priesthood", in *The Book of Ben Sira in Modern Research: Proceedings of the First International Ben Sira Conference 28–31 July 1996 Soesterberg, Netherlands* (ed. P.C. Beentjes; BZAW 255; Berlin / New York: de Gruyter, 1997) 189–222.

Yadin, Y., "The Ben Sira Scroll from Masada. With Notes on the Reading by Elisha Qimron and Bibliography by Florentino García Martínez", in *Masada VI: Yigael Yadin Excavations 1963–1965. Final Reports* (eds. J. Aviram, G. Foerster and E. Netzer; Jerusalem: Israel Exploration Society and The Hebrew University of Jerusalem, 1999) 151–252.

Ziegler, J., *Sapientia Iesu Filii Sirach* (Septuaginta. Vetus Testamentum Graecum Auctoritate Academiae Scientiarum Gottingensis editum, 12/2; 2d ed; Göttingen: Vandenhoeck & Ruprecht, 1980).

Ziegler, J., "Zum Wortschatz des griechischen Sirach," in *Von Ugarit nach Qumran* (FS O. Eissfeldt; eds. J. Hempel and L. Rost; BZAW 77; Berlin: de Gruyter, 1958) 274–87.

Zimmerli, W., *Ezechiel. 2. Teilband. Ezechiel 25–48* (BKAT 13/2; Neukirchen-Vluyn: Neukirchener, 1969).

El Elyon and the Divine Names in Ben Sira

Robert C.T. Hayward
University of Durham

The choice of names and titles for God which ancient Jewish writers, translators, and commentators exercised is both of intrinsic interest, and at the
same time may tell us a good deal, if we have the patience to look and listen,
about the concerns and aims of those Jews whose world was so much bound
up with texts and their reception. The Wisdom book of Jesus Ben Sira offers
plenty in the way of illustration of this state of affairs. Thus Professors Skehan and Di Lella quite properly dub Ben Sira 6:4 as "a good example of the
fluidity of the divine names in the book and its translations," noting that
while Heb. MS C of this verse uses the Tetragram, Heb. MS A and the Syriac
translation have "God";[1] most Gk. MSS read κύριος; and the O-group of
Greek MSS and the Latin translation use the title Most High.[2] This array of
divine designations reflects the textual complexity of the work before us,
where individual manuscripts, especially the surviving Hebrew MSS, often
betray particular nuances in their use of divine titles.[3] Certainly the surviving
Hebrew and Greek witnesses to Ben Sira's book are by now well known as
having their own idiosyncrasies, and for this reason it seems both accurate
and convenient for our purposes in this essay to speak of Hebrew and Greek
traditions, rather than of Hebrew Ben Sira or Greek Sirach *tout court*.[4] For it
will be the Hebrew and Greek material, rather than the Syriac and Latin
translations, which will mostly concern us here as we examine the divine
titles Most High and God Most High, Hebrew עליון and אל עליון, Greek
ὕψιστος and θεὸς ὕψιστος respectively. In the course of this paper, we shall
attempt to offer some rationale for the use of these terms in the Hebrew and

---

1   The Hebrew text of Ben Sira is quoted from Beentjes, Book of Ben Sira; the Greek of
     Sirach from the edition of Ziegler, Sapientia; and the Latin and Syriac versions from
     the edition of Vattioni, Ecclesiastico. Translations are ours.
2   See Skehan – Di Lella, Wisdom, 182.
3   For discussion of the text of Ben Sira, see Wright, Difference, 1–18; Gilbert, Book, 81–
     91; Harrington, Sirach Research, 164–70; Skehan – Di Lella, Wisdom, 51–62; and the
     informative article of Di Lella, Wisdom, 934–36.
4   Observe, for example, the distinctive characteristics of the Masada MS in relation to
     the other Hebrew and Greek witnesses noted by Baumgarten, Notes, 323–27; Strugnell,
     Notes, 109–19; the complex relationship between the Hebrew texts known to us and
     the Greek translation of Ben Sira's grandson indicated by Wright, Difference, 231–50;
     and the remaining possibility that some of the Hebrew text available to us (particularly
     the HT II form) may represent a degree of retrotranslation from Greek or Syriac, as
     noted by Di Lella, Wisdom, 935.

Greek traditions of Ben Sira's Wisdom book; to account for their relatively frequent use as divine titles; and to investigate, as far as time allows, their relationship to other divine Names recorded in the texts.

The divine titles Most High and God Most High are evidently favoured by both Hebrew and Greek traditions of Ben Sira's work, and derive ultimately from the Hebrew Bible, where the titles are not exactly uncommon, but tend to be confined to certain specific circumstances and expressions.[5] It will be of the first importance, therefore, to discover how far the Ben Sira traditions adhere closely to Scriptural models in their use of the terms God Most High and Most High, and to note particularly any instances where they diverge from Scriptural forms of expression. We shall also need to be sensitive to possible modifications of Scriptural language in the use of the titles by both Hebrew and Greek Ben Sira traditions; and we shall have to consider whether some Scriptural associations of these divine designations are simply passed over in the Ben Sira traditions. Throughout this exercise, it will be important to search for a rationale in the use of the title Most High and God Most High. Why does the Wisdom book, at certain key points in its Greek and Hebrew forms, so favour this manner of speaking of God?

1. Hebrew Bible Directly Informs Ben Sira Traditions on God Most High

We may begin with a simple, but particularly important observation. Two verses in the Psalter indicate that עליון may properly be used directly in connection with the Ineffable Name of the God of Israel, the so-called Tetragram. Thus, at Ps 7:18 the author asserts that he will sing to שם יהוה עליון; and again at Ps 92:2 declares in a Psalm for Shabbat טוב להדות ליהוה ולזמר לשמך עליון. Both these verses offer Most High as a direct description of the Name YHWH, whose open utterance was, in Ben Sira's day, restricted to the Temple service in Jerusalem.[6] This close association of the title עליון precisely with the Name of YHWH features again in the Psalter, at Ps 83:19, where people are exhorted precisely to know that God's Name is YHWH, and that He alone is עליון over all the earth. These biblical verses could quite easily justify the use of עליון as a discreet and proper way of referring to the Ineffable Name, indeed as a substitute for the Divine Name itself. In this regard, it is of some interest to note that Ben Sira 43:2 according to MS B reads

---

5   For a recent, exhaustive treatment of the title as found in the Hebrew Bible, with excellent bibliography, see Zobel, עליון, 121–39.

6   On this important point, see Philo, *De Vita Mosis* II. 114; *m. Tamid.* 7:2; *Soṭah* 7:6; and Schürer, History 2, 306–7.

the Tetragram, whereas the Masada MS of the same verse has עליון. As Professor Skehan has noted, the scribe of the Masada Manuscript is very hesitant
to write יהוה or even אלהים; evidently, that scribe regarded עליון as a per-
missible way of referring to the Divine Name.[7] We may recall, in this
connection, that the Qumran *yahad* regulations in 1QS equally avoid use of
the Tetragram or of אלהים, while allowing עליון (1QS 4:22; 10:12; 11:15).[8]
In respect of אלהים, the Bible again provides a rationale for what we find in
1QS, since Ps 57:3 depicts the psalmist as calling out to אלהים עליון, where
Most High appears as a further definition of qualification of God. It is clear,
then that solid Scriptural grounds could be adduced in antiquity for representing the Hebrew Bible's two most common designations for God, YHWH
and אלהים, with the term Most High. Yet, so far as I am aware, there is no
instance of אלהים in the Hebrew MSS of Ben Sira ever being represented by
ὕψιστος in the Greek tradition. The term Most High, it would seem, was there
most associated with the Tetragram.[9]

It might be suggested, then, that verses in the Greek tradition having
ὕψιστος where the corresponding places in Hebrew MSS read the Tetragram
(*e.g.*, MS A 12:2; MS B 43:2; 48:5) are using the term *simply* as a substitute
for that Tetragram. Yet such a suggestion would be too hasty, since there is
evidence that the Greek tradition has exercised careful discretion in its use of
Most High. In this, I would submit, it often takes its cue from the Hebrew
sources available to it. First in this regard we may note the links between the
title Most High and praise, confession, and thanksgiving directed to God described in Psalm verses already quoted. Ben Sira MS B 47:8 tells how King
David rendered thanksgivings to אל עליון, a title which the Greek represents
with ἁγίῳ ὑψίστῳ, "the Holy One Most High".[10] The Greek further juxtaposes thanksgiving and praise with the title Most High at 17:27, where no
Hebrew is extant; and introduces the notion of the people supplicating the

---

7   See Skehan, Divine Name, 18–20.
8   See, *e.g.*, Leaney, Rule, 201–3, 223–26; Knibb, Qumran Community, 134; Skehan, Di-
     vine Name, 14–18, 20–28; and comments on 1QS 8:14 in Charlesworth, Dead Sea
     Scrolls, 37.
9   Statistical information on the occurrences of divine titles in the Hebrew and Greek wit-
     nesses to Ben Sira is set out by Fang Che-Yong, Usus, 159–64, his essay as a whole
     suggesting reasons why differences between Hebrew and Greek witnesses in respect of
     divine titles, where these exist, should have arisen. Haspecker, Gottesfurcht, 48–50,
     61–63, offers further insights based on Fang Che-yong's statistics.
10   God is designated as holy in the Heb. MSS again at 47:10 with reference to His Name;
     at 50:17, where He is called the Holy One of Israel; and at 39:35, where people are ex-
     horted to bless the Name of His Holiness. All these verses are extant in MS B, and,
     along with 47:8, display a strongly liturgical character emphasizing prayer and worship
     directed towards the Name of God, a prominent feature also of Ben Sira's prayer in
     51:1, 11, 12, and 30 (MS B).

Lord Most High at 50:19a, where no divine Name is found in the corresponding Hebrew of MS B. A similar association of ὕψιστος specifically with praise, thanksgiving, and supplication is displayed also in LXX additions to Psalms 13:6 and 65:4, indicating a line of thought about Most High within the Jewish-Greek world of which Greek Sirach may have approved, but one which evidently grows out of the Hebrew Bible itself.[11]

Also arising directly out of the Hebrew Bible is the idea that the Most High is one who may be called upon and invoked. Ps 57:3 makes this clear, and both Hebrew (MS B) and Greek texts of Ben Sira 46:5; 47:5 show Joshua and David as doing just that. In addition, MS B Ben Sira 48:20 has people calling upon עליון in the days of Hezekiah.[12] The Greek rendering of this title as "the Lord, the Merciful" in this verse is most likely determined by the biblical account of the deliverance of the Temple from Assyrian attack in Hezekiah's reign in answer to prayer offered in the Temple (cf. Isa 37:14–20) to the merciful God there present.[13] Thus the title Most High may properly be used in verses speaking of prayer and supplication (Gk. Sir 32/35:21/17; 37:15; 39:5). Next, Ps 50:14 urges votaries to pay their vows to עליון, Scriptural advice which lies behind the wording of Ben Sira 32/35:12/9–15/12 in the Greek tradition with its use of Most High. The Hebrew Bible also informs the Hebrew and Greek forms of Ben Sira 46:5–6, where Joshua's victory as a result of a hail-storm is attributed to the Most High: here, the influence of Ps 18:14 and its parallel in 2 Sam 22:14 with their references to the Most High is unmistakeable.[14] Likewise, Ps 78:35 can talk of אל עליון as Israel's redeemer giving victory over enemies to Israel, providing further Scriptural support for Ben Sira's notion that Most High is one who fights Israel's enemies and prevails in battle. Finally in this list of usages where the Hebrew Bible has evidently laid the foundations for the use of Most High, we may note two other Scriptural verses. The first is a phrase from the Bala`am nar-

---

11   The Hebrew of Ps 13:6 makes the Psalmist declare: "I will sing to the Lord, because He has dealt kindly with me," to which LXX of the verse (Ps 12:6) adds words not represented in the Hebrew, "and I shall sing a psalm to the Name of the Lord Most High." LXX in witnesses A and S2 add to Ps 45:7 the title "Most High" as subject of a sentence which in the Hebrew (Ps 46:7) simply has "He", referring to God, to yield: "the Most High gave forth His voice ..." LXX (S²) of Ps 65:4 add a vocative "O Most High" to a verse urging all the earth to sing to God's Name, a vocative not found in the Hebrew of Ps 66:4.

12   See further Fang Che-Yong, Usus, 163–64, who discusses these verses with reference to their Scriptural background.

13   Note that in 50:19 (Heb. MS B and Greek witnesses) the Temple service offered in Jerusalem is directed precisely to the *Merciful One*. The miraculous deliverance of Temple and city in Hezekiah's day was a resounding demonstration that the Merciful One is indeed one who hears and answers the prayers of the righteous: see 2 Kings 19:15–20. On the mercy of God and related themes, see Marböck, Weisheit, 28–30.

14   See Fang Che-Yong, Usus, 163.

rative which speaks of דעת עליון, "the knowledge of the Most High" (Num 24:16) which consorts well with Ben Sira 42:18 (MS M) and its assertion that the Most High knows all: the text is fragmentary, but the Greek at this point declares that the Most High knows all knowledge. The second is Lam 3:38, which has the phrase מפי עליון. Something very like this Hebrew expression must surely lie behind the Greek text of Sir 24:3, where Wisdom declares that she came forth from the mouth of the Most High.

Well known is the association found in the Hebrew Bible between the title Most High and the holy city Jerusalem and its Temple. Passages such as Ps 46:5 and 87:5 at once come to mind, and clearly inform those verses where עליון refers to the God worshipped in the Jerusalem Temple both in the Hebrew (50:14, 16, 17 MS B), and, even more frequently, in the Greek tradition (50:7, 14, 15, 16, 17, 19, 21). Consequently, Most High is a title used also with reference to offerings made in the Temple (Gk. Sir 7:9; 32/35:21/18; 32/35:8/5). In connection with all this it might be proper to introduce here Gen 14:18–22, where Melchizedek, the priest of God Most High, is described (verse 18) as מלך שלם, king of Salem. It is quite probable that Salem had already been identified in Ben Sira's days as Jerusalem on the basis of Ps 76:3 (*cf.* 1Qap Gen 22:13), in which case the whole episode of Abraham's encounter with that priest-king and the invocations of God Most High would be of some importance to Ben Sira.[15] Indeed, Gen 14:18–22 presents God Most High as one who has rescued Abraham from enemies, as a deliverer in time of trouble, an aspect of the Most High's activities which we have already noted as brought to our attention by Ben Sira in other parts of his work. For reasons which we shall examine presently, Gen 14:18–22 does stand out as being of significance for Ben Sira; but its significance is not straightforward, and for the moment we simply note its general contribution to the use of the divine titles in the Ben Sira traditions.

In all these instances, one can discern more or less clearly the direct influence of the Hebrew Bible on the surviving witnesses to Ben Sira's work. To them, we might even add the Greek of Sir 4:10, where the expression "son of the Most High" (Heb. MS A has "God will call you a son"[16]) strikingly recalls Ps 82:6. But these more or less direct invocations of the biblical usage of God Most High, and the associations of that title with themes and ideas found in the Hebrew text of Scripture itself, represent only a fraction of what

---

15   For the association of the title Most High with the Temple service, see Hayward, Jewish Temple, 56–63. The identification of the Salem of Gen 14:18 with Jerusalem is discussed by Fitzmyer, Genesis Apocryphon, on col. 22 line 13 *ad loc.*; *idem*, Essays, 231–33: "Now this Melchizedek ..."; and see further the traditions noted and discussed by Kugel, Traditions, 278, 283–84, 291–93, who notes the Samaritan identification of it with Mount Gerizim.

16   See Skehan – Di Lella, Wisdom, 167–68.

Ben Sira has to tell us. For in other parts of his work he uses the title God Most High in ways not found in the Bible; and it is to these passages we must now turn. They fall into two categories: those which tend to downplay or slightly diverge from material found in the Hebrew Bible; and those which might be explained as representing a development of biblical thought in line with other known post-biblical tradition. We shall begin by addressing the second of these categories, searching at the same time for reasons why post-biblical writers felt called to "expand" biblical data in the ways they did.

2. Uses of Most High Representing Traditional Development of Biblical Data

Perhaps the most important expressions falling under consideration here are the phrases "Law of the Most High" (Heb. תורת עליון; Gk. νόμος ὑψίστου) and "covenant of the Most High" (Heb. ברית עליון; Gk. διαθήκη ὑψίστου). The first of these is represented in both Hebrew and Greek witnesses at 41:8; 42:2; and 49:4. The Greek form of the phrase occurs at 9:15, where the Hebrew of MS A has a quite different, and possibly corrupt reading;[17] 19:17 and 23:23 where no Hebrew is extant; and 44:20, where the Hebrew of MS B has מצות עליון, "the commandments of the Most High", words actually found in the Greek also at 29:11, for which no Heb. MS remains. Neither "covenant of the Most High", nor "Law of the Most High", is found as such in the Hebrew Bible. In addition, the phrase "covenant of the Most High" is attested only by the Greek traditions of Ben Sira, at 24:23 and 28:7, where no Heb. MSS of these verses survive.[18]

The ultimate source for, and authoritative justification of these phrases would seem to be the Psalter. Speaking of Israel's failure to obey God after He had brought them out of Egypt, Ps 78:56 states: וינסו וימרו את אלהים עליון ועדותיו אל שמרו, "so they tempted and rebelled against God Most High, and did not observe His testimonies." In a similar vein, Ps 107:11 speaks of people who rejected God's precepts, saying: כי המרו אמרי אל ועצת עליון נאצו, "for they rebelled against the utterances of God, and spurned the counsel of the Most High." Verses such as these almost invite the development of a phrase like "the Law of the Most High," since the Torah and the Testimonies are in any case juxtaposed in Scripture (e.g., Neh 9:34), and Hebrew עדות, "testimony", is close in sound to a word from the same verbal root, namely עדות, "precepts", which is contained in the Torah (cf.

---

17 On the textual problem in this verse see Skehan – Di Lella, Wisdom, 218, and Wright, Difference, 308, n. 18.
18 For a possible reconstruction of the Hebrew Vorlage of 24:23, see Skehan, Structures, 365–79, and Wright's critical comments on this endeavour, Difference, 243–45.

Deut 4:45; 6:17, 20). Furthermore, the Ark of the Covenant, which contained the tablets inscribed with words of Torah (Deut 10:1–5; 1 Kings 8:9) is regularly spoken of in Exodus as "the Ark of the testimony", ארון העדות (e.g., Exod 26:33, 34; 27:21). The Ark was ultimately transferred to the Holy of Holies in the Jerusalem Temple where Wisdom takes up her residence and inheritance, according to Sir 24:8.

Thanks to Emile Puech's recent publication of a critical edition of 4Q525 (4QBeatitudes), we can say a little more about the phrase "Torah of the Most High".[19] It is certainly found here (4Q525 2–3 col ii line 4), Puech's edition reading as follows: אשרי אדם השיג *vac* יתהלך בתורת עליון ויכן חכמה לדרכיה לבו, which may be translated as: "happy is the man who has attained to wisdom ... he shall walk in the law of the Most High, and direct his heart to her paths."[20] Puech dates this text to around the middle of the second century B.C.E., suggesting a time between 160 and 140 B.C.E.[21] He notes further occurrences of the phrase in Ben Sira, in *Test. Levi* 13:1; and 11QPs[a] XVIII.12 (where, incidentally, the talk is of Wisdom and the sacrifices offered in the Temple service); but he does not offer suggestions why and how it should have arisen, even though he is clearly aware that it is not a Scriptural phrase.[22] Significantly, Puech also notes that 4Q525 carefully avoids the use of the Tetragram, preferring אל and (ה)אלהים, in contrast with the books of Daniel and Ben Sira, which still use it.[23] This is valuable information; for it strongly suggests that in Ben Sira's usage at least the phrase "law of the Most High" need not be explained as arising out of an early and incipient desire to avoid the Tetragram, but rather corresponds to a usage of the phrase in other nearly contemporary Sapiential works. This suggestion, we believe, will be confirmed by what follows.

The expression "commandments of the Most High" occurs in both Hebrew and Greek traditions, and fits naturally and easily with the notion of the "Torah of the Most High". Like the latter phrase, it grows naturally out of biblical Hebrew passages like Ps 78:17, where Israel is said to have sinned and rebelled against the Most High: a verse like this is best understood as a refusal of Israel to obey divine commandments. Furthermore, the sense that the Most High is one who gives commandments develops naturally enough out of places where the Most High is linked directly to the Name of God in a setting which speaks of משפט and דין, and speaks of God as שופט צדק.

---

19   See Puech, Qumrân Grotte 4, 115–78.
20   See Puech, Qumrân Grotte 4, 122 (and also p. 127) for the Hebrew text; the translation is ours. There are no difficulties in the reading of the manuscript for the phrase which concerns us: see Puech's notes on those readings, pp. 122–23.
21   Puech, Qumrân Grotte 4, 116–19.
22   Puech, Qumrân Grotte 4, 124.
23   Puech, Qumrân Grotte 4, 118.

Such is the purport of Ps 9:3, with its powerful portrayal of the Most High as a monarch dispensing justice in accordance with legal principles decreed by his majesty.

The phrase "covenant of the Most High," however, is less easy to account for. No verse from the Hebrew Bible directly associates the title Most High with any covenant; and the obvious suggestion that the phrase developed by association out of the related terms "Law of the Most High" and "commandments of the Most High" seems lame and unconvincing. In addition, the phrase is confined to the Greek witnesses to Ben Sira's work. These two factors taken together might lead to a suspicion that the phrase "covenant of the Most High" represents a later refinement of Ben Sira's thought, especially since this form of words is not to be found in the Qumran texts, nor in other literature more or less contemporary with Ben Sira.[24] Fortunately, it is possible to show that such suspicion is not well founded, and that the phrase "covenant of the Most High" has what Ben Sira would no doubt have regarded as a firm foundation in Scripture. This begins to become clear when we examine what he has to say about the three major Patriarchs Abraham, Isaac, and Jacob-Israel at 44:19–23, where fortunately Greek and Hebrew witnesses are in our hands. The Hebrew text of Ben Sira 44:19–23 preserved in MS B reads:

(19) Abraham was father of a multitude of nations:
he set no blemish upon his glory.

(20) It was he who kept the commandments of the Most High (מצות עליון):
and who came into covenant (בא בברית) with Him.
In his flesh he cut for him a statute (חק),
and when he was tempted he was found faithful.

(21) Therefore with an oath He established (a covenant) for him,
to bless the nations through his descendants:
To make them inherit (להנחילם) from sea to sea
and from the river to the ends of the earth.

(22) And also for Isaac he established a son (or: thus)
on account of Abraham his father.
The covenant of each First One He gave him:

(23) and blessing rested upon the head of Israel.
And He established him with a blessing (ויכוננהו בברכה) or:
He surnamed him with status of first-born (ויכנהו בבכורה),
And gave to him his inheritance (נחלתו).
Then He set him up as tribes as a division of twelve.

---

24   The reference to the "covenant of the Most High" in 24:23 is found in a passage memorably described by Skehan as "a descent into prose" on Ben Sira's part: see Skehan, Structures, 379.

Throughout the activities described in these verses, it is עליון who is the divine agent. It is the Most High whose commandments Abraham observed, and with whom Abraham came into covenant. Associated with the Most High here is also the covenant of circumcision. It is still the Most High – no other divine title intervenes – who makes Abraham's descendants inherit; incorporates Isaac into the grand scheme of the covenant; brings the blessing to Israel; and ensures the division of Israel into twelve tribes. And the Greek of these verses is very close to the Hebrew, reading as follows:

> (19) Abraham was a great father of a multitude of nations:
> and no blemish was found upon his reputation (*lit.*: glory).

> (20) It was he who observed the Law of the Most High (νόμον ὑψίστου)
> and came into (or: was in, ἐγένετο) covenant with Him.
> In his flesh He established the covenant:
> and in temptation he was found faithful.

> (21) Therefore He established for him with an oath
> that nations should be blessed in his descendants:
> to increase him like the dust of the earth,
> and to exalt his descendants like the stars;
> and to make them inherit from sea to sea,
> and from the river to the farthest part of the earth.

> (22) Also in Isaac He established likewise
> on account of Abraham his father
> the blessing of all men and the covenant.

> (23) He made it rest on the head of Jacob:
> He acknowledged him in his blessings (Syr.*: blessings of the Most High)
> and gave to him in inheritance;
> and divided his portions: in twelve tribes he allotted them.

Apart from the expansion of verse 21 in Greek to include material derived from Gen 13:26; 15:5; and 22:17, Hebrew and Greek agree together remarkably well.[25] Nonetheless, it will be noted that in v. 22 the Greek takes up the notion that the Most High established for Isaac, not a son, but a covenant like Abraham's; while in v. 23 it speaks of the Most High establishing Israel with the blessing, and does not represent the kind of notion found in the margin of MS B, that God surnamed Israel with 'firstbornship'. Nevertheless, there can be little doubt that both Hebrew and Greek versions surveyed here are very close to one another, and that they are particularly indebted to one key passage of Scripture, namely, Deut 32:8–9. The Masoretic Text represents this as follows:

---

25 For the details, see Wright, Difference, 155–56, 178–81, 296, n. 114; and Skehan – Di Lella, Wisdom, 504–5.

בהנחל עליון גוים   בהפרידו בני אדם
יצב גבלת עמים   למספר בני ישראל:
כי חלק יהוה עמו   יעקב חבל נחלתו:

We encounter in these verses, and in Hebrew Ben Sira, the ideas of inheritance expressed by root נחל (Deut 32:8, 9; Sir 44:21, 23); of apportionment featured in root חלק (Deut 32:9; Sir 44:23); and of fixing contained in root נצב (Deut 32:8; Sir 44:23). But Ben Sira has subtly altered the general thrust of Deut 32:8–9. Whereas the latter speaks of the Most High making גוים inherit, and dividing up the sons of Adam, Ben Sira talks of the Most High making *Israel* inherit, and dividing *them* according to their tribes. Furthermore, Ben Sira says all this in reference to covenant, of which Deut 32:8–9 is quite innocent. The גוים remain, even so: Ben Sira makes them an object of blessing, which naturally makes the thoughts of any attentive reader turn to Gen 12:3; 18:18; 22:18; 26:4 and other verses where Abraham and his children are associated with blessings for the nations. Therefore to Genesis we must turn; but not before we have gathered a further point from this Deuteronomic passage.

The verses quoted here, which refer to the Most High making nations inherit; dividing up humanity; and claiming Jacob as His own peculiar portion in the process, are set before us by the biblical writer as proof of an assertion made earlier by that same writer. Speaking to Israel, he has declared that YHWH is אביך הוא עשך ויכננך קנך, "your father who acquired (*or:* created) you: he made you and established you" (Deut 32:6). It is certainly significant that this notion of the Lord's establishing Israel, expressed by some form of the root כון, appears in the body of the text of MS B Ben Sira 44:23, to the effect that the Most High established Israel in blessing when He gave him his inheritance. In that verse, Ben Sira is talking of the Promised Land; and the thrust of his argument throughout the section 44:19–23 is that, by obeying the commandments of the Most High, עליון, Abraham was worthy to enter into covenant with that same Most High who, according to the book Deuteronomy, would allot to Israel her Land as an inheritance for the twelve tribes. To put the matter another way: the inheritance of the twelve tribes is allotted by the Most High, but depends in the first instance on Abraham's obedience to the Most High's commandments. How can this be? And why has Ben Sira expressed himself in such definite and distinctive language?

The answers to these questions begin with Deut 32:6. In that verse, the Lord, who will be directly spoken of as Most High in Deut 32:8, is called not only Israel's father, but her "acquirer" or "creator", Hebrew קנך, a description which cannot fail to recall Gen 14:18–22. In these verses, God is designated, for the very first time in the Hebrew Bible, אל עליון, God Most High, and is further defined as קנה שמים וארץ (Gen 14:19). Now it will be recalled that this part of Genesis describes how Abraham is met by Melchizedek, who is both king of Salem (probably identified as Jerusalem in Ben Sira's day) and priest of God Most High, "acquirer", "possessor", "creator" of heaven and earth. Famously and ambiguously, Gen 14:20 reports that "he gave to him tithe from everything", ויתן לו מעשר מכל. In the very next chapter of Genesis, we learn that God made a covenant with Abraham, promising to grant him the land from the river of Egypt to the great river, the river Euphrates (Gen 15:18). If I am not much mistaken, Ben Sira reasoned along the following lines. Observing the fact that God had made a covenant with Abraham at this particular point in the Scriptural story, he proceeded to ask: on what basis was this covenant made? What had Abraham done to merit such a privilege? The answers to these questions he found in the preceding ch. 14, which reports that Abraham was blessed by Melchizedek as priest of God Most High, and that he paid tithe. It is almost impossible to imagine Ben Sira interpreting his Hebrew Bible to mean that Melchizedek paid tithes to Abraham. As we know from his own writing, Most High is a divine title which Ben Sira associates with God's presence in the Temple in Jerusalem; and, again, the overwhelming probability exists that he understood the Salem of Gen 14:18 to refer to Jerusalem as well. In other words, he could envisage Abraham all those centuries before paying the tithe to the priest of God Most High in Jerusalem, more or less as a pious and God-fearing Jew like Ben Sira himself would do. Here, in all probability, we discover the rationale behind what he wrote in 44:20, that Abraham kept the commandments of the Most High *specifically*, inasmuch as he paid tithe to the priest of God Most High.[26] From Deut 32:6–9 he knew all about the Most High as one who allotted the Land by inheritance and blessing to Abraham's descendants. Consequently, he understood that Gen 15 immediately went on to tell how God rewarded Abraham for his obedience by entering into covenant with him, and that covenant was bound up with the gift of the Land. Thus the divine title עליון is integrated in Ben Sira's thought with covenant, divine commandments (and therefore the Torah), the blessing, and the Land as an inheritance.

So far, we have attempted to expose Ben Sira's inner reasoning behind his use of expressions involving the title Most High which, while not in themselves Scriptural, nonetheless have reasonably clear links with the Bible, and may legitimately be derived from it. But there are aspects of Ben Sira's reflection upon that divine designation which appear to minimize or to down-

---

26 There is a famous gap in the text of *Jub.* at 13:35, which may represent deliberate suppression of material by the scribes; and there is some reason to suppose that the original text told how Abraham had paid tithes to Melchizedek, according to Caquot, Le Livre, 257–64.

play Scriptural aspects of the title Most High. These must be addressed immediately. Thereafter, however, we must consider further "matters arising" out of this section just concluded, which will form the final part of this paper.

3. Ben Sira Downplays Aspects of the Title Most High in Hebrew Bible

We must now consider certain rather subtle differences between Ben Sira and the Hebrew Bible in their use of the expression Most High. As a beginning, we may remain with Gen 14:18–22 and its qualifications of God Most High as "possessor" or "creator" of heaven and earth. Modern research has demonstrated that the root קנה in biblical Hebrew may be understood in a number of ways, as "possess", "purchase", "acquire", or "create";[27] but as far as Gen 14:19 was concerned in antiquity, the participle קנה seems to have been taken to mean "creator". LXX translated it as such, speaking of Abraham as blessed τῷ θεῷ τῷ ὑψίστῳ ὃς ἔκτισεν τὸν οὐρανὸν καὶ τὴν γῆν; and the traditions lying behind the *Book of Jubilees* evidently share this opinion of the word.[28] It is now generally accepted that *Jubilees* received its final form sometime between 160 and 140 B.C.E. The traditions out of which it was composed, therefore, were almost certainly current in Ben Sira's day, only just a generation earlier than the publication of the book.[29] *Jubilees* frequently speaks of God Most High as creator (see, *e.g.*, 7:36; 12:19; 13:16; 20:9; 25:11); and especially illuminating for our purposes is *Jub.* 22:27, which alludes to themes discussed earlier in this essay. Here, Abraham is pictured as blessing Jacob with these words:

> God Most High (is) God of all, and Creator of all, who brought me out from
> Ur of the Chaldees so that he might give me this land to inherit it for ever
> and to raise up a holy seed so that the Most High may be blessed forever.[30]

Two points particularly deserve attention. First, God Most High is designated God of All with special reference to his creative role: this title occurs again at *Jub.* 22:10; 30:18; and 31:32. It had also been used by Ben Sira in both Heb. (MS B) and Gk. of 33/36:1/1a, but not at all in relation to the title God Most

---

27 For the various possible meanings and linguistic history of קנה, see Sarna, Genesis, 382; and Westermann, Genesis 12–36, 205–6.
28 See further Harl, La Bible, 161 (noting the link with Deut 4:32 which LXX forged in their translation of Gen 14:19), and p. 52, where LXX's use of κτίζω in both these verses is expounded.
29 For the composition and date of Jubilees, see Schürer, History 3/1, 312–14; Nickelsburg, Literature, 78–79; *idem*, Bible Rewritten, 101–3; VanderKam, Jubilees, 1030–31. See also Berger, Buch, 295–301.
30 Translated by Wintermute, Jubilees, 99.

High.[31] Secondly, neither Hebrew nor Greek witnesses of Ben Sira's work represent Most High as the subject of verbs of creation, forming, making, or fashioning. Never do these texts speak directly of עליון or ὕψιστος as "creator" or "maker". Nonetheless, Ben Sira does discuss creation and God's activity within it at some length;[32] but his mode of associating creation to the title Most High is tangential, not suggested by the Hebrew Bible. He prefers, it would seem, to speak of "the works of the Most High" if, indeed, he speaks at all of the Most High in the setting of creation. Thus the Masada MS of 43:2 talks of מעשי עליון in respect of the sun, the Greek at the corresponding point in the text reading ἔργον ὑψίστου (Latin: *excelsi*; Syriac: ܪܡܝܐ.ܕ). Heb. MS B, however, differs from the Masada MS at this point in reading "the works of the Lord," using the Tetragram; and the suspicion must arise that the scribe of the Masada document may have altered an original Tetragram into עליון for the sort of reverential reasons outlined by Professor Skehan. The Greek *may* give some support to the originality of the Masada reading; but doubt must inevitably remain. Likewise, the famous statement of 36/33:15 in the Greek that τὰ ἔργα τοῦ ὑψίστου are "two and two, one over against the other," is represented in fragmentary form by the Heb. of MS E where, however, stands written אל [   ]מ.

In fine, the single Hebrew witness to the expression "works of the Most High" may be the product of scribal piety; and the Gk. MSS can often represent a secondary level of understanding of what Ben Sira wrote. The possibility has to be faced that Ben Sira himself wrote a phrase like "the works of the Lord," and that his grandson (or the transmitters of the Greek translations) introduced "the works of the Most High" into the book precisely to ensure that there were indeed verses directly linking the Most High to the creative activity which, they would have believed, Scripture predicated of him at Gen 14:19. But then, *even if* we admit the originality of the phrase in Ben Sira's work, it seems clear that it was used with great restraint in both Hebrew and Greek traditions. Creation is evidently not the foremost idea that comes into the minds of Ben Sira and his tradents when they speak of God Most High. We shall presently suggest a possible reason for this state of affairs.

A similar reticence surrounds Ben Sira's mode of discourse when it comes to the divine title King and the designation Most High. The Psalter (Ps 47:3) is resoundingly clear that YHWH Most High is to be feared, and that He is a great king over all the earth. Only indirectly does Ben Sira associate Most High with the title king, and then only in the Hebrew of MS B. There,

---

31   See also Ben Sira 45:23 (MS B, but not represented in the Gk.) and Sirach 50:22 (where Heb. MS B has "the Lord, the God of Israel"). Skehan – Di Lella, Wisdom, 421, note similar expressions in Psalm 151:4 preserved in 11QPs[a] xxviii.7–8 which I have been unable to trace; and see Marböck, Weisheit, 150.

32   See Haspecker, Gottesfurcht, 150–55, 301–4; and Marböck, Weisheit, 134–54.

the Jerusalem Temple is called "the temple / palace of the King" at 50:2, 7, in a setting which makes it crystal clear that the One who is served in that Temple is עליון (50:14, 16, 17). In the Greek witnesses to this chapter, the title king is simply not found; and at 50:7 the translator has put "Most High" where Hebrew has "King". The Greek, however, seems to have no antipathy towards "king" as a title for God, and makes uses of it at 51:1. Rather, the Greek witnesses seem particularly concerned to emphasise that the God who is served in the Jerusalem Temple is very definitely the Most High, since the title is found no fewer than seven times (50:7, 14, 15, 16, 17, 19, 21). The fondness of the Greek for the title Most High in this chapter is not difficult to explain: the point is being emphasised that the Most High God, a divine title known to and used by pagans far and wide, and carrying with it notions of the supreme deity ruling over all other supernatural forces, is the God of the Jews who is worshipped in the Temple at Jerusalem.[33] Thus the worship of this God in one place has, like Wisdom herself who is resident in His temple, a universal significance.

4. Most High, Temple, and the Land of Israel

Most High, for both Hebrew and Greek forms of Ben Sira's work, is a divine title associated especially on the one hand with God's Law, covenant, commandments, and gift of land as an inheritance to his people in accordance with His promise to the patriarchs; and, on the other hand, with the invocation of God's Name in prayer, praise, confession, supplication, and with His service in the Temple in Jerusalem. The notion that God Most High might be the creator of the cosmos, if present at all, is expressed rarely and obliquely; this aspect of the title is apparently muted, perhaps so that other aspects of it explored here might stand out the more prominently. The most striking of these aspects is Ben Sira's sense of an intimate bond between God's presence in the Temple and the gift of the Land of Israel to the Patriarchs, in which עליון / ὕψιστος plays a determinative role, as we shall now discover. Discussion of this crucial matter is best begun with the commonplace observation that the Temple in Jerusalem was the only place where the Name of God might be pronounced aloud with its proper vocalization: this Temple is the palace of the King, the sanctuary where the Most High is worshipped, and where the blessing with YHWH's Name may be solemnly uttered by the divinely appointed priests (45:15; 50:20).

---

33   See Nock, Gild, 55–69; Harl, La Bible, 160–61; Parker, Hypsistos, 739. The title was regularly associated by pagans with the God of Israel in times later than Ben Sira's: see Mitchell, Anatolia vol. 2, 43–51.

As we know from the Psalter, the one whose Name is YHWH is indeed עליון (Ps 7:8; 47:3; 83:19); and Ben Sira had no hesitation in taking up the biblical datum that the Temple is a house for God's Name, a house for YHWH whose name is qualified as Most High. What he has to say about Solomon's construction of the Temple repays careful attention in Sir 47:13 MS B:

> Solomon ruled as king in days of tranquillity
> And God gave him rest from round about.
> It was he who established a house for His Name   הכין בית לשמו
> And fixed the sanctuary for eternity.   ויצב לעד מקדש

The Greek agrees closely with the Hebrew here, and will concern us later. For the moment, it will be helpful to note how Scriptural terms abound here, while being used in a way not attested in the Bible.[34] Once more, these provide us with clues to what Ben Sira had in mind. The Hebrew Bible indeed makes use of forms of the verb כון to speak of the establishing of the Temple; but never does it suggest that David or Solomon established the sanctuary *tout court*, by using the verb כון in the hiph'il or any other form with house or temple or sanctuary as its direct object. On the contrary, indeed, Exod 15:17 says of the sanctuary (מקדש) that the hands of the Lord established it [מקדש אדני כוננו ידיך], in a verse which represents this founding of the sanctuary as the climax of the Lord's action in bringing Israel to the mountain of His inheritance and planting the nation in the land. Indeed, this is the only verse in Scripture which speaks of anyone having "established" the Temple.[35] Only the Chronicler comes close to Ben Sira; but even he says merely that David and Solomon established certain things "for" or "in respect of" the Temple, using the form הכין followed by the prepositions ל or

---

34   For biblical texts which have most likely influenced Ben Sira's choice of vocabulary here, see further Skehan – Di Lella, Wisdom, 526–27.

35   It should also be noted that this verse speaks of the Lord's *inheritance*, and offers Scriptural proof, if such were needed, for Ben Sira's understanding that the Temple and the Land of Israel are related to one another in terms of the inheritance. Exod 15:17 according to MT reads: תבאמו ותטעמו בהר נחלתך מכון לשבתך פעלת יהוה מקדש אדני כוננו ידיך, and includes also the notion of the planting of Israel in her land, a theme which re-appears in Nathan's oracle to king David concerning the building of the sanctuary recorded in 2 Sam 7:10. According to the Chronicler (1 Chr 15:1, 3, 12), David had established or prepared (root כון being used in all these verses) a place for the Ark of the Covenant, which, of course, was not the Temple itself, but a special tent (1 Chr 15:1). For Ben Sira, there is little doubt that Wisdom, who is Torah, occupies the place of the Ark within the Temple's Holy of Holies: thus the sage's association of the Land of Israel as inheritance, the Temple, and the Torah who is Wisdom resident in the Temple, is strengthened by this further Scriptural support.

בּ.[36] Ben Sira seems to have no such inhibitions: Solomon established the house, the sanctuary which Exod 15:17 presents as an establishment of the Lord Himself.

Furthermore, Scripture never states that Solomon – or anyone else for that matter – "fixed the sanctuary for eternity." The verb נצב never appears in the Bible in connection with Solomon's temple. But this is a word which comes to the fore in the account of Jacob's famous dream at Beth-el, House of God, where he is granted a vision of a ladder "fixed" (מצב) on the earth with its top reaching to the heavens, where YHWH is seen as stationed (נצב) upon it (Gen 28:12–13), promising to Jacob the land on which he is lying as a gift to him and to his descendants (Gen 28:13). And, significantly, we learn later on in that same chapter that Jacob vowed to pay a tithe to God of all that God will give to him (Gen 28:22), should God maintain his promises. It will also be recalled that the great Temple Scroll from Qumran (11QTemp xxix.10) speaks frankly of a covenant which God made with Jacob at Bethel, thus indicating that tithe and covenant could, at any rate in principle, be linked together by other writers in Second Temple times more or less contemporaneous with Ben Sira.[37]

Returning to Ben Sira 44:19–23, we may observe how in those verses Abraham is said to have kept the commandments of the Most High (by paying the tithe), with momentous consequences. He entered into covenant with the Most High; his descendants are privileged to inherit (44:21) from sea to sea; and his grandson Jacob-Israel this same God Most High established with blessing (ויכוננהו בברכה) so as to give him his inheritance. The same Most High then fixed him (ויציבהו) as a people of twelve tribes. In such wise does Ben Sira forge links between God's granting of the Land to the Fathers and the building of the House for His Name by Solomon. It is the same Most High God who "fixed" Jacob in his inheritance, an action appropriate for one who is YHWH, "stationed" (נצב) at the top of the ladder which Jacob had seen "fixed" (מצב) on the earth at the House of God which is Beth-el.

---

36 See, *e.g.*, 1 Chr 22:14; 29:2, 3. The Chronicler does, however, insist that Solomon built the Temple in the very place which David had established for the Ark: see 2 Chr 3:1, noting that he began work on Mount Moriah אשר הכין במקום דויד, "at the place that David had established". See Japhet, Chronicles, 548. No doubt this verse could have played its part, too, in Ben Sira's thoughts about Solomon's actually having "established" the Temple.

37 See Yadin, Temple Scroll vol. 2, 129. The final form of the Scroll is probably best dated to the late second / early first century B.C.E., either late in the reign of John Hyrcanus I or early in that of Alexander Jannaeus: for a convenient digest of various scholarly views on the dating of the scroll, see Schiffman, Temple Scroll, 349–50. The tradition that God had made a covenant with Jacob at Bethel is also made explicit by the Aramaic Targumim PJ, FTP and FTV of Lev 26:42.

5. Concluding Remarks

While Ben Sira's employment of the divine title עליון and its Greek equivalent ὕψιστος is rooted in the Hebrew Bible's choice of this expression to speak of God in particular situations, and as a means of expressing different kinds of divine action and Israel's response to them, the sage was evidently an acute student of the biblical texts and was able to draw from them implications which he did not hesitate to express. Thus while many of the verses of his book which use Most High as a divine title remain within the confines of the biblical usage of that term, other verses bring the title into direct association with religious ideas and concerns which the Bible does not name in connection with it. The Most High appears alongside the Torah, the covenant, the commandments, and the inheritance of the Land by the fathers, while at the same time remaining a title, as it is in Scripture, for the God whose solemn service is observed day by day, year by year, in the Temple in Jerusalem, the Temple built by Jehoshua ben Jehozadaq, unhesitatingly described by Ben Sira in MS B 49:12 as "established for everlasting glory," המכונן לכבוד עולם (once more, the root כון making its appearance).

We have tried to show here the rationale for Ben Sira's understanding of the title Most High. He developed the range of meaning of this title beyond the surface limits for it set by biblical terminology. He achieved this by linking together four fundamental biblical texts, namely Deut 32:6–9; Gen 14:18–22; 15:18, and 28:12–13. These texts share some key vocabulary; and it seems that Ben Sira has drawn upon them to build up a picture of the Most High as the One who granted Israel her land in recognition of Abraham's having kept His commandments by paying tithes to Melchizedek, the priest of God Most High. This same Most High is the One worshipped in the Temple, which is the house for His Name established by Solomon, and then established and prepared for everlasting glory by Jehoshua ben Jehozadaq. It is the Temple of his own day, where Wisdom resides, serving the Lord in the holy tabernacle. From this Temple goes forth the instruction of Wisdom like the rivers of Paradise (24:23–29), to Gentiles as well as Jews; and from this Temple, which is the Temple of the Most High, goes forth blessing in the Name of the God whose Name is YHWH Most High, a blessing first for the Jews who are called by that honourable Name (Ben Sira 47:18 Heb. MS B), and also to the Gentiles, since, according to Ben Sira, the Most High who allotted to the Jewish Patriarchs the land of Israel also promised blessings to the Gentiles, blessings of עליון who is a great King over all the earth (Ps 47:3), blessings of ὕψιστος whom pagans would recognise as supreme ruler of the cosmos.

Bibliography

Baumgarten, J.M., "Some Notes on the Ben Sira Scroll from Masada," *JQR* 57 (1968) 323–27.

Beentjes, P.C., *The Book of Ben Sira in Hebrew: A Text Edition of All Extant Hebrew Manuscripts and A Synopsis of All Parallel Hebrew Ben Sira Texts* (VTSup 68; Leiden: Brill, 1997).

Berger, K., *Das Buch der Jubiläen: Jüdische Schriften aus hellenistisch-römischer Zeit* (vol. 2/3; Gütersloh: Mohn, 1981).

Caquot, A., "Le Livre des Jubilés, Melkisedeq et les dîmes," *JJS* 33 (1982) 257–64.

Charlesworth, J.H. (ed. et al.), *The Dead Sea Scrolls: Hebrew, Aramaic, and Greek Texts with English Translations*, vol. 1: Rule of the Community and Related Documents (Louisville: Knox, 1994).

Di Lella, A.A., "Wisdom of Ben-Sira," in *ABD* 6. 931–45.

Fang Che-Yong, M., "Usus nominis divini in Sirach," *VD* 42 (1964) 153–68.

Fitzmyer, J.A., *The Genesis Apocryphon of Qumran Cave 1: A Commentary,* (2d ed.; Rome: Pontifical Biblical Institute, 1971).

Fitzmyer, J.A., *Essays on the Semitic Background of the New Testament* (London: Chapman, 1971).

Gilbert, M., "The Book of Ben Sira: Implications for Jewish and Christian Traditions," in *Jewish Civilization in the Hellenistic-Roman Period* (ed. Sh. Talmon; JSPS 10; Sheffield: Academic Press, 1991) 81–91.

Harl, M., *La Bible d'Alexandrie. 1 La Genèse* (Paris: Cerf, 1994).

Harrington, D.J., "Sirach Research since 1965: Progress and Questions," in *Pursuing the Text: Studies in Honor of Ben Zion Wacholder on the Occasion of his Seventieth Birthday* (eds. J.C. Reeves and J. Kampen; JSOTSup 184; Sheffield: Academic Press, 1994) 164–70.

Haspecker, J., *Gottesfurcht bei Jesus Sirach. Ihre religiöse Struktur und ihre literarische und doktrinäre Bedeutung* (AnBib 30; Rome: Pontifical Biblical Institute, 1967).

Hayward, C.T.R., *The Jewish Temple: A Non-Biblical Sourcebook* (London / New York: Routledge, 1996).

Japhet, S., *I and II Chronicles* (OTL; London: SCM, 1993).

Knibb, M.A., *The Qumran Community* (Cambridge Commentaries on Writings of the Jewish and Christian World 200 BC to AD 200 2; Cambridge: Cambridge University Press, 1987).

Kugel, J.L., *Traditions of the Bible: A Guide to the Bible as it was at the Start of the Common Era* (Cambridge: Harvard University Press, 1998).

Leaney, A.R.C., *The Rule of Qumran and Its Meaning* (London: SCM, 1966).

Marböck, J., *Weisheit im Wandel. Untersuchungen zur Weisheitstheologie bei Ben Sira* (BBB 37; Bonn: Hanstein, 1971; repr. in BZAW 272; Berlin / New York: de Gruyter, 1999).

Mitchell, S., *Anatolia. Land, Men and Gods in Asia Minor* (2 vols.; Oxford: Clarendon Press, 1993).

Nickelsburg, G.W.E., "The Bible Rewritten and Expanded," in *Jewish Writings of the Second Temple Period* (ed. M. Stone; CRINT 2/2; Assen: van Gorcum, 1984), 89–156.

Nickelsburg, G.W.E., *Jewish Literature between the Bible and the Mishnah* (London: SCM, 1981).

Nock, A.D., "The Gild of Zeus Hypsistos," *HTR* 29 (1936) 55–69 (= repr. in *Arthur Darby Nock. Essays on Religion and the Ancient World* [ed. Z. Stewart; London: Oxford University Press, 1972] 414–43).

Parker, R.C.T., "Hypsistos," in *OCD* (3rd ed.) 739.

Puech, E. (ed.), *Qumrân Grotte 4. XVIII. Textes Hébreux (4Q521–528, 4Q576–579)* (DJD 25; Oxford: Clarendon Press, 1998).

Sarna, N., *The JPS Torah Commentary: Genesis* (Philadelphia: Jewish Publication Society, 5749/1989).

Schiffman, L.H., "Temple Scroll," in *ABD* 6. 348–50.

Schürer, E., *The History of the Jewish People in the Age of Jesus Christ (175 B.C. – A.D. 135)* (vol. 2; rev. and ed.; eds. G. Vermes, F. Millar, and M. Black; Edinburgh: Clark, 1979).

Schürer, E., *The History of the Jewish People in the Age of Jesus Christ* (vol. 3/1; rev. and ed.; eds. G. Vermes, F. Millar, and M. Goodman; Edinburgh: Clark, 1986).

Skehan, P.W., "The Divine Name at Qumran, in the Masada Scroll, and in the Septuagint," *BIOSCS* 13 (1980) 14–44.

Skehan, P.W., "Structures in Poems on Wisdom: Proverbs 8 and Sirach 24," *CBQ* 41 (1979) 365–79.

Skehan, P.W. – Di Lella, A.A., *The Wisdom of Ben Sira: A New Translation with Notes, Introduction and Commentary* (AB 39; New York: Doubleday, 1987).

Strugnell, J., "Notes and Queries on the Ben Sira Scroll from Masada," *Eretz-Israel* 9 (1969) 109–19.

VanderKam, J.C., "Jubilees, Book of," in *ABD* 3. 1030–32.

Vattioni, F., *Ecclesiastico: Testo ebraico con apparato critico e versioni greca, latina e siriaca* (Testi 1; Naples: Istituto Orientale di Napoli, 1968).

Westermann, C., *Genesis 12–36: A Commentary* (trans. J.J. Scullion; London: SPCK, 1985).

Wintermute, O.S., "Jubilees," in *The Old Testament Pseudepigrapha* (2d vol.; ed. J.H. Charlesworth; London: Darton, Longman and Todd, 1985) 35–142.

Wright, B.G., *No Small Difference: Sirach's Relationship to its Hebrew Parent Text* (SBLSCS 26; Atlanta: Scholars Press, 1989).

Yadin, Y., *The Temple Scroll* (3 vols.; Jerusalem: Israel Exploration Society, 1977–1983).

Ziegler, J., *Sapientia Iesu Filii Sirach* (Septuaginta. Vetus Testamentum Graecum auctoritate Societatis Litterarum Gottingensis editum XII/2; Göttingen: Vandenhoeck & Ruprecht, 1965).

Zobel, H.-J., "עליון, ᶜelyon," in *TDOT* 11. 121–39.

"With all your heart"
Praise in the Book of Ben Sira

Jan Liesen
Grootseminarie Rolduc, Kerkrade (NL)

0. Introduction

A cursory look at the literature about the book of Ben Sira suffices to show that praise is not considered a major topic at all. Praise certainly does not receive as much attention as topics like wisdom, fear of God, the Law, creation, history. Yet, it is surprising to see how often praise is mentioned in the concluding paragraphs and chapters of studies about the generally acknowledged main themes. Praise, therefore, somehow does seem to form an important aspect of the book of Ben Sira. It seems that instead of theorising much on praise, the Jerusalemite sage practised it throughout his long book. Vocabulary specifically denoting praise is not very frequent, but the book is permeated with hymns and prayers.[1] One of the reasons, in fact, that the book of Ben Sira is as long as it is, might be that Ben Sira lived up to the advice which he gives in 43:30: *"When you praise the Lord, exalt Him as much as you can."*

1. Status quaestionis

The topic of praise in the book of Ben Sira has not very often been studied directly, but there are a number of studies on the Psalms, which pay attention to the hymnic style and character of certain passages in Ben Sira, some of which are commonly identified as praise. These hymnic sections are studied as if they were psalms by comparing them with the book of Psalms.

The classical form-critical approach identifies literary genres in the Psalter and tries to determine a corresponding Sitz im Leben as an explanation for a particular psalm. Often the Temple and the cult, with all that they entail, are thought to be the environment in which hymns of praise and thanksgiving have their origin. At the time when Gunkel worked out this methodology with regard to the Psalms, it was applied to the Wisdom of Ben Sira by Walter Baumgartner (1914). He offered a classification of hymns and

---

1   Cf. Gilbert, La prière, 227–43.

hymnlike constructions, some of which he identified as praise.[2] Baumgartner, however, assumed that all literary genres fall into two irreducible categories: the lyrical (poetic) and non-lyrical (prosaic) genres. Although he admits (in view of sapiential psalms) that composing hymns is part of a wisdom teacher's activity, he believes that the teaching activity of a sage is the exact opposite of the hymnic activity of a poet. He concludes therefore that the hymnic passages in the book of Ben Sira do not go well together with his wisdom teaching.

This position is completely reversed by the diachronic approach of Ludin Jansen (1937) who detects a double intentionality in psalms that were composed towards the end of the formation of the canonical Psalter and afterwards.[3] On the one hand such late psalms are *prayers* which religiously and spiritually edify the readership and put them in a relationship with God, and on the other hand they are *lessons* in which a teacher, the psalmist, puts himself in relationship with them and conveys religious truths especially concerning the Law. Jansen detaches such late psalms from the cult; their Sitz im Leben is rather the *bet-midrash*, first mentioned by Ben Sira (51:23). He believes that the hymnic passages of Ben Sira are heavily influenced by such late psalms; e.g. he identifies Sir 51:1–12 as a psalm of thanksgiving by an individual, Sir 33/36:1/1a–36:19/13 as a psalm of lamentation by the community, Sir 42:15–43:33 as a hymn, Sir 39:12–35 and 16:24–18:14 as meditation psalms, and Sir 24 as a psalm of praise. He concludes that the redactor of the canonical Psalter must be nearly a contemporary of Ben Sira.

The aspect of a double intentionality in texts of praise returns in the studies of Claus Westermann (1954) who questioned the delimitations of some form-critical categories ('what constitutes a hymn?') and their cultic Sitz im Leben. He complements the form-critical approach with theological considerations.[4] He introduces a distinction between an 'informative' (berichtend) and a 'descriptive' (beschreibend) type of praise, the latter of which would have more cultic affinities, while the former would have its Sitz im Leben in personal experience.[5] The distinguishing characteristic of the descriptive type of praise is that it tries to capture the fullness of God's being with statements that vacillate between his majesty and his mercy.[6] One of the distinguishing characteristics of the informative type of praise is the fact that it can only take place within a community, i.e. in the presence of an audience.

---

2   Baumgartner, Gattungen, 161–98. He distinguished between "vollständige Hymnen" (Sir 24; 39:12–35; 42:15–43:33; 44–50) and "hymnischen Motiven" (Sir 1:1–10; 10:14–18; 16:18; 16:26–17:24; 17:29–30; 18:1–7); Sir 51:1–12 and 51:12a–o are songs of thanksgiving.
3   Jansen, Psalmendichtung.
4   Westermann, Loben (5th ed.; 1st ed. 1954).
5   Westermann, Loben, 18 (with reference to Gunkel).
6   Westermann, Loben, 100–1.

The theological point that Westermann makes is that the descriptive type of praise can only exist within the context of the informative type of praise.[7] In elaborating this model of understanding praise in the Old Testament he made only passing reference to the Wisdom of Ben Sira (esp. Sir 39 and 51), but Westermann's considerations, regarding the nature of what praise is, are pertinent not only to its hymnic parts but also to Ben Sira's book as a whole.

In his detailed study of fear of God in Sirach Josef Haspecker (1967) sees praise as one of the religious attitudes, together with gratitude, love and willingness to bring sacrifices, that are the proper response to God's greatness and goodness.[8] Haspecker finds a connection between the concept of God as creator and two possible human attitudes: either God is mentioned as creator in connection with "turning away one's heart" from him (3:16; 10:12; 38:15), or He is called creator in connection with "turning one's heart", in praise, towards him, which is the very purpose of the hymnic passages (16:26–17:10; 39:12–35; 42:15–43:33).

Several of the texts in Sirach that are considered hymns or songs of praise are studied in detail by Gian Luigi Prato (1975) in the context of the problem of theodicy (39:12–35; 42:15–43:33; 15:11–18:14). Prato comes to the conclusion that for Ben Sira the hymnic format is not a negligible external feature but the only adequate perspective for viewing the complexity of creation and for resolving its bipolarity, i.e. the tension between the 'scientific' objectivity of all created works and their theological value as revealing the Creator God.[9] Praise, then, becomes almost synonymous with the only true sapiential attitude.

In a short but very dense article on Sir 15:9–10 Johannes Marböck (1983) points out that according to Ben Sira praise is the most important God-given task of a sage.[10] The entire didactic function of the sage culminates in praise. This aspect of Ben Sira's teaching is something of a novelty and Marböck situates it in the sage's world view, according to which the whole creation is seen as tapering into praise. Humans have been endowed with heart and mouth and also with wisdom precisely in order to reveal and praise God's greatness in creation (Sir 17:6–10; 17:25–28). Creation (and history) is viewed as a kind of lesson from God (Sir 42:15d לְקֶחוֹ; cf. Sir 4:11)

---

7   Westermann, Loben, 101–2: "Hier scheint mir die Grenze der 'Objektivität' alles theologischen Redens zu liegen. Theologie, d.h. Reden von Gott, Aussagen über Gott kann es nur umfangen vom Loben Gottes geben".

8   Haspecker, Gottesfurcht, 295–309, esp. 302–3: "Dieser Schau des Schöpfers, in der sich Grösse und Güte vereinen, entsprechen die positiven religiösen Haltungen, zu denen Sirach auffordert: Lobpreis (17,10; 39,14ff.35; 43,30–33), Dank (32,13), Liebe (7,30; 47,8), freudiges und freigebiges Opfer (35,7–9)."

9   Prato, Il problema, 85, 206–7, 384.

10   Marböck, Sir 15,9f, 267–76.

to be studied by the sages and then to be passed on to their disciples, and this is done through praise (Sir 50:22–24).

In a recent study on the book of Ben Sira Michael Reitemeyer (2000) proposes the phenomenon of praise (Gotteslob) as a model for understanding the coherence and structure of the entire book, hence the title of his study: "Weisheitslehre als Gotteslob".[11] He distinguishes four "levels" in the book: the first level consists of wisdom poems, hymns, prayers and psalm-like texts and doxological elements. The second level consists of didactic discourses (addressed to an audience in second person singular or plural), connected to the first level by metaphors, catchwords and analogies. Theological reflection makes up the third level and the fourth level consists of the first-person passages. With the texts of the first level a network of keywords, metaphors and basic statements is constructed; on this level Reitemeyer situates the basic framework of the book as well as its doxological tenor.[12] This basic doxological tendency of the book he investigates particularly in two texts: Sir 14:20–15:10 and 39:12–35.

Reitemeyer understands Sir 14:20–15:10 as a psalm which is purposely reminiscent of the Psalter, esp. of Ps 1:2 (הָגָה) and Ps 145:21 (פֶּה – תְּהִלָּה). The human being in search of wisdom described in Sir 14:20–21 is a person who *prays (i.e. recites) the Psalter*.[13] The wise person described in Sir 15:9–10 is a human being who in harmony with creation and its sapiential order praises God reciting the Psalter.[14] From the parallel usage of certain expressions in Sir 15:10 and Ps 145:21 (and its context) Reitemeyer deduces that praise does not only describe the phenomenon of what happens between an

---

11 Reitemeyer, Weisheitslehre.

12 Reitemeyer, Weisheitslehre, 36–37, 90, 408–9. See esp. 37: "Diese Ebenen lassen sich niemals ganz streng auseinanderhalten. ... Es entsteht wohl ein Gerüst im Text."

13 A more fitting parallel for 14:20 / 15:10 would be Ps 49:4. The interpretation of הגה / μελετᾶν in 14:20a *as reciting the psalter* (cf. pp. 129–33, 139, 409) is unlikely because of the explicit complement in 14:20a (wisdom) and the parallel hemistich which focuses on reflection and the next verse which forms a chiasm with 14:20 and which employs verbs denoting *thought* rather than prayerful recitation, התבונן / ἐννοεῖσθαι (see also Sir 6:37ab; cf. Liesen, Full of Praise, 76, 118, 288). Interpreting the psalter as a "new torah" in which wisdom takes shape (p. 139) and situating Ben Sira in the vicinity of the redactors of the psalter (e.g. p. 409), is a circular argument that is not borne out by allusions to Ps 1 and other psalms (e.g. Ps 149 and Sir 39:12–35, cf. Liesen, Full of Praise, 138–39).

14 Reitemeyer, Weisheitslehre, 256: "Wer die neue Tora im Gotteslob des Psalters aufsagt, ahmt jede Situation nach, in der die Tora am Sinai offenbart wurde – macht dieses Geschehen in gewisser Weise 'reproduzierbar', bejaht also in der Tora die ihr zu Grund liegende Schöpfung und Gott. Das hat theologischen Grund darin, dass die am Sinai offenbarte Tora letztlich in der weisheitlichen Ordnung der Schöpfung gründet." Cf. also p. 257: "Wo das Gotteslob aufhört, hört auch das eigentlich* Leben auf" (quoted from Westermann, הלל, 498). – *Anm. d. Hg.: Zitat von Reitemeyer korrekt.

individual and God, but that it has at the same time a teaching and witnessing value. Praising a sage for his wisdom is therefore also praise of God, for in such a wise person God's plan for creation is visible. In Sir 18:27–29 Reitemeyer finds the connection between wisdom, a wise person and praise expressed in a nutshell.[15]

On the basis of Sir 39:12–35 Reitemeyer tries to demonstrate that for Ben Sira praise of God and teaching sapiential insights go inseparably together. He understands the sapiential hymn in particular, and the entire book of Ben Sira in general, as a conscious criticism of Qoheleth's sceptical position of a remote God who cannot be reached, not even in prayer. With the hymn of ch. 39 Ben Sira would want to demonstrate that God can be found in the study of the Torah. Study of the Law comes to full fruition when it enables a person to affirm the world as God's good creation[16] and when, at the same time, it leads a person to praise of God. According to Reitemeyer, the same idea is expressed in the final psalms of the Psalter (Pss 145; 146–150). The proper literary genre of this new kind of wisdom teaching is then the psalms, both the psalm of the canonical Psalter and the psalms composed by Ben Sira (Reitemeyer, 411–12). A person giving praise to God with these psalms becomes a revelation of God's wise order of creation, and praising such prayerful persons is therefore an indirect way of praising God.

From this status quaestionis a bipartite division becomes apparent: a number of studies about praise in Ben Sira are actually part of larger form-critical studies on the Psalms which mention and try to explain Ben Sira as a late example of a certain genre.[17] Baumgartner, Jansen and to some extent

---

15 Reitemeyer, Weisheitslehre, 265.

16 The fundamental problem in the logic of the thesis of the wisdom hymn ("The works of the Lord are all good" – 39:16, 33) appears to be overlooked. Elements which are explicitly meant for vengeance strike indiscriminately both the good and the wicked. This flaw in the reasoning derives from using the concept "work of God" with two different extensions, viz. as referring to God's activity "under the firmament" and as referring to all created elements. Cf. Liesen, Full of Praise, 257–61.

17 The form-critical method is not without problems. Without entering into a discussion about the nature of form criticism, two fundamental positions can be roughly outlined as follows. On the one hand, there is classical form criticism as defined by Gunkel and followed by most form critics down to the present. According to this position form criticism is essentially genre criticism; its basic assumption is that the essential forms of Israelite literature evolved at the stage of oral tradition, since oral tradition was only possible if certain schemata and forms of expression were adhered to. In later times these forms and schemata also conditioned literary composition, so that particular ideas would be expressed through particular literary genres in accordance with the author's intent. Genre therefore represents a particular Sitz im Leben and thereby explains a particular text. On the other hand, there is the position that the interpretation of esp. biblical poetry is not so much concerned with external aspects, such as genre, Sitz im Leben or pattern, but more with internal aspects, i.e. with what the author has done with a general form in a particular text. Careful attention to unique deviations from the

Westermann seem to work on the basis of the assumptions of the classical form-critical method and seek to clarify where Ben Sira fits into the spectrum of literary genres. The answer is, more or less, that Ben Sira utilises the same genres that are found in late canonical and extra-canonical psalms. Haspecker, Prato and Marböck approach the book without a pre-conceived literary form and seek to understand some major theme in the Book of Ben Sira and in the course of doing so they observe that Ben Sira often has recourse to hymnic forms. The reason given for this fact comes down to a theory that for Ben Sira praise is the only adequate mode of expression for speaking about God as He reveals himself in the sapiential order of creation and in the history of Israel. Reitemeyer has a bit of both positions: he takes over the form critical analysis of genres and identifies several psalms in the Wisdom of Ben Sira; on the basis of the similarities between these psalms and the framing psalms of the canonical Psalter he then completely redefines the Sitz im Leben (and meaning) of sapiential praise. He concludes that the kind of wisdom which Ben Sira inculcates in his disciples and readers is already praise.

Another striking conclusion from this status quaestionis is the fact that, while the phenomenon of praise is clearly important for the Book of Ben Sira, no definition or extension of it is given. Reitemeyer presents a lexicographic overview of the relevant terminology and this confirms the impression that praise is something which permeates the entire book.[18] In fact, however, there is no useful definition or delimitation in this overview, for it only labels the language of Ben Sira as doxological language and qualifies all his wisdom teaching as praise.[19]

In spite of this lack of a definition, there is a text which is commonly regarded as praise, and which is commented upon by nearly all interpreters, viz. Sir 39:12–35. In this paper this text will be examined anew in order to understand what praise is for Ben Sira and how it functions in his book.

2. Sir 39:12–35 as Praise of God

There is something curious about the fact that Sir 39:12–35 is commonly regarded as a hymn. While the central part of this text (Sir 39:16–31) is cer-

---

general form explains a particular text. Cf. the discussion by Weiss, Bible, 54–63, 410–16.

18   Reitemeyer, Weisheitslehre, 11–90. For Reitemeyer the terminology of praise is part of what he calls the first level of composition.

19   Reitemeyer, Weisheitslehre, 90: "Auch wenn nicht unbedingt direkt Gotteslob gemeint ist, so erweckt der häufige Gebrauch der entsprechenden Termini den Eindruck einer doxologischen Sprache!"; p. 414: "Es verwundert nicht, dass Sirach sein eigenes Buch, als ein einziges Gotteslob ... versteht ... ".

tainly not a hymn, but rather an *explanation* and an *argument* as to why God's work is good, Ben Sira clearly intends it to be understood as a *hymn*, a (model of) *praise*.[20] He explicitly invites his disciples and readership to praise God with this particular text (Sir 39:14c–15: "and thus say in thanksgiving"), and he concludes his reflexion by repeating the invitation to praise God's name with all one's heart (Sir 39:35). A first important conclusion about praise in Ben Sira, therefore, is that the literary format is not a decisive factor. Apparently, for Ben Sira praise can take the shape of a theodicy poem containing intricate argumentation concerning the goodness of God's work.

If not literary format, then what is the distinguishing characteristic of praise? In Sir 39 it has to be found in the frame of the theodicy poem: Sir 39:12–15, 32–35. It has often been remarked that these framing verses are no simple introduction and conclusion to Sir 39:16–31. Baumgartner classified 39:12–15 as an unhappy mixture of forms, but offered no explanation for the juxtaposition of what he calls an introduction to a mashal and an introduction to a hymn. Haspecker and Prato distinguish different compositional functions for the various elements that make up the framing verses (Haspecker: to organise all towards the central theme of fear of God; Prato: to mark an increase of Wisdom's activity through the sage). Reitemeyer calls Sir 39:12–15 a masterful intermezzo and a part of the 'doxological network' of the book[21] and sees it as a reminiscence of one of the tasks of the sage mentioned in the foregoing autobiographical passage about the wise scribe, viz. "giving thanks to the Lord in prayer" (Sir 39:6d).[22]

The fact is that the introduction and conclusion of the theodicy text have a *double function*: first, they serve as a frame for the text qualifying it as praise, and second, they establish a connection with other texts in the book, esp. with the so-called wisdom passages and first-person-singular passages.[23] These two functions are interconnected, but what interests us here is the first aspect: how do these verses qualify a treatise on the goodness of God's works as praise? Both 39:12–15 and 39:32–35 can be subdivided into three sections:

39:12	self-reference of Ben Sira	39:32	self-reference of Ben Sira
39:13–14b	address of the disciples	39:33–34	summary
39:14c–15	invitation to the disciples	39:35	invitation to the disciples

---

20 Liesen, Full of Praise, 30–39.
21 Reitemeyer, Weisheitslehre, 351: "... ein Meisterwerk thematischer und terminologischer Bündelung ..., die zum einen die Ebenen von Lob und Lehre sowie die des Autors und des Qahal integriert, zum anderen Kontakte zu Schlüsseltexten des Sirach herstellt ...". On how the intertextuality functions, cf. Liesen, Full of Praise, 131–39.
22 Ibidem, with reference to Marböck, Sir 38,24–39,11, 305.
23 A way to read these verses that does justice to the complexity would be to interpret them as a model of communication in which both the sage and the disciple, and even God, have a part to fulfil. Cf. Liesen, Full of Praise, 34–35, 95–97.

The section that *links* the theodicy passage to other texts in the book of Ben Sira is the address of the disciples in 39:13–14b. The vocative ὅσιοι and the images used here ("growing by a stream of water," "spreading fragrance," "blossoming") are all part of an extended wisdom metaphor which Ben Sira has developed as his didactic strategy in the book, esp. in Sir 24.[24] The section that *qualifies* the wisdom hymn *as praise* is the invitation: 39:14c–15 in the beginning and 39:35 in the end. These verses contain the highest concentration of words denoting praise in the entire book.[25] If both functions of the framing verses are covered in this way, where then do the two self-references of Ben Sira, 39:12, 32, fit in? Most commentators argue that these self-references also have a linking function, establishing a connection with other self-references, esp. 24:30–34 and 30/33:16/25–19/27 where the author speaks of his teaching that continued to expand beyond expectation. These references of the author to himself are then understood as clues about how the book came into being in a gradual way.[26] However, while it is very probable that there is a redactional history, it does not explain why Ben Sira thought it good or necessary to make *twice* an allusion to other autobiographical passages, especially considering the fact that the way in which he addresses the disciples already establishes a multiple link with other (wisdom) texts. My suggestion is that these self-references do not only serve to make a link to other texts, but primarily serve to qualify the wisdom poem on the goodness of God's work *as praise*.

A first indication for this interpretation comes from the curious construction of what is commonly called a frame. Just as the explicit invitations, which qualify the hymn as praise, occur *before and after* the theodicy text, so also the self-references come *before and after* this text. One could read that as a pair of inclusions[27], but such combined inclusion is interrupted by 39:33–34 which is not an inclusion. Given the fact that vv. 33–34 are a near literal repetition of key lines from the poem, it makes more sense to read the self-reference (39:32) and invitation to praise (39:35) that come *after* the wisdom poem also as a repetition. It stands to reason that what comes after the theodicy text, viz. 39:32–35, is a short but perfect repetition of *what* Ben Sira holds with regard to the goodness of God's work (vv. 33–34) and of *how* he wants his disciples to understand it (vv. 32, 35). In other words: 39:32–35 repeats in an abbreviated way 39:12–31. A closer look at both self-references brings out that they are indeed repetitions:

---

24   Liesen, Full of Praise, 130–36.
25   Reitemeyer, Weisheitslehre, 88, 350.
26   Cf. Marböck, Structure, 76–77.
27   I understand inclusion as a literary phenomenon whereby one or more elements at the beginning of a text turn up again at the end *of that same* text, thereby marking it as a literary unit.

A   39:12a   Ἔτι *διανοηθεὶς* <u>*ἐκδιηγήσομαι*</u>
    B   39:12b   καὶ ὡς διχομηνία *ἐπληρώθην*
    B*   39:32a   Διὰ τοῦτο ἐξ ἀρχῆς *ἐστηρίχθην*   על כן מראש התיצבתי
A*   39:32b   καὶ *διενοήθην* καὶ ἐν <u>*γραφῇ ἀφῆκα*</u>   והתבוננתי ובכתב הנחתי

Sir 39:12a and 32b both mention the intellectual effort of the sage with the
same verb, διανοεῖσθαι (הִתְבּוֹנֵן / ܐܬܒܝܢ), and the fact that he externalised it
(speaking / writing). Sir 39:12b and 32a both describe Ben Sira's inner state
of mind (full / convinced) and qualify it with a prepositional phrase that
denotes intensity (as the full moon / from the beginning).[28]

A juxtaposition of the summons to praise God also demonstrates that
Ben Sira repeats himself:

14c διάδοτε φωνὴν καὶ αἰνέσατε ᾆσμα
     <u>*εὐλογήσατε* κύριον</u> ἐπὶ πᾶσιν τοῖς ἔργοις αὐτοῦ
15   δότε *τῷ ὀνόματι* αὐτοῦ μεγαλωσύνην
     καὶ ἐξομολογήσασθε ἐν αἰνέσει αὐτοῦ
     ἐν ᾠδαῖς χελυῶν καὶ ἐν κινύραις   [בשי]רות נבל וכלי מינים
     καὶ οὕτως ἐρεῖτε ἐν ἐξομολογήσει   וכן תאמר בתרועה
35   καὶ νῦν ἐν πάσῃ καρδίᾳ καὶ στόματι ὑμνήσατε   מעֻתה בכל לב הרנינו
     καὶ <u>*εὐλογήσατε* τὸ ὄνομα κυρίου</u>   וברכו את שם הקדש

In vv. 14d, 15a Ben Sira mentions "blessing [the Lord]" and "name" and this
is repeated in v. 35b "blessing the name [of the Lord (Heb.: Holy One)]."
What is *not repeated* after the theodicy passage, is all the abundant vocabulary with which Ben Sira marked the wisdom poem as praise, viz. ᾆσμα /
hymn, αἴνεσις / praise, שִׁיר / ᾠδή / song, and תְּרוּעָה / ἐξομολόγησις / thanksgiving. Instead of these various types of praise Ben Sira only mentions the
general ὑμνεῖν / רָנַן with the qualification: "with all [your] heart (Gk.: + and
mouth)." Apparently, this qualification בְּכָל לֵב / ἐν πάσῃ καρδίᾳ suffices to
remind the disciples of the fact that the entire theodicy poem is to be understood as praise; or, in other words: "wholeheartedness" is characteristic of
praise, according to Ben Sira.

The second indication for understanding the self-references of Ben Sira
as markers of praise comes from the contents of both autobiographical statements. Ben Sira qualifies his sapiential activity with expressions of intensity:
"as the full moon" (39:12b) and "from the beginning" (39:32a). As far as
subject matter is concerned the wisdom poem is not praise but a rather
difficult argumentation about the goodness of God's work, yet apparently it

---

28   The reversal of the process of externalization (A) and the internal state of mind (B) in
     39:32 is not a kind of chiasm arching over the text as an inclusion, but is the logical
     consequence of the argumentative quality of a text that seeks to persuade: "*Therefore*, I
     was convinced …".

becomes a celebration, a form of praise, because of the intensity with which Ben Sira presents it. The argumentation of the theodicy may be flawed, and it actually is,[29] but the sage is completely *authentic* in his presentation of it: he is fully convinced of what he writes. Ben Sira can adequately summarise the entire argument in two verses in 39:33–34, but in order to achieve that it leads others to praise he refers to his own conviction "from the beginning" (39:32) and calls for a similar dedication "with one's his heart" on the part of his hearers (39:35).

There is another occurrence of "with all [one's] heart" in combination with praise which sheds more light on this expression, viz. in 47:8 in the praise of the glorious ancestors.[30] All the praiseworthy deeds of King David are characterised in 47:8 as having been accomplished with thanksgiving, giving glory, singing praise with all his heart and with devotion to his Maker. In fact, there are many points of similarity between the description of King David esp. in 47:8–10 and the way in which Ben Sira invites his disciples to praise in the frame of the theodicy text.[31] This congruence in words and phrases reveals something of a pattern. What Ben Sira recommends to his disciples in the frame of the theodicy text, viz. to praise God with all one's heart, is perfectly embodied by King David (except for 47:11a!). During the reign of David all Ben Sira's recommendations of 39:14c–15 were carried out, either by David himself or through his action.[32] When the disciples give praise to God with all their heart (39:35), they resemble David (47:8ac), and therefore, following Ben Sira's recommendations, they too will attain glory. In praising God with the wisdom hymn which Ben Sira composed for them the disciples can picture themselves among the ancestors to whom God granted wisdom (43:33 and 44:1). In short: praising God with all one's heart is praiseworthy and helps one to become wise.

3. Proper Praise

There is yet another way in which the self-references in 39:12, 32 qualify the wisdom poem as praise, and that becomes clear in the light of Sir 15:9–10. Here Ben Sira declares that praise is only proper for a wise person (חָכָם) and

---

29 Liesen, *Full of Praise*, 260.
30 The other occurrence of ἐν ὅλῃ καρδίᾳ in Sir 7:27 is left out of consideration, since it is missing in Hebrew (MS A).
31 Liesen, *Full of Praise*, 136–37.
32 Ben Sira was well aware that not David but Solomon had built the temple (47:13; the temple is significantly called בֵּית לִשְׁמוֹ, cf. 39:15a, 35b), but he attributed the splendour (הֲדָר) of the feasts to David and credited him with giving music an important place in the cult.

that such proper praise is granted by God. The self-references in 39:12, 32 hark back to the immediate context of the wisdom hymn which is a long diptych in which several trades and crafts are compared for the way in which they lead to wisdom. In the second half of this diptych it is the wise scribe who attains wisdom and who is able to bring others to wisdom. The diptych is structured by references about the heart: it is typical of the various craftsmen that they all set their heart on their handiwork (38:26a, 27e, 28g, 30c: διδόναι καρδίαν / where extant: שִׂית לֵב לְ־) and that they are careful about their products (lit. wakeful: ἀγρυπνία / שְׁקִידָה). By contrast, it is typical for the scribe to set his heart on rising early in the morning in a diligent search for God: τὴν καρδίαν αὐτοῦ ἐπιδώσει ὀρθρίσαι / πρὸς κύριον τὸν ποιήσαντα αὐτὸν (39:5ab).[33] In fact, Gk. 39:5b is probably a gloss: it is missing in Syr., and it also disrupts the otherwise regular strophic arrangement, and it is not required by the syntax.[34] Nevertheless, this gloss clearly brings out that the most typical trait of a wise scribe is his total dedication and orientation towards God. The epithet of God in this gloss, "his Maker", also enforces the typification of the scribe because it is reminiscent of the description of David in Sir 47:8cd: he praised God wholeheartedly and loved his Maker.[35] The point of the passage about the wise scribe is that it is autobiographical. When the self-references speak of the intensity with which Ben Sira reflected upon the theodicy poem and how convinced he is of what he wrote, he is actually saying that he is this wise scribe, this wise person (חָכָם), whose heart is wholly set on God. In combination with Sir 15:9–10, it means that his praise is fitting praise, properly uttered in wisdom.

Sir 15:9–10 forms the conclusion to another diptych: 14:20–15:10.[36] The first half of it, 14:20–27, is about a disciple's relationship with personified Wisdom, a relationship which is characterised by endurance on the part of the disciple and intimacy on the part of Wisdom. The second half of the diptych speaks of a God-fearing person and his relationship with Wisdom (15:1–6) and also of his opposite (15:7–8), i.e. the fool and the sinner. Sir 15:9–10 is both formally and content-wise united to the diptych as its conclusion. Sir 15:9 affirms the inappropriateness of praise in the mouth of a רָשָׁע / ἁμαρτωλός, who corresponds to the stupid and proud persons of 15:7–8 who

---

33 Marböck, Sir 38,24–39,11, 293–316.
34 Textcritical evidence shows that some mss have πρὸς κύριον in 39:5a as an object for ὀρθρίζειν, cf. Ziegler, Sapientia, 306. The ὀρθρίσαι – even when undoubtedly focused on God – can do without object in Greek, cf. 32:14 (= Gk. 35:14).
35 Haspecker, Gottesfurcht, 302, already noted a connection between the concept of God as creator and "turning away one's heart" from him (3:16; 10:12; 38:15), or "turning one's heart," in praise, towards him.
36 Haspecker, Gottesfurcht, 140–41; Marböck, Sir 15,9f, 267–76; Prato, Il problema, 381–85.

do not even get to see Wisdom.[37] By contrast, however, praise is fitting in the mouth of a חָכָם, who corresponds to the God-fearing, Law-respecting person of 15:1–6, and such a person is able to instruct (יְלַמְּדֶנָּה) others, in the same way as Wisdom herself instructs, 4:11a (לִמְּדָה). In the reference to himself and in the invitation to praise of 39:12–15 Ben Sira demonstrates that he sees himself as such a חָכָם (cf. 15:10 בְּפֶה חָכָם תֵּאָמֵר with 39:15d כֵּן תֹּאמְרוּ) and that he considers the wisdom instruction of 39:16–31 as a song of praise from which his disciples can learn. At the same time 39:15 recalls for the disciples that their praise of God is only fitting, and only leads them to wisdom, if their life, like that of Ben Sira, corresponds to what they profess, and that means, according to the autobiographical passage about the scribe: respect for and adherence to the Law (38:34cd). Proper wholehearted praise requires a certain wise disposition, otherwise it is not fitting. When summoning his audience to praise Ben Sira inserts some self-references in order to propose a strict parallelism between the disciples and himself, who is a חָכָם. When it comes to praise, the disciples are invited to think of themselves in the light of their wisdom teacher, a person devoted to God.

4. Humble Disposition of the Heart

Contrary perhaps to modern sensibility, the fact that the self-references of 39:12, 32 are very frank does not mean that Ben Sira is not humble. On the contrary, he is humble and he even understands humility as a condition for praising God. This applies both to Ben Sira's self-understanding and to his idea of how wisdom disciples should be. In the autobiographical diptych one of the activities of the wise scribe is his ability to test good and bad among people (39:4d).[38] This highly personal activity provides an opening for Ben Sira to mention what underlies this ability and what is the real characteristic of the ideal scribe, i.e. of himself. The scribe's competence in testing good and bad among people is based on a personal and sustained choice for God (39:5a). Such a dedication and orientation towards God always implies being tested by God. According to the pattern laid out in Sir 2, which is a programmatic chapter,[39] a person who has made a choice for God (cf. 2:1a: *if you come to serve the Lord*) and cleaves to Him (cf. 2:3), will be tested by God

---

37   Sir 15:9 resonates with the invitation of Wisdom in 24:19–22 which culminates in stating that "working with Wisdom" is mutually exclusive with "sinning" (ἁμαρτάνειν).

38   The curious slip into the past tense, ἐπείρασεν, betrays the autobiographical nature of the portrait of the סוֹפֵר.

39   Calduch-Benages, En el crisol, 274.

(cf. 2:1b),[40] and will be(come) aware of his own sins (cf. 2:11, 18) and will seek forgiveness (cf. 2:7, 11, 18). This is precisely what the wise scribe (read: Ben Sira) does: aware of good and bad in himself he *supplicates* before the Most High God and prays for forgiveness (39:5de). The use of δεῖσθαι elsewhere shows that Ben Sira understands supplication as *humbling oneself*, as making oneself dependent on another person (30/33:30/22): parallel with ἐμβλέπειν εἰς χεῖρας; cf. Ps 123:2!). Likewise the use of προσευχή elsewhere demonstrates that Ben Sira understands it as *humbling oneself* (31/34:31/26), but at the same time Ben Sira knows that the prayers of the humble come before the ὕψιστος (cf. 32/35:21/17–18).

Humbling oneself before God is a topic that Ben Sira expatiates on in Sir 3:17–31 and in the process of elaborating it he speaks of humility as a *disposition of the heart*.[41] According to 3:18–20 a wisdom disciple is to *humble* himself with regard to God (3:18: נַפְשֶׁךָ מְעַט מַעֵט / ταπείνου σεαυτόν); and to the *humble* (3:20: לַעֲנָוִים / πραέσιν) God will reveal his plan. In Sir 3:26–27 Ben Sira warns against a "proud heart" (לֵב כָּבֵד), which piles sin upon sin, instead of seeking forgiveness. In 3:28 he evaluates the situation of a scornful or proud person (לֵץ / ὑπερήφανος)[42] as hopeless, without possibility of healing. In 3:29 then Ben Sira presents the disposition of heart that corresponds to humility and that will enable the disciples to attain wisdom. It is only the לֵב חָכָם (καρδία συνετοῦ)[43] which understands the sayings of the wise. Applied to the invitation to praise God wholeheartedly (39:35) and in combination with the admonition that proper praise befits only the wise (15:9–10) it means that according to Ben Sira praise should be done in humility, in acknowledgement of God's greatness and of one's own need for forgiveness.

---

40 See also 37:27: a test of the self is what Ben Sira warns the Wisdom disciple to prepare for, and such a testing leads to discernment of (good and) bad.

41 Cf. the admonitions of 1:28–30, which are enclasped by sayings about the deceitful heart / mind; the exclamations about timid hearts in 2:12–13; and especially the instructions about the heart in 2:2, 17 which constitute an inclusion for the teaching of Sir 2.

42 A proud-hearted person (3:28: לֵץ / ὑπερήφανος; cf. 11:30: לֵב גֵּאֶה / καρδία ὑπερηφάνου) is someone who turns good into evil (11:31). He is the opposite of a wise person, cf. 35/32:18 which opposes אִישׁ חָכָם ⟺ לֵץ. Wisdom is far from such a person (15:8a) and also the disciple must be careful with him (8:11), and avoid him, in order not to learn from him and become like him (13:1b).

43 For 3:29 we follow MS A; Gk. reads for 3:29b: "and the ear of the hearer is the desire of the wise man" [ἀκροατής can also mean "disciple, pupil", and in a technical sense "reader"]. In MS A the two hemistichs give better parallels, and Gk. can be understood as being derived from it: Gk. misunderstood the adjective חָכָם for a person, and consequently adapted 3:29b.

5. Conclusion

The fact that praise is at the same time somehow present on every page of
Ben Sira's book and yet remains elusive, is well demonstrated in Sir 51:1–12,
which is commonly recognised as a hymn of thanksgiving. In this personal
prayer Ben Sira explicitly thanks and praises God for his deliverance: 51:1,
11, 12. The subject matter of this prayer, however, seems to have little to do
with giving thanks or praise: it is rather a long list of hardships that Ben Sira
overcame with God's help. Westermann has drawn attention to the fact that
like many languages Biblical Hebrew has no root to express gratitude. הוֹדָה
which is usually translated as "to thank" is never used in the Bible to express
gratitude between two human beings.[44] When in the Old Testament gratitude
between persons is meant, the verb בֵּרֵךְ, to bless, is used. When gratitude
towards God is at stake, the counterpart of "please" is not "I thank you", but
"I praise you". Westermann explains this situation by the extension that the
verb "to praise" has: it is so vivid and has so wide a meaning that it includes
gratitude. Biblical praise is not in the first place an inner feeling towards God,
as modern man would understand gratitude as something within himself, but
it is an externalisation towards God of this feeling. Praise is essentially an answer to what God has done and it takes the shape of doing something back,
viz. enumerating what He has done. In biblical praise God is always the
grammatical subject (either in 2nd or 3rd person), not the person who is
grateful towards God. Instead of saying "thank you, God" biblical authors
exhaust themselves in descriptions of what God has done, and precisely that
is praise.[45]

For Ben Sira, too, praise is external, active, as in 39:15d: "Say thus";
praise is something that you do. Praise in Ben Sira is an externalisation, it is
an answer to God, and in order for it to be a valid answer that rings true, it
has to be uttered wholeheartedly and with a humble heart, i.e. a certain way
of life should correspond to it. Praise is, therefore, also an inner attitude and
in this Ben Sira shows himself to be a late representative of the biblical tradition. For Ben Sira praise is practically equivalent to true wisdom (cf. 19:20–
22) and he thinks it can be learned from a wise and sensible person (cf.
19:29), like himself.

---

44 Westermann, Loben, 20–24.
45 A similar situation occurs with the verb אָהַב, "to love". The Song of Songs is all about
    the love of two persons; it takes the literary form of a dialogue but neither one ever
    says "I love you"; instead both he and she go to great lengths in describing the lovable
    qualities of the other, and therein they demonstrate their love (for this observation I
    thank Joachim Becker).

Bibliography

Baumgartner, W., "Die literarischen Gattungen in der Weisheit des Jesus Sirach," *ZAW* 34 (1914) 161–98.

Calduch-Benages, N., *En el crisol de la prueba. Estudio exegético de Sir 2,1–18* (ABE 32; Estella: Verbo Divino, 1997).

Gilbert, M., "La prière des sages d'Israel," in *L'expérience de la prière dans les grandes religions. Actes du Colloque de Louvain-La-Neuve et Liège (22–23 Novembre 1978)* (eds. H. Limet and J. Ries; Homo Religiosus 5; Louvain-la-Neuve: Centre d'Histoire des Religions, 1980) 227–43.

Haspecker, J., *Gottesfurcht bei Jesus Sirach. Ihre religiöse Struktur und ihre literarische und doktrinäre Bedeutung* (AnBib 30; Rome: Pontifical Biblical Institute, 1967).

Jansen, H.L., *Die spätjüdische Psalmendichtung, ihr Entstehungskreis und ihr "Sitz im Leben". Eine literaturgeschichtlich-soziologische Untersuchung* (Skrifter utgitt av det Norske Videnskaps-Akademi i Oslo: 2, Historisk-Filosofisk Klasse 3; Oslo: Dybwad, 1937).

Liesen, J., *Full of Praise. An Exegetical Study of Sir 39:12–35* (JSJSup 64; Leiden: Brill, 2000).

Marböck, J., "Sir 15,9f. – Ansätze zu einer Theologie des Gotteslobes bei Jesus Sirach", in מקור חיים Meqor hajjim (FS G. Molin; ed. I. Seybold; Graz: Akademische Druck- u. Verlagsanstalt, 1983) 267–76.

Marböck, J., "Sir 38,24–39,11: Der schriftgelehrte Weise. Ein Beitrag zu Gestalt und Werk Ben Siras," in *La sagesse dans l'Ancien Testament* (2d ed.; ed. M. Gilbert; BETL 51; Leuven: Peeters, 1993), 293–316, 421–23.

Marböck, J., "Structure and Redaction History of the Book of Ben Sira. Review and Prospects," in *The Book of Ben Sira in Modern Research. Proceedings of the First International Ben Sira Conference 28–31 July 1996, Soesterberg, Netherlands* (ed. P.C. Beentjes; BZAW 255; Berlin / New York: de Gruyter, 1997) 61–79.

Prato, G.L., *Il problema della teodicea in Ben Sira. Composizione dei contrari e richiamo alle origini* (AnBib 65; Rome: Pontifical Biblical Institute, 1975).

Reitemeyer, M., *Weisheitslehre als Gotteslob. Psalmentheologie im Buch Jesus Sirach* (BBB 127; Berlin: Philo, 2000).

Weiss, M., *The Bible from Within. The Method of Total Interpretation* (Jerusalem: Magnes, 1984).

Westermann, C., *Das Loben Gottes in den Psalmen* (5th ed.; Göttingen: Vandenhoeck & Ruprecht, 1977).

Westermann, C., "הלל *hll* loben," *THAT* 1. 493–502.

Ziegler, J., *Sapientia Iesu Filii Sirach* (Septuaginta. Vetus Testamentum Graecum auctoritate Academiae Scientiarum Gottingensis editum, XII/2; 2d ed; Göttingen: Vandenhoeck & Ruprecht, 1980).

God and Men in Israel's History:

God and Idol Worship in *Praise of the Fathers* (Sir 44–50)

Teresa R. Brown
Church Divinity School of the Pacific, Berkeley, California

In *Praise of the Fathers*, Ben Sira uses the history of Israel to demonstrate that God is the creator, sustainer, and most importantly, the ultimate judge and arbiter of the nation's conduct. This reprise of the nation's history was not compiled to review or preserve the events of the past, but as a teaching tool for Ben Sira's own time. Writing as a sage in Jerusalem in the late Second Temple period, Ben Sira uses the stories of Israel's famous past heroes to admonish his contemporaries to learn from the nation's past failures. At a time when the Jews in Jerusalem were in danger of abandoning their covenant with God and following the practices of Hellenism, Ben Sira urged them to be faithful to the Law and not seek wisdom in foreign places. Evidence of these warnings is found throughout the book of Sirach,[1] but it is heavily concentrated in *Praise of the Fathers*.

In chapters 44–50, Ben Sira compares and contrasts the good men of Israel with the sinners, idol-worshippers and fools who disregarded the Law and brought God's punishment on the people. Ultimately, the message of *Praise of the Fathers* is that Israel must be faithful to the commandments, and in particular to the first commandment. Exclusive worship of Yahweh posed a continuing problem for Israel, even though, as history demonstrates, when Israel worshipped idols, God's punishment was severe.

Even though the message of *Praise of the Fathers* was mentioned earlier in the text: "Consider the ancient generations and see: who ever trusted in the Lord and was put to shame?" (2:10), it is easy to miss Ben Sira's comparison of the "good guys and the bad guys" in Israel's history. After all, the poem begins with the statement: "I will now praise the men of *hesed*, our fathers in their generations." There is no apparent ambivalence in this opening, no hint that it will be anything but a hymn of praise, and there is effusive praise for many of the men in this poem. However, there are also descriptions of men and their actions that could never be mistaken for praise. Despite this, almost no scholars have commented on the condemnations in this poem.

It is odd that Ben Sira begins this poem with the statement that he will praise men of Israel, and then condemns many of those about whom he writes. In this paper I argue that the literary style Ben Sira uses effectively in

---

1   For example, 3:22–24; 11:29–34; 12:10–18; 13:13, 15–20; 16:1–4; 35/32:20–24; 37:12; 41:8–9; 42:2.

Praise of the Fathers is antithetical parallelism that juxtaposes opposites. This literary technique is based upon a pedagogy that reinforces positive behavior by emphasizing the negative results of the opposite behavior. It is a common practice in wisdom literature, particularly in Proverbs.

> A wise son makes his father glad; but a foolish son is a grief to his mother (10:1)
> The slack hand impoverishes; but the diligent enriches (10:4)
> Blessings are for the head of the just; but a rod for the back of a fool (10:6)

While synonymous parallelism may be more common in Sirach, antithetical parallelism is also found:

> A wise man makes himself popular by few words, but fools pour forth their blandishments in vain (20:13)
> The fool steps boldly into a house, while the well-bred man remains outside (21:22)
> Fools thoughts are in their mouths, wise men's words are in their hearts (21:26)

Since *Praise of the Fathers* is not just about the genuine heroes of Israel, I suggest that in this poem Ben Sira uses the sinners, idol-worshippers and fools of the past to contrast their behaviour against those who kept the Law. This contrast serves as a literary device to further enhance the virtue of the men of *hesed.*

There are two examples of Ben Sira's contrasting good and bad behavior in the mention of a single individual. For example, Ben Sira praises David's defeat of Goliath (47:4), his victories against the Philistines (47:7), and his respect for the proper worship of God (47:8). Ben Sira credits David with setting the calendar for the annual feasts (47:10), writing the psalms (47:8), and arranging for the Temple singers to honor God (47:9). However, David's faults are not ignored; Ben Sira notes: "The Lord took away his sins, and exalted his power forever" (47:11). David is a sinner – undoubtedly a reference to his plan to have Uriah the Hittite murdered in battle – but God forgives David's sins.

Solomon is also the recipient of both praise and condemnation. Ben Sira extols Solomon's world-renowned wisdom (47:14) as the author of wisdom texts (47:17), his skills as a ruler (47:13a, b and 16), and his erecting of the Temple in Jerusalem (47:13c, d). But he also blames Solomon for the division of the kingdom and the eventual exile of the people by both the Assyrians and the Babylonians (47:20–22). The specific reason Ben Sira gives for Solomon's failing is that he allowed his many foreign wives to bring their idols with them when they came to Israel (47:19, 20). Furthermore, as the Deuteronomist relates, Solomon built altars for these gods, and in his old age, he himself was an idol-worshipper at the altars of these foreign gods (1 Kgs 11:4–8), breaking the first of the commandments God gave to Moses at Sinai. Solomon is, on the one hand, praised by Ben Sira for building the Temple where God is present to the nation and where the people worship, and, on the other hand, reviled as the one who turns away from the worship of one God.

Of other men Ben Sira condemns in this poem, there is no balance of texts offering praise. For example, Solomon was succeeded by his son, of whom Ben Sira says:

> Solomon rested with his fathers and left behind him one of his sons,
> Ample in folly and lacking in understanding,
> Rehoboam, whose policy caused the people to revolt. (47:23a–c)

There is no way these words could ever be construed as praise, or Rehoboam considered a man of *hesed*. This description of Rehoboam also contains a second antithesis for Solomon: the man, legendary for his wisdom, fathered a son who is described as a fool who lacks understanding. Despite Rehoboam's lack of ability to lead the people, however, Ben Sira places the actual blame for the division of Israel on Solomon for his idol worship.

Next mentioned is Jeroboam who "caused Israel to sin and gave to Ephraim a sinful way" (47:23e). Israel and Ephraim are specific references to the northern kingdom and the Baal worship at local sanctuaries that began under Jeroboam is depicted in the Books of Kings. It was for their sin of idol worship that the north was led into exile (Sir 48:15). The text specifically says "the people did not repent" (48:15a), which appears to indicate the blame was placed on the entire nation. However, Israel's king was given the responsibility of being the spiritual as well as the political leader of the nation. According to Deuteronomy, the king was to have a copy of the law that he was to read throughout his life in order to keep the commandments faithfully (Deut 17:14–20). Idol worship was dependent upon the king's allowing altars or shrines to be erected in the country.

What about Judah? In a brief text that serves as the introduction to the passage about Hezekiah, Ben Sira states that even though Judah continued to be ruled by Davidic kings, not all of them were faithful to Yahweh and idol worship occurred in the south as well as the north (48:15e–16). The two southern kings who receive special mention and praise from Ben Sira are Hezekiah and Josiah. Although the biblical text (2 Kgs 18–20) praises Hezekiah first for his faithfulness to God, particularly for removing the vestiges of idol worship, as well as for his military and political accomplishments (also 2 Chr 29–32), Ben Sira is strangely silent regarding Hezekiah's contributions to the reformation of cultic practices and emphasis on keeping faithful to the Law, despite the fact Hezekiah made extensive liturgical reforms (2 Chr 29–31), besides Hezekiah's destruction of the sites dedicated to idol worship.

Instead, Ben Sira chooses to praise Hezekiah for preventing the destruction of Jerusalem in spite of the Assyrian siege (48:17–21). In saving Jerusalem, Hezekiah preserved the Temple where the nation worshipped God. Additionally, the picture of Hezekiah as an ideal king is enhanced by the mention of the close relationship between Hezekiah and the prophet Isaiah (48:20c, d). Unlike the northern kings who ignored the warnings of Elijah and Elisha (48:1–14), Hezekiah followed the direction of Isaiah. Finally, Hezekiah "did what was pleasing to the Lord and held to the ways of David his father" (48:22). This positive reference to David's kingship is further indication that David had attained a reputation for piety in Ben Sira's time.

Hezekiah was followed by two kings who allowed idol worship, Manasseh and Amon (2 Kgs 21:2–9, 19–22). This meant the nation was once again ready for reform when Josiah took the throne. Ben Sira praises Josiah who "inherited our apostasy, put an end to Baal worship, his heart was completely given to God. In the time of wickedness he procured *hesed*" (49:2–3). While this praise is lavish, it is also very generalized. For instance, Ben Sira makes no specific mention of the discovery of the scroll that led to Josiah's reforms (2 Kgs 22:8–11).

Next, Ben Sira's attention turns from individuals to the southern kings as a group: "Except for David, Hezekiah and Josiah, all of them were corrupt. The kings of Judah abandoned the torah of the Most High to the end. He gave their power to others; their glory to a godless foreign nation" (49:4–5). Like the mention of David's piety in the text on Hezekiah, here Ben Sira again makes it clear that even though David has sinned, he is one of the three good kings of Judah. This parallels the Deuteronomist's opinion: "Asa did what was right in the sight of the Lord, as his father David had done" (1 Kgs 15:11). My conclusion is that there is a difference between the sin Ben Sira accuses David of, and the sins of the other kings. God forgave David's sins of adultery with Bathsheba and the conspiracy to murder Uriah the Hittite. What is most important in this poem is that David never engaged in idol worship, the sin Ben Sira considers the most serious in the nation's history.

Ben Sira's is actually stricter in designating who was a good king; his list of the kings worthy of praise is smaller than the biblical text will allow. Both Asa (2 Chr 14:2) and his son, Jehoshaphat (1 Kgs 22:43; 2 Chr 17:3–6) are called good kings. Perhaps Ben Sira did not also praise Asa and Jehoshaphat because the biblical narrative says they were not able to wipe out all idol worship in spite of their efforts (1 Kgs 15:14; 22:44; 2 Chr 15:17; 20:33). While the Deuteronomist and Chronicler were willing to ignore these transgressions of Asa and Jehoshaphat, Ben Sira was not as generous.

Even though Ben Sira does not mention the names of all the kings he considered wicked, the saying that only David, Hezekiah and Josiah were good guys means all the other kings, those from Judah as well as Israel, were corrupt. They abandoned the Law, and although specific details are not mentioned, it seems clear that the sin Ben Sira considered most significant was idol worship.

There is another, more cryptic, reference to sinners or bad guys in this poem praising the men of *hesed*. This is the text about the judges in 46:11–12.

> The judges, each by his name,
> Everyone who did not worship false gods
> And did not turn away from God,
> May his memory be blessed!
> May their bones receive fresh life from their final resting place
> And their names, being made new,
> Take on a new splendor in their sons.[2]

Is it Ben Sira's intention in this text to praise all the judges, or are we to use the criteria in the passage to determine which judges are being praised? I suggest that because Ben Sira spells out what makes a judge praiseworthy, and some of the judges do not meet the criteria, the reader is challenged to name the good judges.[3] These literary characteristics are commonly found in riddles, and I would like to treat Sir 46:11–12 as a riddle. The source of information about the judges is in the biblical text.

Riddles are classified as a form of wisdom writing because they depend on hidden clues that arc only available to those who are in the know and recognize the hidden meaning cleverly disguised in common language.[4] Riddles also have a pedagogic role. They allow the teacher to test the student's ability to analyze data, not merely memorize details. The riddles in the Samson story in Judges are well-known examples of the literary form.[5]

If this is a riddle, the clues are that the judges who are deserving of praise are those who did not turn from Yahweh to worship idols, and those who are survived by a large number of descendants.[6] Looking at the biblical text, it is easy to eliminate many of the men whose stories are told there, be-

---

2   Translation is that of the paper's author.

3   Other scholars have noted some of the judges do not merit the praise of this text. Snaith, Ecclesiasticus, 230, says Gideon and Samson must be excluded; the former because he made an idol, and the latter because he rebelled against God. Petraglio, Il libro, 186–90, uses the evidence of the biblical text to say Abimelech, Jephthah and Samson were not men of esteem. Skehan – Di Lella, Wisdom, 520, suggest that these verses about the judges should be read as hyperbole, rather than literal praise.

4   Crenshaw, Samson, 99–111.

5   Samson asks a riddle (Judg 14:14) and the Philistine's answer is also given in the form of a riddle (Judg 14:18). Samson's responses to Delilah's questions about the source of his strength may also be a riddle. I believe that Jotham's fable (Judg 9:7–21) is another riddle.

6   The judges I considered for this comparison are Gideon, Jephthah and Samson. Ehud (Judg 3:12–30) is never referred to as a judge. Deborah (Judg 4:1–5:31) is a woman, and it is clear from his choice of characters in Israel's history that Ben Sira intended to mention only males. Barak is referred to as a judge in some manuscripts of 1 Sam 12:11 and the author of Hebrews 11, but is not given that title in the book of Judges, so he is not considered here.

cause without this ability to compare the two texts, the reader would have to assume Ben Sira intends to praise all the judges.

Starting with the criterion of idol worship, the literary structure of Judges is based on a cycle of repeating events: when Israel is obedient to Torah, all goes well; then Israel begins to worship the gods of the Canaanite neighbors; God punishes Israel with an enemy nation that overpowers and enslaves Israel; Israel suffers under the foreign power; Israel cries out to Yahweh for help and repents; God raises up a judge to lead the Israelites against the foreign nation, restore proper worship and preside over the nation for a period of peace before the cycle starts over again. Considering this repeating cycle, it is not unexpected to find evidence of idol worship in Judges, and the biblical text indicates that Gideon, Jephthah and Samson have ties to idol worship, and thus cannot meet one of the criteria for praise.

The second criterion is a man who had many descendants. Gideon's sons were all killed under violent circumstances, except Jotham who fled to the mountains to escape the same fate. We know that Jephthah had only one child, his only daughter, who he killed to fulfill a foolish vow. In spite of the many, foreign, women, in Samson's story, there is no indication he ever fathered any children. These three major judges cannot meet either criterion required for them to be praised.

There are other, lesser-known, judges from Israel's history, and there are some interesting things to note about the descendants of some of these minor judges (Judg 10:1–5; 12:8–15). Following Abimelech's death, Tola judged the nation for 23 years. Next came Jair of Gilead who judged for 22 years. He had 30 sons who rode on 30 donkeys and had 30 towns. Presumably those towns were filled with his descendants. Following Jephthah, Ibzan judged for seven years. He had 30 sons and 30 daughters who married outside their clan and made alliances for their father who brought in 30 brides for his sons. After Ibzan, Elon judged for 10 years. He was followed by Abdon who ruled for eight years and had 40 sons and 30 grandsons who rode on 70 donkeys. Abdon's prosperity extended beyond his progeny even to his livestock! Even though most people would not recognize the names of these judges, they are a sharp contrast to the major judges who were heirless.

Additional antithetical texts in this poem deal with men who were involved in the liturgical life of the nation. Many of the men who whom Ben Sira praises are lauded for their liturgical duties in the Temple. In addition to the liturgical contributions of David and Solomon, and the reforms of Hezekiah and Josiah, Ben Sira produced the lengthy praise of Aaron (45:6–22) that emphasizes the role of the priests in worship, and is reinforced in the depiction of the high priest Simon in chapter 50. These men and their faithfulness to the proper worship of God are the antithesis of idol worship that brought about the downfall of the kingdom and the exile. Ben Sira uses it as a warning to his contemporaries not to let this happen again.

What I hope to have documented is that in this so-called poem of praise to the men of *hesed* there are numerous references to men who were sinners, idol-worshippers and fools. The distinguishing factor between the "good guys and bad guys" is idol worship. It is only those men who supported the monotheism of Israel that Ben Sira considered praiseworthy. In his own context, Ben Sira was hardly unaware that Jerusalem contained not only the Temple of Yahweh, but altars where the Greek pantheon was worshipped. He saw the presence of these foreign altars as being as dangerous to the Jews as Baal worship had been in the time of Jeroboam. Using a history of Israel based on its heroes as a polemic against idol worship is in character with the task of a sage. Ben Sira's choice to put both the good guys and bad guys in *Praise of the Fathers* displays a creative literary side to his genius.

Bibliography

Crenshaw, J.L., *Samson, a Secret Betrayed, a Vow Ignored* (Atlanta: Knox Press, 1978).

Petraglio, R., *Il libro che contamina le mani. Ben Sirac rilegge il libro e la storia d'Israele* (Theologia 4; Palermo: Augustinus, 1993).

Skehan P.W. – Di Lella, A.A., *The Wisdom of Ben Sira: A New Translation with Notes, Introduction and Commentary* (AB 39; New York: Doubleday, 1987).

Snaith, J.G., *Ecclesiasticus or the Wisdom of Jesus, Son of Sirach* (CBC; Cambridge: University Press, 1974).

Two Approaches: Simon the High Priest and YHWH God of Israel / God of All in Sirach 50

Otto Mulder
Almelo, Netherlands

From his portrayal of Simon, it is abundantly clear that to an appreciable degree Ben Sira personally identifies with him as a contemporary and kindred spirit, particularly in opposing inner divisiveness arising from differences in the interpretation of the Torah and other forms of revelation, as well as in the appraisal of the Temple and of the priestly ordinances related to calendars and festivals. Both men aimed at the consolidation of the Temple, which Ben Sira describes by depicting the glory of Simon, surrounded by a crown of priests, arranging the ordinances in service of the sacrifice. He summarises the interaction between Simon and YHWH in the voice of the hymn, in the light of great value, in the blessing and in the doxology. The Greek version of this text exhibits remarkable differences[1].

1. Methodology in the Inquiry into Ben Sira

The inquiry into the Praise of the Fathers in the book of Ben Sira (Jesus Sirach) has been carried out for the most part on the basis of text compilations based on the Greek version and in recognition of the fact that Ben Sira has been greatly influenced by Hellenism.

Based on two distinct approaches, I have opted for an independent and separate analysis of the Hebrew and Greek texts employing a variety of methods and combining the insights of literary analysis with classic historical-critical exegesis. The starting point of my study concerning Simon in Sirach 50 is the Hebrew version in MS B. The Greek version is understood to be an independent adaptation by the grandson of Ben Sira dating from the year 132 BC.

From the perspective of textual criticism, the importance of the manuscript MS B – which dates from the early Middle Ages – has been confirmed by new photographic material obtained of this manuscript from the Cairo Geniza discovered by Schechter in 1896.

---

1   Mulder, Simon. New bromide photographs of pages T-S 16–314 recto / verso and T-S 16.315 recto are printed on p. 80, 82, 84. An English translation of my dissertation will be published in 2002 in the Supplements to the Journal for the Study of Judaism.

In Sir 50:21b for instance the first word of this colon is illegible. Schechter's proposed reading העם כלו *the people all of them* cannot be discerned in the facsimile or the photo. In all probability, ספר discerns an א in the facsimile of the second word of this colon leading him to read אל, which occurs as the divine name 61 times in the book of Ben Sira.[2] Upon closer inspection, the vague contours of [...]ר[...]מ would appear to be present. For this reason I propose the following reading of 21b: מברכי אל מפניו. This rare verbal form מבֹרְכֵי, a *pu'al* participle 3. per. pl. in status const. of ברך, can be found in Num 22:6; Ps 37:22; 1 Chr 17:27. Evidence for this solution is based on the idiom of Ben Sira. A nominal form in combination with אל is frequent in Sirach. In 42:17 one finds קדושי אל *the holy ones of God* a parallel employing a participle with the same form as מברכי אל. 50:21ab in translation: *And once again they fall down, a second time [the blessed of God] before his face.* This reading *[the blessed of God] before his face* is comparable with Gk.

2. Sirach 50 and the Structure of the Praise of the Fathers

Sirach 50 is the concluding segment of the Praise of the Fathers. Interpretations thereof vary considerably. Gilbert considers 50 and 51 to be later additions.[3] Skehan – Di Lella propose a subdivision into parts I (1–23), II (24–43), III (44:1–50:24) together with a conclusion (50:25–28/29) and the appendix 51.[4] Jüngling focuses attention on the *"Ich-Passagen des Autors"* (16:24–25; 24:30–34; 30/33:25/16–27/19; 39:12; 42:15 and 44:1). He insists on the unity of 39:12–50:22(26) and the disengagement of 50:27–29 (51:1–30) as epilogue.[5] Schrader is inclined to see the book as the work of a disciple who posthumously compiled available fragments and added the conclusion in 50:27–29.[6] Marböck leaves the question of multiple redactions and editions open together with the question of Ben Sira's own involvement in the compilation of his work in various stages from 35/32:14 onwards. He is correct, however, in wondering why this arrangement could not have been the work of Ben Sira himself.[7]

---

2   ספר, 63.
3   Gilbert, Wisdom Literature, 283–324.
4   Skehan – Di Lella, Wisdom.
5   Jüngling, Bauplan, 89–105.
6   Schrader, Leiden, 69.
7   Marböck, Structure, 61–79.

Ben Sira structures this historical narrative by adding demarcation texts which he inserts at the beginning and at the end of each segment. He avails himself of various literary forms. In Sirach 44–50 a structural ordering of the text is visible in the annotations that provide the framework for the three parts in which the history of Israel is being related after the introduction 44:1–15:

Part I: from Enoch to Phinehas (44:16–45:25d) with an exhortatory blessing (45:25e–26c)
Part II: from Joshua to Solomon (46:1–47:21b) with a confirmation of the promise (47:22a–f)
Part III: from Solomon to Nehemiah (47:23–49:13) with an announcement of judgment (48:15a–16b), a concluding retrospective (49:4a–6b), followed by an evocation (49:14a–16b), which refers back to the origin in Adam (49:14–16).

All this ends in 50:1–28 with climactic reference to Simon, the High Priest. In exalted terms Ben Sira sings the praises of Simon (50:1–24) and concludes with autobiographical forms: an invective "Scheltrede" and an epilogue in which he reveals his identity by name (50:25–28).

The structure of Sirach 50 can be summarised in eight literary units:

1. Sir 50:1–4   Simon as builder,
2. Sir 50:5–10   Simon as High Priest,
3. Sir 50:11–14   Simon officiating at the sacrifice,
4. Sir 50:16–19   Simon at the feast,
5. Sir 50:20–21   Simon and the High Priestly blessing,
6. Sir 50:22–24   Doxology,
7. Sir 50:25–26   Ben Sira's *Invective,*
8. Sir 50:27–28/9   Ben Sira's epilogue and blessing.

In light of the evidently well-planned and harmonious lay-out of the Praise of the Fathers, it seems reasonable to assume that Ben Sira was an independent author who portrayed the history of Israel in his own manner. His purpose is evident in the demarcation texts which serve as a guide for his representation of history in a reworking of the traditions surrounding the personalities involved, particularly with respect to Simon. It also seems reasonable to consider 50:1–28 as Ben Sira's most personal contribution.

3. Divine Names in the Praise of the Fathers of All Time

In this structural composition, divine names in Greek differ substantially and numerically from Hebrew. The use of divine names in both versions of Sir 50:1–28 (Gk. 29) can be summarised as follows:

50:1–10:	in	7a:		Gk.	ὕψιστος
50:11–15:	in	13b:	Heb.	ייי	Gk. κύριος
		14b:	Heb.	עליון	Gk. ὕψιστος παντοκράτωρ
		15d:		Gk.	ὕψιστος παμβασιλεύς
50:16–19:	in	16d:	Heb.	עליון	Gk. ὕψιστος
		17c:	Heb.	עליון	Gk. κύριος
		17d:	Heb.	קדוש ישראל	Gk. παντοκράτωρ θεός ὕψιστος
		19a:		Gk.	κύριος ὕψιστος
		19b:	Heb.	רחום	Gk. ἐλεήμων
		19c:		Gk.	κόσμος κυρίου
50:20–21:	in	20c:	Heb.	ייי	Gk. κύριος
		20d:	Heb.	ייי	Gk. ἐν ὀνόματι αὐτοῦ
		21b:	Heb.	אל	Gk. ὕψιστος
50:22–24:	in	22a:	Heb.	ייי אלהי ישראל	Gk. ὁ θεός πάντων
50:25–29:	in	28a:	Heb.	ייי	Gk.
		29b:		Gk.	κύριος
		29d:		Gk.	κύριος

The difference bctween the Hebrew and the Greek versions is noteworthy in Sir 50:11–24: Simon officiating at the sacrifice, at the feast, in the blessing and in the doxology.

4. Simon the High Priest in Relation to God

4.1 Remarks on 50:11–15: Simon in Function of the Sacrifice

In 50:11–14 Simon ascends in his garment of honour and in his vestment of glory towards the elevated altar. In this function, he bestows splendour on the whole temple, on the walled enclosure of the sanctuary (11d). He presides at the order of the sacrifice (12b). He takes the portions from the hands of his brothers מיד אחיו, in Gk. ἐκ χειρῶν ἱερέων *priests* (12a). They surround him as a crown of sons עטרת בנים, in Gk. στέφανος ἀδελφῶν *a crown of brothers* (12c), as seedlings of the cedars in Lebanon, as willows from the river bank, all the sons of Aaron כל בני אהרן, in Gk. πάντες υἱοὶ Ααρων *all the sons of Aaron* (13a), before the whole assembly of Israel כל קהל ישראל, in Gk. πάσης ἐκκλησίας Ισραηλ *the whole assembly of Israel* (13c). His service at the altar is thus complete.

With respect to the portrayal of Simon among all the sons of Aaron and the whole assembly of Israel in 50:11–14, the difference between Heb. and Gk. is very small.

The four cola inserted in Gk. 50:15a–d disrupt the harmony of the literary structure of 3x7 lines in 50:5–19. The characterisation of the names of God ὑψίστου παντοκράτορος (14b) and ὑψίστῳ παμβασιλεῖ (15d) evolves into a more transcendental definition, such as παντοκράτορι θεῷ ὑψίστῳ (17d) and κυρίου ὑψίστου (19a).

4.2 Remarks on 50:16–19: Simon at the Feast

Characteristic here is the reproduction of the liturgy in the temple with the trumpets, the mighty flourish, the remembrance, the worship, the song, the light and the prayer, all of which would appear to be pointing to the feast of Rosh Hashanah.

In 50:16a one group בני אהרן הכהנים *the sons of Aaron, the priests* blow on the trumpets. In Gk., however, only υἱοὶ Ααρων *the sons of Aaron* do so. By blowing and sounding a mighty flourish, the priests summon the remembrance of the Most High.

The verb זכר leads beyond the feast of Yom Kippur and ultimately to the rejection of the O'Fearghail's solution which speaks of the "Daily Whole-Offering"[8]. On the contrary, זכר points to *a day of remembrance with the flourishing trumpets*, which is explicitly referred to in the Temple Scroll שבתון זכרון תרועה מ... *a day of sabbath rest, a day of remembrance with the flourishing trumpets* (11Q19 column XXV.3).

This day can be identified with the first day of the seventh month (Ezek 45:18), which can be further associated with the beginning of the New Year (Ezek 40:1), בראש השנה at *Rosh Hashanah*. In the synagogue, this day is called: "The Day of Remembrance" or "The Day of the Sound of the Trumpet". We will argue, therefore, that the day in question is the "Sitz im Leben" of Simon and, moreover, of the entire Praise of the Fathers, which was probably written with this specific purpose in mind. The use of the verbs in 50:1–21 tends to suggest that Ben Sira wrote his book during Simon's lifetime.

In his description of Simon at the feast, Ben Sira draws attention away from the priests in 50:16a–d and towards the people of Israel in 50:17a–19b. He draws attention in his figurative itinerary to the exceptional designation כל בשר יחדו *all the people together*, in Gk. πᾶς ὁ λαὸς κοινῇ (17a). This word combination is rare in Tenak and can be found elsewhere only in Job 34:15 and Isa 40:5. Ben Sira clearly employs כל to present a vast and inclusive perspective on God's universalism which includes all humanity without exception. There is an apparent boundary within the sanctuary between the exterior forecourt where everyone is welcome and the interior forecourt

---

8   O'Fearghail, Sir 50:5–21, 301–6.

which is restricted to those who belong to the people of Israel. The expression כל בשׂר יחדו enjoys a significant association with the content of the notion היחד *ha-yahad* found in the literature of Qumran[9]. The attitude of honour and respect for YHWH points to the ultimate aim of the entire sacrificial event during the feast: the remembrance of that which is essential for all human persons who live in his light.

The worship of the Most High and the Holy One of Israel has its focus in this remembrance. Everything is brought together for everyone in the presence of God. This is apparent from the characteristic use of the word כל, which is repeated 5 times in 4 word combinations:

13a	כל בני אהרן	all the sons of Aaron	Gk. πάντες υἱοὶ Ααρων
13c	כל קהל ישׂראל	the whole assembly of Israel	Gk. ἔναντι πάσης ἐκκλησίας Ισραηλ
17a	כל בשׂר יחדו	all the people together	Gk. πᾶς ὁ λαὸς κοινῇ
19a	כל עם הארץ	all the people of the land	Gk. ὁ λαὸς
20b	כל קהל ישׂראל	the entire congregation of Israel	Gk. ἐπὶ πᾶσαν ἐκκλησίαν υἱῶν Ισραηλ

All together! Simon included! The target group in Gk. 50:20b is more limited: υἱῶν Ισραηλ. This combination is lacking in the Septuagint. Ben Sira's grandson lived in the year 132 BC in a context in which the formation of groups was more accentuated. This is apparent, for example, in his reference to two distinct groups of Samaritans (50:26ab).

On the day of remembrance all people together are actively involved in the event of worship in which the remembrance itself is realised. The flourish of the trumpets signals the actual presence of עליון *the Most High* (17c)[10], קדושׁ ישׂראל *the Holy One of Israel* (17d)[11].

In the history of exegesis, Gk. has tended to be determinative of the theological understanding of Ben Sira's book of wisdom. Emphasis is firmly

---

9   Stegemann, Qumran Essenes, 83–166. "The new organizational term created by the Teacher (of Righteousness) for his unification of all Israel as far as he could reach it was *ha-yahad* (in and after the intersacerdotium). This was a new term, inaugurated neither from the past nor from the hellenistic term *to koinon*, which mainly designated local societies, or single communities. The Teacher's term *ha yahad* basically had other connotations: *Ha-yahad* meant a confederation of all existing Jewish groups, their union in a new religious body, which had never existed before. The *yahad* should represent all Israel. At that time, *ha qahal* was understood to designate mainly cultic assemblies, not an organizational body. The term *ha-am* would automatically include every Jew by birth." Stegemann's final conclusion is that the Essenes were indeed the main Jewish Union of the late Second Temple times (p. 155).

10   Kraus, Psalmen. "Der Universalismus in der Theologie der alttestamentlichen Psalmen ist nicht das Spätprodukt eines religiösen Entwicklungsprozesses innerhalb der Geschichte Israels, sondern vielmehr ein im Typos der Verehrung des 'höchsten Gottes' bereits vorgegebenes Element der kanaanäischen Welt" (p. 197).

11   Fang Che-Yong, Usus, 153–68. In Gk. "Deus Israel apparet Deus universalis."

placed on God's all-inclusive power in Gk. 17d: προσκυνῆσαι τῷ κυρίῳ αὐτῶν παντοκράτορι θεῷ ὑψίστῳ *to worship their Lord, the Almighty God, the Most High.* In addition, a striking emendation is implemented in Gk. 50:19a: the people ὁ λαὸς besought the Lord, the Most High κυρίου ὑψίστου.

The divine name in the introduction to the doxology in Gk. 50:22a is even more at variance with Heb.: Καὶ νῦν εὐλογήσατε τὸν θεὸν πάντων *And now bless the God of all.*

The theological vision of God clearly takes on a more universal and transcendent character,[12] one which is more at home in an all-inclusive theology in which YHWH becomes the God of all people and all things, the Most High and the Almighty, who is all and governs all (17d).

In the vision of God in Heb. 50:18ab two terms are employed קוֹלוֹ and נֵרוֹ which, while accentuating the immanence of עֶלְיוֹן and קְדוֹשׁ יִשְׂרָאֵל, also raise a number of questions. The word combination נתן קוֹלוֹ *he raises his voice* (18a) is common in prophetic speech and in songs of thanksgiving after battle (2 Sam 22:14; Joel 2:11; 4:16; Amos 1:2; 3:4; Hab 3:10 and Ps 18:14) and is similar to the expression *he let his voice be heard* (Isa 30:30; 42:2 and Ezek 19:9). In these contexts, however, YHWH is usually the acting subject.

In the Praise of the Fathers this expression of the presence of YHWH is regular. YHWH lets his voice be heard to Moses on Sinai (45:5a). He is present in the temple in the sound of the golden bells worn by the High Priest as a remembrance for his people (45:9de). The voice of YHWH is heard from heaven in the mighty thunder (46:17b). Given the semantic background of קוֹלוֹ, therefore, the customary interpretation of 50:18a based on Gk. with the choral song of the Levites should be lightly emended. From the perspective of syntax, therefore, הַשִּׁיר can be interpreted as an internal object accusative[13] which is qualified by the act. In translation: *and He raises his voice in the song.*

The history of exegesis exhibits even more variety with respect to 50:18b. Ryssel considers נֵרוֹ *his light* to refer to the lights on the west side of the temple square. In column IX of the *Temple Scroll*, the priests take care of the lamps according to the regulations (Lev 24:4). Hayward initially favours the Menorah but later rejects this idea on the basis of *Tamid.*[14] Smend ultimately argues: "Der Fehler יַעֲרִיכוּ hat aber auch das sinnlose נֵרוֹ herbeigeführt."

---

12 Hengel, Judentum, 544.
13 Joüon, Grammar, 451.
14 Hayward, Jewish Temple. He translates "they set in order His lamp" (p. 43) and comments: "If the Hebrew represents what Ben Sira wrote, he has either reported the details of the ritual out of order, or the half-verse itself is misplaced in the present text; but it must be admitted that the Hebrew may be corrupt, and that the Greek version should be preferred." (p. 59). See also Smend, Weisheit, 488.

In spite of the variety of interpretations, it should be noted that the facsimile as well as the photograph are totally clear with respect to the reading נרו. Any emendation, therefore, must be judged far fetched and arbitrary, as is evident from the interpretation in Gk. 50:18 with the Levites: καὶ ἤνεσαν οἱ ψαλτῳδοὶ ἐν φωναῖς αὐτῶν ἐν πλείστῳ ἤχῳ ἐγλυκάνθη μέλος *and the singers joined in harmony, the song resounded with the most melodious echoes*. In Gk. 50:19c the word κόσμος requires explanation. While it commonly means *order, world and universe*,[15] the present context suggests the contrary *hymn of praise*.

Semantic analysis reveals that 50:18–19 constitutes a continuation of the discourse. As in 18a, it is possible that the Most High is the subject here and that נרו with suffix 3. per. sg. refers to *his light*. The noun המון may refer to the assembled crowd (17a, 19a). The verb ערך, is used in מערכות *the regulations* (12b, 14a) and in the *hiph'il* 3. per. pl. *to contrast, assess*. The frequent occurrence of this verb in Leviticus 27 is striking. It refers in this instance to the assessment which took place in the temple on a daily basis and had a significant role to play with respect to merchandise, livestock, marriage and divorce. 'Arak. 9.1 ordains that the assessment for the New Year festival should be done with rejoicing (Lev 25:15).

"All the people together" (17a) is the subject of העריכו (3. per. pl.). As High Priest, Simon is included as part of כל בשר יחדו in the remembrance and in the high estimation of the light of YHWH. The text returns once again to the individual in the prayer (בתפלה) before the face of רחום *the Merciful One*. This name for God is unique in the Praise of the Fathers. In Tenak, however, this divine name occurs with striking frequency in summaries of Israel's history.[16]

4.3 Remarks on Sir 50:20–21: Simon and the High-Priestly Blessing

The connection with the preceding verses (50:16–19) is immediately apparent from the structure. Simon thus forms the primary link. The second link is to be found in the more detailed specification of the subject in 21 with respect to כל בשר יחדו *all the people together* in 17ab. A third link is established by the divine names עליון and קדוש ישראל together with the twofold mention of ייי.

---

15   Hayward, Jewish Temple, supposes that the translator, like the original author, relates Tamid to the stability and order of the universe (κόσμος), the sacrifice in the Temple serving to establish to perfection God's order for the world (p. 79).

16   In Tenak: Exod 34:6; Deut 4:31; Pss 78:38; 86:15; 103:8; 111:4; 112:4 and 145:8; Joel 2:13; Jonah 4:2; Neh 9:17, 31; 2 Chr 30:9.

The concord between Simon and ייי is most striking in 20cd in which Simon recites the blessing. The name ייי is on his lips. Tenak contains frequent evidence of synthetic thinking, whereby a single body part is used to express the attitude of a person in his / her entirety.[17]

Simon is related to Phinehas in 50:24b and is thus placed in a climactic third position in the line of High Priests after Aaron. Ben Sira establishes a chain of covenants[18] in which the relationship between Phinehas and Simon is confirmed in 50:24.

In relation to אל מפניו (50:21b), the twofold mention of ייי (50:20cd) is clearly intended to underscore the value of the blessing in which Simon reveals his glory. The verb פאר (imperfect *hithpa'el* 3. per. sg. m.) in 50:20d is thus to be explained in this context. The blessing of ייי and the name of ייי are related to the presence of the תפארת *the glory* (49:16; 50:1, 11b) and are expressed in a verbal form. Simon is acting subject at this juncture. If one maintains the reading יתפאר, Simon's active role in the mediation of the name ייי takes on a different perspective to that found in the history of exegesis of the Praise of the Fathers. Smend considers the repetition of ייי appropriate in connection with the reading התפאר (perfect *hithpa'el* 3. per. sg. m.) and he translates: *"mit dem Namen des Herrn stand er herrlich da"*.

Lévi's translation: *"glorifié par le nom de Dieu"* places Simon in a passive role. Ryssel offers a reflexive translation *"und des Namens Jahwes rühmte er sich,"* Box *"and he glorified himself with the name of the Lord"* with the accent on the instrumental function of the name.

Hayward translates in the passive: *"and in the Name of the Lord he was glorified."*

The verb פאר and the noun תפארת (49:16b and 50:1a, 11b) function here as key concepts. YHWH is always subject of פאר in Tenak. Although Simon is acting for the last time as subject in 50:20d: ובשם ייי יתפאר *and in the name of YHWH he reveals his glory*, there is absolutely no question at this juncture of self-aggrandisement. Ben Sira is familiar with this consideration and provides a new interpretation of such involvement as a responsible individual[19] in the concretisation of God's glory. This is apparent in the case of the physician (38:6) who acquires insight from God: להתפאר בגבורתו *in order to reveal his glory through his strength* (38:25). In similar fashion, Simon reflects God's glory in a worthy manner in his function as High Priest and the qualities he brings to it.[20] A similar interactive process is evident in 50:9c in which Simon *is aware that he is bound.*[21]

---

17   Wolff, Anthropologie, 23; Schroer – Staubli, Körpersymbolik.
18   Von Rad, Gottesvolk, 9–108.
19   Kaiser, Mensch, 1–22.
20   Hengel, Judentum, 256.
21   Neusner, Mishnah, 304 (Rosh Hashanah 3.8).

4.4 Remarks on 50:22–24: Doxology

The literary form of descriptive praise in Heb. is changed into a prayer of entreaty in Gk. This literary unit in Heb. with five bicola and the form of a doxology begins with עתה *now*. Such an appeal is a characteristic introduction to
the praise of the God of Israel. The colon 22ab is written across the entire
width of the page and serves, from a codicological point of view, as a *catch-
line* indicating a new beginning.

YHWH is described in more detail via the epexegetical genitive as ייי
אלהי ישׂראל *God of Israel*. He is the acting subject (22b–24d) in five verb
forms (50:22b–23b) and is indirectly involved on three further occasions in
the abiding character of his mercy, in the lasting character of the covenant
with Phinehas and in the fact that the latter shall not be broken for Simon and
his descendents (50:24).

Virtually every translation adopts the subjunctive mood, whereby 50:22–
24 is read as a prayer of entreaty (in 1. per. pl.) instead of a doxology (in 2.
per. pl.). From the perspective of *Formgeschichte*, the segment represents descriptive praise of YHWH, the God of Israel, who works wonders. The descriptive praise lacks the characteristic adversative ו of the prayer of entreaty
which is used to establish contrast.[22] Under normal circumstances, the content of descriptive praise in both Tenak and the Akkadian psalms is placed in
the context of direct speech. Thanksgiving does not belong to the forms of
expression typical of this genre while adoration, praise, honour, glorification
and service are generally characteristic thereof.[23]

In the discourse of Gk., God's dealings with *us* (22c–24b) follow the
opening appeal (22ab) in seven cola. This 1. per. pl. refers to human persons
in general or to the people. The accent on *us* (7x 1. per. pl.) suggests a different literary concept, a different vision of the intended addressees and a different temporal aspect (4x) *the days*. Ben Sira's grandson thoroughly modifies
the doxology (50:22–24), removing theological weight from the expectations
for the future. The hope that YHWH 'will be in peace among you' is reduced
to 'peace in our days'. With the omission of Phinehas and Simon, the accent
is shifted to 'ourselves' and 'our days'.

---

22 Westermann, Loben. The descriptive praise (p. 97) starts with an imperative call to
    praise and continues in the unfolding of God's majesty and goodness in a variety of ex-
    pressions which flow and overflow with words (p. 100).
23 Westermann describes a later form of this style with one motive: God's majesty (Psalm
    150), creation (Psalm 8; 19; 104; 139). This form can be found in the hymn of praise in
    Sir 39:12–35, which begins (12–15 in Gk.) and ends with מעשׂה אל כלם טובים *All
    the works of the Lord are good* (33a). Characteristic is the enumeration of the utmost
    importance of human life.

The difference in concept between the prayer of entreaty and descriptive praise is evident in Gk. This prayer expresses urgent human need in the fact that the God of all, who does great things, who prolongs our days, who acts according to his mercifulness, will give us a joyful heart and peace as of old (Gk. 50:23). All this was in fact the reality which Ben Sira described in his portrayal of the days of Simon. For his grandson, however, who we can date around 132 BC, all this was nothing more than a future for which he could only long.

On the contrary, Ben Sira introduces in his praise a universal vision of אדם, the human person in the general sense, and thus establishes a relationship with 49:16 in the form of an *inclusio* around Simon in his glorious deeds in 50:1–21 as a whole. In terms of content, it is significant that YHWH gives the תפארת *glory* to Adam (49:16) and Simon according to his most profound רצון *kindness* (22d).

The key concept ברית פינחס *covenant with Phinehas* is of vital importance within the structure of the text for the moment of instruction. The word combination as such is not found elsewhere in Tenak. This priestly covenant is established from the time of Aaron (45:15cd), for as long as the heavens endure. It is typical of Ben Sira's wisdom that the spatial entities of heaven and earth do not function as a traditional theme but that the heavens serve rather as a temporal entity. Via the temporal expression כימי שמים *as long as the days of the heavens endure* Ben Sira establishes a historical association between Simon, Aaron and Phinehas. He appeals to his audience with unique word combinations in 50:24 and via the transition from אדם 3. per. sg. in 22c to לכם 2. per. pl. in 23a.

In a personal appeal to *you* Ben Sira allows for his audience's endorsement of the words of praise on the basis of the experience of salvation which has been achieved in Simon and is assured for the future on account of God's promise of continuity.

Rather than Moses or Aaron, it would appear that Phinehas is the key figure in the Praise of the Fathers, serving as he does as an example for Simon. Phinehas' zeal לאלוהי כל *for the God of all* and his voluntary action (45:23ef) is expressed in his active engagement on the basis of his own choice and responsibility.

Significant differences are evident in the standard commentaries when the point of departure is based on Gk. instead of Heb. Phinehas in fact disappears from view. Peters interrupts the text after 24ab and emends 24b: ובימיו יושענו *"Und er helfe uns in seinen Tagen!"* and for these reasons considers 24cd to be a gloss. He detects a particularistic tendency in Heb. 50:22a which speaks of YHWH, the God of Israel instead of God of all as in Gk.

The call to praise in 50:22–24 is characterised by a striking codico-logical form.[24] The cola 50:22ab are written across the full width of the ma-nuscript and serve thus to demarcate the text. The opening line 50:22ab is written over the concluding line (l. 18 B XIX verso, line 18).

From the perspective of content, the imperative ברך in combination with the divine name ייי אלהי ישראל as introduction to the descriptive praise is unique, in spite of the fact that it appears quite familiar.

Ben Sira addresses his appeal to the entire community of Israel and postulates a position thereby which becomes clear when compared with 1 Chr 29:10–19.

In his song, David offers exuberant praise of YHWH. Everything, even the temple building, stems ultimately from God and is realised by the people. The king lays claim to an upright heart because his people have given every-thing freely and it is for this reason that he calls upon YHWH, God of our fathers Abraham, Isaac and Jacob (29:17–18). The opening words of 1 Chr 29:10: ברוך אתה יהוה אלהי ישראל אבינו *blessed are You, YHWH, God of our father Israel* differs with respect to the divine name. This leads to a striking distinction in terms of the theological content of the vision of God. The distinction is clearly apparent when compared with the appeal of Ben Sira: ברכו ייי אלהי ישראל *bless YHWH, the God of Israel*.

Chronicles speaks of Israel as "our father," thus referring to Jacob and the ancient ideal of an uninterrupted tribal covenant. Ben Sira, in contrast, sees Jacob from a traditional perspective as a theme typical of prophetic preaching (49:10c). Elsewhere, he envisages Jacob as a totality (36:17/11; 46:10), or as Israel as a whole כל קהל, thereby establishing a different limit to the community. Although the difference might appear to be rather subtle, the practical elaboration thereof is significant. This vision of the temple and the place of king David is typical for the Chronicler's perception of history. David institutionalises the community, rooted in the fatherhood of Israel, and limits himself thereby to native born Israelites. This Chronistic vision forms the basis of Ezra's theological concept of the holy congregation.

In opposite position, Ben Sira represents a trend rooted in prophecy and wisdom which envisages Israel's election in universal terms. He does not even mention Ezra and is critical of the particularistic concept of the holy na-tion.

---

24   Beit-Arié, *Hebrew Codicology.*

5. Conclusion

There is indeed no small difference between Heb. and Gk.[25] Two generations later the Greek version suggests the Hellenistic notion of a *Beispielreihe* or *encomium*. Judged on its own merits, the Hebrew version points to the context of Torah, which, being identified with wisdom, leads to life. The basic principle is the fear of YHWH. In this context Simon demonstrates his glory in the Temple in the name of YHWH, the God of Israel, and represents the climax of the "Praise of the Fathers of all time" in the universal concept of the priesthood with all the sons of Aaron in the temple and all the people together and the entire congregation of Israel at Rosh Hashanah.

Bibliographie

Beit-Arié, M., "Hebrew Codicology," in *The Makings of the Medieval Hebrew Book. Studies in Paleography and Codicology* (Jerusalem: Magnes Press, 1993) 41–74.

Box, G.H. – Oesterley, W.O.E., "The Book of Sirach," in *The Apocrypha and Pseudepigrapha of the Old Testament in English, with Introductions and Critical and Explanatory Notes to the Several Books I. Apocrypha* (ed. R.H. Charles; Oxford: Claredon Press, 1976 [1913]) 268–517.

Fang Che-Yong, M., "Usus nominis divini in Sirach," *VD* 42 (1964) 153–68.

Gilbert, M., "Wisdom Literature," in *Jewish Writings of the Second Temple Period. Apocrypha, Pseudepigrapha, Qumran Sectarian Writings, Philo, Josephus* (ed. M.E. Stone; CRINT 2/II; Assen / Philadelphia: van Gorcum, 1984) 283–324.

Hayward, C.T.R., *The Jewish Temple: A Non-Biblical Sourcebook* (London: Routledge, 1996).

Hengel, M., *Judentum und Hellenismus. Studien zu ihrer Begegnung unter besonderer Berücksichtigung Palästinas bis zur Mitte des 2. Jh.s v. Chr.* (2d ed.; WUNT 10; Tübingen: Mohr, 1973).

Joüon, P., *A Grammar of Biblical Hebrew* (trans. T. Muraoka; SubBi 14; Rome: Pontifical Biblical Institute, 1991).

Jüngling, H.W., "Der Bauplan des Buches Jesus Sirach," in *Den Armen eine frohe Botschaft* (ed. J. Hainz; FS F. Kamphaus; Frankfurt a.M.: Knecht, 1997) 89–105.

Kaiser, O., "Der Mensch als Geschöpf Gottes. Aspekte der Anthropologie Ben Siras," in *Der Einzelne und seine Gemeinschaft bei Ben Sira* (eds. R. Egger-Wenzel and I. Krammer; BZAW 270; Berlin / New York: de Gruyter, 1998) 1–22.

Kraus, H.-J., *Psalmen* (4th ed.; BKAT XV/1, Neukirchen-Vluyn: Neukirchener, 1972).

Lévi, I., *L'Ecclésiastique ou La Sagesse de Jésus, fils de Sira. Texte original hébreu édité traduit et commenté. Deuxième partie (III,6, à XVI,26; extraits de XVIII, XIX, XXV et XXVI; XXXI,11, à XXXIII,3; XXXV,19, à XXXVIII,27; XLIX,11, à fin.)* (vol. 2; Bibliothèque de l'École des Hautes Études; Sciences Religieuses 10/2; Paris: Leroux, 1901).

Marböck, J., "Structure and Redaction History of the Book of Ben Sira. Review and Prospects," in *The Book of Ben Sira in Modern Research. Proceedings of the First In-*

---

25   Wright, Difference.

ternational Ben Sira Conference 28–31 July 1996, Soesterberg, Netherlands (ed. P.C. Beentjes; BZAW 255; Berlin: de Gruyter, 1997) 61–79.

Mulder, O., *Simon, de hogepriester, in Sirach 50* (Almelo: Mulder, 2000).

Neusner, J., *The Mishnah: A New Translation* (New Haven: Yale University Press, 1988).

O'Fearghail, F., "Sir 50:5–21: Yom Kippur or the Daily Whole-Offering?," *Bib* 59 (1987) 301–6.

Peters, N., *Der jüngst wiederaufgefundene hebräische Text des Buches Ecclesiasticus, untersucht, herausgegeben, übersetzt und mit kritischer Note versehen* (Freiburg: Herder, 1902).

von Rad, G., "Das Gottesvolk im Deuteronomium," in *Gesammelte Studien zum Alten Testament II* (TB 48; München: Kaiser, 1973 [1929]) 9–108.

Ryssel, V., "Die Sprüche Jesus', des Sohnes Sirachs," in *Die Apokryphen des Alten Testaments* (ed. E. Kautzsch; APAT I; 4th ed.; Darmstadt: Wissenschaftliche Buchgesellschaft, 1975) 230–475.

Schrader, L., *Leiden und Gerechtigkeit: Studien zu Theologie und Textgeschichte des Sirachbuches* (BBET 27; Frankfurt a.M.: Lang, 1994).

Schroer, S. – Staubli, T., *Die Körpersymbolik der Bibel* (Darmstadt: Wissenschaftliche Buchgesellschaft, 1998).

ספר בן סירא / The Book of Ben Sira. Text, Concordance and an Analysis of the Vocabulary (The Historical Dictionary of the Hebrew Language), Jerusalem 1973.

Skehan, P.W. – Di Lella, A.A., *The Wisdom of Ben Sira: A New Translation with Notes, Introduction and Commentary* (AB 39; New York: Doubleday, 1987).

Smend, R., *Die Weisheit des Jesus Sirach* (Berlin: Reimer, 1906).

Stegemann, H., "The Qumran Essenes – Local Members of the Main Jewish Union in Late Second Temple Times," in *The Madrid Qumran Congress: Proceedings of the International Congress on the Dead Sea Scrolls, Madrid 18–21 March 1991* (eds. J. Trebolle Barrera and L. Vegas Montaner; STDJ 11; Leiden: Brill, 1992) 83–166.

Westermann, C., *Das Loben Gottes in den Psalmen* (3d ed.; Göttingen: Vandenhoeck & Ruprecht, 1963).

Wolff, H.W., *Anthropologie des Alten Testaments* (3d ed.; München: Kaiser, 1977).

Wright, B.G., *No Small Difference: Sirach's Relationship to its Hebrew Parent Text* (SBLSCS 26; Atlanta: Scholars Press, 1989).

Ben Sira's Praise of the Fathers:
A Canon-Conscious Reading

Alon Goshen-Gottstein
Bet Morasha, Jerusalem

1. Introduction

I first discovered Ben Sira's Praise of the Fathers about a decade ago, while studying the transformations of the biblical concept of covenant in Second Temple literature. I had never previously been so possessed by a text. The more I studied, the more there was to the text. The text took me over, increasingly unfolding new insights and presenting me with previously unseen aspects of its construction. It seemed to have a life of its own, and I felt granted the privilege of entry into what had previously been concealed. I became aware of the structure of the work, as well as of the meaning and wealth of association of so many of its details, with additional details taking on greater meaning as my study progressed. I felt, and still do feel, a debt to this work, perhaps to Ben Sira himself, to share the great wealth that presented itself to me in studying this work. Yet, nearly a decade later, I have not succeeded in capturing in writing what my eyes and heart have found in this work. Various academic and administrative projects have repeatedly delayed my ability to do justice to the work, according to my own ability. While the work always remains with me, cooking on a back burner, so to speak, I realize that some time will pass before I am able to fully devote myself to organizing and presenting the insights gained while studying the Praise. Rather than postpone any publication of these insights till I can treat them with the level of detail I feel they deserve, I have gladly accepted this kind invitation to share these ideas with the scholarly community, in a preliminary form.[1] I am acutely aware of the great gap between what a short essay can capture and the kind of careful attention that can only be expressed in a monograph. My goal in the present article is to share the main thesis that has become obvious to me in reading the work. Once that thesis is established, the entire Praise must be reread in its light, thereby further corroborating the thesis. Further elaboration of the text and reflections on its religious significance must await a more detailed study.

---

1   I have previously presented these ideas at the eleventh World Congress of Jewish Studies, Jerusalem, 1993, and at the SBL annual meeting, (Washington DC) 1993.

2. The Praise of the Fathers – Purpose and Genre

Ben Sira's Praise of the Fathers spans chs. 44–49 of the work. It is framed on either side by an additional praise: ch. 50 is praise for the High Priest Simeon, while 42:15 till the end of ch. 43 is a praise of God's work in creation. The Praise of the Fathers is thus situated within a series of works of praise. In interpreting the Praise one should not divorce it from the praises that frame it. But how exactly is the Praise to be understood, particularly when one considers its situation in relation to the praises that precede and follow it?

One direction that has been taken in the history of the interpretation of this text is to see in this list of biblical figures precisely that – a list. Some writers have suggested that the Praise of the Fathers functions as a list, providing a pedagogic purpose, by setting up on a pedestal Israel's heroes, offering them as subjects for emulation.[2] According to such an understanding, the purpose of such an edifying list of educational examples is to strengthen the religious identity and commitment of the hearers or readers of this text.

But to what extent can we really claim that the list serves such an ideologically and religiously strengthening function?[3] We have lists that function as exhortations for ideal religious behavior from roughly the same period as the Praise of the Fathers. 1 Macc 2:49–61 is a case in point. A list of examples is brought, beginning with Abraham, and including, among others, Joseph, Phinehas, Elijah and Daniel. Like the Praise of the Fathers, here too we are presented with a list of great biblical personalities. However, the author is very clear regarding the moral to be drawn from these examples. These are all examples of faithfulness in times of hardship, and of steadfast belief in the face of the adversary. There is a clear logic underlying the choice of members in the list. The list's members are chosen because they exemplify its pedagogic purpose. Now, in the case of the Praise of the Fathers no similar underlying logic can be immediately discerned. Ben Sira himself does not tell us why he includes the various people he does in the Praise. There is no moral that is drawn from the list, and in fact one is hard pressed to offer anything but the most general description that these are Israel's "greats". Surely, if this list fulfilled a pedagogic or ideological purpose, more than just a list of Israel's "greats" should be expected.

Moreover, a comparison of the length of Matityahu's speech in 1 Maccabees and of that of the Praise is telling. Matityahu's speech is fairly short. It does not exceed 15 verses, sustaining its argument through the various examples offered. The Praise of the Fathers, by contrast, spans six entire chapters of Ben Sira's book. I think more of Ben Sira's skills as a writer than to sug-

---

2   Siebeneck, Bones, 411–28; MacKenzie, Ben Sira, 312–27.
3   The following point is made *contra* Lee, Studies, 48.

gest that his pedagogic point was lost in the lengthy meanderings through the various examples of an unspecified religious virtue!

More convincing is the suggestion that the Praise is to be understood in terms of history. Such an understanding also makes better sense of the Praise of Creation and the Praise of Simeon that frame the Praise of the Fathers. Thus, a praise of creation leads to a telling of Israel's history in terms of praise. This in turn culminates in the Praise of Simeon the High Priest, who from this perspective may be taken as a culminating moment of Israel's history. The Praise of the Fathers is thus seen as a history. Yet this is not a history in any sense previously known in the writings of Israel. It is, in terms of later historical thinking, a history of great people. But should a list of great biblical figures really be taken as a form of historical writing? The present article will argue against a historical reading of the Praise. Indeed, in approaching the Praise from a historical viewpoint we may be distorting something fundamental to the Praise, and blinding ourselves to its true concerns.

History is an attempt to impose structure, give meaning, and find patterns and directions in a set of events and happenings. Writing history is not a neutral descriptive act, certainly not in a religious culture, such as the one in which someone like Ben Sira operated. If we argue that the Praise of the Fathers is a history of some sort, we must suggest the logic underlying the historical processes narrated by Ben Sira: What is the structure of history, what is its goal? Additionally, historical writing, especially when it covers such a vast scope as does the Praise of the Fathers, tends to divide history into periods. Periodization, structure and purpose are challenges that a historical reading of the Praise must address. Most writers have encountered great difficulties in offering a consistent historical reading of the Praise. The most important exponent of a historical reading of the Praise is Burton Mack, in his *Wisdom and the Hebrew Epic*. Mack is aware of these challenges, and attempts to address them. According to Mack, history finds its fulfilment in the historical moment depicted in Ben Sira ch. 50, representing the High Priest Simeon serving in the Jerusalem temple. This moment functions as the telos of the entire Praise, suggesting a sense of fulfilment and completion of history in this cultic setting.[4]

Yet how does such a history compare to the classical historical thinking that finds expression in the Hebrew Bible? The most common pattern of historical thinking is the deuteronomic one. History is controlled by religious behavior, determined by covenantal stipulations, and plays out the centrality of the covenant as constitutive of Israel's identity and hence of its history. Accordingly, Israel's history is one of sin and repentance, returning cyclically

---

4   I will not enter in the present context into a detailed discussion of Mack's thesis. The value of my suggestion should be judged on the basis of the reading of the relevant texts. I hope to offer a more detailed critique of Mack's reading in a future version of my study.

to covenantal faithfulness. Repentance is a key element in this pattern of thinking. History is the arena in which God's relationship with Israel is made manifest, and the covenantal blessings and curses, indicative of Israel's faithfulness to the covenant, find expression in the historical arena. Covenant is thus a major structuring concept of religious thought, finding primary expression in the arena of history. Such patterns of historical thought are found in various biblical works, including works of the early Second Temple period, like Nehemiah ch. 9.

It is obvious that if we speak of history in the Praise of the Fathers it is not in this sense that we can speak of it. Ben Sira's Praise is not, like Nehemiah ch. 9, a story of sin, repentance and God's pedagogy with Israel. Repentance does not appear anywhere in the Praise, surely a curious omission if the Praise were any kind of history.[5] But more significantly, the Praise is not a story of God's relationship with Israel at all. It is a story, rather: a list, of great people, presented in sequence, thus creating a narrative-like impression, without really offering any narrative. Ben Sira addresses almost exclusively righteous people as his heroes, and sinners find only a very secondary place in the Praise. An impression of an ideal and glorious past is suggested, despite Ben Sira's mention of Israel's sins. It is this impression that led those scholars mentioned above to consider the Praise as a list of examples, rather than as in some way historically significant.

That the Praise is not intended as history accounts best for the fact that various biblical events are not mentioned in it. There is no clear reference to the Judean exile, nor to the return from the exile, even though figures from the early Second Temple period are mentioned in the Praise. In this context we can recall the omission of Ezra from the Praise, which has occupied scholarly attention.[6] Various biblical stories are also lacking from the Praise, particularly stories of Israel's sins, as narrated in the Torah, but also as they are told in the prophets. Assuming the Praise is some kind of history would necessitate an accounting for the various omissions that a historical perspective might have expected to find in the text.

One could, of course, claim that the Praise is a history of a different sort. Yet, if indeed this was a history of great men, more thought should be given to the genre and the form in which Ben Sira chose to express his historical reflections. For it is a pretty unique form of expression in which individuals are praised. Praise is traditionally reserved for God.[7] Ben Sira himself obviously

---

5   The only reference to repentance is in the opening of ch. 48, where lack of repentance
     is singled out (48:15).
6   See below, n. 46.
7   The problem of the distinction between praise of humans and praise of God has informed earlier attempts to define the genre of the Praise and its biblical precedents. See
     Lee, Studies, 25–29.

uses praise in a wider sense.[8] But what is it that allows Ben Sira to move from a praise of God to the praise of humans? A partial answer may be found in the juxtaposition of the Praise of the Fathers to the Praise of Creation. If the Praise of Creation is a form of praising God through his creatures, the Praise of the Fathers could be seen as an extension of that praise, moving chronologically from creation to history. Yet, we cannot ignore the fundamental change in focus, when humans and their excellence are the subject of the praise, and not the power of God, expressed in his handiwork. The fact is that God is not praised throughout the Praise of the Fathers as the maker of humans,[9] but human heroes are the objects of Ben Sira's praise.

The uniqueness of the praise, when compared with earlier biblical literature, has led scholars to seek other literary sources for its formation. Significantly, the alternative sources have been outside Judaism, and conform to the understanding that Ben Sira is operating in a hellenistic milieu, and hence borrows from Jewish as well as from hellenistic literary traditions. A key candidate for Ben Sira's literary inspiration has been the Greek encomium.[10] This suggestion incorporates earlier understandings that saw in the work a set of moral examples, the so-called *Beispielreihe*.[11] The question is what enabled Ben Sira to assimilate these literary forms into his world view. Is it simply an indication of Ben Sira's hellenization? What changes have taken place in his native Jewish world view that have allowed the integration of such literary forms? In other words, what has taken place in Ben Sira's religious world view that allows him to focus upon people, even great and excellent people, making them the objects of his praise, without it being conceived as improper in terms of religious sensibilities? We cannot imagine Ben Sira as someone who simply imports foreign literary forms, thereby producing changes in his own religious context. Imports must be planted in fertile and receptive soil. What is it about Ben Sira's Judaism that enables him to receive this literary form, and to devote a significant portion of his book to

---

8   See the article by Jan Liesen in the present volume.
9   The idea that the praise of the heroes does ultimately point back to the praise of God can be found in the Praise. See the conclusion of ch. 45 and 50:22. However, this addresses a particular group, the priestly group, and comes at the conclusion of two significant subdivisions. It is not the case that all human praise is expressly related to the praise of God.
10 See Lee, Studies, as well as Mack's work.
11 See Lee, Studies, 32–48. It seems to me, however, that Lee's suggestion that the Praise functions as an encomium does not depend on understanding the function of the gallery of greats in terms of an example list. If examples are indeed fundamental to the form of the encomium, and if the present article's thesis that an appeal to past figures does not serve pedagogic purposes is accepted, then Ben Sira's degree of borrowing of a hellenistic form is significantly reduced. We would still need to account for what enables Ben Sira to praise humans, rather than God. However, the question would no longer be framed in terms of intercultural borrowing.

them? In order to understand how praise functions for Ben Sira, let us begin
by examining the precise boundaries of the different units within Ben Sira's
series of praises.

3. The Praise of the Fathers: Canonical Traces

Having noted that the Praise of the Fathers is framed by two other praises, we
turn our attention to the transition points between the praises. We note that at
these transition points Ben Sira applies a particular literary technique, that he
applies nowhere else in the Praise, except in one other instance, which I consider significant for the present argument. Ben Sira indicates transition, while
maintaining continuity, by echoing a term, found in the conclusion of an earlier section, in the opening of the following section.

The Hebrew of 44:1 refers to אנשי חסד. We lack the Hebrew for 43:33.
But it has been reconstructed back from the Greek either as אנשי חסד,[12] or as
חסידים.[13] The Praise of the Fathers concludes in 49:16: ועל כל חי תפארת
אדם, the word תפארת being echoed immediately in the opening of the Praise
of Simeon in 50:1: גדול אחיו ותפארת עמו.[14]

There is one other occurrence of this literary technique within the
Praise.[15] 45:26 concludes with וגבורתכם לדורות עולם, echoed immediately
in the opening of 46:1: גבור בן חיל. While the textual reading is not beyond
doubt,[16] there is little doubt that this passage serves as a conclusion and a

---

12   Smend, Weisheit; Kahana, דברי.
13   Segal, ספר. There is no Syriac for the latter part of ch. 43.
14   This leads me to reject the odd division proposed by Ska, L'éloge, 191, according to
     which 49:11 is read as the beginning of a new section of the Praise, including and con-
     cluding with the Praise of Simeon. The suggestion puts the carriage before the horse.
     Since Ska is interested in upholding a canonical reading of the Praise, he defines the
     sections of the Praise according to what he assumes is the canonical division of Scrip-
     ture, thereby ignoring the internal literary indications of the Praise – the method of
     echoing here noted, as well as the inclusio of 44:16 and the concluding verses of ch. 49.
     Ska comments on the concluding passage being problematic. It is, however, only
     problematic inasmuch as Ska approaches it with preconceived notions. I am perfectly
     happy with 49:14–16 as a return to the starting point of the Praise, and as an opportu-
     nity for mentioning figures who were not mentioned in the Praise because they did not
     fit into its thematic framework.
15   Compare:
     4:10 (Heb.) "son" / 4:11 "her sons"
     15:9 (Heb.) "from God" / 15:11 "from God"
     19:17 (Gk.) "Law" / 19:20 "Law".
16   I follow Segal's (ספר) reconstruction, echoing the earlier suggestion of Cowley –
     Neubauer, Original Hebrew; that seems to me the only way of making sense of the He-
     brew, despite the fact that the facsimile is not perfectly clear. This reconstruction is re-
     jected by Smend, Weisheit. The recognition that this is the closure of a unit within the

transition point. The latter part of v. 25 and v. 26 turn from third person to second person address, offering a blessing and a prayer for the priestly family. This conclusion is very similar, in content, in form and in language to the concluding prayer of ch. 50, and is indeed fitting for the conclusion of a literary unit.[17]

Why does Ben Sira introduce a break at this point? An examination of what precedes this transition point and of what follows it reveals an obvious fact: the transition occurs at the point at which Ben Sira concludes his reference to personalities of whom we hear in the Torah, and before he embarks on a description of personalities of whom we hear in the prophetic corpus. The transition point thus reflects the transition from Torah to Prophets, the two parts of the canon, known to have existed in Ben Sira's times.[18]

Once we become aware of the canonical dimension of the arrangement of the Praise,[19] many other facts corroborate the canonical concerns of the Praise. While the earlier part of the Praise, devoted to the Torah, makes no mention of the individual books of the Torah, the later part of the Praise, that addresses the Prophets, seems to make it a point to relate to all books in the prophetic corpus. This is particularly striking in view of the fact that concerning some of these books Ben Sira really has nothing to say. Thus, 46:11–12 relates to the Judges, without really saying anything relevant concerning them, except for the fact that they are mentioned and blessed. Similarly, the twelve prophets are mentioned in 49:10, with little being learned from them.[20] If the point were moral example, or the telling of history, there is no point in mentioning these minor figures. However, if the point is to redescribe the prophetic canon, as part of a wider project in which Ben Sira is en-

---

praise, which can be established on grounds other than the technique of echoing, lends further support to this reading, once it is recognized that Ben Sira uses this technique in transition points. Skehan – Di Lella seem to accept this reading as well, though it is rendered, like the Syriac, in terms of rule. See Skehan – Di Lella, Wisdom, 514.

17   The Praise of Creation also concludes with a second person exhortation to the praise of God (see 43:30).

18   I shall not enter here into a discussion of whether the canon in Ben Sira's time was divided into two or into three parts. The present reading of the Praise of the Fathers would best fit a bipartite division of the canon. See Leiman, Canonization, 150–51 and Sheppard, Wisdom, 14 n. 59. In any event, the basic understanding that a canon is reflected seems to me indisputable, contrary to Mack, Wisdom, 224–25. A review of recent discussions of this subject is found in Ska, L'éloge, 182–85.

19   The scholar who has been most aware of the canonical dimensions of the Praise is Ska, L'éloge, 181–93. However, Ska sees the canonical division as providing periodization within an essentially historical framework in which the Praise is understood. His thesis is thus a variation on the conventional reading of the Praise, as exemplified by the work of Mack.

20   Interestingly, in both cases Ben Sira speaks of the flourishing of their bones. Promise of resurrection allows Ben Sira to mention these heroes while saying very little concerning them.

gaged, then all parts of the canon must be addressed, even where there is little
to say concerning the individual works or the figures related to those works.

The cases of the judges and the twelve minor prophets are telling in another way as well. If Ben Sira wanted to make honorable mention of individual heroes in Israel's history, he should have referred to individual figures by
name. What is the point of referring to works by their title? Why not list the
prophets or the judges individually? It seems to me the answer lies in the fact
that Ben Sira is more interested in describing the canon than he is in describing individual lives. For this reason he refers in the case of these collections
to both works by their titles, rather than by reference to their individual heroes and their virtues.

If we realize that Ben Sira's intent is to describe the canon, then of
course the Praise functions as an important source of knowledge regarding
the shape of the canon in Ben Sira's time.[21] To take an example: Job is listed
in 49:9, following reference to Ezekiel, prior to mention of the twelve prophets. One could of course reason that Ben Sira places Job following Ezekiel,
since Ezekiel himself mentions Job.[22] However, the Hebrew text seems to refer to Job as איוב נביא.[23] It would seem that Job is not mentioned only as a
righteous person, but is taken to be a prophet. Once it is recognized that Ben
Sira's interests focus on a description of the canon, it is possible to view the
mention of Job in this section as indication that the book of Job was part of
the prophetic corpus,[24] possibly even in the location assigned by Ben Sira.

Ben Sira's canonical awareness has been the focus of the work of Gerald
Sheppard, who has described Ben Sira as "canon-conscious."[25] The scriptural

---

21   This has, of course, long been known. See Leiman, Canonization, and Beckwith, Old
     Testament. The present thesis presents Ben Sira as actively and consciously describing
     the canon, rather than simply providing us information in passing.

22   Ezek 14:14. Accordingly, the linguistic subject of וגם הזכיר, in 49:9 would be Eze-
     kiel. However, one would be hardpressed to extend the subject of the phrase to 49:10,
     where the twelve prophets are mentioned. That 49:9 and 10 both open in the same way,
     וגם, may therefore lead us to dissociate 49:9 from Ezekiel, and to see it as a general
     reference to the canon. Could this be another brief allusion to God, as linguistic subject
     of the Praise? (See following discussion). The last such allusion was found in 49:5.

23   Thus Smend, Weisheit, and ספר.

24   To limit reference to Job as prophet to Ben Sira's understanding of Ezek 14:14 and 20
     would raise the question of Ben Sira's understanding of Daniel, who is also mentioned
     in the same chapter in Ezekiel. Beckwith, Old Testament, 73, raises the possibility that
     Ben Sira indeed considered Daniel a prophetic work. I prefer to understand the refer-
     ence to Job as growing out of its canonical context, rather than out of his mention in
     Ezek 14. Accordingly, that no mention is made of Daniel points to the lack of canonical
     status of the book at the time. Beckwith himself also raises this possibility, but makes it
     dependent upon an alternative reconstruction of 49:9.

25   Sheppard, Wisdom, 109. The term "canon-consciousness" is itself derived from Seelig-
     mann, Voraussetzungen, 152.

canon shapes religious consciousness and informs how key concepts are understood and presented. Sheppard himself has spelled out the implications of his reading of Ben Sira as canon-conscious with regard to earlier parts of the book, but has not addressed the Praise of the Fathers. Sheppard was concerned with how the concept of wisdom was transformed in light of canonical awareness. The Praise of the Fathers does not feature wisdom in a central position, and hence fell outside the purview of Sheppard's work. Once we are aware of the degree to which Ben Sira is indeed canon-conscious, the fact that he structures a significant unit of his book, the Praise of the Fathers, along canonical lines should not occasion great surprise.

The suggestion that the Praise of the Fathers is an attempt to describe the canon, and is part of a wider canonical consciousness that characterizes the work of Ben Sira, allows us to return to the question of the purpose of the Praise. It seems to me that canonical awareness is the framework in which the Praise is best understood, rather than historical awareness. Ben Sira's goal is not to tell the stories through any particular unfolding logic. His goal is not to offer pedagogic example and moral precedent. Rather, his concern is to describe the canon, and this he does through highlighting the great heroes and fathers whose lives are recorded in the canon. In the course of this description some moral example and some history may find expression in a secondary manner. Most of the figures chosen are exemplary figures, and hence the memory of their virtue can always serve a beneficial pedagogic purpose. Following the sequence of biblical books also creates a narrative sequence that has some historical semblance, even if no historical logic is uncovered. However, both pedagogy and history are secondary to Ben Sira's true concern, which is to describe and reflect upon the meaning of the canon. If we focus on either pedagogy or history we lose sight of Ben Sira's true concerns. To the extent that posing historical questions and addressing the text with historical awareness might lead us astray from Ben Sira's true purpose, it is better to put the historical perspective aside altogether, and to attempt to uncover what Ben Sira's true concerns were, and in what way his description of canon is more than just a description. For Ben Sira does not only describe the canon. As I shall presently suggest, the Praise functions as an extended reflection and meditation upon the meaning of the canon. I believe our interpretive energies should be devoted to unearthing the associations that Ben Sira attaches to the different parts of the canon, thereby exposing the meaning the canon held for Ben Sira. I believe this is his ultimate concern, and it is significant enough to cause us to leave aside the perspectives that were hitherto brought to the discussion of this text.

This allows us also to return to the question of how a new literary genre, praising human personalities, rather than God, could grow on faithful Jewish soil. I believe the canonical perspective helps us account for this novelty as well. Reflecting upon canon is reflecting upon Scripture. To consider the meaning of canon is to engage in a meditation upon Scripture. Once Scripture and its study emerge as central religious concepts, numerous patterns for approaching Scripture are possible. One can tell the story as story, but as Scripture one can find various ways of configuring Scripture, of finding new links and associations between its parts, and of uncovering hidden connections between its components. Scripture as object of reflection invites ever new ways of conceptualizing and addressing it in its entirety and in the relationship between its components. Later rabbinic literature presents us with a great wealth of how different parts of Scripture are interrelated by the rabbis, and how new associations and structures emerge from reflection upon Scripture. A similar process takes place already in the work of Ben Sira. While the process of revelation has not been declared over, and while Ben Sira himself may have entertained thoughts of his own work entering the scriptural canon,[26] canon has been sufficiently formed to allow meditation and reflection upon its components and their relationship. In other words, both Scripture and its canonical divisions have been formed in such a way as to permit the kind of religious activity later known as תלמוד תורה, the study of Torah. The Praise of the Fathers is thus an expression of this type of activity.

Scripture functions as an alternative religious focus to God. If a God-focused orientation leads to directing praise to God, a scripturally oriented perspective allows for a more expansive use of praise. In the framework of the study of Scripture, Ben Sira is free to introduce organizational principles that are novel. They neither fit classical patterns of history writing, nor do they follow patterns of moral pedagogy. Praise of great men is made possible because underlying it is the activity of study and reflection upon Scripture. What is of greatest significance for Ben Sira is not what is said about any of the individuals, though that of course is also important. Rather, what is central for him is the way in which the accumulation of statements concerning figures of old fits into wider patterns that give meaning to Scripture and to the structure of the canon. I therefore suggest that praising the lives of the nation's fathers is one of any number of strategies that could have been taken by Ben Sira, and which allow him to offer his listeners and readers reflections upon Scripture. It is the reflection upon the meaning of Scripture that is thus the true concern of the Praise of the Fathers.

4. The Torah – Sign of the Covenant

Once we realize that Ben Sira's project in the Praise of the Fathers is to describe canon, and to provide meaning for canonical divisions, we must dis-

---

26   See the conclusion of ch. 24.

cover in what way Ben Sira accomplishes his task. Sensitivity to word play and to word choice plays a major role in providing an answer. What Ben Sira has to say regarding the meaning of the canonical division will become apparent when we consider the types of things narrated in the earlier part of the Praise, especially when these are compared with the content of the latter part of the Praise. To the extent that we can find themes and terms that are exclusive to one part of the Praise, and are absent from the other, this will provide us with a key to the meaning ascribed by Ben Sira to the different parts of the canon.

The historical reading of the Praise has taken its clue from a footnote of Haspecker.[27] Haspecker noted the concentration of covenantal language in the first part of the Praise. This observation led him to see in the first part of the praise the historical foundations of Israel's covenant with God, while the second part of the Praise is devoted to the struggle to uphold the covenant. There are several difficulties with this understanding. First, nowhere in the first part of the Praise do we encounter a covenant made with the entire people. Even the descriptions of the Sinai event do not emphasize the making of the covenant. More significantly, it is not the people as a whole, but Moses who is featured in the context of Ben Sira's description of the events at Sinai, in 45:1–5. And perhaps most significantly, the term covenant does not appear in the context where we would most expect it, namely in the context of the Sinai covenant.

The Praise of the Fathers focuses upon individuals, praising them and extolling their virtues. While it is reasonable to assume the wider national background as the context for the Praise, it is important to be mindful of the fact the people as such are not the subject of the Praise, and hence ברית must be understood as in some way different from the conventional description of the making of historical covenants with the People of Israel.

There is a second, and no less significant, difficulty in the historical reading that flows from Haspecker's suggestion. If the story of the Praise is that of making covenants and the ensuing struggle to fulfill them, the absence of ברית from the second part of the Praise is striking.[28] That this is no accident will be seen from an examination of 45:25, where the covenant with David is mentioned. The mention is clearly secondary to the context. Following a hasty incidental mention, Ben Sira immediately returns to his proper subject matter – Aaron. Why mention David at all at this point? After all, Ben Sira will devote extensive attention to David in ch. 47. The answer seems to me that Ben Sira wishes to concentrate all references to ברית in the earlier part of the Praise, and to avoid mention of the covenant in the second part of

---

27   Haspecker, Gottesfurcht, 85 n. 94.
28   Beentjes, Hezekiah, 79, fails to explain the significance of this fact, even though he recognizes it is not accidental.

the Praise. He therefore pushes mention of the Davidic covenant into a hasty reference, apropos of another covenant under discussion, leaving a fuller presentation of David to the later part of the Praise. The combination of the particular uses of ברית in the earlier part of the Praise and its complete absence from the second part lead me to seek a different explanation for the uses of ברית in the Praise, thereby reinforcing the canonical understanding that has already started to come to light.

Ben Sira's work is characterized by careful and deliberate choice of words, by word play and by associations of words into clusters that convey meaning. In light of this premise, borne out by the study of the Praise as well as of other parts of the book, we must reflect upon the meaning of the concentration of the term ברית in the first part of the Praise and its absence in the second. Given that the first part of the Praise addresses the Torah, the first of the two orders of Ben Sira's canon, we are led to consider the relationship between the Torah and ברית. The association of Torah and ברית is readily available in other parts of the book, thus confirming the suggestion that the choice of ברית in the first part of the Praise is not accidental. ברית, for Ben Sira, is synonymous with Torah. Sir 24:23 provides ample proof for this association, even if the Hebrew original has been lost. We are led to conclude that Ben Sira concentrates his references to ברית in the earlier part of the Praise because ברית is suggestive or indicative of the meaning of the subject of the first part of the Praise – the Torah. If so, the mention of ברית is not accidental to Ben Sira's descriptions of the heroes of the first part of the Praise, but is rather fundamental to their description, as heroes of the first part of the canonical order of Scripture.

But if this is the case, we should expect to find ברית mentioned concerning each and every one of the heroes of the first part of the Praise. Why then are certain heroes not referred to in terms of ברית? Ben Sira's associative word plays provide us with synonyms to ברית, that fulfill the same function that ברית would. In particular, we should note the use of אות in the earlier part of the Praise. אות and ברית obviously belong to the same semantic field, as can be seen from several biblical associations of the two.[29] For Ben Sira they also function as related terms. The most obvious indication for this is in 44:17–18. בבריתו חדל מבול is followed by באות עולם נכרת עמו. Not only do we have here a parallelism between ברית and אות, but we clearly see that אות is equivalent to ברית through the choice of verb applied to it – כרת, a verb used biblically in relation to ברית. Once this equivalence is recognized, we can say that all heroes in the first part of the Praise are de-

---

29   See Gen 9:12, 13, 17; 17:11.

scribed in relation to ברית[30] or its equivalent expression. Thus, Enoch in 44:16 is described as אות דעת. Moses performs אותות, thus linking this figure too with the semantic field that governs the presentation of this part of the Praise.[31] Also the "bad guys" in the first part of the Praise are tied in semantically by use of אות. Thus, that God brings upon Dathan and Abiram an אות, in 45:19, is contextually appropriate.[32]

If deliberate choice of words characterizes the first part of the Praise, we must ask what does Ben Sira understand by this choice of words, and what is the subtle message that he delivers through his word choice. I suggest Ben Sira makes the following point: The Torah is ברית in the deepest sense, and all the heroes that are addressed as part of the description of this part of the canon are described in terms of ברית. What is told of them suggests the fuller meaning of ברית, thus highlighting the meaning of this part of Scripture, and bringing to light what is characteristic of it. According to this suggestion, ברית is a divine gift, an expression of the action of God, not of human action. It endows the receiver with special status, leading him to partake of divine glory and status. This is the religious significance of the Torah as the word of God and the gift of God to Israel. It is an endowment of divine status and the reception of a divine gift, rooted in divine action and initiative. Such an understanding effectively precludes a historical understanding of ברית. Rather than the historical covenant made between God and Israel, leading to the historical struggle to uphold the covenant, emphasizing human commitment and responsibility, Ben Sira applies ברית as the one-sided endowment of

---

30 Abraham in 44:20; Jacob in 44:22; Aaron in 45:15, Phinehas in 45:24 and David in 45:25.

31 45:3. Both Smend, Weisheit, and Segal, ספר translate σημεῖα as אותות. There is no Greek for the Hebrew אותות in 48:12. It is still somewhat perplexing that the receiving of Torah is not related to the term ברית, and אותות is only expressed in a secondary context. It seems that Ben Sira intentionally avoided reference to ברית in the case of the giving of the Torah. It seems Ben Sira wanted to avoid the association of ברית with covenant in the conventional national sense, preferring instead the particular sense of ברית used in the Praise, which I shall spell out shortly. He therefore preferred to address Sinai as a moment of giving Torah and commandments, thus placing an obligation upon the people, rather than the one-sided endowment of status, which characterizes his own use of ברית in the earlier part of the Praise. Moses is thus tied to the thematic concerns of the first part of the Praise through a secondary word play, rather than through the primary association with Sinai.

32 While there is no use of ברית in the second part of the Praise, we do encounter one use of אותות in the second part, with regard to Elisha, in 48:12. Significantly, Sinai is not mentioned in relation to the giving of the Torah by Moses in ch. 45, but is mentioned in ch. 48 with regard to Elijah. Does Ben Sira's choice of words suggest an affinity between Moses and the prophetic duo of Elijah and Elisha?

God. This endowment is immediately realized in the lives of its recipients, and finds expression in their unique status. Such emphasis precludes the historical perspective of covenant as ground of battle for faithfulness, replacing it with the stability and accomplishment of the one-sided divine gift. The meaning of this suggestion will become clearer when it is juxtaposed with the themes that emerge from the second part of the Praise. But before attending to those, let us note some of the characteristic terms and modes of expression in the first part of the Praise, that support the suggestion I have just made.

One of the most striking facts about the first part of the Praise of the Fathers is the way in which the heroes of the first part are described. Rather than describe them or their actions directly, Ben Sira continuously describes God's actions. The linguistic subject of the first part of the Praise is God, and not the heroes Ben Sira describes. The entire narrative describes what God does to those heroes, rather than what the heroes themselves accomplish. While there are short secondary digressions that place the individual hero as the subject of a brief phrase, the running narrative has God as its subject.[33] That this is deliberate emerges from a comparison with the second part of the Praise. In the second part we no longer encounter this phenomenon, and the linguistic subject of the various expressions are the heroes themselves and not God. It must, therefore, be characteristic of the meaning that Ben Sira ascribes to the first part of the Praise, and hence to the meaning he attributes to covenant and to the Torah, the subject of the first part of the Praise.

---

33   The opening verses of the Praise may be an exception. While they are short, it seems God is not the subject of the verses. This is true for Enoch, for Noah and for Abraham, up to the point in verse 20 when God makes a covenant with him, from which point onward God becomes the linguistic subject. At the same time, the references to these heroes do not really make them the proper subject of the sentences. Instead, Ben Sira uses the passive form, rather than the active form that serves for the rest of the first part of the Praise. By using the passive form, Ben Sira can still point to God as the hidden subject, without expressly invoking the active form in relation to God. Why would Ben Sira adopt this strategy? Perhaps because these heroes precede Israel, and Ben Sira does not wish to accord them the same status that he later accords Israel's heroes. In calling his work שבח אבות עולם, Ben Sira may intend reference to more than Israel's heroes, yet he still might wish to distinguish between these heroes and Israel's heroes. The subtle distinction between passive and active forms of expression may serve this purpose. A comparison of 44:18 and 20 is telling. Whereas in the case of Noah we read: באות עולם נכרת עמו, concerning Abraham we read: בברית עמו ובא, thus describing God in an active form. In fact, it is only from that point onward that the Praise develops its third person singular running narrative. It is as though the making of a covenant with Abraham was the first instance of true covenantal divine action. Perhaps this is also suggestive of the meaning of Torah, whose true beginnings are only with Abraham.

That ברית, and hence the Torah, are a one-sided action of God, a status-endowing gift, can be seen from some of the descriptions in the first part of the Praise. The case of Aaron is perhaps most characteristic. Since Aaron serves as the paradigm for Phinehas and later for the Praise of Simeon, which functions as a focal or receiving point of the entire praise, it can be taken as paradigmatic in its usage. The description of Aaron is one of endowing with status. Aaron is described as receiving the divine Glory (45:7), and as being chosen (v. 16). This is suggestive of the meaning of ברית throughout.

Perhaps the most suggestive way of expressing the uniqueness of the first part of the Praise is through the term ברכה, suggesting a divine blessing, a movement grounded in God Himself, stretching toward Israel. We find ברכה only in the first part of the Praise.[34] The combination of concepts: covenant, glory, blessing, all point to one-sided divine action, that endows the recipient with special status, partaking of a divine gift.[35] This cluster of concepts is particular to the first part of the Praise. I suggest therefore that it addresses not only the heroes of the first part of the Praise, but also the implied subject of the first part – the Torah itself. By describing the heroes of this part of the Praise in this manner, Ben Sira is also offering us his understanding of the uniqueness of the Torah, and what distinguishes it from the body of prophetic writings. The Torah is the action of God. It is a one-sided gift of God, endowing Israel with special status, allowing Israel to share in divine glory and blessing.

---

34   44:23 and in the margins of MS B to 45:7. A call to bless God is only found in the first part, and then again in the Praise of Simeon (see 45:15 and 25). I consider 46:11 formulaic, and not an instance of actively invoking a blessing as in the earlier part.

35   It should be noted that כבוד is not exclusive to the first part of the Praise, even though its active uses of endowment with glory are. To the extent that 44:2, in the prologue to the Praise, spoke of the heroes as receiving divine glory, this is fulfilled only with regard to heroes of the first part of the Praise (compare also 45:25). While none of the heroes in the second part receive divine glory, the term does occur frequently enough to not allow us to see the use of כבוד as one of the distinguishing features of the first part of the Praise. Closer examination reveals that all uses of כבוד are related to the temple and its worship. (The only exceptions are 44:19 and 47:20, which are mirror images of one another. This mirror image may account for the use of כבוד in 47:20). The continuity of כבוד with regard to the temple is understandable, considering the entire work leads to a praise of a High Priest at the moment of worship. Thus, if Scripture is approached in an analytic movement, distinguishing between its different components, the temple functions in the Praise as a complementary force, unifying its different parts. Further examination of the themes of worship and sacrifice in the Praise will have to await a later study.

5. The Prophets – Human Action and Religious Speech

Canonical awareness is more explicit in the second part of the Praise than in the first. While the first part of the Praise was devoted to the Torah, there was no effort to relate to the different books of the Pentateuch. Unlike the first part of the Praise, that was governed by a key concept that bears strong relationship to the Torah, the second part of the Praise is not governed by one key concept. What we do find in it is systematic reference to the entire prophetic corpus and indication of the sequence of prophetic books in Ben Sira's canon. Thus Joshua is followed by the Judges and by Samuel, in accordance with the biblical sequence. Given the canonical perspective that informs the composition of the Praise, we recognize that Ben Sira integrates the Psalms into his canonical description through the figure of David, as indeed he does following this with the Solomonic works, that are addressed through the figure of Solomon.[36] The Book of Kings is addressed in what follows, however not as the history of kings, but as the history of prophets.

That prophets and prophecy are at the center of Ben Sira's attention emerges from Ben Sira's special accents. Joshua is treated as a prophet (46:1). Because the Judges were not prophetic figures, almost nothing is said of them in 46:11–12, except for a short reference that is designed to include them in Ben Sira's description. They are not integrated into the governing theme of prophecy.[37] Samuel's prophetic status is highlighted throughout Ben Sira's presentation. It is particularly interesting to see how Ben Sira introduces David. David is introduced through reference to Nathan the prophet, who frames David's career, from the prophetic perspective (47:1). This is a very odd way to introduce David, unless prophecy is itself the principal theme, as it is in this work. Solomon is integrated from several perspectives. The first is the canonical perspective, that allows Ben Sira to refer to the Solomonic works. The second is the temple, which is a major concern of the Praise.[38] The third is the necessary historical background of Solomon's sins, that led to the splitting of the kingdom and to the subsequent unfolding of the story. However, what is important in this story again is the place of the prophets. Ben Sira devotes attention to Elijah and Elisha, rather than to a host of kings who are not mentioned. Hezekiah is assumed under the prophetic inspiration and saving power of Isaiah (48:20–25).

---

36   In another study I hope to support the suggestion that in 47:15–17 Ben Sira is referring not only to Proverbs, but to the Song of Songs as well.

37   The one unequivocal instance of prophecy in the book of Judges is Deborah. Ben Sira could have concentrated upon her. It is probable that Ben Sira's attitude to women is the source for this omission. See Trenchard, Ben Sira's View, and Di Lella, Women, 39–52.

38   As noted above, the present analysis will not do justice to the centrality of the temple in the Praise.

If each of the chs. from 46–48 was devoted to one or two figures, ch. 49 addresses no less than 14 figures, and this if we count the twelve prophets as one. References in this chapter, which is also the shortest of this part of the Praise, are much briefer and do not seek to develop a full-blown image of the prophetic figures. Ben Sira seeks to establish three things in this short chapter: the destruction of the temple, mention of the remaining prophets who occupy the latter part of the prophetic canon, and reference to the building activity of figures at the beginning of the Second Temple period.[39] The destruction is the necessary background for the building activity Ben Sira immediately describes. Mention of other prophets allows Ben Sira to complete his survey of the prophetic corpus, even though little attention is devoted to the later prophetic works.

It is clear that Ben Sira's concerns in the second part touch upon prophecy and the prophetic corpus. This is obvious both from the fact that Ben Sira describes the contents of the entire prophetic corpus and from the fact that in presenting the books of the earlier prophets, Ben Sira focuses upon the prophetic status of the heroes, or shapes the stories in such a way as to feature prophets at center-stage. However, in contradistinction to the first part, where covenant emerged as the controlling concept, that allowed Ben Sira to present the Torah in a particular light, the second part does not offer such a clear conceptual framework. For Ben Sira's understanding of the meaning of the prophetic corpus to emerge, we must therefore analyze some of the themes that appear in the second part of the Praise, as well as some of the differences between the first and the second part. An account of these will allow us to uncover Ben Sira's understanding of the meaning of the prophetic corpus, and of what distinguishes the Prophets from the Torah.

One of the important features that distinguish between the first and second parts of the Praise is the linguistic (rather than the thematic) subject. The Praise of the earlier part of the canon highlighted God's actions. It was God who was the subject of the narrative flow of the earlier part of the Praise. By contrast, the second part of the Praise highlights human action. Nowhere in the second part of the Praise does Ben Sira adopt the continued reference to

---

39   Reference to building activity begins already with Hezekiah in 48:17. Ben Sira also uses ch. 49 to mention those biblical figures, from the book of Genesis, whom he did not incorporate into the first part of the Praise. These include both the earlier generations, Adam, Seth, Shem, Enosh and Joseph. The case of Joseph offers further proof to the claim that the first part of the Praise is governed by the centrality of the covenant. Those heroes whom Ben Sira feels the need to mention, but who do not fall within the thematic concerns of the first part of the Praise are thus relegated to its conclusion. This forms a kind of inclusio, expanding the specific inclusio of Enoch, referred to both at the opening of the Praise (44:16) and in its conclusion (49:14). I believe this reading adequately responds to the points raised by Carr, Canonization, 39, based upon which Carr rejects the understanding that Ben Sira had before him a canonical collection of prophets.

God as the subject of the Praise. This part of the Praise extols human action, not divine. This distinction is quite significant. If underlying the division of the Praise into two parts is the distinction between Torah and Prophets, we may have here a key to the meaning ascribed by Ben Sira to the division of Torah and Prophets. The Torah is an expression of divine action, while the Prophets are more of an expression of human activity.

Attention to the particular kind of human activity reported in the second part of the Praise is significant. Let us begin by noting those instances in the second part of the Praise in which we do encounter divine action. It seems that where we have divine action in the second part of the Praise, it is in response to human prayer. The first hero of the second part, Joshua, calls to God, and God answers, thereby allowing Ben Sira to speak of God's actions in miraculously intervening in Joshua's wars (46:5–6). A similar pattern is found in the case of Samuel, where divine miraculous action follows Samuel's prayer (46:16–18).

The next person to pray is David (47:5). However, David's prayer is not followed by divine action, but by human appreciation of his might. Instead, divine action with regard to David appears at the end of the section, where God is described as forgiving David's sin, and establishing his kingdom (47:11). Immediately prior to this reference to God's action we find repeated mention of David's songs, composed for God's glory. Reference to David as poet and author of the Psalms takes up four bicola in verses 8–10 of ch. 47. Ben Sira thus seems to portray God's actions in the case of David as a reaction to David's liturgical activity, in the composition of the Psalms. Ben Sira thereby seems to suggest that David's sin is forgiven not on account of his repentance, but on account of his prayer, as expressed in the Psalms.[40] A final instance of divine action in response to human prayer is found in 48:20, where following the people's prayer during the siege of Jerusalem by Rabshakeh, the people call in prayer, and God again intervenes miraculously and saves them.[41]

---

40   Contrast this with the treatment of Solomon. Both Solomon and David sin and both compose biblical works, including works of praise. David's works are presented as the prayer that brings about God's forgiveness. Solomon's works, by contrast, are the product of his youth (47:14), and his sin is the product of his old age. His books cannot therefore be the cause of God forgiving his sins.

41   There are only two further instances of divine action in the second part of the Praise. Both of these are short, and serve as bridges, leading from one historical period to the other. The first is in 47:22, where Ben Sira describes the splitting of the Davidic kingdom. Yet, due to His promise to David, God does not destroy his lineage. The second instance is a brief reference to God in 49:5, where Israel's power and glory are given to other nations. In both instances the reference is to broad historical movements, and not to specific historical actions of God. Perhaps more importantly, in both instances a keyword is used that is associated with the first part of the Praise. In 47:22 חסד is used, which is clearly associated with the first part of the Praise, see 44:1, 10. Note also 46:7

It is important to note that divine action is not necessary in order to justify the miraculous. The entire passage on Elijah and Elisha (48:1–14) highlights their power to perform miracles, without making any reference either to God as actor or to prayer. Miracles could have been described as expressions of human power in other instances as well. The association of human prayer and divine action is thus intentional. I believe it suggests something significant about the second part of the canon. The second part of the Praise, addressing the prophetic corpus, presents prayer as an activity typical of the heroes in this part of the Praise.

The suggestion that prayer is significant in providing the religious meaning of the prophetic works gains weight when we note that none of the heroes in the earlier part of the Praise are described as praying. We know that Abraham and Moses prayed. They could be taken as paradigms of prayer and of the miraculous intervention of God in Israel's life. What is told of Joshua and Samuel could have easily been told of them. Yet Ben Sira chooses to not refer to them in this light. That prayer is found only in the second part of the Praise and not in the first seems therefore highly significant. It is best understood as part of Ben Sira's attempt to give meaning to this part of the canon.

Let us reflect further upon how prayer provides for Ben Sira a key to the religious significance of the prophetic works. We should note that Ben Sira devotes a much greater portion of the second part of the Praise to the figures of the so-called former prophets (Joshua, Samuel, David) than to the classical prophets: Isaiah, Jeremiah and Ezekiel, all of whom get the briefest mention. If the purpose of the second part of the Praise is to relate to the prophets, why did Ben Sira devote so little attention to the great prophets, telling instead the stories of conquest and battle? I believe this is due to the fact that in composing the Praise, Ben Sira is struggling with the religious meaning of the

---

where Ben Sira tells a tale of Joshua that is not in the Prophets, but in the Torah. The choice of חסד here seems intentional. Ben Sira seems to signal that he has briefly shifted back to a story from the Torah, by clearly communicating that this event occurred in the days of Moses, and is hence marked by חסד. In this light it seems reasonable to interpret 49:3 as a reference to the finding of the Torah in the days of Josiah. This leaves us with only one additional use of חסד in the second part, the one under discussion in 47:22. If God is faithful to his covenant with David, then His action is in keeping with covenantal fidelity. That brings Ben Sira thematically back to the first part of the Praise. Hence, divine action seems intentionally accompanied by חסד, to suggest that we have here an additional inroad of the first part of the Praise into the second. The other instance of divine action, in 49:5, is accompanied by כבוד, which as we have already noted is characteristic, if not exclusive, of the first part. I believe these two exceptions do not upset the governing principle that God does not usually act in the second part of the Praise unless in response to human prayer. Ben Sira seems to be aware of when he deviates from this rule. Not only are the references very brief and general, they are also accompanied by linguistic indications that Ben Sira is aware of his deviations.

prophetic corpus. The religious significance of Jeremiah and Isaiah is obvious and needs little elaboration. They are prophets because their prophetic activity is easily recognizable, as visionaries and mediators of the divine word. But what is it that makes the book of Joshua a work of prophecy? The questions that the earlier books of the prophetic canon place before Ben Sira are far more challenging, and this is why he goes to greater lengths to provide them with religious meaning. We have already seen how Ben Sira casts Joshua as a prophet, and how David is discussed only after Nathan is presented as the prophet in his days. It seems to me that the attempt to uncover the religious significance of this part of Scripture is not limited to the association of the heroes with prophets. Ben Sira also portrays these heroes in moments of prayer, thereby suggesting prayer as a kind of prophetic activity. Prayer is thus a means of endowing this part of canon with religious significance. Prayer is the human speech, directed at God, just as Torah is the divine speech, addressed to humans. One way of making sense of the bipartite division of Scripture is through the distinction between two dimensions of speech, flowing between God and Israel. The prophets are those who speak to God, in response to His speech. Hence, prayer is constitutive of the prophetic experience.[42] Ben Sira introduces prayer into this part of the Praise because it helps uncover the prophetic significance of the second part of the canon.[43]

While prayer is typical and constitutive of the second part of the Praise, it is not the only theme featured in it. Two elements seem to appear repeatedly in Ben Sira's descriptions of prophetic times: forms of power and ways in which these are related to the use of religious speech. In addition to prayer, the second part of the Praise points to other forms of religious use of language. Let us examine the various sub-sections of the second part of the Praise.

The opening verse of the second part of the Praise, 46:1, designates Joshua as prophet and mighty hero. It seems to me this opening phrase captures key elements that will appear throughout the second part of the Praise. Joshua's heroic deeds are spelled out in the chapter. We have already noted how Joshua calls out to God. Samuel too is both prophet and judge. His appointing of kings takes place as an expression of the word of God, בדבר אל (46:13). Reference to his speech occurs once again in his appointment of

---

42   There is, of course, biblical precedent for the image of the prophet as the one who prays (see Gen 20:7).

43   The implication of this suggestion is that Ben Sira may have conceived of the Psalms as a kind of prophetic work, since it is a form of prayer to God. If indeed Ben Sira had only two parts to his canon, he may have included reference to works that we do not consider to be prophetic under the rubric of prophetic works. Prayer may have enabled him to do so. David is presented as praising God in 47:8–10. In the case of Solomon, praise is mentioned in 47:15, although Proverbs is not necessarily to be taken as prophetic.

David (46:15), and he too is portrayed in prayer (46:16). His prayer is related to the conquest of enemies.[44] David is clearly a hero of might. Ben Sira's portrayal of David in ch. 47 highlights two themes: David's power, which is later expressed in his conquest of enemies, and his composition of songs of praise for God. David too prays, as we noted above.

Unlike David, Solomon is not portrayed as powerful. While we have reference to his speech, expressed in his wisdom (47:14–17), his power is expressed only in his wealth, or in the very fact that he is king. However, Solomon may be the exception that proves the rule. Ben Sira highlights the uniqueness of Solomon's times as times of peace, and the construction of the temple during such times (47:13). The avoidance of the expressions of power may thus be deliberate. Instead, Solomon is designated in terms of his great name, and by his sharing in the divine name (47:16, 18). As will be seen elsewhere, in those instances in which Ben Sira does not highlight the two themes of power and religious speech, he features instead reference to the name of the hero. Name or memory (זכר, שם) thus function as a third motive in this section, filling in gaps when Ben Sira does not employ the other two motives.

The section on Elijah and Elisha certainly presents power, though not of a military nature. Both Elijah and Elisha are designated as prophets. Emphasis on the power of speech, both theirs and God's, appears several times in the passage.[45] A different kind of power is associated with these two prophets – the power to perform miracles, to change the laws of nature, and to overcome death.

The section on Hezekiah and Isaiah presents us again with different kinds of power. On the one hand we encounter the power to overcome the camp of Assyria, by force of prayer (48:20–21). But we also find another kind of power associated with Hezekiah. The opening verse (48:17), punning on Hezekiah's name, states:

יחזקיהו חזק עירו, בהטות אל תוכה מים
ויחצב כנחשת צורים, ויחסום הרים מקוה

Unlike David, where Nathan is first mentioned as a lead in to the description of David, here Hezekiah is mentioned prior to the mention of Isaiah, who appears only later, when God answers their prayer, and delivers them by the hands of Isaiah (48:20). This change is significant. It stems, in part, from Ben Sira's need to pun upon Hezekiah's name as a source of strength. It can also be accounted for by the fact that unlike the case of Nathan and David, where Nathan was inserted somewhat artificially, in order to relate David's kingship to the prophetic office, in the present instance the prophet receives significant

---

44   V. 18. The subject of the verse can be either Samuel or God.
45   Ch. 48, verses 1, 3, 12.

independent treatment later in the passage, thereby allowing Hezekiah to stand on his own. In any event, another kind of strength is expressed here. This is the strength of building and fortification, strengthening the city and building a *mikveh*, a water gathering, within the city. The significance of this description in the overall structure of the praise will become obvious when we consider the Praise of Simeon in ch. 50. Different types of strength find expression in the different sub-sections of the Praise. In this case, where physical military strength is lacking – Assyria are not defeated by military power, but by a divine plague – another form of strength is expressed.

This is the last of the longer treatments of biblical figures. Ch. 49, as we have noted, consists of shorter references to specific figures. References to prophets are obvious in the present context, and need no explanation. Less obvious are the references to builders in the latter part of the chapter, where Zerubbabel, Jeshua son of Jozadak and Nehemiah are mentioned. The concerns here no longer seem to be canonical.[46] Rather, builders follow the precedent of Hezekiah, in providing a background for the activities of Simeon the High Priest, the subject of the Praise in ch. 50.[47] Thus, Ben Sira introduces an additional focus to his presentation. Alongside mention of prophets, and the heroes of the prophetic canon, Ben Sira makes special mention of builders, as preparation for the Praise of Simeon.

One other element appears in the second part of the Praise, to which I have already alluded. In several instances Ben Sira does not seem to have anything significant to say about the heroes, or at least does not relate the figures to the themes that govern the second part of the Praise. In these instances Ben Sira simply makes mention of the name and memory of these figures. This is how he treats the Judges (46:11–12) and Josiah (49:1–3). Ben Sira refers to only three kings as righteous kings: David, Hezekiah, and Josiah (49:4). While the descriptions of David and Hezekiah fit the wider patterns I presented above, Josiah is referred to as a righteous king, but neither in relation to prayer and prophecy, nor in relation to power.[48] As I suggested above, this may also be the case with regard to Solomon.

Reference to the heroes' name and memory is significant in one particular aspect – it highlights the focus upon them as human, emphasizing their human achievement and individuality. The alternative to human name is, of course, the divine name. It is significant that the only reference to name in the

---

46 A fact that may be supported by the lack of mention of Ezra. I agree with Ska's understanding of this lack. See Ska, L'éloge, 191–92.

47 This renders unnecessary the suggestion of Vermeylen, Pourquoi, 195–214.

48 As I mentioned above, this may be because Ben Sira alludes in 49:3 to the story of the finding of the Torah and the consequent reforms. If so, thematically Josiah fits into the first part of the Praise. Hence, Ben Sira does not describe him in terms characteristic of the second part of the Praise, preferring instead to simply refer to his name and memory.

first part of the Praise is to God's name, while the second part of the Praise is the only one in which the human name of the hero is singled out.[49] This corroborates the distinction already seen from the linguistic evidence, where the first part of the Praise focuses properly on God, while the second part focuses upon the human heroes. The distinction between human and divine thus appears once again as a feature distinguishing the two parts of the Praise from one another.

All this leads us to the following generalization, regarding the difference between the two parts of the Praise. The first part is devoted to the Torah, the word of God. Its proper subject is therefore God himself. By contrast, the second part is devoted to the Prophets. The distinction between Torah and Prophets emerges as the distinction between the divine and the human. What characterizes the prophets is human action and human power. Various types of power are represented, including military power, building power and the power to perform miracles. These manifestations of human power are not autonomous, and they bear a strong relationship to God, by virtue of appeal to him and to his word. Whether through prayer, or in some other way, the heroes in the second part manifest power in association with God, in what is at times a dialogical relationship and at other times a relationship in which divine speech and power are extended to the human agent. The divine thus manifests itself through the human in speech and in power, finding expression in multiple arenas of life. The prophets and the prophetic corpus thus give expression to the reality of God as it finds expression through human reality. It is the power of religiously hallowed speech that provides the link between the human and the divine.

A further distinction comes into focus as an extension of the distinction between divine and human. There is a different sense of time that governs the first and the second parts of the Praise. The first part of the Praise, depicting divine action, refers to time in terms of eternity. There are no less than 6 oc-

---

49   For use of divine name in the first part, see 45:15. God's name does appear in the second part of the Praise, but only as object of worship, in particular in the context of the temple (see 47:10 and 47:13). Solomon comes close to being associated with the divine name in 47:18, but Ben Sira avoids reference to the name of God, a term he uses in all other instances. Concerning memory, there is one occurrence of it in the first part, in 45:1. Either Ben Sira is less strict with his use of memory than he is with his use of name, despite the parallelism, or else Moses is an exception, being a bridge between the first and second parts of the Praise, by virtue of his prophetic office (compare 46:1). It is interesting that reference to the זכר of Moses is made as the second part of the verse describing his being beloved of God and men. This may not be accidental. In all the above I exclude discussion of the prologue to the Praise, in ch. 44. Following my analysis of the Praise, a reading of the prologue should be offered that indicates awareness of different classes of heroes, corresponding to the different parts of the Praise. Such a reading would conform to the suggestion according to which name, and probably memory, are characteristic of heroes of the second part of the Praise.

currences of עולם in the first part of the Praise.[50] There are no references to the times of individual figures in the first part, and the entire presentation happens in some eternal continuous present-time. Significantly, none of the figures are introduced as living in particular times, the בימי being completely absent from the first part. By contrast, בימי is a key term in the second part. As soon as Joshua is introduced, we learn that something happened in his days, בימיו (46:1). Various other references are found in the second part.[51] Other terms are also found in the second part suggesting a time-bound awareness.[52] Perhaps one should also note in this context that in the first part there are no temporal connections between the descriptions of the heroes. While Ben Sira is clearly aware of the temporal sequence, and presents his heroes in this sequence, their presentation is not a function of such sequence.[53] By contrast, the second part has many temporal links between its parts, as well as temporal distinctions within some of the sub-sections. A distinction is made regarding Samuel's activities in life and after death (46:20). A similar distinction is later introduced concerning Elisha (48:14). Distinctions between youth and later age are introduced for David and Solomon (47:4, 14). Temporal sequence is highlighted with regard to David (47:1), Solomon (47:12), the movement following Solomon's death (47:23), Elijah (48:1), and sins following this period (48:15). From ch. 46 till the end of ch. 48 we are presented with a chronological sequence,[54] with one link following

---

50   This does not include references in the prologue. These are 44:18 and 45:7, 13, 15, 24, 26. See in addition לדור ודור in 44:16. עולם does appear in the second part of the Praise, and perhaps is not an exclusive marker of the first part. Nevertheless, with the exception of חרפת עולם in 47:4, the contexts are reminiscent of the first part: the eternal covenant with David, incorporated into the first part through the brief allusion 45:25, in 47:11 and the glory of the temple in 49:12. We have already seen that reference to the temple cuts across the distinctions otherwise made between the two parts of the Praise. For 48:25 see below, n. 55.

51   The first reference is followed by a reference to the days of Moses in 46:7. The hero is still Joshua, and not Moses, who properly belongs to the first part of the Praise. Other cases are 47:13; 48:12, 18; 49:3. The only reference in the first part is in 45:15: כימי שמים. This, of course, is more of a parallel to עולם than a proper reference to a particular time. Once again, the prologue takes on new significance in light of the present distinction. See 44:2 and 7.

52   See 46:19 and 20 and 48:10 for עת. The term does appear, however, also in 44:17, in relation to Noah.

53   There is obviously some temporal sequence in the reference to Abraham's descendants, in ch. 44, but that is the only suggestion of passage of time or of sequence in the first part.

54   Further thought should be given to the relationship between chronological sequence and historical awareness. I have claimed that Ben Sira is not doing history in the Praise. The chronological flow of the second part of the Praise must be considered in relation to this claim. Obviously, chronology is one component of historical awareness. It is

another, with the appropriate terms connecting the different links.[55] Nothing of the sort is found in the first part of the Praise, despite the fact that there is an implied historical sequence there as well. There is instead an eternal quality in the list of personalities presented in the first part. We are confronted with a gallery of great figures all of whom radiate eternity, rather than with a historical sequence of people, following one another in historical procession.[56] That the first part concludes with the words לדורות עולם is thus representative of the quality of the first part as expressing eternity.[57] The first and second parts of the Praise can thus be captured in terms of eternity and time. The distinction between divine and human is mirrored in the distinction between eternal and time-bound. This distinction adds further significance to Ben Sira's reflection on the meaning of the canonical division of Torah and

---

not, however, sufficient in and of itself to establish history as Ben Sira's concern in the Praise. That chronological awareness is particular to the second part of the Praise suggests it is a part of a larger awareness, rather than the conditioning perspective. Furthermore, most of the sequential presentation is intended to explain the circumstances leading to the destruction and rebuilding of the temple. Whatever degree of historical awareness is expressed in Ben Sira's poem, it seems to be centered around the temple, and around providing a background to events related to it, including the work of Simeon the High Priest, as reported in ch. 50. Chronology thus serves as background to understanding a particular moment in time, rather than a wider understanding of the flow of history and its deeper logic.

55   Ch. 49, while still time-bound in its consciousness, is no longer part of this narrative, because of the short references typical of this chapter. In view of the fact that ch. 48 is the conclusion of this time-bound sequence, it is interesting to note that the concluding verse of the chapter (v. 25) refers to עולם. The conclusion of the time-bound is in pointing back to the eternal, the proper subject of the first part. That the narrative pattern changes in ch. 49 supports my suggestion that for Ben Sira the earlier prophetic books presented more of a challenge than the later ones. The carefully constructed sequence corresponds to the period of the earlier prophetic books. The latter works are not part of this sequence, and are only briefly alluded to. This suggestion poses a difficulty, concerning the mention of Josiah at the beginning of ch. 49. Josiah should have been part of the earlier narrative sequence. The narrative sequence may have been broken because Ben Sira is leading to the summary of righteous kings in 49:4, and is not interested in the narrative itself. See also previous note. An alternative understanding is that the historical sequence ends at 48:15. From 48:16 Ben Sira presents the kings according to virtue, and not according to a historical sequence. Two righteous kings are presented, each in relation to a prophet – Hezekiah and Isaiah, Josiah and Jeremiah. Note, however, that no direct link is established between Josiah and Jeremiah, except for being mentioned in the same paragraph.

56   The closest to a historical presentation is 44:23. However, no temporal terms are used here. The move from Aaron to Phinehas and to David makes no indication of distinction of time period.

57   The most probable reading is that the address in 45:25–26 is to the priests who hear Ben Sira's praise. If one were to understand that Ben Sira is turning to the figures he has just described, the point would be even more powerful.

Prophets. Torah expresses the timeless divine realm. Prophecy expresses the human, time-bound, as it responds to, and as it associates with, the divine.

Torah and Prophecy thus emerge as distinct realms. The canonical division expresses a major religious distinction between the two parts of canon, corresponding ultimately to the distinction between the divine and the human. What Ben Sira has offered us is thus a reflection upon the meaning of the canonical division into two parts. The wider structure of the canon presents us with separate emphases upon the eternal word of God and the time-bound word of man, addressed to God, or uttered in association with God. Through how Ben Sira structures the two parts of the Praise he provides us with insight as to the meaning of the division of the canon into two. This is the earliest reflection upon the meaning of this canonical division, attempting to clarify the religious significance of the division between Torah and Prophets.

6. The Praise of Simeon

Scholars who have understood the Praise as history have emphasized the continuum of figures appearing in the Praise of the Fathers, culminating in Simeon. Simeon is grafted onto the gallery of Israel's greats, thereby bringing history to its fulfilment. "Not only is the history of Israel followed right into Ben Sira's own time, but the resolution of all of the major themes suggests that the history of promise and formation finally is being actualized".[58]

The canonical understanding that I have offered necessitates a different understanding of the relationship between the Praise of the Fathers and the Praise of Simeon. The end of ch. 49 clearly signals the end of Ben Sira's engagement with canonical materials. All figures dealt with up to that point are biblical figures. By returning to the starting point of the biblical story – the figure of Adam, Ben Sira draws to a close the survey of biblical greats by returning to the point of origin, thereby indicating the end of his treatment of biblical materials. The echoing technique, to which I referred earlier, provides further indication that Ben Sira concludes a unit, moving on to a different, if related, unit. The meaning of the transition between ch. 49 and ch. 50 is thus the move from scriptural reference to a contemporary reference to Simeon the High Priest. But if we do not understand this transition in terms of historical continuity and fulfilment, how are we to make sense of the continuity between the Praise of the Fathers and Praise of Simeon? We must account for this transition in a way that will respect both the break and separation between the two praises and the obvious continuity there is between them.

---

58   Mack, Wisdom, 55.

The recognition that the Praise of the Fathers has two distinct parts, each with its own unique thematic emphasis, reflecting a bipartite division of scriptural canon, is significant for understanding how Ben Sira presents Simeon. Unlike the historical understanding, a canonical reading does not allow us to see in Simeon a part of the previous story. He can, however, be presented as an expression and a realization of the biblical virtues expressed in the praise of the two parts of the biblical canon. The unique features of both parts of the biblical canon, expressed through the thematic particularity of the two parts of the Praise of the Fathers, are fulfilled in the person of Simeon. Simeon is thus a fulfilment not of history but of the ideal religious types representative of Scripture in its entirety. Rather than a story that simply has its next chapter, the canon functions as a source of signification, endowing later reality with meaning. The closure of the canon and its autonomous standing allow it to find expressions in ongoing life. The meaning is derived precisely from the fact that the canon is complete, and its message is self-standing. This self-standing reality can then be realized and fulfilled, as a blessing, as a sign, or as the fulfilment of scriptural reality in and of itself.

The process of the realization of Scripture in a person or in a particular reality seems to be inherent in how Scripture is understood in Second Temple and later Judaism. Scripture is not understood in isolation from reality, but in relation to it, always seeking to find specific representation and realization in individuals and circumstances. The Gospels' reading of the life of Jesus as the fulfilment of Scripture is a prime example of the same attitude to Scripture. So is the rabbinic habit of proclaiming the applicability of a particular verse to a person or a situation.[59] Paradoxically, Scripture's autonomous status and closure allow it to remain open to reality, inviting its actualization in the lives of people. The closure of Scripture does not mean a rupture with history. Yet reality is not integrated by means of a historical continuum. Rather, Scripture functions as a hermeneutical lens, by means of which later life is understood and interpreted. As Gerald Sheppard's work indicates, the implications of a canon-conscious perspective are hermeneutical. Scripture offers the hermeneutical lens by means of which later reality is conceived.

The case of Simeon the High Priest provides a beautiful illustration for how canonical awareness shapes the image of contemporary reality. Simeon is understood in terms that grow directly out of the earlier treatment of canonical materials. Ben Sira seeks to describe him as the ideal person. He does this by appeal to the typology he has already established in the Praise of the Fathers. This typology classifies different types of personalities and activities, corresponding to the different parts of Scripture. Simeon is then described as someone possessing the ideal and representative qualities of the heroes of both parts of the Praise of the Fathers. Simeon is presented in a way that sug-

---

59   See, for example, *Ta'an.* 3.8.

gests he is a synthesis of the two types, corresponding to the Torah and the Prophets. He thus provides in his person an integration of what are otherwise distinct features, representing different forms of religious perfection.

Had we stuck to a purely historical reading, the conclusion that Simeon is the most perfect man, the fulfilment of all that preceded, would have been inevitable. However, because we are dealing with the implementation of Scripture in a hermeneutical movement to the life of a person, the conclusion should not be that Simeon is the most perfect, greater in perfection than Moses, Aaron, Elijah and all the other greats mentioned in Ben Sira's poem. Instead, he is perfect because the perfection established independently in Scripture, and serving perpetually as a benchmark for the ideal life, finds such perfect and harmonious expression in his person. Scripture sets the standard by which Simeon is measured, and favourably so.

Let us now examine what is told of Simeon, and see the ways in which his praise echoes themes from both parts of the Praise of the Fathers. Ben Sira begins his presentation of Simeon with a clear time-bound reference to building activities that took place in Simeon's time. No less than four references are made to the time and the generation of Simeon in the first three verses of Simeon's Praise. In Simeon's days the building was strengthened, the ramparts were fortified, and a מקוה was dug. The continuity with building activity reported in the second part of the Praise of the Fathers is obvious. Particularly striking is the correspondence to Hezekiah. מחזק עירו in 50:4 echoes חזק עירו, reported of Hezekiah in 48:17. Reference to מקוה is explicit in both. Simeon's building activity obviously continues the building activity reported of several figures at the end of ch. 49 as well. That strength is significant to the description of Simeon emerges from the fact that the verb חזק is repeated twice in the opening verses. Unlike the case of Hezekiah in 48:17, this is not the fruit of punning. It therefore reflects what is central to Ben Sira in his portrayal of Simeon.

Following this, we find a description of Simeon's splendor and glory at the time of worship.[60] The beauty of the High Priest is, of course, reminiscent of the description of Aaron at the end of the first part of the Praise of the Fathers. There is, however, one significant element that appears in the Praise of Simeon that is lacking in the description of Aaron.[61] Nowhere in the de-

---

60 This has usually been taken as reference to the Yom Kippur service, though other suggestions have been made as well. See the paper by Otto Mulder in the present volume.

61 I will not enter here into a full analysis of Simeon's Praise. Some elements, such as the poetic descriptions in vv. 6–10, are best understood against the background of the Praise of Creation in chs. 42–43. A fuller appreciation of the sequence of praises and their internal allusions is beyond the present scope. I attach great significance to the movement from the Praise of Creation to the Praise of the Fathers, culminating in the Praise of Simeon.

scription of Aaron is there any reference to prayer, or to sound, speech and song that are pronounced as part of the temple service before God.[62] Aaron is glorious on account of his vestments, and his service in the temple is exclusively by means of the sacrificial order, with all its components. Simeon is not represented simply as a latter-day Aaron. Rather, we note that alongside his sacrificial activity there is also activity of prayer, and activity involving speech and sound. Trumpets sound (v. 16), a great and mighty sound is sounded before God (v. 17), song is offered (v. 18), and the people pray before God. This is not directly reported of Simeon. It does, however, introduce elements that are typical of the second part of the Praise of the Fathers into his Praise.

While the description of Simeon introduces elements that are typical of the second part of the Praise of the Fathers, one cannot mistake the fact that his presentation is essentially modelled on the examples of Aaron and Phinehas, figures representing the first part of the Praise of the Fathers. This is true of the description of the temple worship and of the splendor and glory of Simeon. It becomes even more obvious in the concluding verses of the Praise. Verses 22–24 echo the concluding verses of the first part of the Praise of the Fathers, at the conclusion of ch. 45. Both conclusions open with the formula ועתה ברכו נא את יי. Both contain a prayer for the granting of the wisdom of heart. The language used in the concluding verses of Simeon's Praise echoes language typical of the first part of the Praise of the Fathers. Here, and only here for the first time since we left the description of the Torah and moved on to a description of the prophetic canon, do we encounter ברית. We also encounter again חסד. Verse 24 – ויקם, חסדו שמעון עם יאמן לו ברית פינחס, is thus a return to the first part of the Praise of the Fathers, suggesting Simeon should be seen not only as an example of ideal activities of the second part of the Praise of the Fathers, but also as an ideal expression of the first part. Indeed, we find a return to the form of linguistic expression typical of the first part of the Praise, shifting the subject from Simeon himself to God as the author of actions. When God is praised in verse 22, saying המגדל אדם מרחם ויעשהו כרצונו, we should not construe this as a denial of free choice, and the shifting of the agency of action onto God.[63] Rather, we have here a return to the linguistic pattern typical of the first part of the Praise of the Fathers, that presents God, rather than the human person, as the subject. To speak of Simeon in these terms is to say that his perfection shares in

---

62   It is interesting, in this context, to recall the work of Israel Knohl, who has addressed the fact that worship during the First Temple period seems to have been carried out in silence. See Knohl, Sanctuary.

63   A fuller appreciation of this phrase leads us to considerations of the relationship between the Praise of Simeon and the Praise of Creation, which, as stated, are beyond the scope of this presentation.

the kind of perfection brought about only by God, as representative of his own action, captured in the Torah. Simeon is thus the synthesis of human and divine action, of the perfection typical of Torah as well as of the perfection representative of the Prophets. His perfection is thus synthetic.

That the Praise of Simeon concludes with a blessing of faithfulness that is כימי שמים serves as a counterpoint to the opening verses of Simeon's Praise, in which the time bound quality of his actions was emphasized. What began as completely time-bound and corresponding in quality to the perfection of the prophetic canon concludes with the eternal, divine-based perfection, continuous with the perfection of the Torah, as captured in the covenants made at that time, with Aaron and Phinehas. Appeal to the covenant does not suggest that the ongoing battle, throughout Israel's history, has finally been won. Rather, the perfection of the hero at hand is described in accordance with patterns and ideals representative of the fundamental canonical division. Accordingly, we return for the first time to the covenantal gift of God, typical of the Torah. Simeon is thus the perfect man because he is seen as perfect through the lens of Scripture, and through the categories through which it is perceived, bringing those to their harmonious integration. Ultimately, Simeon is perfect because the totality of Scripture is the mark and the representation of perfection, both human and divine.

7. Future Work

I hope I have succeeded in proving that a new approach must be adopted towards the reading of Ben Sira's Praise of the Fathers. Once it is accepted that the Praise of the Fathers must be read against the background of awareness of the structure and content of the biblical canon, a range of textual and theoretical issues present themselves. The reading I have offered suggests what is the backbone of Ben Sira's presentation. There are numerous textual details that have not been part of my presentation, and which deserve further attention, as part of a careful close reading of the Praise, in the suggested new light. Particular attention must be paid to the prologue of the Praise, and to how it fits the suggested understanding. We have noted that the Praise of the Fathers is situated between the Praise of Creation and the Praise of Simeon. While I have suggested how Simeon's Praise is tied into the Praise of the Fathers, we have not yet looked at the Praise of Creation, nor at how the entire sequence must be read as one continuum. All these textual considerations must await future work.

The chapters I have analyzed occupy more than 15 percent of Ben Sira's book. Their location at the end of his work raises the question of their import in the overall structure of his book. This in turn raises the question of the relationship between the ideas expressed in the Praise and other parts of Ben Sira's work. In light of the new reading of the Praise, other parts of the book should be examined, both for parallels and for additional expressions of Ben Sira's canonical awareness. I believe the suggested reading of the Praise allows us to frame new categories in light of which other parts of the book may be read. For example: the distinction between prayer and Torah study, as distinguishing the different parts of the Praise, should motivate a more detailed investigation of these two themes and their relationship in other parts of the work.

I have ignored in my presentation a key element in the Praise of the Fathers. As I noted, the Temple and its worship play a major role in the Praise. Once the centrality of the Temple is recognized, interesting questions concerning the economy and hierarchy of religious values in Ben Sira's world emerge. What can be said concerning the relationship between Torah study, such as underlies the entire logic of the Praise, and Temple worship? And what kind of historical awareness informs Ben Sira's work? My argument has been that scriptural awareness has, to a large extent, displaced historical awareness, and that therefore reading the Praise through a historical lens distorts its true concerns. Can the decline in historical awareness be documented in other parts of the book? To what extent is it related to the rise in scriptural awareness, and to what extent is it a consequence of other factors? How are the changes in the historical notion of covenant, so central to the Hebrew Bible as well as to the Praise, yet so different in their respective uses, indicative of wider changes in historical awareness? And what is the relationship between the cosmic awareness, expressed in various places in Ben Sira's work and the possible decline in historical awareness? Cosmos, history, Scripture and Temple are configured in interesting and novel ways in Ben Sira's work. The Praise of the Fathers allows us a peek into new religious configurations, that set Ben Sira apart from earlier biblical tradition, and that make him much more similar to later rabbinic literature. The entire complex of themes here noted, and their particular configurations, thus serve as an indicator for the evolution of Judaism from its biblical to rabbinic phases, with Ben Sira providing us with a window upon these transitions as they take place. The questions emerging out of my reading of the Praise of the Fathers are thus significant not only for the text itself, nor are they limited to an understanding of the thought of Ben Sira. Ultimately, they touch upon cardinal questions that concern the growth and development of Judaism in late Second Temple period.

One final set of questions should not be forgotten. What is the function of the formation of the biblical canon upon the shifts and transformations here alluded to? Can the emerging new balance of ideas, concepts and values be traced to the recent phenomenon of scriptural canonization? What new religious possibilities are opened up through the creation of canon, and to what extent can we find in Ben Sira an important test case for the very meaning of canon? As the earliest Jewish reflection on the meaning of canon, Ben Sira allows us not only to ask how canon works and what it means, but also what shifts and transformations in religious world view can be attributed to the formation of canon.

All these challenging ideas seem to me to grow out of the suggested new reading of the Praise of the Fathers. Clearly, the work has just begun. May Ben Sira's own words, ch. 39, v. 6, be applied to the completion of this work.

Bibliography

Beckwith, R.T., *The Old Testament Canon of the New Testament Church* (London: SPCK, 1985).

Beentjes, P.C., "Hezekiah and Isaiah: A Study on Ben Sira xlviii 15–25," in *New Avenues in the Study of the Old Testament: A collection of Old Testament Studies* (ed. A.S. van der Woude; Oudtestamentische Studiën 25; Leiden: Brill, 1989) 77–88.

Carr, D.M., "Canonization in the Context of Community: An Outline of the Formation of the Tanak and the Christian Bible," in *A Gift of God in Due Season: Essays on Scripture and Community* (FS J.A. Sanders; eds. R.D. Weis and D.M. Carr; JSOTSup 225; Sheffield: Academic Press, 1996) 22–64.

Cowley, A.E. – Neubauer, A., *The Original Hebrew of a Portion of Ecclesiasticus (XXXIX.15 to XLIX.11) together with the Early Versions and an English Translation* (Oxford: Clarendon Press, 1897).

Di Lella, A.A., "Women in the Wisdom of Ben Sira and the Book of Judith: A Study in Contrasts and Reversals," in *Congress Volume, Paris 1992* (ed. J.A. Emerton; VTSup 61; Leiden et al.: Brill, 1995) 39–52.

Haspecker, J., *Gottesfurcht bei Jesus Sirach. Ihre religiöse Struktur und ihre literarische und doktrinäre Bedeutung* (AnBib 30; Rome: Pontifical Biblical Institute, 1967).

Kahana, A., בן־סירא שמעון דברי ב' כרך החיצונים הספרים (2d ed.; Tel Aviv: Masada, 1955–56).

Knohl, I., *The Sanctuary of Silence: The Priestly Torah and the Holiness School* (Minneapolis: Fortress Press, 1995).

Lee, Th.R., *Studies in the Form of Sirach 44–50* (SBLDS 75, Atlanta: Scholars Press, 1986).

Leiman, S.Z., *The Canonization of Hebrew Scripture: The Talmudic and Midrashic Evidence* (Transactions of the Connecticut Academy of Arts and Sciences 47; Hamden: Archon, 1976).

Mack, B.L., *Wisdom and the Hebrew Epic: Ben Sira's Hymn in Praise of the Fathers* (CSHJ; Chicago: University Press, 1985).

MacKenzie, R.A.F., "Ben Sira as Historian," in *Trinification of the World*, (FS F.E. Crowe; eds. T.A. Dunne and J.M. Laporte; Toronto: Regis College Press, 1978) 312–27.

Seeligmann, I.L., "Voraussetzungen der Midraschexegese," in *Congress Volume, Copenhagen 1953* (VTSup 1; Leiden: Brill, 1953) 150–81.

ספר בן סירא / *The Book of Ben Sira: Text, Concordance and an Analysis of the Vocabulary* (The Historical Dictionary of the Hebrew Language; Jerusalem: Academy of the Hebrew Language, 1973).

Segal, M.Z., השלם בן־סירא ספר (2d rev. ed.; Jerusalem: Bialik, 1958).

Sheppard, G.T., *Wisdom as a Hermeneutical Construct: A Study in the Sapientializing of the Old Testament* (BZAW 151; Berlin / New York: de Gruyter, 1980).

Siebeneck, R.T., "May Their Bones Return to Life! Sirach's Praise of the Fathers," *CBQ* 21 (1959) 411–28.

Ska, J.L., "L'éloge des Pères dans le Siracide (Si 44–50) et le canon de l'Ancien Testament," in *Treasures of Wisdom: Studies in Ben Sira and the Book of Wisdom* (FS M. Gilbert; eds. N. Calduch-Benages and J. Vermeylen; BETL 143; Leuven: Peeters, 1999) 181–93.

Skehan, P.W. – Di Lella, A.A., *The Wisdom of Ben Sira: A New Translation with Notes, Introduction and Commentary* (AB 39; New York: Doubleday, 1987).

Smend, R., *Die Weisheit des Jesus Sirach erklärt* (Berlin: Reimer, 1906).

Trenchard, W.C., *Ben Sira's View of Women: A Literary Analysis* (BJS 38; Chico: Scholars Press, 1982).

Vermeylen, J., "Pourquoi fallait-il édifier des remparts? Le Siracide et Néhémie," in *Treasures of Wisdom: Studies in Ben Sira and the Book of Wisdom* (FS M. Gilbert; eds. N. Calduch-Benages and J. Vermeylen; BETL 143; Leuven: Peeters, 1999) 195–214.

Ben Sira und die Frühe Stoa

Zum Zusammenhang von Ethik und dem Glauben an eine göttliche Providenz

Ursel Wicke-Reuter

Der systematische Theologe Christoph Schwöbel weist in einem im Jahre 2001 erschienenen Aufsatz darauf hin, dass sich die Ethik in einer "Orientierungskrise" befindet.[1] Wichtig an dieser Diagnose ist besonders die in ihr enthaltene Voraussetzung, dass nämlich die Ethik nicht nur Orientierung gibt, sondern *selbst* der Orientierung bedarf, dass sie sich folglich "*de facto* schon immer an etwas orientiert."[2] Im Anschluss an den Philosophen Alasdair MacIntyre vertritt Schwöbel die Auffassung, die Ethik habe ihren eigenen Orientierungsrahmen preisgegeben, woraus die gegenwärtige Krise resultiere. So sei der Versuch der Aufklärung, "eine unabhängige rationale Rechtfertigung der Sittlichkeit zu entwickeln," gescheitert.[3] Ohne eine Vorstellung davon, was die Bestimmung des Menschen, was Sinn und Ziel seiner Existenz ist, so die These, verliere die Ethik ihr Fundament und damit zugleich ihre Orientierungskraft.[4] Zur Wiedergewinnung dieser Basis sei es daher notwendig, neu über den Zusammenhang zwischen "Sein und Sollen" nachzudenken, zwischen dem also, was der Mensch faktisch ist und worin die seiner Bestimmung gemäße sittliche Aufgabe liegt. Die Rückbesinnung auf historische Modelle mit dem Ziel einer "Freilegung und Klärung von *Prämissen* ethischer Verständigung"[5] scheint einen wichtigen Beitrag auf diesem Wege zu leisten.

Vor diesem Hintergrund erhält die Vergegenwärtigung des Ansatzes der Stoa und Ben Siras eine überraschende Aktualität. Bei beiden wird die Ethik im Rahmen der Lehre von einer Welt und Mensch umfassenden Providenz Gottes begründet. Diesen Zusammenhang möchte ich im folgenden als ein Ergebnis meiner Dissertation vorstellen.[6]

---

1 Schwöbel, Einführung, 1ff.
2 Schwöbel, Einführung, 1.
3 Schwöbel, Einführung, 5.
4 Vgl. Schwöbel, Einführung, 7f.
5 Forschner, Handeln, 3.
6 Sie trägt folgenden Titel: *Göttliche Providenz und menschliche Verantwortung bei Ben Sira und in der Frühen Stoa* (BZAW 298; Berlin / New York: de Gruyter, 2000).

1.

Der Gedanke liegt nahe, dass in der Weltkultur des Hellenismus, durch welche kommunizierenden Kanäle auch immer, zwischen dem jüdischen Glauben und der griechischen Philosophie und Literatur trotz aller Unterschiede doch irgendwelche geistigen Beziehungen oder Einflüsse bestanden haben. Im Falle Ben Siras wurde die Frage bereits zu Beginn des vorigen Jahrhunderts gestellt. Sie erhielt zwei entgegengesetzte Antworten: Während R. Smend sen. auf der einen Seite eine antihellenistische Tendenz bei Ben Sira glaubte feststellen zu können,[7] meinte I. Lévi auf der anderen Seite zahlreiche Entlehnungen aus der griechischen Literatur nachweisen zu können.[8] Ein wichtiger neuer Impuls ging in der Mitte des vorigen Jahrhunderts von Martin Hengel aus, der in seiner bahnbrechenden Arbeit mit dem Titel "Judentum und Hellenismus" auch dem Sirachbuch ein Kapitel widmete.[9] Hengel griff erneut die von Smend vertretene These auf, indem er die Auffassung vertrat, in einer antihellenistischen Polemik liege geradezu der Grundzug des Werkes. Allerdings schloss Hengel griechische Einflüsse dabei nicht aus. Mit großer Umsicht ordnete er das Sirachbuch dem geistesgeschichtlichen Kontext seiner Zeit zu und zeigte damit, wie sehr Ben Sira selbst ein Kind des Hellenismus war. Explizit wies er u.a. auf gedankliche Berührungen mit der Stoa hin,[10] die er allerdings ebenfalls dem Kontext der von ihm als antihellenistisch gedeuteten Polemik Ben Siras zuwies.[11]

Da der Hellenismus nicht nur eine die damalige Welt umspannende, sondern auch eine *plurale* Kultur war, musste mit dieser These, selbst wenn ihr eine partielle Berechtigung zukommen sollte, nicht schon alles gesagt sein. Eine Abwehr der materialistischen Philosophien Demokrits und Epikurs wäre immerhin denkbar.[12] Ganz anders liegen die Dinge jedoch im Blick auf die Frühe Stoa. Allein die zeitliche Nähe der Lebenszeit Ben Siras zum Wirken der Schulgründer Zenon, Kleanthes und Chrysipp lässt eine gewisse Affinität zwischen beiden zumindest als vorstellbar erscheinen.[13] In der Tat lassen sich zahlreiche gedankliche Berührungspunkte finden, die eine wie auch immer geartete Begegnung Ben Siras mit stoischem Gedankengut wahrscheinlich erscheinen lassen. Einige Beobachtungen in dieser Richtung hat R.

---

7   Vgl. Smend, Weisheit, XX–XXIV.
8   Vgl. Lévi, L'Ecclésiastique, LX–LXVII.
9   Hengel, Judentum, 241–75, vgl. auch 284–92.
10 Vgl. Hengel, Judentum, 265–69.
11 Vgl. Hengel, Judentum, 268, 270.
12 Vgl. Hengel, Judentum, 256.
13 Die Schule der Stoa wurde im Jahre 301 oder 300 v.Chr. von Zenon gegründet. Nach seinem Tod im Jahre 262 oder 261 trat Kleanthes an seine Stelle, schließlich wurde Chrysipp von 232 oder 231 an bis zu seinem Tod im Jahre 208 oder 204 Schuloberhaupt, vgl. Long, Philosophy, 109, 113. Die Epoche der so genannten Frühen oder Alten Stoa ist damit an ihr Ende gelangt.

Pautrel in einem im Jahr 1963 erschienenen Aufsatz zusammengetragen,[14] ebenso J. Marböck im Rahmen seiner Studie "Weisheit im Wandel".[15] Zu nennen sind u.a. das Gesetz, die Frage der Verantwortung des Menschen, die Ordnung des Kosmos bzw. der Schöpfung.

Wie bereits Pautrel festgestellt hat, setzt jedoch die fragmentarische Überlieferung der stoischen Schriften der Frühzeit dem Vergleich mit Ben Sira eine Grenze:[16] Die Werke von Zenon, Kleanthes und Chrysipp sind fast vollständig verloren, so dass die Forschung auf das sekundäre Zeugnis von antiken Doxographien sowie von Zitaten und Paraphrasen stoischer Gedanken in den Werken anderer antiker Autoren zurückgreifen muss. Der Nachweis einer literarischen Abhängigkeit Ben Siras von der Frühen Stoa ist unter diesen Bedingungen nahezu ausgeschlossen. Daher setzt der Vergleich einen methodischen Ansatz voraus, der statt von einzelnen Redewendungen und motivischen Parallelen von komplexen gedanklichen Zusammenhängen auszugehen hätte. Dieser Weg wurde in der vorliegenden Arbeit versucht.

Auf eine kurze Formel gebracht, lässt sich die gewählte Methode als eine Verknüpfung von theologischer Exegese und vergleichender Systematik einordnen, wobei die Weisheitstraditionen auf beiden Seiten als Brücken dienen. Als Ergebnis hat sie gczeigt, dass sich Ben Sira an nicht wenigen Stellen dem Einfluss stoischer Gedanken geöffnet hat, dies aber in der Weise, dass er sich unter dem griechisch-hellenistischen Einfluss den eigenen alttestamentlich-jüdischen Traditionen nicht entfremdete. Interesse verdient dabei besonders die Beobachtung, in welchem Maß sich der jüdische Gelehrte argumentativ den Stoikern nähert, wenn es darum geht, Antworten auf Fragen zu formulieren, die ihm die eigene jüdische Tradition im Kontext der – damals – "modernen" Diskussionslage aufgegeben hat. Wenn man die inhaltlich verwandten Stellen miteinander vergleicht, so ist kaum zu übersehen, dass Ben Sira die Auseinandersetzung mit dem Fremden für die eigene Position fruchtbar gemacht hat. So gelang es ihm, den Glauben der Väter im Kontext der geistigen Herausforderungen des Hellenismus neu zu begründen. Die Eigenständigkeit in diesem Aneignungsprozess geht so weit, dass Sirach gelegentlich sogar stoische Vorstellungen in gedankliche Zusammenhänge überträgt, die der stoischen Philosophie selbst fremd sind, ja, die geradezu im Widerspruch dazu stehen.

Ein markantes Beispiel hierfür ist die Frage nach der innerweltlichen Gerechtigkeit, auf die ich unten eingehen werde (s.u. Abschnitt 5).

---

14   Ben Sira, 535–49.
15   Vgl. Marböck, Weisheit, 143ff, 170f.
16   Vgl. Pautrel, Ben Sira, 540.

2.

Die systematische Frage, die im Zentrum des Vergleichs steht, ist die nach dem Verhältnis zwischen der göttlichen Allmacht und der Verantwortung des Menschen. Diese Problemkonstellation ist das thematische Bindeglied zwischen Ben Sira und den Stoikern. Für beide ist der Gedanke der sittlichen Vervollkommnung des Menschen von entscheidender Bedeutung. Bei den Stoikern verwirklicht sie sich in der Tugend, bei Ben Sira in der Nachfolge der Weisheit, in Gottesfurcht und im Gehorsam gegen das göttliche Gesetz. Beide, Sirach und die Stoiker, stehen nun in gleicher Weise vor der Aufgabe, die Annahme der Verantwortlichkeit des Menschen mit der Vorstellung von Gott als der alles bestimmenden Wirklichkeit in Einklang zu bringen.

Der stoische Lösungsansatz geht von dem Gedanken der göttlichen Providenz aus, der Vorstellung also, dass alles im Kosmos von einem göttlichen Urheber vernünftig und zweckmäßig eingerichtet ist. Allem Anschein nach hat sich der Siracide hiervon anregen lassen. Sowohl bei Ben Sira als auch in der Stoa ist die Lehre von der göttlichen Providenz mit der Begründung der Ethik eng verknüpft. Dies möchte ich im Folgenden erläutern. Ich beginne mit der Stoa.

3.

Die Lehre von der göttlichen Providenz hat bei den Stoikern ihren Ort in der so genannten Physik, der Naturlehre also. Dabei ist die Erkenntnis wichtig, dass die stoische Naturlehre in ihrem Kern eine *rationalistische Theologie* darstellt.[17] In ihrem Zentrum steht die Auffassung, dass die Natur, die Physis, ein göttlich-rationales Prinzip ist und als solches den Kosmos durchdringt und gestaltet. Sie ist der Logos, der die gesamte Materie durchwaltet[18] – in der lateinischen Fassung: mundus est deus.[19] So verbürgt die göttliche Natur in gleicher Weise die *Einheit* des Kosmos wie seine *vernünftige Struktur*. Die Stoiker beschreiben diesen Aspekt der göttlichen Physis durch den Begriff der Pronoia (lateinisch: providentia), was sowohl Voraussicht als auch Fürsorge bedeutet. Die göttliche Natur bewirkt in ihrer Eigenschaft als Pronoia, dass ausnahmslos alles im Kosmos vernünftig und zweckmäßig eingerichtet ist. Nichts ist ohne einen Nutzen für das Ganze, alles erfüllt einen bestimmten

---

17 Vgl. hierzu Long – Sedley, Philosophers, 267; Forschner, Ethik, 246ff.
18 Vgl. von Arnim, Stoicorum Veterum Fragmenta (im folgenden zitiert als SVF I–IV plus Fragmentnummer), SVF II 1021, 1022, 1024.
19 Vgl. SVF II 641.

Zweck – selbst das, was auf den ersten Blick als sinnlos oder überflüssig erscheint.[20]

Am eindrucksvollsten zeigt sich diese rationale Ordnung an der Bewegung der Himmelskörper. Aber auch die irdischen Erscheinungen lassen erkennen, dass sie alle einer höchsten Vernunft folgen. Dies zeigt sich beispielsweise an den Tieren und Pflanzen, die von der Natur mit den Anlagen zur Erhaltung und Fortpflanzung ausgestattet wurden.[21] So hat die göttliche Allnatur den Kosmos als ein teleologisch durchstrukturiertes Ganzes hervorgebracht. Ihr Logos durchwaltet den Kosmos, der folglich als durch und durch rational zu gelten hat.

Allerdings besitzt der Kosmos eine hierarchische Struktur: Denn nicht alles partizipiert in gleicher Weise an der göttlichen Vernunft. So ist auf der niedrigsten Stufe das Anorganische angesiedelt, dann folgen Pflanzen, danach die Tiere. An der Spitze schließlich steht der Mensch. Nur er ist selbst zum Gebrauch der Vernunft in der Lage.[22] Der Mensch ist sozusagen aktiver Teilhaber an der göttlichen Vernunft. Die Stoiker gehen daher soweit, von einer Gemeinschaft zwischen Göttern und Menschen zu sprechen[23] und ihn, den Menschen, als das 'göttliche Geschlecht' zu bezeichnen.[24] Diesem Umstand verdankt es sich, dass alles im Kosmos auf den Menschen hin ausgerichtet und zu seinem Nutzen bereitgestellt ist.[25]

Aber auch der Mensch selbst hat einen Zweck zu erfüllen. Seine Aufgabe ist es, das Werk der göttlichen Natur erkennend zu betrachten und ihrem Gesetz zu folgen. Cicero überliefert diesen Gedanken in einer knappen Formel:

> *homo ortus est ad mundum contemplandum et imitandum.*
> Der Mensch ist dazu geboren, das Weltall zu betrachten und nachzuahmen.[26]

Der Zusammenhang zwischen stoischer Ethik und dem Naturbegriff der Stoa wird hier greifbar: Die Natur selbst ist es, die den Menschen zur Tugend und damit zur Wahrnehmung von Verantwortung leitet. Die Voraussetzung hierfür besteht in der Einsicht, dass der Kosmos als das Werk der göttlichen Pronoia vernünftig und "gut" ist. Aus der Betrachtung der Natur kann der Mensch folglich den Weg zur Sittlichkeit finden.[27] Der Schlüssel liegt dabei

---

20 Vgl. SVF II 1106–26.
21 Vgl. SVF II 708–37; III 178.
22 Vgl. SVF II 458 und Lapidge, Cosmology, 171.
23 So deuten die Stoiker den Kosmos als eine Stadt, die von Göttern und Menschen bewohnt wird, wobei die Götter gebieten und die Menschen ihrem Gebot Folge leisten, vgl. SVF II 528; III 333–39.
24 Vgl. SVF I 537.
25 Vgl. SVF II 1152–63.
26 Vgl. SVF II 1153.
27 Vgl. hierzu auch Forschner, Handeln, 8f.

in der stoischen Identifikation von Vernunft und Natur. So wird die Natur als "Vernunftnatur" zum Maßstab für das Gute.

Im Anschluss an diesen Naturbegriff entwickeln die Stoiker ihre Auffassung vom Gesetz: Das Gesetz, der *Nomos*, ist für die Stoiker *natürliches Gesetz*.[28] Die Natur als die reine, göttliche Vernunft "gebietet," was recht ist und verbietet das Gegenteil. So ist das universale Gesetz, das den Kosmos lenkt, zugleich das Maß des rechten Handelns, kosmische und sittliche Ordnung werden in eins gesetzt. Cicero überliefert folgende Definition:

> Das wahre Gesetz ist die rechte Vernunft, die mit der Natur übereinstimmt. Es ist von universaler Geltung, unveränderlich und von ewiger Dauer. Es ruft zur Pflicht, indem es befiehlt, und hält vom Frevel fern, indem es verbietet.[29]

Der Mensch verwirklicht seine Bestimmung geradezu im Gehorsam gegen das Gesetz, man kann daher sagen: die Sittlichkeit ist der Inbegriff des Menschseins des Menschen. Von dort ist es nur noch ein kleiner Schritt zum so genannten stoischen Telos, dem Ziel der Ethik, das vor allem in seiner lateinischen Übersetzung weite Verbreitung gefunden hat: "secundum naturam vivere" ist ein Leitspruch der Stoiker, den fast jeder Gelehrte kennt, oder auf Deutsch:

> *Daher erklärte Zenon als erster in dem Buch über die Natur des Menschen, dass das Ziel das Leben im Einklang mit der Natur ist, was dasselbe ist wie das tugendgemäße Leben. Denn dazu führt uns die Natur ... Denn unsere [einzelnen] Naturen sind Teile der Natur des Ganzen. ... Darin besteht die Tugend des Glückseligen und der gelungene Lauf des Lebens, dass man alles in Übereinstimmung des eigenen Genius mit dem Willen des Allherrschers tut.*[30]

4.

Liest man das Werk Ben Siras vor dem Hintergrund dieser stoischen Naturlehre, so stößt man zunächst auf einen Unterschied: Ben Siras Vorstellung von Gott als dem Schöpfer unterscheidet sich fundamental vom stoischen Gottesbegriff, wonach das Göttliche ein der Welt immanentes Prinzip darstellt. Dagegen hält Ben Sira an der Trennung von Gott und Welt fest. Gott bleibt im Gegenüber zur Schöpfung.[31]

---

28 Der stoische Begriff vom natürlichen Gesetz steht im Kontext der griechischen Auseinandersetzung um das Verhältnis von Natur und Gesetz, das in der sophistischen Antithese von Physis und Nomos seinen Kristallisationspunkt besaß. Vgl. dazu Forschner, Ethik, 9–24; Heinimann, Nomos; Wicke-Reuter, Providenz, 181–97.
29 SVF III 325.
30 SVF III 4.
31 Vgl. auch Hengel, Judentum, 268 und Wicke-Reuter, Providenz, 56.

Sieht man jedoch von diesem Unterschied einmal ab, so öffnet sich der
Blick für erstaunliche inhaltliche Parallelen. Auch für Ben Sira hat die Vorstellung eine fundamentale Bedeutung, dass Gott in weiser Voraussicht alles
in der Schöpfung aufeinander abgestimmt und für alles Vorsorge getroffen
hat. Der Gedanke begegnet folglich an mehreren Stellen des Buches, vor allem in den großen Hymnen auf Gott als den Schöpfer.[32]

Man kann nun einwenden, dass bereits im Alten Testament die Vorsehung Gottes eine beachtliche Rolle spielt. Beispielhaft sei auf die Josephsge-
schichte hingewiesen.[33] Neu ist bei Ben Sira jedoch die Universalisierung
entsprechender Ansätze im Alten Testament. Während dort Gottes providen-
tielles Handeln nur in einzelnen erzählerischen Zusammenhängen zur Sprache kam, wird der Gedanke durch den Siraciden generalisiert und systemati-
siert. Dabei entwickelt Ben Sira die Vorstellung von einer universal verstandenen, Schöpfung und Geschichte umfassenden Vorsehung Gottes.[34] Wie die
Stoiker vereint er dabei Voraussicht und Fürsorge. So ist von Gottes Allwissenheit nicht mehr nur im Blick auf einzelne Ereignisse oder das jeweils ak-
tuelle Geschehen die Rede. Vielmehr steht für Ben Sira fest, dass Gott *alles*
Sein vor seiner Erschaffung wissend vorweggenommen hat:

Alles war ihm bekannt, ehe es geschaffen wurde. (Sir 23,20)[35]

Oder in 39,20 stellt Ben Sira fest:

Von Ewigkeit zu Ewigkeit geht sein Blick;
gibt es eine Grenze für seine Hilfe?
Nichts ist zu klein und gering bei ihm,
und nichts ist zu wunderbar und stark vor ihm. (Sir 39,20)

In Vorwegnahme des Künftigen hat Gott alles in der Schöpfung wohl geord-
net und sinnvoll aufeinander bezogen. Ben Sira bringt den Gedanken zusammenfassend auf folgende Formel:

Die Werke Gottes sind alle gut,
und für jeden Zweck trägt er Sorge zu seiner Zeit. (Sir 39,16.33)

Mit dem allgemeinen Begriff des "Zwecks" erreicht Ben Sira in seinen Ausführungen einen Grad der Abstraktion, der dem traditionellen weisheitlichen
Denken in seiner Konkretheit und Aspekthaftigkeit eher fremd ist. Es verdient dabei besondere Aufmerksamkeit, dass der hebräische Begriff für den
Zweck (צֹרֶךְ) im Alten Testament lediglich ein einziges Mal belegt ist (2Chr

---

32   Vgl. Sir 16,17–18,14; 39,12–35; 42,15–43,35 und dazu neben den einschlägigen Kom-
      mentaren Prato, Il problema, 62–208, 262–99; Marböck, Weisheit, 134–54.
33   Vgl. die Pointe in Gen 50,19f und dazu Kaiser, Gott I, 183ff.
34   Vgl. dazu insgesamt Wicke-Reuter, Providenz, 57f, 75–79.
35   Zur Übersetzung und Textkritik sämtlicher Sirachstellen vgl. Wicke-Reuter, Providenz.

2,15) und hier in einer anderen, unspezifischen Bedeutung erscheint.[36] Die Vermutung liegt nahe, dass es sich bei der Verwendung der Wurzel צרך für den "Zweck" im Kontext der Schöpfungstheologie um eine originäre Interpretationsleistung des Siraciden handelt.

Sirach zeigt nun, dass sich Gottes vorausschauende Fürsorge bis ins Kleinste erstreckt. So erläutert er an den fundamentalen Lebensgütern, wie Gott von Beginn an alles für einen bestimmten Zweck vorgesehen und geschaffen hat – freilich mit einer wichtigen Unterscheidung:

(25) Gutes teilte er den Guten zu von Beginn an,
aber den Bösen Gutes und Böses.
(26) Das Allernotwendigste für das Leben des Menschen
ist Wasser und Feuer und Eisen und Salz,
das Mark des Weizens, Milch und Honig,
das Blut der Traube, Öl und Kleidung.
(27) All dies dient den Guten zum Guten,
aber für die Bösen wendet es sich zum Schlechten. (Sir 39,25–27)

In ähnlicher Weise sehen auch die Stoiker einen Beweis für die Umsicht der göttlichen Pronoia darin, wie sie das für die Grundbedürfnisse des Menschen Notwendige bereitstellt.

Chrysipp lobt die Vorsehung sehr, weil sie Fische und Vögel und Honig und Wein hervorgebracht hat.[37]

Resümierend stellt Ben Sira in einem anderen Hymnus fest:

Und nichts davon hat er umsonst hervorgebracht. (Sir 42,24b)

Eine ähnliche Formulierung wird von Chrysipp überliefert:

Nichts hat die Natur vergeblich hervorgebracht.[38]

Wie bei den Stoikern, so erhält der Gedanke der göttlichen Providenz auch bei Ben Sira seine besondere Relevanz für die Begründung der Sittlichkeit. Entsprechend nimmt die Anthropologie im Rahmen seiner Schöpfungslehre einen breiten Raum ein. Besonders augenfällig ist dies in dem Lehrgedicht in Sir 16,17–17,24.[39] Der Siracide setzt sich hier mit folgendem Einwand auseinander. Ein hypothetischer Gegner stellt in Abrede, dass Gott sich um das Treiben der Menschen kümmere. Daraus zieht er den Schluss, dass sich ein Handeln nach Gottes Gebot weder positiv noch negativ "auszahle": sowohl Lohn als auch Strafe, so die Argumentation, bleiben aus (16,17–23). Ben Sira

---

36 So bezeichnet צרך hier den "Bedarf." Vgl. dazu ausführlich Wicke-Reuter, Providenz, 71.
37 SVF II 1160.
38 SVF II 1140.
39 Vgl. hierzu neben den einschlägigen Kommentaren Prato, Il problema, 262–87; Marböck, Weisheit, 136ff; Wicke-Reuter, Providenz, 143–70.

weist diesen Einwand mit Entschiedenheit zurück. In einem langen Gedicht bringt er den Nachweis für die Sorgfalt, mit der Gott sich seiner Schöpfung fortwährend annimmt. Er belegt dies zunächst mit dem Hinweis auf die Ordnung am gestirnten Himmel, die sich im Gehorsam der Gestirne spiegelt:

bis in Ewigkeit werden sie [scil. die Gestirne] nicht ungehorsam gegen sein Wort. (Sir 16,28b)

Dieser anthropomorphen Formulierung kann man bereits einen Vorgriff auf den Abschnitt über den Menschen entnehmen: Die von Gott geschaffene Ordnung besteht fort im Gehorsam der Geschöpfe, die damit indirekt zu ihrer Aufrechterhaltung beitragen. Die Aussage deutet somit darauf hin, dass auch im Denken Ben Siras eine Parallele zwischen kosmischer und sittlicher Ordnung besteht.[40]

Nach einem kurzen Blick auf die Welt der Pflanzen und der Tiere in 16,29f wendet sich der Autor schließlich dem Menschen zu (ab 17,1). Die Darstellung ist dabei von vornherein zugespitzt auf die Stellung des Menschen im Gesamt der Schöpfung und auf die Aufgabe, die ihm aus dieser Stellung erwächst. Vergleichsweise ausführlich geht Sirach auf die Befähigung des Menschen zur Erkenntnis ein:

(6) Er bildete Zunge, Augen und Ohren,
und ein Herz zum Nachdenken gab er ihnen.
(7) Mit verständiger Erkenntnis erfüllte er sie,
und Gut und Böse zeigte er ihnen. (Sir 17,6f)

Ähnlich wie bei den Stoikern ist damit zugleich eine bestimmte Zwecksetzung für den Menschen verbunden, wie aus den Versen 8–10 hervorgeht:

(8) Er pflanzte sein Auge in ihr Herz,
um ihnen die Größe seiner Werke zu zeigen,
(9) damit sie von seinen Wundern erzählten
(10) und seinen heiligen Namen priesen. (Sir 17,8–10)

Es ist folglich die Bestimmung des Menschen, dass er die Größe der göttlichen Werke erkennend betrachtet und im Lobpreis seiner Bewunderung Ausdruck verleiht.

Vollends erfüllt der Mensch seine Aufgabe jedoch erst, wenn er der Einsicht in das Wunder der Schöpfung den Gehorsam gegen das göttliche Gebot folgen lässt, wie aus dem Folgenden hervorgeht (17,11–14). Auch das Gesetz hat Gott dem Menschen zur Erkenntnis vorgelegt:

(11) Er gewährte ihnen Erkenntnis
und gab ihnen das Gesetz des Lebens zum Besitz.
(12) Einen ewigen Bund richtete er mit ihnen auf
und zeigte ihnen seine Gesetze. (17,11f)

---

40 Diesen Aspekt hat vor allem Prato, Il problema, 298f betont.

Die Begründung für den Gehorsam gegen das göttliche Gebot wird somit in der Schöpfungstheologie verankert: Wie bei den Stoikern verwirklicht auch bei Ben Sira der Mensch seine geschöpfliche, "natürliche" Bestimmung, indem er nach dem Gesetz Gottes lebt.

Die Parallele zu der bereits genannten stoischen Formel ist kaum zu übersehen. Zur Veranschaulichung sei sie noch einmal wiederholt:

Der Mensch ist dazu geboren, dass er das Weltall betrachtet und nachahmt.[41]

Der Stoiker Kleanthes nennt in seinem Zeushymnus noch eine dritte Aufgabe des Menschen, nämlich den Lobpreis der Götter,[42] so dass sich auch bei den Stoikern die Trias von Einsicht, Lob und Nachfolge des göttlichen Gesetzes findet.

Es wäre nun allerdings ein Fehlschluss, würde man das Gesetz bei Sirach, ähnlich dem stoischen Nomos, als ein natürliches Gesetz ansehen, das als Ausdruck der göttlichen Vernunft in der Natur enthalten und über die Vernunft prinzipiell allen Menschen in gleicher Weise zugänglich ist. Trotz aller Annäherung an die Stoa bleibt das Gesetz bei Sirach positives, geoffenbartes Gesetz: Es ist mit dem Dekalog und darüber hinaus mit der gesamten Gesetzgebung im Pentateuch identisch.[43] Dennoch berührt sich Ben Siras Gesetzesbegriff mit dem stoischen: Bei beiden ist das Gesetz, hier das göttliche, dort das natürliche, von der göttlichen Vernunft bzw. der Weisheit Gottes erfüllt. Der schöne Hymnus in Sir 24 gibt darüber reichlich Auskunft.[44] Und wie bei den Stoikern entspricht es der natürlichen Bestimmung des Menschen, nach dem Gesetz zu leben. So ist das göttliche Gebot kein beliebigwillkürliches, sozusagen heteronomes Gesetz. Vielmehr ist es auch bei Ben Sira der Inbegriff einer göttlichen Ordnung, die die Grundlage der menschlichen Gemeinschaft bildet. Als solches richtet es die Sittlichkeit unter den Menschen auf.

---

41 SVF II 1153.
42 Vgl. SVF I 537.
43 Darauf weist zu Recht Schnabel in seiner Untersuchung zum Verhältnis von Gesetz und Weisheit hin, vgl. Schnabel, Law, 84ff. Seine Folgerung, dass eine Berührung zwischen dem siracidischen und dem stoischen Gesetzesbegriff daher von vornherein ausgeschlossen sei (vgl. ebd.), ist jedoch nicht zwingend: Der Charakter des jüdischen Gesetzes als geoffenbartes, positives Gesetz schließt seinen Anspruch auf die Repräsentation einer universalen Weisheit nicht aus. So lässt sich auch das Gesetz Ben Siras als Ausdruck einer göttlichen, kosmisch-universalen Ordnung interpretieren.
44 So gipfelt dieses Weisheitsgedicht in der Ineinssetzung von Weisheit und Gesetz (Sir 24,23–29), vgl. dazu Schnabel, Law, 71f; Marböck, Weisheit, 77ff; Wicke-Reuter, Providenz, 214–19 und zur Identifikation von Weisheit und Gesetz bei Ben Sira insgesamt Hengel, Judentum, 284–92; Schnabel, Law, 69–92; Marböck, Weisheit, 85–96; ders., Gesetz, 1–21 (= 1995, 52–72); Boccaccini, Middle Judaism, 81–99; Collins, Wisdom, 46–61; Wicke-Reuter, Providenz, 197–223.

5.

Eingangs habe ich angedeutet, dass sich Ben Sira gedankliche Ansätze der Stoiker aneignet und sie dabei stellenweise ihrem ursprünglichen Sinnzusammenhang entfremdet (s.o. Abschnitt 1). Dies möchte ich abschließend am Beispiel der innerweltlichen Gerechtigkeit erläutern.

Sowohl Ben Sira als auch die Stoiker haben sich mit der Frage nach dem individuellen Leid auseinandergesetzt, jedoch in unterschiedlicher Deutung. Gerade die stoische Lehre von der göttlichen Providenz ist immer wieder in die Kritik geraten.[45] Die Auffassung, dass der göttliche Logos alles durchdringt und in seiner Eigenschaft als Pronoia den Kosmos in schönster Ordnung und Zweckmäßigkeit gestaltet, lässt die Frage nach dem Bösen zu einem brennenden Problem werden. Ist Gott die Ursache des Bösen?

Die Stoiker beantworten die Frage im Horizont ihrer eigenen Pronoia-Lehre: Da alles im Kosmos einen besonderen Zweck hat und zur Harmonie des Ganzen beiträgt, gibt es nichts wirklich Schlechtes. Was dem Menschen als das Böse erscheint, ist in Wahrheit ein unverzichtbarer Bestandteil des Ganzen.[46] Es ist unvermeidbar für die Verwirklichung der besten aller möglichen Welten. Wäre der Mensch in der Lage, das Ganze zu überblicken, dann würde er erkennen, welche Funktion das Böse erfüllt.

Aber versagt diese Erklärung nicht angesichts von unverschuldetem Leid, so möchte man fragen? Die Stoiker antworten hierauf mit dem Hinweis auf das "Ziel" der Ethik: Nur wer im Einklang mit der Natur lebt, erlangt die Tugend und damit zugleich die Glückseligkeit.[47] Der "Weise", der dieses Ziel erreicht hat, begreift sich folglich als Teil des rational geordneten Ganzen. Daher nimmt er die Schläge des Schicksals als Ausdruck einer höheren Vernunft hin. Er kann das persönliche Geschick als Beitrag zur kosmischen Harmonie betrachten, so dass sein individuelles Ergehen letztlich unbedeutend wird. Diese Schicksalsergebenheit des Weisen ist ein Ausdruck seiner inneren Autonomie.[48]

Die Stoiker gehen sogar noch einen Schritt weiter: Nach ihrer Auffassung kann als gut und böse im eigentlichen Sinne nur das sittlich Gute bzw. Böse gelten.[49] Da die Eudaimonia, die Glückseligkeit, allein von der Tugend, dem sittlich Guten abhängt, können äußere Lebensumstände wie Krankheit oder Armut der Glückseligkeit des Menschen keinen Abbruch tun.[50]

---

45 Vgl. SVF I 159; II 1168, 1169, 1172, 1183.
46 Vgl. SVF II 1182.
47 Vgl. SVF III 4, 16, 582–84.
48 Vgl. dazu Wicke-Reuter, Providenz, 39f, 48f.
49 Vgl. SVF III 29–37 und Forschner, Ethik, 171–82.
50 Vgl. dazu Forschner, Handeln, 47; ders., Ethik, 167.

Es liegt auf der Hand, dass Ben Sira diese Ansicht nicht teilt. Er hält an der alttestamentlichen Gleichung von Gerechtigkeit und Leben fest[51] und vertritt die Auffassung, dass jeder Mensch das ihm nach seinem religiös-sittlichen Verdienst Zustehende erhält.[52] Anders als die Stoiker beschränkt er dabei das Gute bzw. Böse nicht auf die Sittlichkeit. Für ihn ist beides für ein gelingendes Leben notwendig, sowohl das sittlich Gute als auch die Güter wie Wohlstand, Gesundheit u.ä. Darin erweist sich gerade Gottes Gerechtigkeit, dass die Güter gerecht verteilt werden. So legt Ben Sira dar, dass Gott bereits in der Schöpfungsordnung die Voraussetzungen dafür geschaffen hat, wie wir bereits gesehen haben:

Gutes teilte er den Guten zu von Anfang an,
ebenso den Bösen Gutes und Böses. (Sir 39,25)

Wichtig ist dabei jedoch die Unterscheidung:

All dies dient den Guten zum Guten,
aber für die Bösen wendet es sich zum Schlechten. (Sir 39,27)

Mit dieser Differenzierung kann Ben Sira die im Denkhorizont einer innerweltlichen Vergeltung schwierige Beobachtung integrieren, dass auch schlechte Menschen reichlich an den Gütern der Schöpfung partizipieren.

Allerdings ist das Vertrauen in die Wirksamkeit dieses Prinzips im Umkreis Ben Siras offenbar brüchig geworden. In einer unüberschaubaren Welt ließ sich der Glaube an einen gerechten Ausgleich im Diesseits nur mehr schwerlich festhalten. Das Leid des Gerechten wurde daher zum Anlass, die Güte der Schöpfung und die Gerechtigkeit des Schöpfers in Frage zu stellen. Gerade vor diesem Hintergrund wird für Ben Sira der Gedanke einer alles umgreifenden göttlichen Providenz bedeutsam. Mit dem Hinweis auf die Güte des Ganzen vermag Ben Sira der Erfahrung von Ungerechtigkeit eine andere Wirklichkeit entgegenzusetzen. In diesem Sinne vergewissert Ben Sira seine Leser:

(16) Die Werke Gottes sind alle gut,
und für jeden Zweck trägt er Sorge zu seiner Zeit.
(21) Keiner soll sagen: "Warum ist dies, wozu jenes?",
denn das Alles ist für seinen Zweck bestimmt.
Keiner soll sagen: "Dies ist schlechter als das",
denn das Alles wird sich zu seiner Zeit als trefflich erweisen. (39,16.21)

Freilich hält Ben Sira, im Unterschied zu den Stoikern, dennoch an der Erwartung fest, dass jedem Menschen das ihm Zukommende zuteil wird. Um beides miteinander zu verbinden, führt er in den Gedanken der Zweckmäßigkeit hier auf ganz eigene Weise die weisheitliche Kategorie vom rechten

---

51 Vgl. dazu Kaiser, Gott I, 350.
52 Zum Gedanken der göttlichen Vergeltung bei Sirach vgl. Dommershausen, Vergeltungsdenken, 37–43 und Wicke-Reuter, Providenz, 125–31.

Zeitpunkt ein. So wie die Stoiker widrige Einzelerfahrungen von der Harmonie des Ganzen her deuten, so transzendiert der Siracide eine als ambivalent
erfahrene Gegenwart auf die Zukunft hin, in der sich Gottes Gerechtigkeit
erweisen wird. Zwar ordnet Ben Sira die Güte des Ganzen nicht dem Einzel-
schicksal über. Aber die erkennbare Ordnung und Harmonie der Schöpfung
wird quasi zum Unterpfand für das Vertrauen, dass zu seiner Zeit auch dem
einzelnen Gerechtigkeit widerfahren wird. Es ist daher von besonderer Bedeutung, dass Ben Sira sein Werk mit einer Verheißung beschließt:

Verrichtet euer Werk in Gerechtigkeit,
und er wird euch euren Lohn geben zu seiner Zeit. (51,30)

Bibliographie

von Arnim, H. (ed.), *Stoicorum veterum fragmenta* (4 vols.; Leipzig: Teubner 1903–24; repr.
    Stuttgart: Teubner, 1964).
Boccaccini, G., *Middle Judaism. Jewish Thought, 300 B.C.E. to 200 C.E.* (Minneapolis:
    Fortress Press, 1991).
Collins, J.J., *Jewish Wisdom in the Hellenistic Age* (OTL; Louisville: Westminster John
    Knox, 1997).
Dommershausen, W., "Zum Vergeltungsdenken des Ben Sira," in *Wort und Geschichte* (FS
    K. Elliger; eds. H. Gese and H.P. Rüger; AOAT 18; Neukirchen-Vluyn: Neukirche-
    ner Verlag, 1973) 37–43.
Forschner, M., *Die stoische Ethik. Über den Zusammenhang von Natur-, Sprach- und Mo-*
    ralphilosophie im altstoischen System (2d ed.; Darmstadt: Wissenschaftliche Buch-
    gesellschaft, 1995).
Forschner, M., *Über das Handeln im Einklang mit der Natur. Grundlagen ethischer Ver-*
    ständigung (Darmstadt: Wissenschaftliche Buchgesellschaft, 1998).
Heinimann, F., *Nomos und Physis. Herkunft und Bedeutung einer Antithese im griechischen*
    Denken des 5. Jahrhunderts (Schweizerische Beiträge zur Altertumswissenschaft 1;
    Basel: Reinhardt, 1945; 5th repr.; Darmstadt: Wissenschaftliche Buchgesellschaft,
    1987).
Hengel, M., *Judentum und Hellenismus. Studien zu ihrer Begegnung unter besonderer Be-*
    rücksichtigung Palästinas bis zur Mitte des 2. Jh. v.Chr. (WUNT 10; 2d ed.; Tübin-
    gen: Mohr, 1973).
Kaiser, O., *Der Gott des Alten Testaments. Theologie des AT I: Grundlegung* (UTB 1747;
    Göttingen: Vandenhoeck & Ruprecht, 1993).
Lapidge, M., "Stoic Cosmology," in *The Stoics* (ed. J.M. Rist; Major Thinkers Series 1;
    Berkeley et al.: University of California, 1978) 161–85.
Lévi, I., *L'Ecclésiastique ou La Sagesse de Jésus, fils de Sira. Texte original hébreu édité*
    traduit et commenté. Deuxième partie (III,6, à XVI,26; extraits de XVIII, XIX, XXV
    et XXVI; XXXI,11, à XXXIII,3; XXXV,19, à XXXVIII,27; XLIX,11, à fin.) (vol. 2;
    Bibliothèque de l'École des Hautes Études; Sciences Religieuses 10/2; Paris: Le-
    roux, 1901).
Long, A.A., *Hellenistic Philosophy. Stoics, Epicureans, Sceptics* (Classical Life and Letters;
    London: Duckworth, 1974).

Long, A.A. – Sedley, D.N., *The Hellenistic Philosophers* (vol. 1: *Translations of the Principal Sources, with Philosophical Commentary*; Cambridge: University Press, 1987; 5th repr.; 1992).

Marböck, J., "Gesetz und Weisheit. Zum Verständnis des Gesetzes bei Jesus Ben Sira", *BN NF* 20 (1976) 1–21 = in *Gottes Weisheit unter uns. Zur Theologie des Buches Sirach* (ed. I. Fischer; Herders Biblische Studien 6; Freiburg: Herder, 1995) 52–72.

Marböck, J., *Weisheit im Wandel. Untersuchungen zur Weisheitstheologie bei Ben Sira* (BBB 37; Bonn: Hanstein, 1971; repr. in BZAW 272; Berlin / New York: de Gruyter, 1999).

Pautrel, R., "Ben Sira et le Stoïcisme," *RSR* 51 (1963) 535–49.

Prato, G.L., *Il problema della teodicea in Ben Sira. Composizione dei contrari e richiamo alle origini* (AnBib 65; Rome: Pontifical Biblical Institute, 1975).

Schnabel, E.J., *Law and Wisdom from Ben Sira to Paul: A Tradition Historical Enquiry into the Relation of Law, Wisdom, and Ethics* (WUNT 2/16; Tübingen: Mohr, 1985).

Schwöbel, Ch., "Einführung: Woran orientiert sich Ethik?," in *Woran orientiert sich Ethik?* (eds. W. Härle and R. Preul; Marburger Jahrbuch Theologie 13; Marburg: Elwert, 2001) 1–13.

Smend, R., *Die Weisheit des Jesus Sirach erklärt* (Berlin: Reimer, 1906).

Wicke-Reuter, U., *Göttliche Providenz und menschliche Verantwortung bei Ben Sira und in der Frühen Stoa* (BZAW 298; Berlin / New York: de Gruyter, 2000).

Divine Will and Providence

James K. Aitken
University of Reading

> Even so said the Holy One, blessed be He: "If I
> create the world on the basis of mercy alone, its
> sins will be great; on the basis of judgement alone,
> the world cannot exist. Hence I will create it on
> the basis of judgement and of mercy and may it
> then stand!" Hence the expression *Adonai Elohim*.
> (*GenR* 12:15)

An ancient Jewish tourist of late antiquity might pause before the inscriptions at the great synagogue in Sardis, one of the most striking Jewish buildings of the time and symbolic of the integration of Jews into their local environment.[1] The synagogue, perhaps only to be bettered by the legendary Alexandrian synagogue (*t.Sukkah* 4:6),[2] was decorated with mosaics and paintings, and it was adorned with marble *menoroth*, of which nineteen have been discovered, including one made or dedicated by a certain Socrates, a Jew with the most Greek of all names. The dedicatory inscriptions also discovered attest to the life of the Jews in the ancient city, and our tourist might be struck by the frequent use of the Greek term πρόνοια, found or restored in eleven of the 79 extant texts.[3] He may deduce that it is a circumlocution for God, designated in one text with similar wording as παντοκράτωρ θεός, and that furthermore it denotes the care and treatment exercised by God, since πρόνοια commonly designates in inscriptions human oversight and planning.[4] Is it, he wonders as he stands there, the result of the education of these acculturated Sardian Jews, living in such a centre with its neo-Platonic connections,[5] that they have resorted to such a circumlocution? Have they drunk of the Sardian

---

1   The interpretation of the synagogue has been explored by, *inter alios*, Kraabel, Impact 178–90. Many of Kraabel's essays, including this one, have been conveniently gathered in Overman – MacLennan, Diaspora Jews.

2   "Rabbi Judah said, 'Whoever has never seen the double colonnade of Alexandria of Egypt has never seen the great glory of Israel in his entire life'." The imagery of the Tosefta passage is discussed by Fine, Holy Place, 43–45.

3   All the Greek inscriptions have now been published by Kroll, Greek inscriptions, 5–55. Kraabel has reproduced the "providence" inscriptions in his article "Pronoia at Sardis", 75–96.

4   Cf. Kraabel, Pronoia, 79.

5   See Foss, Sardis, 22–27.

philosophical air and, as Kraabel feels, invented a unique Jewish term for God that is in tune with their Lydian surroundings?

Such questions pertaining to a 900-year-old late antique Jewish community, not far from the coast of Asia Minor, may seem a long way from our Jerusalem sage of the second century BCE. It remains an open question, however, whether the Sardian πρόνοια is a designation for God, and whether our tourist would have recognized his Jewish tradition in those words. It is also debatable whether we can detach a theological understanding of πρόνοια from its frequent use in philosophical writings, and therefore whether the inscriptions denote merely a belief in a philosophical determining principle or more specifically a belief in the control of the Jewish God. Certainly the discovery of similar inscriptions in the ancient synagogue of Philippopolis (now Plovdiv, Bulgaria) does indicate that not everything is to be ascribed to Sardis's unique philosophical environment.[6] But if we cannot be sure of the level of influence in such an acculturated city as Sardis, we are on less stable terrain when it comes to Ben Sira. A long Jewish tradition of divine providence, found in a number of writers, would have contributed to the formation of the Sardian inscriptions, and Ben Sira plays a part in that tradition. The precise position that he holds on providence, however, is not clear, and the degree to which he has been influenced by Greek thought in his formulation of ideas remains disputed. Here we will consider some neglected evidence in Ben Sira's discussion of providence, namely his interest in divine will as one of the controlling principles over the universe. The question of Hellenistic influence on this concept will be touched upon but no certain conclusion on it will be given.

The extent of Hellenistic influence in Jerusalem at the time of Ben Sira remains a debatable point, since the presence and awareness of the Greeks, Ptolemies and Seleucids, whilst undoubtedly attested in the period, do not necessarily prove the acceptance of the Greek intellectual tradition. We should distinguish between the material presence of Greeks, be it knowledge of the language or trading contacts, from the reading and studying of their thought. In the case of Ben Sira he does seem to have drawn, whether consciously or not, on literary forms and quotations found in Greek literature, but it is difficult to determine in every instance how much he has been influenced.[7] And the complexity of anyone's identity, or for that matter of Jewish identity in the Greco-Roman period, does not allow for simple conclusions or for simplified polarities. It is noticeable that when discussing the possible in-

---

6   As noted by Rajak, Jews, 460–61, and mentioned only in passing by Kraabel, Pronoia, 87. The Plovdiv inscriptions have been published by Kesjakova, Ancient synagogue, 20–33.

7   The problem of determining the likelihood of any influence has been demonstrated recently by Mattila, Ben Sira, 473–501. On the question of Ben Sira's opposition to Hellenism, see Aitken, Interpretation, 193–95.

fluence of Stoic thought on Ben Sira, some scholars have wanted to suggest that he did not draw his ideas directly from the Stoics, but that he was only in some way aware of their notions.[8] Such ambiguity reflects the problem that much of Ben Sira's language is biblical or can be seen as a natural outcome of reading the Bible, and yet at the same time is similar to Greek philosophical notions. Has Ben Sira's view of God and divine providence been shaped by the cultural climate in which he lived?

1. Providence in Jewish Tradition

Within Jewish-Greek literature it is possible to find a few examples of πρόνοια that at least confirm the existence of a belief in divine providence in Jewish tradition before Sardis, even if not the circumlocution.[9] The word is remarkably absent from the Septuagint (including the Greek Sirach), except in those books originally penned in Greek, but by the time of Philo and Josephus it had become a catchword to explain the actions of God and the cause of historical events. And yet as early as the second century BCE,[10] in the *Letter of Aristeas* we find a Greek philosopher praising the Jewish conception of Providence (§ 201), and it plays a role in the Greek portions of Daniel and in 2 Maccabees. Later it was to become an integral part of martyrdom in 4 Maccabees. One of the more important pieces of evidence is Josephus's description of the Jewish parties at his time. Josephus alleges that the Essenes believed in providence or rather "determinism" (εἱμαρμένη), the Sadducees in free will (ἐπ' ἀνθρώπων ἐκλογῇ), and the Pharisees in both (*B.J.* 2.163 [on Pharisees], 164 [on Sadducees]; *A.J.* 18.13 [on Pharisees], 18 [on Essenes])]. In contrast to Josephus's rigid categorisation (which corresponds to the distinction between the Epicureans and the Stoics), the situation was probably more complex than that. The concepts are not to be seen as mutually exclusive, but instead it is probably correct to think that they all believed in both free will and determinism, with varying degrees of emphasis.[11] Speculation over the place of man in the world, the control over the universe

---

8   E.g. Marböck, Weisheit (1971), 94, 145 [now reprinted as BZAW 272, 1999]; Winston, Theodicy, 240.
9   References can be found in Kraabel, Pronoia, 84–88; Trebilco, Communities, 41–43; Frick, Providence, 6–15; Rajak, Gifts, 232–36; idem, Jews, 459–60.
10   There is no certainty over the dating of *Aristeas*, but the consensus tends towards a date in the second century. See Hadas, Aristeas, 3–54, who provides extensive discussion of the evidence.
11   So Sanders, Dead Sea Sect, 29. Urbach, Sages, 255–56, argues that it should not be attributed purely to Josephus's philosophical categorisation, but that the Dead Sea Scrolls display an interest in predestination which would corroborate Josephus's description of the Essenes.

and divine action all seem to have been part of intellectual life in the ancient period, and they remain areas of inquiry to this day. The similarities so often drawn between Greek, Hebrew and Egyptian writers on these subjects, especially in discussions of sapiential literature, are probably to be accounted for more by human interest in the world than by a common source or knowledge of each other's literature.[12] As a sapiential theme it understandably might also be found in the Mishnaic tractate 'Aboth, where possible confirmation exists that people held on to a concept both of free will and of determinism. In the words of R. Akiba:

All is foreseen (הכל צפוי), but freedom of choice (רְשׁוּת) is given; and the world is judged by goodness, yet all is according to the magnitude of the deed.[13]

This aphorism has been taken as indicative of the contradiction between God's omniscience and human free-will, Maimonides seeing it as an attempt to resolve the contradiction, and other commentators interpreting it as a postulation of the two principles.[14] Nevertheless, it has also been argued that the expression "all is foreseen" denotes the seeing by God of all the actions of mankind rather than divine foreknowledge (cf. 'Aboth 2.1). Even if this is the correct interpretation the ambiguity did permit different interpretations, and the presence of the contradiction in later Rabbinic literature is clear (e.g. GenR 12:15]).

This contradiction of believing in free will and determinism at the same time has also been a noted part of Ben Sira's thought, and might indicate his lack of an attempt to produce a systematic philosophy in the manner of the Stoics.[15] Part of the problem in studying providence in Jewish literature, and particularly at the time of Ben Sira, is determining what sort of providence we are looking for, how to distinguish it from questions of theodicy[16] and to what extent it involves a deterministic worldview. One aspect of providence concerns the government of the world, including God's concern for the needs of mankind. A second aspect, however, is the "divine plan", involving the judging by God of humans according to their deeds. Central to the discussion

---

12 Mattila, Ben Sira, 475, rightly puts it: "When it comes to the notion of thoroughgoing divine providence shared by these various divergent traditions of the Hellenistic world, it is probably impossible to determine precisely who influenced whom, how, when, or where".

13 m.Aboth 3:16. This is the verse numbering of Danby, Mishnah, 452, whose translation has been modified here. According to Herford's system (Ethics, 88–89) it is verse 19. For a textual variant at the end of the saying see the discussion of Herford.

14 For a summary of opinions on the passage, see Urbach, Sages, 257–58.

15 See in general Maier, Mensch. The most detailed study of Providence in Ben Sira, and its parallels with Stoic ideas, is the recent work by Wicke-Reuter, Providenz.

16 On the consequences of a belief in providence for theodicy see Winston, Theodicy, 241–43.

of providence in Ben Sira have been passages that demonstrate both the free
will of mankind and God's pre-ordained structure of the universe, each of
which is argued for by Ben Sira. The writer seems to have varied his argument in accordance with the immediate context and his implied opponents.[17]
He holds, for example, that humans are endowed with free will, a belief that
Hengel argues was in response to the determinism of Qoheleth and the Epicureans,[18] and therefore that God is not to be held responsible for evil. It is the
יצר of mankind that is the cause (15:11–20),[19] even if elsewhere he argues
that God is the source of the differences between the just and the unjust
(36/33:10–13]).[20] Ben Sira seems to have different viewpoints when speaking
about mankind, to whom he attributes responsibility for their own actions,
and when speaking about Creation, which he sees as harmonious. God's concern for his Creation is a traditional biblical notion, but Ben Sira may have
incorporated it into a rational formula that requires all parts of Creation to
conform to his cosmic authority.[21] God's works have been arranged in good
order (16:26–27; 39:12–35) and the works of Creation all have their own purpose (cf. the use of צורך – 39:16),[22] and will be revealed in their time
(39:17).[23] This is summarized in the well-known passage on the dualism
inherent in nature (36/33:14–15; 42:24–25), which is probably the strongest
piece of evidence for the influence of Greek thought.[24] It seems that Ben Sira
would have held that God has ordered the world, and everything is embedded
in his cosmology (cf. 41:3–4),[25] but that humans are still to be considered responsible for their actions. A certain tension exists between his belief in a
harmonious creation and the need to absolve God of responsibility for human
evil.

This tension arises from the consideration of the second aspect of providence, comprising the judging of mankind according to their deeds. It does,
however, arise from the question of how God intervenes into a world that he
has ordered and created in harmony. Ben Sira's portrayal of God has been

---

17 So Collins, Wisdom, 83.
18 Hengel, Judaism, 141–42. Cf. Frick, Providence, 9–10.
19 The most detailed discussion of יצר is by Hadot, Penchant mauvais, 9–31, who argues
    that it is a neutral inclination with a propensity for good or evil.
20 Maier, Mensch, 98–115, suggests that Ben Sira in chapter 15 is arguing against oppo-
    nents and tries to absolve God of any responsibility. He is followed in this by Collins,
    Wisdom, 83. See also Gilbert's article in this volume.
21 E.g. Pautrel, Ben Sira, 543; Middendorp, Stellung, 29; Kaiser, Rezeption, 46.
22 On the frequent use of this Hebrew noun in Ben Sira, see Hengel, Judaism, 141–45,
    who suggests its frequency is motivated by anti-Epicurean intentions; Marböck, Wei-
    sheit, 141; Prato, Il problema, 395–96; and Aitken, Background, 77 n. 7.
23 Everything having a purpose and time is of course a biblical idea, and not Ben Sira's
    rationalistic invention (see Mattila, Ben Sira, 478). Compare Qoh 3:1.
24 See on the role of this passage in his theodicy, Prato, Il problema, 13–61.
25 Cf. Middendorp, Stellung, 28.

shown to place special emphasis on the role of God within human lives, further developing themes from the Bible. The human free will and the ordered system of Creation do not prevent God from such involvement in the lives of humans. J. Fichtner has argued that Ben Sira transformed the early Israelite wisdom literature, with its silence about divine mercy, into a nationalized wisdom, in which the older religious traditions are integrated with sapiential concerns and the theme of divine mercy is given a central role.[26] He has been followed in this by J. Coert Rylaarsdam and by J. Crenshaw.[27] The latter finds the arguments of Fichtner to be for the most part correct. Crenshaw argues that even if one can trace a belief in mercy in the earlier wisdom tradition, it is Ben Sira who feels the need to emphasize it (see especially 16:11, 12). The reason for this, Crenshaw feels, is the uncertain situation under the taxation and control of the Ptolemies, exacerbated by the appearance of the Seleucids and rising Hellenistic influence.[28] People needed the reassurance that God would have mercy on those who kept to his ways and turned away from sin, in a time when "belief in the moral order became highly problematic". Fichtner and his successors have noted an important feature of God that could be said to transcend the tension in the book between God's control and human culpability. There have in fact been few studies that have considered the nature of God as presented in the literature of this period, beyond those analysing the questions of theodicy or monotheism. G.F. Moore is an exception to this, but relies too much on rabbinic evidence that is hard to date.[29] And yet a better understanding of the portrayal of God should allow us to appreciate how some of the tensions inherent in the problem of free-will can be resolved. We shall, therefore, concentrate on the actions of God in his treatment of mankind (the first aspect of providence as noted above), and in particular what becomes an important theme in the book of Ben Sira, divine will. We will discuss in the conclusion the reason for Ben Sira's interest, but it should be noted that Crenshaw's interpretation of a need for reassurance, exacerbated by rising "Hellenism", is dependent on E. Bickerman's presentation that was influential on Hengel of a religious crisis in the period. There is in fact little evidence of such a crisis before the Maccabees, and furthermore such a view has perhaps hindered our appreciation of the powerful presentation of God in the literature.[30]

---

26   Fichtner, Weisheit. On "mercy" in Ben Sira, see also the paper by Beentjes in this volume.
27   Rylaarsdam, Revelation; Crenshaw, Concept, 191–205 [Reprint 1–18].
28   Ibid., 204–5.
29   Judaism vol. I, 357–442.
30   In a forthcoming article "Pre-Maccabees" I shall explore the origins of such a view and discuss in greater detail the presentation of God in the extant literature of the Persian and early Hellenistic periods.

2. Providence as God's Concern for Mankind

The term providence in theological discussion can denote both a specific determinism for the universe or more generally divine care over the world and its creatures, as it seems to mean at Sardis. This double sense is embedded in the origins of the term itself. The Greek verb προνοέω can denote "to provide for, take thought for" (see LSJ: 1490–91) and the noun πρόνοια "care, thought (for)". The term "divine providence" seems to have first been used in Greek by Herodotus (3.108.2: τοῦ θείου ἡ προνοίη) and then Sophocles (*Oedipus at Colonus* 1180: πρόνοια ... τοῦ θεοῦ). Plato developed the notion in philosophy, applying the term in Book 10 of the *Laws* both to a world soul guiding the universe but also to God's care for all things.[31]

Debate on Ben Sira has often centred on the question of theodicy and determinism, but providence has a wider sense than that. Although we are influenced in our understanding of providence by modern theological concerns and by the influence of Greek thought itself, we should ask what someone versed in the biblical text would understand by it. This is not to say that Ben Sira was a biblical scholar and nothing more, but to propose that the Bible was important for his understanding. It can be argued that the biblical conception of God in control of affairs was reached by analogy with human affairs.[32] Kingship is a likely source for such an analogy, and this is well demonstrated by the presentation of God as lord over the nations in the Psalms. It is not a philosophical notion of God having a plan throughout history, but a belief that God treats his people and ensures justice in the manner of a king. Certainly Ben Sira's view of the structure of Creation suggests a more developed understanding of providence than this simple biblical view, and his emphasis that all will be fulfilled in the time (39:17) implies some sort of goal that is not so explicit in the Bible. But did Ben Sira elaborate on the biblical image of the care of God for his people? And how does this divine action relate, if at all, to the understanding of providence elsewhere in book? In trying to answer these questions, our observations can only be cursory given the limited space, but attention will be drawn to how Ben Sira's words address the relationship between God and mankind. The power of language to have a force on its recipients, in this case Ben Sira's readers, in order to define and enforce their relationship with God will be considered. If we can better appreciate the effect of language within its context we can maybe infer something of the effect that Ben Sira's work would have had in shaping the Jewish understanding of God.

---

31   See Frick, Providence, 5–6.
32   So Rogerson, Doctrine, 541–42.

The locus classicus for Ben Sira's view of human free will is 15:11–16:14.[33] Humans are encouraged by the writer not to attribute blame for their problems to God. Instead they should recognize that from the creation of mankind free choice was given (15:14–15):

> It was he, from the first (מראש), when he created humankind (אדם)
> who made them subject to their own free choice (יצר).
> If you choose (חפץ), you can keep his commandment;
> fidelity is the doing of his will (רצון).[34]

The passage proceeds to present the choice that is available to humans between fire and water, and life and death, adopting the language from Deuteronomy 30:19. The human inclination provides the opportunity to make a choice (חפץ), that choice being the sapiential theme reiterated throughout the work of Ben Sira, namely keeping God's commandment. The consequences of the ethical choice are life or death. This human choice is emphasised in the text by the use of the verb חפץ three times in the space of a few verses (15:15, 16, 17). It might be possible to detect a distinction drawn by Ben Sira, in contrast to the use in the biblical Psalms, between חפץ, which is applied to humans, and רצון, which mostly although not exclusively is applied to God.[35] The will of humans must be orientated towards the will of God, any choice being made by humans having to conform to the preference of God if the human is to escape punishment.

A variant in the manuscript tradition makes a parallel with the Genesis creation account, already implied in the choice of the verb ברא and the double-meaning of the designation of אדם. MS A and Bmg substitute MS B's מראש with the expected מבראשית, echoing the first word of Genesis. It is not easy to determine which is the original reading, since, although it is more likely that a scribe would correct the text to reflect Genesis than to remove such an allusion through the writing of מראש, the latter can be seen as a defective reading of מבראשית. It contains some of the same letters, and all that is required is for the initial *beth* to be omitted and for the ending to be truncated to bring about the reading מראש. Whichever we prefer, it is clear that the presence of the verb יצר "to fashion" in Genesis (2:7, 8, 19) instigated the belief that the inclination (first mentioned in Genesis 6:5) was instilled in mankind during creation (cf. below on the pun on the verb and noun in Ben

---

33 This is the division of the passage advocated by Prato, Il problema, 229–31, and Wicke-Reuter, Providenz, 107–11.

34 Translation from Skehan – Di Lella, Wisdom, 267, based on MS B with MS A providing the text for damaged portions of the manuscript. A and Bmg make the connection with Genesis 1 more explicit in their choice of Hebrew (see ibid., 271), as will be discussed below. The additional stich in MS A seems to have arisen from a resemblance to the Syriac of 4:19 (see Di Lella, Hebrew Text, 127–29).

35 Hadot, Penchant mauvais, 195–96.

Sira 36/33:13). The double *yod* in the verbal form at Genesis 2:7 certainly in later times gave rise to the view of two inclinations (*Tg. Ps.-J.* Gen 2:7; *GenR* 14:4; *b. Ber* 61a). The reference to the creation contributes to Ben Sira's purpose of absolving God of any responsibility for evil, by drawing attention to God's giving humans choice from the very beginning. It also recalls the first choice given to mankind, namely whether or not to eat of the fruit of the tree, a choice that will incur death (Gen 2:17). Life or death is the choice that Ben Sira says is before each person.

It should be borne in mind that for Ben Sira Wisdom, who takes root and flowers like many exotic plants, is compared to the Torah. If the plants in chapter 24 are those of the garden of Eden (cf. Ezek 31:9), then there may be a reference to the tree of life from Gen 2:9 and 3:22 in Ben Sira's portrayal of Wisdom.[36] Although the phrase "tree of life" is not to be found in chapter 24, nor even the "Torah of life" (cf. Sir 17:11; 45:5), we are nevertheless told in *Tg. Neof.* to Gen 3:24 that the Law is the tree of life (cf. Prov 11:30; 13:12; 15:4), a concept that would have fitted Ben Sira's introduction to Wisdom as Torah very well. The connection between the Law and trees is revealed by *Neof.* and *Ps.-J.* to Exod 15:25, where Moses is shown by the Lord a tree and then, according to the Targumim, taught some of the commandments. This verse (Exod 15:25) is accordingly paraphrased by the fragment Targum (Paris MS 110) as "... the Law which is comparable to the tree of life". If such an idea may be seen in the text of chapter 24, it would explain the progression made with apparent ease by Ben Sira from the exotic plants to the Torah and the waters of Eden. It would also account for the emphasis on the choice to keep the commandment (מצוה) in 15:15.

The allusions to Genesis, some of which are certainly intended even if we cannot be certain how many or how precisely we should interpret them, establish the existence of the יצר from the beginning of creation. They also thereby establish the necessity for keeping the commandments to avoid death, which might recall the disputed allusion at Ben Sira 25:24 to Eve as the first sinner who introduced death into this world.[37] The keeping of the commandment is presented as being equivalent to performing God's will, a common biblical term, but one that seems to have special significance given its contrast to חפץ. Although רצון is mentioned but once in this passage, it seems likely that it was generally a concept of note for Ben Sira. This is observable on a purely statistical level when we find seventeen occurrences in the extant Hebrew sources, a striking frequency already commented upon by G.

---

36   Bonnard, Sagesse, 74; Marböck, Weisheit, 74.
37   Despite Levison's attempt to interpret this passage differently (Eve, 617–23), it does seem to allude to Eve's guilt (cf. Skehan – Di Lella, Wisdom, 348–49).

Shrenk.[38] To this should be added the possibly seven cases of the word in the *Vorlage* of the Greek translation in places where we no longer have an extant Hebrew text.[39] Even given these figures, how can we be sure that Ben Sira is imputing a theological significance for the divine will? The word רצון is after all not unknown in wisdom literature, appearing frequently in Proverbs (twelve times) and the Psalms (thirteen times). The answer lies in two pieces of evidence: first, the importance of the concept and of the word רצון in contemporary Jewish thought, and, second, the semantic development detectable in Ben Sira and other Hebrew literature of the time.[40]

3. רצון in the Dead Sea Scrolls

The evidence of literature from the same time as Ben Sira is often overlooked in studies of the sage, but its importance cannot be overstated. The Dead Sea Scrolls in particular, since they are extant for the most part in Hebrew and permit therefore of easy comparison, provide valuable evidence of Jewish thought in the second and first centuries BCE. Perhaps owing to their association with a Jewish sect they have not been discussed so much in this connection.[41] However, whilst many of the texts are not sectarian at all, even

---

38 Shrenk, εὐδοκέω, 2, 743–44, who gives a figure of 23 occurrences, adding to the Hebrew those places where εὐδοκία occurs without an extant Hebrew text (on the problems of such calculations see the next note). My analysis has found the following seventeen instances in the Hebrew (including the repetition at 4:27): 4:12^A, 27 (MS A only = 8:14); 8:14^A; 11:17^A; 15:15^{A,B}; 16:3^{A,B}; 32/35:20/16^B; 35/32:11^B, 12^{B,F}, 14^{B,F}; 36/33:13^E; 36:22/16–17^B; 39:18^B; 42:15^{B,Mas}; 43:26^B; 48:5^B; 50:22^B.

39 To determine instances where the Hebrew might have had the word, but is now either missing or corrupt, is an extremely problematic task. Taking the evidence of the Greek alone we find that רצון is translated most frequently by εὐδοκία (as elsewhere in the LXX), but also by εὐφροσύνη (4:12), θέλημα (16:3), δόξα (8:14) and ἔλεος (50:22). At the least one can identify likely occurrences of Hebrew where the Greek has εὐδοκία at 1:27; 2:16; 18:31; 29:23; 31/34:22/18b; 32/35:5/3 and 41:4. For this last instance the Hebrew has תורה, which may well be the original reading that has been interpreted by the Greek translator. The evidence is further complicated by εὐδοκία being the equivalent not only of רצון in the extant Hebrew of Ben Sira (see Hadot, Penchant mauvais, 194).

40 Hadot's study (Penchant mauvais, 193–96) concentrates on the distinction in Ben Sira between the human and divine will, relying on the Greek translation (and the LXX Psalms) for the most part. Here our attention will be on the semantic development in the Hebrew that Hadot does not discuss, and on the consequences for the providential treatment of mankind by God.

41 Those studies that do explicitly compare the Scrolls and Ben Sira include Lehmann, Ben Sira, 103–16; idem, 11QPs^a, 239–51; and Aitken, Apocalyptic, 181–93. One

those that are still reflect beliefs current in Judaism in the later Second Temple period.[42] Ben Sira's use of words and concepts should be seen in the context of their use by other authors of the time. That way we may better appreciate what he might have understood by his selection of words, reflecting ideas and usages current in his time.

The case at hand is the sage's preference for the word רצון. In Qumran Hebrew this occurs at least 144 times, approximately twice as frequently as the cognate verb.[43] In a similar fashion to Ben Sira a distinction is sometimes drawn between רצון and חפץ. In 1QS, 1QM and 1QH the will of God is always denoted by רצון, and human will, in contrast, by חפץ. The Damascus Document is not consistent, however, in this.[44]

In Qumran Hebrew רצון had already come to denote the guidance of God over human affairs. This has led Mansoor to suggest that predestination was a prominent theme,[45] but this is perhaps saying too much. It denotes God's care over humanity and mankind's resulting dependence on God, but not necessarily a predetermined order. The guidance extends to the created order such that the times and seasons are dependent on God's will (e.g. 1QM 18:13–14; 1QH 13[5]:4; cf. Sir 43:26). The theme is most prominent, however, in the dependence upon God's will of all facets of human life, from the physical to the moral. Human perfection is said to be dependent on it (1QH 17[10]:5–7), as are human understanding (1QH 14[6]:12–13), election (1QH 15[7]:14–15[18–19]) and justice.[46] There seems to have been a development from the biblical presentation, where רצון in the Hebrew Bible most often denotes what is "acceptable" (e.g. a sacrifice), and can be used of what pleases either a human or God. It is found twelve times in Proverbs, where it denotes either what is acceptable in the sight of God (e.g. Prov 11:1, 20), or the favour of God that the righteous seek (e.g. Prov 8:35). Ben Sira is not reliant on this sapiential precursor for his understanding of the term, reflecting instead the contemporaneous Qumran documents.

---

should also note the work discussing the contribution both sources make to our understanding of the Hebrew of the time: e.g., Muraoka – Elwolde, Sirach.

42   This obvious point is made by Hempel, Qumran Communities, 43–53. Barr overstates the case when he says, "The Scrolls make clear to us the extent of a Jewish *sectarianism*, and thereby a world of conflict and criticism, closely linked with the transmission and interpretation of biblical and other authoritative religious books" (Concept, 580).

43   The figures are my own calculations, of course must remain provisional until we have a definitive concordance to the Scrolls.

44   See Segalla, La volontà di Dio in Qumran, 379–80. Cf. also idem, La volontà di Dio nei LXX, 121–43.

45   Mansoor, Thanksgiving Hymns 162 n. 9.

46   Further examples can be found in Segalla, La volontà di Dio in Qumran.

4. רצון in Ben Sira

In Ben Sira רצון can denote, as it does in the Hebrew Bible, human pleasure or more strongly human caprice (Sir 8:14 [= 4:27];[47] 16:3;[48] 18:31 [Gk.]; 32/35:20/16; 35/32:11, 12) and the favour of God sought by the righteous (1:27 [Gk.]; 4:12; 11:17; 35/32:14). However, Ben Sira uses it most frequently of the will by which God acts, a meaning unattested in Proverbs. Shrenk, who describes this as a "striking development of the Hebrew", glosses the word in this sense as "divine ordination or resolve". It is specifically identified when God has an active role in choosing, guiding, or creating. In 48:5 Elijah is said to have brought a dead man back to life by the רצון ייי. A reciprocal relationship is implied in 36:22/16–17 where the plea is to hear the prayer of "your servants" כרצונך על עמך "according to [or 'by', Bmg] your pleasure over your people".

The divine רצון is also presented as being active within the created order. The creatures of God's creation perform his רצון at the utterance of his word (43:26), and in similar fashion at 39:18 and 42:15[49] his will in creation is achieved by his mere command. In 39:18 the power and immediate effect of his will are emphasised in a section that concentrates on the omnipotence of God. Strikingly the רצון is there in parallelism with God's salvation (תשועה), relating God's will and command with his saving acts. As we shall see below, this theme appears elsewhere in Ben Sira. It transpires that רצון is used of God when he is active, in a way not found in Proverbs. Perhaps a close analogy is Isa 60:10 where God declares that in his mercy he is favourable to his people, or the use of רצון in Pss 30:8 or 51:20. Certainly in Ben Sira the active use of רצון is clear (as it is also found in Rabbinic Hebrew),[50] and this is an important feature of certain passages touching on his view of providence.

---

47 In MS A this verse has been inserted also before 4:28.
48 MS B adds אל after רצון in 16:3, perhaps aware of the frequency of רצון applied to God in Ben Sira. Lévi, L'Ecclésiastique, 113, finds the omission of the divine complement odd and wonders if the expression, which is omitted in Greek, is an explanatory gloss.
49 42:15 could be interpreted in different ways. The options are presented by Skehan – Di Lella, Wisdom, 487.
50 E.g., Segal, ספר בן סירא, 348, quotes the morning prayer for women: שעשני רצונו.

5. Ben Sira 50:22

A neglected occurrence of the word רצון is in a passage that could be described as a summary of the actions of God. Ben Sira's blessing that concludes his review of history is presented almost as if it comes from the mouth of Simon the High Priest himself, appearing immediately after the description of Simon's blessing the people (50:22):

עתה ברכו נא את ייי אלהי ישראל המפלא לעשות בארץ
המגדל אדם מרחם   ויעשהו כרצונו

Now[51] bless the Lord the God of Israel, He who works wonders on earth,
He who magnifies mankind from the womb and treats him according to his will.[52]

Most commentators have said little about this verse, other than it inspired Martin Rinckart's hymn "Nun danket alle Gott", and that it continues the theme of the role of God in the history of Israel.[53] Attention has rather been focussed on the important verses following, which expound the continuation of the covenant with Phinehas. But the words of 50:22 are significant, since they formulate very carefully, almost in a credal manner, Ben Sira's understanding of divine action. The liturgical origin of these words cannot be excluded, despite our uncertainty over the details of the liturgy at this time. Its positioning after the description of the high priestly blessing would suggest this. The appearance of the formula ברכו־נא in Late Biblical Hebrew in a similar context to Simon's blessing of the people (1 Chr 29:20; cf. Neh 9:5), although attested only once, also suggests it was used in a formal manner, even though the formula with ברוך became much more frequent in Qumran Hebrew. The use of ברכו in the refrains of the Psalms should be noted too (e.g. Pss 66:8; 68:26; 103:20). Furthermore, one Qumran fragment has been preserved that contains very similar wording to the blessing in Ben

---

51 The particle עתה may be indicating the conclusion of the section (so Skehan – Di Lella, Wisdom, 549; cf. Prov 8:32), but both עתה and נא are found in blessing and cursing formulae, and may be a focussing particle, drawing attention to the content of the blessing (cf. Zatelli, Pragmalinguistics, 60–74; Aitken, Semantics). In such a case, there is no suitable English rendering, but for convenience the standard "now" has been preserved in the translation here.

52 There are some translation problems with a number of words in this verse. These shall be discussed in turn further below.

53 E.g. Rybolt, Sirach, 108; Skehan – Di Lella, Wisdom, 554; Sauer, Jesus Sirach, 341. The observation seems to go back to Box – Oesterley, Book of Sirach, 511. Petraglio, Il libro, 408–9, notes the universalistic nature of the reference to the earth rather than to Israel.

Sira, and thereby implies that Ben Sira could be using the language of contemporary prayer:

4Q503 13–16:14   ברו[ך] אל ישראל המפל[י]א

Blessed be the God of Israel who works wonders

The praise of God's wonders (פלאות) is frequent in the Qumran blessings
and prayers (e.g. 4Q437; 4Q438; 4Q504 8 *recto* 3), and this may suggest that
Ben Sira is employing known prayer terms in his text.[54] This is important in
itself for the development of prayer in the Second Temple period, but it
should not make us think that what Ben Sira has written is merely formulaic.
He had to choose out of the prayer tradition what he thought suitable, and his
wording conforms to interests that he expresses elsewhere in the book.

According to MS B Ben Sira calls for a blessing of ייי אלהי ישראל
"the Lord, the God of Israel", but, as has often been pointed out, this results
in a stich that is too long for the parallelism. Perhaps on comparison with
4Q503 13–16:14 we should read only אלהי ישראל, but a suggested
emendation would be to read only אלהי הכל "God of all" (cf. Gk. τὸν θεὸν
πάντων),[55] which is the term for God at 33/36:1/1a and 45:23, or perhaps
ייי הכל (cf. 45:25). This latter expression is of course related to the
statement that God is "the all" (הוא הכל, 43:27; cf. 4QD^b 18.5.9).[56] It
expresses the immanence of God, who is thus involved in human affairs as
much as the figure of Wisdom. Such immanence is implied elsewhere in the
text such as in 42:16b on the glory of the Lord filling creation,[57] but a
reminder of it here is appropriate before the enumerating of his actions.

Ben Sira proceeds to identify God as one who works wonders on earth
(המפלא לעשות בארץ), a general designation of the power of God. The
Psalmists, for example, praise God for his wonders, Ps 136:4 even stating
that he alone actually works such wonders. The wonders can also denote specifically those of the Exodus narrative (e.g. Ps 78:12) or form part of the
promising of a covenant (Exod 34:10). In Ben Sira, when referring to God,
the wonders mostly seem to denote the mysteries of Creation (e.g. 42:17;
43:29), but here with the reference to the earth that does not seem to be the
case. The significance of Ben Sira denoting God as one who performs wonders is that he thereby generalizes the very specific historical actions of the
"Praise of the Fathers". He presents the consistency in time and space of
God's actions, predicated on his past saving actions. It is therefore significant

---

54   See Prato, Il problema, 162–64, for a discussion of the related expression "to recount
     (all) the wonders" in Ben Sira and Qumran.
55   E.g. Segal, ספר בן סירא, 348; Skehan – Di Lella, Wisdom, 549.
56   The comparison with 4QD^b was first suggested by M. Kister.
57   See Kister, לפירושו, 353–55. On the significance of the expression "God of all", see
     Collins, Wisdom, 88–89.

too that in the important discussion in chapters 15 and 16, he refers to God's past actions (16:6–10). It suggests a stability in the actions of God, and also implies the combining of the traditional ahistorical presentation of God in sapiential literature with the saving God of historical literature.

The phrase המגדל אדם מרחם "He who magnifies mankind from the womb" has similarities with other verses in Ben Sira, but no exact equivalent. The noun רחם in its four appearances (including this one) in the book is always preceded by the preposition מן. In 40:1 the expression מרחם, forming part of a proverbial maxim that God sets before humans trouble from birth until death, has little bearing on 50:22. Likewise the expression מרחם [תה]ום at 51:5 is of no concern to us here. The one possible relevant verse is the reference to the appointing of Jeremiah as prophet "from the womb" (49:7: מרחם נוצר נביא), an obvious allusion to Jer 1:5, but this verse is without the Piel verb גדל.[58] The appointing of Jeremiah is also a one-off event for him, whereas the magnifying of mankind in 50:22 implies the establishing of a permanent, preordained state. It may be that Ben Sira is emphasizing here the worth of each human, who is either magnified or praised by God from birth. This would be a further indication that God is not responsible for evil, and that it is human choice to commit evil. It would, therefore, seem to be continuing the argument with Ben Sira's implied opponents of 15:11–20 that God is not to blame. It does, however, contradict the theme of 36/33:7–15 that God causes people to walk in different paths, and, in contrast to 35/32:14–15, it does not imply any dualism in nature or mankind.

In turning to the final phrase of 50:22 we find ambiguity in how to read it. Is there a *waw* consecutive in ויעשהו כרצונו or not? If there is, then the past tense of the verb might refer to the creation of man ("And has made him"),[59] an important subject in some passages in Ben Sira. The cause of evil is attributed at 15:14 to the יצר placed in man by God – it is God's choice at creation that gave man choice. There the verb is ברא, as Gen 1:1, and not the עשה of 50:22, although עשה is used frequently of the Creator in Ben Sira. And although the next verse (15:15) contains the noun רצון (humans may choose to follow God's will) it is in the common biblical use with God's will as the equivalent to (and here in parallelism with) the commandment. It seems to be different from 50:22, but it does portray the relationship between God and man in an interesting way. God gives man a יצר so that man can follow God's רצון – it expresses a reciprocal relationship between God and mankind.

The second important passage for our theme that contains a reference to the creation of mankind is 36/33:10–13:

---

58   The Piel can be reconstructed at 43:28 and at 49:11 (only the *lamedh* is visible in MS B), in both of which instances it denotes "to praise".
59   This is the translation of Hayward, Jewish Temple, 43.

10 So, too, all people are clay,
        for from earth humankind (אדם) was formed;
        ...

13 Like clay in the hands of a potter (יוצר),
        to be moulded according to his pleasure (רצון),
        So are people in the hands of their Maker,
        to be requited according as he judges.[60]

These verses seem to be much closer to the possible meaning of 50:22,
portraying God as deciding by his will (רצון) the character of each person.
But this predestinarian tendency may not be the only possible meaning for
50:22. If the sequence is not to be interpreted as a *waw* consecutive, then the
present tense of וייעשהו would refer to his ongoing treatment of mankind, as
we translated it above.[61] If the tense of the verb is to be consistent with the
series of participles preceding it, then the present would also seem the more
likely. The Greek translation does indeed render it by the present participle of
ποιέω. We would accordingly have a picture of God performing the great
deeds of history and treating mankind according to his רצון. It would be a
fitting conclusion to a work that places so much emphasis on the divine resolve,[62] and would underline the continual providential treatment of mankind
that had been illustrated in the "Praise of the Fathers".

6. A Dialogical Relationship

The examples reflect a broader picture that could be illustrated by further references and closer analysis. Given these aspects of Ben Sira's depiction of
God, can we answer the question, What kind of God? We have drawn attention to some of the principles upon which God acts for humans. There does
seem to be a development of the biblical concept of divine רצון and an emphasis on the status accorded to mankind by God. This seems to provide a
metanarrative of the relationship between God and mankind in which the language is a representation or mediation of the power of the divine. The portrayal is one of a complex reality between mankind and God, and we should
perhaps not envisage God as entirely controlling human destiny. Ben Sira

---

60 Translation from Skehan – Di Lella, Wisdom, 394, based on Hebrew MS E and in part
     the Greek.
61 Cf. Sauer, Jesus Sirach, 338.
62 Shrenk, εὐδοκέω, 743, classifies 50:22 as a general example of God's will, which he
     distinguishes from those that denote "divine resolve". Its positioning, however, in a
     concluding blessing with key theological terms would suggest that the noun may have a
     stronger force, closer to its use in important passages elsewhere in the book.

tempers his arguments that he produces in some places by a picture of a God who is responsive to the situation. The establishment of the יצר in mankind and the choice to fulfill the commandments in obedience to the covenant – a primary message of Ben Sira is "fear of the Lord" – allows for some human response to God. There is a process of exchange, humans having the choice and God working by his רצון, assigning roles to each party on mutual moralizing grounds. The assurance that God will maintain mercy and show forgiveness is preserved through historical narratives and civic pride, expressed both in passages such as 16:6–10 and in the "Praise of the Fathers" itself.

The covenant represented public commitments on the part of God as well as mankind, and it is perhaps no surprise that 50:22, which we discussed, is the introduction to the prayer for the continuation of the covenant with Phinehas. Throughout the book God is shown as establishing a typology of statuses and privileges, the status of mankind with the choice to do good or ill, and the privilege of being a part of Israel. Through this dialogue of covenant the people are collaborators, God allowing room for negotiation and mutual accommodation. God responds to people's good behaviour, and the people respond to the benefaction, real or perceived, that Ben Sira portrays God as mercifully giving. Hence the final result was not predetermined and the language of beneficence, of mercy and delight rather than of power was to both parties' profit. One might offer a simple functionalist explanation of all this, that Ben Sira praises God unconditionally and that therefore the cause of evil is to be attributed to mankind. But his theology is shaped through language and the portrayal of human-divine interaction, and he avoids mere celebration of divine splendour. There is some parity between the human and divine in the nature of the giving of choice, and the emotional activities of God.

Finally, it is not always necessary to identify a *Sitz im Leben* for every piece of literature, but it can be informative. We might suggest a different setting for Ben Sira that would have produced such notions other than Crenshaw's proposal of a time of instability. John Rogerson has suggested that the biblical presentation of divine providence is modelled on the image of the king dispensing justice and ruling by decision. In Ben Sira's time, under the Hellenistic kings, there was a tradition of euergetical language, of benefaction by the kings of cities and peoples, recorded in letters and decrees. The promise of care for the city and people was extended, and notions such as *eunoia* and *eucharistia* were the principles on which these decrees declare the king will operate. Recent research has shown how these decrees are not to be seen as mere benefaction by the king, but involve a reciprocal relationship between the king and the city.[63] It is to the mutual benefit of each that the city receives largesse, and is able also to offer thanks to the king who gives it.

---

63   This has been explored in Ma, Antiochos III, *passim*.

Freedom, for example, by the ruler's grant imposed the assumption of a ruler's authority and control (he could take back what he gave), but he required that freedom to be maintained by the city, otherwise he would not be able to offer benefits in the first place. There is a vocabulary for presiding values, that expresses exchange in terms of cordiality and courtesy, and perhaps this is reflected too in Ben Sira's picture of divine action. The pleasure with which God acts and grants privileges to mankind asserts his authority, but at the same time he gives room for humans to make a reciprocal response. What this means for providence is that there is a greater narrative of divine behaviour, which transcends some of the more problematic passages that appear to contradict each other in the presentation of divine selection of human paths. Our Jewish tourist in Sardis may see in *pronoia* both a Greek concept and the biblical tradition, but would certainly feel how apt it is to call God *pronoia*, encapsulating divine concern for humans. Perhaps he would have offered up a little prayer on seeing it, using the words of Ben Sira 50:22.

Bibliography

Aitken, J.K., "Apocalyptic, Revelation and Early Jewish Wisdom Literature," in *New Heaven and New Earth. Prophecy and the Millennium: Essays in Honour of Anthony Gelston* (eds. C.T.R. Hayward and P.J. Harland; VTSup 77; Leiden: Brill, 1999) 181–93.

Aitken, J.K., "The Proposed Aramaic Background to Mk 9:11," *JTS* 53/1 (2002) 75–80.

Aitken, J.K., "The God of the Pre-Maccabees: Representation of the Divine in the Persian and Hellenistic Periods," in *The God of Israel* (ed. R.P. Gordon) forthcoming.

Aitken, J.K., "Biblical Interpretation as Political Manifesto: Ben Sira in His Seleucid Setting," *JJS* 51 (2000) 191–208.

Aitken, J.K., *The Semantics of Blessing and Cursing in Ancient Hebrew* (Leuven: Peeters Press, 2003).

Barr, J., *The Concept of Biblical Theology: An Old Testament Perspective* (Minneapolis: Fortress Press, 1999).

Bonnard, P.E., *La Sagesse en Personne annoncée et venue: Jésus Christ* (Paris: Éditions du Cerf, 1966).

Box, G.H. – Oesterley, W.O.E., "The Book of Sirach", in *APOT vol. I* (ed. R.H. Charles; Oxford: Clarendon Press, 1913) 268–517.

Collins, J.J., *Jewish Wisdom in the Hellenistic Age* (OTL; Louisville: Westminster John Knox Press, 1997).

Crenshaw, J.L., "The Concept of God in Old Testament Wisdom", in *Urgent Advice and Probing Questions: Collected Writings on Old Testament Wisdom* (Macon: Mercer University Press, 1995) 191–205 = In *Search of Wisdom: Essays in Memory of John G. Gammie* (repr.; eds. L.G. Perdue, B.B. Scott and W.J. Wiseman; Louisville: Westminster / John Knox Press, 1993) 1–18.

Danby, H., *The Mishnah. Translated from the Hebrew, with Introduction and Brief Explanatory Notes* (London: Oxford University Press, 1933).

Di Lella, A.A., *The Hebrew Text of Sirach: A Text-Critical and Historical Study* (Studies in Classical Literature 1; The Hague: Mouton, 1966).

Fichtner, J., *Die altorientalische Weisheit in ihrer israelitisch-jüdischen Ausprägung. Eine Studie zur Nationalisierung der Weisheit in Israel* (BZAW 62; Giessen: Töpelmann, 1933).

Fine, S., *This Holy Place: On the Sanctity of the Synagogue during the Greco-Roman Period* (Notre Dame: University of Notre Dame Press, 1997).

Foss, C., *Byzantine and Turkish Sardis* (Archaeological Exploration of Sardis: Monographs 4; Cambridge: Harvard University Press, 1976).

Frick, P., *Divine Providence in Philo of Alexandria* (TSAJ 77; Tübingen: Mohr Siebeck, 1999).

Hadas, M., *Aristeas to Philocrates: Letter of Aristeas* (Jewish Apocryphal Literature; New York: Harper, 1951).

Hadot, J., *Penchant mauvais et volonté libre dans la Sagesse de Ben Sira (L'Ecclésiastique)* (Brussels: Presses Universitaires, 1970).

Hayward, C.T.R., *The Jewish Temple: A Non-Biblical Sourcebook* (London: Routledge, 1996).

Hempel, C., "Qumran Communities: Beyond the Fringes of Second Temple Society," in *The Scrolls and the Scriptures: Qumran Fifty Years After* (eds. S.E. Porter and C.A. Evans; Sheffield: Sheffield Academic Press, 1997) 43–53.

Hengel, M., *Judaism and Hellenism: Studies in Their Encounter in Palestine During the Early Hellenistic Period* (trans. J. Bowden; London: SCM Press, 1974).

Herford, R.T., *The Ethics of the Talmud: Sayings of the Fathers, Edited with Introduction, Translation and Commentary* (New York: Schocken Books, 1962).

Kaiser, O., "Die Rezeption der stoischen Providenz bei Ben Sira," *JNSL* 24 (1998) 41–54.

Kesjakova, E., "The ancient synagogue of Philippopolis" [Bulgarian with French summary], *Archeologia* [Sofia] 1 (1989) 20–33.

Kister, M., "לפירושו של ספר בן־סירא," *Tarbiz* 59 (1990) 303–78.

Kraabel, A.T., "The Impact of the Discovery of the Sardis Synagogue," in *Sardis from Prehistoric to Roman Times: Results of the Archaeological Exploration of Sardis 1958–1975* (eds. G.M.A. Hanfmann et al.; Cambridge / London: Harvard University Press, 1983) 178–90.

Kraabel, A.T., "Pronoia at Sardis," in *Studies on the Jewish Diaspora in the Hellenistic and Roman Periods* (eds. B. Isaac and A. Oppenheimer; Te'uda 12; Tel-Aviv: Ramot Publishing, 1996) 75–96.

Kroll, J.H., "The Greek Inscriptions of the Sardis Synagogue," *HTR* 94 (2001) 5–55.

Lehmann, M.R., "Ben Sira and the Qumran Literature," *RQ* 3 (1961) 103–16.

Lehmann, M.R., "11QPsª and Ben Sira," *RQ* 11 (1983) 239–51.

Lévi, I., *L'Ecclésiastique ou La Sagesse de Jésus, fils de Sira. Texte original hébreu édité traduit et commenté. Deuxième partie (III,6, à XVI,26; extraits de XVIII, XIX, XXV et XXVI; XXXI,11, à XXXIII,3; XXXV,19, à XXXVIII,27; XLIX,11, à fin.)* (vol. 2; Bibliothèque de l'École des Hautes Études; Sciences Religieuses 10/2; Paris: Leroux, 1901).

Levison, J.R., "Is Eve to Blame? A Contextual Analysis of Sirach 25:24," *CBQ* 47 (1985) 617–23.

Ma, J., *Antiochos III and the Cities of Western Asia Minor* (Oxford: Oxford University Press, 1999).

Maier, G., *Mensch und freier Wille: Nach den jüdischen Religionsparteien zwischen Ben Sira und Paulus* (WUNT 12; Tübingen: Mohr [Siebeck], 1971).

Mansoor, M., *The Thanksgiving Hymns* (STDJ 3; Leiden: Brill, 1961).

Marböck, J., *Weisheit im Wandel. Untersuchungen zur Weisheitstheologie bei Ben Sira* (BBB 37; Bonn: Hanstein, 1971; repr. BZAW 272; Berlin / New York: de Gruyter, 1999).

Mattila, S.L., "Ben Sira and the Stoics: a Reexamination of the Evidence," *JBL* 119 (2000) 473–501.

Middendorp, Th., *Die Stellung Jesu Ben Siras zwischen Judentum und Hellenismus* (Leiden: Brill, 1973).

Moore, G.F., *Judaism in the First Centuries of the Christian Era: the Age of the Tannaim* (Cambridge: Harvard University Press, 1927).

Muraoka, T. – Elwolde, J.F. (eds.), *Sirach, Scrolls and Sages: Proceedings of a Second International Symposium on the Hebrew of the Dead Sea Scrolls, Ben Sira and the Mishnah, Held at Leiden University, 15–17 December 1997* (STDJ 33; Leiden: Brill, 1999).

Overman, J.A. – MacLennan, R.S. (eds.), *Diaspora Jews and Judaism: Essays in Honor of, and in Dialogue with, A. Thomas Kraabel* (South Florida Studies in the History of Judaism 41; Atlanta: Scholars Press, 1992).

Pautrel, R., "Ben Sira et le Stoïcisme," *RSR* 51 (1963) 535–49.

Petraglio, R., *Il libro che contamina le mani: Ben Sirac rilegge il libro e la storia d'Israele* (Theologia 4; Palermo: Augustinus, 1993).

Prato, G.L., *Il problema della teodicea in Ben Sira: Composizione dei contrari e richiamo alle origini* (AnBib 65; Rome: Pontifical Biblical Institute, 1975).

Rajak, T., "The Gifts of God at Sardis," in *Jews in a Graeco-Roman World* (ed. M. Goodman; Oxford: Clarendon, 1998) 229–39.

Rajak, T., "Jews, Pagans and Christians in Late Antique Sardis: Models of Interaction," in *The Jewish Dialogue with Greece and Rome: Studies in Cultural and Social Interaction* (AGJU 48; Leiden / Boston / Köln: Brill, 2000) 447–62.

Rogerson, J., "Can a Doctrine of Providence Be Based on the Old Testament?," in *Ascribe to the Lord: Biblical and Other Studies in Memory of Peter C. Craigie* (eds. L. Eslinger and G. Taylor; JSOTSup 67; Sheffield: JSOT Press, 1988) 529–43.

Rybolt, J.E., *Sirach* (CBC 21; Collegeville: Liturgical Press, 1986).

Rylaarsdam, J.C., *Revelation in Jewish Wisdom Literature* (Chicago: University of Chicago Press, 1946).

Sanders, E.P., "The Dead Sea Sect and Other Jews: Commonalities, Overlaps and Differences," in *The Dead Sea Scrolls in Their Historical Context* (ed. T.H. Lim with L.W. Hurtado, A.G. Auld, A. Jack; Edinburgh: Clark, 2000) 7–43.

Sauer, G., *Jesus Sirach: Übersetzt und erklärt* (ATDA 1; Göttingen: Vandenhoeck & Ruprecht, 2000).

Segal, M.Z., ספר בן־סירא השלם (2d rev. ed.; Jerusalem: Bialik, 1958).

Segalla, G., "La volontà di Dio in Qumran," *RB* 11 (1963) 379–80.

Segalla, G., "La volontà di Dio nei LXX," *RB* 13 (1965) 121–43.

Shrenk, G., "εὐδοκέω, εὐδοκία", in *TDNT vol. 2* (ed. G. Kittel; Grand Rapids: Eerdmans, 1964) 738–50.

Skehan, P.W. – Di Lella, A.A., *The Wisdom of Ben Sira: A New Translation with Notes, Introduction and Commentary* (AB 39; New York: Doubleday, 1987).

Trebilco, P.R., *Jewish Communities in Asia Minor* (SNTSMS 69; Cambridge: Cambridge University Press, 1991).

Urbach, E.E., *The Sages: Their Concepts and Beliefs* (Cambridge: Harvard University Press, 1979).

Wicke-Reuter, U., *Göttliche Providenz und menschliche Verantwortung bei Ben Sira und in der Frühen Stoa* (BZAW 298; Berlin / New York: de Gruyter, 2000).

Winston, D., "Theodicy in Ben Sira and Stoic Philosophy," in *Of Scholars, Savants, and Their Texts* (ed. R. Link-Salinger; New York: Lang, 1989) 239–49.

Zatelli, I., "Pragmalinguistics and Speech-Act Theory as Applied to Classical Hebrew," *ZAH* 6 (1993) 60–74.

Jüdische Wirkungsgeschichte

Theology and Non-Theology in the Rabbinic Ben Sira

David S. Levene
University of Leeds

The quotations from the Book of Ben Sira in early rabbinic literature exhibit considerable – and well-known – oddities.[1] Their relationship to the text (both the transmitted Greek, Latin and Syriac translations and the Hebrew versions discovered at Cairo, Masada and Qumran) is complex, with some areas of overlap, but also with substantial variations from what is known elsewhere. Moreover, the apparent status of the book in the Rabbis' eyes varies dramatically from outright hostility to being placed on the same level as undisputed scripture. The object of this paper is to argue that part of what generates these divergent responses to Ben Sira is rabbinic awareness of its theology – even though it is not the most overtly theological sections of the work that are quoted and discussed by the Rabbis. Although quotations from Ben Sira are found in midrashic and other rabbinic literature, many of these are post-Talmudic: I shall be confining myself in this paper to the explicit references to the book in the two Talmuds.

The first thing that needs to be observed is that the type of passage that is quoted from Ben Sira hardly gives a balanced picture of the work. Overwhelmingly what are quoted are aphoristic proverbs taken without context. There is not a single quotation from the last portion of the book, the praise of Jewish heroes in chs. 44–50. Nor are there even any quotations from the overtly theological portions of the book: none, for example, from the discussion of wisdom and freedom of choice in chs. 14–18. The focus is instead on maxims providing practical advice for living a proper life.[2] This is one reason (though far from the only one)[3] that it has been suggested that the text of Ben Sira that the Rabbis were using was not the book in the form that we have it today, but rather a florilegium of maxims taken from it.[4]

---

1   My interest in the Rabbinic quotations of Ben Sira was originally stimulated by a Usenet discussion with Amitai Halevi and Alan Pfeffer, and my thanks go to both of them. I should like in particular to thank Jeremy Corley for inviting me to give this paper and for his assistance during its production, and to all those at the Ben Sira conference who offered suggestions, especially James Aitken, Alon Goshen-Gottstein and Stefan Reif.

2   Cf. the comments of Wright, Considerations (consulted on 1 March 2001).

3   Another is that certain of the quotations conflate verses from different parts of the book: this is the case, for example, with the quote at *b. B. Qam.* 92b (on which see further below), which combines the first part of 27:9 with the second of 13:15. See more generally Wright, Considerations; idem, B. Sanhedrin 100b, 41–50.

4   Such florilegia certainly existed at a later period: MS C from the Cairo Geniza is an example.

However, postulating such a florilegium does not satisfactorily account for all the aspects of the treatment of the book in the Talmuds. As I said above, the responses to the book are considerably divergent. At the one extreme stands *b. B. Qam.* 92b, which in collecting proof-texts for a point offers a conflation of two verses from Ben Sira as coming from the *Ketubim* – in other words, the "Writings" that form the third part of sacred scripture. At the other stands the discussion between R. Joseph and Abaye in *b. Sanh.* 100b on whether the book of Ben Sira falls under the category of ספרים החיצונים (literally "external books"), which, according to R. Akiva in the Mishnah (*Sanh.* 10:1), if a Jew reads he loses his portion in the World to Come. R. Joseph argues that it does, and cites a number of passages from the book in support of this position; however he ultimately concludes (in the standard Vilna text) that מילי מעלייתא דאית ביה דרשינן להו ("we may expound to them the good things that it contains"). There is, however, an alternative textual reading, according to which R. Joseph states אי לאו דגנזוה רבנן להאי סיפרא כי הני הוי דרשינן להו – "*if the Rabbis had not hidden this book, we would have expounded to them.*"[5] The difference is a significant one: both versions accept that there are good things in the book, but according to the standard reading, it *is* permitted to read them, whereas according to the variant text it is not.[6] It seems likely that this latter reading is the older one: the standard text bears every mark of being an alteration designed to harmonise the discussion here with the undeniable fact that elsewhere in the Talmud verses from Ben Sira are quoted entirely unproblematically – including these very same verses at *b. Yebam.* 63b (on which see further below).

The peculiarity of R. Joseph's position, which the Talmud here seems broadly to endorse, cannot be overemphasised. It should be pointed out first of all that this debate between him and Abaye is not primarily concerned with the "canonicity" of the book.[7] The question of "canonicity" may raise its head with the idea that the Rabbis chose to "hide" it despite its value,[8] but that is not the focus of the discussion.[9] The issue at stake here is not whether the book should form part of scripture, but whether it should be read at all; and on the view that it should not be, disobedience will lose the Jew his share in the World to Come. Some scholars have sought to explain this by arguing

---

5   Rabbinovicz, Sefer, *ad loc.*
6   There is a third alternative reading: אף על גב דגנזו רבנן להא סיפרא – '*Although* the Rabbis hid this book &c.' – whose implications in this context are similar to those of the Vilna text (Rabbinovicz, Sefer, *ad loc.*).
7   On the problematic concept of "canonicity" in early Judaism, see e.g. Barr, Holy Scripture, esp. 41–64.
8   For the precise meaning of the term in Talmudic literature, and its relationship to questions of canonicity, see Leiman, Canonization, 72–86.
9   Compare *t.Yad.* 2:13, where the book is listed as one that does not "defile the hands." On the relationship between "defiling the hands" and canonicity, see Leiman, Canonization, 102–20.

that this is not considering private reading, but public exposition;[10] but while it is possible that this was what is intended by the original Mishnaic statement, by the time of the Talmuds that possibility appears to be excluded by *y. Sanh.* 10:1, which makes a clear distinction between actively banned books and books permitted for casual reading:

רבי עקיבא אומר: אף הקורא בספרים החיצונים כגון סיפרי בן סירא
וסיפרי בן לענה. אבל סיפרי המירום וכל ספרים שנכתבו מיכן והילך
הקורא בהן כקורא באיגרת. מאי טעמא? ויותר מהמה בני היזהר וגו׳
להגיון ניתנו ליגיעה לא ניתנו.

> R. Akiva said: "Also he who reads external books" – for example, the books of Ben Sira and the books of Ben La'anah. But the books of Homer[11] and all the books written subsequently, one who reads in them is like someone reading in a letter. Why? *And furthermore, my son, beware* &c. [Ecclesiastes 12:12]: they were given for casual reading but were not given for study.

Hence Ben Sira, on the view adopted by R. Joseph, falls into a category well outside the books that are merely unacceptable for public exposition – that would, after all, presumably be true of Homer also. The book is, according to that view, unacceptable for all purposes.[12]

The problem is that none of the passages from Ben Sira that are quoted in support of R. Joseph's position seem naturally to warrant such an extreme response. Abaye quotes a series of maxims from Ben Sira which might be thought possibly to justify the ban, but none of them seem obviously unacceptable, and each of them he then proceeds to demonstrate actually accords with statements made either in the Torah or in the book of Proverbs or by the Rabbis. Finally, the Talmud quotes a passage which appears to have no such parallels, and which must therefore be taken as the justification:

אלא משום דכתיב זלדקן קורטמן, עבדקן סכמן, דנפח בכסיה לא צחי.

---

10 So e.g. Ginzberg, Observations, 129–31; Bloch, Outside Books, 87–108; Haran, Problems, 247–51 similarly argues that the ban is on reciting the book with a formal chant.

11 For the identification of "Hameros" of this and other rabbinic passages with Homer, see especially Lieberman, Hellenism, 105–14.

12 See further on this topic Leiman, Canonization, 86–91. He offers two possible interpretations of *y. Sanh.* 10:1, one of which (his "Solution B") he appears slightly to prefer: to interpret להגיון as applying to Ben Sira and meaning "for *recitation*," and hence to conclude that oral exposition was allowed, and that it was only the writing and reading of a text that was forbidden. However, his reasons for this are partly in order to provide a satisfactory interpretation of the abbreviated parallel passage in *Qoh. Rab.* 12:12, a late work whose value as evidence for the correct interpretation of the Talmud is accordingly relatively slight. This solution also makes a distinction between reading a text and oral recitation which seems hard to explain, especially in a culture where many people's access to texts would precisely be in oral rather than in written form. Leiman's "Solution A," which interprets להגיון as applying to Homer, is thus to be preferred.

אמר במאי איכול לחמא, לחמא סב מיניה. מאן דאית ליה מעברתא
בדיקניה כולי עלמא לא יכלי ליה.

> But because it is written: "A thin-bearded man is acute, a thick-bearded one is a
> fool; he who blows in his cup is not thirsty; he who says, 'With what shall I eat
> my bread?' take the bread away from him; if one has a parting in his beard, no
> one at all will overcome him."

This rather ludicrous set of maxims in fact does not correspond to anything in our surviving texts of Ben Sira. Rashi's understanding of the
passage, which is surely correct, is that the reason it is quoted is to
demonstrate the book's triviality, and hence that it is not worth reading. But
this apparent solution simply accentuates the problem. It is not of itself
surprising that maxims from Ben Sira found in the Talmud should not appear
in the transmitted text, given the general mismatch between the texts referred
to above – there are indeed other examples of such unattested maxims,
including one earlier in this very passage. It is a little more worrying that a
whole set of such maxims should be quoted in a context which is seeking to
justify the dismissal of the book – maxims, indeed, which not only do not
appear in the transmitted text, but which are entirely out of character with
anything that we are familiar with in that text. Nor does mere triviality any-
way seem an adequate reason for condemning those who read the book to
losing their place in the World to Come, especially when other books are not
subjected to a comparable ban. And postulating a florilegium, while it explains reasonably satisfactorily the textual variation, makes it harder rather
than easier to understand R. Joseph's reported attitude, since there would
appear to be less in a set of disconnected practical maxims to generate opposition than there would be in a book of more wide-ranging historical and
theological interest.[13]

Were it the case that the Talmudic rabbis had a wider understanding of
the book than the bare selection of quotations would imply, the issues at stake
in this debate would be easier to understand: the book's acceptance or rejection would be based, as one might expect *a priori*, on theological grounds –
this chapter of the Talmud is after all precisely the one which discusses acceptable theological limits for Jews. Yet the debate as it is actually conducted
appears to be based on entirely different grounds: there is a mismatch be-

---

13 Leiman, Canonization, 97–102 argues that the original ban was not because of the con-
    tent of Ben Sira *per se*, but because of its use in sectarian circles, which rendered it a
    threat to rabbinic Judaism. This is of course possible, although it is hard to see why
    such a comprehensive ban would be necessary to counter this unless the actual content
    of Ben Sira contained aspects that would render it especially serviceable to non-rab-
    binic sects. However, the Talmudic discussion, at any rate, is premised on the reason
    for such a ban being the content of the book – which leaves the problem of what in the
    content would be thought to justify actual suppression, rather than simply ignoring the
    text.

tween the terms of debate and the conclusions drawn. This very fact might lead us to hypothesise that the debate as it stands in the Talmud is not an accurate record of the actual issues under discussion, but rather a construct designed to reach the desired conclusions, but where the compilers were either unable or unwilling to quote the actual verses upon which the decisions were being made, perhaps because to do so might precisely draw attention to the passages that were potentially unacceptable.

This argument, however, depends upon the Rabbis actually being aware of Ben Sira in something approaching the form in which we have it, and moreover upon their being acquainted with it sufficiently closely to respond to its theology. This would not, of course, be incompatible with the idea that they were employing a florilegium as the primary source for many of their quotations, for which there is strong evidence (see n. 3 above): such a florilegium could perfectly well exist side by side with a sequential text (as indeed it does in the Geniza).[14] But it would still require that, despite the absence of direct quotations from the theologically charged portions of Ben Sira, the Rabbis should be aware of the theological range of the text. Is there any evidence for this?[15]

It is, as I said above, perfectly true that what is quoted from Ben Sira in the Talmuds are apparently merely decontextualised maxims; moreover, some of those quotations appear in contexts where nothing more than a decontextualised maxim is appropriate, as in the quotation of Sir 11:1 in the story of Alexander Jannai and Shimon ben Shetach at y. Ber. 7:2.[16] However, a surprisingly high proportion of them appear in contexts that, like b. Sanh. 100b, themselves have a strong theological cast. This is the case with the other extended collection of quotations from Ben Sira in the Talmuds: that found at b. Yebam. 63b. These quotations are in fact largely identical (though with some differences in wording and order) to the 'acceptable' quotations from Ben Sira that R. Joseph offered at b. Sanh. 100b (cf. above):

---

14 For the possibility of multiple forms of the text of Ben Sira being simultaneously available to the Rabbis see Wright, Considerations. The fact that t.Yad. 2:13 and y. Sanh. 10:1 (quoted above) both refer to the books of Ben Sira may be relevant in this context; cf. Leiman, Canonization, 184 n. 413.

15 The appropriate methodology for the study of the Talmuds and other Rabbinic texts is highly controversial, and those who approach them with different assumptions reach radically different conclusions. As will become apparent, my general sympathies are with those scholars who see the redacted texts as broadly coherent unities, at least within particular tractates, chapters or sugyot; this position is above all associated with the voluminous writings of Neusner, (e.g. Integrity); for an example of a similar approach, but with a more "literary" focus comparable to the one I adopt, see Kraemer, Reading. However, this approach has been much criticised in other scholarly circles; see for a recent example Cohen, (ed.), Synoptic Problem, especially the essays by Goldenberg and Becker.

16 The quotation here has in fact been "contaminated" with the first part of Prov 4:8, which is the proof-text quoted in the parallel passage at b. Ber. 48a.

כתוב בספר בן סירא: אשה טובה מתנה טובה. בחיק ירא אלהים
תנתן. אשה רעה צרעת לבעלה. מאי תקנתיה? יגרשנה ויתרפא
מצרעתו. אשה יפה אשרי בעלה מספר ימיו כפלים. העלם עיניך
מאשת חן פן תלכד במצודתה. אל תט אצל בעלה למסוך עמו יין
ושכר, כי בתואר אשה יפה רבים הושחתו ועצומים כל הרוגיה.
רבים היו פצעי רוכל המרגילים לדבר ערוה, כניצוץ מבעיר גחלת.
ככלוב מלא עוף כן בתיהם מלאים מרמה. אל תצר צרת מחר
כי לא תדע מה ילד יום, שמא מחר בא ואיננו, נמצא מצטער על
העולם שאין שלו. מנע רבים מתוך ביתך ולא הכל תביא ביתך.
רבים יהיו דורשי שלומך גלה סוד לאחד מאלף.

It is written in the book of Ben Sira: "A good woman is a good gift; she will be given into the embrace of the God-fearer [26:3]. An evil woman is a plague to her husband. What is the solution? Let him divorce her and be healed from his plague [cf. 25:23–26]. A beautiful woman is a joy to her husband; his number of days shall be doubled [26:1]. Avert your eyes from a charming woman [9:8] lest you are caught in her net [9:3]. Do not go in to her husband to mix with him wine and beer [9:9], for in the face of a beautiful woman many were destroyed and the mighty are all her slain [9:8]. Many are the wounds of the spice-peddler [11:29], which lead him to obscene things as a spark lights the coal [11:32]. *As a cage full of birds, so are their houses full of guile* [Jer 5:27]. Do not worry about tomorrow's trouble, *for you do not know what a day will beget* [Prov 27:1]. Perhaps tomorrow will come, and he will be no more, and consequently has worried about a world that is not his [cf. 30:23]. Keep many from within your house and do not bring everyone into your house [11:29]. Many are those who seek your welfare; reveal a secret to one in a thousand [6:6]."

This rather disparate collection of maxims at first sight looks rather strange. It was unproblematic in *b. Sanh.* 100b, where after all it was only being offered as a more or less random set of examples of "good things" to be found in the book. It is less obviously clear how they are appropriate in *b. Yebam.* 63b, which has no comparable justification.

If one examines the context of the discussion in *b. Yebam.*, however, some outlines of an answer begin to emerge. The initial quotations from Ben Sira, concerning the difference between a good and a bad wife, pick up and reinforce a set of maxims on the same topic attributed to Raba a few lines earlier, which in turn comments on a set of anecdotes about the marriages of certain of the Rabbis. This passage, at any rate, seems entirely appropriate to the general discussion in this part of the Talmud. This then leads very naturally into a discussion of one's relationship with women more generally, with warnings against inappropriately mixing with other men's wives. One can find more detailed similarities also; for example, the recommendation to divorce a bad wife has earlier been stated as advice of Raba (citing as a proof-text Prov 22:10).

A broader consideration of the Talmud here, however, reveals more of significance than simply a general overlap of topic. In the Talmud the discussions of good wives and bad wives are both highly discursive, with looping digressions generated out of comments or phrases, in the course of which their maxims are given strongly theological overtones. Out of the discussion of good wives, it is argued that through Abraham and Sarah's offspring (with the input of the proselytes Ruth and Naamah) the whole world is blessed, because all blessings come through Israel. Conversely, punishment comes into the world because of Israel alone – which leads back into the accounts of bad wives, who are compared to Gehinnom. A proof-text concerning bad wives (Deut 32:21) is then applied by another rabbi to the Zoroastrians, who persecute the Jews – but whose persecutions are linked to Jewish sins. Specifically, the Zoroastrians are said to have exhumed the Jewish dead, and this is then generalised into a wider comment about evil men not being buried, but being killed in order that they should not sin and so find themselves in Gehinnom. Although the argument is complex and goes through many stages, the association of good and bad women with themes of reward and punishment more widely, and specifically with life and death, is a point that it repeatedly returns to. It is noteworthy that one of the passages then quoted from Ben Sira (26:3) directly refers to the good wife as being divine reward for the God-fearing man; but also that in a verse just before in the text (25:24) – which the Talmud does *not* quote – one finds the famous statement of fundamental female responsiblity for sin and death (ἀπὸ γυναικὸς ἀρχὴ ἁμαρτίας καὶ δι' αὐτὴν ἀποθνῄσκομεν πάντες).[17] That precise idea is not part of the theology that the Talmud itself is bringing in at this point,[18] but the general association is shared by both texts. The point is not that the Talmud by quoting Ben Sira is seeking to endorse his theology, but rather that the fact that the two texts make comparable associations of topics suggests that the Talmud was not selecting its quotations from Ben Sira simply as useful but disconnected maxims: their appropriateness rests precisely in an awareness of their wider theological backgrounds.

This point is reinforced more strongly by the continuation of the Talmud's arguments. Directly following the set of quotes from Ben Sira, the discussion moves back to the conclusion of the central topic of this section. The Mishnah here upon which the Talmud is commenting concerns the duty of a Jew to produce children: the initial question under discussion was how many children it is necessary to produce to fulfil the *mitzvah* (and what counts as "children"); from here the discussion moved to the necessity of marriage, and

---

17   Cf. Skehan – Di Lella, Wisdom, 348–49.
18   This view is sometimes found elsewhere in rabbinic writings, most notably at *Ber. Rab.* 17:8; however it is no less common to attribute the blame to Adam and to see Eve entirely as a victim. On the portrayal of Eve in rabbinic literature, see Boyarin, Carnal Israel, 80–94.

hence to the role of the good and the bad wife considered above. Now, immediately subsequent to the quotation from Ben Sira, the topic of propagation resumes, but does so at a far more fundamental level, with justifications provided for the entire *mitzvah* – and provided in essentially theological terms. It begins with a recapitulation of an earlier statement that the Messiah will not come until all unborn souls (currently in *Guf*) have been born.[19] This then leads to an argument that someone who does not produce children is like someone who sheds blood and / or like someone who lessens the *d'mut* (the divine image of God in man). Ben Azzai, who supports this, is criticised for hypocrisy (since he was childless),[20] but defends himself with the words ומה אעשה, שנפשי חשקה בתורה, אפשר לעולם שיתקיים על ידי אחרים ("but what am I to do, since my soul is in love with Torah, and it is possible for the world to be preserved by others?"). Finally it is concluded that if there are ever fewer than 22,000 Jews, then the *shechinah* – the Divine Presence of God – departs from Israel, in which case anyone who has failed to produce children is *chayev mitah* (liable for a theoretical death penalty).

What is the relevance of this to Ben Sira? The last quotations from him, directly before this concluding discussion in the Talmud, have left the topic of women, and instead have moved to a set of three maxims, all of which are broadly concerned with keeping oneself apart from others. The second and third of these state that one should not allow people into one's house, and should maintain one's secrets; the first is that one should not worry about tomorrow, since if one dies, one has worried about a world which is not one's own (נמצא מצטער על העולם שאין שלו). Their implicit themes thus contrast very radically with the theology of the discussion in the Talmud that succeeds them, which is precisely concerned with every Jew's responsibility towards each other and to future generations. The contrast is especially noticeable with the first maxim (which is also, it may be noted, the one that is the furthest from anything that survives in the transmitted text of Ben Sira): the idea that the future world is not one's own is picked up in Ben Azzai's argument that as a lover of Torah he is forced to leave propagation to others (the reference to allowing others to "preserve the world" is particularly pointed in the light of Ben Sira); nevertheless the thrust of the passage is to reject Ben Azzai's position, and to maintain the necessity for all Jews to care for the future by leaving successors behind them. It is also worth noting that the quote from Ben Sira incorporates from Prov 27:1 the phrase לא תדע מה ילד יום ("you do not know what the day will beget") – the metaphor is striking in the context of the Talmud, since it is precisely by "begetting" that the Talmud is arguing that one discharges properly one's responsibility towards

---

19   This was originally quoted at 62a in the context of the question whether a man who has
      children who died can be regarded as having fulfilled the duty of propagation.
20   Cf. *b. Soṭah* 4b.

the future, both in terms of preserving the Divine within the world in its different aspects, and ultimately by bringing on the Messiah.

Putting this together, it looks very much as if this apparently random set of maxims that the Talmud quotes here from Ben Sira is in fact anything but random. They play an important linking role in the argument, by offering a set of ideas about the proper relationship between the individual and his fellows, and hence his responsibility to the community at large – but a set of ideas which can be shown to contain theological implications which the Talmud can then controvert, when it brings the argument back to the ultimate point at issue, the necessity that people by producing children each individually take responsibility for all others in the present and the future alike. It is true that the passages that are quoted from Ben Sira are not of themselves explicitly stating these points; however, read in the context of the book as a whole, the theological undertones that the Talmud identifies do not seem out of line with Ben Sira's general thought – it is noticeable, for example, that Ben Sira at 30:4–5 and 44:11–15 appears to identify the benefit of having children in terms of the "survival" that they can provide for the individual parent rather than in terms of the duty that is performed to the community as a whole, and one may also observe that at 16:1–4 he argues that it is better to die childless than have evil offspring. This is not to say that the Talmud is necessarily drawing directly from a sequential text: in particular, with the antepenultimate maxim the combination of language which seems especially pointed in this argument and the absence of a close parallel in the transmitted text must lead us at least to suspect that it may have been heavily adapted to suit this context. But the general conclusion must be that the Rabbis in quoting maxims from Ben Sira are responding to them not merely as a set of maxims, but fundamentally as a theological text, whose theological implications are not there merely to be accepted, but which form part of a theological dialectic within the wider Talmudic argument.

That Ben Sira is often being read by the Rabbis primarily theologically may be illustrated by a further example: *b. Ḥag.* 13a. The topic here is the ban in the Mishnah (*Ḥag.* 2:1) on discussing מעשה בראשית [i.e. the mystic details of God's creation of the universe] in the presence of more than one other person. The Talmud first considers the precise scope of the ban, and concludes that a single individual may have expounded to him the six days of creation, but not the period before, or indeed what is above or below the created universe – but then it moves into a lengthy discussion of apparently the very things that it is not permitted to discuss, with an extended account of what precisely was created on the first day, the attributes of God that were employed to create it, the order of creation of heaven and earth, the pillars on which the earth rests, and the nature of the seven heavens. The discussion then, however, concludes by placing this as the limit of permitted enquiry:

עד כאן יש לך רשות לדבר, מכאן ואילך אין לך רשות לדבר, שכן
כתוב בספר בן סירא: במופלא ממך אל תדרוש ובמכוסה ממך אל
תחקור, במה שהורשית התבונן, אין לך עסק בנסתרות.

> Thus far you have permission to speak, further than this you do not have per-
> mission to speak, for thus it is written in the Book of Ben Sira [3:21–22]: "Do
> not expound the things that are concealed from you, and do not investigate the
> things that are hidden from you. Think upon the things that are permitted to
> you; you have no business with the things that are secret."

The section then closes with an account of the evil king of Babylon denounc-
ed in Isaiah 14 (whom Jewish tradition identified with Nebuchadnezzar), who
ignored this principle (cf. Isa 14:14), sought to ascend to the level of God,
and was accordingly punished.

The context in the Talmud gives Ben Sira's dictum a central role in this
theological argument. The contradiction between the ban upon expounding
creation and the apparent exposition of creation is manifest; it is Ben Sira
who effects the reconciliation, by defining for the Rabbis that the matter hitherto under discussion is not in fact the sort of topic that is banned.[21] As we
saw with b. Yebam., these verses in Ben Sira do not of themselves precisely
contain the theological implications that the Talmud is employing them for,
since they occur as part of a general discussion of the necessity for humility,
rather than as a precise attempt to mark out appropriate and inappropriate
limits for enquiry. But at the same time, as we also saw with b. Yebam., the
underlying theology that the Talmud identifies here is not out of line with
Ben Sira's thought in general.[22] Although he does at 3:21–22 indicate that
there should be limits placed on speculative enquiry, this is stated in a general
context that places the works of God in creation within the broad purview of
the writer, which associates the divine attributes of Wisdom above all with
the work of creation, which sees Wisdom indeed as existing prior to creation,
but which does not allow the precise nature of Wisdom itself to be explored
(cf. 1:1–6) – this is of course the point from which Ben Sira's work begins.
The detail of the Talmudic argument is hardly present, but there is a sufficiently broad overlap to suggest that the Talmudic selection of Ben Sira as an
appropriate conclusion to its argument is not a result of decontextualised selection of a random maxim. We might also note that the Talmud, when discussing earlier in the passage the attributes of God that created the world,
places wisdom as the first of them (b. Ḥag. 12a): naturally there are other
sources in Scripture for this idea (not least the Book of Proverbs, which is indeed what is cited by the Talmud as a proof-text), but the broad congruence
between it and Ben Sira is still noteworthy. Here too we can see Ben Sira

---

21   Cf. Urbach, Sages, 193.
22   There is a similar tension in this work between the claim that God has revealed secret
     knowledge to mankind (e.g., 42:19) and the denial that his secrets are accessible (e.g.,
     43:31–32); see on this tension N. Calduch-Benages in this volume.

being cited not merely as a disconnected maxim, but as part of a complex of theology that the Talmud is exploring in this passage.

The parallel discussion in *y. Ḥag.* 2:1 introduces further considerations. The Ben Sira quotation here comes in not as part of the discussion of the ban on teaching מעשה בראשית, but of the next clause in the Mishnah, which bans teaching מעשה המרכבה [the vision of the 'chariot' in Ezekiel] even to a single individual.[23] The Talmud begins by providing various anecdotes about Rabbis who had studied this topic, culminating with the famous story (cf. also *b. Ḥag.* 14b) of the four rabbis who entered פרדס: Ben Azzai (who went mad), Ben Zoma (who died), R. Akiva (who emerged safely) – and "Acher" (lit. "another") who became an apostate. "Acher," the Talmud explains, was in fact Elisha ben Abuyah,[24] and then introduces a long account of his wrongdoings, his expositions of the Torah in spite of those wrongdoings, the reasons for his apostasy, and his ultimate deathbed repentance, along with the attempt of his former pupil R. Meir to ensure him his place in the World to Come (all of this is paralleled in *b. Ḥag.*, but in a separate argument at a later point – 14b–15b). After his death his daughters came to R. Judah the Prince seeking charity; R. Judah was initially reluctant, but they appealed to him:

ר׳ אל תבט במעשיו הבט בתורתו. באותה השעה בכה ר׳ וגזר
עליהן שיתפרנסו אמר מה אם זה שיגע בתורה שלא לשום שמים
ראו מה העמיד מי שהוא יגע בתורה לשמה על אחת כמה וכמה.

"Rabbi, don't look at his deeds, but look at his Torah." At that moment Rabbi [Judah the Prince] wept and decreed on them that they should be provided for. He said: "See what this man produced, who laboured in Torah not for the sake of heaven; if so, how much the more one who labours in Torah for its own sake!"

Immediately after this, the quotation from Sir 3:21–22 is introduced – but with slightly different wording (see below):

ר׳ אלעזר בשם בר סירה: פליאה ממך מה תדע? עמוקה משאול מה
תחקור? במה שהורשיתה התבונן אין לך עסק בנסתרות.

R. Eleazar in the name of Bar Sira: "What is hidden from you, why do you seek to know? What is deeper than Sheol, why do you investigate? Think upon the things that are permitted to you; you have no business with the things that are secret."

This then leads into a set of further warnings along similar lines. First, Rav quotes Ps 31:19, interpreting the injunction against lips הדברות על צדיק to refer to those who speak about "the righteous one of the world" things

---

23   For an extensive study of מעשה המרכבה in Talmudic literature based on different underlying assumptions (cf. n. 15 above) see Halperin, Merkabah.

24   There is an extensive recent study of Elisha ben Abuyah in rabbinic literature which I have been unable to consult: Goshen-Gottstein, Sinner.

that he keeps hidden, and the reference to "pride and contempt"(בגאוה
ובוז) to mean those who have the arrogance to boast about explaining
מעשה בראשית; R. Jose ben Chaninah then argues that if one loses one's
share in the world to come for getting glory at his neighbour's expense, one
should do so even more for doing so at the expense of חי עולמים – the "Life
of Worlds." From here the argument moves back into a discussion of מעשה
בראשית, with a consideration of the precise limits of the ban and the manner
of creation that parallels the discussion in the Babylonian Talmud (see
above).

It can immediately be seen that although the elements of the discussion
in the two Talmuds are broadly identical, the order of the argument, and
hence the role that Ben Sira plays in that argument, are substantially different
from one another. Whereas in the Babylonian Talmud the quotation from Ben
Sira caps and rounds off the discussion of מעשה בראשית, and the account
of מעשה המרכבה and Elisha ben Abuyah is reserved for a separate discussion, in the Jerusalem Talmud the discussion begins from מעשה המרכבה,
and then moves via Elisha ben Abuyah into a consideration of מעשה
בראשית.[25] Here too, however, the Ben Sira quote comes at a crucial point:
the point where the transition is being made between these separate themes. It
thus serves both as a conclusion to the story of Elisha ben Abuyah, and as an
introduction to the discussion of מעשה בראשית.

What is then the precise significance of the quote in the Jerusalem Talmud's argument? The obvious point is that, unlike in the Babylonian Talmud,
it is not there to offer a solution to the problem of the appropriate limits of
enquiry; rather it appears to be commenting upon Elisha ben Abuyah in particular, just indeed as the comments of Rav and R. Jose ben Chaninah are.
Elisha ben Abuyah, it appears, is being presented as someone who has sought
out hidden things which he should not, and who has arrogantly attempted to
expound matters in despite of God. In this respect it may be noted that the
original context of the passage as it appears in Ben Sira makes the quotation
here more directly apposite than in the Babylonian Talmud: as mentioned
above, that section of Ben Sira is concerned with the need for humility – and
that is of course precisely the point that is then picked up by the comments of
Rav and R. Jose ben Chaninah, which immediately succeed it.

But the role of the quotation in the argument goes further. It is noticeable
that the treatment of Elisha ben Abuyah in the Talmud is more ambivalent
than a bare account of his story might make it appear. Although he is an

---

25   Becker, Sammelwerke, 17–18 sees a sharp break and a new section of the Talmudic
     discussion beginning with the Ben Sira quote; however nothing in the text marks such a
     break, and the quote (as well as the one that succeeds it) is apposite in the context of
     what went before as well as those which come after; note the rather different analysis
     of Neusner, Talmud, 50.

apostate, and is described as (among other things) advising the Romans how to compel Jews to break the Sabbath, the origin of his apostasy is not presented as wilfulness, but – in two of the alternative versions that the Talmud introduces – the result of his failure to understand the nature of reward and punishment: he saw a man who let a mother bird go when taking the young but nevertheless died (contrary to what is promised in Deut 22:6–7), and saw the severed tongue of R. Judah the Baker in a dog's mouth, and concluded that there was no divine reward and no resurrection of the dead. His failure to understand moreover extends to his own position: he believes that he is barred from repentance, although ultimately on his deathbed is taught otherwise by R. Meir, who persuades him to repent, and concludes that his own intercession on his behalf will ensure Elisha a place in the World to Come. The focus of the story as it is told in the Talmud is thus above all on theodicy: for all his knowledge of the Torah, that is what Elisha ben Abuyah failed to comprehend.

In the light of this, the Ben Sira quotation takes on some extra dimensions. Although Elisha ben Abuyah did not, as it seems, understand theodicy, others in the story are presented as doing so, and as having a better understanding of this aspect of the world despite their inferiority in knowledge of Torah: not only R. Meir and R. Judah the Prince, but even his daughters. The direct juxtaposition of the story of the daughters' approach for charity to R. Judah the Prince with Ben Sira is interesting if one recollects that immediately before the quote in at least some versions of Ben Sira's text, one finds (3:19) a comment that God לְעֲנוִים יְגַלֶה סוֹדוֹ ("will reveal his secret to the poor / lowly").[26] In both Ben Sira and the Talmud, being barred from looking into what is beyond oneself is compatible with an apparently lesser person having the insights that one lacks oneself.

More significantly still, the verse from Ben Sira, as noted above, appears in a slightly different wording to that found in the Babylonian Talmud (which is closer to the Hebrew text of MS A and the Greek translation); the chief difference is that the second clause asks why search "what is deeper than Sheol." This has the effect of aligning it more closely with the story of Elisha ben Abuyah as outlined above: the reference to Sheol brings into sharper focus the fact that the central point is concerned with reward and punishment after death. This theme is then in turn picked up by the discussion of מֵעֲשֵׂה בְרֵאשִׁית; the work of creation is directly connected with the same theme of reward and punishment:

העוֹלָם הזה נברא בה"א והעוֹלָם הבא נברא ביו"ד. מה ה"א פתוח
מלמטן רמז לכל באי עוֹלם שהן יורדין לשאול. מה ה"א יש לו נקודה
מלמעלן משעה שהן יורדין הן עולין. מה ה"א פתוח מכל כך פותח

---

26 It is found in this form in the Hebrew MS A, as well as in G II and in the Syriac; see
    the note of Skehan – Di Lella, Wisdom, 159.

פתח לכל בעלי תשובה. מה יו"ד כפוף כך יהיו כל באי העולם כפופין.

This world was created by ה and the World to Come by י. Just as ה is open un-
derneath, it is an indication that all who enter the world will go down to Sheol.
Just as ה has a stroke upwards, once they have gone down they will go up. Just
as ה is open on all sides, so is a gate open to all penitents. Just as י is bent, so
shall all who enter the world be bent.

The quotation from Ben Sira, with its explicit reference to Sheol, thus links
the two parts of the discussion: it indicates the dangers of Elisha ben
Abuyah's search into what is hidden, but it connects that with Elisha's particular failing, which was to understand the divine justice upon which the
universe rests. Once again, therefore, a quotation from Ben Sira is playing a
significant role in a theological discussion; but in this respect the theological
role that the Talmud implicitly assigns to the quotation is, as was also seen
with *b. Yebam.* 63b and *b. Ḥag.* 13a, not one that is based upon its actual
meaning within Ben Sira's own work. Here, unlike those previous cases, the
theology that the Talmud is presenting is less obviously close to Ben Sira's
own wider position; while he is certainly interested in questions of
theodicy,[27] it is less clear that he accepts the specific doctrines of posthumous
reward and punishment; however, the process of translation and revision of
his text has introduced a certain amount of material of this sort into it,[28] and if
the Rabbis did indeed possess a sequential text, it is likely to have contained
similar accreted material.

The conclusions that this study leads to are thus to a certain degree para-
doxical. The context and use that the Talmuds make of the quotations from
Ben Sira strongly suggest that the rabbis did not see him merely as a convenient source of practical wisdom, but as an author who is fundamentally
concerned with issues that one might call "theological." Moreover, at least
some of the "theological" use that is made of him assigns a position that is
fairly easy to identify with positions that Ben Sira actually adopted in his
work. At the same time, the verses *themselves* do not express these positions
in their original context; it is only through the process of quotation and re-
contextualisation that they acquire their new meanings (sometimes via what
appears to be a certain degree of tacit adaptation to enable them to fit the
Talmudic context more closely). In other words, the general positions that
Ben Sira is used to endorse in the Talmud suggest rabbinic awareness of his
wider thought, yet the actual selection of quotations does not.

This paradox, however, sheds some useful light upon the contradictory
rabbinic attitudes to Ben Sira with which I began my discussion. In *b. Sanh.*
100b, as discussed above, there seems to be a mismatch between the relatively innocuous quotations that R. Joseph introduces from Ben Sira, and the

---

27   See generally on this topic Prato, Il problema.
28   See Skehan and Di Lella, Wisdom, 83–87.

extreme conclusions that he draws from those quotations. We can now see that the underlying phenomenon is precisely the same: in places where one would naturally expect explicit theological statements, what one finds instead are simple maxims – which however are treated by the Talmud as if they *were* theological statements. In effect, there appears to be throughout an element of displacement, with practical maxims standing in for and substituting for theology. This very fact of displacement, of course, means that the underlying motives for it are unstated and so hard to determine. But one natural explanation might be that, although the Rabbis did have access to a more or less "complete" text of Ben Sira, and hence were responding to his thought in broadly "theological" terms, nevertheless aspects of his writing generated enough suspicion among at least some of the Rabbis that there was a reluctance to quote from the theological portions directly. Instead, they selected maxims that could be treated to the same effect, a process which would of course be assisted by the employment of florilegia (see above). The Ben Sira of the Talmuds is thus simultaneously both a theological and a non-theological author: only non-theological portions are quoted, but in such a way as to treat the actual theology at one remove.

In the absence of direct statements, it is harder still to decide what in the theology of Ben Sira might have generated rabbinic opposition, such that they were unwilling to engage with it directly. Any answer can only be speculative: one possibility might be the strong personification given to Wisdom, especially in ch. 24, which might be thought to adumbrate dangerously the Christian tendency to provide seemingly independent existence to particular aspects of God;[29] it is also, of course, possible that the various alterations and accretions that we know the text of Ben Sira underwent include versions with problematic theological statements that no longer survive. But whatever answer is given, the least that one may reasonably conclude is that the Rabbis knew more about Ben Sira's thought than the bare list of Talmudic quotations would suggest.

Bibliography

Barr, J., *Holy Scripture: Canon, Authority, Criticism* (Oxford: Oxford University Press, 1983).

Becker, H.-J., *Die großen rabbinischen Sammelwerke Palästinas. Zur literarischen Genese von Talmud Yerushalmi und Midrash Bereshit Rabba* (TSAJ 70; Tübingen: Mohr Siebeck, 1999).

Bloch, J., "Outside Books," in *Mordecai M. Kaplan Jubilee Volume: English Section* (ed. M. Davis; New York: Jewish Theological Seminary of America, 1953) 87–108.

---

29   Cf. the comments of Kearns, Ecclesiasticus, 545–46. On the significance of the development of hypostatised Wisdom in Ben Sira, and its subsequent suppression in Rabbinic writings, see Hengel, Judaism, vol.1, 153–75; cf. also Urbach, Sages, 37–65.

Boyarin, D. *Carnal Israel: Reading Sex in Talmudic Culture* (Berkeley: University of California Press, 1993).

Cohen, S.J.D. (ed.), *The Synoptic Problem in Rabbinic Literature* (BJS 326; Providence: Brown University, 2000).

Ginzberg, L., "Some Observations on the Attitude of the Synagogue towards the Apocalyptic-Eschatological Writings," *JBL* 41 (1922) 115–36.

Goshen-Gottstein, A., *The Sinner and the Amnesiac: The Rabbinic Invention of Elisha ben Abuya and Eleazar ben Arach* (Stanford: Stanford University Press, 2000).

Halperin, D.J., *The Merkabah in Rabbinic Literature* (AOS 62; New Haven: American Oriental Society, 1980).

Haran, M., "Problems of the Canonization of Scripture," *Tarbiz* 25 (1956) 245–71 [Hebrew].

Hengel, M., *Judaism and Hellenism: Studies in Their Encounter in Palestine during the Hellenistic Period* (2 vols; trans. J. Bowden; London: SCM, 1974).

Kearns, C., "Ecclesiasticus, or the Wisdom of Jesus the Son of Sirach," in *A New Catholic Commentary on Holy Scripture* (2d ed.; eds. R.C. Fuller, L. Johnston and C. Kearns; London: Nelson, 1969) 541–67.

Kraemer, D., *Reading the Rabbis: The Talmud as Literature* (Oxford: Oxford University Press, 1996).

Leiman, S.Z., *The Canonization of Hebrew Scripture: The Talmudic and Midrashic Evidence* (Transactions of the Connecticut Academy of Arts and Sciences 47; Hamden: Archon, 1976).

Lieberman, S., *Hellenism in Jewish Palestine* (Texts and Studies of the Jewish Theological Seminary of America 18; New York: Jewish Theological Seminary of America, 1950).

Neusner, J., *The Integrity of Leviticus Rabbah: The Problem of the Autonomy of a Rabbinic Document* (BJS 93; Chico: Scholars Press, 1985).

Neusner, J., *The Talmud of the Land of Israel: A Preliminary Translation and Explanation* (vol. 20: *Hagigah and Moed Qatan*; Chicago: University of Chicago Press, 1986).

Prato, G.L., *Il problema della teodicea in Ben Sira: Composizione dei contrari e richiamo alle origini* (AnBib 65; Rome: Pontifical Biblical Institute, 1975).

Rabbinovicz, R., *Sefer Dikdukei Soferim* (Munich: Roesl, Huber, 1867–86).

Skehan, P.W. – Di Lella, A.A., *The Wisdom of Ben Sira: A New Translation with Notes, Introduction and Commentary* (AB 39; New York: Doubleday, 1987).

Urbach, E.E., *The Sages: Their Concepts and Beliefs* (trans. I. Abrahams; Jerusalem: Magnes, 1975).

Wright, B.G., "B. Sanhedrin 100b and Rabbinic Knowledge of Ben Sira," in *Treasures of Wisdom: Studies in Ben Sira and the Book of Wisdom* (FS M. Gilbert; eds. N. Calduch-Benages and J. Vermeylen; BETL 143; Louvain: Peeters, 1999) 41–50.

Wright, B.G., "Some Methodological Considerations on the Rabbis' Knowledge of the Proverbs of Ben Sira," ftp://ftp.lehigh.edu/pub/listserv/ioudaios-l/Articles/bwsira

Prayer in Ben Sira, Qumran and Second Temple Judaism:
A Comparative Overview

Stefan C. Reif
Cambridge Universitz Library

Treatment to Date

On first applying myself to the actual preparation (as distinct from the broad consideration) of the contents of this paper, it occurred to me that the challenge was not a daunting one. The topic was such an obviously important one, with broad ramifications, that there would be no shortage of earlier studies that could easily serve as guides and precedents and my task would merely be to copy the overall picture that had previously been painted, with an additional flourish here and an occasional highlight there. I therefore confidently undertook the necessary bibliographical search for comprehensive and systematic presentations of the whole topic represented in my title and was soon faced with an interesting result. Not only was there no close study of the liturgical content of Ben Sira in the broader context of the Jewish worship of his day but neither was there any concise summary of how Ben Sira relates to matters of prayer, worship and liturgy throughout his book. Although this state of affairs meant that I was obliged to research, think and write for myself to a degree that I had not expected, it was at the same time personally encouraging since it justified my choice of topic and provided the opportunity of making at least some first moves towards the provision of what was undoubtedly a *desideratum*. While no scholarly predecessor had wholly covered the ground I had proposed to examine, there were undoubtedly studies that had addressed, or touched on, certain aspects of the topic and it was clear that my initial responsibility would therefore be to summarise some such work, to assess aspects of its character and to illustrate my remarks with a few examples.[1]

It should be stated at the outset that, given the limitations placed upon the size of the papers presented here, my approach in meeting this first obligation will have to be highly eclectic and the treatment will need to be broadly thematic rather than tightly chronological, permitting me to give the flavour of some of what has been written without engaging in anything like a

---

1   I am grateful to Dr. Jeremy Corley, of Ushaw College, Durham, and to Dr. Renate Egger-Wenzel, of the Institut für Alt- und Neutestamentliche Wissenschaft at the University of Salzburg, for their kind initiative in inviting me to deliver a paper on this topic at the Durham conference of July, 2001, and for their devoted work in arranging the conference and the publication of its papers.

thorough bibliographical analysis. Given that Ben Sira's period is dominated
by the Second Temple, it is not inappropriate to commence with a note to the
effect that almost all the commentators on his book place stress on the Jerusalem cult and the author's devotion to this central element of Jewish life in
the Judean state of his day. As will shortly become clear, not all of them succeed in doing so without betraying what are to my mind some specific and
gratuitous elements of tendentiousness. For his part, Coggins, while stressing
how highly Ben Sira regards the role of the priest both historically and con-
temporarily, justifiably and judiciously raises the issue, as so many others do,
of whether he may even himself have been a priest, citing the main evidence
for this contention but remaining unconvinced that it is persuasive.[2] More remarkably and questionably, Oesterley, having traced overall reverence, delight and zeal in Ben Sira's attitudes to Temple rituals and priestly functions,
also somehow manages to detect in them a weakening of the commitment to
the Jerusalem cult. Basing himself on verses that say no more than that sacrifice, to be efficacious, has to be sincere and pious, rather than mechanical and
hypocritical, he argues, in a leap of scholarly as well as theological faith, that
Ben Sira "is, in effect, offering a plea for the abandonment of material sacrifice" and concludes that "he never directly affirms the atoning effect of sacrifices."[3] To his credit, Lange, in a weighty article, focuses more cautiously on
alleged polemics regarding the cult and on the relative dates of Ecclesiastes
and Ben Sira.[4]

For other scholars, it is Ben Sira's relationship with later rabbinic liturgy
that is of the greatest relevance and importance. At the beginning of the
twentieth century, Elbogen was anxiously searching for parallels between
Ben Sira and the rabbinic 'amidah and listed various phrases that seemed to
him to qualify, and a similar line was later pursued later by Idelsohn.[5] For
Gevaryahu, Ben Sira was to be seen as a typical formulator of prayers in his
day and this activity to be linked with the presupposed existence of the synagogue. He also identified liturgical themes such as threats from the non-Jew-
ish world, exile and redemption.[6] Rivkin, on the other hand, will have none
of this supposition about the existence of the synagogue and uses Ben Sira to
argue powerfully that there was no such institution in the middle of the Second Temple period.[7] In his introduction to the books of the Apocrypha, Brockington does cover the hymns and praises of Ben Sira fairly well but here

---

2   Coggins, Sirach, 49.
3   Oesterley, Wisdom, lxxi–lxxii.
4   Lange, Diskussion, 113–59.
5   Elbogen, Gottesdienst, 29–31, 43, 48, 50, 53–54, 68, 73, 244 and 278; Hebrew edition,
     22–23, 31, 34, 37, 39, 41–42, 54, 58, 185 and 208; English edition, 26–27, 35, 38, 43,
     45, 47, 49, 62, 66, 194 and 217; Idelsohn, Liturgy, 20–22 and 110.
6   Gevaryahu, Shimon Ben-Sira, 256–74.
7   Rivkin, Ben Sira, 320–54.

too he most certainly has other theological fish to fry, indulging himself in a statement of his own spiritual preferences rather than a fair assessment of Ben Sira's religious values, or indeed those of his contemporary co-religionists. "One might think", he writes, "that such an attitude would have lifted Ben Sira above the level of nationalism and led him to think in terms of universalism as did some of the prophets before him. That was evidently far more than the ordinary Jew could reach."[8]

A most useful treatment is provided by Johnson in a short but important monograph on apocryphal and pseudepigraphical prayer in which many of the relevant sources are listed throughout the study.[9] The book of Ben Sira does not, however, receive individual attention in that work but is cited only within the larger context, a policy I myself followed in my volume on the history of Hebrew prayer.[10] Integral links between different aspects of religious expression is another topic that is found by some scholars in their examinations of liturgical developments in the period under discussion. Newman, for example, sees the role of exegesis in the penitential prayers of the Second Temple period and points out the literary models used in prayers, including some by Ben Sira.[11] She does not, however, pay any attention to the rabbinic liturgy or to the evidence from Qumran. In his careful and useful review of recent research, Reiterer has little to cite in the area of liturgy but does stress the connection between the different theological areas as portrayed in the work of Jolley. As the latter scholar puts it, "Torah is to be used in study and worship as the guide to how one should live ... Torah and wisdom are inseparably linked together in Sirach in a synergistic relationship."[12] As will become apparent in the body of this paper, I am greatly dependent here on Segal's ספר בן־סירא השלם and on Skehan – Di Lella's Wisdom of Ben Sira and it will therefore perhaps be appropriate to cite both these works before I conclude this short summary of work done.[13] In his introduction, Segal barely refers to prayer at all but does deal with sacrifices. He points out that Ben Sira values these highly and honours the priesthood but that, at the same time, he views both these institutions within the total Jewish religious context.[14] Di Lella also notes the centrality of cult and prayer for Ben Sira

---

8   Brockington, Introduction, 71–84, with the cited piece on p. 83.
9   Johnson, Prayer, 7, 11, 16, 20, 25–26, 28–29, 36, 38, 40–43, 46, 48–50, 54–59, 61–62 and 66.
10   Reif, Judaism, 45–46 and 346.
11   Newman, Praying, 73, 114, 133, 137, 153, 160–63, 177, 179, 182, 194, 213, and 238.
12   Reiterer, Review, 23–60, citing Jolley, Function, on p. 50.
13   Segal, ספר בן־סירא; Skehan – Di Lella, Wisdom. The Hebrew and English texts used in this article have been cited from these two volumes respectively. For text-critical reasons these texts do not exactly match. The alternative verse citations are those given in Arabic rather than in Hebrew numerals in Segal's volume.
14   Segal, ספר בן סירא, introduction, 33–34.

and their place in his total religious outlook. He argues not just that social justice is part of this outlook for Ben Sira but that it is "more important and central", perhaps going a little further in this connection than I, or some others, might wish to do[15].

Current Approach

Given the summaries just offered of what has, or has not, been accomplished to date, it should be clear that it would now be useful for students of Ben Sira if such literature could be supplemented by the provision of a critical overview of the total liturgical picture capable of being drawn on the basis of the relevant Ben Sira texts. There are also additional reasons why such an analysis would be timely. Until a little over a decade ago, the study of Jewish liturgical history had been something of a "Cinderella" in the broader field of Hebrew and Jewish studies, a state of affairs that led numerous scholars, myself included, to call, at about that time, for the subject to receive the attention it truly deserved.[16] Whether as a result of such a call, or for other reasons, just such a development has taken place and a much larger number of books and articles, containing more extensive and more varied treatments of the field, have made their appearance and stimulated considerably more debate.[17] Among the periods that have received particular attention have been the Second Temple period and the early Christian centuries and the time has now surely come to set Ben Sira in such context. Furthermore, the new availability of many Qumran texts has provided insights into areas previously known only to a limited degree and liturgy has been a particular beneficiary of the publication, translation and study of such texts. As will shortly be noted, a number of recently published volumes have greatly illuminated the liturgical activities recorded at Qumran.[18] This has meant that instead of guessing at the nature of Jewish prayer and worship during and immediately after the Second Temple period, we now have some definite and relevant data on which to base our speculations. What I therefore propose to do in the next part of this paper is to summarise the central liturgical content and ideology of Ben Sira by way of some major textual examples, before moving on to the consideration of other elements to be found in remaining texts, and a comparison of these findings with the broader liturgical situation.

---

15   Skehan – Di Lella, Wisdom, introduction, 87–88.
16   My own contribution to this appeal was an article entitled "Jewish Liturgical Research: Past, Present and Future", 161–70.
17   For excellent bibliographical guidance to these, see Tabory, Prayer.
18   See my discussion of evidence from Qumran, below. See now also the new publication by Davila, Works.

Major Texts

1. Simeon the High Priest and Public Worship (50:16–24) [50:23–36]

Hebrew text (H^B)

23. ויריעו וישמיעו קול אדיר	להזכיר לפני עליון:
24. כל בשר יחדו נמהרו	ויפלו על פניהם ארצה:
25. להשתחות לפני עליון	לפני קדוש ישראל:
26. ויתן השיר קולו	ועל המון העריכו נרו:
27. וירנו כל עם הארץ	בתפלה לפני רחום:
28. עד כלותו לשרת מזבה	ומשפטיו הגיע אליו:
29. אז ירד ונשא ידיו	על כל קהל ישראל:
30. וברכת ייי בשפתיו	ובשם ייי יתפאר:
31. וישנו לנפל שנית	ל.....מפניו:
32. עתה ברכו נא את ייי אלהי ישראל	המפליא לעשות בארץ:
33. המגדל אדם מרחם	ויעשהו כרצונו:
34. יתן לכם חכמת לבב	ויהי בשלום ביניכם:
35. יאמן עם שמעון חסדו	ויקם לו ברית פינחס:
36. אשר לא יכרת לו ולזרעו	כימי שמים:

English text

16. [The sons of Aaron would sound a blast, the priests on their trumpets of beaten metal;]
    A blast to resound mightily as a reminder before the Most High.
17. Then all the people with one accord would quickly fall prostrate to the ground
    In adoration before the Most High, before the Holy One of Israel.
18. Then hymns would reecho, and over the throng sweet strains of praise resound.
19. All the people of the land would shout for joy, praying to the Merciful One,
    As the high priest completed the service at the altar by presenting to God the sacrifice due;
20. Then coming down he would raise his hands over all the congregation of Israel;
    The blessing of the Lord would be upon his lips, the name of the Lord would be his glory.
21. Then again the people would lie prostrate, receiving the blessing from the Most High.
22. And now, bless the God of all, who has done stupendous things on earth;
    Who makes humans grow from their mother's womb, and does with them according to his will!
23. May he grant you wisdom of heart, and may he abide among you as peace;
24. May his kindness towards Simeon be lasting; may he fulfil for him the covenant with Phinehas
    So that it may not be abrogated for him or for his descendants, while the heavens last.
23. [May he grant us joy of heart and may there be peace in our days in Israel, as in the days of old.] (Greek)
24. [May his kindness remain constantly with us and may he save us in our days.] (Greek)

Summary

After the wine libation has been offered, the priests ceremonially sound the trumpets and all the people[19] involve themselves in the act of divine worship by prostrating themselves before God. Prayer and song (led by the Levites?) accompany the latter part of the cultic ritual and when the high priest has concluded his ministrations at the altar he blesses the people, apparently still at that stage with the literal use of the tetragrammaton,[20] and they then once more prostrate themselves.[21] Ben Sira invites the priests (or, less likely, the people?) to praise God for the wonders of creation and prays for wisdom (or, according to the Greek, for joy and kindness) and peace for them, as well as for an eternal priesthood, to which he shows himself, throughout the passage, closely attached.[22]

2. Parents, Cult, Priesthood, Tithes and Charity (7:27–36) [7:28–38]

Hebrew text (H^A)

ואם תחוללך אל תשכח:	[בכל לבך כבד אביך	.28
ומה תגמל להם כגמולם לך:]	זכר כי מהם היית	.29
ואת כהניו הקדיש:	בכל לבך פחד אל	.30
ואת משרתיו לא תעזב:	בכל מאודך אהב עושך	.31
ותן חל]קם כאשר צוותה:	כבד אל והדר כהן	.32
זבחי] צדק ותרומת קדש:	לחם אברים ותרומת [יד	.33
למען תשלם ברכתך:	וגם לאביון [הושי]ט יד	.34
וגם ממת אל תמנע חסד:	תן מתן לפני כל חי	.35
ועם אבלים התאבל:	אל תתאחר מבוכים	.36
כי ממנו תאהב:	אל תשא לב מאוהב	.37
ולעולם לא תשחת:	בכל מעשיך זכור אחרית	.38

---

19   Given the parallel with v. 17 [v. 24], the Hebrew עם הארץ does not here convey the sense of a privileged group, as it does in the Hebrew Bible (e.g. Gen 23:7 and 2 Kgs 11:14), but is more akin to its later rabbinic meaning of "the general public".

20   Contrast *y. Yoma* 3:7, 40d.

21   For variations in the order and content of the ritual, compare 2 Chr 29:27–29 and *m. Tamid.* 6.3–7.3.

22   See also, e.g., 45:6–22 [45:9–40] and 50:5–21 [50:6–31]. For a broader exegetical study of Simon the High Priest and chapter 50, see O. Mulder's forthcoming volume, *Simon the High Priest in Sirach 50*, to be published by Brill as a supplement to the *Journal for the Study of Judaism*.

English text

27. With your whole heart honor your father; your mother's birth pangs forget not.
28. Remember, of these parents you were born; what can you give them for all they gave you?
29. With all your soul fear God, revere his priests.
30. With all your strength love your Maker, neglect not his ministers.
31. Honor God and respect the priest; give him his portion as you have been commanded:
    The flesh of sacrifices, contributions, his portion of victims, a levy on holy offerings.
32. To the poor also extend your hand, that your blessing may be complete;
33. Give your gift to anyone alive, and withhold not your kindness from the dead;
34. Avoid not those who weep, but mourn with those who mourn;
35. Neglect not to care for the sick – for these things you will be loved.
36. In whatever you do, remember your last days, and you will never sin.

Summary

Respect for God and one's parents is set alongside honour for the priest and meeting one's obligations to him in the matters of tithes and his share of the sacrifices.[23] This is immediately followed by instructions to assist the poor, the unfortunate and those in mourning,[24] all of this in order to ensure that one's life is blessed and one is loved.[25] The reference to the מתים may be to the dying,[26] or to the dead, who need burial,[27] or to the leper,[28] but amounts in all cases to an act of kindness.

3. Correct Nature and Wider Context of Worship (7:8–15)

Hebrew text (H^A)

כי באחת לא תנקה:	אל תקשור לשנות חט 8.
[ובהקריבי לאל עליון יקח:]	[אל תאמר לרב מנחתי יביט 9.
הי כאל נחלקה:	אל תאיץ בצבא מלאכת עבדה 10.

---

23 Whether one points אֲבָרִים or אַבָּרִים (under the influence of Ps 78:25), the reference is still to some aspect of what is due to the priests; see also Sir 45:6–26 [45:9–50]. The pointing אֲבָרִים is in itself controversial; see Reif, Shabbethai Sofer, 149 and 259–60. On the matter of respecting parents, see also Sir 3:1–16 [3:1–15]. Kister has important comments on this passage, particularly as it relates to Deut 6:5, in his article "Notes", 183–86.

24 The concern with playing a part in mourning practices is also reflected in other texts; see n. 45 below.

25 For another passage in which the major Torah precepts are holistically regarded as worship, see Sir Sir 34/31:21–36:22/16.17 [34:19–36:17].

26 As in 2 Kgs 20:1: כי מת אתה ולא תחיה.

27 As in Gen 47:29: ועשית עמדי חסד ואמת אל נא תקברני במצרים.

28 As in *b. Ned.* 64b on Num 12:12: מצורע דומה למת.

וּבִצְדָקָה אַל תִּתְעַבֵּר: אַל תִּתְקְצַר בַּתְּפִלָּה   11.
זְכֹר כִּי יֵשׁ מֵרִים וּמַשְׁפִּיל: אַל תָּבֻז לְאֱנוֹשׁ בְּמַר רוּחַ   12.
וְכֵן עַל רֵעַ וְחָבֵר יַחְדּוּ:   אַל תַּחֲרוֹשׁ חָמָס עַל אָח   13.
כִּי תִקְוָתוֹ לֹא תִנְעַם: אַל תַּחְפֹּץ לְכַחֵשׁ עַל כָּחַשׁ   14.
וְאַל תִּישָׁן דָּבָר בַּתְּפִלָּה: אַל תָּסוֹד בַּעֲדַת שָׂרִים   15.

English text

8.   Do not plot to repeat a sin; not even for one will you go unpunished.
9.   Say not, "He will appreciate my many gifts; the Most High will accept my offerings."
10. Be not brusque in your prayers; neither put off doing a kindness.
11. Laugh not at an embittered person; there is One who exalts and humbles.
12. Contrive no mischief against your brother, nor against your friend and companion.
13. Take no pleasure in telling lie after lie; it never results in good.
14. Do not hold forth in the assembly of the elders, nor repeat yourself when you pray.
15. Hate not laborious work; work was assigned by God.

Summary

Persistent sinners are advised that offerings in the Temple may not bring forgiveness of sin. People are instructed not to show contempt for their less for-
tunate fellows or to plan violence or deceit against them. Nor should they
chatter indiscreetly[29] in important company. Within the context of these ethical prescriptions, there are also warnings about giving the appropriate attention to prayer[30] and charity and, possibly also (if the phrase מלאכת עבודה is
so explained), to manual labour.

4. David's Role in Composing Hymns and Music at Specific Times (47:8–11) [47:11–17]

Hebrew text (H^B)

לְאֵל עֶלְיוֹן [בְּדָבָר כָּ]בוֹד: בְּכָל מַעֲשֵׂהוּ נָתַן הוֹדוֹת   11.
וּבְכָל [יוֹם הַלְלוּ תָמִי]ד: בְּכָל לִבּוֹ אוֹהֵב עוֹשֵׂהוּ   12.
וְ[קֹ]וֹ[ל] [מִזְמוֹר בַּנְּבָל]ים תִּקֵּן: נְגִינוֹת שִׁיר לְ[פְנֵי מִזְבֵּחַ   13.

---

29   Deriving the verb in 14a [15a] from the root סוד in the sense of "conversing inti-
     mately", as in Sir 9:15 [9:21], Jer 23:18–22 and Job 15:8.
30   It is possible that 14b [15b] alludes to the gratuitous repetition of prayer which Ben
     Sira is condemning as much as its exaggerated abbreviation but there is no indication
     that fixed formulae are here presupposed. Kister may be right in seeking a sense that is
     a better parallel to the first half of the verse and opting for a meaning of שנה דבר simi-
     lar to Prov 17:9 and pointing תְּפִלָּה and not תִּפְלָה; see Kister, Genizah Manuscripts,
     40–41. See also the contribution of F.V. Reiterer to this volume.

14. [נתן] ל[ח]גים הדר   ויתקן מועדים שנה בש[נ]ה:
15. בה[ללו] את שם קדשו   לפני בק[ר] ירון משפט:
16. [גם] ייי העביר פשעו   וירם לעולם קרנו:
17. [וי]תן ל[ו] חק ממלכת   וכסאו הכין על ירושלם:

English text

8. With his every deed he offered thanks; of God Most High he proclaimed the glory.
    With his whole heart he loved his Maker
9c. and daily had his praises sung;
10a. He added beauty to the feasts
10b. and solemnised the seasons of each year
9a. With string music before the altar,
9b. providing sweet melody for the psalms
10c. So that when the Holy Name was praised,
10d. before daybreak the sanctuary would respond.
11. The Lord forgave him his sins and exalted his strength forever. He conferred on him
    the rights of royalty and established his throne in Israel.

Summary

David loved and praised God and composed songs and music for special occasions. He composed hymns for recitation in the sanctuary, expressing himself liturgically every morning.[31] Because of this, his sin was forgiven, he
was granted success, and his dynasty was permanently established in Jerusalem.[32]

5. The Scribe has Liturgical as well as Intellectual Duties (39:5–8) [39:7–12]

Hebrew text (Segal's retroversion)

7. לב ישית לשחר עושהו   ולפני עליון יתחנן:
8. ויפתח פיו בתפלה   ועל עונותיו יעתיר:
9. אם אל עליון ירצה   רוח בינה ימלא:
10. הוא יביע דברי חכמה   ויודה לייי בתפלה:
11. הוא יכין עצה ודעת   ובמסתריו יתבונן:
12. הוא יביע מוסר שכל   ובתורת ייי יתפאר:

---

31 The Hebrew text has משפט, with the possible meaning of "custom" or "form", while a
    Hebrew gloss, and the Greek, read מקדש. David is to such an extent idealised as the
    most outstanding example of one who conducts the praise of God that his role here is
    clearly identified (or confused?) with that of the high priest.

32 Less central attention is given to Jerusalem in the Greek and Syriac, which refer more
    generally to Israel.

English text

5. His care is to rise early to seek the Lord, his Maker, to petition the Most High,
    To open his lips in prayer, to ask pardon for his sins.
6. Then, if it pleases the Lord Almighty, he will be filled with the spirit of under-
    standing;
    He will pour forth his words of wisdom and in prayer give praise to the Lord.
7. He will direct his counsel and knowledge aright, as he meditates upon God's mys-
    teries.
8. He will show the wisdom of what he has learned and glory in the Law of the
    Lord's covenant.

Summary

The scribe is expected to develop intellectually, to understand God's mysteries, and to express himself intelligently and ethically. He should at the same
time, however, appreciate that all this is intended as a religious exercise. He
should also therefore humbly and enthusiastically seek and praise God,[33] pray
for the forgiveness of his sins, and take pride in mastering (and teaching?) the
Torah.

6. Prayer and Fasting Require Repentance (31/34:30/25–31/26) [34:26–28]

Hebrew text (Segal's retroversion)

.26   טובל ממת ושב ונוגע בו   מה יועיל ברחיצתו:

.27   כן אדם צם על חטאיו   ושב והולך ועושה אלה:

.28   תפלתו מי ישמע   ומה יועיל בתעניתו:

English text

30. If a person again touches a corpse after he has bathed, what did he gain by the
     purification?
31. So with a person who fasts for his sins, but then goes and commits them again:
     Who will hear his prayer, and what has he gained by his mortification?

Summary

Just as there is no point in undergoing purification through ritual immersion
and then immediately attracting impurity, so fasting and praying for forgive-

---

33 *Pace* Segal (ספר בן סירא, 259) and Skehan – Di Lella (Wisdom, 452), there is no
    clear indication in this text that the reference is necessarily to the composition of formal
    prayers (such as are found in the later rabbinic tradition, according to Segal); the author
    may just as well have spontaneous prayer in mind.

ness[34] cannot be efficacious if one sets about sinning again. The subsequent three bicola parallel ethical behaviour and the offering of sacrifices and appear to equate their religious value (32/35:1/1a–5/3).

7. Successful Prayer at Sennacherib's Invasion (48:19–21) [48:26–29]

Hebrew text (H^B)

ויחילו כיולדה:	‎[אז נ]מוגו בגאון לבם	.26
ויפרשו אליו כפים:	‎[ויקראו] אל אל עליון	.27
ויושיעם ביד ישעיהו:	‎[וישמע] בקול תפלתם	.28
ויהמם במגפה:	‎[ויך במ]חנה אשור	.29

English text

19.   The people's hearts melted within them; they were in anguish like that of childbirth.
20.   But they called upon the Most High God and lifted up their hands to him;
      He heard the prayer they uttered, and saved them through Isaiah.
21.   God struck the camp of the Assyrians and routed them with a plague.

Summary

When they were terrified by Sennacherib's hosts, not only Hezekiah but "they" (Isaiah? all the people?) prayed to God and raised their hands in worship. God heard their prayer and rescued them, through Isaiah, by striking the Assyrians with a plague that sent them on their way in confusion.[35]

8. Prayer for the Rescue of God's People Israel (33/36:1/1a–36:22/17) [36:1–17]

Hebrew text (H^B)

ו[שים] פחדך על כל הגוים:	הושיענו אלהי הכל	.1
ויראו את גבורותיך:	הניף על עם נכר	.2
כן לעינינו הכבד בנו:	כאשר נקדשת לעיניהם בנו	.3
כי אין אלהים זולתך:	וידעו כאשר ידענו	.4

---

34   Note the close association here of the acts of fasting and praying and their joint contribution to the forgiveness of sin; see also Sir 18:15–23 [18:14–22].

35   The textual variants presupposed in the texts before the Greek and the Syriac translators modify the description of the prayer and the response to it but without significant alteration of the liturgical significance of the passage. As to the matter of who was praying, see H. Eshel – E. Eshel, 4Q448, 651.

5. חדש אות ושנה מופת	האדר יד ואמץ זרוע וימין:
6. העיר אף ושפוך חמה	והכניע [צר] והדוף אויב:
7. החיש קץ ופקוד מועד	כי מי יאמר לך מה תעשה:
8. [באף אש יאכל שריד	ומרעי עמך ימצאו שחת:]
9. השבת ראש פאתי מואב	האומר אין זולתי:
10. אסוף כל שבטי יעקב	ויתנחלו כימי קדם:
11. רחם על עם נקרא בשמך	ישראל בכור כיניתה:
12. רחם על קרית קדשך	ירושלם מכון שבתיך:
13. מלא ציון את הודך	ומכבודך את היכלך:
14. תן עדות למראש מעשיך	והקם חזון דבר בשמך:
15. תן את פעלת קוויך	ונביאיך יאמינו:
16. תשמע את תפלת עבדיך	כרצונך על עמך:
17. וידעו כל אפסי ארץ	כי אתה אל [עולם]:

English text

1. Come to our aid, God of the universe,
2. And put all the nations in dread of you!
3. Raise your hand against the foreign folk, that they may see your mighty deeds.
4. As you have used us to show them your holiness, so now use them to show us your glory.
5. Thus they will know, as we know, that there is no God but you.
6. Give new signs and work new wonders;
7. Show forth the splendor of your right hand and arm;
8. Rouse your anger, pour out wrath,
9. Humble the enemy, scatter the foe.
10. Hasten the ending, appoint the time when your mighty deeds are to be proclaimed:
11. Let raging fire consume the fugitive, and your people's oppressors meet destruction;
12. Smash the heads of the hostile rulers, who say, "There is no one besides me!"
13. Gather all the tribes of Jacob,
16. That they may inherit the land as in days of old.
17. Show mercy to the people called by your name: Israel whom you named your firstborn.
18. Take pity on your holy city, Jerusalem, the foundation for your throne.
19. Fill Zion with your majesty, your temple with your glory.
20. Give evidence of your deeds of old; fulfil the prophecies spoken in your name,
21. Reward those who have hoped in you, and let your prophets be proved true.
22. Hear the prayers of your servants, for you are ever gracious to your people;
Thus it will be known to all the ends of the earth that you are the eternal God.

Summary

Ben Sira prays for God to demonstrate his power and reputation in a miraculous way, as he did in the past, and to save his people Israel by swiftly destroying their most arrogant enemies. In this way, the other peoples of the world will recognize his uniqueness. With his special affection, God should ingather the exiles of his people, Israel, and show his glory in Zion and Jerusalem. By answering such prayers, God will testify to the reliability of the prophetic message and the world will recognize his universal divinity.[36]

9. Hallel in the style of Psalm 136 from time of the Zadokite high priesthood (51:12i–xvi) [51:21–35]

Hebrew text (H^B)

.21	הודו לייי כי טוב	כי לעולם חסדו:
.22	הודו לאל התשבחות	כי לעולם חסדו:
.23	הודו לשומר ישראל	כי לעולם חסדו:
.24	הודו ליוצר הכל	כי לעולם חסדו:
.25	[הוד]ו לגואל ישראל	כי לעולם חסדו:
.26	[הו]דו למקבץ נדחי ישראל	כי לעולם חסדו:
.27	הודו לבונה עירו ומקדשו	כי לעולם חסדו:
.28	הודו למצמיח קרן לבית דוד	כי לעולם חסדו:
.29	הודו לבוחר בבני צדוק לכהן	כי לעולם חסדו:
.30	הודו למגן אברהם	כי לעולם חסדו:
.31	הודו לצור יצחק	כי לעולם חסדו:
.32	הודו לאביר יעקב	כי לעולם חסדו:
.33	הודו לבוחר בציון	כי לעולם חסדו:
.34	הודו למלך מלכי מלכים	כי לעולם חסדו:
.35	וירם קרן לעמו	תהלה לכל חסידיו
	לבני ישראל עם קרובו	הללויה:

English text

i.   Give thanks to the Lord, for he is good, for his mercy endures forever;
        Give thanks to the God of [our] praises, for his mercy endures forever;
        Give thanks to the Guardian of Israel, for his mercy endures forever;
        Give thanks to him who formed all things, for his mercy endures forever;

---

36   Of particular significance for Jewish liturgical history is the occurrence here of theological themes, as well as elements of phraseology and vocabulary, that are broadly reminiscent of later rabbinic liturgy. This is especially true of vv. 1/1a–6/5a, 13a.16b/10, 13–19, 22 [vv. 1–4, 7, 10–13 and 16–17] and Segal (ספר בן סירא, 226–29) notes the similarities, perhaps without drawing sufficient attention to the fact that there are also important variations of detail; see also Kister, "Notes", 164–66. The Greek refers to "Aaron's blessing" at the end of the passage (v. 22 [v. 16]) but there is insufficient reliability about the authenticity of this text as a reflection of the original to permit any liturgical conclusions.

v.   Give thanks to the Redeemer of Israel, for his mercy endures forever;
      Give thanks to him who has gathered Israel's dispersed, for his mercy endures forever;
      Give thanks to him who rebuilt his city and his sanctuary, for his mercy endures for-
      ever;
      Give thanks to him who makes a horn to sprout for the house of David, for his mercy
      endures forever;
      Give thanks to him who has chosen the sons of Zadok as his priests, for his mercy en-
      dures forever;
x.   Give thanks to the Shield of Abraham, for his mercy endures forever;
      Give thanks to the Rock of Isaac, for his mercy endures forever;
      Give thanks to the Mighty One of Jacob, for his mercy endures forever;
      Give thanks to him who has chosen Zion, for his mercy endures forever;
      Give thanks to the King of the kings of kings, for his mercy endures forever;
xv.   He has raised up a horn for his people, be this his praise from all his dutiful ones,
      For the children of Israel, the people close to him. Praise the Lord!

Summary

Even if, as many scholars have suggested, this hymn of praise may not have
been composed by Ben Sira himself, it must still date to a period no later than
152 B.C.E. since it mentions the Zadokite dynasty of priests that came to an
end at that date. It is not the verses borrowed from the book of Psalms, and
the similarity to Psalm 136, that are particularly noteworthy in this context,[37]
but the liturgical phraseology. With the exception of the reference to the
Zadokites, all the expressions have precise parallels or at least equivalents
in the rabbinic liturgy, especially the *'amidah*.[38]

10. Praise God for his Bounty (35/32:11–13) [32:17–18]

Hebrew text (H^B)

17. פטר לביתך ושלם רצון   ביראת אל ולא בחסר כל׃
18. ועל כל אלה ברך עושך   המרוך מטובתו׃

English text

11.   [When it is time to leave, tarry not;] be off for home without delay,
12.   [And there enjoy doing as you wish,] but without sin or words of pride.
13.   Above all, give praise to your Maker, who showers his favors upon you.

---

37   These are discussed at length by Skehan – Di Lella (Wisdom, 569–71).
38   See Segal, (סירא בן ספר, 356–57) and Skehan – Di Lella (Wisdom, 571). Segal ar-
     gues that this psalm was composed by Ben Sira himself, used for public worship in his
     day, and then omitted from the text when no longer liturgically relevant. To be more
     cautious, the evidence permits us to say no more than that the psalm had a liturgical
     function in the middle of the second pre-Christian century.

Summary

Ben Sira advises his readers to maintain the appropriate courtesies when paying visits. He appears to counsel the recitation of a blessing acknowledging God's bounty and the wording has minor similarities to the rabbinic grace after meals.[39]

11. Blessing God on Seeing a Rainbow (43:11) [43:13]

Hebrew text (H^B)

13. ראה קשת וברך עושיה   כי מאד נאדרה [בכב]וד:

English text

11. Behold the rainbow! Then bless its Maker, for majestic indeed is its splendor.

Summary

The manifestation of God's power in the natural world is the theme of 42:15–43:33 [42:21–43:38] and the specific reference to the glories of the rainbow includes an exhortation to praise God for having created it.[40]

Other Texts

Other, generally shorter, texts deal with more specific items in the liturgical field. Ben Sira takes the idea of the hymn further than its prototype in Psalms which is probably why some have sought to identify Greek elements, such as the *encomium,* in its structure.[41] He treats the genre more consistently and systematically and devotes specific sections to the praise of God, creation, wisdom, and the historical heroes of the Jewish people.[42] In addition to such hymns, there are also prayers to God that request encouragement, that are of the supplicatory variety, and that make specific appeals.[43] Among such ap-

---

39   It seems fairly clear from the text that the author has in mind the recitation of a blessing thanking God for the food one has just eaten but there is no indication here that the reference is necessarily to a formal, authoritative or communal benediction.

40   Rabbinic custom includes blessings in appreciation of natural phenomena and this practice is clearly adumbrated here; but the caution expressed in the previous footnote is again relevant.

41   See, e.g., Lee, Studies.

42   Sir 39:15–35 [39:20–47] and 16:24–18:14 [16:28–18:13]; 42:15–43:11 [42:21–43:13]; 24:1–29 [24:1–30] and 14:20–15:10 [14:23–15:10]; 44:1–45:26 [44:1–45:50].

43   Sir 37:15 [37:21]; 17:24–32 [17:19–27]; see also text 6 above.

peals are requests for strength in avoiding sin in general and slanderous talk in particular.[44] Mourning customs are presupposed but caution is advised with regard to their possible exaggeration[45] and there is no indication of formal or standardised prayer-texts for such *rites de passage*. In order to improve the degree of efficacy of one's prayers, one should genuinely repent and make efforts to be wholly sincere, as well as forgiving others and avoiding anger.[46] The clear impression is given that the wise and the poor have better prospects in this connection.[47] Links are regularly made between prayer and other religious duties such as Torah, cult and respect for others.[48] It is also suggested that good health is dependent on prayer as well as on doctors.[49] In the context of relating the activities of Jewish historical heroes, it is regularly noted that they prayed when circumstances demanded and the expression that occurs and recurs is קרא אל אל עליון.[50]

Summary of Liturgical Content

Ben Sira had a high opinion of the Temple and the priesthood and a strong conviction about their central role in Jewish religious practice. He incorporates many of the liturgical elements recorded in the Hebrew Bible but with the addition of a greater public involvement in and around the Temple Mount and perhaps of a development of the musical aspect of liturgy. He prefers a holistic approach to Jewish liturgy that makes a close association between Torah, ritual, social precepts, wisdom, prayer and charity, all of them by necessity requiring high degrees of conviction and sincerity. He makes extensive use of the hymn of praise as a way of expressing his commitment to the central elements of the Jewish religious tradition and also appears to employ the benediction to acknowledge welcome developments. He formulates personal supplications and appeals to God with a common use of language and vocabulary that mimics and borrows those of the Hebrew Bible but undoubtedly goes beyond it. He provides no evidence of any fixed set of texts that represents formal prayer regularly recited on particular occasions; that is to say, he does not testify to a fixed liturgy outside the Temple.

---

44   Sir 22:27–23:21 [22:32–23:35].
45   Sir 7:34 [7:36] (in text 2 above); 22:6–12 [22:6–11]; 38:16–23 [38:16–25].
46   Sir 17:29 [17:24]; 21:1–3 [21:1–4]; 28:2–5; see text 6 above.
47   Sir 15:9–10; 21:5 [21:6]; see text 5 above.
48   Sir 3:1–16 [3:1–15]; 45:4–5 [45:5–8]; see also texts 2–3 above.
49   Sir 38:9–15.
50   Sir 46:5 [46:7]; 47:5 [47:6]; 48:20 [48:27] (in text 7 above); see also similar expressions in 50:16–17 [50:23–25] (in text 1 above), 7:9 (in text 3 above), 47:8 [47:11] (in text 4 above), 39:5–6 [39:7–9] (in text 5 above), and 46:16 [46:27].

Evidence from Qumran

As is well known, much new material from Qumran has been made available in recent years. What overall picture does it give of the liturgical situation as reflected in these Scrolls? Here I am particularly indebted to the pioneering work of Rabin,[51] the parallels suggested by Weinfeld[52] and the careful studies of Nitzan,[53] Schuller,[54] Chazon[55] and Falk[56]. I have myself also written an article on the subject scheduled for publication in a volume containing a series of papers given at a conference at the Orion Centre of the Hebrew University of Jerusalem early in the year 2000.[57] There is now a wealth of evidence to indicate that many of the hymns and prayers found there represent the religious activities of the "common Judaism" of the Second Temple period. Although more work has to be done on explaining such phenomena as the occurrence of different prayers for the same occasion, it can no longer be doubted that communal prayer at fixed times predated tannaitic Judaism and that the content, language, form and function of rabbinic prayer cannot justifiably be regarded as totally innovative. The *hodayot* reflect the experiences and teachings of the Qumranic sect and they exist in a variety of collections. Words and expressions in the non-canonical psalms have their equivalents in other Hebrew texts of the late Second Temple and early post-destruction periods and there are elements of Aramaic influence. The close relationship with aspects of the rabbinic liturgical evidence is also noteworthy. We encounter familiar, national notions such as the divine love of Israel, the choice of Jerusalem, the special status of Zion, and the uniqueness of the Davidic kingdom. There are also broader theological themes that the two groups have in common such as God's great name, creation and calendar, the closeness of the supplicant to God, and the removal of Satanic and evil power.[58] There are many individual words, in both verbal and nominal forms, and numerous

---

51 Rabin, Background, 144–61, with a later Hebrew version published in *Qoveṣ Ma'amarim Bilshon Ḥz"l*, 355–82; Investigation, 163–71.
52 Weinfeld, Traces, 15–26; Prayers for Knowledge, 186–200; Question, 495–96; Grace, 15–23; Grace after Meals in Qumran, 427–40; Prayer, 241–58; Song, 131–57.
53 Nitzan, Qumran Prayer.
54 Schuller, Psalms; Observations, 133–43; Psalm of 4Q372 1, 67–79; Prayer, 153–71; Cave Four, 137–50; Use, 207–22.
55 Chazon, Prayers, 265–84; Manuscripts, 207–14; (with Bernstein), Introduction, 9–13; Hymns, 244–70; Liturgy, 7–17.
56 Falk, Prayer, 852–76; Festival Prayers.
57 The tentative title is "The Second Temple Period, Qumran Research and Rabbinic Liturgy: Some Contextual and Linguistic Comparisons" and the volume, edited by E.G. Chazon, is scheduled for publication by Brill in 2002. The summary contained here is based on that article and on the work of the scholars cited in the previous six footnotes.
58 See e.g. 4Q504 (4QDibHamᵃ) as in Baillet, Qumrân Grotte 4 III, 137–68 and García Martínez – Tigchelaar, Dead Sea Scrolls, 1009–19. See also Lehmann, Writings, 13–18.

short phrases, that the literatures of Qumran and the Rabbis share. There are
also parallel uses of verses and of sections of the psalms. Other specific features of the Judean scrolls are that they supplement biblical content with apocalyptic material and reformulate apocalyptic myths in the biblical style, as
well as expressing the sanctity of the sabbath by the use of ritual poetry.

Conclusions

It should by now have become apparent that the Qumran approach and that of
the Rabbis have a little more in common with each other than either or both
of them have with Ben Sira. They both presuppose a practice to recite regular
prayers at specific times while there is no mention of such a custom in Ben
Sira. Sabbaths and festivals feature strongly in both of them and there are poetic formulations for special occasions, while these characteristics do not appear in Ben Sira. Apocalyptic elements, angelology and eschatology appear
to play a more significant role at Qumran and with the Rabbis than in Ben Sira's composition. On the other hand, Ben Sira's holistic liturgical approach is
more reminiscent of that of the Rabbis than that of Qumran and his devotion
to the Temple cult is followed at least in theory by rabbinic Judaism. Similarly, Ben Sira links Torah and wisdom with prayer in a manner that calls to
mind the later views of the Rabbis. All three sources have in common the use
of hymns of praise, supplicatory prayers and benedictions, as well as the occurrence of words and phrases that are in essence biblical but subsequently
take on special forms and meanings. They also share as central themes in
their entreaties the notions of the election of Israel, the status of Zion, the holiness of Jerusalem, the return of the Davidic dynasty, and the manifestation
of God's great power now and in the future. What therefore seems likely is
that the Rabbis ultimately borrowed extensively from the kinds of circles
which produced Ben Sira and the Dead Sea Scrolls, and from some others,
but, in the matter of detailed liturgical expression, they championed a fresh
order, style and distinctive formulation. Ben Sira undoubtedly takes the matter of worship beyond that of most of the Hebrew Bible but does not reflect
the same liturgical intensity as that found at Qumran. He thus sets the tone
for some rabbinic developments but is apparently not the source for various
others.[59]

59   I prepared this article for publication during a period as a Fellow of the Center for Ad-
     vanced Judaic Studies at the University of Pennsylvania in Philadelphia, September –
     December 2001. I am most grateful to the Center, its Director Professor David Ruder-
     man, and his dedicated staff, for their kind invitation and their generous assistance.

Bibliography

Baillet, M., *Qumrân Grotte 4 III (4Q482–4Q520)* (DJD 7; Oxford: University Press, 1982).

Brockington, L.H., *A Critical Introduction to the Apocrypha* (Studies in Theology; London: Duckworth, 1961).

Chazon, E.G., "Hymns and Prayers in the Dead Sea Scrolls," in *The Dead Sea Scrolls after Fifty Years: A Comprehensive Assessment*, vol. 1 (eds. P.W. Flint and J.C. Vander-Kam; Leiden, Boston and Köln: Brill, 1998), 244–70.

Chazon, E.G., "New Liturgical Manuscripts from Qumran", *Proceedings of the Eleventh World Congress of Jewish Studies, Jerusalem, 1993*, Division A (Jerusalem: World Union of Jewish Studies, 1994), 207–14.

Chazon, E.G., "Prayers from Qumran and their Historical Implications," *DSD* 1 (1994) 265–84.

Chazon, E.G., "The *Qedushah* Liturgy and its History in Light of the Dead Sea Scrolls," in *From Qumran to Cairo: Studies in the History of Prayer* (ed. J. Tabory; Jerusalem: Orhot, 1999), 7–17.

Chazon, E.G. – Bernstein, M.J., "An Introduction to Prayer at Qumran", in *Prayer from Alexander to Constantine: A Critical Anthology* (ed. M. Kiley *et al.*; London and New York: Routledge, 1997), 9–13.

Coggins, R.J., *Sirach* (Guides to Apocrypha and Pseudepigrapha; Sheffield: Academic Press, 1998).

Davila, J.R., *Liturgical Works* (Eerdmans Commentaries on the Dead Sea Scrolls 6; Grand Rapids: Eerdmans, 2000).

Elbogen, I., *Der jüdische Gottesdienst in seiner geschichtlichen Entwicklung* (Frankfurt a.M.: Kaufmann, 1931; reprint, Hildesheim: Olms, 1962); Hebrew edition התפילה בישראל בהתפתחותה ההיסטורית (eds. J. Heinemann, I. Adler, A. Negev, J. Petuchowski and H. Schirmann; Tel Aviv: Devir, 1972); English ed., *Jewish Liturgy: A Comprehensive History* (English trans. and ed. by Raymond P. Scheindlin; Philadelphia, Jerusalem and New York: Jewish Publication Society of America and Jewish Theological Seminary of America, 1993).

Eshel, H. – Eshel, E., "4Q448, Psalm 154 (Syriac), Sirach 48:20, and 4QpIsaa," *JBL* 119 (2000) 645–59.

Falk, D.K., "Prayer in the Qumran Texts", in *The Cambridge History of Judaism*, vol. 3, *The Early Roman Period* (eds. W. Horbury, W.D. Davies and J. Sturdy; Cambridge: University Press, 1999), 852–76.

Falk, D.K., *Daily, Sabbath and Festival Prayers in the Dead Sea Scrolls* (STDJ 27; Leiden, Boston and Köln: Brill, 1998).

García Martínez, F. – Tigchelaar, E.J.C., *The Dead Sea Scrolls Study Edition*, vol. 2 (Leiden, Boston and Köln: Brill, 1998).

Gevaryahu, H., "Shimon Ben-Sira: The Image of a Jerusalem Scholar," in *David Gross Anniversary Volume* (ed. S. Kodesh [Hebrew]; Jerusalem: Hamatmid, 1983), 256–74.

Idelsohn, A.Z., *Jewish Liturgy and its Development* (New York: Holt, 1932).

Johnson, N.B., *Prayer in the Apocrypha and Pseudepigrapha: A Study in the Jewish Concept of God* (JBLMS 2; Philadelphia: SBL, 1948).

Jolley, M.A., "The Function of Torah in Sirach" (Louisville KY: Southern Baptist Theological Seminary dissertation, 1993).

Kister, M., "Genizah Manuscripts of Ben Sira," in *The Cambridge Genizah Collections: Their Contents and Significance* (ed. S.C. Reif; Cambridge: University Press, 2002), 36–46.

Kister, M., "Some Notes of Biblical Expressions and Allusions and the Lexicography of Ben Sira," in *Sirach, Scrolls and Sages* (eds. T. Muraoka and J.F. Elwolde; STDJ 26; Leiden, Boston and Köln: Brill, 1999), 183–86.

Lange, A., "In Diskussion mit dem Tempel: Zur Auseinandersetzung zwischen Kohelet und weisheitlichen Kreisen am Jerusalemer Tempel," in *Qohelet in the Context of Wisdom* (ed. A. Schoors; BETL 136; Leuven: University Press, 1998), 113–59.

Lee, T.R., *Studies in the Form of Sirach 44–50* (SBLDS 75; Atlanta: Scholars Press, 1986).

Lehmann, M.R., "The Writings of Ben Sira, the Dead Sea Scrolls and Temple Worship in the Liturgy of Yom Kippur," in *Piyyut in Tradition*, vol. 2 (eds. B. Bar-Tikva and E. Hazan [Hebrew]; Ramat Gan: Bar-Ilan University, 2000), 13–18.

Newman, J.H., *Praying by the Book: The Scripturalization of Prayer in Second Temple Judaism* (SBLEJL 14; Atlanta: Scholars Press, 1999).

Nitzan, B., *Qumran Prayer and Religious Poetry* (STDJ 12; Leiden, New York and Köln: Brill, 1994), translated by Jonathan Chipman from the Hebrew original *Ha-Tefillah Ve-Ha-Shirah Ha-Datit Mi-Qumran Be-Ziqatan La-Miqra* (Ph.D. dissertation, Tel Aviv University, 1989).

Oesterley, W.O.E., *The Wisdom of Jesus the Son of Sirach or Ecclesiasticus in the Revised Version with Introduction and Notes* (Cambridge: University Press, 1912).

Rabin, C., "The Historical Background of Qumran Hebrew," in *Scripta Hierosolymitana* 4 (Jerusalem: Magnes, 1965), 144–61; repr. in *Qoveṣ Ma'amarim Bilshon ḥz'l*, vol. 1 (ed. M. Bar-Asher; Jerusalem: Akademon, 1972), 355–82.

Rabin, C., "The Linguistic Investigation of the Language of Jewish Prayer," in *Studies in Aggadah, Targum and Jewish Liturgy in Memory of Joseph Heinemann* (eds. J.J. Petuchowski and E. Fleischer; Jerusalem and Cincinnati: Magnes and Hebrew Union College, 1981), Hebrew section, 163–71.

Reif, S.C., *Judaism and Hebrew Prayer* (Cambridge: University Press, 1993).

Reif, S.C., "The Second Temple Period, Qumran Research and Rabbinic Liturgy: Some Contextual and Linguistic Comparisons," in *Liturgical Perspectives: Prayer and Poetry in Light of the Dead Sea Scrolls* (ed. E.G. Chazon; Leiden, Boston and Köln: Brill; forthcoming 2002).

Reif, S.C., "Jewish Liturgical Research: Past, Present and Future," *JJS* 34 (1983) 161–70.

Reif, S.C., *Shabbethai Sofer and his Prayer-book* (Cambridge: University Press, 1979).

Reiterer, F.V., "Review of Recent Research on the Book of Ben Sira," in *The Book of Ben Sira in Modern Research* (ed. P.C. Beentjes; BZAW 255; Berlin and New York: de Gruyter, 1997), 23–60.

Rivkin, E., "Ben Sira and the Nonexistence of the Synagogue: A Study in Historical Method," in *In the Time of Harvest: Essays in Honor of Abba Hillel Silver on the Occasion of his 70th birthday* (ed. D.J. Silver; New York and London: Macmillan, 1963), 320–54.

Schuller, E., "The Cave Four Hodayot Manuscripts: A Preliminary Description," *JQR* 85 (1994) 137–50.

Schuller, E., "Some Observations on Blessings of God," in *Of Scribes and Scrolls: Studies on the Hebrew Bible, Intertestamental Judaism and Christian Origins presented to John Strugnell on the Occasion of his Sixtieth Birthday* (eds. H.W. Attridge, J.J. Collins and T.H. Tobin; Lanham, New York and London: University Press of America, 1990), 133–43.

Schuller, E., "Prayer, Hymnic and Liturgical Texts from Qumran," in *The Community of the Renewed Covenant: The Notre Dame Symposium on the Dead Sea Scrolls* (eds. E. Ulrich and J. VanderKam; Christianity and Judaism in Antiquity 10; Notre Dame: University of Notre Dame, 1994), 153–71.

Schuller, E., "The Psalm of 4Q372 1 within the Context of Second Temple Prayer," *CBQ* 54 (1992) 67–79.

Schuller, E., *Non-Canonical Psalms from Qumran: A Pseudepigraphic Collection* (HSS 28; Atlanta: Scholars Press, 1986).

Schuller, E., "The Use of Biblical Terms as Designations for Non-Biblical Hymnic and Prayer Compositions," in *Biblical Perspectives: Early Use and Interpretation of the Bible in Light of the Dead Sea Scrolls* (eds. M. Stone and E.G. Chazon; Leiden, Boston and Köln: Brill, 1998), 207–22.

Segal, M.Z., השלם בן-סירא ספר (2d rev. ed.; Jerusalem: Bialik, 1958).

Skehan P.W. – Di Lella, A.A., *The Wisdom of Ben Sira: A New Translation with Notes, Introduction and Commentary* (AB 39; New York: Doubleday, 1987).

Tabory, J., *Jewish Prayer and the Yearly Cycle: A List of Articles* (supplement to *Kiryat Sefer* 64; Jerusalem, 1992–93) and *Reshimat Ha-Ma'amarim Odot Batei Kenesset* [= *List of Articles about Synagogues*] (Ramat Gan and Jerusalem: Bar Ilan University and Hechal Shelomo, 2000).

Weinfeld, M., "Grace after Meals at the Mourner's House in a Text from Qumran," *Tarbiz* 61 (1992) 15–23.

Weinfeld, M., "Grace after Meals in Qumran," *JBL* 111 (1992) 427–40.

Weinfeld, M., "Prayer and Liturgical Practice in the Qumran Sect," in *The Dead Sea Scrolls: Forty Years of Research* (eds. D. Dimant and U. Rappaport; STDJ 10; Leiden, New York, Köln and Jerusalem: Brill, Magnes and Ben-Zvi, 1992), 241–58.

Weinfeld, M., "The Prayers for Knowledge, Repentance and Forgiveness in the Eighteen Benedictions – Qumran Parallels, Biblical Antecedents and Basic Characteristics," *Tarbiz* 48 (1979) 186–200.

Weinfeld, M., "On the Question of Morning Benedictions at Qumran", *Tarbiz* 51 (1982) 495–96.

Weinfeld, M., "The Angelic Song over the Luminaries in the Qumran Texts," in *Time to Prepare the Way in the Wilderness: Papers on the Qumran Scrolls by Fellows of the Institute for Advanced Studies of the Hebrew University, Jerusalem, 1989–90* (eds. D. Dimant and L.H. Schiffman; STDJ 16; Leiden and New York: Brill, 1995), 131–57.

Weinfeld, M., "Traces of *Qedushat Yozer* and *Pesukey De-Zimra* in the Qumran Literature and in Ben-Sira," *Tarbiz* 45 (1975–76) 15–26.

Anhang

Originalität des Ben Sira?

Ein unveröffentlichter Beitrag Rabbi Altmanns

Renate Egger-Wenzel
Universität Salzburg

Dieser kurze Beitrag will Herrn Altmanns nicht edierten, handgeschriebenen Entwurf zu einem Artikel bezüglich der Originalität des ab 1896 in der Kairoer Geniza entdeckten H-Textes von Ben Sira vorstellen. Das Manuskript wurde im Sommer 2000 im Zuge der Umstellung der Stiftsbibliothek St. Peter, Salzburg, auf EDV in einem Dublettenraum gefunden und verblieb im dortigen Archiv. Es befand sich in einem Exemplar von Peters, Liber Iesu Filii Sirach, welches die Signatur D79.606 erhielt.

Nach den im Buch liegenden diversen handschriftlichen Notizzetteln zu urteilen, handelt es sich um ein Exemplar, das sich im persönlichen Besitz des Salzburger Siraforschers Andreas Eberharter[1] befunden haben muss. Das darin entdeckte Manuskript Altmanns kann frühestens auf das späte Jahr 1906 datiert werden, da Herr Altmann auf eine von ihm selbst verfertigte, aber im Band namentlich nicht bezeichnete Rezension zu Ginzberg, Randglossen, 609–25 verweist, die in der Zeitschrift für Hebräische Bibliographie X. Jahrgang, September-Oktober, No. 5 des Jahres 1906 erschienen ist. Wahrscheinlicher ist aber eine Datierung ab 1907, da erst ab dieser Zeit Herr Altmann als Rabbiner in Salzburg tätig war[2] und scheinbar im Kontakt mit dem ansässigen Alttestamentler der Theologischen Fakultät stand.

Im folgenden wird der Text des Artikels geboten, wie er sich im Manuskript darstellt. Die in runden Klammer hochgestellten Zahlen verweisen auf Anmerkungen Altmanns, die im Text später folgen und Linien getrennt sind:

(rechte Seite)
1 RABBINER ADOLF ALTMANN, SALZBURG.[3]

Über das Streichbare des Buches (ben) Sirach.
Von Professor H.P. Chajus[4] (Pirinzi, (wahrscheinlich des Verfassers Pseudonym)
(1)
a.d.u.

---

1   Eberharter wurde am 12. Okt. 1865 in Zell am Tiller in Tirol geboren und starb am 24.4.1932 in Salzburg. Zwischen 1901 und 1932 war er Professor für Altes Testament an der Theologischen Fakultät der Universität Salzburg.

2   "He served as rabbi in Salzburg (1907–1915) where he wrote the two-volume 'Geschichte der Juden in Stadt and Land Salzburg' (1913, 1930), which is still the authoritative work on the subject, and in Merano" (aus EncJud [CD-ROM Edition]).

3   Gedruckter Briefkopf.

5 Schon mehreremal habe ich meine Meinung geäussert, dass die Abschnitte
   3–38, 50 u weiter des hebräischen Sirach, laut wie sie in Ägypten entdeckt
   wurden, (herausgegeben von Herrn Schächter[5]) in der grossen Mehrzal
   nicht dem Orginale des Buches entstammen [(2)].
   Nur stellenweise bekommt man von diesem Buche den Eindruck
10 zuzugeben, dass so u nicht anders der jerusalemische Schriftsteller
   im 3. Jahrh. vor christl. Zeitrechnung geschrieben hat.
   Im allgemeinen aber sind wir gezwungen zu sagen, dass es von
   Gefäss in Gefäss geleert wurde u der ursprüngliche Geruch verdunstet ist.
   Fragt man mich aber: welcher Übersetzung also entstammt das
15 Hebräische das wir besitzen, so kann ich keine präcise Antwort geben.
   Im ganzen grossen ist es übereinstimmend mit dem Syrischen, doch
   sehr viel ist es (das Hebr.) auch dem ungleich.
   Es lässt sich auch nicht behaupten, dass die fraglichen Stellen einen
   anderen syrischen Text *Copie*[6] hatten, als den vor uns liegenden.
20 Auch lässt sich nicht denken, dass es aus dem Griechischen geschöpft ist,
   wozu der vielen Schriftstellen die dem Griechischen folgen.
   Vielleicht jedoch, dass sein Ursprung eine aramäische Übertragung
   dieses Sektierer Buches war, die verloren ging, von der aber Fragmente in älteren Werken sich vorfinden [(3.)]
25 Allenfalls soll diese Ansicht nicht mehr als eine Vermutung sein.
   Was ich aber mit diesem Artikel bezwecken will ist, zu beweisen, dass
   die Behauptung: das Werk wie es der Feder des Iosua, Sohn des
   Simon, Sohn Eliesers entsprang, vollkommen identisch ist mit
   der Gestalt, die das vor kurzer Zeit entdeckte Hebräische aufweist, eine
30 Unmöglichkeit ist.

(linke Seite)

1 (1) Siehe meine Bemerkungen in der Zeitschrift für hebr. Bibliographie X p. 134. folg.[7]
   (dort habe ich auch meine früheren Abhandlungen verzeichnet.)
   Gelegentlich will ich hier dem was ich dort sagte, Einiges hinzufügen, dass
   3,12 erweist, dass die textliche Lesart *(Copie)* des Griechischen gerechtfertigt ist:
5 u betrübe ihm nicht bei seinem Leben (nicht wie im Syrischen u Hebräischen:
   u verlasse ihm nicht solange du lebst)
   Man widerlege meine Ansicht nicht mit dem, was Herr Israel Levi
   (Rev. et juives 1902 vol 44.293.)[8] beweisen wollte, dass der Verfasser
   des Buches Tobiah (3,4)[9] sich des ben Sirach bedient habe, wie er

---

4 Der Autor bezieht sich entweder auf den Artikel Notes critiques, 31–36 oder מחקרים
   לבן־סירא, 109–15 von Chajes-Florenz. – Die folgende Runde Klammer wird im Manuskript geöffnet, aber nicht geschlossen.
5 Vermutlich handelt es sich um Schechter – Taylor, Wisdom.
6 Die kursiv formatierten Worte sind nachträgliche Einfügungen.
7 Vgl. Altmann, Review of Ginzberg, Randglossen, 134f.
8 Lévi, Quelques citations, 291–94 zitiert Tob 4,3 (*Er rief ihn also und sagte: Mein Sohn,
   wenn ich gestorben bin, begrab mich! Lass deine Mutter nicht im Stich, sondern halte
   sie in Ehren, solange sie lebt. Tu, was sie erfreut, und mach ihr keinen Kummer!*; Zitat
   in kursiv ist der Einheitsübersetzung entnommen, andernfalls folgt ein Vermerk) und
   nimmt Bezug auf Sir 3,12: בני התחזק בכבוד אביך ואל תעזבהו כל ימי חייך
   (Mein Sohn, mach dich stark in der Ehre deines Vaters und verlass ihn nicht alle Tage
   deines Lebens; eigene Übersetzung).

10   im Hebräischen lautet. Seine Beweise sind nicht zwingend. Das
    Gegenteil ist der Fall. In der Fext-Lesart[10] *Copie* A. heisst es: ὑπεριδης[11] etc. etc.
    und in der Lesart C. εγκατλιπης[12] etc. etc.
    So auch in der lateinischen Übersetzung (derelinquere .. contristari)
    was beweist, dass den Übersetzern ein Grundtext des Tobiah in zwei
15   Lesarten *Copien* vorlag u einige nahmen in ihrem Texte beide auf.
    (auf die Abhandlung des Herrn Levi machte mich mein Schüler, Herr
    M. Kalu,[13] Rabbiner in Verona aufmerksam)
    (2) Wohl weiss ich, dass heute fast alle Forscher in der Ansicht übereinstimmen, das
    Hebräische gut zu heissen u anzunehmen. Das meine Zweifel aber trotzdem
20   aufrecht bleiben, will ich sie den gelehrten Lesern vorlegen.
    Allerdings muss ich auch eingestehen, dass ich mich nicht in alle
    Bücher u Abhandlungen über diesen Gegenstand vertieft habe.
    Wenn sich nun Mancher, worauf ich hinweise, irgendwo vorfinden
    sollte, so wolle mir verziehen sein.
25   (3) Mein Beleg für diese Meinung ist nicht nur die Stelle im Talmud Synhedrium
    100. S 2. aramäisch: "lasse Sorge dir nicht ins Herz steigen, denn Menschen
    über Menschen tötet die Sorge"[14] (im Hebräischen 30,21–23.: "liefere deine
    Seele nicht der Sorge aus, [...][15] denn viele tötet die Sorge ..)
    aber auch *in* Tansonfans[16] (Randkomentar zum Talmud a.d.U.)
30   (es ist mir nicht bekannt *ob* auf das schon hingewiesen wurde)
    Im Traktat Erubin 63. S.1.[17] unter der Spitzmarke "Rabbi Hamnuna[18]"
    heisst es: " ---- denn es sagt Raw[19] zu Rabbi Hamnuna, mein Sohn, von dem
    was du besitzest lasse es dir gut gehen" (aramäisch). Im Talmud selbst aber Erubin

---

9   Hier ist wohl ein Zahlensturz passiert. Es muß Tob 4,3 heißen.

10   Schreibfehler, eigentlich: "Text-Lesart".

11   Nach Hanhart, Tobit, steht im Haupttext ὑπερίδῃς (ὑπεροράω – übersehen, verachten).

12   Hanhart, Tobit, zitiert als Variantlesart die Minuskelhandschrift 319 Athos, Βατοπαι-
    δίου, 513; geschrieben 1021 ἐγκαταλειπης (ἐγκαταλείπω – zurücklassen, im Stich las-
    sen).

13   Aufgrund der Zweideutigkeit im handschriftlichen Entwurf ist nicht festzustellen, ob
    der Name "Ralu" oder "Kalu" geschrieben wird.

14   Vgl. Synhedrin (2. Hälfte) 100b (in Goldschmidt, Babylonische Talmud 9, 83): "... laß
    keinen Kummer in dein Herz dringen, denn starke Männer tötete der Kummer, ...", wo-
    bei in der Fußnote ein Hinweis auf Spr 12,25 steht (*Kummer im Herzen bedrückt den
    Menschen, ein gutes Wort aber heitert ihn auf*). Vor dieser Stelle wird die Frage disku-
    tiert, ob Ben Sira ein ketzerisches oder nur externes Buch ist. Je nachdem steht es unter
    Leseverbot oder ist zu lesen erlaubt (vgl. bes. Jerusalemer Talmud).

15   Nicht gekennzeichnete Auslassung in der Sira-Stelle 30,21–23.

16   Vermutlich sind die Tosafot gemeint.

17   Unter dieser Stellenangabe findet sich kein Hinweis auf den oben angegebenen Inhalt
    und in Folge auch keine Kommentierung in den Tosafot.

18   Es handelt sich um Hamnuna Saba, den Älteren, der ein Schüler von Rab war, und die-
    sem als Leiter der Schule in Sura nachfolgte (vgl. Sanh. 17b). Auch er gehörte zu den
    babylonischen Amoräern (vgl. Kaplan, Hamnuna, 1247).

19   Hier meint Altmann vermutlich "Abba Arikha, 'der Lange', wohl wegen seiner unge-
    wöhnlichen Körpergröße, eigentlich Abba, gewöhnlich einfach Rab genannt", der der
    ersten Generation der babylonischen Amoräer zuzurechnen ist und einen Jüngerkreis in
    Sura am Eufrat um sich sammelte. Er starb im Jahr 247; Stemberger, Einleitung, 92.

54. S.1 heisst es ~~aber~~ (hebräisch): "von dem was du besitzest lasse es dir gut gehen."[20]
übereinstimmend

Im Anschluss seien einige kritische Bemerkungen an das Manuskript von Rabbi Altmann angebracht. Des weiteren wird Altmann in der Originalitätsdebatte nach Auffindung der ersten hebräischen Fragmente von 1896/7 positioniert.

Altmann benennt (rechte Seite Z. 6) die von Schechter herausgegebenen Abschnitte des H-Textes von Sir mit "3–38,50." Es handelt sich um Kapitelangaben, die der Ausgabe von Schechter – Taylor, Wisdom, am nächsten kommen und aus dem Jahr 1899[21] stammen. Dabei übersieht Altmann allerdings einige Passagen. Es ist daher nicht eindeutig zu entscheiden, welche Veröffentlichungen Schechters Altmann konkret vorgelegen sind.[22]

Altmann will beweisen, dass als Verfasser des in der Kairoer Geniza gefundenen Textes (rechte Seite Z. 27/28) keinesfalls "Iosua, Sohn des Simon, Sohn Elieser" (vgl. Chag 13a) in Frage kommt und bezeichnet zudem dessen Werk als " Sektierer Buch" (rechte Seite Z. 23). Damit übernimmt er etwas

---

20   Vgl. Erubin V,i 54 (in Goldschmidt, Babylonische Talmud 2, 161): "Rabh sprach zu R. Hamnuna: 30Mein Sohn, hast du was, so lasse es dir gut bekommen, denn in der Unterwelt gibt es kein Vergnügen mehr, und auch der Tod verspätet sich nicht". Die Fußnote 30 im Text enthält einen Hinweis auf Sir 14,11.12.19. Goldschmidt zitiert hier irrtümlich v19, meint aber v18. Möglicherweise ist inhaltlich passend mit Hinweis auf v11 auch v16 zu berücksichtigen (vgl. *Sir 14,11 Mein Sohn, wenn du imstande bist, pflege dich selbst; soweit du kannst, lass es dir gut gehen! 12 Denk daran, dass der Tod nicht säumt und die Frist bis zur Unterwelt dir unbekannt ist. ... 18 Wie sprossende Blätter am grünen Baum – das eine welkt, das andere wächst nach –, so sind die Geschlechter von Fleisch und Blut: das eine stirbt, das andere reift heran.* – Babylonian Talmud, Tosafot zu Erubin V,i 54: היטב ה לך יש אם בני המנונא לרב רב ליה אמר בשאול חוק לבני אניח תאמר ואם התמהמה למות ואין תענוג בשאול שאין לך נובלין והללו נוצצין הללו השדה לעשבי דומי האדם בני לך יניד מי). Dieses Carpe-diem-Zitat wird in den Tosafot nicht auf Ben Sira zurückgeführt, sondern den Rabbinen zugeschrieben. Der Kontext handelt davon, dass man die Tora wie ein Genussmittel in sich aufsaugen soll, als sei sie nach dem Tode nicht mehr verfügbar.

21   Vgl. Reiterer, Text, 29f (siehe auch Anm. 22): "MS A: 3,6b. 8a–18b. 20a–4,4a°. 5a–15b. 17a.c–5,9b°. 10a–6,17b. 19a–22b; 27,5a–6b; 6,25a–b. 27a–7,8b°. 15a–b. 10a–26b. 29a; 11,34b°; 12,2a–5c°. 6a–b°. 7a–13,6b°. 7a–14°. 16a–16,9b°. 10a–b°. 11a–22b°. 23a–26b;
      MS B: 30,11a–34 / 31,11b; 35/32,1c–36 / 33,3b; 32/35,11a / 8a–33 / 36, 10b / 7b. 12a / 9a–36,23d / 18d; 37,27a–38,18b. 20a–27b; 49, 12c–15b°. 16a–50,14b.16a–23b°. 24a–29b°; 51,1a–b°. 2a–d°. 3a / 2f–3d / 3c°. 4a–6b°. 7a–13b. 15a–b°. 16a–30d°."

22   Da der Entwurf Altmanns wohl frühestens 1907 entstanden ist und er sich vornehmlich auf die Fragmente der Kairoer Geniza bezieht, kommen nur noch folgende Veröffentlichungen Schechters in Frage, die sich allerdings auch nicht mit den Kapitelangaben treffen: Schechter, Fragment, 1–15 ("MS B: 39,15c–17b / 16d°. 18a–31b°. 32a–40,1d. 3a–7b"); ders., Genizah Specimens, 197–206 (Sir 49,12–50,22 ohne MS-Angabe); ders., Further Fragment, 456–65 ("MS C: 4,23°. 30a–31b; 5,4a–7d. 9a–13b; 36,24a / 19a; 25,8a–d°. 13a–b. 17a–24b; 26,1a–2a").

ungenau den Namen des Autors aus Γ (Sir 50,27: Ἰησοῦς υἱὸς Σιραχ Ελεαζαρ ὁ Ἱεροσολυμίτης), indem er vor Eleasar Sohn einfügt, und verbessert Sirach anhand von H^B mit Simon bei Positionsvertauschung von der ersten beiden Glieder des Namens:

לשמעון בן ישוע בן אלעזר בן סירא   Sir 50,27

שמעון בן ישוע שנקרא בן סירא אלעזר בן   Sir 51,30

שמעון בן ישוע בןסירא[23]

Weiters bezieht er – geht man von der Häufigkeit der im Talmud zitierten Stellen aus – im Sinne von bSanh 100b eine Minderheitenposition, die Ben Sira als ketzerisches Buch unter Leseverbot stellt (vgl. KohR XXII,11 und jSanh 28a). Dagegen steht die häufigere gebäuchliche rabbinische Zitationsweise[24] des Talmud, die Sirazitate mit כתוב בספר בן סירא ("Geschrieben steht im Buch Ben Sira") oder ähnlichen Formulierungen einführt, was darauf hindeutet, dass das Buch Ben Sira analog zu anderen biblischen Büchern behandelt wurde und auch ähnliche Autorität genoss.

Der in Kairo aufgefundene H-Text entspricht nach Meinung Altmanns keineswegs dem Original des Sektier Buches Sira. Es weist zwar Ähnlichkeiten mit Syr. auf, ist aber nicht als Übersetzung von dort her zu verstehen, auch nicht von untereinander abweichenden Manuskripten. Da Syr. erst in den letzten zehn Jahren für das Verständnis des Sirabuches an Bedeutung gewonnen hat, ist die damalige Beobachtung Altmanns interessant.[25]

Weiters kann nach Auffassung von Altmann der H-Text keine Rückübersetzung aus Γ sein, wie später auch Ziegler vermutet hat.[26] Er nimmt an, dass der Kairoer Text auf eine aramäische Übersetzung des verlorenen H-Textes von Sira zurückgeht, ist sich aber nicht ganz sicher. Mit dieser Position ist Rabbi Altmann in der Originalitätsdebatte an der Seite von D.S. Margoliouth einzuordnen, der annimmt, dass es sich um eine Rückübersetzung – z.B. aus dem Persischen – handelt.[27]

Allerdings sind nach dem heutigen Forschungsstand[28] die wieder entdeckten H-Texte aufgrund des Vokabelschatzes und der Formbildungen dem klassischen Hebräisch zuzurechnen.[29] Lediglich neuere Formbildungen

---

23   Vgl. die Diskussion in Reiterer, Text, 1–10, bes. 6.
24   Vgl. Chag 13a; Jeb 63b; Ket 110b; BB 98b; 146a; Ned 16b.
25   Vgl. Bickell, Sirachtext, 251–56 und später Di Lella, Hebrew Text, 106–42; ders., in Di Lella – Skehan, Wisdom, 58, die für manche Teile sehr wohl Rückübersetzungen aus Syr. vermuten; siehe auch Rickenbacher, Weisheitsperikopen, 40.
26   Ziegler, Beiträge, 281–84.
27   Vgl. Margoliouth, Origin, und die ganze Diskussion nach 1886 siehe Reiterer, Text, 16–25.
28   Vgl. insbesondere die Ergebnisse der Leidener Tagungen von 1995, 1997 sowie 1999 in Israel: Muraoka – Elwolde, Hebrew; dies., Sirach und dies., Diggers.
29   So schon Rüger, Text, 115.

in Einzelfällen und wenige Aramäismen weisen auf eine Weiterentwicklung hin, die sich ähnlich wie in Qumran darstellt. Daher ist es äußerst unwahrscheinlich, dass es sich beim Kairoer Geniza Text um eine Übersetzung aus dem Aramäischen handelt. Es ist ursprüngliches Hebräisch.

Bibliographie

Altmann, A., Review of L. Ginzberg, "Randglossen zum hebräischen Ben Sira," in *Orientalische Studien* (FS Th. Nöldeke II; ed. C. Bezold; Gießen: Töpelmann, 1906) 609–25: *Zeitschrift für hebräische Bibliographie* 10,5 (1906) 134f.

The Babylonian Talmud (repr. 1st ed.; Jerusalem: Makor, 1968–1972).

Bickell, G., "Der hebräische Sirachtext eine Rückübersetzung," *WZKM* 13 (1899) 251–56.

Chajes-Florenz, H.P., "Notes critiques sur le texte hébreu de l'Ecclésiastique," *Revue des études juives* 40 (1900) 31–36.

Chajes-Florenz, H.P., "סירא‎-לבן מחקרים‎," *Haḳedem* 1 (1907) 109–15.

Di Lella, A.A., *The Hebrew Text of Sirach: A Text-Critical and Historical Study* (Studies in Classical Literature 1; The Hague: Mouton, 1966).

Encyclopaedia Judaica: The most comprehensive authoritative Source on the Jewish World (version 1.0; CD-ROM; Jerusalem : Judaica Multimedia Israel, 1997).

Goldschmidt, L., *Der Babylonische Talmud* (vol. 9; Berlin: Biblion, 1967).

Hanhart, R. (ed.), *Tobit* (Septuaginta VIII/5; Göttingen: Vandenhoeck & Ruprecht, 1983).

Kaplan, Z.,"Hamnuna," *EncJud* 7. 1247f.

Lévi, I., "Quelques citations de l'Ecclésiastique," *Revue des études juives* 44 (1902) 291–94.

Margoliouth, D.S., *The Origin of the 'Original Hebrew' of Ecclesiasticus* (London: Parker, 1899).

Muraoka, T. – Elwolde, J.F. (eds.), *Diggers at the Well: Proceedings of a Third International Symposium on the Hebrew of the Dead Sea Scrolls and Ben Sira Held in October 1999 at Ben-Gurion-University of the Negev* (STDJ 36; Leiden: Brill, 2000).

Muraoka, T. – Elwolde, J.F. (eds.), *The Hebrew of the Dead Sea Scrolls and Ben Sira: Proceedings of a Symposium Held at Leiden University 11–14 December 1995* (STDJ 26; Leiden: Brill, 1997).

Muraoka, T. – Elwolde, J.F. (eds.), *Sirach, Scrolls, and Sages: Proceedings of a Second International Symposium on the Hebrew of the Dead Sea Scrolls, Ben Sira, and the Mishnah, Held at Leiden University, 15–17 December 1997* (STDJ 33; Leiden: Brill, 1999).

Peters, N., *Liber Iesu Filii Sirach sive Ecclesiasticus hebraice secundum codices nuper repertos vocalibus adornatus addita versione latina cum glossaria hebraico-latino* (Freiburg: Herder, 1905).

Reiterer, F.V., "Text und Buch Ben Sira in Tradition und Forschung. Eine Einführung," in *Bibliographie zu Ben Sira* (ed. F.V. Reiterer; BZAW 266; Berlin / New York: de Gruyter, 1998) 1–42.

Rickenbacher, O., *Weisheitsperikopen bei Jesus Sirach* (OBO 1; Freibourg: Vandenhoeck & Ruprecht, 1973).

Rüger, H.P., *Text und Textform im hebräischen Sirach: Untersuchungen zur Textgeschichte und Textkritik der hebräischen Sirachfragmente aus der Kairoer Geniza* (BZAW 112; Berlin: de Gruyter, 1970).

Schechter, S., "A Fragment of the Original Text of Ecclesiasticus," *Expositor* 5,4 (1896) 1–15.

Schechter, S., "A Further Fragment of Ben Sira," *JQR* 12 (1899/1900) 456–65.

Schechter, S., "Genizah Specimens. Ecclesiasticus," *JQR* 10 (1898) 197–206.

Schechter, S. – Taylor, Ch., *The Wisdom of Ben Sira. Portions of the Book Ecclesiasticus, from Hebrew Manuscripts in the Cairo Genizah Collection Presented to the University of Cambridge by the Editors* (Cambridge: University Press, 1899).

Skehan P.W. – Di Lella, A.A., *The Wisdom of Ben Sira: A New Translation with Notes, Introduction and Commentary* (AB 39; New York: Doubleday, 1987).

Stemberger, G., Einleitung in den Talmud und Midrasch (Beck-Studium; 8th ed.; München: Beck, 1992).

Ziegler, J., "Zwei Beiträge zu Sirach. II. Zu מכוער Sir 11,2 und 13,22," *BZ* NF 8 (1964) 281–84.

Jesus Sirach und das Luthertum des 16. Jahrhunderts.

Über Inhalt und Funktion eines schlesischen Katechismus von 1561

Eve-Marie Becker
Universität Erlangen

1.

Die sog. apokryphen atl. Schriften[1] wurden im Zuge der Reformation endgültig vom atl. Kanon separiert und damit zu deuterokanonischen Schriften deklassiert.[2] Doch erscheint M. Luthers Sirach-Übersetzung[3] 1532/33 zunächst als Separatdruck bzw. als "Klein-Oktav mit Randglossen"[4] und wird zwischen 1533 und 1545 allein in Wittenberg mindestens zwölfmal aufgelegt.[5] Im Herbst 1534 ist Jesus Sirach, dessen Text gegenüber dem Erstdruck nahezu unverändert blieb,[6] dann "in hochdeutscher Fassung ... in der Wittenberger Vollbibel"[7] den apokryphen Schriften zugeordnet. Die theologische Bedeutung dieser Schriften blieb im Protestantismus aber dennoch gewahrt, auch wenn dies angesichts unserer modernen protestantischen Wahrnehmung der sog. apokryphen Schriften erstaunen sollte. Denn die frühjüdische Schrift Jesus Sirach scheint in der gegenwärtigen Wirklichkeit evangelischer Kirchen kaum mehr bedeutsam zu sein: Im Unterschied zum Katechismus der

---

1   Die Klassifizierung der apokryphen atl. Schriften als ebensolche apokryphe Schriften findet sich bereits bei Hieronymus, vgl. Volz, Luthers Stellung, 93f.

2   Hierbei ist jedoch anzumerken, dass Luther den Begriff der Apokryphen erst 1534 innerhalb der sog. Vollbibel verwendet, vgl. auch WA DB 12/2. Denn während Luther in seinen frühen Vorlesungen (1513–1518) durchaus die atl. Apokryphen und so auch Jesus Sirach zitiert, beginnt der eigentliche hermeneutische Streit über deren Bedeutung und Normativität einerseits erst im Zuge der Auseinandersetzung mit Eck über die Fegefeuerlehre des 2Makk bei der Leipziger Disputation 1519, vgl. dazu Lohse, Entscheidung, 218ff und 228. Andererseits nimmt A. Karlstadt 1520 eine Unterteilung der atl. Apokryphen in Hagiographen, zu denen auch Jesus Sirach zählt, und völlig apokryphen Schriften vor, vgl. Volz, Luthers Stellung, 97f.

3   Im Unterschied zu den meisten übrigen apokryphen Schriften ist Jesus Sirach zumindest in Teilen von Luther selbst unter der Mitarbeit von Cruciger übersetzt worden, vgl. Lohse, 228.

4   Vgl. Volz, Bibelübersetzungen, 1203 und ders., Luthers Stellung, 105 oder auch Sauer, Jesus Sirach, 484 und Grimm, Luthers Übersetzung, 379 (Zitat ebd.). Vgl. auch WA DB 12,LXXIIIff.

5   Vgl. WA DB 12,XV.

6   Vgl. WA DB 12,XLIII.

7   Volz, Luthers Stellung, 105.

Katholischen Kirche (1993) kennt nämlich der sog. Evangelische Erwachsenenkatechismus (⁶2000) das Buch Jesus Sirach offenbar nicht.[8]
Nun geht aber unsere moderne protestantische Vernachlässigung des Siraciden gerade nicht darauf zurück, dass er im reformatorischen Kanon,[9] der
seinerseits nur einen Reflex auf die bereits bestehenden Grenzen des hebräischen Kanons darstellte, zu den apokryphen Schriften zählte.[10] Denn das Sirachbuch erfreute sich in der reformatorischen Literatur auch unabhängig von
der Frage der Kanonizität einer hohen Wertschätzung.

Ernst Koch hat 1990 in einem umfangreichen Beitrag, der von der Si-
rachforschung nicht genügend rezipiert wurde, auf die Bedeutung alttestamentlicher Spruchweisheit, zu der auch Teile der sog. atl. Apokryphen und
damit Jesus Sirach zählen, in der lutherischen Theologie des 16. Jhs. hingewiesen. Die Schrift Jesus Sirach kann sogar bis in das 18./19. Jh. hinein – neben den Psalmen – als die am häufigsten edierte und interpretierte biblische
Schrift überhaupt bezeichnet werden.[11] So dienten insbesondere Texte aus
den Büchern der Weisheit Salomos und Jesus Sirachs der Auslegung bei diversen Leichenpredigten im Bereich der Wittenberger Reformation.[12] Die
Interpretation des Sirach-Buches[13] begegnet aber nicht nur im Bereich von
Kasualpredigten[14] oder den Predigten in Wochengottesdiensten.[15] Daneben
entstanden neue griechische oder lateinische Textausgaben,[16] oder einzelne
Verse aus dem Sirach-Buch wurden – bis ins 19. Jh. hinein[17] – in Motetten-

---

8 Vgl. dazu auch Becker, Jesus Sirach Deutsch, 18–20. Während der katholische
   Katechismus vor allem in seinem dritten, ethisch geprägten Teil Jesus Sirach vielfältig
   zitiert, fehlt der Siracide im Stellen- und Sachregister des evangelischen Katechismus
   völlig.
9 Vgl. Reiterer, Bibliographie, 16.
10 Zudem wird die Sonderexistenz des Buches Jesus Sirach gerade durch die fehlende
   hebräische Textgeschichte vom 12.–19. Jh. maßgeblich gefördert.
11 Vgl. Koch, Philosophia, 714f.
12 Vgl. Koch, Philosophia, 708 und Anm. 19 mit Verweis auf eine Predigtsammlung von
   J. Spangenberg von 1545. "Funffzehen Leichenprediget / So man bey dem Begrebnis
   der verstorbnen / jnn Christlicher gemein thun mag ...," bei VD 16 vol. 19, 400f (S
   7804ff).
13 Im Folgenden führe ich einige der bei Koch, Philosophia, 707ff in Bezug auf das Sirach-Buch genannten Beispiele an.
14 So etwa bei Hochzeiten, vgl. P. Jenisch: "Vir lehrhaffte Hochzeitspredigten," Leipzig
   1609 bei Koch, Philosophia, 707 und Anm.12.
15 Vgl. die Sirach-Predigten von F. Rhote, Teil 1 und 2, Leipzig 1587, bei Koch, Philosophia, 707 und Anm. 2 und 3. "Das Buch Jesus Syrach Jm Latein ECCLESIAS-
   TICUS. Auff Deutsch / Dje Geistliche Zucht genandt / Jn hundert vnd zwey vnd drei-
   sig Predigten erkleret / vnd auff die Lehre des heiligen Catechismi gerichtet ...," bei VD
   16 vol. 17,415f (R 3211f).
16 Vgl. bei Koch, Philosophia, 707.
17 J. Brahms hat in seinen sog. Vier Ernsten Gesängen Sir 41 vertont und dabei das Buch
   Jesus Sirach "als Teil des lutherschen Kanons gelesen," Loader, Johannes Brahms,
   264.

Zyklen vertont[18] oder zum Zwecke der Erinnerung als Gebäudeinschriften, auf Hausbesen, Trinkgläsern oder Epitaphien niedergeschrieben.[19] Zu eben demselben Zweck der Erinnerung erstellte sogar eine Frau, die Regensburger Mädchenschulmeisterin Magdalena Heymair, eine Reimfassung des Sirach-Buches[20]. "Der eigentliche kirchliche Ort der Auslegung der Spruchweisheit" und so auch Jesus Sirachs liegt jedoch im "Wirkungsbereich der Wittenberger Reformation" in der Katechismusunterweisung.[21] Bei diesen katechetisch ausgerichteten Auslegungen[22] ist zumeist ein ständiger Bezug zum Dekalog erkennbar. Außerdem gelangt die Schrift Jesus Sirach durch diese katechetische Verwendung dauerhaft in den Schulunterricht des 16. und 17. Jhs.[23]

Die gründliche Arbeit Kochs erwähnt allerdings einen schlesischen Sirach-Katechismus aus dem Jahr 1561 nicht, den ich in der Universitätsbibliothek in Erlangen fand und den ich im Folgenden als Beispiel für die lutherische Rezeption des Sirach-Buches im 16. Jh. vorstelle.

2.

Am 19. April 1561, dem ersten Todestag Philipp Melanchthons († 19.4. 1560), beschließt *Petrus Vincentius* (1519–1581), ehemals Student Luthers und Melanchthons und gegenwärtig Rektor der Universität in Wittenberg, seine Vorrede auf einen Katechismus, den ein ihm bekannter Prediger im schlesischen Brieg (heute: Brzeg) mit Namen Esaja Tribauer zu der Schrift Jesus Sirach zusammengestellt hat:[24]

Das buch Jesus Syrach / nach ordnung der heubtartickel Christlicher lere/in Frage und Antwort gestellet / Durch Ern Elaiam Tribawer / Predigern zum Brigk in Schlesien.
Mit einer Vorrede M. Petri Vincentii Bratislawiensis.
Wittemberg. Gedruckt durch Hans Lufft. 1561.

---

18   Vgl. Koch, Philosophia, 716.
19   Beispiele dazu bei Koch, Philosophia, 712. Im übrigen gehört gerade die Spruchweisheit zum üblichen Potential der Stadtreformation.
20   Vgl. bei Koch, Philosophia, 712. M. Heymair, "Das Bu(e)chlein Jesus Syrach inn Gesange verfasset / vnd der lieben Jugend zu gutem in Truck gegeben ...," Regensburg 1573/1578, bei VD 16 vol. 9, 126 (H 3442f).
21   Koch, Philosophia, 709. Vgl. dazu P. Glaser: "Der gantze text der dreyen Bücher Salomonis / Der Sprüchwörter. Dess Predigers. Der Weisheit. Vnd dess Buchs Syrachs ...," Leipzig 1572, vgl. Koch, Philosophia, 717, Anm. 22.
22   Vgl. des weiteren bei Koch, Philosophia, 709f und Anm. 9 und 34: D. Chytraeus, Wittenberg 1565 oder E. Sarcerius, "IN IESVM SYRACH, INTEGRA SCHOLIA, IN VSVM SCHOlasticae ...," Frankfurt / Main 1543, bei VD 16 vol. 18, 101 (S 1724).
23   Vgl. Koch, Philosophia, 709f.
24   Signatur in der Universitätsbibliothek Erlangen: Trew Sx 545.

Dieser Katechismus mitsamt seiner Vorreden gewährt uns einen partiellen, aber charakteristischen Einblick in die Rezeptionsgeschichte des Buches Jesus Sirach im Luthertum des 16. Jahrhunderts.

Der Wittenberger Eloquenz- und Dialektik-Professors P. Vincentius, der selbst biografisch immer auch im Schuldienst stand und dessen Breslauer und Görlitzer Schul- und Studienordnungen "zu den besten" des 16. Jhs. zählen,[25] ist an dem Sirach-Katechismus E. Tribauers sicher vorwiegend aus ebensolchen katechetischen Gründen interessiert. Denn er versteht das Buch Jesus Sirach selbst als eine "erklerung der zehen gebot,"[26] das durch die Tribauer'sche Zusammenordnung besonders der Belehrung der Jugend dienen kann.

Was wissen wir über den *Verfasser* dieses Sirach-Katechismus? Der in Iglau / Mähren geborene Esaja T. Tribauer[27] ist uns nun nicht nur als Schreiber dieses Sirach-Katechismus, sondern daneben als Verfasser verschiedener anderer Schriften, die zumeist zwischen 1561 und 1571 in Wittenberg gedruckt wurden, bekannt.[28] Darunter finden sich polemische[29] und seelsorgerliche Schriften[30] und analog zu dem Sirach-Katechismus eine weitere katechismusartige Auslegung der Sprüche und des Predigers Salomo.[31] Der Prediger E. Tribauer widmete sich in seinem Schrifttum also besonders der Auslegung atl. Weisheitsliteratur und deren lehrhafter Unterweisung.

Wir fragen nun weiter nach der *Gestalt* der Schrift. Der knapp 200 Seiten umfassende Sirach-Katechismus enthält drei Vorreden (Bl. 2–12), den Tribauer'schen Katechismus in 80 Artikeln (Bl. 13–197), der tituliert ist als "Das Buch Jesus Syrach. In frag und antwort gestellet," sowie ein abschließendes "Register" als Inhaltsverzeichnis über diese 80 verhandelten Artikel (Bl. 198–199).

Der Katechismus E. Tribauers lässt sich – ähnlich einer protestantischen Dogmatik – in wesentlich drei Teile, einen theologischen, einen ethischen und einen eschatologischen Teil, untergliedern: Während Tribauer in den Ar-

---

25 Schimmelpfennig, Vincentius, 735.

26 So P. Vincentius in seiner Vorrede, Bl. 4.

27 Vgl. Allgemeine Deutsche Biographie vol. 38, 595. P. Vincentius spricht zudem in seiner Vorrede zum Katechismus eine deutliche Empfehlung für E. Tribauer gegenüber der Stadt Iglau aus, in der Tribauer dann 1571 tatsächlich als Prediger tätig ist.

28 Vgl. VD 16 vol. 20, 516f (T 1919 – T 1928).

29 Tribauer setzt sich in der Schrift: "Ein Klein Hand bu(e)chlein wider die enttzuckten vnd vergeisterten Schwenckfelder ...," Regensburg 1571 (vgl. VD 16 vol. 20, 516, T 1924) mit den Schwenckfeldern auseinander. Aus dieser Auseinandersetzung ist das bei Wackernagel, Kirchenlied, 544f aufgeführte Lied "Ein gesang wider die Teufflische vnnd verfu(e)rische Sect der Schwenckfelder" erhalten.

30 Es handelt sich hierbei z.B. um eine Trostschrift für Eltern angesichts des Todes ihrer Kinder, vgl. VD 16 vol. 20, 517 (T 1927).

31 "Die Spru(e)che vnd der Prediger Salomo / nach ordnung der Hauptartickel Christlicher Lere / in Frag vnd Antwort gestellet Durch Esaiam Tribawer Prediger zum Brieg in Slesien Gedruckt zu Witteberg durch Lorentz Schwenck 1563," vgl. Verzeichnis vol. 20, 516 (T 1921/1926).

tikeln 1–6 Aspekte der Gotteslehre thematisiert, ist er sonst in seinem Katechismus überwiegend mit ethischen Fragen befasst: mit dem Leben des frommen Menschen (Art. 7–17), mit einer Haustafel-Ethik (Art. 18–27), mit Gottlosigkeit und Lebensgenuss (Art. 28–39), Freundschaft und Feindschaft (Art. 40–45) und mit verschiedenen Fragen zum Leben angesichts von Gesetz und Gerechtigkeit (Art. 46–71). In den neun letzten Artikeln (72–80) bereitet er einen eschatologischen Schluss vor.[32] Im 75. Artikel ("Vom Tod") behandelt Tribauer nicht nur die Eigenschaft und die Funktion des Todes, sondern verinnerlicht mit der Frage "Was wirkt in uns den Tod?" den Wirkungsbereich des Todes und geht schließlich auch auf seelsorgerliche ("Wie soll sich ein Mensch über einen verstorbenen Freund in Traurigkeit trösten?") und rituelle Aspekte ("Was sind wir dem toten Leichnam schuldig?") ein. Dagegen umfasst der 77. Artikel ("Vom Ende aller Dinge") lediglich zwei kurze Fragen, die ebenso lakonisch beantwortet werden.[33] Die Artikel 78 ("Von Arznei") und 79 ("Von Tischzucht"), die wesentlich auf Sir 34/31,12ff bzw. 38 Bezug nehmen, kann Tribauer offensichtlich nicht sinnvoll den zuvor im ethischen Teil thematisierten Fragen zuordnen. So nimmt er diese beiden für Sirach charakteristischen Themen vor dem resümierenden Artikel 80 ("Von den Stücken, die Gott und den Menschen wohlgefallen und missfallen") am Ende seines Katechismus' auf.

Die *Struktur* der Artikel, in welcher Tribauer Frage und Antwort einander zuordnet, ist im gesamten Katechismus nahezu identisch: Jeder Artikel ist fortlaufend nummeriert und ähnlich einem Locus communis mit einer Themenangabe überschrieben. Der Tribauer'sche Katechismus knüpft mit dieser Loci-Struktur einerseits an die mit den Loci communes Melanchthons gesetzte Tradition protestantischer Dogmatik an.[34] Andererseits ist die Schrift durchaus dem klassischen Typus des reformatorischen Katechismus' verpflichtet. Denn jeder Artikel enthält unterschiedlich viele Fragen und Antworten. Diese Antworten bestehen zumeist aus einem Merksatz, der gleichsam die vorweggenommene Summe der darauf folgenden Textstellen aus dem Sirachbuch darstellt. Die jeweils kaum mehr als wenige Verse umfassenden Textstellen stammen aus der Sirach-Übersetzung Luthers, am Rand ist das jeweilige Kapitel notiert. Indem Tribauer das Sirach-Buch in dieser eklektizistischen Weise als Spruchsammlung verwendet, wendet er die Be-

---

32 Vgl. dazu auch den Beitrag von Wischmeyer, Theologie und Anthropologie im Sirachbuch im vorliegenden Band.

33 Bl. 193: Frage: "Worauf soll man in allen Dingen sehen?" Antwort: "Auf das Ende." Frage: "Werden auch alle Dinge ein Ende nehmen?" Antwort: "Alles Zeitliche wird vergehen."

34 Vgl. Melanchthon, Loci communes 1521.

merkungen Luthers zur Entstehung von Jesus Sirach in seiner eigenen Schrifthermeneutik an.[35]

Im 14. Artikel ("Vom Gebet und Danksagung") berücksichtigt Tribauer zudem die literarische Form des Sirach-Textes, indem er verhältnismäßig umfangreich die Gebete Jesus Sirachs selbst (Kap. 23; 36; 50) zu Wort kommen lässt (Bl. 52ff). Der kürzeste Artikel im Tribauer'schen Katechismus (Art. 22) enthält lediglich eine Frage und eine Antwort und ist dem "Vieh" gewidmet.[36] Im deutlich umfangreichsten Artikel 1 (Bl. 13–26) traktiert Tribauer die Frage nach "Gott und seinen Werken" und weicht hierbei zudem von der sonst üblichen Strukturierung seiner Artikel ab. Denn hier charakterisiert Tribauer in zusätzlichen acht Leitsätzen, die an die Sprache der Psalmen erinnern, das Wesen und die Eigenschaften Gottes und verweist dabei auf Textbelege aus dem Sirach-Buch.

3.

So spiegelt die *Sirach-Interpretation* E. Tribauers nicht nur eine exzellente Textkenntnis wider, mit der er die Textbelege thematisch zusammenordnet, was im übrigen auch P. Vincentius in seiner Vorrede lobt.[37] Vielmehr zeigt sich besonders daran, dass Tribauer im wesentlichen alle im Sirach-Buch behandelten Themen aufgreift[38] und im Verlauf seines Katechismus' auf die jeweiligen Sirach-Kapitel Bezug nimmt, dass er das Buch Jesus Sirach selbst zur Grundlage einer zugleich seelsorgerlichen, dogmatisch-lehrhaften und praktischen Unterweisung für das Leben eines Christen vor Gott und in der Welt zu nehmen imstande ist.

Deutlicher noch lässt sich schließlich den zwei *Vorreden* zum Tribauer'schen Katechismus entnehmen, wie die reformatorischen und nachreformatorischen Theologen diese frühjüdische Schrift interpretierten und welche Funktion sie ihr für die Theologie und die kirchliche Unterweisung zuer-

---

35 Luther versteht die Schrift Jesus Sirach ihrerseits als Zusammenlesung vieler verschiedener Sprüche, vgl. WA DB 12,147,1ff.

36 Bl. 74: Frage: "Wie soll sich ein Hausvater gegen sein Vieh verhalten?" Antwort: "So es gut und nützlich ist, soll es warten, pflegen und behalten." Es folgen Textbelege aus Sir 7 und 33.

37 Vgl. P. Vincentius, Bl. 6. Damit die Schrift Jesus Sirach aber besonders für junge Menschen verständlich ist, habe E. Tribauer die schönen Sprüche Sirachs "so bis anher on ordnung durch einander versteckt und vermenget sind gewesen / in locos communes, das ist / ordentlich nach den heubtartickeln Christlicher lere gefasset und zusamen gezogen / was zusamen geho(e)ret / und einerley materien ist / das man dasselbe bey einander finden / lesen und betrachten mu(e)ge."

38 Vgl. dazu das Register Bl. 198f etwa mit dem Inhaltsverzeichnis bei Skehan – Di Lella, Wisdom, XIIIff.

kannten. E. Tribauer stellt unmittelbar vor seinen Katechismus die Vorreden Luthers auf das Buch Jesus Sirach von 1533, die Luther 1545 in neuer Sprachfassung beibehalten hat (Bl. 9–12). Für Luther ist Jesus Sirach "ein nu(e)tzlich Buch, fur den gemeinen Man"[39] und ein Leben in der Welt bzw. ein "Buch von der Hauszucht,"[40] womit sich Luther an den Titel der deutschen Nürnberger Ausgabe A. Kobergers (1483) anlehnt.[41]

Petrus Vincentius hebt in seiner Vorrede (Bl. 2–8) nicht nur die Leistung E. Tribauers hervor, die Sprüche Jesus Sirachs in "ein ordnung gefast" zu haben (Bl. 3). Vielmehr schätzt Vincentius die sentenziöse Weisheit des Siraciden, die darin den heidnischen Autoren überlegen sei, da in deren Schriften nichts über "Gottes furcht / glaube / lieb / hoffnung / rechter anruffung / von Gottes verheissung etc." enthalten ist (Bl. 5f). Das Sirach-Buch dagegen ist für Vincentius eine christliche Erklärung der "gemeinen lere im Christlichen Catechismo / von Gottes wort / glauben und rechten guten wercken" (Bl. 6) und insofern nicht nur für die Belehrung der Jugend nützlich.

Die Rezeption des Sirach-Buches in der lutherischen Theologie konzentriert sich folglich vornehmlich auf zwei Bereiche: Zum einen wird die weisheitliche Spruchform als intellektuelles Potential für eine vernunftorientierte katechetische Unterweisung sowohl der Jugend als auch der gemeinen "Hausperone" (Bl. 4) empfunden, was der Intention des Siraciden durchaus entspricht (vgl. z.B. Sir 50,29ff). Sirach bietet gleichsam das Material für eine vernünftige Belehrung des Gottesfürchtigen.[42] Zum anderen führt die Applikation der siracidischen Weisheit in die Ethik christlichen Lebens hinein: Sie ordnet dem Glauben die Werke, d.h. vor allem die Befolgung der Zehn Gebote, sinnvoll zu und ermöglicht in seelsorgerlicher Hinsicht, "lebenssichernde Strukturen" zu stärken und den Menschen "Hilfen in den Bedrohungen durch Krankheit, Krieg, Hunger und Chaos"[43] an die Hand zu geben.

Es zeigt sich aber zudem eine Entwicklung im hermeneutischen Umgang mit Sirach von Luther zur lutherischen Theologie der folgenden Generation: Damit, dass Tribauer seinem Katechismus insgesamt nämlich einen dogmatischen Aufriss gibt, stellt er die siracidische Weisheit letztlich in eine soteriologische Perspektive und geht über die Bewertung Luthers, Jesus Sirach sei ein nützlich zu lesendes Buch, hinaus. Die intellektuell-ethische Dimension

---

39   WA DB 12,147,16.
40   WA DB 12,146,20 oder 147,20f.
41   Vgl. auch Lohse, Entscheidung, 230f und WA DB 12,144 Anm. 2: "In der mittelalterlichen deutschen Bibelübersetzung lautet seit der Nürnberger Ausgabe Anton Kobergers (1483) die Überschrift: '... hebt an das buch ecclesiasticus. das ist das buch der geystlichen zucht'".
42   Vgl. auch Luther, WA DB 12,147,16ff.
43   Koch, Philosophia, 712.

der Sirach-Rezeption wird somit in der lutherischen Theologie der nächsten Generation um eine eminent dogmatische erweitert.

4.

E. Tribauer beschließt seine Katechismus-Ausgabe (Bl. 197) mit dem Verweis auf die im Buchschluss Sirachs selbst enthaltene Leseanweisung. Wie nämlich schließt Sirach sein Buch (Sir 50,29–31)? "Mit einer vermanung das man sein buch gern lesen wolle. Diese Lere und Weisheit / hat in dis buch geschrieben Jesus der Sohn Syrach von Jerusalem / und aus seinem hertzen solche lere geschu(e)ttet. Wol dem / der sich hierin ubet / und wers zu hertzen nimet / der wird weise werden / Und wo er darnach thut / so wird er zu allen dingen tu(e)chtig sein / Denn des Herrn liecht leitet in."

Bibliographie

Allgemeine Deutsche Biographie (vol. 38; Leipzig: Duncker & Humblot, 1894).

Becker, E.-M., "'Jesus Sirach Deutsch.' Über die Chancen und Schwierigkeiten einer modernen deutschen Übersetzung," *Deutsches Pfarrerblatt* 102 (2002) 18–20.

Evangelischer Erwachsenenkatechismus. Glauben – erkennen – leben (6th rev. ed.; eds. M. Kießig et al.; Gütersloh: Gütersloher Verlagshaus, 2000).

Grimm, W., "Luthers Übersetzung der alttestamentlichen Apokryphen," *TSK* (1883) 375–400.

Katechismus der Katholischen Kirche (München: Oldenbourg / Benno / Paulusverlag et al., 1993).

Koch, E., "Die 'Himmlische Philosophia des heiligen Geistes.' Zur Bedeutung alttestamentlicher Spruchweisheit im Luthertum des 16. und 17. Jahrhunderts," *TLZ* 115 (1990) 705–20.

Loader, J.A., "Johannes Brahms, Agnostizismus und andere Weisheiten," in *Begegnung mit Gott. Gesammelte Studien im Bereich des Alten Testaments* (ed. J.A. Loader; Wiener Alttestamentliche Studien 3; Frankfurt a.M.: Lang, 2001) 257–68.

Lohse, B., "Die Entscheidung der lutherischen Reformation über den Umfang des alttestamentlichen Kanons," *Evangelium in der Geschichte. Studien zu Luther und der Reformation* (FS B. Lohse; eds. L. Grane, B. Moeller and O.H. Pesch; Göttingen: Vandenhoeck & Ruprecht, 1988) 211–36.

D. Martin Luthers Werke. Kritische Gesamtausgabe. Die Deutsche Bibel 1522–1546 (vol. 12: *Die Übersetzung des Apokryphenteils des Alten Testaments*; Weimar: Böhlau Nachfolger, 1961) (= WA DB 12).

Melanchthon, Ph., *Loci communes 1521. Lateinisch-Deutsch. Übersetzt und mit kommentierenden Anmerkungen versehen v. H. G. Pöhlmann* (ed. Lutherischen Kirchenamt der Vereinigten Evangelisch-Lutherischen Kirche Deutschlands VELKD; Gütersloh: Mohn, 1993).

Reiterer, F.V. (ed.), *Bibliographie zu Ben Sira* (BZAW 266; Berlin / New York: de Gruyter, 1998).

Sauer, G., *Jesus Sirach (Ben Sira)* (JSHRZ III/5; Gütersloh: Mohn, 1981).

Schimmelpfennig, A.S., "Vincentius," *Allgemeine Deutsche Biographie* 39. 735–36.

Verzeichnis der im Deutschen Sprachbereich erschienenen Drucke des XVI. Jahrhunderts
(eds. Bayerischen Staatsbibliothek in München in Verbindung mit der Herzog
August Bibliothek in Wolfenbüttel I. Abteilung. Verfasser-Körperschaften-
Anonyma; Stuttgart: Hiersemann, vol. 9 1987, vol. 17 1991, vol. 18 1992, vol. 19
1992, vol. 20 1993) (= VD 16).

Skehan P.W. – Di Lella, A.A., *The Wisdom of Ben Sira: A New Translation with Notes, Introduction and Commentary* (AB 39; New York: Doubleday, 1987).

Volz, H., "Bibelübersetzungen IV. Deutsche Bibelübersetzungen," *RGG*³ 1. 1201–07.

Volz, H., "Luthers Stellung zu den Apokryphen des Alten Testaments," *Luther-Jahrbuch* 26
(1959) 93–108.

Wackernagel, Ph., *Das deutsche Kirchenlied. Von der ältesten Zeit bis zu Anfang des XVII.
Jahrhunderts. Mit Berücksichtigung der deutschen kirchlichen Liederdichtung im
weiteren Sinne und der lateinischen von Hilarius bis Georg Fabricius und Wolfgang Ammonius* (vol. 5; Hildesheim: Olms, 1964; reprint ed. Leipzig, 1877).

Progress Report:

Three Leiden Projects on the Syriac Text of Ben Sira

Wido van Peursen
Leiden University

1. Introduction[1]

In the last decade Leiden University has become an important centre for the study of Ben Sira. As to the Hebrew text, Professor T. Muraoka of the Department of Near Eastern Studies gave a great incentive to the study of the language of Ben Sira. Already before he came to Leiden in 1992 he had published on the book of Ben Sira and had prepared a Japanese translation of it. In December 1995 he organised the *First Leiden Symposium on the Hebrew of the Dead Sea Scrolls and Ben Sira,*[2] which in December 1997 was followed by the *Second Leiden Symposium on the Hebrew of the Dead Sea Scrolls and Ben Sira.*[3] Professor E. Qimron, who was involved in the preparations for this second symposium, organised together with Professor Muraoka the third symposium on this subject, which was held at the Ben Gurion University of the Negev in Beer Sheva in October 1999.[4] The participants of these symposia agreed that a fourth symposium should be organised, although the plans for it are still in an initial phase. The present writer was happy to prepare a PhD dissertation on the verbal system in the Hebrew text of Ben Sira under the supervision of Professor Muraoka in the years 1995–1999 (thesis successfully defended on 2 November 1999).

As to the Syriac text, the main centre of the study of Ben Sira is the Peshiṭta Institute Leiden, which is part of the research program *The Hebrew Bible and its Ancient Versions* of the Faculty of Theology. At the moment there are three ongoing projects on the Syriac text of Ben Sira within the larger context of research projects on the Old Testament Peshiṭta as a whole.

---

1   The author wishes to express his gratitude to Prof. Dr. T. Muraoka and Dr. K.D. Jenner for commenting on earlier versions of this paper. The investigations which resulted in the present article were supported by the Netherlands Organisation for Scientific Research (NWO).
2   See Muraoka – Elwolde, Hebrew.
3   See Muraoka – Elwolde, Sirach.
4   See Muraoka – Elwolde, Diggers.

2. The Critical Edition of the Syriac Text

In 1959 the Peshiṭta Institute Leiden started working towards the preparation
of the critical edition of the Syriac translation of the Old Testament, the
Peshiṭta. The edition is published under the auspices of *The International Organization for the Study of the Old Testament* (IOSOT). The publication of
this edition as well as the preparatory work and the continuing research related to it are part of an international project, coordinated and partly also carried out by the Peshiṭta Institute Leiden. At the moment this edition is three-
quarters complete and it is expected to be fully completed in 2010 AD.

The edition of the Syriac text of Ben Sira is in preparation. It will appear
in volume IV, 1 of the edition, together with the books of Ruth, Susanna,
Esther, and Judith. The preparation of this edition is in the hands of the di-
rector of the Peshiṭta Institute, Dr. K.D. Jenner, and the present writer. They
will build on the work done by some other scholars who were involved in the
study of the Syriac text of Ben Sira but for various reasons did not have the
opportunity to continue the work. Special mention should be made of the
collations made by Dr. M.M. Winter, who is well-known for his studies on
the origin of Ben Sira in Syriac[5] and his concordance on the Syriac text of
Ben Sira.[6]

In accordance with the policy followed throughout the Peshiṭta edition,
the edition of the Syriac text of Ben Sira will mainly follow the text of the
Codex Ambrosianus (7a1). For the book of Ben Sira we do not have fifth- or
sixth-century manuscripts, so that this manuscript, together with 7h3 and the
small portion of text in the palimpsest 7pk2, is the oldest direct textual witness we have. In the Leiden Peshiṭta edition emendations in the main text are
given in the first critical apparatus, while the second apparatus gives variants
in the other ancient manuscripts up to the twelfth century.

Part V of *The Old Testament in Syriac* will consist of a concordance to
the Peshiṭta, edited by Dr. P.G. Borbone, Dr. K.D. Jenner, and the present
writer. The first volume of this work, the concordance to the Pentateuch, appeared in 1997. Volume 2, the concordance on the Historical Books, is in
preparation. The sixth and final volume will probably be completed before
the last volume of the text edition. The present writer will be involved in the
preparation of the Ben Sira material for this concordance. A by-product of the
concordance is a preliminary, digitalised Syriac dictionary in simplified form.
The work is being done in cooperation with the *Concise Aramaic Lexicon* at
Cincinnati.

Plans have been made to produce also an *editio minor* of the Peshiṭta,
which will contain both the Old Testament and the New Testament in one

---

5   Winter, Origins.
6   Winter, Concordance.

volume. The Old Testament will be prepared at the Peshiṭta Institute Leiden; the New Testament will be edited by Dr. A. Juckel from the Evangelisch-Theologischen Fakultät of the Westfälische Wilhelmus-Universität Münster. Unlike the *editio maior*, which basically gives a Basic Textus Receptus (BTR-text), the *editio minor* will be a critical edition.[7] Hence the *editio minor* will not be a mere abridged version of the *editio maior*, but a text that is basically different, because it is based on a different approach to the text.

3. The Translation of Ben Sira in the New English and Annotated Translation of the Syriac Bible (NEATSB)

In 1998 the *International Organization for the Study of the Old Testament* (IOSOT) authorized the Peshiṭta Institute Leiden to prepare an edition of a new and annotated translation of the Syriac Bible into English. The aim of this edition, called "New English and Annotated Translation of the Syriac Bible" (NEATSB), is to facilitate the use of the Peshiṭta and to provide access to the Syriac theological literature, especially that of the commentaries on the Bible and of liturgy. Three general editors ware appointed: Dr. K.D. Jenner (Leiden), Prof. Dr. J. Joosten (Strasbourg), and Dr. A. Salvesen (Oxford). In 2001 Dr. R.B. ter Haar Romeny (Leiden) and Prof. Dr. G. Greenberg (London) join the editorial board. The work is being carried out in cooperation with the Department of Biblical Research of the Bar-Ilan University in Ramat Gan. In order to start the preparations for this edition officially a seminar at the Peshiṭta Institute Leiden was held on 4 and 5 February 1999, chaired by Dr. D.J. Lane (Leeds University). At this seminar some preliminary samples were presented.[8] The participants agreed that the annotated translation should contain the following items:

1. An introduction to each book that discusses the general relation between the Peshiṭta and its *Vorlage* (for most biblical books the translators will start with the working hypothesis that the Peshiṭta was translated from a Hebrew text that was more or less identical with the Masoretic Text) and the character of the translation ('translation technique'). The introduction will also deal with recurrent phenomena in the translation that should otherwise be mentioned (over and over again) in the annotations.

2. An English translation of the Syriac Bible. The NEATSB will not indicate divergences from the Masoretic Text by means of italics, underlined

---

7   On the BTR-text, see especially Koster, Peshiṭta. On the decisions that have been made in the preparation of the *editio maior*, see Old Testament in Syriac. General Preface.

8   A general report of the meeting has been published in *Hugoye* 2/2 (1999; http://syrcom.cua.edu/Hugoye/Vol2No2/index.html). For J. Joosten's contribution to the seminar see Joosten, Materials.

text, brackets or any other diacritics, both for practical reasons (an elaborate use of different formats may be confusing or distracting for the reader) and because of theoretical and methodological considerations (the relation between the Masoretic Text and the Peshiṭta is often too complicated to be captured by straightforward indications of 'plus', 'minus', etc.). An exception may be made for Chronicles, where the major differences from the Masoretic Text may be italicised. Symbols referring to the annotations will be avoided as well. In the annotations there will be lemmata taking up words from the translation.

3. Annotations. The annotations should provide information about significant divergences from the Masoretic Text (in relation to the other ancient versions), significant variant readings in the Peshiṭta manuscripts, and significant information about the reception history. Where useful, also Jewish (non-Syriac) traditions can be included. Textual and informative notes will be given in one apparatus.

In the preparation of each book at least two persons will be involved, probably in the model of a translator and a counter reader. The whole project may take about ten years. Preferably the translated books will be published in separate fascicles. At a later stage these fascicles can be gathered into several volumes, like one for the Pentateuch, one for the Minor Prophets, etc. As far as Ben Sira is concerned, the present writer has finished a preliminary English translation of the Syriac text and has started to make the annotations.

4. Research Project: Language and Interpretation in the Syriac Text of Ben Sira: A Comparative Linguistic and Literary Study

4.1. The Computer Assisted Linguistic Analysis of the Peshiṭta (CALAP)

In 1999 the Peshiṭta Institute Leiden and the Werkgroep Informatica of the Free University in Amsterdam started a joint research project called "Computer Assisted Linguistic Analysis of the Peshiṭta" (CALAP). This project is supported by the Netherlands Organisation for Scientific Research (NWO). The aim of the project is threefold: a description of the linguistic characteristics of the Peshiṭta on morphological, syntactical and lexical levels; a detailed description of the translation technique of the Peshiṭta by comparing this translation with the Masoretic Text; and a contribution to the study of the syntax and lexicography of classical Syriac.

A computer-assisted analysis makes it possible to give a consistent description of the language of the Peshiṭta and to make a systematic comparison with the Masoretic Text. A database that provides systematic access to the linguistic data for Hebrew, in most cases the source language of the Peshiṭta translation, is available at the Free University; a database that provides access to the target language, Syriac, is being developed.

The first constituent project of CALAP, which started in 1999, is the analysis of the book of Kings; the second constituent project, which started in 2000, concerns the analysis of the Syriac Ben Sira. At the moment the CALAP team consists of six members. Dr. K.D. Jenner (Leiden University) and Prof. Dr. E. Talstra (Amsterdam, Free University) perform the direct, daily supervision of the project; Dr. J.W. Dyk and Dr. P.S.F. van Keulen work on the analysis of Kings; Mr. C. Sikkel is involved in the adaptation of available computer programs and the development and implementation of new programs; the present writer has been participating in the project since March 2000 and is responsible for the analysis of the book of Ben Sira.

The CALAP project is supported by an Executive Committee and an Advisory Board. The Executive Committee comprises the aforementioned Dr. K.D. Jenner and Prof. Dr. E. Talstra, as well as Dr. P.G. Borbone (Turin) and Dr. D.M. Walter (USA-Elkins). The guidance and final responsibility for CALAP rests with this Executive Committee. The members of the Advisory Board are Prof. Dr. J. Joosten (Strasbourg), Prof. Dr. A. van der Kooij (Leiden), Prof. Dr. T. Muraoka (Leiden), and Dr. G. Khan (Cambridge).

4.2. The Ben Sira Constituent Project

The aims of the research of the CALAP project mentioned in the preceding paragraph provide the framework for the constituent project on Ben Sira. However, in some respects the aims of this part of the CALAP project have been formulated differently, because the relationship with the Hebrew and Greek versions is more complicated than with most of the other biblical books and because Ben Sira represents a different type of literature than Kings. The aim of this constituent project has three components: a description of selected phenomena in the Syriac of Ben Sira, in relation to the literary genres in which they occur; a comparison of these phenomena with similar or related phenomena in the Syriac of Kings, in order to investigate possible differences between biblical Syriac prose and biblical Syriac poetry; and a comparison with related phenomena in the Hebrew textual witnesses in order to determine what parameters in the Syriac text can be taken into consideration for constructing a model of the Hebrew text that formed the basis for the Syriac translation.

Accordingly, the project will start with a literary-critically and syntactically consistent description of the text of the Syriac Ben Sira. The syntactic annotation of the CALAP system offers the possibility of a consistent description of the Syriac text. The main focus in the grammatical description will be on the larger units (groups of words, parts of speech, verses, and larger textual units), the hierarchical relation between them (word-order, explicit or implicit subject, direct and indirect object, references between clauses, parallel and chiastic structures, types of subordination in dependent and nominal clauses) and the markers of the character of these relations. Since Ben Sira is a poetic text, it will also be investigated whether the translator(s) aimed at a certain degree of independent poetic creativity. This might be manifested in literary and compositional qualities that linguistically and macro-syntactically cannot be fully explained from the Hebrew or Greek text. This approach, however, is not complete. In order to identify the poetic qualities of the Syriac of Ben Sira as effectively as possible, the text will be compared with a clear-cut prose text. For this purpose the text of Kings has been chosen, which is studied in the other constituent project of CALAP.

4.3. Methodology

The computer-assisted analysis concerns a systematic analysis on several levels. The following levels can be distinguished.

1. Word level. On this level the analysis concerns segmentation of Syriac words into morphemes in accordance with the morphological paradigm established for CALAP, and an analysis of word forms on the basis of grammatical functional deductions from this paradigm.

2. Phrase level. On this level words are combined into phrases (e.g., noun + adjective); this entails the lexicographical analysis (determination of the lexical class), the morphosyntactic analysis (systematic adaptation of word classes in certain environments, e.g., participle > adjective, adjective > noun), and the analysis of phrase-internal relations (e.g., regens-rectum, attribute, modifier).

3. Clause level. Phrases are combined to form clauses or simple sentences (e.g., conjunction + verb + determinate noun phrase + prepositional phrase), at which level syntactic functions will be assigned (predicate, subject, obligatory and optional constituents, distinction between verbal and nominal clauses).

4. Sentence level. This level concerns the combination of clauses to form sentences (e.g., verbal clause + infinitive clause), at which level, too, syntactic functions will be assigned (e.g., determining object clauses, attributive clause).

4.4. An Example of the Morphological Analysis in the CALAP System

The following detailed example may illustrate the way in which forms are analysed in the CALAP database. It concerns the analysis of Sir 1:15 on word level. The Syriac text reads:

ܡܪܚܡ ܐܢܫܐ ܥܡܗܘܢ܆ ܥܡ ܘܐܬܩܢܬ ܥܠܡܐ ܡܢ ܘܡܗ ܕܩܘܫܬܐ ܥܡ ܐܝܟ "she is with the man of truth and she was established from of old; and with their descendants her mercy is established".

In the the encoded text of the CALAP database this becomes <M >NC/~> HJ D-QWCT/~> W-HJ MN <LM/~> @>T@TQN||[T== W-<M ZR</+HWN @>T@Q(W&JM||[XSD/+H=

In this example we find the following symbols, which are employed to segment each Syriac word into morphemes:

1. / separates the noun lexeme from the nominal ending indicating emphatic, absolute, or construct state, as in >NC/~>, QWCT/~>, <LM/~>, ZR</+HWN, and XSD/+H=. In the morphological paradigm forms like ZR</+HWN, and XSD/+H= are analysed as ZR</ and XSD/, that is, construct nouns with zero-ending, to which personal pronouns are attached (marked by +, see below).

2. ~ is the emphatic marker, which occurs in >NC/~>, QWCT/~>. With this symbol it is possible to distinguish, for example, the emphatic state masculine from the absolute state feminine. Thus the adjective ܫܦܝܪ "beautiful" can be analysed as CPJR/~> (emphatic state masculine) or as CPJR/> (absolute state feminine) and a noun like ܡܠܟܐ can be encoded as MLK/~> "king" (emphatic state) or MLK/> "queen" (absolute state).

3. @@, which occurs in @>T@TQN||[T== and @>T@Q(W&JM||[marks the so-called passive stem formation prefix, the Eth-prefix in Ethpeel, Ethpaal, and Ettaphal. In an imperfect form, like ܢܬܒܪܟ "he will be blessed" in Sir 1:13, we get !N!@(>T@BRK[, where (indicates that the letter following this symbol, the Alaph, is a paradigmatically expected but absent letter (see below).

4. | indicates the so-called final (reduplicated) verbal stem element. It distinguishes Pael from Peal and Ethpaal from Ethpeel. The interpretation of ܐܬܬܩܢܬ as an Ethpaal is based on the lexicon, since the form itself allows also for the interpretation as an Ethpeel.[9]

5. [separates the verbal lexeme from the verbal personal endings, as in @>T@TQN||[T==. In a form like @>T@Q(W&JM||[the ending is analysed as a zero-morpheme.

6. T== is the verbal ending for the 3rd person feminine singular. In the perfect the ܬ-ending occurs in the 1st person singular, the 2nd person masculine singular and the 3rd person feminine singular. These three endings are marked with T, T=, and T== respectively. Thus in @>T@TQN||[T== the

---

9   In this case we disagree with Winter, Concordance, 651, who analyses this word as an Ethpeel.

choice for T== rather than T or T= is based on contextual considerations because of the feminine singular subject.

7. + marks the personal suffix pronoun attached to the noun, as in ZR</+HWN and XSD/+H=. Here, too, the = is used to distinguish morphemes that have the same form. +H= indicates the suffix pronoun 3rd person feminine singular, +H the masculine suffix pronoun of the 3rd person singular.

8. (indicates a paradigmatically expected but absent letter; & signifies a paradigmatically unexpected letter. Hence the combination (W&J in @>T@Q(W&JM|[indicates that we find a Yodh where we expect a Waw. We consider the Waw as the paradigmatically expected letter, because that is the letter which occurs in the quotation form in the lexicon, where we find QWM (ܩܘܡ).

4.5. Two Characteristics of the CALAP System

Two characteristics of the system employed in the CALAP project deserve to be mentioned. In the first place, the system follows a strictly bottom-up approach, starting on the level of graphemes and ending on the level of text linguistics. This means that the levels mentioned in § 4.3 above are analysed in the order indicated there, and that the analysis on a subsequent level can only start when the analysis of the preceding level is completed.

In the second place, the system works with encoding rather than lemmatization. In the example above, one can see how each Syriac word is segmented into morphemes. An advantage of this system is that both the surface form of the word and the abstract morphemes can be retrieved. Thus we find in the perfect 3rd person masculine plural the usual form ܟܬܒܘ but also ܟܬܒܘܢ and ܟܬܒ. These forms are analysed as KTBW, KTB[W&N, and KTB[(W respectively. In these three encodings both the abstract morpheme of the 3rd person masculine singular, that is [W (ܘ-), and the surface forms, that is -ø, -W (ܘ-), and WN (ـܘܢ), are reflected. This means not only a practical advantage, namely that one can retrieve both the surface forms to see how they are analysed and the abstract morphemes to see what their surface forms are, but it also implies that the morphological paradigm can be revised if necessary. Thus in the case of the above-mentioned examples of ܟܬܒܘ and ܟܬܒ, we can remark that for the verbal endings we started with the paradigm found in traditional grammars and take the zero-ending in ܟܬܒ as the 3rd person masculine singular morpheme and the ܘ-ending in ܟܬܒܘ as the 3rd person masculine plural morpheme. The Peshitta manuscripts, however, quite often have the zero-ending where we expect ܘ and *vice versa*. This phenomenon is so frequent that it is hard to dismiss all the examples as scribal errors. At the moment we cannot rule out the possibility that the fluctuation of ܟܬܒ and ܟܬܒܘ should be considered a morphological, rather than an orthographical phenomenon. This would lead to an important change in the morphological paradigm, because it implies that the zero-ending and the ܘ-ending are allomorphs marking the 3rd person masculine (both singular and plural). In the CALAP system such a reinterpretation of the material can be formally registered in the database by changing the definition of the function of the morphemes under discussion. Since the lemmatization is done automatically on the basis of the morphological encoded text and a formal paradigm containing a functional description of the morphemes, there is no need to change the lemmatization in all separate instances manually.

4.6. Schedule

The Ben Sira consistuent project of CALAP is a four-year project. It should result in the publication of some articles and a monograph entitled *Language and Interpretation in the Syriac Text of Ben Sira* on the formal, linguistically characteristic differences between biblical Syriac prose and biblical Syriac poetry (comparison of the Syriac version of Ben Sira with that of Kings), as well as the text-historical and text-critical position of the Syriac Ben Sira. Some articles related to the research project of the present writer have appeared.[10]

Bibliography

Joosten, J., "Materials for a Linguistic Approach to the Old Testament Peshiṭta," *Journal for the Aramaic Bible* 1 (1999) 203–18.

Koster, M.D., *The Peshiṭta of Exodus. The Development of its Text in the Course of Fifteen Centuries* (SSN 10; Assen/Amsterdam: Van Gorcum, 1977).

Muraoka, T. – Elwolde, J.F. (eds.), *Diggers at the Well: Proceedings of a Third International Symposium on the Hebrew of the Dead Sea Scrolls and Ben Sira Held in October 1999 at Ben-Gurion-University of the Negev* (STDJ 36; Leiden: Brill, 2000).

Muraoka, T. – Elwolde, J.F. (eds.), *The Hebrew of the Dead Sea Scrolls and Ben Sira: Proceedings of a Symposium Held at Leiden University 11–14 December 1995* (STDJ 26; Leiden: Brill, 1997).

Muraoka, T. – Elwolde, J.F. (eds.), *Sirach, Scrolls, and Sages: Proceedings of a Second International Symposium on the Hebrew of the Dead Sea Scrolls, Ben Sira, and the Mishnah, Held at Leiden University, 15–17 December 1997* (STDJ 33; Leiden: Brill, 1999).

The Old Testament in Syriac according to the Peshiṭta Version. General Preface (Leiden: Brill, 1972).

van Peursen, W.Th., "Morphological and Syntactical Issues in the Syriac Text of 1 Kings 1," in *Bible and Computer. The Stellenbosch AIBI–6 Conference. Proceedings of the Association Internationale Bible et Informatique "From Alpha to Byte", University of Stellenbosch, 17–21 July 2000* (ed. J. Cook; Leiden: Brill, 2002) 99–112.

van Peursen, W.Th., "The Alleged Retroversions from Syriac in the Hebrew Text of Ben Sira Revisited: Linguistic Perspectives," in *Kleine Untersuchungen zur Sprache des*

---

10   Van Peursen, Issues, and idem, Retroversions.

Alten Testaments und seiner Umwelt (Vol. 2; ed. R.G. Lehmann; Waltrop: Spenner, 2001) 47–95.

Winter, M.M., *A Concordance to the Peshiṭta Version of Ben Sira* (Monographs of the Peshiṭta Institute Leiden 2; Leiden: Brill, 1976).

Winter, M.M., "The Origins of Ben Sira in Syriac (Part I) (Part II)," *VT* 27 (1977) 237–53, 494–507.

Opferterminologie in Ben Sira

Friedrich V. Reiterer

Die folgende Aufstellung bietet einen ersten Überblick über das Material. Wollte man eine umfassende Sammlung bieten, müsste man die griechischen, hebräischen und syrischen Belege je als Ausgang nehmen[1] und die Parallelen dazuordnen. Im großen und ganzen wurde hier Γ der deutschen Übersetzung zugrunde gelegt.

7,31d	Abgabe	ἀπαρχή ἁγίων	ותרומת קדש	
32/35,8a/5a	Altar	θυσιαστήριον		ـلَܬ...! ܕܩܘܪ̈ܒܢܝܗܘܢ
47,9a	Altar	θυσιαστήριον	לפני מזבח[2]	-
50,14a	Altar	βωμός	מזבח	ܡܕܒܚܐ
50,11c	Altar	θυσιαστήριον	מזבח	
50,15c	Altar	θυσιαστήριον		ܡܕܒܚܐ
50,19c	Altardienst	vgl. 50,19d λειτουργία	לשרת מזבח	
31/34,23b/19b	Brandopfer	θυσία		ܕܩܘܪ̈ܒܢܝܗܘܢ
50,19d	Dienst	λειτουργία	vgl. 50,19c לשרת מזבח	
45,15e	Dienst tun	λειτουργέω	לשרת	ܠܡܫܡܫܘ
50,14a	Dienst tun	λειτουργέω	לשרת	ܠܡܫܡܫܘ
24,15d	Duft	ἀτμίς		ܪܝܚܐ
38,11a	Duft	εὐωδία	....	
39,14a	Duft	ὀσμή		ܪܝܚܐ
45,16c	Duft	εὐωδία	ריח ניחח	ܒܣܡܐ
49,1a	Duft	σύνθεσις θυμιάματος	קטרת סמים	ܐܝܟ ܒܣܡܐ ܕܗܪ̈ܘܡܐ
50,15d	Duft	ὀσμή εὐωδίας		ܪܝܚܐ ܒܣܝܡܐ
3,14b	erbauen	ἀντὶ ... προσανοικοδομέω	תנתע	ܡܬܒܢܝܐ

---

1 Zum Beleg für die anstehenden Probleme vergleiche man z.B. 32/35,8a/5a: Obwohl kein H-Beleg gegeben ist, weist ܩܘܪ̈ܒܢܝܗܘܢ ܠܬ... (vgl. die Emendationsvorschläge) darauf hin, dass Syr kein Verständnis für die Opfervorstellungen hatte. Dadurch scheint gesichert, dass in Syr im Verhältnis zu H jüngeres Stadium vorliegt.

ܩܘܪ̈ܒܢܝܗܘܢ ܠܬ... ܕܟܐܢܐ ܩܘܪ̈ܒܢܝܗܘܢ   προσφορὰ δικαίου λιπαίνει θυσιαστήριον
Lag u. Moss: ܩܘܪ̈ܒܢܝܗܘܢ.   oblatio iusti inpinguat altare

2 Segal, ספר, z.St.

30,18b	Erschei-nungsort	τάφος	לפני גלול	ܩܒܪܐ
45,20c	Erstlinge	ἀπαρχή πρωτογενημάτων	ראשית קדש[3]	ܪܫܝܬܐ ܕܩܘܕܫܐ
31/34,31d/26d	Fasten	ταπεινόω		ܕܨܐܡ
32/35,8a/5a	fett machen	λιπαίνω		ܨܠܘܬܐ !
38,11b	Fett	λίπανον	דשן	
47,2a	Fett	στέαρ	כחלב	ܬܪܒܐ
45,16b	Fettstücke	κάρπωσις	וחלבים	ܟܠܘܬܐ ܘܕܒ̈ܚܐ
7,9a	Gabe	δῶρον		ܕܩܘܪ̈ܒܢܝ
31/34,21/18a	Gabe	προσφορά		ܨܠܘ̈ܬܗܘܢ
31/34,23a/19a	Gabe	προσφορά		ܨܠܘ̈ܬܗܘܢ
32/35,10b/7b	Gabe	ἀπαρχή		ܒܡܘܗ̈ܒܬܟ
38,11b	Gabe	προσφορά	דשן (ערוך)	
			vgl. כנפי הוניך	
45,21a	Gabe	θυσία κυρίου	אשי ייי	
32/35,12a/9a	geben	δίδωμι	תן	ܗܒ
7,10a	Gebet	προσευχή	תפלה	ܒ̈ܠ ܨܠܘܬܟ
7,14b	Gebet	προσευχή	תפלה	ܒ̈ܠ ܨܠܘܬܟ
21,5a	Gebet	δέησις		ܨܠܘܬܗ
31/34,31c/26c	Gebet	προσευχή		ܨܠܘܬܗ
36,22a/16a	Gebet	δέησις	תפלת	ܨܠܘܬܐ
39,5d	Gebet	προσευχή		ܦܘܡܗ ܒܨܠܘܬܐ
39,6d	Gebet	προσευχή		ܬܫ̈ܒܚܬܗܘܢ
50,19b	Gebet	προσευχή	בתפלה	
51,11c	Gebet	δέησις		
7,31c		δόσις βραχιόνων	ותרומת יד	ܪܫܝܬܐ ܕܐܕܪ̈ܥܐ
32/35,9b/6b	Gedenkopfer	μνημόσυνον		ܘܕܘܟܪܢܗܘܢ
38,11a	Gedenkopfer	μνημόσυνον σεμιδάλεως	אזכרה אזכרתה	
45,16c	Gedenkopfer	μνημόσυνον	אזכרה	
30,19a	Götzen	κάρπωσις εἰδώλῳ	יטב לאללי[4]	ܨܠܡܐ
30,18b	Götzenbild	τάφος	לפני גלול	ܩܒܪܐ
32/35,2/1b	Heilsopfer	σωτήριον		ܦܘܩܕܢܐ
46,16c	Milchlamm	ἀρνὸς γαλαθηνοῦ		ܐܡܪܐ ܕܚܠܒܐ
31/34,22/18b	Opfer	δώρημα		ܩܘܪ̈ܒܢܝܗܘܢ
32/35,1/1a	Opfer	προσφορά		ܦܘܠܚܢܐ
32/35,9a/6a	Opfer	θυσία		ܡܘܗܒܬܗ
45,14b	Opfer	! ἐνδελεχῶς	תמיד	

3 Vgl. Peters, Text, z.St.
4 Vgl. Schechter – Taylor, Wisdom, z.St.

46,16c	Opfer	προσφορά	עלתו	ܡܩܪܒܬܗ
41,21b	Opferanteile	μερίς καὶ Δόσις	מחלקות מנה	
47,2a	Opferfleisch	σωτήριον	מקדש	ܩܘܕܫܐ
30,18b	Opfergabe	θέμα βρωμάτων	תנופה מצגת	ܡܐܟܘܠܬܐ ܕܡܝܬܝܢ
32/35,8a/5a	Opfergabe	προσφορά	-	ܩܘܪܒܢܘܗܝ
32/35,15a/11b	Opfergabe	θυσία	זבח	ܩܘܪܒܢܐ
45,16b	Opfergabe	κάρπωσις	עלה	ܥܠܘܬܐ
50,14b	Opfergabe	προσφορά ὑψίστου	מערכות עליון	ܫܘܘܬܐ ܕܩܘܕܫܐ
7,9b	opfern	προσφέρω		ܡܩܪܒ
31/34,21/18a	opfern	Θυσιάζω		ܥܠܘܬܗܘܢ
31/34,24a/20a	opfern	θύω		ܢܟܣ
50,15b	opfern	σπένδω		ܘܢܣܟ
50,12a	Opferstücke	μέλος	נתחים	ܗܕܡܐ
7,29b	Priester	ἱερεύς	כהניו	ܟܗܢܘܗܝ
7,31	Priester	ἱερεύς	כהן	ܠܟܗܢܘܗܝ
50,1	Priester	ἱερεύς	הכהן	ܟܗܢܐ
51,12u	Priester		לכהן	
45,15e	Priester sein	ἱερατεύω	לכהן	
46,13d	Priester sein		מכהן	ܟܗܢܐ
45,7b	Priesteramt des Volkes	ἱερατεία λαοῦ	vgl. 45,7c ויׁשרתהו	
45,20d	Schaubrote	ἄρτος ἐν πρώτοις	חלקו	ܘܦܬܘܪܐ ܕܠܚܡܐ
7,31d	Schlachtopfer	θυσία ἁγιασμοῦ	זבחי צדק	
7,31c	Schuldopfer	ἀπαρχή ... περὶ Πλημμελείας	לחם אברים	ܠܚܡܐ ܕܩܘܪܒܢܐ
32/35,3/2	Speiseopfer	σεμίδαλις		ܩܘܪܒܢܐ
45,14	Speiseopfer	θυσία	מנחתו[5]	
50,9a	Speiseopfer	πυρεῖον	מנחה	ܦܬܘܪܐ
32/35,5b/3b	Sühne	ἐξιλασμός		
3,30b	sühnen	ἐξιλάσκομαι	תכפר	ܬܚܣܐ
45,16d	sühnen	ἐξιλάσκομαι	לכפר	ܘܠܡܚܣܝܘ
45,23f	sühnen	ἐξιλάσκομαι	יכפר	ܚܣܐ
45,14a	verbrennen	ὁλοκαρπόομαι	קטר	
32/35,11b/8b	weihen	ἁγιάζω	הקדש	ܐܘܦ !
39,14a	Weihrauch	λίβανος		ܒܣܡܐ
49,1	Weihrauch	σύνθεσις θυμιάματος	קטרת סמים	ܦܬܘܪܐ ܕܒܣܡܐ
50,9	Weihrauch-feuer	πῦρ καὶ Λίβανος	אש לבונה	ܢܘܪܐ ܕܠܒܘܢܬܐ
24,15d	Weihrauch-wolken	λιβάνου ἀτμίς		

5 Vgl. Peters, Text, z.St.

24,15b	Wohlgeruch	εὐωδία		ܐܢܒ
32/35,8b/5b	Wohlgeruch	εὐωδία		
32/35,11b/8b	Zehnte	δέκατος	מעשר	

Errata et Corrigenda

Pancratius C. Beentjes

P.C. Beentjes, The Book of Ben Sira in Hebrew. A Text Edition of all Extant Hebrew Manuscripts and a Synopsis of all parallel Hebrew Ben Sira Texts. VTS 68. Leiden: Brill, 1997.

Part I. Text

p. 23	Sir 3,15 (A)	כחס read:	כחם
p. 24	Sir 3,28 (A)	כי between מנטע and רע must be deleted	
	Sir 4,2 (A)	רֶוֶה read:	רֶוַח
	Sir 4,7 (A)	עיד read:	עוד
p. 27	Sir 6,1 (A)	עליו read:	עליך
	Sir. 6,2 (A)	עיליך read:	עליך
p. 28	Sir 6,22 (A)	כמשה read:	כשמה
p. 29	Sir 6,37 (A)	יביך read:	יבין
	Sir 6,37 (A)	איות read:	איותה
	Sir 7,7 (A)	אל אל read:	אל ואל
p. 30	Sir 7,11 (A)	מרום read:	מרים
	Sir 7,13 (A)	תנעס read:	תנעם
p. 31	Sir 7,34 (A)	מבובים read:	מבוכים
	Sir 8,2 (A)	כן read:	פן
p. 32	Sir 9,1 (A)	אשה read:	אשת
p. 35	Sir 10,22 (A)	וזר read:	וזד
	Sir 10,26 (A)	תתכחם read:	התחכם
p. 36	Sir 11,8 (A)	וּבְחוֹך read:	וּבְתוֹך
	Sir 11,9 (A)	תאר read:	תאחר
p. 37	Sir 11,14 (A)	והביך read:	והבין
	Sir 11,17 (A)	ין [...] חל[.] read:	ין[...]חל[.]
	Sir 11,19 (A)	נכה read:	נכח
p. 38	Sir 11,30 (A)	בוצו read:	בוצע
p. 39	Sir 12,12 (A)	אסרי read:	אמרי
	Sir 12,14 (A)	תעבר read:	תבער
	Sir 12,15 (A)	להצלך read:	להצילך
p. 40	Sir 12,15 (A)	יתכלכ read:	יתכלכל

	Sir 12,17 (A)	כאשר	read:	כאיש
	Sir 13,1 (A)	וחבר	read:	וחובר
	Sir 13,7 (A)	יארך	read:	יראך
p. 43	Sir 14,18 (Am)	twofold אחר	read both as:	אחד
p. 44	Sir 15,17 (A)	ומות	read:	מוות
p. 49	Sir 10,22 (B)	יראת	read:	יראֹת
p. 52	Sir 15,15 (B)	רצון	read:	רצֹון
p. 54	Sir 30,13 (B)	עליו	read:	עולו
	Sir 30,13 (B)	יתלע בך	read:	יתלעבך
	Sir 30,19 (Bm)	יטֿן	read:	יעֿן
p. 59	Sir 32,14 (Bm)	רצון	read:	רצוץ
	Sir 32,18 (B)	זר	read:	זד
	Sir 32,18 (Bm)	זר	read:	זד
p. 63	Sir 36,24 (Bm)	קינה	read:	קונה
p. 66	Sir 38,12 (Bm)	צוכיך	read:	צרכיך
	Sir 38,12 (Bm)	ולא	read:	ואל
p. 70	Sir 40,15 (B)	עֿן	read:	על
p. 75	Sir 43,4 (B)	שלוח	read:	שולח
	Sir 43,5 (B)	עשהו	read:	עושהו
	Sir 43,5 (Bm)	וליון	read:	עליון
p. 77	Sir 43,32 (B)	ראתי	read:	ראיתי
p. 89	Sir 50,16 (B)	חצצרות	read:	בחצצרות
p. 92	Sir 51,12c (B)	ושראל	read:	ישראל
p. 95	Sir 41,16 (C)	לשמר	read:	לשמור
	Sir 20,23 (C)	שונה	read:	שונא
p. 102	Sir 37,24 (D)	ויאשרוהו	read:	ויאשריהו
p. 105	Sir 33,4 (E)	תגיתה	read:	תגיה
p. 107	Sir 33,27 (E)	מרוד	read:	ימרוד
p. 109	note 73	hywh hrwtst	read:	תסתורה והיה
p. 110	Sir 32,18b (F)	זר	read:	זד
p. 116	Sir 41,18b (M)	תגבר	read:	תגור
p. 119	Sir 43,17 (M)	ופרח	read:	יפרה
p. 120	Add: Sir 43,29 (M)		יֿי[............]	[........................]
	Add: Sir 43,30 (M)		ש אל[.........]	[........................]
p. 123	Sir 6,22 (2Q18)	כה	read:	כח
p. 125	Sir 51,18 (11QPsᵃ)	ולא	read:	ולוא

Part II. Synopsis

p. 133	Sir 6,22 (A)	כמשה	read:	כשמה
	Sir 6,22 (2Q18)	כה	read:	כח
p. 137	Sir 10,22 (A)	וזר	read:	וזד
p. 140	Sir 11,8 (A)	וּבְתוֹך	read:	וּבְתוֹך
	Sir 11,9 (A)	תאר	read:	תאחר
p. 143	Sir 15,15 (A)	אל	read:	אם
	Sir 15,17 (A)	ומות	read:	מוות
p. 150	Sir 32,18b (B)	זר	read:	זד
	Sir 32,18b (F)	זר	read:	זד
p. 156	Sir 37,24 (D)	ויאשרוהו	read:	ויאשריהו
p. 164	Sir 41,16 (C)	לשמר	read:	לשמור
p. 165	Sir 41,18b (M)	תגבר	read:	תגור
p. 172	Sir 43,17 (M)	ופרח	read:	יפרה
p. 177	Sir 51,18 (11QPs[a])	ולא	read:	ולוא

p. 173 Add:

	MS B	MS M
Sir 43,29	ונפלאות דבריו אד מאד[......]נו[ן	[.........] [.............]י"ו
Sir 43,30	רימו קול בכל תוכלו יכ יש עוד [.....]ל[...]	[.........] [......]ש אל

Abkürzungsverzeichnis[1]

Allg.	allgemein	Kap(p).	Kapitel
Anm.	Anmerkung	Lag	de Lagarde
Anm. d. Hg.	Anmerkung des/r Heraus-	LXX	Septuaginta
	geber/in	Moss	Mossul
Art.	Artikel	MS	Manuskript
AT	Altes Testament	n.Chr.	nach Christus
atl.	alttestamentlich	Nr.	Nummer
bes.	besonders	Pap.	Papyrus
bzw.	beziehungsweise	Pl.	Plural
ca.	circa	Qal	Grundstamm
ders.	derselbe	Syr.	Syrisch / Peshitta
d.h.	das heißt	S.	Seite
d.i.	das ist	sc. / scil.	scilicet
dies.	dieselbe(n)	sen.	Senior
ebd.	Ebenda	s.o.	siehe oben
EDV	Elektronische Datenverar-	sog.	so genannt
	beitung	St.	Sankt
EÜ	Einheitsübersetzung	s.u.	siehe unten
f(f)	folgende(r)	u.	und
FS	Festschrift	u.a.	und andere
FN	Fußnote	u.ä.	und ähnliche
G	Septuaginta	u.ö.	und öfter
Γ	Ben Sira - griechisch	usw.	und so weiter
ΓII	Überarbeitung von ΓI	v.Chr.	vor Christus
H	hebräischer Text	v(v)	verse(s)
H^A	Handschrift A	V(v)	Vers(e)
H^B	Handschrift B	Vulg.	Vulgata
H^{Bm}	Handschrift B, Marginalie	vgl.	vergleiche
H^C	Handschrift C	Z.	Zeile
Hg.	Herausgeber	z.B.	zum Beispiel
insg.	insgesamt	z.St.	zur Stell
Jh.	Jahrhundert		

---

[1] Englische Abkürzungen folgen *The SBL Handbook of Style: For Ancient Near Eastern, Biblical, and Early Christian Studies* (eds. P.H. Alexander, J.F. Kutsko et al.; Peabody: Hedrickson, 1999).

Index of Passages[1]

---

[1]   Die Doppelzählung im Buch Sira erfolgt nach Ziegler / Rahlfs.

Numbers

Num 5,9 ....159f
Num 6,19 161
Num 6,20 161
Num 10,10 162
Num 11,21 122
Num 12,12 327
Num 14,27f 122
Num 15,20f 159
Num 16,35 122
Num 18,8 ....150, 159f
Num 18,11 .... 150, 159
Num 18,12 159
Num 18,18 161
Num 18,19 ....150f
Num 18,20 150
Num 18,29 159
Num 22,6 222
Num 24,16 184
Num 25,2 162
Num 25,6ff 172
Num 25,12 172
Num 28,24 165
Num 31,29 159
Num 35,2 154
Num 35,2–5 154

Deuteronomy

Deut 1,31 34
Deut 2,14ff..........................122
Deut 4,29 143
Deut 4,31 .... 112, 114, 228
Deut 4,45 186
Deut 5 67
Deut 5,10 43
Deut 6,1f.............................15
Deut 6,4–9 67
Deut 6,5 .... 143, 327
Deut 6,5f........................43, 57
Deut 6,17 186
Deut 7,9 43
Deut 7,34 150
Deut 9,4f...............................5
Deut 10,1–5 186
Deut 10,9 150
Deut 10,12 ....43, 143
Deut 10,12f.........................15
Deut 10,15 150
Deut 11,1 43
Deut 11,13 ....43, 143
Deut 11,22 43
Deut 11,25 144
Deut 11,26ff.........................5
Deut 11,31f..........................5

Deut 12,6.................146, 159,
.... 161f, 165
Deut 12,11................146, 159,
.... 161f, 165
Deut 12,12.........................150
Deut 12,17.................146, 159,
.................................161, 165
Deut 12,27.........................162
Deut 13,4....................43, 143
Deut 13,18.........................101
Deut 14,27.........................150
Deut 14,29.........................150
Deut 17,14–20.................216
Deut 18,1........................ 149f
Deut 18,1ff.........................149
Deut 18,3.........................150
Deut 18,3f.........................149
Deut 18,4.........................159
Deut 19,9............................43
Deut 21,18–21....................33
Deut 22,6f 317
Deut 24,9.........................150
Deut 26,2.........................159
Deut 26,10.........................159
Deut 26,16.........................143
Deut 27,26............................57
Deut 28................................48
Deut 28,1ff............................57
Deut 29,29a.........................94
Deut 30,2......................... 143f
Deut 30,6....................43, 143
Deut 30,10.........................143
Deut 30,15.........................120
Deut 30,15–20.................5, 47
Deut 30,16....................15, 43
Deut 30,19.........................120
Deut 30,20............................43
Deut 32,6...................34, 189
Deut 32,6–9...............190, 196
Deut 32,8............43, 128, 189
Deut 32,8f 188f
Deut 32,9.........................189
Deut 32,21.........................311
Deut 32,38.........................162
Deut 33,19.................146, 162

Joshua

Josh 14,3 154
Josh 14,3f...........................154
Josh 14,4 ....147, 154
Josh 15,13 147
Josh 18,7 147
Josh 22,5 143
Josh 22,23 162
Josh 22,27 162

Josh 23,14......................... 143

Judges

Judg 3,12–30 218
Judg 4,1–5,31 218
Judg 7,8 146
Judg 9,7–21 218
Judg 10,1–5 219
Judg 12,8–15 219
Judg 14,14 218
Judg 14,18 218
Judg 20,10 146

1 Samuel

1Sam 2,29......................... 159
1Sam 7,3........................... 143
1Sam 10,8......................... 162
1Sam 11,7......................... 144
1Sam 12,11....................... 218
1Sam 12,20....................... 143
1Sam 12,24....................... 143
1Sam 16,5......................... 162
1Sam 22,10....................... 146

2 Samuel

2Sam 7,10......................... 194
2Sam 7,14........................... 35
2Sam 22,14............... 183, 227
2Sam 24,14........ 101, 106, 114

1 Kings

1Kgs 2,4 143
1Kgs 3,26 101
1Kgs 5,9 7
1Kgs 5,10–13 8
1Kgs 8,9 186
1Kgs 8,23 143
1Kgs 8,48 143
1Kgs 8,50 101
1Kgs 11,4–8 215
1Kgs 14,8 143
1Kgs 15,11 217
1Kgs 15,14 217
1Kgs 18,48 143
1Kgs 22,43 217
1Kgs 22,44 217

Isaiah

Jeremiah

Lamentations

Ezekiel